The Baltic Sea

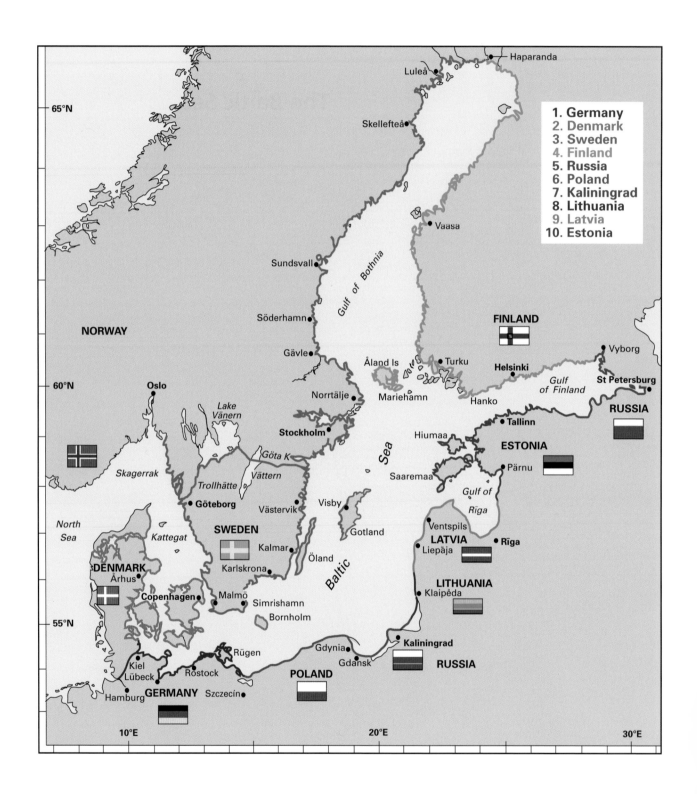

The Baltic Sea

**Germany, Denmark, Sweden,
Finland, Russia, Poland, Kaliningrad,
Lithuania, Latvia, Estonia**

 RCC PILOTAGE FOUNDATION

Imray Laurie Norie & Wilson

Published by
Imray Laurie Norie & Wilson Ltd
Wych House The Broadway
St Ives Cambridgeshire PE27 5BT England
www.imray.com
2010

First edition 1992
Second edition 2003
Third edition 2010

© Text: Royal Cruising Club Pilotage Foundation 2010
© Plans: Imray Laurie Norie & Wilson Ltd 2010
© Photographs as credited 2010

ISBN 978 184623 187 2

British Library Cataloguing in Publication Data.
A catalogue record for this title is available from the
Britiah Library.

The plans have been reproduced with the permission of
the Swedish Maritime Administration - Stockholm,
Finnish Hydrographic Service - Helsinki, BSH German
Hydrographic Office - Hamburg. This product has been
derived , in part, from products owned by Kort and
Matrikelstyrelsen. Licence no. G.10-2002

The last input of technical information was March 2010.

Printed in Great Britain by Butler Tanner and Dennis
Ltd, Frome, Somerset.

CORRECTIONAL SUPPLEMENTS

This pilot book may be amended at intervals by the issue
of correctional supplements. These are published on the
internet at our web site www.imray.com (and also via
www.rccpf.org.uk) and may be downloaded free of
charge. Printed copies are also available on request from
the publishers at the above address. Like this pilot,
supplements are selective. Navigators requiring the latest
definitive information are advised to refer to official
hydrographic office data.

ADDITIONAL INFORMATION

Additional information may be found under the
Publications page at www.rccpf.org.uk. This includes a
downloadable waypoint list, links to Google maps,
additional photographs and mid season updates when
appropriate. Passage planning information may also be
found on that website.

CAUTION

Whilst the RCC Pilotage Foundation, the authors and the
publishers have used reasonable endeavours to ensure the
accuracy of the content of this book, it contains selected
information and thus is not definitive. It does not contain all
known information on the subject in hand and should not be
relied on alone for navigational use: it should only be used in
conjunction with official hydrographic data. This is particularly
relevant to the plans, which should not be used for navigation.

The RCC Pilotage Foundation, the authors and the publishers
believe that the information which they have included is a useful
aid to prudent navigation, but the safety of a vessel depends
ultimately on the judgment of the skipper, who should assess all
information, published or unpublished.

The information provided in this pilot book may be out of date
and may be changed or updated without notice. The RCC
Pilotage Foundation cannot accept any liability for any error,
omission or failure to update such information.

To the extent permitted by law, the RCC Pilotage Foundation, the
authors and the publishers do not accept liability for any loss
and/or damage howsoever caused that may arise from reliance on
information contained in these pages.

POSITIONS

All positions in the text are to WGS 84 datum. They are
supplied as aids to help orientation and to assist in locating and
maintaining transits referred to in the book. As always, care
must be exercised to work to the datum of the chart in use.

WAYPOINTS

The RCC Pilotage Foundation consider a waypoint to be a
position likely to be helpful for navigation if entered into some
form of electronic navigation system for use in conjunction with
GPS. In this pilot they have been derived from electronic charts.
They must be used with caution. All waypoints are given to
datum WGS 84 and every effort has been made to ensure their
accuracy. Nevertheless, for each individual vessel, the standard
of onboard equipment, aerial position, datum setting, correct

entry of data and operator skill all play a part in their
effectiveness. In particular it is vital for the navigator to note
the datum of the chart in use and apply the necessary
correction if plotting a GPS position on the chart.

Our use of the term 'waypoint' does not imply that all vessels
can safely sail directly over those positions at all times. Some –
as in this pilot – may be linked to form recommended routes
under appropriate conditions. However, skippers should be
aware of the risk of collision with another vessel, which is
plying the exact reciprocal course. Verification by observation,
or use of radar to check the accuracy of a waypoint, may
sometimes be advisable and reassuring.

We emphasise that we regard waypoints as an aid to
navigation for use as the navigator or skipper decides. We
hope that the waypoints in this pilot will help ease that
navigational load.

PLANS

The plans in this guide are not to be used for navigation – they
are designed to support the text and should always be used
together with navigational charts.

It should be borne in mind that the characteristics of lights
may be changed during the life of the book, and that in any
case notification of such changes is unlikely to be reported
immediately. Users should consult the *Admiralty List of
Lights*.

All bearings are given from seaward and refer to true north.
Symbols are based on those used by the British Admiralty –
users are referred to *Symbols and Abbreviations (NP 5011)*.

Contents

The RCC Pilotage Foundation

In 1976 an American member of the Royal Cruising Club, the late Dr Fred Ellis, indicated that he wished to make a gift to the Club in memory of his father, the late Robert E. Ellis, of his friends Peter Pye and John Ives and as a mark of esteem for Roger Pinckney. An independent charity known as the RCC Pilotage Foundation was formed and Dr Ellis added his house to his already generous gift of money to form the Foundation's permanent endowment. The Foundation's charitable objective is 'to advance the education of the public in the science and practice of navigation' which is at present achieved through the writing and updating of pilot books covering many different parts of the world.

The Foundation is extremely grateful and privileged to have been given the copyrights to books written by a number of distinguished authors and yachtsmen including the late Adlard Coles, Robin Brandon and Malcolm Robson. In return the Foundation has willingly accepted the task of keeping the original books up to date and many yachtsmen and women have helped (and are helping) the Foundation fulfill this commitment. In addition to the titles donated to the Foundation, several new books have been created and developed under the auspices of the Foundation. The Foundation works in close collaboration with three publishers – Imray Laurie Norie and Wilson, Adlard Coles Nautical and On Board Publications – and in addition publishes in its own name short run guides and pilot books for areas where limited demand does not justify large print runs. Several of

the Foundation's books have been translated into French, Spanish, German and Italian.

The Foundation runs its own website at www.rccpf.org.uk which not only lists all the publications but also contains free downloadable pilotage information.

The overall management of the Foundation is entrusted to trustees appointed by the Royal Cruising Club, with day to day operations being controlled by the Director. All these appointments are unpaid. In line with its charitable status, the Foundation distributes no profits, which are used to finance new books and developments and to subsidise those covering areas of low demand.

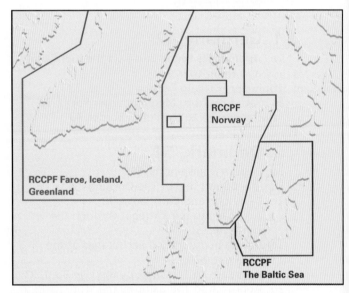

PUBLICATIONS OF THE RCC PILOTAGE FOUNDATION

Imray
Faroe, Iceland and
 Greenland
Norway
The Baltic Sea
Channel Islands
North Brittany and
 the Channel Islands
Isles of Scilly
North Biscay
South Biscay
Atlantic Islands
Atlantic Spain & Portugal
Mediterranean Spain
 Costas del Sol and Blanca
 Costas del Azahar,
 Dorada & Brava
 Islas Baleares
Corsica and North
 Sardinia
North Africa
Chile

Adlard Coles Nautical
Atlantic Crossing Guide
Pacific Crossing Guide

On Board Publications
South Atlantic Circuit
Havens and Anchorages
for the South American
Coast

The RCC Pilotage Foundation
Supplement to Falkland
Island Shores
Guide to West Africa
Argentina

RCCPF Website
www.rccpf.org.uk
Supplements
Support files for books
Passage Planning Guides
ePilots

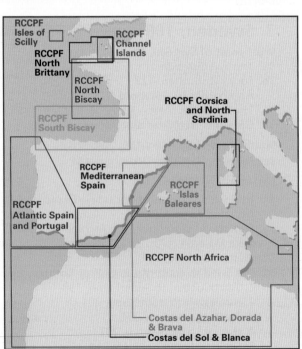

Foreword

The Baltic Sea is vast and diverse in every sense. This book sets out to provide the cruising yachtsmen with the background details necessary to plan extended cruising throughout the region whether it is to the popular well developed areas or the more remote parts where the only company is the wildlife. Our earlier book has now been much enhanced, updated and extended to include the west coast of Sweden and the whole of the Gulf of Bothnia. All areas of the Baltic Sea are now covered. Although the pilotage information for each country is much greater than hitherto, particularly in Denmark and Germany thanks to Jeremy Parkinson's practical research, it would be impractical to mention the thousands of harbours and anchorages in all these differing countries. However, all key facts for each country are provided along with details of the local guides and how to source them.

No work of this type and complexity could be prepared without the dedicated attention of a team of volunteers. Their names and the areas they covered are listed on this page. Mike Lewin-Harris had the courage to lead the team from the start, Willie Wilson at Imray personally prepared the work from the early input and Mike Redfern took up the difficult challenge to project manage the latter aspects of the work. They have had excellent support from the authors who have all worked tirelessly on their individual major projects – The Pilotage Foundation congratulates them all.

The Pilotage Foundation would welcome feedback from sailors who cruise the differing countries of the Baltic as this will help us remain aware of the changes taking place over the life of the book. Comments or photographs of major events may be published on the Pilotage Foundation's website which also includes considerable worldwide pilotage information. Comments or photographs of major events may be published on the Pilotage Foundation's website (www.rccpf.org.uk) which also includes considerable worldwide pilotage information. This includes the *Baltic Passage Planning Guide* which may prove helpful to those sailing there for the first time.

One could spend a lifetime cruising this fascinating sea. We hope this book will help you enjoy your adventures there.

Martin Walker
Hon Director, RCC Pilotage Foundation
April 2010

Acknowledgements

This third edition of *The Baltic Sea* draws heavily on the earlier work by Barry Sheffield and Oz Robinson and then by Anne Hammick and her supporting team; it would not have been possible without the

CONTRIBUTING EDITORS

Germany *Jeremy Parkinson*
Denmark *Jeremy Parkinson*
Sweden
Introduction *Michael Lewin-Harris*
Øresund *Michael Lewin-Harris*
West Coast *Bruce Weir*
Göteborg *Bruce Weir*
The Bohuslän *Mike Redfern*
The Göta Canal *Bruce Weir*
South Coast *Michael Lewin-Harris*
East Coast *Michael Lewin-Harris*
The Gulf of Bothnia *Mike Redfern*
Finland
Introduction and mainland *Tony and Jill Vasey*
The Gulf of Bothnia *Mike Redfern*
The Åland Islands *Mike Redfern*
Russia *Jeremy Parkinson & Vladimir Ivankiv*
Poland *Jeremy Parkinson*
Kaliningrad *Jeremy Parkinson & Vladimir Ivankiv*
Lithuania *Graham & Fay Cattell*
Latvia *Graham & Fay Cattell*
Estonia *Graham & Fay Cattell*

very major commitment and determination of the contributing authors listed below. The scale of their task has been considerable.

All books benefit from wider experience and the authors have been fortunate and grateful to have received input from the following: Tom Aitken, Lennart Andreasson, Jake Backhus, Arnis Berzins, Anthony Browne, Peregrine Bruce, Henry Buchanan, Dan Darwall, Stuart Carnegie, Max Ekholm, Baz Ennels, Lars Fasth, John Gilmour, Anthony Fawcett, Andrew Fleck, Thorry Gunnersen, Staffan Jonsson, Mariola Kijewska, Stephen Lennane, Peter Mason, Jim Mottram, Dave and Lorna Price, David Reynolds, John Sadd, Stephan and Margarita Strobel, David and Philippa Thorne, Kalevi Westersund, Simon and Jill Vines, Tom and Dorothy Wadlow. If anyone has been omitted I hope they will accept our apologies. Only a selection of the numerous photographs received could be included but all helped inform the authors and many will be published on the Pilotage Foundation website as a supporting file to this book.

Our major proof readers have been Kit Power, John Sadd and Sandy Watson and the Pilotage Foundation team have provide some additional support. Preparing this book has been a complicated task and would have been impractical without the interest, encouragement and dedication of Willie Wilson and his hard working team at Imray.

The RCC Pilotage Foundation is grateful to them all – and also to their partners who so often provide active help and support but whose names do not appear here.

Martin Walker
April 2010

Tacker o Tag chandlery on quay at Ystad. It stocks everything and is like a maritime museum *S. Carnegie*

Passathafen at Travemünde *J.Mottram*

Brightly painted German buoys *E. Redfern*

A visit from the border guards, Latvia *E. Redfern*

Bows-to mooring in the Swedish Archipelago *E. Redfern*

Cruise boat on the Göta Kanal *E. Redfern*

Introduction

General information

The overall objective of this guide is to provide a general introduction to the Baltic Sea, including the approaches, to enable yachtsmen contemplating a visit to the area to form a view of its merits as a cruising ground. It aims to give an overall impression of the countries on the shores of the Baltic, to provide basic pilotage information for selected harbours and to indicate potentially interesting lesser ports worthy of exploration. It also deals with the practical and administrative problems likely to be encountered during a visit to the area. However it neither attempts nor claims to be comprehensive – the information for each area contains suggestions for further reading, and for yachtsmen's guides in particular. No attempt has been made to list all the many general tourist guides relevant to each area, which may be found on the shelves of any good bookshop.

The sequencing adopted in the second edition has been retained in the third but with increased coverage of Denmark and the west coast of Sweden a pragmatic approach has had to be taken in those areas. With the majority of readers likely to approach from the south it was decided to take the whole of the Swedish west coast from Falsterbo in the south to the Norwegian border in the north. This includes both Danish and Swedish sides of the Øresund. The rest of Denmark from Skagen and through the Bælts has been written north to south to accommodate the many readers approaching from the Skagerrak. Inevitably, at some stage in the cruise part of the book will have to be followed in reverse, but it is hoped that this order will prove convenient for the greatest number of yachtsmen. In no way is it intended to reflect the interest or merits of individual countries.

The Baltic Sea
(Compiled by Stephen Lennane)

For those used to the Atlantic, the English Channel and the North Sea, the Baltic is excitingly different. A continental inland sea and one of the largest areas of brackish water in the world, it has unique features which will appeal to yachtsmen who want a change from the temperate maritime climate of Britain and the near continent, their familiar scenery, and the crowds of yachts that abound their shores.

Created by a depression in three million year old bedrock, the Baltic region has been affected by glaciation, most recently 11,000 years ago, and is still in constant change. The land once pressed down by the ice is beginning to rise, especially in the north of the area and, with land-rise occurring at about one metre per century, surveys carried out in the century before last may no longer accurately reflect the depths. In the south there is no land rise and the sea is gradually gaining on the low-lying coast. The central and northern Baltic is characterised by rocky archipelagos, the southern and eastern areas by long sandy beaches and lagoons.

Because of the inflow from the rivers there is a decrease in salinity in the water, which becomes almost fresh at the top of the Gulf of Bothnia. Together with the cold winter climate this produces a challenging environment for both plants and animals. There is a decrease in both size and diversity, and only a quarter of the number of fish species are found in the Gulf of Bothnia as are found in the Kattegat. In total the Baltic is home to about 100 species of fish, of which the important ones are cod, herring and salmon, with some flatfish. Cod stocks have diminished substantially in recent years. There are three varieties of seal – grey, common and ringed – as well as porpoises, though the latter are now rare. Waterfowl abound in the lakes of the south and there are white-tailed eagles and ospreys further north.

The drainage basin of the Baltic is home to some 85 million people, giving rise to environmental problems. These have been compounded by the particular difficulties arising from the demise of the Soviet Union. The waste from the uranium processing plant in eastern Estonia is only metres from the sea. Alarming levels of untreated sewage were not uncommon around St Petersburg but in late 2009 it was reported that the St Petersburg water utility company had upgraded the wastewater treatment technique resulting in a significant reduction of pollution inputs to the Baltic Sea. The growth of marine algae on the surface of the Baltic Sea during the summer months is becoming a significant environmental problem and the cause has yet to be identified although the run-off of agricultural fertilisers is suspect. It is significant that the flow of water through the Kattegat and from the rivers is so slow that it takes about 25 years for the waters of the Baltic to be replaced.

In response to this realisation the Helsinki Commission was set up in the early 1970s to protect the marine environment of the Baltic Sea, through intergovernmental cooperation between the then seven Baltic coastal states. The Helsinki Convention, the world's first anti-pollution measure covering an entire sea, was signed by all seven in 1974 and came into force six years later. In 1992 a new convention was signed, again by all the states bordering the Baltic Sea (by now numbering nine), as well as the European Community, and this came into force in January 2000. Its obligations and benefits are now being felt.

The Baltic coastline has been populated since the ice receded some 11,000 years ago, and the earliest archaeological remains date from 4000BC. By the time of the Bronze Age, around 1200BC, individual groups had become established and later the Roman writer Tacitus mentions 'Baltic Tribes'. From 200AD the inhabitants of the central Baltic island of Gotland – the Goths – began to spread south through Poland and Russia into northern Italy. Their eastward movement was halted by the Huns near the Black Sea and, turning southwest, they conquered Rome in 410AD.

By the 9th century the people of the north were again casting their influence beyond the Baltic. The Vikings became prominent and powerful, due both to their ships and navigational abilities and to the entrepreneurial approach they took to other people's property. In addition to raids on eastern Britain and voyages to Iceland, Greenland and possibly North America, they also travelled via the Russian rivers all the way to Greece, which they called the Eastern Empire. Trade was established with the Byzantines of the Black Sea region, the main Baltic trade goods being amber, wax, fur and charcoal.

During the 10th century German and English missionaries expanded the reach of Christianity, building churches on what had been pagan sites, and in the year 1000 German traders established a base

Changing Europe at the Solidarity Museum in Gdańsk
E. Redfern

Smorgesborg in Copenhagen *E. Redfern*

on Gotland. By the 11th century Lithuania had become the last remaining pagan culture in Europe.

Later the trade routes forged by the Vikings were taken over by Hansa merchants from Wismar, Rostock and Lübeck, who banded together partly in an effort to protect their ships from piracy (*hansa* may be translated to mean 'armed group'). Part of their power came from control of the herring fisheries, vital to Catholic Europe, and when fully fledged the Hanseatic League dominated trade from King's Lynn in the west to Novgorod in the east. The merchants also benefited from the development of the Baltic cog, a ship which, with a centre-mounted rudder and shallow draught, carried five times the cargo of the Viking ship. Not good to windward, these ships followed the seasonal variation of winds and sailed in convoys making an annual circuit. The profusion of modern ferry services across the Baltic, an area where until recently land travel has often been difficult or impossible, is a reminder of this trade. These routes remain a useful and interesting way for yachtsmen to travel to and from an over-wintering yacht.

Two Baltic products traded for many centuries will be of particular interest to yachtsmen. Stockholm tar, produced from the slow burning of the roots of pine trees, has always been used as a preservative for wood and rigging and gives old ships their distinctive smell. Also associated with pine or spruce trees is amber, the fossilised resin from forests growing some 30 to 40 million years ago. Large quantities of amber are to be found in the southeast corner of the Baltic, notably in Poland, Kaliningrad and Lithuania, where it can be picked up on the beaches or bought in local shops (but beware of fakes).

The political and military history of the Baltic over the last 500 years is complicated, with the changing influences at various times of Sweden, Germany and Russia, and the accompanying wars. The power of the Hanseatic League was counteracted by the 1397

Children in the Baltic

(Contributed by Andrew Fleck)

If impending parenthood is threatening your sailing, or your five-year-old has lost interest in the topless bus on the Isle of Wight, then give serious consideration to the Baltic. Its major drawback is the distance from most British harbours, but for those who can organise a delivery trip with friends prior to the family holiday, the distance should not be an insurmountable obstacle. Alternatively, each year many British yachts lay up in the various yards throughout the region, thereby extending their cruise to several years. A brief glance at the atlas shows innumerable islands which offer many short days' sailing – plenty to satisfy young crew who enjoy the excitement of weighing anchor, rapidly changing scenery and arrival at a new port. In the western Baltic, busy Danish fishing harbours and fine sand beaches provide interest for rainy days and sunshine alike. When harbourside activities pall, excellent local transport services connect to castles and museums, swimming pools or theme parks. All of these are easily researched through efficient local tourist offices.

By contrast, the plethora of sparsely developed islands that characterise the west and east coasts of Sweden, and the spread of islands in the Åland and Finnish archipelagos, make Denmark seem quite suburban. These waters give unparalleled opportunities for exploration. It is also hard to imagine a more perfect environment in which youngsters might learn to sail, since the waters are sheltered and tideless and the winds and weather systems more constant than in Britain. Older children who want to swim and sunbathe will find a crystal-clean environment, with more hours of summer sunshine than in Britain. The Swedish and Finnish islands have fewer cultural and man-made attractions than Denmark, but for those looking for peaceful anchorages in which the whole crew can amuse themselves this is definitely the place to be!

In an area so rich with opportunities it would be unwise to recommend any single anchorage. However, for a comprehensive description of almost every possible option (albeit in Swedish) accompanied by rather more useful aerial photographs and chartlets, the *Naturhamnar på Ostkusten* guide from the Svenska Kryssarklubben (Swedish Cruising Club) is a sound investment. If it is your intention to cruise eastern Sweden and then return, give some thought to crossing the country via the Göta Canal which runs from Mem, just south of Nyköping, in the east to Göteborg in the west. This has the obvious advantage that you do not retrace your steps, and introduces further variety into the cruise. It also has the significant bonus of bringing the crew, young or older, west to Göteborg in sheltered conditions, from which the Kiel Canal is less than a week's cruise away, largely through the Danish archipelago.

Irrespective of the precise details of the cruise, remember that Scandinavia is above all a child-friendly area. It is entirely normal for families to dine out with children, so that restaurants cater for their needs, be it with high chairs and toys or by bringing the youngest their meal first. Your fellow diners are more likely to smile at the normal antics of a toddler than to exude that air of intolerance which so quickly turns a long-anticipated meal into a running disaster that cannot be terminated too soon. And finally, if it all goes wrong and a trip to the pharmacy, doctor or hospital is required, you will encounter the highest level of professionalism and excellent spoken English.

If all this fails to tempt the weary parent, consider the fact that the absence of tides means that no early starts are required in order make the next tidal gate!

The Baltic provides plenty to interest young children – here at Seglinge in the Åland Islands *A. and A. Fleck*

union of Norway, Denmark and Sweden – the Kalmar Union. This lasted until Gustav Vasa became King of Sweden in 1523, when Sweden became the dominant power. In the late 18th century the German influence then became greater under Frederick the Great of Prussia, and the Baltic became a German lake.

As may be expected, the Royal Navy played significant parts from time to time, notably at the Battle of Copenhagen when Nelson famously used his blind eye, against Russia and its Finnish grand duchy during the Crimean War, and in the First World War when British submarines were used with effect. The Kiel Canal, opened in 1895, was built to enable the German fleet to pass directly between the Baltic and the North Sea without having to run the gauntlet of the Kattegat.

After the Second World War the Soviet Union leased Finland's Porkkala peninsula, so controlling the eastern part of the Gulf of Finland and the approaches to St Petersburg. Until the disintegration of the Soviet Union the eastern part of the Baltic was effectively a Russian preserve. Kaliningrad has always been important to Russia as its only Baltic

The sauna experience

(Contributed by John Dare, sauna enthusiast)

For many people a wonderful extra to cruising in the Baltic is the sauna experience. Almost everywhere one goes – hotels, marinas, yacht clubs and even fairly remote islands – one will find a sauna to enjoy. After a few days at sea, particularly if the weather has been a little unfriendly, there are few things more pleasant than a relaxing sauna bath. It is a great delight to get warm, clean and relaxed all at the same time.

So what happens? The sauna experience varies from the well-organised facility with showers, jacuzzis and swimming pools adjacent, to the little sauna hut in the woods with a simple, wood-burning stove. The latter are perhaps the most enjoyable, particularly if they are on the edge of the water with a lovely view as they often are. In any case the experience is basically the same. First, wash yourself in the shower, sea, pool or other available water. Then sit and relax in the sauna and the heat (most likely between 60°C and 90°C) should have you perspiring freely in five minutes or so. A first stay of around ten minutes serves most people, but step out for a break if you feel at all uncomfortable. During the break the most traditional thing to do is to enter the sea, which you will find remarkably refreshing. Then return to the sauna for some more heat and repeat as you wish. Also, during the break, especially where you have the sauna to yourself, it is very relaxing to simply sit outdoors enjoying a snack or perhaps a cold beer. Remember, the essence of the experience is to relax and take your time – a hurried sauna is a waste of time.

There are no hard and fast rules about sauna etiquette, but a few general guidelines should be observed. Drinking and eating in the sauna is not done. Traditionally saunas are mixed, but in busy or more public places you will come across designated hours for men and women, or even different saunas for each. Normally saunas are taken naked, but if modesty dictates you can certainly wrap a

A typical Finnish sauna *P. and G. Price*

towel around yourself or even wear a swimsuit - and you should, of course, respect the privacy of others using the sauna before you. If you are using a wood-burning sauna you will doubtless find wood and wood-cutting tools close to hand, and you are expected to replace the wood you have used. Saunas by definition are clean places, and you should certainly leave the area as clean as you found it. In some marinas use of the sauna is included in your harbour dues while in other places a charge is made, and it may sometimes be necessary to book, usually for one hour. The situation varies and one simply has to enquire.

Above all, saunas are social places to be enjoyed with friends and/or family. The sauna experience is an essential part of the Baltic cruise, so relax and enjoy it!

port not to be closed by ice for much of the winter, and remains a part of Russia despite its isolated position between Poland, Belarus and Lithuania.

With political tensions eased, the future of the Baltic as a trading area continues to increase and it is attracting a growing number of visitors. Those interested in culture will be amply rewarded if they persevere to St Petersburg and there visit the Hermitage Museum, the Kirov ballet and the opera. An annual opera festival takes place at Savonlinna on the Saimaa Lakes, while in Sweden the court theatre at Drottningholm on Lake Mälaren, a few miles from Stockholm, is world famous. At Göteborg there are pontoons alongside the new opera house and one can return to the cockpit for refreshments during the interval!

All in all, the Baltic is quite as outstanding a cruising area as is the Mediterranean, and the yachtsman who ventures there will be well rewarded and, perhaps, slow to leave.

Health risk

A risk which is unlikely to be known to British yachtsmen concerns two diseases carried by some ticks. Not all ticks are infected but those which are may be encountered in coastal regions (as well as in a wide swathe across Europe). The only areas which do not appear to be affected are west and north Sweden and Denmark (except Bonholm). The diseases are TBE (tick-borne encephalitis) and Lyme Disease. It is possible to be vaccinated against TBE but not Lyme Disease (which can only be treated afterwards with antibiotics). Refer to www.tbe-info.com.

Languages

Each country has its own language which, except in the case of German, is unlikely to be spoken by the English visitor. The most useful second language is English – it is very widely understood in Denmark, Sweden and Finland and, unless one is fluent, there is little point in attempting more than a polite word or two in the national language. In Russia there are usually enough English speakers amongst customs officials and yacht club administrators to deal with most problems, and even the captains of Russian patrol boats can manage enough English for a straightforward interchange of information. German is also widely spoken, other than in Sweden.

Currency

At the time of writing only two Baltic countries – Germany and Finland – have converted to the Euro, though this is almost certain to increase.

Brightly-painted houses at Degerby in the Åland Islands *E. Redfern*

Details of the other seven are given in the relevant country's text. Numerous internet sites provide current exchange rates. In practice the Euro is accepted very widely in tourist areas.

ATMs (automatic teller machines) are to be found in all countries including the St Petersburg region of Russia. Only Kaliningrad still appears to rely on exchange bureaux, which may be unwilling (or unequipped) to accept 'plastic'.

Credit and debit cards are becoming ever more widely used throughout the region. But it is always prudent to check the situation before committing oneself. In Denmark any transaction using a credit or debit card attracts a charge. Obtaining cash and using this for payment is the cheapest option. Again, a more detailed breakdown will be found in the relevant country's text.

The custom around the Baltic is for harbours to fly the flags of visiting yachts. These are at NJK Helsinki *E. Redfern*

Water quality and launderettes

Water is available on the pontoons of the vast majority of Baltic yacht harbours, and where this is not the case it is noted in the text. Quality is generally good, other than in Russia (both the St Petersburg and Kaliningrad regions) where visitors are recommended to boil tap water before drinking – or to arrive with tanks already full.

Many yacht harbours have on-site launderettes, which may need to be booked in advance. However British yachtsmen (or women) may be taken aback by how long the machines take. They are often very 'green' and operate at much lower temperatures than their UK equivalents, taking two hours or more for a standard wash.

Provisioning and alcohol

Daily needs can be met in every country bordering the Baltic Sea. The indoor markets are excellent and outstanding but expensive in Stockholm and Helsinki. Availability has rapidly improved in Poland, Lithuania, Latvia, Estonia and Russia. It goes without saying, however, that few if any shops will be found near the more remote anchorages, and that any cruising yacht should be capable of self-sufficiency for extended periods of time.

If, having transited the Kiel Canal, one is headed towards Denmark, Sweden and Finland, considerable savings are to be made by provisioning the boat before leaving Germany. At present shopping facilities remain somewhat better in Schleswig–Holstein (effectively Kiel to Travemünde) than in Mecklenburg–Vorpommern (Wismar eastwards), but these differences are evening out.

Particular savings are to be made on alcohol, which is extremely expensive in both Sweden and Finland. Note that crew under the age of 20 cannot take alcohol into Sweden.

If following the southern route – via Poland, Kaliningrad, Lithuania, Latvia and Estonia – daily needs will be met by shops and supermarkets, with the added interest of many open markets selling fresh food and other products at prices lower than those in the shops. Alcohol is generally cheaper than in the northern countries, and some of the local liqueurs are well worth sampling. However alcohol should NEVER be bought in markets or from kiosks – stick to commercially labelled and sealed bottles.

The shopping situation in Russia has improved dramatically since the break up of the Soviet Union, and almost all basic commodities are now available at prices which appear cheap to Western visitors. A few specific suggestions regarding shopping in Russia will be found on page 275.

Telephones

Telephone systems are dealt with on a country by country basis. Sufficient to say that no problems should be encountered in making international phone calls to or from any country bordering the Baltic Sea, including but expensively, both the St Petersburg and Kaliningrad areas of Russia

Mobile phone coverage on land is generally good, though this may not be the case a few miles offshore. UK network companies make varying charges for international calls and it is worth checking these before departure – and also whether any special deals are available. Recent EU legislation has resulted in lower costs to receive and to make calls, the charges being the same throughout the EU Baltic region. In the case of a long cruise it may be worth considering investing in a single or multi country SIM card. Most economic of all may be a Skype telephone for use via wireless broadband.

Throughout much if not all of the region the emergency services (police, ambulance and fire brigade) can be reached, free of charge, by dialling 112.

Email

Internet – and therefore email – access is very widespread. Many harbours and public libraries provide

Planning and navigation

Reaching the Baltic

Extensive detail is available from www.rccpf.org.uk then follow 'Passage Planning Guides'. In summary the quickest approach to the Baltic from southern England is through the Kiel Canal, the entrance to which can be reached in a few days from south or east coast harbours. Once through the Canal the British Kiel Yacht Club, run by the British Army, makes visitors welcome, and Kiel is a good place to store ship for a long cruise.

Visitors from Scotland or northern England may prefer to reach the area via the Kattegat, while it is also possible to go through Limfjord or the Eider River and Gieselau Kanal without unstepping masts.

Finally, many yachts traverse the Göta Kanal at either the beginning or the end of their cruise, in order to 'complete the circle'.

Cruise planning

The northern side of the Baltic and the Gulf of Finland can be explored very comfortably on a day-sailing basis, but ports along the southeastern shores are more widely spaced and some passages may be more than 100M. If the aim is to get to Russia or Estonia a more direct passage may be taken, calling perhaps only at Bornholm, southern Sweden or Gotland.

For the round trip, the choice is between the two obvious options. An argument for going anticlockwise is that the navigation and yachting facilities of the south and east shores of the Baltic are the lesser known quantities and best visited first so that towards the end of the cruise, when time begins to run out, the yacht is in the area with the better established yachting and communications facilities. The chief argument for sailing in a clockwise direction is that for many the entire purpose of the cruise is to explore the Swedish and Finnish islands. Clearing out for Russia, though theoretically possible from Estonia, is also a great deal easier from the northern side of the Gulf of Finland.

Admiralty charts 259 (the Baltic Sea on a scale of 1:1,500,000), 2816 (the Baltic Sea – Southern Sheet at 1:750,000), 2817 (the Baltic Sea – Northern Sheet and Gulf of Finland at 1:750,000) and possibly 2252 (the Gulf of Bothnia at 1:750,000) are likely to be found useful in the early planning stages.

the service, sometimes free or for a small charge. The situation in individual countries is covered in the text.

Where Wi-Fi is not available those with computers on board may find it most convenient to access the internet via their own mobile phone. This is surprisingly straightforward, given the appropriate phone and the correct software and cable but can be very expensive. If reliant on public computers there is the choice of a web-based service providers such as hotmail or yahoo, or accessing one's UK account via a site such as Googlemail.

Travel

By air

The countries surrounding the Baltic Sea are well served by both national and budget airlines. Individual country details are given in the text, but the following résumé of airports handling flights either direct to the UK or entailing only one change may be helpful when planning crew changes or visits home.

Germany – Hamburg, Lübeck and Berlin
Denmark – Esjberg, Århus and Copenhagen
Sweden – Göteborg (Landvetter) and Malmö in the west, and on the east coast Ronneby (for Karlskrona), Kalmar, Visby (Gotland), Arlanda, Skavsta or Västerås (for Stockholm) and, further north, Örnsköldvik, Umeå and Luleå
Finland – Vaasa, Mariehamn, Turku and Helsinki, plus Lappeenranta and Savonlinna on the Saimaa Lakes
Russia – Pulkovo-2 for St Petersburg (Pulkovo-1 handles domestic flights) and Kaliningrad (via Copenhagen or Hanover)
Poland – Warsaw, Gdańsk and Kraków
Lithuania – Vilnius, Palanga and Kaunas
Latvia – Rīga
Estonia – Tallinn.

By land

Again, details for individual countries will be found in the text, but in general it may be said that both rail and coach services are good throughout the Baltic area. It takes about 24 hours from London to Copenhagen and 36 hours to Stockholm or Poland by rail, whilst the interesting train/ferry journey from London to Helsinki takes around 60 hours, as does St Petersburg via Berlin and Warsaw. Few of the major ports in this guide are not on national rail networks, and those which are not can be reached by coach or ferry. The Thomas Cook European Rail Timetable, published monthly, remains an invaluable guide for planning rail travel in Europe and Scandinavia.

Coach services generally take longer than the equivalent distance by train, but are often considerably cheaper and may therefore appeal to younger crewmembers.

By sea

Ferries between the UK and Baltic ports are most likely to be of interest to those whose cruise extends over several seasons, when driving out with a laden car at the beginning of each season may make good economic sense.

Currently Sweden's DFDS Seaways, www.dfdsseaways.com, runs the only direct services, from Harwich to Esbjerg (Denmark), and Newcastle to Bergen, Norway. However, for those who prefer to make a shorter channel crossing and then drive to a Danish, German or Polish port the choice is vast, with so many ferries dashing across the Baltic that one wonders there is enough space! A Google search will reveal a host of ferry operators.

The best overall website is www.ferrylines.com which gives up to date news on what is happening – new services, closures etc.

Websites and the internet

The internet is an outstanding resource when researching a Baltic cruise. Websites detailing individual countries, towns and harbours are listed in the text – most of an exceptionally professional standard, often with English translation, video graphics etc. Very few fail to include an email address for the harbour and/or civic authorities, through which specific questions can be raised. The internet is also an excellent source of weather information, as detailed on pages 366–371.

Some of the more general sites relevant to the area as a whole include:

www.helcom.fi – the website of the Baltic Marine Environment Protection Commission (Helsinki Commission or HELCOM). Essential reading for all yachtsmen planning a Baltic cruise
www.cruising.org.uk – the homepage of the Cruising Association, which has long had strong links with the Baltic. Parts of the site are restricted (by password) to CA members only
www.imray.com – the website of Imray Laurie Norie & Wilson Ltd, including a full list of charts, publications and free, downloadable supplements
www.rya.org.uk – the homepage of the Royal Yachting Association
www.hmrc.gov.uk – homepage of HM Revenue and Customs

Formalities and paperwork – the yacht

Where the term *ship's papers* is used in the text it is presumed to include:

- A registration document, either under Part 1 of the Merchant Shipping Act of 1995 or the Small Ships Register (SSR), or the national equivalent;
- A VAT receipt or exemption (the EU Single Administrative Document);
- evidence of marine insurance, specifying in detail what areas are covered;
- A VHF Ship's Radio Licence
- Yachts sailing in German waters must carry a copy of the rules *Prevention of Pollution from Ships' waste disposal overboard. Rules laid down in Annex V of MARPOL 73/78.*

In addition the yacht should be equipped with both a motor-sailing cone and anchoring ball to display as required.

No difficulties should be encountered in keeping a VAT-paid yacht in any of the European Union countries indefinitely.

Non EU-registered yachts can, at present, stay in the EU for a maximum of 18 months, after which they must clear out of the EU tax area and clear back in. No minimum time has been specified between exit and re-entry. However the rules do change from time to time, and the owner of a yacht in this position would be wise to keep abreast of them. Details from HM Revenue and Customs, www.hmrc.gov.uk.

British yachtsmen are made very welcome in most Baltic countries and, in addition to the appropriate courtesy flag, it is well worth displaying a good-sized ensign. Discussion continues as to whether a plain red should be flown in areas where a blue ensign, defaced or otherwise, may cause confusion, but there are few in any country who will not recognise the Union flag quartering at the hoist.

Formalities and paperwork – those aboard

Customs and immigration requirements are considered in the individual country sections. All countries require a valid passport for each person aboard. Only Russia still requires citizens of the United Kingdom to obtain a voucher and confirmation to apply for a visa in order to visit – see page 274. Details of embassies and consulates are included in the text, and nationals of other countries are advised to check their visa situation well before leaving home. Non-Europeans need to be aware that any visit of over 90 days requires a Schengen visa which must be obtained in their country of permanent residence.

At least one person aboard must hold the VHF Operator's Certificate of Competence, with GMDSS endorsement if appropriate. If planning to visit Poland, Lithuania, Latvia, Estonia or Russia the skipper will also need an International Certificate of Competence. The rules are that skippers of boats which are flagged in the Baltic States require a 'driving licence' but skippers of vessels whose flag state does not require them to have such qualifications, are not required to have such in these countries. Nevertheless it is wise for all crew members to carry whatever certificates they do hold.

In the UK the ICC is administered by the Royal Yachting Association, Ensign Way, Hamble, Southampton SO31 4YA ☎ 0845 345 0400 *Fax* 0844 556 9516 *Email* enquires@rya.org.uk www.rya.org.uk, and is available at a cost of £40, but free to members. An examination may have to be taken if an equivalent certificate is not already held – full details, including application form, appear on the RYA website.

Appropriate health insurance may be a wise investment, while EU nationals should also carry a European Health Insurance Card which has replaced the E111. (see the Department of Health's leaflet Health Advice for Travellers, obtainable from post offices, travel agents or by telephoning ☎ 0800 555 777), which entitles one to free medical treatment under a reciprocal agreement with the National Health Service.

Climate and weather

The sailing season is from June through to September, but July and August are the best months when the sea has warmed up and the almost constant daylight, together with moderate and steady winds, provide good cruising conditions. The sea temperature at the junction of the Gulfs of Finland and Bothnia rises from about 6°C in May to 15°C in August, when it reaches some 17°C off St Petersburg and as much as 24°C amongst the islands of Sweden and Finland. The middle reaches of the Baltic, south of Gotland, are warmest in September at 14–15°C.

Mean air temperatures during June, July and August are around 20°C at both ends of the Baltic but can be much higher in sheltered waters and inland – take a swimsuit and T-shirts as well as oilskins and sweaters.

The average annual precipitation is roughly equivalent to that of East Anglia. Poor visibility is least likely to occur in summer – possibly one day in ten when there is less than 1M in the worst areas, which are at the entrance of the Baltic, around Gotland, The Gulf of Bothnia and a patch northwest of the Estonian island of Hiiumaa. Elsewhere, visibility of less than 1M occurs on about one day in twenty.

Winds tend to be moderate and gales rare. The overall tendency is for winds to be from south through to west, but they are fairly evenly distributed and the weather patterns are such that winds often become established for four or five days in the same direction.

Notwithstanding the above, which is based on meteorological data collected over a number of years, it is clear that weather patterns throughout the Baltic area appear to be less predictable than was the case a few decades ago. Extremes of winter cold are unlikely to affect the cruising yachtsman directly. The eastern Baltic countries of Finland, Russia, Estonia, Latvia, Lithuania and Poland can experience summer temperatures around 30°C.

Tides, currents and sea level

There is no appreciable tide within the Baltic, but prolonged winds in one direction and changes in atmospheric pressure can produce significant variations in depth. The datum of charts of the Baltic is generally mean sea level, not the lowest astronomical tide.

Because the Baltic collects more fresh water than evaporates from its surface there is a weak but steady surface outflow of low density, less saline, water through the Kattegat into the North Sea, partially balanced by a return flow of more saline water at a lower level. Within the Baltic surface currents are weak and tend to run towards Denmark, parallel to the associated coastline. Wind patterns can produce their own surface currents. Currents can flow in almost any direction, even upwind, since their direction is influenced not only by the wind but also by the shapes of the basins.

Following a blow which upsets sea levels, surface and submarine currents may be markedly different.

In extreme wind conditions, which are unlikely to occur in summer, surface currents of four knots and local sea level aberrations of 2m have been noted. This effect is particularly marked in the eastern end of the Gulf of Finland – notably in the shallow approaches to St Petersburg – and in the northern extremes of the Gulf of Bothnia. Long term prediction is not possible and the best course is to consider the effect of the weather pattern of the previous days on the surface of the water – and ask locally when in doubt.

The geodetic base (horizontal datum)

Caution Positions of lights and other marks given in this publication have been taken from a variety of sources and will not necessarily agree exactly with positions obtained from a GPS receiver. In particular, the position given beneath each harbour name is included purely to facilitate planning and is NOT intended as a waypoint.

Buoyage

The IALA System A has been adopted by all countries. In Finland and Sweden both cardinal and lateral buoys may not have topmarks, having to be identified by colour alone. This can present difficulties if sailing towards the sun and thus can be as strong a determinate of when to sail as tides in The Channel. In both countries transits are much used, most often a vertical yellow stripe against a red background – see photo page 239 – though sometimes a much less visible black and white. It should not be forgotten that in early season the harsh winter weather may have removed top marks or complete buoys.

Coastal navigation

Those more used to coastal sailing may be surprised at just how tiring the intricate navigation of Sweden and Finland's narrow inner passages can become, particularly for a small crew. Many couples find that, with one person steering and the other navigating, a short day – maybe only four to six hours – is often plenty.

In complex areas a supply of small removable adhesive markers (many favour little red arrows) enables one to keep track of one's position on the chart with ease. Each island looks much like its neighbour, as do the buoys on the chart, but with this simple tool one can, if distracted, find one's place again at a glance. Many navigation buoys are small by UK standards and a good pair of binoculars is essential.

Berthing systems and etiquette

Marina berthing in the Baltic differs from that in the UK and adjacent waters in a number of ways.

Firstly, few marinas or yacht harbours monitor VHF and, if contact is to be made with harbour officials before arrival, mobile phone is generally the best bet.

Secondly, a dedicated 'arrivals pontoon' is almost unknown and it is perfectly acceptable to enter any vacant berth. In some harbours a red or green marker at the head of each berth indicates whether the occupant is expected to return that day, but in the majority the skipper is expected to arrive, secure, check with the harbour staff, and then move if necessary.

The growing popularity of 'boating' is putting pressure on harbour space so that finger pontoons are often being installed in place of stern buoys. Where the latter still exist pick up is easier with the aid of a long handled metal hook available from most chandleries. Particularly in Sweden the fingers are most likely to be of the thin metal boom variety as pictured below. Although supported by a small float at the outer end they are not designed to bear the weight of a person. So enthusiastic crew jumping onto these booms will have a wet and possibly dangerous arrival! Locally available clips are the easiest way to secure to the small metal rings on these fingers.

Mooring in a 'box' may be more of a problem. In this case the berth is entered between two posts, to which the stern lines are secured – and which will often be no more than 3m apart. The posts are either wood or lengths of railway line covered with plastic pipe or, in some cases steel pipe filled with concrete. The first two have a degree of give and can sometimes be 'sprung' apart. The art is to judge the width of the gap in relation to that of the yacht, with

The 'split' pulpit and hook-on boarding ladder seen throughout the Baltic which greatly ease access from bows to mooring *A. Hammick*

A rocky foreshore on the coast East of Helsinki *E. Redfern*

fenders rigged but not over the side as this would make the boat even wider. Two stern lines – preferably of floating material – with large bowlines should be taken forward so that they can be passed over the poles on entering. Occasionally, in larger berths, a second set of posts will be provided amidships for springs. Many local yachts are built with wooden rubbing strakes, which allow passage between piles without damage to topsides, and if undertaking a major fit-out prior to an extended Baltic cruise it might be wise to consider following suit. (A cheap but practical alternative is to drape a heavy warp along the topsides when entering a narrow 'box'). In some marinas there is helpful width signage.

Having entered the berth the foredeck crew must get ashore smartly with the bow lines – no easy task for the less agile, particularly from a modern yacht with high freeboard and very probably a furling headsail in the way. For this reason a split pulpit is the norm in Scandinavian waters, often backed up by a removable bow ladder. With a little ingenuity it might be possible to adapt a conventional 'topsides' boarding or swimming ladder for the task, though it would still be necessary to clamber over the pulpit itself. A DIY or gardener's stool can ease subsequent landing and boarding.

Anchoring

Anchoring is generally less traumatic than berthing, and the idyllic anchorage with bow secured to a convenient rock – sometimes almost within touching distance – and an anchor out astern is almost a Baltic cliché. But do not forget to ease the bow lines and make up the stern line for a quiet night. Popular spots may already be equipped with rings if no trees are handy. Some yachtsmen advocate carrying a few climbers' pitons and a hammer but this practice causes damage and cannot be encouraged. A drum and roller fixed to the pushpit will ensure that the stern anchor rode, only part of which need be chain, feeds out smoothly. A single-piece anchor such as the Bruce is generally favoured, both for its holding power and as being easier to manhandle.

Practicalities

Fuel

Diesel fuel is readily available throughout the Baltic, other than in Kaliningrad. However a minority of yacht harbours do not yet have diesel pumps on site and a few 20 litre containers may prove useful. In Sweden many fuel points are either card or banknote (20 and/or 50 kronor) operated – instructions are generally given in English and German in addition to Swedish. Throughout the area fuel may sometimes have to be paid for in cash rather than by credit card – check the position before filling up. Tax-free fuel is not available. If leaving the UK with tax paid red diesel in their tanks skippers should carry receipts showing that tax has been paid. Red diesel should only be in the boat's tanks and not in cans.

Further details regarding individual harbours are included in the text.

Refuse disposal and holding tanks

Among the environmental protection measures specified by the Baltic Marine Environment Protection Commission (also known as the Helsinki Commission or HELCOM, www.helcom.fi) are strict rules forbidding the overboard disposal of refuse and controlling the discharge of sewage.

The former should present no problems, and the requirement for separation of refuse for disposal and recycling is commendable. In response, most yacht harbours have a number of clearly labelled bins.

Although not a legal requirement for visiting craft, in practical terms it is becoming increasingly difficult to exist without a holding tank capable of connection to a pump out system which is found in many harbours, often at the fuel berth. The rules are complex and changing but the discharge of sewage or 'black water' within a certain distance of the shore is now widely illegal. In some cases this is 12M but see individual countries for some information and check at your first port of call.

A rubbish collectin barge in Stockholm *skärgård P. & G. Price*

Bottled gas

Many yachtsmen have been heard to mutter that one subject the EU might usefully address would be the standardisation of bottled gas cylinders and connectors. Pending this it remains a problem if cruising in the area.

Most British yachts use butane, either *Camping Gaz* or *Calor Gas*. The former is sometimes available in northern latitudes where propane, which is stored at higher pressure and has a much lower freezing point, is standard. This higher pressure requires both a stronger cylinder and individual pressure release valve which is why it is dangerous to fill a butane bottle with propane. It should be noted that the familiar British rule that 'blue bottles = butane and orange bottles = propane' does not hold true around the Baltic where blue bottles are likely to contain propane. *Camping Gaz* is readily available in Germany and Denmark. Otherwise it is available in a few places i.e. Sweden – Kalmar and Stockholm, Finland – Helsinki, NJK Blekholmen and Latvia – Rīga.

Calor Gas is not available in either form outside the UK. Skippers of boats using *Calor* propane would be well advised to take sufficient supplies for the entire voyage as it is not legally possible for these bottles to be refilled elsewhere in the EU. If carrying more than one bottle then safe storage is essential to ensure that any leakage ventilates outside the vessel rather than into the bilges. It may be possible to refill propane bottles in Russia

The alternative to carrying extra bottles during a longer cruise in the Baltic is to purchase a local bottle and direct connecting regulator but to remember that refills can then only be obtained in that country of origin.

One way to conserve gas is to cook on an open fire whenever possible – the food often tastes better too! However do not light fires or portable barbecues on bare rock as this may crack and split and NEVER on grass where fire may spread. The best bet is on sand or pebbles. Alternatively in most marinas it will be possible to plug in an electric kettle or other appliance not exceeding 2kw. A pressure cooker will reduce fuel usage to a minimum.

Electricity

A 220 volt electricity supply is available in most yacht harbours throughout the Baltic. Many pontoons are now fitted with the familiar circular, blue, European standard connectors – older facilities generally have ordinary continental 2-pin plugs, though others may occasionally be met with. If correct polarity is vital to your system it is wise to have fitted a polarity metre and a short reversed polarity lead available.

It is advisable to carry a very long connecting cable, as some berths may be at a distance from the nearest socket. A residual current device (RCD) to trip the supply if any leakage occurs to earth – such as are sold for use in UK gardens – may provide an additional safety measure if the yacht is connected to an aged harbour circuit.

Chandlery

A well-found cruising yacht should, within reason, carry all necessary chandlery and spares aboard. However this is a council of perfection and if a specific item is needed there is an excellent chance of running it to earth. Not surprisingly, the best stocked yacht chandleries – the equal of any in Europe – are to be found in Finland and Sweden (including Gotland), closely followed by Germany and Denmark. Poland has well-stocked chandleries in Gdynia. In Estonia there are good chandleries at Pirita (Tallinn) and Pärnu as well as at Rīga, Latvia and Klaipėda, Lithuania. There are also several newly-established chandleries in St Petersburg. There is an increasing interest in yachting in Kaliningrad and they have their own sailing club so chandlery may be available.

Repairs and laying up

It would be invidious to recommend individual boatyards in a book which may still be in circulation a decade from now. When company names and contact details are given in the text this is purely to record their existence and should not be taken as any form of endorsement except where specifically stated.

Having said that, there are a great many excellent yards all around the Baltic, and current recommendations should be sought from marina managers or, preferably, yacht club personnel. As a rule prices tend to be higher in the west and north than in the south and east. Electrical storms are relatively common in the eastern Baltic, and electrical equipment should be unplugged if the yacht is to be left for any length of time. The only problems are the shortage of cradles for visiting yachts and the increasing pressure on space. Undercover storage is not necessary – most local boats are outside, some with masts up. But it is essential to make early enquiries and also to check with insurance companies in good time.

Radio communications and weather information

This information can be found in the Appendix at pages 363 and 365.

1. Germany

The provinces (*Länder*) of the Federal Republic of Germany have well-marked individual characteristics and strong local governments (in some ways a *Länd* can be considered as analogous to a State in the USA). Germany's Baltic coastline falls naturally into two parts – the former West German province of Schleswig-Holstein and the former East German province of Mecklenburg-Vorpommern. Neither has any dramatic physical feature, but each has considerable interest in other respects.

The western segment, from Flensburg to Travemünde, has excellent yachting centres. It is an agricultural country with scattered farms, hillocks, small valleys, lakes and estuaries leading to important ports such as Kiel and the historic and beautiful city of Lübeck.

The eastern part offers that slightly mysterious fascination of what was until relatively recently forbidden territory. Despite the tremendous rebuilding efforts since reunification, today's visitor will still encounter reminders of life as it was under communist rule but can also enjoy a countryside where wildlife has been left undisturbed. The coast has spits, bars and islands enclosing irregular inland seas known as Bodden, often backed by sand dunes planted with Norway spruce. There are a number of historically significant towns, each with its own character.

Economically, Schleswig-Holstein depends largely on agriculture and service industries, including the maintenance of a considerable volume of shipping in transit. The mainstays of Mecklenburg-Vorpommern are agriculture, fishing and tourism, together with shipbuilding at Rostock and Wismar. There is very little manufacturing industry apart from that associated with shipping. The tourist industry has been established since the end of the 19th century when the extensive beaches of the province became popular.

The cultural and economic differences between Schleswig-Holstein and Mecklenburg-Vorpommern are overlaid by the economic success of the former West German economy contrasted with the economic failure of the old East German system. However, these differences are steadily eroding as the benefits of reunification spread through the former East Germany.

Although English is widely used throughout the rest of Germany, especially among the business community, in Mecklenburg-Vorpommern, as a result of its isolation, relatively little English is spoken.

History

Schleswig-Holstein has been for centuries a no-man's-land between Denmark and greater Germany, and both parties have used force to establish their claims. It became a province of Prussia in the last part of the 19th century, but following a plebiscite after the First World War the border was changed and the northern part given to Denmark, an arrangement which left significant minorities on the wrong side of the border. Nevertheless, Schleswig-Holstein remained a political unit and, while it was part of the British zone of occupation after the Second World War, its status was changed to that of an autonomous German Länd.

In Mecklenburg-Vorpommern (Vorpommern is the remains of the former province of Pomerania, most of which now lies in Poland) there was a marked contrast between the development of the trading towns and that of the countryside. In the middle of the 13th century, the volume of trade and the dangers attending it led Wismar to join Rostock and Lübeck in a union designed to protect it from piracy on the lawless Baltic. From this the Hanseatic League emerged, to develop into one of the world's most powerful trading cartels. But neither the wealth nor the ideas behind the social development of the Hanseatic towns filtered outwards to the countryside and, up to 1918, Mecklenburg was the most backward part of Germany, with large estates whose owners forcibly repressed agricultural workers. Even after that date there was serious trouble between labourers and landowners, leading to the area becoming a centre of reaction and later a stronghold for Hitler's National Socialists. The large estates were eventually broken up in 1945 through legislation introduced when Mecklenburg was part of the USSR's zone of occupation but under communist rule there was little economic advance until after 1991 when East and West Germany were re-united.

Practicalities

Time

Germany uses UT+1 in winter and UT+2 in summer.

Money

Germany uses the Euro. Cash dispensers are widespread.

Shopping

The availability and choice of consumer goods in Schleswig-Holstein is as extensive as anywhere in Europe. The facilities in Mecklenburg-Vorpommern are not yet as highly developed, but are catching up rapidly and prices tend to be lower.

Most shops are closed on Saturday afternoons and on Sundays.

As prices throughout Germany are lower than in Scandinavia, yachts bound in that direction might well consider stocking up with non-perishable stores before leaving Germany. This applies particularly to beer, wines and spirits as these are expensive in Denmark and even more so in Sweden. (See page 110 for Swedish tax-free allowances).

Public holidays

Official public holidays in Germany include: 1 January, Good Friday, Easter Sunday and Monday, 1 May (Labour Day), Ascension Day (May), Whit Sunday and Monday (May or June), 3 October (German Unification Day), 24–26 December, 31 December. A number of regional holidays are also held.

Communications

Telephone communication facilities are excellent. To make an international call dial 00 followed by the country code, area code (omitting any initial 0) and number. The country code for Germany is 49. Phone boxes are mostly card-operated although some are dual card/cash. Phone cards are readily obtainable.

There is good mobile phone coverage and internet cafés are widely available. Wi-Fi is now installed at most larger marinas.

Travel

There are major airports serving the Baltic coast area at Hamburg, Lübeck and Berlin.

There are good train services throughout Germany and on to Poland, and excellent express coach services from London to Hamburg and Travemünde.

Ferry services operate on the following routes: Kiel – Klaipėda, Kiel – Oslo, Kiel – Göteborg, Puttgarden – Rødby; Travemünde – Trelleborg ; Travemünde – Helsinki; Travemünde – Rīga; Rostock – Gedser; Rostock – Trelleborg, Rostock – Helsinki, Rostock – Ventspils, Sassnitz/Mukran – Trelleborg; Sassnitz/Mukran – Baltysk, Sassnitz/Mukran – Klaipėda.

Holding tanks

These are required in all vessels over 10·5m LOA or 2·8m beam. Foreign vessels are exempt if only staying in Germany for one season.

1. GERMANY

Internet sites

www.germany-tourism.de – the homepage of the German National Tourist Office, with all the usual links, weather information etc. Includes pages on both Schleswig-Holstein and Mecklenburg-Vorpommern. English version.

www.visits-to-germany.com – a general tourist site, but with attractive graphics and much of interest. English version.

www.dwd.de – website of the German Meteorological Office.

www.bsh.de/ – the website of the German Hydrographic Office, including an (apparently complete) listing of German charts and official publications. Impeccable English version.

www.kiel-canal.de – website of the (commercial) United Canal Agency but with some history, webcams etc. English version.

www.luebeck-tourism.de – tourist guide to Travemünde and Lübeck, with full English translation.

www.all-in-all.com – an excellent site covering the Mecklenburg-Vorpommern region, with English translation and many useful links.

www.warnemuende.com – the Warnemünde/Rostock city homepage.

www.ycstr.de – homepage of the Yacht Club of Strelasund, in German only.

www.ruegen.de – a very useful website covering Rügen island, with links to many of its towns and villages. Full English translation.

www.peenemuende.de – homepage of the Peenemünde museum, in German only.

www.stettiner-haff.de – website of the Stettiner Haff (Zalew Szczeciński), in German only.

Formalities

EU citizens do not need visas, but passports must be held and British yachts should carry the usual registration papers. It is sensible for the skipper to have a Certificate of Competence (see page 8), although it would be unusual for this to be inspected. Appropriate radio licences should also be carried. (Note that a motor-sailing cone should also be available and displayed when appropriate, as failure to do so can lead to an immediate fine). Children under 15 are not permitted to steer a vessel in German waters.

Customs clearance is not necessary when coming from another EU country, unless non-EU nationals are aboard. There are customs clearance posts on the Baltic coast at Laboe (in Kieler Förde), Travemünde, Wismar, Warnemünde, Barhöft (on the west side of the northern arm of the Strelasund), Stralsund and Ueckermünde.

There should be no difficulty in keeping a VAT-paid yacht in Germany indefinitely. It does not matter in which country the VAT has been paid, but proof of payment is likely to be needed. Non EU-registered yachts can stay in the EU for a maximum of 18 months.

Customs enquiries ☏ +49 (0)351 44834 530
Email enquiries.english@zoll.de

The Germany Embassy in London is located at 23 Belgrave Square, London SW1X 8PZ ☏ 020 7824 1300 *Fax* 020 7824 1449
Email consularl@german-embassy.org.uk

The Consulate General (to which visa enquiries should be addressed) is round the corner at 1–6 Chesham Place, Belgrave Mews West, London SW1X 8PZ ☏ 020 7824 1463 *Fax* 020 7824 1449 *Email* pass@lond.diplo.de

The website for both is www.london.diplo.de/Vertretung/london/en/Startseite.html

The British Embassy is located in Berlin, at Wilhelmstrasse 70, 10117 Berlin ☏ +49 (0)30 204570
http://ukingermany.fco.gov.uk/en

There is also an Honorary Consul in Kiel at Maklerstrasse 11–14, 24159 Kiel ☏ +49 431 331971.

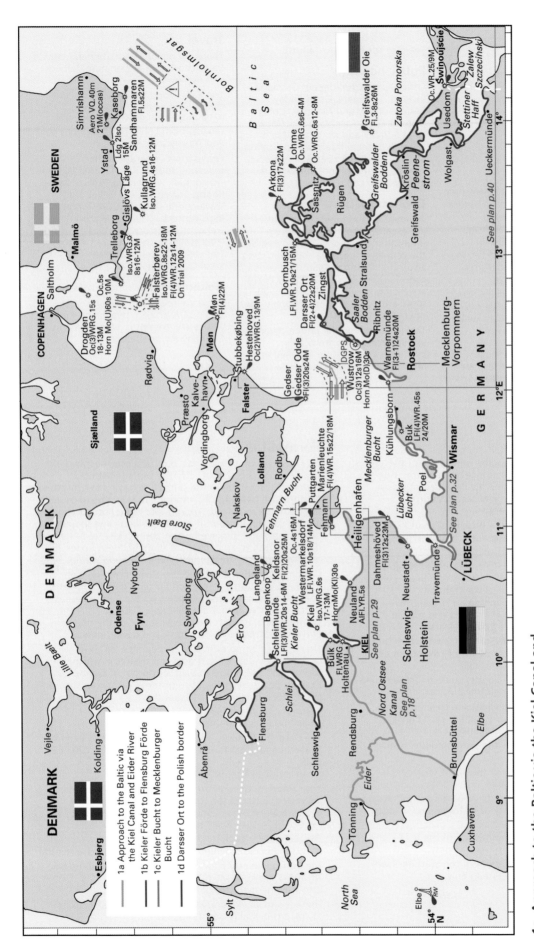

1a. **Approach to the Baltic via the Kiel Canal and the Eider river, 17**

1b. **Kieler Förde to Flensburg Förde, 23**

1c. **Kieler Bucht to Mecklenburger Bucht. 30**

1d. **Darsser Ort to the Polish border, 43**

Cruising

The cruising areas

The area between Flensburg and Kiel has well-developed yachting facilities. Flensburg and the Schlei are rewarding and will intrigue readers of the *Riddle of the Sands* as the area where the heroes of that classic spy story, Davies and Carruthers, began their adventure in the *Dulcibella*.

The coast east of Kiel is low-lying and well populated. Yachts aiming for the Mecklenburg area will sail past the mammoth Heiligenhafen yacht harbour before passing under the impressive Fehmarnsund bridge (clearance 23m, but winds from north or east can raise sea level by up to 1·5m) connecting Fehmarn island to the mainland. Those heading for southern Sweden will skirt the northern coast of Fehmarn. Neither route holds much of shore interest, but Travemünde and Lübeck are both extremely enjoyable places to visit.

East of Wismar the coast features hills and woods for some 6M but then flattens out. Further east it is again wooded between Warnemünde and the promontory of Darsser Ort. Inland lies the Mecklenburg lake district, densely wooded and boasting more than a thousand lakes. This unspoilt region is ideal for walking, cycling or indeed exploring by boat, via a system of shallow canals linking major lakes.

The coastline is low lying and seemingly featureless from seaward, but appearances are deceptive – immediately behind the tree-lined spits and sandbars forming much of this coast lie the Bodden – large unspoilt lagoons, often bordered by immense expanses of reeds, and remarkable for their birds, isolation, shoal waters and small fishing ports. Although being increasingly discovered by yachtsmen, they still have a special ambience derived from their isolation and the unsophisticated lives of the people who dwell in the villages and farms around their shores.

For navigation in the Bodden German charts (and perhaps one of the German pilot books) are necessary, and the small craft folios, which are increasingly available in electronic form as well as on paper, are clear and accurate.

Behind the coasts of Darss and Zingst lie three Bodden which may be entered from the eastern end: Barther, Bodstedter and Saaler. Dredged, buoyed channels 19m to 25m wide are maintained with depths of 3·2m up to Barth and 2·4m beyond (the offshoot to Prerow carries 2·1m, that to Wustrow 1·5m and that to Ribnitz 1·6m). But it must be remembered that, depending on the winds and atmospheric conditions, sea levels may change by as much as +2m to −1m.

The coastal islands of Hiddensee, Rügen and Usedom, with their long, wide, sandy beaches alternating with steep cliffs, are fast becoming a popular but far from overcrowded holiday area – secluded fishing villages and breeding grounds for swans, geese and other wild birds are still to be found.

Behind the western and northern coasts of Rügen is another area of Bodden which can be entered from the north or the south, with depths of 3m in the dredged channels, but very shoal and sometimes stony outside them.

At the southern tip of Hiddensee lies the entrance to the Strelasund, the buoyed channel which separates the island of Rügen from the mainland. Just inside the entrance is a major breeding ground for wild geese and swans, which may be seen in their thousands.

The clearly-marked channel winds past the small yacht and fishing harbour of Barhöft (where the SAR vessel is stationed now that its former harbour at Darsser Ort is closed) to the charming town of Stralsund, which is undergoing considerable restoration and is also an excellent shopping centre. The double lifting road and rail bridge, the Ziegelgrabenbrücke, leads through to the Strelasund south, which meanders through marshes and meadows to Stahlbrode and Palmer Ort where the comparatively deep (8m) Greifswalder Bodden begins.

The small islands of Ruden and Greifswalder Oie lie off the eastern entrance of the Greifswalder Bodden, the shores of which hide a number of small harbours tucked into inlets.

To the south the Peenestrom, a well-buoyed, landlocked channel, leads through green countryside past Peenemünde (of wartime V1 and V2 fame) and inside the island of Usedom. There are two opening bridges, at Wolgast and Zecherin, to negotiate on the way. The opening times of these bridges appear to vary from year to year, but can be obtained from the harbour office at Stralsund or the harbourmasters of most of the smaller ports in the area. Dredged depths are 6m as far as Wolgast and 2·5m beyond. South of Wolgast, on the east side of the Peenestrom lies the Achterwasser, an extensive area of water with several small attractive harbours.

The seaward side of Usedom, from Peenemünde to the approaches to Świnoujście, is generally low – less than 60m – and featureless, with no harbours. The best marks are the churches of Zinnowitz, Heringsdorf and Ahlbeck (the border lies about 1·5M southeast of Ahlbeck church).

At the southern end of the Peenestrom yachts emerge into a large inland sea known as the Stettiner Haff in German or the Zalew Szczeciński in Polish. It is an attractive and sheltered cruising area with 3m to 5m depths. It is crossed by a string of yellow buoys marking the border with Poland.

Yacht services and chandlery

Mooring fees are considerably lower than in the UK, and in ports with few facilities there may well be no charges at all for overnight mooring.

Berthing will generally be in one of three forms, most commonly the 'box' (see *Berthing systems and etiquette*, page 9), which can prove problematical for a beamy yacht and for the single-handed. (The suspension of a couple of fattish ropes of the right length along the upper topsides will prevent many a scrape in short-handed yachts). Other possibilities

Charts and chart packs

Admiralty charts, or their German equivalents, are excellent for yachts on passage. However for more leisurely cruising, and particularly to explore the area between Darsser Ort and the Polish border, three series of chart packs are available – the Sportschiffahrtskarten 3000 series published by the German Hydrographic Office, the NV series and the *Sportbootkarten* series, published by Delius Klasing. Both are also sold digitally.

The German Hydrographic Office (BSH) *Sportschiffahrtskarten 3000 Series* covers all of the German Baltic Coast but the sets for Rugen (3006), the Peenestrom and Stettiner Haf (3007) and the Zalew Szczecinski and Szczecin (3020) are particularly useful.

There are two excellent series of chart packs (size A2) which are readily available in Denmark. They are published annually and come with electronic versions on CD and complementary piot books.

The Nautische Veröffentlichung series:
Serie 1 Fünen – Kiel
Serie 2 Lübeck – Bornholm – Kopenhagen
Serie 4 Rügen – Bodengewässer – Stettin
Serie 6 Poland – Litauen – Lettland
NOK Nord-Ostsee Kanal. A chart (A2) of the Kiel Canal.

The Delius Klasing *Sportbootkarten* series:
Satz 1: Kieler Bucht, Mecklenburger Bucht, Schlei – 12 charts and 78 harbour plans covering the coast as far east as Warnemünde.

Satz 2: Mecklenburg, Vorpommern, Bornholm – 10 charts and 85 harbour plans covering the coast from Darsser Ort to the Polish border.

The advantages of the series type of chart are that one pack covers a large area and many harbour plans are included. However some people find the combination of large-scale and small size somewhat inconvenient and prefer to use normal charts.

Pilots and cruising guides

In English
The Baltic Pilot Volumes I and II (NP 18 and 19) are useful for reference, but they are not ideally suited to the needs of the yachtsman.
Imray/Cruising Association *Cruising Almanac*. Imray Laurie Norie & Wilson Ltd. This has very limited coverage of German Baltic ports.
Brian Navin's *Cruising Guide to Germany and Denmark*, published by Imray Laurie Norie & Wilson Ltd in 2006 (3rd edition) is useful.

In German
There are several pilot books available in German covering the Baltic coast, including:
Ostseeküste Travemünde bis Flensburg by Jan Werner published by Delius Klasing as companion to their Satz 1 chart series, and *Ostseeküste Travemünde bis Stettin* by Jan Werner published by Delius Klasing as companion to their Satz 2 chart series.
Der NV Hafenlotse, Volumes 1 and 4, published by Nautische Veröffentlichung (complements Serie 1 and 4 of their charts).
Sejlerens Marina Guide Volume 4, Ostsee, Nordsee, Elbe and Weser revised annually and available free at Marina offices.
Hafenhandbuch Vols Ostsee 1 and Mecklenburg-Vorpommern und Polen published by Delius Klasing.
See the *Appendix*, page 361, for sources.

are bows-to with the stern secured to a buoy, alongside a jetty or, in recently-built marinas, against a finger pontoon. The concept of visitors' berths is uncommon, and a temporarily vacant berth will usually be indicated by a green plaque at its head. A red one indicates that it is reserved and that its owner will soon be returning. VHF communication with marinas is no longer permitted so that any queries about berthing or facilities must be conducted over the telephone.

In Schleswig-Holstein yachts are well provided for. Chandlery, fuel and bottled gas (including *Camping Gaz*) are readily available.

In Mecklenburg-Vorpommern facilities are less well developed, but are improving fast. Obtaining fuel and bottled gas is no longer a problem. Chandlery is available in the major harbours.

Radio communications and weather information

The coast has continuous VHF coast radio station coverage, the stations being remotely controlled from Bremen. VHF Channels are Flensburg 27, Kiel 23, Lübeck 24, Rostock 60 and Arkona 66. Weather forecasts in slow German are issued on these channels at 0745, 0945, 1245, 1645 and 1945 LT. Vital navigational warnings are broadcast on VHF Ch 16 every Hour and H+30 until cancelled.

NAVTEX is perhaps the best and most reliable method of receiving weather information in English. See Appendix on page 371.

The website of the German Weather service dwd.de gives forecasts and charts under 'boating'. It also has a useful 3-day forecast for winds and wave heights.

Marina Offices are another good source of weather forecasts.

Fehmarnsund bridge at sunrise *B. Sheffield*

1a. Approach to the Baltic via the Kiel Canal and the Eider river

The Kiel Canal

The Nord-Ostsee Kanal, also known as the Kiel Canal, is one of the major routes from the North Sea into the Baltic, and is a formidable feat of engineering. Built so that the German fleet could move between the Baltic and the North Sea without having to pass through the Kattegat, it was opened in 1895. It is just over 53M (98·5km) long with a minimum bridge clearance of 39·6m (130ft). It is very wide, and dredged to 11m. Near Rendsburg, roughly halfway along the canal, is one of the last remaining transporter bridges in the world. Its moving section passes across the canal at a height of 12m.

There are two pairs of locks at each end – the western at Brunsbüttel, at the entrance from the Elbe, and the eastern at Holtenau (a suburb of Kiel) where the canal enters Kiel Hafen. At Brunsbüttel yachts are usually directed to the southern lock, and at Holtenau to the northern lock, except in winter.

If approaching from the west, the waiting area is to the southeast of the moles (see plan), where one can secure to one of the two posts, or simply drift around until able to enter. Contact should be made with the lock on VHF Ch 13 (Callsign *Kiel Kanal 1*). A confusing array of lights may be displayed from the locks, but the various combinations of green and white can be ignored as applying only to shipping. Those relevant to yachts are: fixed red = no entry; white over red = prepare to enter; fixed white = yachts may enter. A loudspeaker also instructs yachts regarding entry. Traffic messages for east-going vessels are broadcast on VHF Ch 02 at H+15 and H+45, and for west-going vessels on VHF Ch 03 at H+20 and H+50.

In the locks, mooring is to floating wooden staging with freeboard of only a few centimetres, so fenders need to be touching the water (a small covered tyre which does not float is invaluable). The rise and fall is very small at both ends and there is no turbulence – indeed, it is generally not even possible to distinguish whether the lock is being filled or emptied.

It is essential to keep well clear of commercial shipping whilst in the canal, generally by keeping to the starboard side. Even so it is wise to keep well clear of the bank, as passing ships can create a great deal of wash which may even ground a yacht. A good watch should also be kept for the many ferries which cross the canal along its length, and have right of way over yachts. Should three vertical red lights be seen all yachts should keep to starboard and stop, usually to allow a large vessel to pass.

1. GERMANY

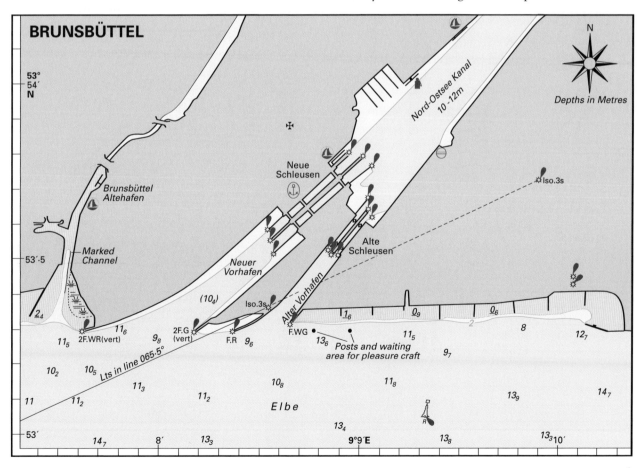

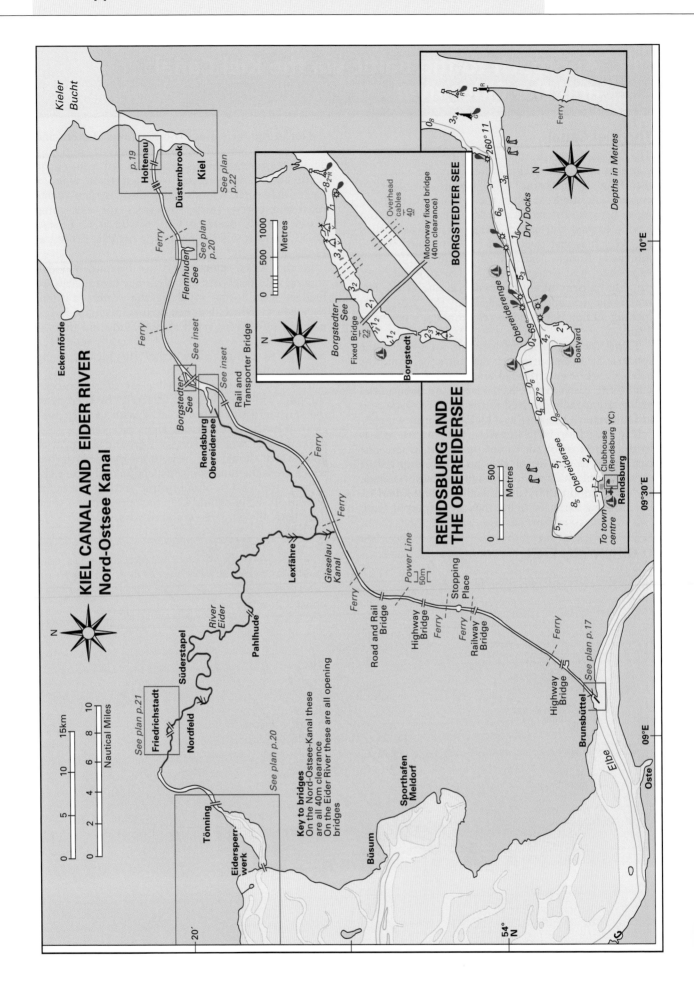

KIEL CANAL AND EIDER RIVER
Nord-Ostsee Kanal

Kieler Bucht

Eckernförde

Kiel

Düsternbrook

p.19 Holtenau

See plan p.22

Ferry

Flemhuder See

See plan p.20

Ferry

See inset

Rail and Transporter Bridge

Borgstedter See

Rendsburg
Obereidersee

See inset

Ferry

River Eider

Süderstapel

Pahlhude

Lexfähre

Gieselau Kanal

Ferry

Ferry

See plan p.21

Friedrichstadt

Nordfeld

See plan p.20

Tönning

Eidersperr-werk

Key to bridges
On the Nord-Ostsee-Kanal these are all 40m clearance
On the Eider River these are all opening bridges

Sporthafen Meldorf

Büsum

Road and Rail Bridge

Power Line

Highway Bridge

Stopping Place

Ferry

Railway Bridge

Highway Bridge

Brunsbüttel

See plan p.17

Ferry

Elbe

Oste

RENDSBURG AND THE OBEREIDERSEE

Borgstedter See

Overhead cables 40

Motorway fixed bridge (40m clearance)

BORGSTEDTER SEE

Borgstedter See

Fixed Bridge 22

Borgstedt

Metres
0   500   1000

Depths in Metres

Dry Docks

Boatyard

Obereiderenge

260° 11

87°

69°

Obereidersee

Clubhouse (Rendsburg YC)

Rendsburg

To town centre

Metres
0   500

15km
0   5   10   15km
Nautical Miles
0   2   4   6   8   10

20´

54° N

09°E

09°30´E

10°E

The modest canal dues are payable at the Holtenau (eastern) end, at the harbour office on the central island before the yacht leaves the lock. Charts can be bought at Holtenau at Kapitän Stegmann's office which is on the south side of the locks. Unfortunately it is forbidden to traverse the canal on foot across the locks so that it is necessary to moor alongside the quay at Tiessenkai just east of the locks and walk back to the foot ferry.

Although the canal can be traversed in one day at a speed of five knots (the maximum speed is 8·1 knots or 15km/h), it is quite an effort to do so as hand-steering is required throughout. Lightly-crewed yachts may well find it more pleasurable and practical to make an overnight stop (see below). Motorsailing is permitted, providing a speed of at least 3·25 knots (6km/h) is maintained. Sailing only and tacking are not permitted. If opting to motorsail, the regulation downward-pointing cone must be displayed.

Yachts are not permitted to proceed through the canal between sunset and sunrise or in bad visibility, and will not be locked in unless there is time to reach one of the authorized mooring places, marked by yellow buoys. Lockmasters will provide details of the latest permitted mooring places. If intending to spread the passage over two days the best place to lie overnight is probably the yacht harbour at Rendsburg, about 1·5M inside the entrance to the Obereidersee at Km66 (35·6M) from Brunsbüttel, 17·4M from Holtenau). The yacht harbour is at the head of the bight, near the Rendsburg Yacht Club (www.regatta-verein-rendsburg.de) and convenient for the town centre and mainline station. It has good facilities including fresh water, fuel, a restaurant, food shops and a chandlery. Another attractive spot is in the entrance to the Flemhuder See at Km 85·5 (48M and 7M respectively) where an anchorage carrying about 2·5m depth is marked out by four yellow buoys. Other permitted places include

Sharing the Kiel Canal *J. Parkinson*

The Holtenau locks at the east end of the Kiel Canal
J. Parkinson

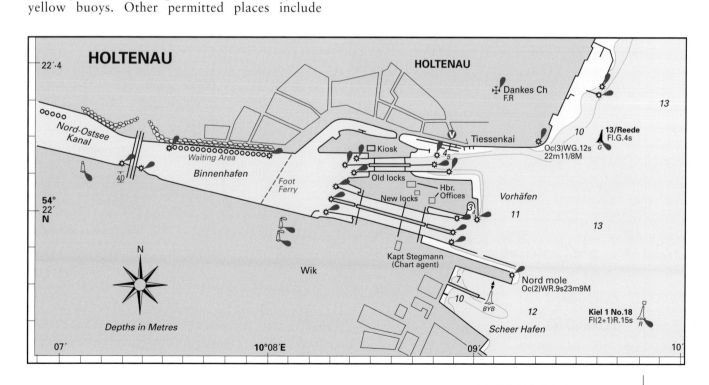

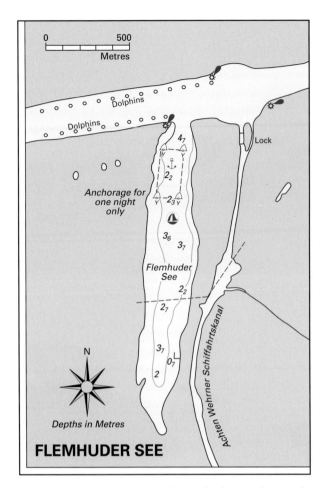

0 500
Metres

Dolphins
Dolphins

Lock

4₇
2₂
Anchorage for one night only
2₃
3₆
3₇
Flemhuder See
2₂
2₇
3₇
0₇
2

Achten Wehrner Schiffahrtskanal

N

Depths in Metres

FLEMHUDER SEE

Transporter bridge near Rendsburg *J. Parkinson*

Approach to the Baltic via the Eider River

The slow-flowing and meandering River Eider is an alternative mast-up route to the Baltic for those with time to spare. However it does not by-pass the Kiel Canal entirely as one has to join the Kiel Canal just past the 40km mark via the mile-long Gieselau Kanal. However it is a very attractive route and enables one to visit the interesting towns of Tönning and Friedrichstadt. It is 85M from the entrance to the river to Holtenau as opposed to 54M from Brunsbüttel to Holtenau. There are four locks and four opening bridges and apart from the Eidersperrwerk lock, which is manned continuously, they are not manned at night and only at set times on Sundays and public holidays. The river is tidal as far as the lock at Nordfeldt.

It is 21M from Helgoland to the Eider River Landfall buoy at 55°14'·5N 08°27'·6E and from

Brunsbüttel either just inside the locks on the north side but this is rather noisy or 1km further east on the same side in more rural surroundings but with no facilities. (Between the two is a fuel berth for yachts). Other places are Dückerswisch Siding at 20·5km, Oldenbüttel Siding at 40·5km and the Borgstedter See with entrances at 67·5 and 70kms. Another possibility is the entrance to the Gieselau Kanal on the waiting pontoon just before the lock at 40·5Kms.

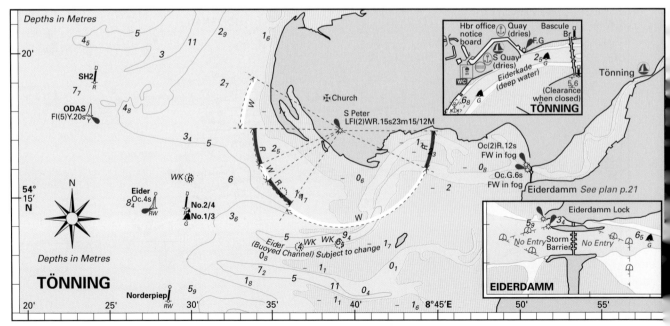

Depths in Metres

TÖNNING

EIDERDAMM

Eiderdamm *See plan p.21*

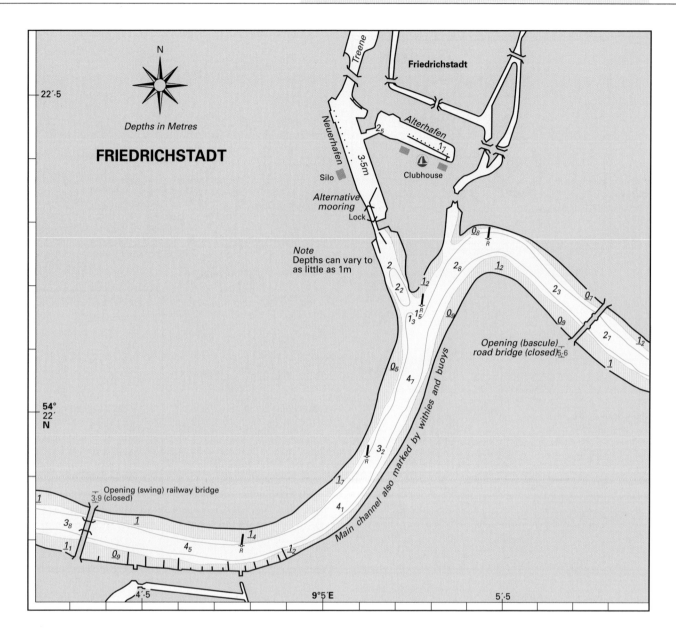

there another 16M along the shallow buoyed channel to the lock at Eidersperrwerk. ☏ +49 4833 45350, VHF Ch 14. There is a waiting basin on the seaward side and a quay on the landward side of the lock. The lock does not operate after HW+0230 as the sluices are then opened and there is a 2–5 knot current to seaward.

It is essential to arrange to tackle the buoyed approach channel during the second half of the flood and to avoid the route altogether in strong onshore winds because of the bar (1·5–3m). HW at Eidersperrwerk is HW Helgoland +0120.

Once through the Eidersperrwerk lock it is another 5M to Tönning by unlit buoyed channel but if it is getting late there is a good anchorage in the river just out of the channel north of Red Buoy No. 66.

Tönning

This is an attractive old fishing town and berthing is possible alongside in the river. The quays in the inner harbour channel mostly dry at LW. Basic facilities but no fuel berth.

Friedrichstadt

This town was built by the Dutch when they were brought in to sort out the drainage problems of the area in the 17th century. Consequently the town has a very Dutch appearance with a network of canals, bridges and gabled houses. Berth in the Neuerhafen in 3m or the Alterhafen in 1·7m by going through the lock but the approach to the lock can carry as little as 1m at LW. Basic facilities.

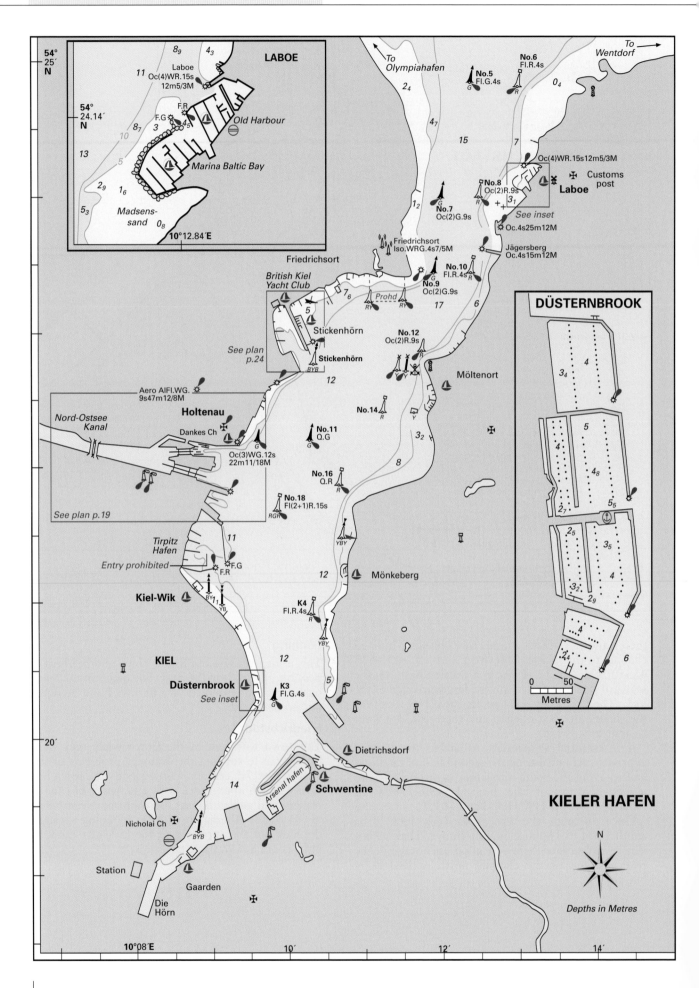

LABOE

54° 25′ N

Laboe
Oc(4)WR.15s
12m5/3M

54° 24.14′ N

F.R

F.G

Old Harbour

Marina Baltic Bay

Madsenssand

10°12.84′E

To Olympiahafen

To Wentdorf

No.5 Fl.G.4s

No.6 Fl.R.4s

Oc(4)WR.15s12m5/3M

No.8 Oc(2)R.9s

Laboe

Customs post

Oc.4s25m12M

Jägersberg Oc.4s15m12M

No.7 Oc(2)G.9s

Friedrichsort Iso.WRG.4s7/5M

No.10 Fl.R.4s

No.9 Oc(2)G.9s

Prohd

Friedrichsort

British Kiel Yacht Club

Stickenhörn

Stickenhörn

See plan p.24

No.12 Oc(2)R.9s

Möltenort

DÜSTERNBROOK

Aero AlFl.WG. 9s47m12/8M

Holtenau

Nord-Ostsee Kanal

Dankes Ch

Oc(3)WG.12s 22m11/18M

No.11 Q.G

No.14 R

No.16 Q.R

No.18 Fl(2+1)R.15s

See plan p.19

Tirpitz Hafen

Entry prohibited

Kiel-Wik

Mönkeberg

K4 Fl.R.4s

KIEL

Düsternbrook
See inset

K3 Fl.G.4s

KIELER HAFEN

Nicholai Ch

Station

Gaarden

Die Hörn

Dietrichsdorf

Arsenal hafen

Schwentine

N

Depths in Metres

0   50
Metres

1b. Kieler Förde to Flensburg Förde

Kieler Förde including Kiel

54°21'N 10°10'E

Distances (from Kiel)
Heiligenhafen 35M, The Schlei 25M, Flensburg Förde 50M, Travemünde 65M, Gislövs Läge 130M, Copenhagen 145M, Stubbekøbing 85M

Charts
UKHO 2113, 2341, 2344, 2469
German 30, 32, 33, 34

Lights
1215 **Kiel light tower** 54°30'N 10°16'·5E
Iso.WRG.6s29m17–13M 071°-R-088°-W-091·3°-G-148·5°-W-220°-R-246·5°-W-295°-R-358°-W-025·5°-G-056° Horn Mo(KI)30s Racon Red round tower, white band on grey base 33m. Floodlit

1230 **Friedrichsort** 54°23'·4N 10°11'·6E Iso.WRG.32m7–5M
171·5°-G-196°-W-202° 209°-R-224°-W-280°-G-300°-W-032°-G-090° + F.Y. 019°-vis-039° 188°-vis-209° + F.W.6M 202°-vis-209° White round tower, green bands on gallery and base 32m. Floodlit

The marina breakwater south head, 1M southwest, is also lit

1248 **Scheerhafen** (Holtenauer Schleusen, S side)
54°21'·8N 10°09'·1E Oc(2)WR.9s23m9M
159°-R-192°-W-214°-R-288°-W-003° Red beacon, white band, grey lantern, masonry base 20m

1246 **Nord-Ostsee Kanal** (Holtenauer Schleusen, N side)
54°22'·2N 10°09'·2E Oc(3)WG.12s22m11/8M
217°-G-224°-W-270°-G-354°-G(unintens)-012°-W(unintens)-039° Red round tower 20m

Harbour communications
Port Office ① +49 4319 011173, *VHF* Ch 11 (0730–1600 LT),) +49 1716 497373 (outside office hours)
www.port-of-kiel.de
Kieler Förde/Kiel Canal Vessel Traffic Service
① +49 4313 603456 *VHF* Ch 22

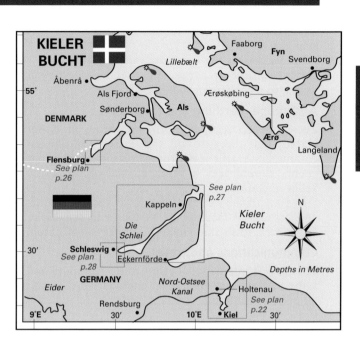

General

Kieler Förde is the approach to Kieler Hafen, a Solent-like area with Kiel, a major naval base, a commercial port and easily the largest yachting centre in the Baltic, at its head. Holtenau, the eastern end of the Kiel Canal, lies on the western side of Kieler Hafen, and there are numerous yacht harbours around its shores.

Kiel has a superb shopping centre – modern, busy and with great variety. For yachts entering the Baltic it is an excellent place to store ship for the whole Baltic cruise or to have repairs carried out and, having first-class travel facilities, it is an ideal place for crew changes.

Approach

Approach waypoints:
From north or northwest 54°30'N 10°15'E
From east or northeast 54°28'N 10°20'E

It should be noted that there are military firing ranges between Kieler Förde and Heiligenhafen. They are likely to be in use on weekdays, but not at weekends. When in use AlFl.YR.5s lights are shown on towers on the shore at 54°26'N 10°19'E and

54°23'N 10°56'E and at five other locations in between. Range control boats are stationed at the east and west ends of the range in use to intercept yachts and pass instructions to them on VHF Ch 16. A situation broadcast by Todendorf Naval Coastal Radio Station is broadcast at 0730, 1100, and 1530 LT Monday–Friday (and exceptionally at 0730 and 1100 on Saturdays) on VHF Ch 11 announced five minutes beforehand on VHF Ch 16.

Major landmarks at the entrance to Kieler Förde are the Kiel light tower and (in daylight) the impressive German Navy war memorial just north of Laboe. The förde is very well buoyed throughout, but there is a large area of shoal water extending from the shore near the naval war memorial. Friedrichsort light 1230 is a prominent landmark when approaching the British Kiel Yacht Club at Stickenhörn. The entrance to the canal is about 1M further south.

The port-hand of the two Kieler Bucht light structures, marking the Baltic approach to Kiel *A. and A. Fleck*

Formalities

Yachts arriving from the North Sea will, if necessary, already have cleared customs at Cuxhaven or Brunsbüttel. Those coming from Scandinavia or the Baltic do not normally require clearance, but it is available at Laboe.

For yachts leaving Germany, outward clearance is also obtainable at Laboe, but is only necessary if sailing to a country outside the EU.

Anchorage, berthing and facilities

There are no restrictions on anchoring in Kieler Hafen, but because of the heavy volume of commercial traffic it is strongly recommended that yachts should seek a berth at one of the many yacht harbours.

In view of the extensive choice of yacht harbours and associated facilities to be found in the Kieler Förde area, this section merely highlights a selection.

Communications and travel

The nearest international airports are Hamburg and Lübeck. There are good train and coach services to all parts of Europe.

Tiessenkai at Holtenau

54°22'N 10°09'E

Tiessenkai is a small yacht harbour on the north bank immediately outside the Holtenau entrance to the canal. Mooring is mostly rafted alongside staging. Although there are few facilities apart from two small chandleries, there are a couple of restaurants near the quay in Holtenau, outside the lock gates, and this is a convenient place from which to prospect the canal. Customs post. The chart agent, Kapitän Stegmann, is to be found on the south side of the Holtenau locks (see under Holtenau in the section on the Kiel Canal) in a small trading estate, together with Elna, a marine electronics company. Water and electricity available and showers with a key from the lockmaster.

The British Kiel Yacht Club *J. Parkinson*

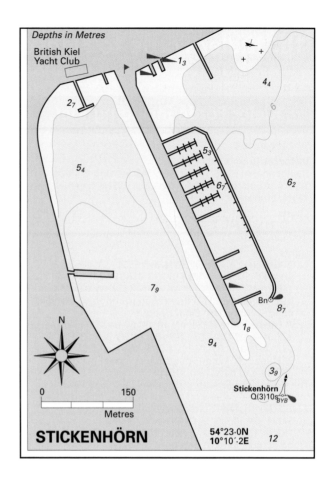

STICKENHÖRN

British Kiel Yacht Club (BKYC)

54°23'N 10°10'E

Many British yachts (other nationalities are also welcome) are likely to berth at the British Kiel Yacht Club at Stickenhörn. The BKYC is a British Combined Services establishment, situated adjacent to a German naval air station

If intending to stay at the BKYC it is best to call Sailtrain on VHF Ch 06 well before arrival to ask for instructions, ℡ +49 431 398833 or *Email* jettyman@bkyc.de www.bkyc.de. Turn into the

harbour leaving Stickenhörn east cardinal buoy to starboard – the BKYC is at the far end. Berthing on the T-shaped jetty is bow- or stern-to with long lines to posts in large boxes.

Water and electricity are available on the jetty and there are showers and toilets in the clubhouse, together with a bar and a cafeteria. Weather forecasts are posted daily on the BKYC notice board and there is a well-equipped boatyard nearby.

Shopping is not easy, but a supermarket and other shops for everyday supplies, banks and restaurants can be found in Friedrichsort, about 20 minutes' walk away. On the other hand it is pleasant to take one of the frequent ferries from Friedrichsort pier to wherever one wishes to visit in the fjord. *Camping Gaz* can be purchased from some petrol stations in the vicinity of the BKYC and fuel is obtainable at Laboe.

Düsternbrook

54°20'N 10°09'E
Situated about 1·5M south of the canal entrance.
Düsternbrook Sporthafen ✆ + 49 4312 6048 40
www.sporthafen-kiel.de

This is the nearest harbour to the excellent shopping centre of Kiel, which can be reached on foot via the promenade and the Oslokai. Constructed for the 1938 Olympics, it has 288 berths in 2–4m and all normal marina facilities including Wi-Fi. It is a good base from which to stock up or change crews. Large yachts berth in the northernmost basin. The Kieler Yacht Club ✆ + 49 4431 85021 www.kyc.de, has its headquarters on the other side of the main road and welcomes visiting yachtsmen. There is a very large and well-stocked chandlery in Kiel town centre.

Laboe

54°24'N 10°13'E

Laboe is a pleasant small town with an old fishing and yacht harbour ✆ +49 4343 427556 and a new Marina Baltic Bay ✆ +49 4343 421151 built immediately south of it on the eastern side of Kieler Förde. Beware the frequent ferry traffic from the inner side of the outer mole of the old harbour. It is best not to round the molehead too closely. It is a convenient place to obtain fuel. Customs and immigrations services are available (see *Formalities* above) as well as a boatbuilder and sailmaker. Laboe is the closest place from which to visit the conspicuous U-Boat Memorial.

Strande

54°26'N 10°10'E
Strande ✆ +49 4349 8988, (0800–1200 and 1600–1800 LT), is situated on the western side of Kieler Förde, about 4M north of Holtenau. Like Laboe, it is a good place to obtain fuel as well as being worth considering in its own right as a pleasant first or last night stop in the Baltic. Good bathing beach. Close by is the Olympiahafen marina ✆ +49 4313 71021, *Mobile* +49 172 8024352 built for the 1972 Sailing Olympics. It has all facilities.

General

This lovely fjord forms the boundary between Germany and Denmark and in fact the boundary line runs along the middle of the shipping channel in such a way that the porthand buoys are in Germany and the starboardhand ones are in Denmark. There are numerous small towns, harbours and opportunities for anchoring along its shores and at its head is the attractive city of Flensburg nearly 28M from the open sea.

Flensburg *J. Parkinson*

Approach

Approach waypoints:
From north and northeast 54°50'·5N 10°07'E
From south and southeast 54°45'N 10°05'E
From these waypoints appropriate courses lead to Kalkgrund Lt which is left to port and from there a westerly course leads to the start of the channel buoys which eventually lead to Flensburg.

Berth

The nearest marina to the city is the privately run Stadthafen which has box berths for 168 yachts. It can be very crowded but sometimes one is able to berth in the middle of the marina on the jetty

reserved for fishing boats in which case one pays the dues to the fishermen and not to the marina office. Depths are 4m on the outside but only 1m at the inside berths. However, depths at Flensburg can increase up to 4m in prolonged easterly gales and reduce by up to 2m in similar conditions from the west. There are other marinas nearby and one can usually find a berth somewhere but this may necessitate motoring round to look for an empty space with a green plaque at its head. On the west shore of the harbour are the Watersports Club marina (WSV Galwik), the Niro-Petersen marina and opposite the Stadthafen is a small marina for traditional yachts while tall ships berth at the quay just to the north of them.

Facilities

The Stadthafen has water/electricity on the jetties and showers/toilets near the office. There is a restaurant and laundry. All other services are available somewhere.

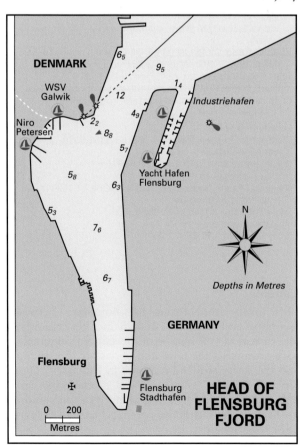

Die Schlei

54°40'·27N 10°02'·2E (Entrance)

Distances
Flensburg 35M, Sønderborg 20M, Eckernförde 19M, Kiel 22M, Marstal 22M

Charts
German Small Craft Chart Set 3003
Danish 195

Lights
N Mole Hd 54°40'·3N 10°02'·2E LFl(3)WR.20s14m14M
White round tower, black band
Ldg Lts 107·5 *Front* 54°40'·4N 10°02'E Oc.W.4s6m9M
White mast Rear 90m from front Oc.W.4s8m9M White Mast

Harbour communications
Schleimünde Marina ✆ +49 4642 4972
Mobile +49 172 721 5366
www.schleimuende-hafen.de
Maasholm Marina ✆ +49 4642 6571
www.maasolm.de
Kappeln Stadthafen ✆ +49 04642 1830
www.kappeln.de
Kappeln Yachtzentrum ✆ +49 4642 1563
Mobile +49 170 451 7172
www.yachtzentrum-kappeln.de
Arnis Wassersportgemeinschaft ✆ +49 4642 4421
www.wsg-arnis.de
Lindaunis Marina ✆ +49 4641 7317
www.camping-lindaunis.de
Brodersby Marina ✆ +49 4622 2188
www.marina brodersby.de
Schleswig Wiking Yachthafen ✆ +49 4621 35666
www.wiking-yachthafen.de
Schleswig Stadthafen ✆ +49 4621 8010
www.schleswiger-stadtwerke.de

General

This beautiful fjord is 20M long and offers sheltered sailing in lovely surroundings. There are many choices of marina, some urban, some with yachtyard facilities and some in very rural surroundings with few facilities. All tastes are catered for within short distances. And there are many anchoring

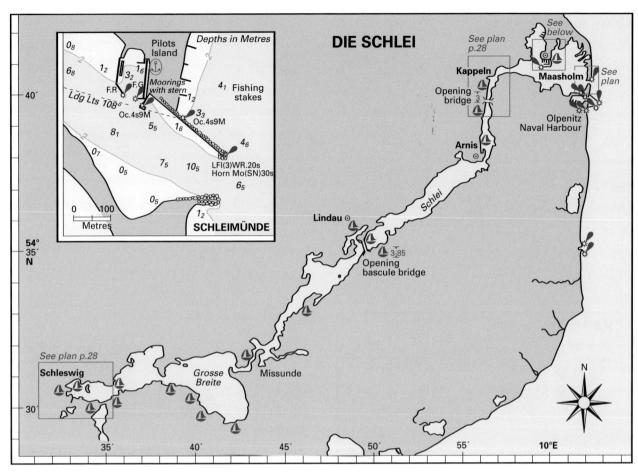

DIE SCHLEI

Depths in Metres

Pilots Island

F.R F.G Moorings with stern

Ldg Lts 108°

Oc.4s9M

Fishing stakes

Oc.4s9M

LFl(3)WR.20s
Horn Mo(SN)30s

Metres

SCHLEIMÜNDE

Kappeln

Opening bridge

Arnis

Schlei

Lindau

Opening bascule bridge

See plan p.28

Schleswig

Grosse Breite

Missunde

See plan p.28

See below

Maasholm

See plan

Olpenitz Naval Harbour

opportunities out of the buoyed channel but depths must be closely watched as there is much shallow water and depths can vary suddenly and unpredictably (see below).

Depending on wind conditions there may be quite strong currents up to four knots in the narrows in extreme conditions and depths and clearances can also be affected by 1–2m. This can make berthing problematical in some places.

There is a double road and rail bridge at Kappeln (closed clearance 3·3m). It opens 15 minutes before every hour from 0545 to 2145 (April–October). The electric cables just north of Kappeln have a clearance of 26m. And there is another lifting bridge at Lindaunis. which opens on request. In Germany and Denmark vessels fly international code flag 'N' in the rigging to indicate that they are waiting for a bridge to open.

Approach

Approach waypoint 54°40′N 10°03′·5E

The approach is straightforward on 287° from the Schlei landfall RW buoy Oc.4s at 54°40′·05N 10°03′·4E and follow the buoyed channel through the narrow entrance between the piers. The channel is dredged to 5m. Do not confuse the entrance to the Schlei with the more prominent entrance to the Olpenitz naval harbour, to which entrance is forbidden, 0·75M further south.

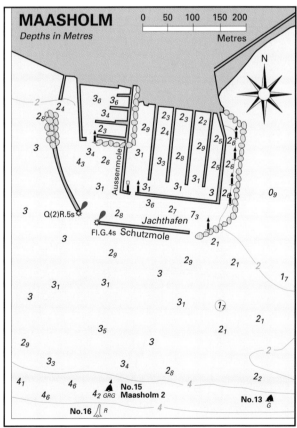

MAASHOLM
Depths in Metres

Metres

Aussenmole

Q(2)R.5s

Fl.G.4s Schutzmole

Jachthafen

No.15
GRG Maasholm 2

No.16 R

No.13
G

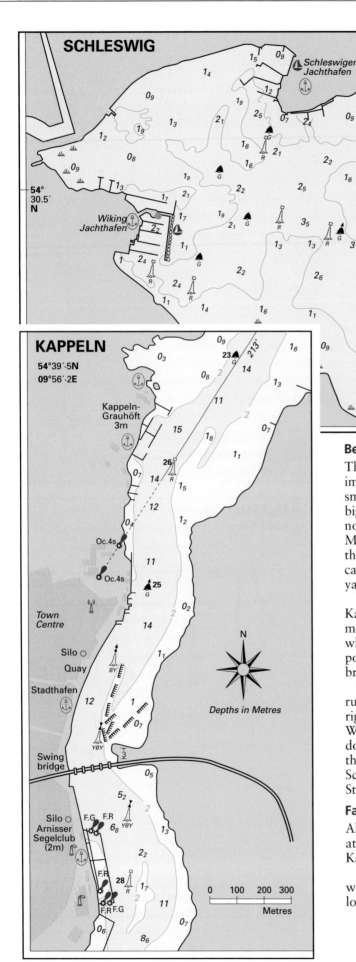

SCHLESWIG

KAPPELN

54°39′·5N
09°56′·2E

Depths in Metres

Berthing

The first of many marinas is at Schleimünde immediately inside the northern entrance mole. It is small and has basic facilities but no shops. A much bigger marina with all facilities and again on the northern side is 1·5M from the entrance at Maasholm. Berth in box berths in the *yachthafen* on the starboard side of the entrance or larger yachts can berth on the outside of the southern jetty of the yacht basin. Fuel berth.

The first major town on the passage up-river is Kappeln which has a big choice of marinas but the most convenient berth for visitors is the Stadthafen where one berths in box berths with bow to a pontoon on the west side of the river just before the bridge. It has basic facilities and a fuel berth closeby.

Upriver of Kappeln the scenery becomes more rural but continues to have a big choice of marinas right up to Schleswig where the main marina is the Wiking Yachthafen which has all facilities. It is dominated by a huge octagonal apartment block. On the north side of the river at Schleswig is the Schleswiger Yachthafen and the much smaller Stadthafen further east.

Facilities

All the marinas have basic facilities but several are attached to yacht yards such as the Yachtzentrum at Kappeln.

Schleswig has an interesting Viking Centre as it was from here that the Vikings used to haul their longships overland to the North Sea.

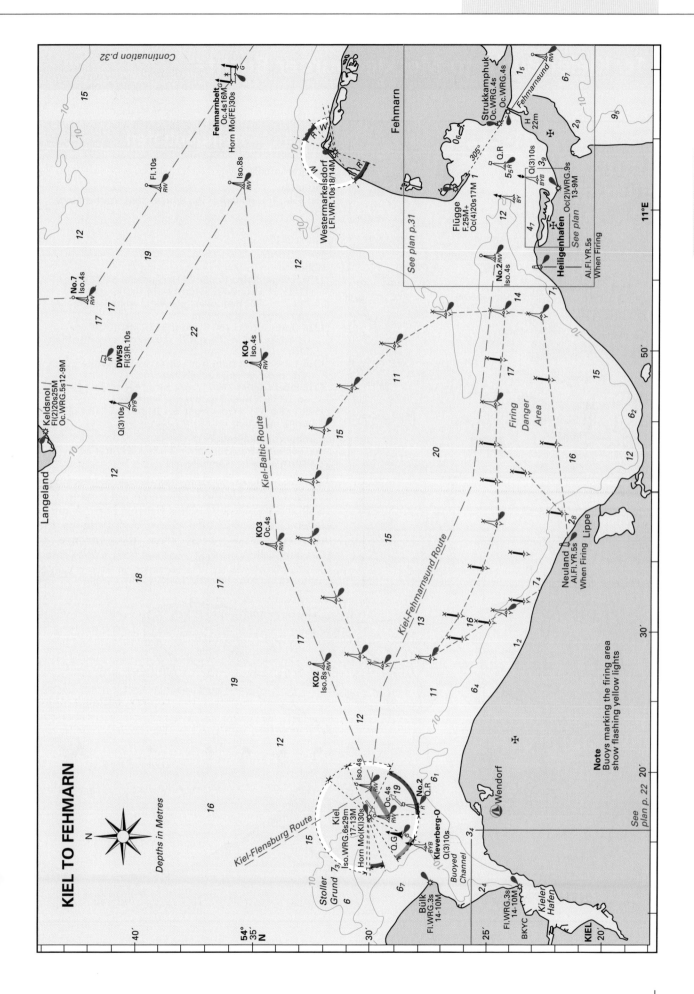

KIEL TO FEHMARN

N

Depths in Metres

54° 35' N

Continuation p.32

Fehmarnbelt Oc.4s16M
Horn Mo(FE)30s

Fl.10s
RW

Westermarkelsdorf
LFl.WR.10s18/14M

Strukkamphuk Oc.WRG.4s
Oc.WRG.4s

Fehmarn

See plan p.31

Flügge
F.25M+
Oc(4)20s17M

Q.R
5R
5R
BY
Q(3)10s
3g
BYB

Heiligenhafen Oc(2)WRG.9s
13·9M
See plan

Al.Fl.YR.5s
When Firing

Fehmarnsund

Iso.8s
RW

No.7 Iso.4s
RW

DW58
R
Fl(3)R.10s

No.2 Iso.4s
RW

KO4 Iso.4s
RW

Keldsnol
Fl(2)20s25M
Oc.WRG.5s12·9M

Q(3)10s
BYB

Langeland

Kiel-Baltic Route

KO3 Oc.4s
RW

Firing
Danger
Area

Neuland Al.Fl.YR.5s
When Firing
Lippe

Kiel-Fehmarnsund Route

KO2 Iso.8s
RW

Wendorf

Note
Buoys marking the firing area
show flashing yellow lights

See
plan p. 22

Kiel-Flensburg Route

Iso.4s
RW

Kiel
Iso.WRG.6s29m
17·13M
Horn Mo(KI)30s

Oc.4s
RW

No.2 Q.R
R

Q.G
G
BYB

Kleverberg-O
Q(3)10s
Buoyed
Channel

Stoller
Grund

Büik
Fl.WRG.3s
14·10M

Fl.WRG.3s
14·10M
BKYC

Kieler
Hafen

KIEL

11°E

1c. Kieler Bucht to Mecklenburger Bucht

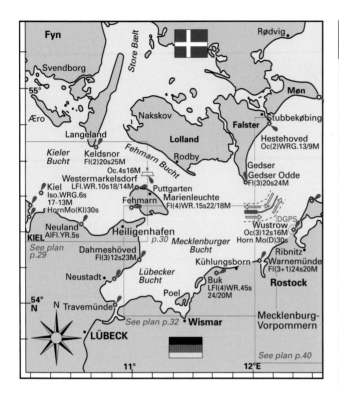

Heiligenhafen

54°23'N 11°00'E

Distances
Kiel 35M, Travemünde 33M, Wismar 38M, Warnemünde 43M

Charts
UKHO 2117
German 43, 31

Lights
1328 **Heiligenhafen** (S side of Heiligreede) 54°22'·2N 11°01'·2E Oc(2)WRG.9s16m13–9M 100°-G-206°-W-212·2°-R-250° Red tower, platform, white lantern, red and white dwelling 13m
1336 Outer Ldg Lts 268·5° *Front* 54°22'·4N 10°59'·6E Oc.4s13m17M White g with red border on white mast 11m
1336·1 *Rear* 312m from front Oc.4s19m17M White v with red border on grey warehouse
1329 Inner Ldg Lts 279·2° *Front* 54°22'·6N 10°59'·1E Iso.3s13m17M Red g on white mast 14m
1329·1 *Rear* 195m from front, Iso.3s13m17M Red v on white mast 16m

Harbour communications
Heiligenhafen Harbourmaster ① +49 4362 5034 24
www.marina-heiligenhafen.de

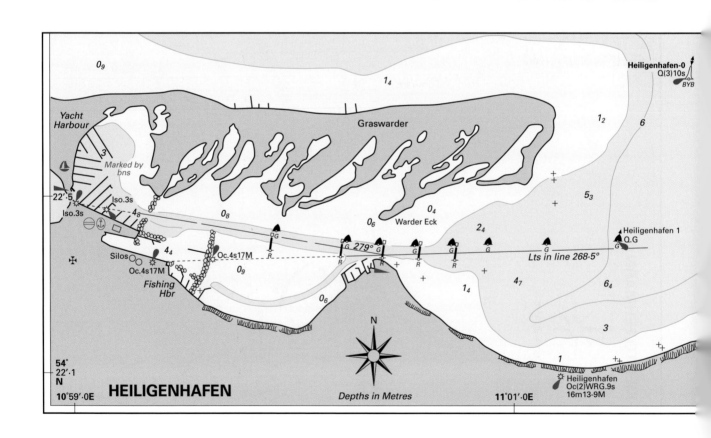

General

See note regarding Firing Ranges under Kieler Förde on page 23–4.

Heiligenhafen is a major yacht and fishing harbour strategically placed for yachtsmen making eastwards from Kieler Förde. In strong northeasterly conditions the approach may become unpleasant, and in these circumstances it may be preferable to seek a harbour on Fehmarn Island such as Orth (54°27′N 11°03′E) or Burgtiefe (54°25′N 11°12′E) and Burgstaaken (54°25′N 11°11′E) in the Burger See to the east of Fehmarnsund bridge.

Approach and entrance

Approach waypoint 54°24′N 11°03′E

Approach is made in the white sector of Heiligenhafen light on a bearing of approximately 210° to pick up the outer leading lights in the vicinity of Heiligenhafen No. 1 buoy. By day a useful guide to the entrance is the 134m radar tower about a mile south-southwest of Heiligenhafen light. By night this tower has red lights. After following the outer leading lights for about 0·7M the inner leading lights will be picked up.

Anchorage and berthing

It is possible to anchor off Heiligenhafen light in five or 6m in suitable conditions but most yachts will wish to continue to the main yacht harbour. Alternatively it may be possible to find an alongside berth in the old harbour to the south of the yacht harbour.

Formalities

The harbourmaster's office is between the yacht harbour and old harbour.

Facilities

Heiligenhafen is a small holiday town with all shopping facilities convenient to the harbour, where a full range of services are available for yachts. Wi-Fi. There is a fuel berth in the marina.

Communications and travel

Being a holiday resort, and on the way to Fehmarn Island, it would be possible to reach Kiel or Lübeck by coach.

Fehmarnsund

This is the channel between the island of Fehmarn and the mainland. It is crossed by a combined rail and road bridge with a clearance of 23m. but this can vary by up to 2m depending on wind conditions. Clearance is indicated at water level on each side of the bridge. There are sometimes currents up to four knots if there have been persistent strong winds from the east or west.

The approach from the west is wide and straightforward but from the east the channel is very narrow and closely buoyed. It carries a depth of 5m.

Lights
From West:
1288 **Flügge** 54°26′·5N 11°01′E Oc(4)W.20s38m17M Red octagonal tower with white bands and red dwelling
1300 **Fehmarnsund Bridge** 54°27′·17N 11°06′·17E Oc.WRG.4s23m8–5M 074·5°-G-086°-W-094°-R-108°
From East:
1288 Ldg Lts 305°
Front **Strukkamphuk** 54°24′·6N 11°05′·7E Iso.WR.3s7m White round tower
Rear **Flügge** 3·3M from front F.W.37m25M Red octagonal tower with white bands and red dwelling. Intense light on Ldg Line

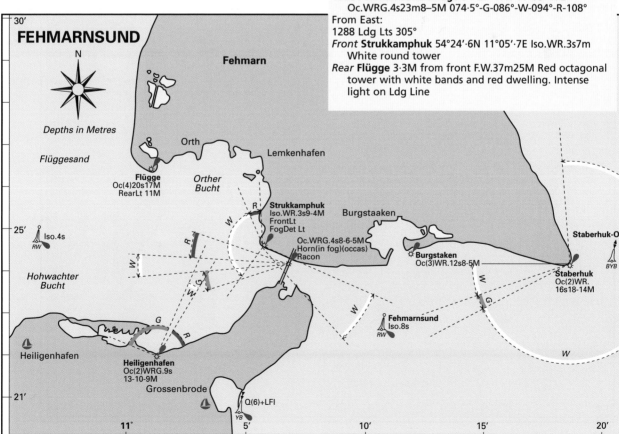

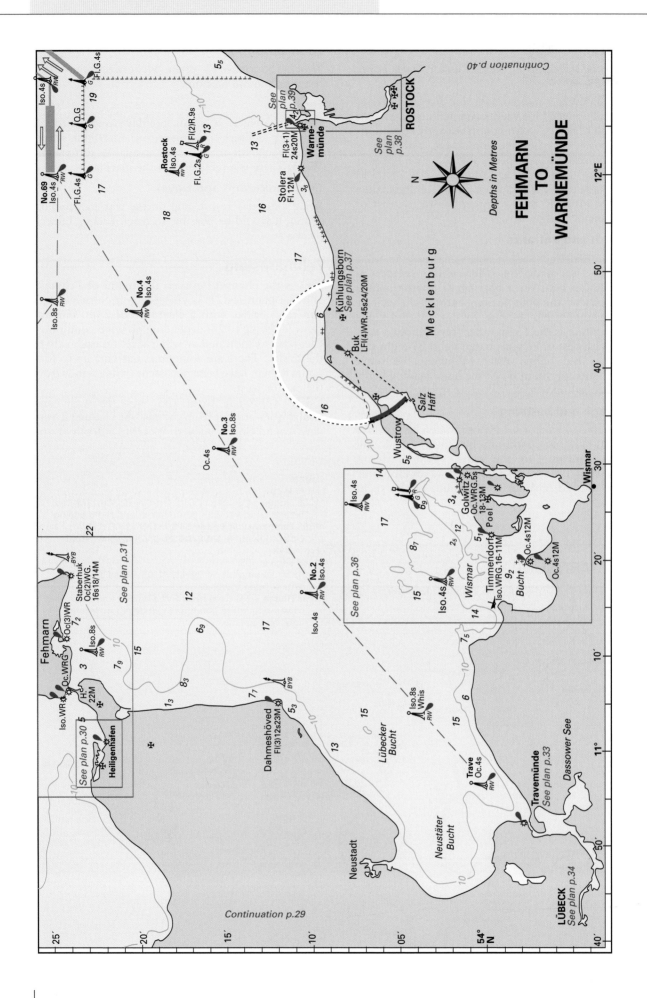

FEHMARN
TO
WARNEMÜNDE

Depths in Metres

Travemünde (including Lübeck)

53°57'N 10°47'E

Distances (to Travemünde)
Kiel 65M, Heiligenhafen 35M, Wismar 25M

Charts
UKHO 2117, 2354, 2355
German 36, 37, 35, 51, 52

Lights
1360 **Travemünde** (Hochhaus) 53°57'·8N 10°53'E
Fl.WR.4s114m19/15M 165°-R-214°-W-234°-R-245°
Building 118m
1370 **Priwall Ldg Lts 215·9°** *Front* 53°57'·5N 10°53'·2E
Oc(2)9s14m17M White ▲ with red border on white
mast 13m
1370·1 *Rear* 380m from front Oc(2)9s24m17M
White ▼ with red border on white framework tower
21m
1362 **North molehead** 53°57'·8N 10°53'·4E
Oc.RG.4s10m6/5M+F.Y in fog 123°-R-201°-G-066°
White tower, black bands with glass bricks 9m Floodlit

Harbour communications
Travemünde Port Authority ☎ +49 4502 74362
VHF Ch 16, 19
Travemünde/Lübeck Vessel Traffic Service ☎ +49 4502
84750 *VHF* Ch 13 (broadcasts every three hours from
0600–2100 LT)
Trave Bridge (Herrenbrüke) *VHF* Ch 13
Lübeck Hubbrucken VHF Ch 18
Passathafen Marina ☎ +49 4502 6396
Böbs Werft Marina ☎ +49 4502 5051
www.boebs-werft.de
Marina Baltica ☎ +49 4502 86010
www.marina-baltica.de

General

Travemünde is the outer port for Lübeck. It is a
holiday resort and a busy ferry and commercial port
with three major yacht harbours. Its shopping centre
is adequate though not extensive. Travemünde is an
ideal base from which to visit Lübeck by public
transport.

Approach

Approach waypoint 54°05'N 11°03'E

The most prominent landmark is a 37-floor tower
block (with Travemünde light on the top)
immediately north of the harbour entrance, visible
from a considerable distance out to sea.

The fairway leading into the harbour is well
buoyed, with powerful leading lights on a bearing of
216°. The frequent arrivals and departures of ferries
also serve to indicate the harbour entrance.

Anchorage

Anchoring outside the entrance to the Trave is
unwise because of the many large rocks left over
from the ice age and anchoring in the river is
impracticable because of the heavy commercial
traffic but it is possible in the Potenitzer Wiek or in
the Dassower See. Higher up the river there are
various bays on the south side and at Silk on the
north after the river curves westward.

Berthing

There are three major yacht harbours – the
Passathafen, immediately to port on entry behind the
permanently-moored square-rigger *Passat*, or the
Marina Baltica and adjacent Böbs Werft marina,
both about half a mile further in on the starboard
hand. All carry depths of up to 7m.

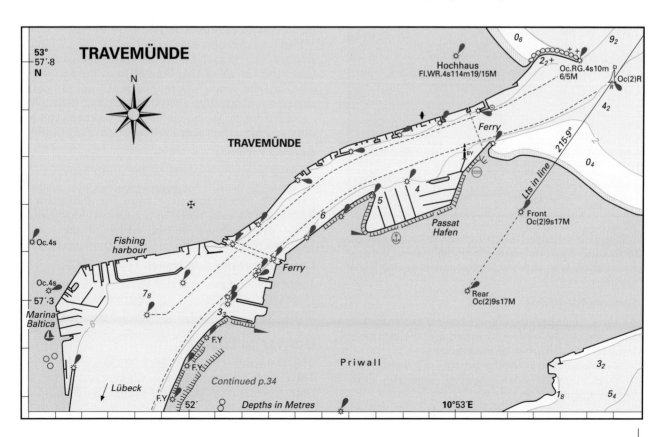

Continued p.34

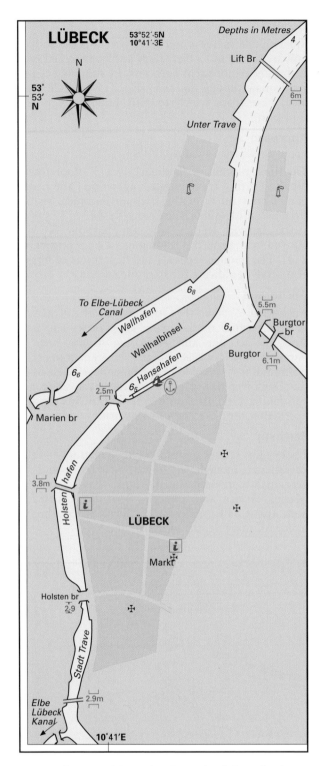

Historic ship harbour at Lübeck *M. Stroebel*

Hansa Marina at Lübeck *M. Stroebel*

It is also possible to berth in the fishing harbour, to starboard just before reaching the Marina Baltica, where there is a more traditional ambience but fewer facilities.

Services for yachts

All three yacht harbours have excellent facilities. The Passathafen has Wi-Fi and is perhaps slightly more attractive visually, but all are efficient.

There is a crane at the Passathafen if it is necessary to step the mast after emerging from the Elbe-Lübeck Canal.

Marina Baltica can accommodate yachts up to 30m length and 5m draught. It has boat-building facilities with engineers and onshore storage.

Fuel can be obtained at either of two bunker stations, one on each side of the river close to the car ferry, and *Camping Gaz* bought from the hardware store in the town centre. There is no full-scale chandlery shop, but there are several boatyards equipped for most repairs. Weather forecasts can be obtained from the yacht harbours or Lübeck Radio.

General facilities

There is a shopping centre on the north bank, about 10 minutes' walk from Marina Baltica and a short ferry ride across the river from the Passathafen. Banks, restaurants, hotels and a tourist information office will be found in the centre of the town. Customs post.

Communications and travel

There are good bus and rail services to Lübeck and Hamburg, where there are international airports. Ferries to Trelleborg, Helsinki and Rīga.

Upriver to Lübeck

The Hanseatic city of Lübeck, 11M up the River Trave from Travemünde, is easily reached by bus or train from Travemünde, and should not be missed.

The city has a population of 200,000 and it is full of historic buildings which have been painstakingly restored and maintained following the bomb damage of the Second World War. There is also an interesting historic-ship harbour, the Hansahafen, where a number of carefully preserved old ships lie.

If it is decided to visit by boat, the surroundings are pleasant as far as the marinas at Herreninsel and Schlutup, about halfway to Lübeck. From there the river becomes increasingly industrialized, but it is possible to get close to the centre of the city and berth in the southern corner of the Hansahafen where there is a small marina with basic facilities either alongside at the quay or on the pontoon.

Wismar

53°54′N 11°26′E

Distances
Travemünde 25M, Warnemünde 35M

Charts
UKHO 2217, 2359
German 1641

Lights
1386 **Timmendorf** 53°59′·5N 11°22′·6E
Iso.WRG.6s21m16–11M 049°-W-054·5-G-073°-W-079°-R-125°-G-135°-W-137°-R-196°-G-202·5°-W-211·5°-R-220° White round tower, red and brown top, white lantern, red cupola, with white dwelling 21m
1398 **Gollwitz N** 54°01′·4N 11°28′E
Iso.WRG.4s13m19·14M 162·3°-G-164·5°-W-166°-R168·3° White tower with red and green lantern on white building
1382 **Hohen Wieschendorf** Ldg Lts 180·3° Front 53°57′·6N 11°20′E Oc.4s20m15M White lattice mast 16m
1382·1 *Rear* 1500m from front Oc.4s39m16M White v with red surround on white lattice mast 21m
1387·8 **Walfisch** Ldg Lts 123·9° Front 53°56′·7N 11°25′·1E Oc(2)9s10m7M Red and white g on white tubular metal mast 10m
1387·9 *Rear* 1·35M from front, Oc(2)9s30m7M Red and white tubular metal mast 30m
1392 **Wismar** Ldg Lts 149·9° Front 53°54′N 11°27′·1E Oc.R.4s28m12M Framework tower on promontory on west side of harbour 26m
1392·1 *Rear* 700m from front Oc.R.4s46m12M Framework tower 43m

Harbour communications
Harbour Office ☏ +49 3841 4520 (0700–1530 Monday–Friday, 0800–1200 LT Saturday) Outside office hours ☏ +49 3841 2510
Wismar Vessel Traffic Service VHF Ch 12 (broadcasts on VHF Ch 12 every 3hrs from 0630–2130 LT in German or English on request)
Wismar Alten Hafen ☏ +49 3851 441327
Wismar Westhafen ☏ +49 3841 389005
Mobile +49 1624 20355 www.westhafen.net
Wismar Brunkowkai ☏ +49 3841 441327

General
Wismar, a historic town of some 60,000 inhabitants, is principally engaged in shipbuilding and repairs. The old town has remarkable baroque and Gothic architecture and the Alte Markt is a reminder of the greatness of the Hanseatic League. It is one of the largest squares in Germany, with many gabled houses including the 'Alte Schwede', built in 1380

though taking its name from the pub opened there in the late 19th century, a reminder that Wismar belonged to Sweden in the 17th and 18th centuries. The old town has a preservation order and much restoration has been carried out, though of the medieval fortifications only the Wassertor and bits of the town wall remain. The church of St Nicholas and the museum in the Schabbel-haus are worth visiting.

An attraction of Wismar from the yachtsman's viewpoint is that one naturally berths within easy walking distance of the centre of this small (by comparison with Lübeck and Rostock) and memorable town although in 2008 extensive redevelopment was about to take place on the land between the Alten Hafen and the Brunkowkai which will make those berths noisy for some time into the future.

From Wismar, ships of the 'White Fleet' (Weisse Flotte) take an hour to run to the island of Poel, which is popular for its beaches. Poel also has a museum illustrating the island.

Schwerin, on the edge of the Mecklenburg Lake District, is some 30km by rail from Wismar. Its castle, inspired by Chateau Chambord, was the seat of the Dukes of Mecklenburg until they were thrown out in 1918 – it is both amazingly grand and unsatisfactorily dull, though its gardens and orangery are pleasant enough. Outside the town, Schweriner See is, at 65km², the largest of many lakes which contribute to a pretty countryside.

Approach
Approach waypoints:
From north or east 54°05′N 11°26′·6E (Grossestief)
From west 54°02′·5N 11°18′E (Offentief)

The Grossestief channel is entered about 3M north of the island of Poel on about 165° (in the white sector of Gollwitz N light) before swinging west at the second pair of channel buoys on to 230° south of Hannibal Shoal. Thereafter the channel is marked by buoys and leading lights.

An alternative approach, from the Offentief landfall buoy with about 5m depth, crosses between the Hannibal and Lieps shoals northwest of Timmendorf light. It is marked by a pair of unlit buoys and is in a white sector of Timmendorf light.

The mooring on the north side of the south jetty at Kirchdorf *J. Parkinson*

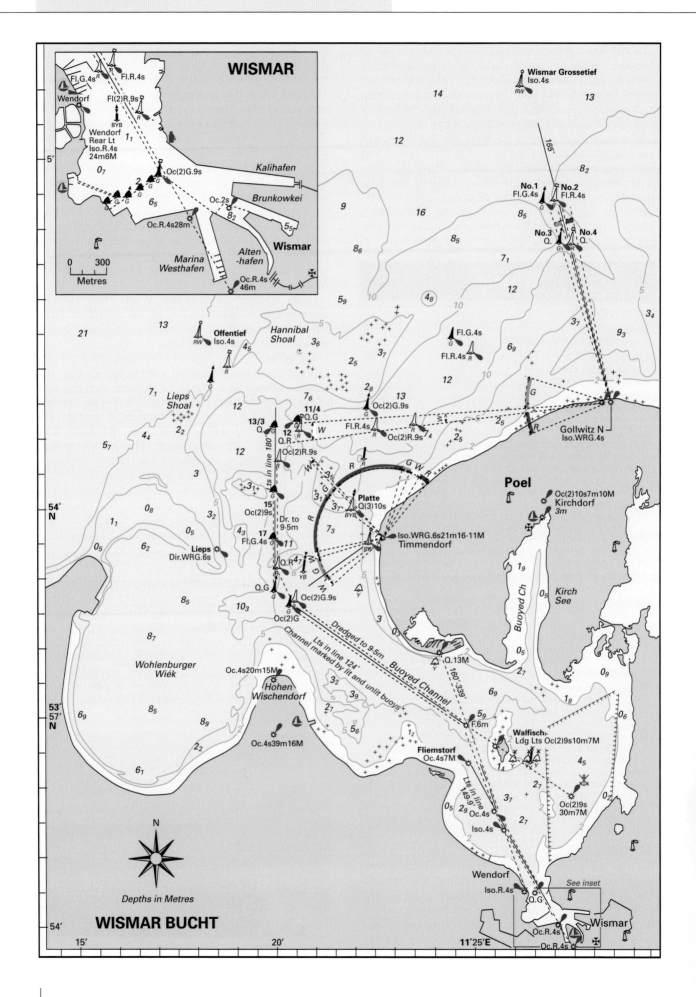

WISMAR

Fl.G.4s   Fl.R.4s
Wendorf   Fl(2)R.9s
BYB
Wendorf
Rear Lt
Iso.R.4s
24m6M
0₇
Oc(2)G.9s
Kalihafen
Brunkowkei
Oc.2s
Oc.R.4s28m
8₂
5₅
Wismar
Marina   Alten-
Westhafen   hafen
Oc.R.4s
46m

0   300
Metres

Wismar Grossetief
Iso.4s
RW

14   13

12

8₂

No.1   No.2
Fl.G.4s   Fl.R.4s

9   16
8₅
8₅   No.3   No.4
8₆   Q.   Q.
7₁
12
5₉   10   4₈   10   3₇   9₃

21   13   Offentief
RW   Iso.4s
4₅   Hannibal
Shoal   3₆   Fl.G.4s
Fl.R.4s   6₉
Lieps   2₅   3₇
Shoal   7₆   2₈   13
7₁   11/4   Oc(2)G.9s
12   PQ.G   W   12   10
13/3   12   Fl.R.4s
Q.   Q.R   Oc(2)R.9s 7₄   2₅
Oc(2)R.9s   2₅   2
4₄   2₂   R   R   G   W   R
5₇   12   15   R   3₅   G W R
3   Oc(2)9s   G   3₇   Platte   Poel   Oc(2)10s7m10M
0₈   3₂   Dr. to   7₃   Q(3)10s   Kirchdorf
54°   9.5m   BYB   3m
N   1₁   17   Iso.WRG.6s21m16-11M
0₅   Fl.G.4s 11   Q.R   Timmendorf   1₉
Lieps   4₃   YB   Kirch
6₂   Dir.WRG.6s   Q.G   See
0₅   Oc(2)G.9s   0₅
8₅   Oc(2)G   Buoyed Ch   0₅
10₃   0₅   2₇
8₇   Dredged to 9.5m Buoyed Channel   3   0₉
Channel marked by lit and unlit buoys   Q.13M   6₉   1₈
Wohlenburger   Lts in line 124°   Y
Wiék   Oc.4s20m15M   3₂   5₉   0₆
Hohen   3₉   Walfisch
8₅   Wischendorf   2₇   Ldg Lts Oc(2)9s10m7M
6₉   8₉   5₆   1₂   4₅
2₂   Oc.4s39m16M   Fliemstorf   2₇
6₁   Oc.4s7M   Lts in line   Oc(2)9s
49.9°   30m7M
0₅   2₉   Oc.4s   3₇
Iso.4s

N   Wendorf
Iso.R.4s   See inset
Q.G   Wismar
Depths in Metres   Oc.R.4s
Oc.R.4s

WISMAR BUCHT

165°
160°-339°
F.6m

Anchorage

Anchor outside the shipping channel with appropriate warning signals as there is considerable commercial shipping in Wismarbucht. If visiting Kirchdorf on the island of Poel do not consider anchoring in the dredged approach channel as the holding is bad in very soft mud and ferries take up most of the fairway. Visiting yachts can moor alongside on the north side of the south jetty in 2m at the outer end.

Berthing

In Wismar visiting yachts can berth alongside on the east side of the Alten Hafen but this is more suitable for larger vessels. Berthing for yachts is available at the Westhafen or Brunkowkei marinas which are not much further from the city centre.

Services for yachts

Water, electricity and shower/toilet facilities are available at both marinas although facilities at Brunkowkei are minimal. There are laundry facilities at Westhafen and there is a fuel station on the north side of the harbour basin between the oil jetty and the chemical works. Weather forecasts are available on request from the harbourmaster's office.

There is no yacht chandlery or sailmaker and no specialist facilities for yacht repairs, although the ship repair yard could no doubt be approached in connection with serious problems.

General facilities

Groceries, gas and most other supplies are available in the town centre, where there is a tourist information office and banks, restaurants and hotels abound.

Communications and travel

There are good train services to Hamburg, Berlin and Rostock.

Vessels in the Alten Hafen at Wismar *J. Parkinson*

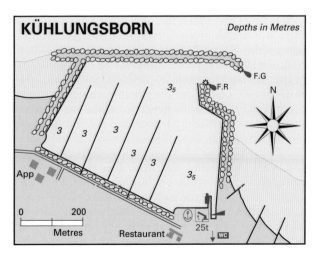

Kühlungsborn

53°09'N 11°47'E

Distances
Wismar 27M, Heiligenhafen 30M,
Warnemunde 12M, Gedser 25M, Stralsund 64M

Charts
UKHO 2365, 2117
German 163, 1671

Lights
1400 **Buk** 54°07'·9N 11°41'·6E LFl(4)WR.45s95m24–20M
    Red and brown round tower, red cupola
Kuhlungsborn E Mole Head FR.6m4M Red Mast
N Mole Head FG.6m4M Green Mast
1404 **Warnemunde** 54°10'·9N 12°05'·1E Fl(3+1)W.24s 34M
    20M White round tower with black bands, two
    galleries, copper cupola

Communications
Harbourmaster ① +49 38 2934 1055
    Mobile +49 151 12110565 www.kuehlungsborn.de

General

A large new marina with several hundred berths has been built just to the east of Kühlungsborn, the largest seaside resort in Mecklenburg, amongst much new housing development.

Approach

Approach waypoint 54°09'·5N 11°46'·5E

Straightforward by day or night from a northeasterly direction and round the eastern end of the north breakwater.

Berth

Berth at new pontoons in 3·0 to 3·5m

Facilities

Water/electricity on the pontoons. Showers/toilets. Laundry, Diesel berth. Shops, restaurants, banks all available in the town.

From Kühlungsborn the Molli, a steam railway which has a gauge of only 90cm and is a great tourist attraction, runs through Heiligendamm to Bad Doberan. Heiligendamm was established in 1793 as a spa – it is known as 'The White Town by the Sea' because of its white-painted, period buildings.

Warnemünde (with Rostock)

54°11'N 12°05'E

Distances
Wismar 35M, Kühlungsborn 12M, Rostock 6M,
Darsser Ort 30M, Stralsund 54M

Charts
UKHO 2365, 2370
German 163, 1671, 1672

Lights
1404 **Warnemünde**, W side of entrance 54°10'·9N
 12°05'·1E Fl(3+1)24s34m20M White round tower,
 black bands, two galleries, copper cupola 31m
1415 **Petersdorf Ldg Lts** 161·6° *Front* 54°08'·7N 12°06'·8E
 Oc.R.4s24m12M Striped metal mast, red top 21m
1415·1 *Rear* 1260m from front Oc.R.4s45m15M Striped
 metal mast, red top 33m
1405 **West molehead**, E arm 54°11'·2N 12°05'·2E
 Iso.G.4s14m6M Horn Mo(WN)30s Green tower, white
 band, two galleries 12m Floodlit
1405·1 **East mole** 54°11'·2N 12°05'·5E Iso.R.4s14m6M Red
 tower, white band, two balconies 12m Floodlit

Harbour communications
Warnemünde/Rostock Vessel Traffic Service ✆ +49 381
 2067 1141/2 *VHF* Ch 73, 16 (vessels must maintain a
 listening watch on VHF Ch 73 – broadcasts on VHF Ch
 73 every two hours from 0515–2115 LT in German,
 English on request)
Rostock Port Authority ✆ +49 38 1381 8710
 VHF Ch 10
Alter Strom ✆ +49 3815 1864
Hohe Düne Yachthafen ✆ +49 0381 5040 8080
 www.yachthafen-hohe-duene.de

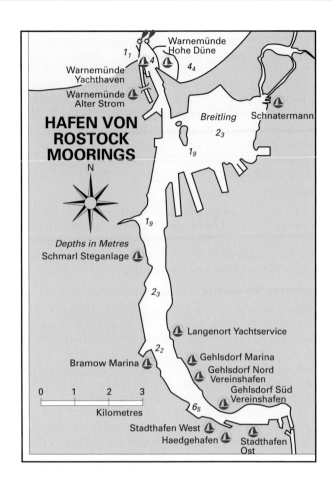

General

Warnemünde, a holiday resort and ferry terminal,
still maintains an inshore fishing fleet which ties up
with yachts in the Alter Strom alongside gabled
houses. It lies at the entrance to the huge,
commercial but ancient Hanseatic port of Rostock,
whose docks and shipyards stretch for 15M due
south from Warnemünde along the River Warnow.
Warnemünde is a good base from which to visit
Rostock by train.

Approach and entrance

Approach waypoint 54°13'N 12°04'E

The harbour mouth is very obvious both by day and
by night, and is equipped with powerful leading
lights. There are no hazards outside the harbour, and
there is a well-buoyed fairway extending some 7M
out to the Rostock fairway buoy but beware of
commercial traffic which must not be obstructed.

The harbour mouth is divided into two, the
eastern side being the deep-water channel to the
commercial port and to Rostock, whilst the western
side leads to the yacht harbour and the fishing port.
On the east side of the entrance the very grand Hohe
Düne development has been built with its own large
and well appointed marina. This has its own
straightforward entrance as in the plan on page 39.
Immediately inside the western entrance of the main
harbour there are again two channels, the eastern
one leading past the entrance to the yacht harbour
before rejoining the deep-water channel, and the
western one being the Alter Strom, which is much
used by fishing boats and tourist vessels. At night,
beware several unlit dolphins at the seaward end of
the dividing wall between the yacht harbour and the
Alter Strom.

Anchorage

Do not anchor in this busy waterway.

Berthing

The Alter Strom which is much the most picturesque
and convenient area in which to berth is now very
congested with fishing boats and tourist vessels.
Yachts may have difficulty finding a berth and may
have to raft up to a fishing boat. Maximum draught
3·1m. It is uncomfortable in onshore winds.

The Yachthafen to the east of the Alter Strom is
fairly convenient but is subject to surge in onshore
winds and from ships passing in the main channel. It
has box berths and the entrance carries a depth of
only 2·2m.

The Hohe Düne marina is more expensive but one
berths at pontoons which are well sheltered. It is a
short walk and a ferry ride to reach the town.

Services for yachts

Water, electricity, toilets and showers are available in
the Alter Strom, Yachthafen and at Hohe Düne. Fuel
berths in the Alter Strom and Hohe Düne. *Camping
Gaz* from SchiffService Warnow Werkstatte
Warnemünde (who are also Volvo Penta agents) in
the Alter Strom. There is a crane capable of lifting

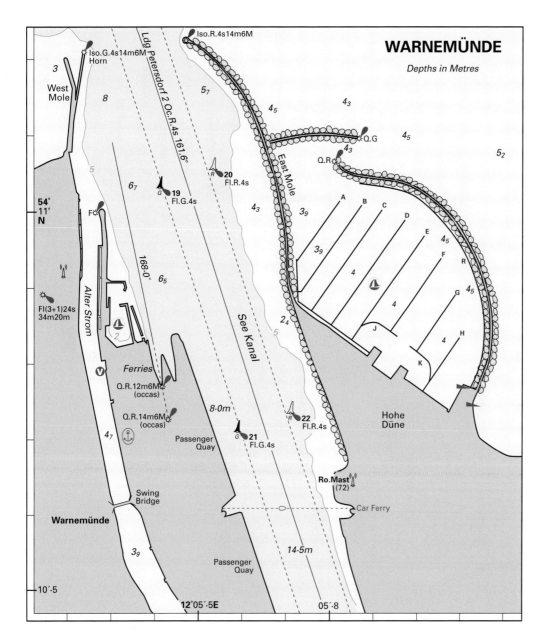

2·5 tonnes at the yacht harbour, and a larger one capable of handling 40 tonnes at Hohe Düne.

General facilities

Provisions are available from nearby shops, and there are stalls selling pancakes, hot dogs and other forms of fast food on the Alter Strom. Since this is a holiday resort, there is a very wide range of restaurants, hotels and banks to choose from. The Hohe Düne has a luxury hotel and a large choice of restaurants, cafés and bars on the marina-side.

Communications and travel

There is a regular ferry sailing to Gedser in Denmark, Trelleborg in Sweden and Ventspils in Latvia while the centre of Rostock is no more than 10 minutes by the S-bahn railway.

Hohe Dune Marina at Warnemünde *J. Parkinson*

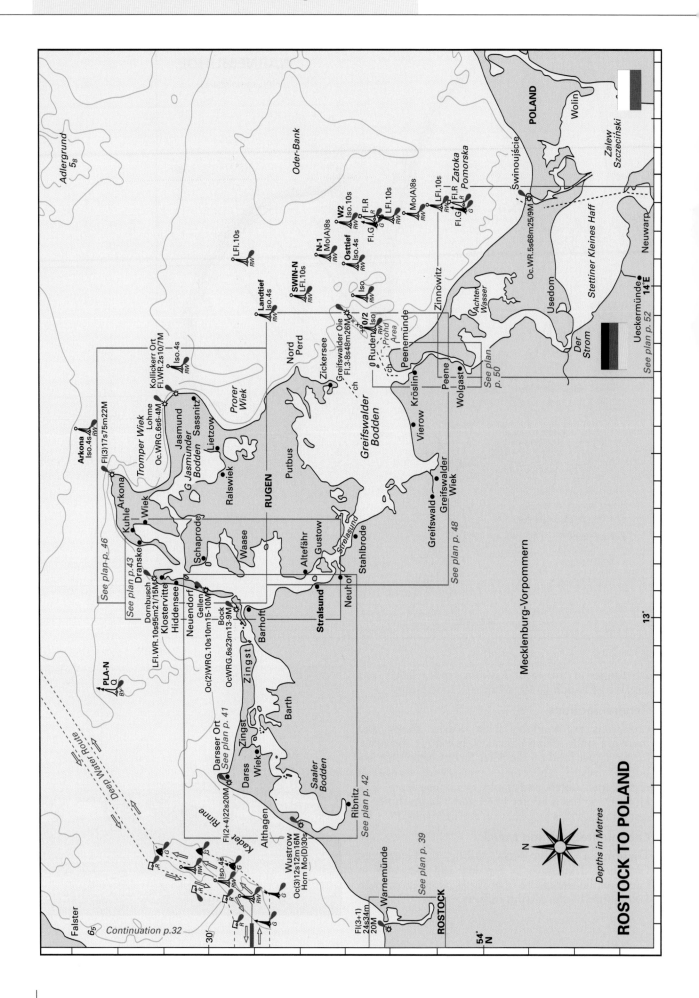

POLAND

Wolin

Zalew Szczeciński

Adlergrund 5₈

Oder-Bank

Fl.LFl.10s RW

Fl.G Fl.R *Zatoka Pomorska*

Mo(A)8s RW LFl.10s RW

W2 Iso.10s RW

Fl.R

N-1 Mo(A)8s RW

Osttief Iso.4s RW

Fl.G RW Fl.G

SWIN-N LFl.10s RW

Iso.4s RW

Landtief Iso.4s RW

Oc.WR.5s68m25/9M

Neuwarp

Stettiner Kleines Haff

Iso. RW

Greifswalder Oie Fl.3-8s48m26M

0/2 Iso.

Prohd Area

ch

0 Ruden RW

ch

Peenemünde

Zinnowitz

Achter Wasser

Usedom

Der Strom

Uckermünde

14°E

See plan p. 52

Kollickerr Ort Fl.WR.2s10/7M RW

Iso.4s RW

Nord Perd

Zickersee

Kröslin

Vierow

Peene

Wolgast

See plan p. 50

Kuhle

Lohme Oc.WRG.6s6-4M

Jasmund Sassnitz

Lietzow

Prorer Wiek

Tromper Wiek

Arkona Iso.4s RW

Fl(3)17s75m22M

Arkona

Wiek

G. Jasmunder Bodden

Schaprode

Ralswiek

Putbus

RÜGEN

Greifswalder Bodden

Greifswald

Greifswalder Wiek

See plan p. 48

Waase

Altefähr

Gustow

Stahlbrode

Strelasund

Neuhof

See plan p. 46

See plan p. 43

Dranske

Dornbusch LFl.WR.10s95m21/15M

Klostervitte Hiddensee

Neuendorf

Gellen

Bock Oc.WRG.6s23m13-9M

Barhöft

Stralsund

Neuhof

PLA-N Q BY

Oc(2)WRG.10s10m15-10M

Zingst

Barth

Ribnitz

Saaler Bodden

See plan p. 42

Darsser Ort *See plan p. 41*

Darss Wiek

Zingst

Althagen

Fl(2+4)22s20M

Rinne

Kadet

Wustrow Oc(3)12s12m16M Horn Mo(D)30s

POLAND

Mecklenburg-Vorpommern

13°

Depths in Metres

N

ROSTOCK TO POLAND

Falster 6₅

Continuation p.32

-30'

Iso.4s RW

Warnemünde

See plan p. 39

Fl(3+1)24s34m 20M

ROSTOCK

54° N

Deep Water Route

Fishing boats in the Alter Strom with the visitors' berths further out at Warnemünde *J. Parkinson*

Upriver to Rostock

From Warnemünde yachts can take the well-marked main channel 6M upriver to Rostock, the largest town in the area and notable for its numerous fine buildings, many of which survive despite heavy bombing during the Second World War. The centrepiece is the Marienkirche, an immense gothic edifice built over a period of 400 years, which houses a late 15th-century astronomical clock and a famous baroque organ.

Pilotage is straightforward, past the shipyards and docks, though the passage is best made in daylight due to numerous unlit buoys and projecting wooden jetties. Around Gehlsdorf there are a number of small yacht harbours along the east bank of the river, but these are not well situated for exploring Rostock, see plan on page 38. Beyond Gehlsdorf the river runs east/west and a variety of berthing options are available on the south (city) bank. The first is in the Haedge Hafen by the Rostocker Segelverein. Further upstream, between the conspicuous Volks Theater and A.G. Getreide buildings, there are more small marinas until one reaches the town quay (Stadthafen Ost).

All normal shopping facilities, hotels, banks and restaurants are available in the town centre, and the town has good rail connections with Berlin and Hamburg.

Outside Rostock is the open air Klockenhagen Museum illustrating a regional farmhouse and farming. It is possible to take the train further afield, from Warnemünde to Rostock and on to Bad Doberan, which has the Doberaner Munster, a great brick church built by the Cistercians between 1294 and 1368.

Warnemunde to the entrance to the Strelasund

Mecklenburger Bucht Traffic Separation Scheme

It should be noted that there is a Traffic Separation Scheme between Falster (Denmark) and the German coast between Warnemünde and Darsser Ort (see plan page 40).

Darsser Ort

Approach waypoint 54°30′N 12°35′E
54°28′N 12°32′E
Charts UKHO 2365, 2601; chart 162)

In 2008 this harbour was closed because of silting in the entrance channel and there is doubt as to whether it will be re-opened. However in 2004 it was also closed and re-opened after similar doubt and so it is retained in the book in case it is re-opened as it is a useful stop between Warnemünde and Stralsund which are 54M apart. A yacht which had hoped to berth there in 2008 was warned not to go within 1M of the entrance.

The harbour was once an East German patrol boat base and is situated in a nature reserve. The SAR vessel which was stationed there has now been moved to Barhöft. On account of its strategic position it used to be a popular and often crowded harbour, but has minimal facilities apart from two jetties. Yachts moor bow to a jetty and stern to a buoy. Anchoring is not allowed.

Having avoided the shoal off the point of Darsser Ort, marked by east and west cardinal buoys, the approach to Darsser Ort is straightforward and well marked by lateral buoys, but very narrow and subject to silting. In 2005 after dredging the entrance carried a depth of 3·5m.

The nearest shopping facilities are at Prerow about 2M from the harbour.

A hazard of visiting Darsser Ort is attack by hordes of mosquitoes which breed in the surrounding reeds. Despite this there is a popular nudist camp on the coast 400m to the southeast!

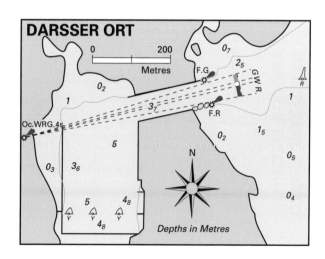

1. GERMANY

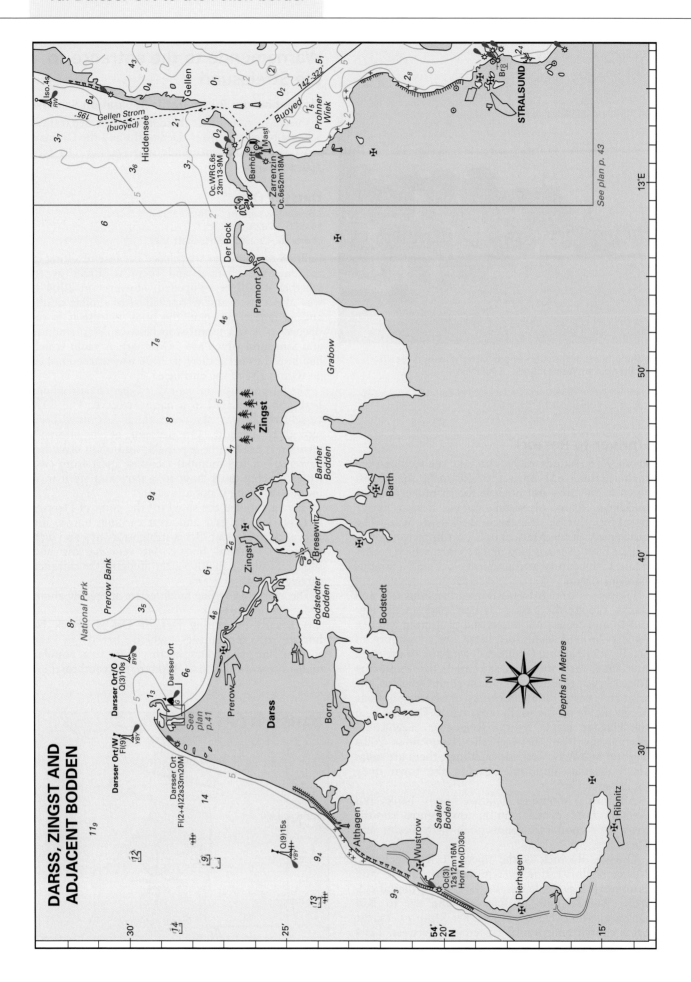

**DARSS, ZINGST AND
ADJACENT BODDEN**

Gellen

Hiddensee

Gellen Strom
(buoyed)

Iso.4s
RW

Buoyed

142°-322°

Prohner
Wiek

STRALSUND

See plan p. 43

13°E

Oc.WRG.6s
23m13-9M

Barhöft

Zarrenzin
Oc.6s52m18M

Der Bock

Pramort

Zingst

Grabow

Barther
Bodden

Barth

Bresewitz

National Park

Prerow Bank

Zingst

Darsser Ort/O
Q(3)10s
BYB

Darsser Ort

See
plan
p.41

Prerow

Darss

Bodstedter
Bodden

Bodstedt

Born

Darsser Ort/W
Fl(9)
YBY

Darsser Ort
Fl(2+4)22s33m20M

Q(9)15s
YBY

Althagen

Wustrow

Saaler
Bodden

Oc(3)
12s12m16M
Horn Mo(D)30s

Dierhagen

Ribnitz

N

Depths in Metres

30'

25'

54°
20'
N

15'

30'

40'

50'

1d. Darsser Ort to the Polish border

In order to get from Darsser Ort to Poland, the quickest route is probably to stay offshore and leave the island of Rügen to starboard. Assuming the harbour of Dasser Ort remains unavailable (see above) this involves a passage of around 100 miles from Warnemünde to Sassnitz, the first good harbour on the outer side of Rügen Island, with a further 40 miles to Świnoujście, the nearest port in Poland. Unless you are contemplating a long passage to the Gulf of Gdańsk this makes little sense, and would entail missing the Boddens and Haffs sheltered by the islands and sometimes likened to the Norfolk Broads on a grand scale.

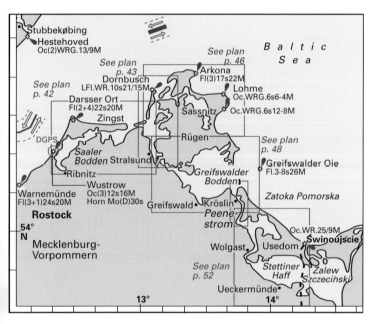

Saaler Bodden, Bodstetter Bodden, Barther Bodden and Grabow

There are no harbours between Darsser Ort and the entrance to the Strelasund. The coast shields an extensive area of shallow Bodden, which are entered from the Strelasund just north of the small fishing and yacht harbour of Barhöft (54°26′N 13°02′E). The Bodden are well buoyed and contain a number of charming little harbours, but it is essential to have the large-scale charts of the area to get to them (e.g. BSH Sportschiffahrskarten *3008*). To access the western Bodden (Saaler and Bodstetter) it is necessary to pass through the swing bridge at Bresewitz, which in 2008 opened only twice daily at 0930 and 1830 LT, less often in winter.

Barth

54°22′N 12°43′E

Yachtsmen wishing to sample this area might consider a visit to Barth at the head of the Barther

Bodden, where there are a couple of well-equipped marinas and all the facilities of an interesting small town close at hand.

The Northern Approach to the Strelasund

The Strelasund offers the opportunity for yachtsmen to take an interesting route inside Rügen island, via Stralsund, to Greifswalder Bodden and is a short-cut to the northern entrance of the Peenestrom channel which leads to the Stettiner Haff (Zalew Szczecinski).

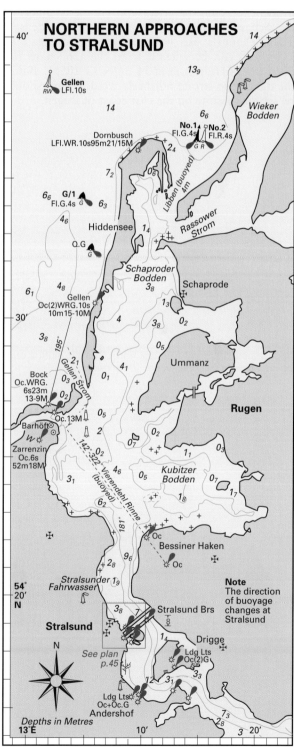

The northern approach via the Gellenstrom west of Hiddensee island, starts at the Gellen Landfall Buoy (54°38'·4N 13°02'·6E) although from the west it is more practical to enter the channel at No. 1 G buoy (54°36'·3N 13°14'·7E) or in quiet conditions at No. 7 G buoy (54°30'·5N 13°03'·1E) in the western W sector of the Gellen Light (54°30'·5N 13°04'·5E Oc(2)WRG.10s10m15–10M white round metal tower, red top, stone base) although it would be unwise to attempt this approach to Stralsund in the dark as not all the channel buoys are lit. The latter approach to No. 7 G buoy carries a minimum depth of 3m. In strong onshore winds it would be prudent to reach the Strelasund via the channels of the Schaproder Bodden in the lee of Hiddensee. These channels are well-marked and dredged to 2·5m and can be entered from the Libben to the northeast of Hiddensee at 54°36'N 13°10'·9E. But in the dark or in strong northerly winds course should be set for Sassnitz on the east coast of Rügen.

Stralsund

54°19'N 13°06'E

Distances
Warnemünde 51M, Świnoujście 50M, Szczecin 85M

Charts
UKHO 2365
German 162, 1622, 1579, 1511

Lights
Approach
1440 **Darsser Ort** 54°28'·4N 12°30'·2E Fl(2+4)22s33m20M
　 Round red tower, brown cupola and building 35m
2576 **Zarrenzin Ldg Lts 195·1°** *Front* 54°26'·9N 13°01'·4E
　 Oc.WRG.6s23m13–9M 089°-W-180°-R-191°-W-290°-G-
　 308°-W-069° White framework tower, red lantern and
　 gallery with white roof, grey stone base, white stripe
　 23m
2576·1 *Rear* 1·3M from front Oc.6s52m18M White metal
　 framework tower, red bands and lantern, white
　 cupola 24m Visible on leading line only
2592 **Kap Arkona** 54°40'·8N 13°25'·9E Fl(3)17s75m22M
　 Red lantern on yellow round tower with two galleries
　 35m
Channel
2575·9 **Bock Ldg Lts 322·1°** *Front* 54°27'N 13°02'E
　 Oc.6s12m13M 302°-vis-342° White framework tower,
　 red lantern and gallery with white roof, grey stone
　 base, white stripe 13m
2576 *Rear* 700m from front, as above. A back bearing on
　 322·1° can be used when heading south towards
　 Stralsund

Harbour communications
Stralsund North Vessel Traffic Service ☏ +49 38
　 31249511/2 *VHF* Ch 16, 67 (vessels must maintain a
　 listening watch on VHF Ch 16 or 67 – broadcasts on
　 VHF Ch 67 every two hours from 0635–2235 and at
　 0235 LT).
Stralsund Vessel Traffic Service ☏ +49 38 3125 4215
　 VHF Ch 11 (0700–2000 Monday–Friday, 0700–1300 and
　 1800–2000 LT weekends and holidays)
Citymarina Harbourmaster ☏ +49 38 3144 4978
　 www.rundtoern-marinas.com

Approaching Stralsund from the north. The city marina can be seen behind the breakwater *J. Parkinson*

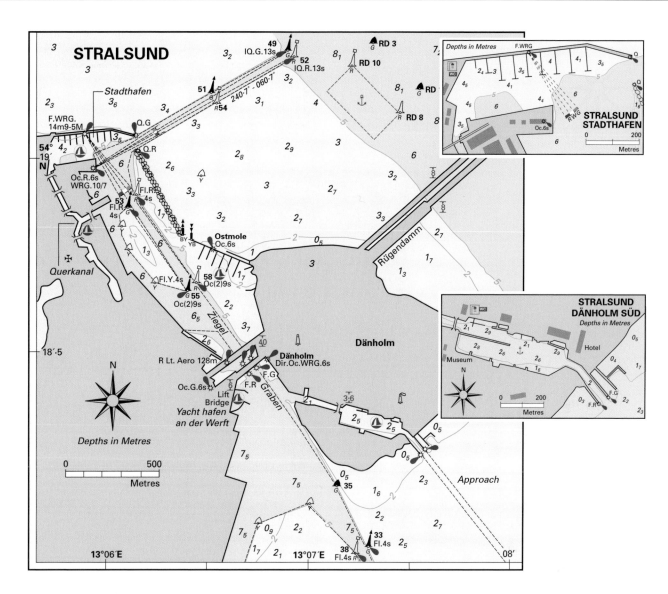

It was founded in 1209 and joined the Hanseatic League in 1293. Like Wismar, it was under Swedish control in the 17th and 18th centuries and came under Prussian control in 1815. It was very badly damaged in British and US air raids during the Second World War, a memory which lies not far below the surface. However the fine Town Hall survived, and over its windows on the market side can be seen the arms of Hamburg, Lübeck, Wismar, Rostock, Stralsund and Greifswald. The three parish churches of St Mary, St James (Jacobikirche) and St Nicholas demonstrate the prosperity of the town – especially the last, which was started in the 13th century and largely rebuilt after a fire in 1662. The eclectic maritime museum, which also contains a considerable tropical aquarium, is concerned with the biology and geology of the coast.

This is an attractive port and holiday resort, full of old-world charm and with many historic buildings, cobbled streets and a lively open-air market. A vast amount of high-quality restoration work has been completed and more is being done. There are many good, modern shops.

Approach

The port lies on the west bank of the Strelasund, the narrow channel between the island of Rügen and the mainland, where the small island of Dänholm provided a convenient bridging point. Whether coming from the north or the south it is necessary to navigate through this channel, which is tortuous but very clearly marked and well lit. There is sometimes a small current in the Strelasund, with a direction and strength dependent on wind conditions over the southern Baltic.

The approach from the north is via the Gellenstrom (see above) and this leads eventually into the Strelasund via channels dredged to 4·5m. If intending to continue south to the Greifswalder Bodden, it will be necessary to enter Stralsund harbour to pass through the opening bridge, whether or not one stops at Stralsund itself. In 2008 this bridge opened five times daily at 0520, 0820, 1220, 1720, 2130 but times seem to vary slightly from year to year so a check should be made at harbour offices or by calling Stralsund Traffic.

Approaching from the south, the channel divides around the island of Dänholm (see plan above), the

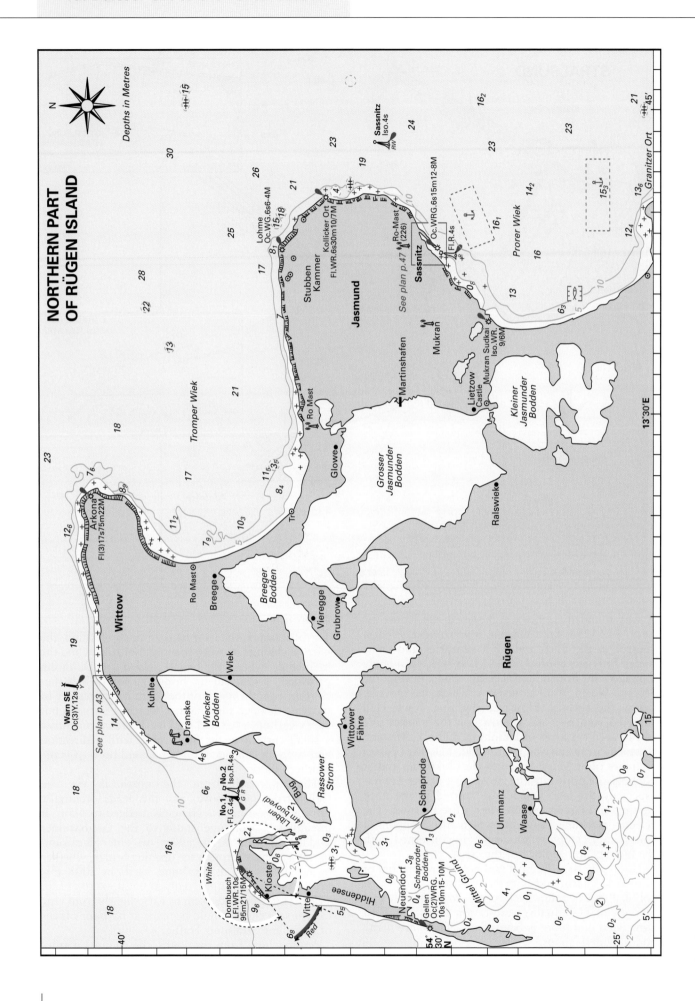

NORTHERN PART OF RÜGEN ISLAND

Depths in Metres

western fork (the Ziegel Graben) leading to the town through twin lifting road and rail bridges (see above for opening times). If it is necessary to wait for the bridge it is usually possible to find a temporary berth at the Yachthafen an der Werft, on the western side of the Strelasund just south of the bridge. The new fixed motorway bridge just north of the lifting bridge has a clearance of 40m. The longer part of the railway bridge connecting Dänholm to the larger island of Rügen does not open, and has a fixed height of 8m.

The direction of buoyage changes at the bridges.

Anchorage

There are numerous anchorages outside the fairway, but appropriate signals must be displayed.

Berthing

Visiting yachts normally moor to pontoons in the Stadthafen which lies immediately to starboard after entering the harbour through the northern entrance. There are 240 berths, mostly alongside finger pontoons, but they are uncomfortable in southeasterly winds. Yachts may also be permitted to moor alongside the commercial quays midway between the north and south entrances, provided that no larger vessels are expected.

The Yachthafen an der Werft, the yacht harbour immediately south of the twin lifting bridges, has few visitors' berths and it is usually difficult to find a place, especially for yachts of more than 2·5m beam. Although it is not as close to the town centre as the Stadthafen, and has a railway line close by, in some ways it is a more pleasant harbour.

Other possibilities are the basin at the south end of Dänholm island, which is accessed from the eastern fork (the main channel) of the Strelasund, or the yacht club at the northern end of Dänholm, to the north of the bridge. However both entail a long walk into the town centre. It is also possible to berth in the Querkanal close to the town centre but this has a depth of only 1·5m and is accessed through an opening bridge which has fixed opening times.

The twin opening bridges at Stralsund *J. Mottram*

Services for yachts

Water, electricity and Wi-Fi are available on the Citymarina pontoons, with showers and toilets on Pontoon 8 and near the harbourmaster's office. The Yachthafen an der Werft also has showers and toilets.

There is a chandlery on the quay north of the Querkanal, where *Camping Gaz* cylinders may be exchanged, and fuel from a jetty a little further south (operating times vary – enquire in advance).

General facilities

There is a small general store opposite the harbourmaster's office at the Stadthafen, and sometimes a mobile fish stall on the quay, but otherwise all shops, banks and restaurants are in the town centre, within easy walking distance from the Stadthafen and about 1·5km from the Yachtclub an der Werft.

Communications and travel

There are good train services to Berlin and Rostock, but it should be noted that there are two railway stations, which can be very confusing.

Rügen

For yachtsmen equipped with detailed German charts, Rügen offers numerous opportunities to discover a variety of small yacht harbours tucked away in the corners of the Bodden on Hiddensee and the northern part of Rügen all reached by closely buoyed and dredged channels.

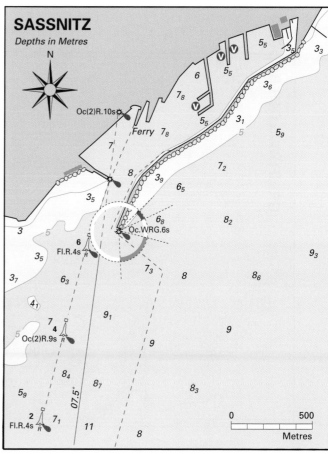

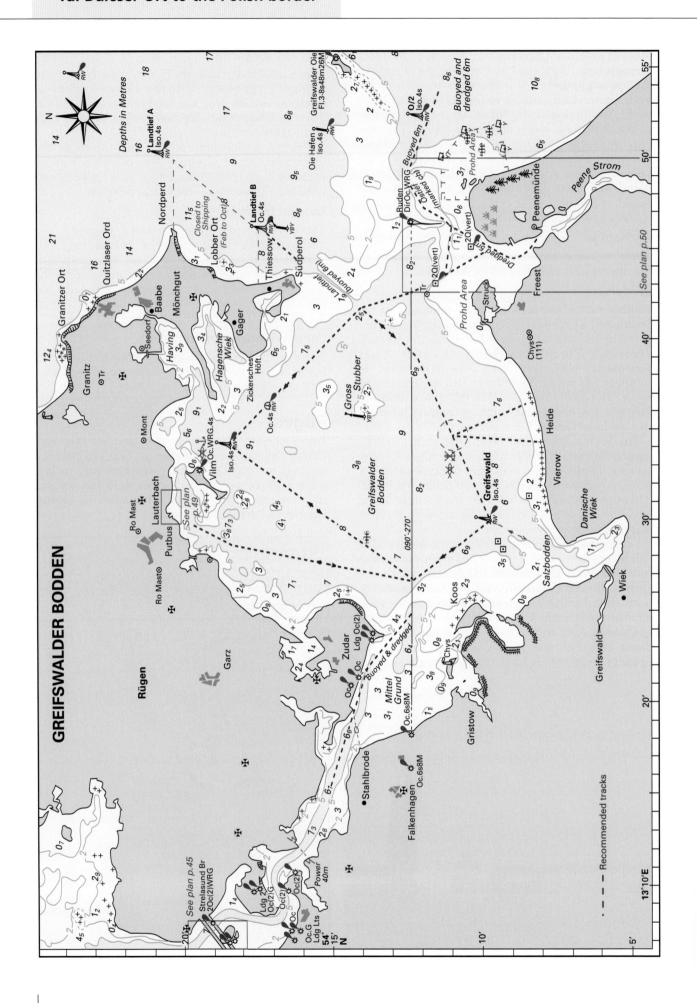

GREIFSWALDER BODDEN

Depths in Metres

N

RW

Landtief A
Iso.4s
RW

Nordperd

Quitzlaser Ord

Granitzer Ort

Granitz

Seedorf

Baabe

Mönchgut

Having

Hagensche Wiek

Gager

Zickersches Höft

Mont

Vilm Oc.WRG.4s

Iso.4s RW

Oc.4s RW

Gross Stubber
YBY

Greifswalder Bodden

Closed to Shipping
(Feb to Oct)

Lobber Ort

Landtief B
Oc.4s
RW
YBY

Thiessow
RW

Südperol

Landtief
(buoyed 6m)

Greifswalder Oie
Fl.3·8s48m26M

Oie Hafen
Iso.4s

O/2
Iso.4s
RW

Buoyed 6m and
dredged 6m

Buoyed and
dredged 6m

Prohd Area

Ruden
DirOc.WRG
Ostief ch
(marked ch)

2Q(vert)

2Q(vert)

Tr

Prohd Area

Struck

Freest

Peenemünde

Peene Strom

See plan p.50

Dredged 5m

Chys
(111)

Heide

Vierow

Danische Wiek

Wiek

Greifswald

Salzbodden

Greifswald
Iso.4s
RW

Koos

Ro Mast

Lauterbach

See plan p.49

Putbus

Ro Mast

Rügen

Garz

Zudar
Oc
Oc
Oc(2)
Ldg Oc(2)

Buoyed & dredged

Mittel Grund

Oc.6s8M

Gristow

Chys

Falkenhagen
Oc.6s8M

Stahlbrode

See plan p.45

Strelasund Br
2QOc(2)WRG

Ldg Oc(2)G
Oc(2)
Oc(2)

Power 40m

Oc.G Ldg Lts

54° 15'N

13°10'E

090°-270°

Recommended tracks

Sassnitz

54°30′N 13°38′E
Admiralty chart 2365
German charts 162, 151, 1516

The only harbour of any consequence on the 'outside' of Rügen is Sassnitz, which lies on the east coast. Although still an active fishing port, all of the ferry activity has now transferred to a new ferry port at Neu Mukran some 3M to the southwest. For the yachtsman it offers a secure and well-appointed staging port with a new City-marina planned. The Port Authority can be contacted on ☏ +49 38 3926 9010 *VHF* Ch 15 69 and the marina on ☏ +49 38 3926 9020 www.stadhafen-sassnitz.de

Greifswalder Bodden

The southern end of the Strelasund leads into Greifswalder Bodden, a large body of mostly navigable water to the south of Rügen.

From the eastern end of Greifswalder Bodden there are two alternatives:

• Via one of the two dredged channels through to the open Baltic, either northeast for Sweden and Bornholm or southeast for Świnoujście and the Polish coast;

• Or – and the more interesting – via the Peenestrom channel through to the Stettiner Haff (Zalew Szczeciński), a lake some 30 miles long straddling the German/Polish border from which there is access back into the Baltic (see page 293).

Lauterbach

54°21′N 13°30′E
UKHO charts 2365
German charts 151, 1511, 1578

Lauterbach is on the south coast of Rügen island and has a 300 berth marina with box berths at two pontoons with 2·9 to 3·4m depths behind the eastern breakwaters. ☏ +49 38 301 8090, www.im-jaich.de. Fuel berth in the communal harbour where there are also some berths for visitors.

It is worth considering for the opportunity to visit Putbus, about 1·5km inland, which was once a highly fashionable summer resort with a theatre and Prince Putbus' palace. Surviving from those days are a park and a circular terrace of fine houses.

A supermarket and other shops will be found a short walk along the road to Putbus.

Seedorf

54°21′N 13°39′E
UKHO chart 2365
German charts 151, 1511, 1578

Seedorf, ☏ +44 383 03736, also on the south coast of Rügen island, is a beautiful natural harbour in unspoilt country, with some 40 berths amongst the reeds. It is approached by buoyed channel with minimum depth of 2–6m. There are no facilities, but it is the harbour from which to visit the Jagdschloss, Prince Putbus' amazing hunting 'lodge' in the Granitz wood. Although a 4km walk, the schloss is well worth the effort and those who do not suffer from vertigo will be rewarded with a fine view over the island from the tower. On the way one may also encounter a narrow-gauge steam train which runs in a loop around this part of the island.

Greifswald/Greifswald Wieck

54°06′N 13°27′E
UKHO chart 2150
German chart 151, 1511

In the southwest corner of Greifswalder Bodden lies the attractive harbour of Greifswald Wieck, with simple facilities and shopping in Wieck on the north bank. At the top of the harbour a wooden drawbridge, which opens about every hour (times on the bridge), allows yachts to access the university town of Greifswald some 2·5M up the river Ryck. At Greifswald yachts lie alongside in the Museumhafen along with many historic boats close to the town centre. The town itself is modern having been heavily bombed during the Second World War.

Museumhafen. Greifswald   J. Parkinson

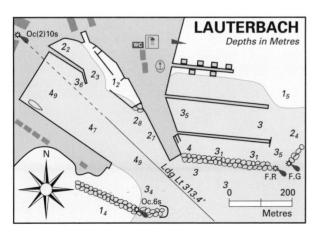

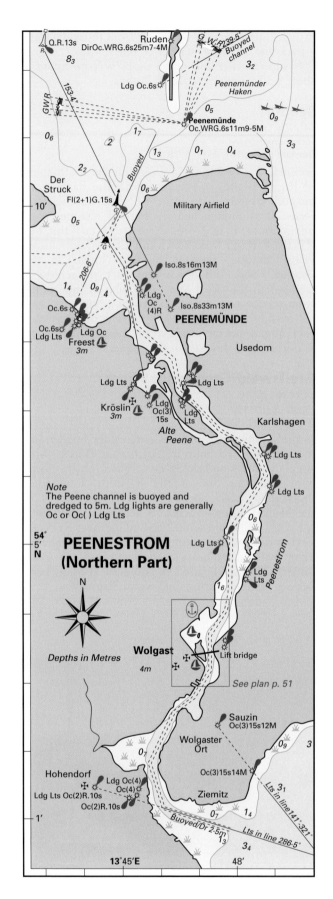

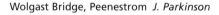

Ruden and Greifswalder Oie

54°12′N 13°46′E and 54°15′N 13°54′E
ULKHO chart 2365
German charts 151, 1511, 1512, 1578

Small island addicts may wish to visit Ruden and Greifswalder Oie in the eastern approaches to Greifswalder Bodden. Neither has any facilities. Ruden, now a nature reserve which can be walked around, still has the remains of missile tracking facilities which were installed to observe the trials of V1 and V2 missiles launched from Peenemünde. Greifswalder Oie is simply an unspoilt island which is also a nature reserve and subject to restrictions.

Peenemünde and the northern Peenestrom

The northern end of the Peenestrom passes Peenemünde, the German wartime research and development site for the V1 and V2 missiles, which some consider to be the birthplace of space flight. The site, now a museum, is well worth a visit for those with an interest in military history or engineering. An old Russian submarine is berthed in the harbour which has basic facilities but no fresh water.

Opposite Peenemünde, on the west bank of the Peenestrom, is the large modern marina at Kröslin (54°07′N 13°45′E), with finger pontoons and good repair and servicing facilities. The marina is well sheltered and a yacht could safely be left there for an extended period. A small supermarket and other shops are to be found in the nearby village.

Birdlife is abundant on the Peenestrom and one is unlucky not to see white-tailed sea eagles.

Wolgast Bridge, Peenestrom *J. Parkinson*

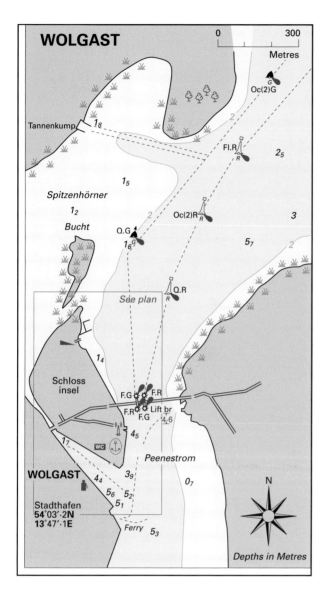

1. GERMANY

Wolgast Stadthafen *J. Mottram*

Wolgast

54°03′N 13°47′E

UKHO charts 2150

German charts 151, 1512, 1513

Wolgast is an attractive small town, recently much restored. South of the bridge, yachts can berth on the town quay in about 3m on the south side of

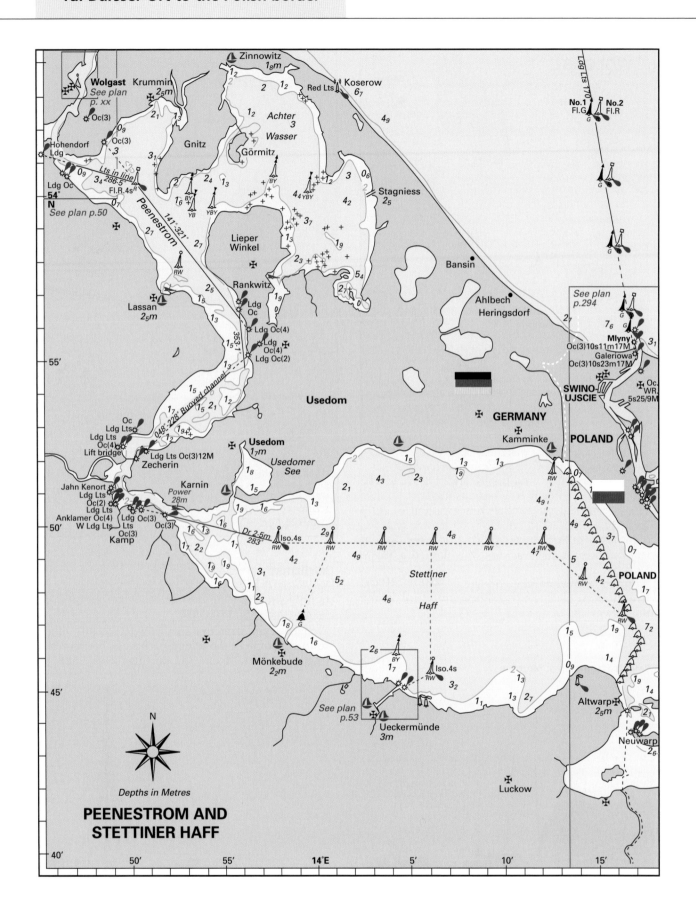

PEENESTROM AND
STETTINER HAFF

Depths in Metres

Schlossinsel provided commercial vessels are not expected. It is only a short walk from the town centre. There are basic facilities with a chandlery nearby, as well as the usual domestic shops. North of the bridge there is a small marina also on Schlossinsel but further from the town. Diesel is available from a fuel barge.

In 2008 Wolgast Bridge opened five times daily at 0545, 0845, 1245, 1645, 2045 but, as at Stralsund and Zecherin, times seem to vary slightly from year to year and should be checked.

Information is broadcast by Wolgast Vessel Traffic Service on *VHF* Ch 09 every two hours from 0715–2115 LT. The port can be contacted on ☎ +49 38 3625 1137.

The southern Peenestrom

From Wolgast southwards the channels are lit mainly by leading lights which are usually only operated when commercial traffic is expected, but the dredged channel is narrow and the buoys are mostly unlit so that navigation in the dark would undoubtedly lead to groundings. Far better to anchor in one of the many suitable places and wait for the dawn. The channel opens out into a lake, the Achterwasser, which can be explored with a large-scale chart (see plan page 52) and due care. The southern end narrows to a channel dredged to 2·5m which is marked by unlit buoys, and to leave it is to be instantly stuck in soft, glutinous mud.

Zecherin Bridge is another timegate and in 2008 opened five times daily at 0535, 0935, 1135, 1635, 2035 but as at Stralsund and Wolgast times seem to vary slightly from year to year and should be checked.

Two miles below this bridge at Karnin is the derelict lifting span, now permanently raised, of the old railway spanning the Peenestrom. The approach spans were bombed during the war and no trace can now be seen. The main channel now passes south of the remains. Once past this old relic the way is clear into the Stettiner Haff (Zalew Szczeciński).

Stettiner Haff

There are several small picturesque harbours around the lake but beware of the abundant fishing stakes. Do not pass between them as they may be joined to one another by underwater nets. End stakes carry a red and white diamond, the white side pointing to clear passage and the red to the obstructed side.

It used to be mandatory to report to a Polish customs launch moored close to the buoys marking the border with Poland when crossing into Polish waters but as from 2008 this formality is no longer required.

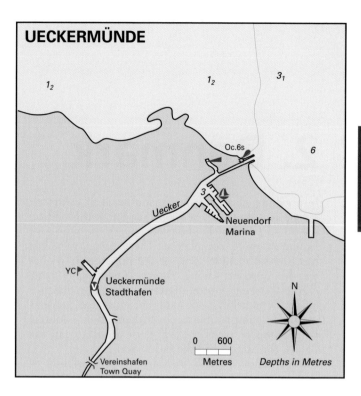

UECKERMÜNDE

Ueckermünde
53°45'N 14°04'E
German chart 1513

Ueckermünde offers a good opportunity to obtain stores or yacht services close to the Polish border. Approaching vessels are requested to report to the Port Control ☎ +49 39 771 3181, *VHF* Ch 14, by making contact 10 minutes before reaching the landfall buoy UE at 53°45'·4N 14°05'·9E and again before departure.

After an attractive tree-lined entrance there is large new marina associated with a housing development on the port hand, near Neuendorf, but it is nearly 1·5km to the nearest shopping in Neuendorf/Ueckermünde Ost.

A mile further up the Uecker on the starboard hand lies a second yacht harbour carrying a depth of 1·8m where there are two sailing clubs with visitors' box berths some of which are on the west side of the river in deeper water. These berths are a short walk from the small town of Ueckermünde. The town quay beyond the yacht harbour is used by commercial vessels but yachts can lie alongside for a short stay on the north side, upriver of the ferry terminal. There are no facilities but there is a boatyard above the bridge and Ueckermünde is a good place to stock up with gas before entering Poland as there is a large gas station on the far side of the town (beyond the Lidl supermarket) selling various types of gas including *Camping Gaz*.

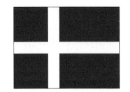

2. Denmark

In previous editions only the southeast of Denmark has been covered in The Baltic Sea but in this edition the RCC Pilotage Foundation covers the whole of Denmark more completely. The guiding principle has been to include some of the principal harbours on the popular sailing routes. These have been chosen as being approximately 30M sailing distance apart. Denmark has so many harbours and marinas it would be impossible to cover them all in a volume which aims to cover the whole of the Kattegat, the Baelts, the Sound and the Baltic Sea.

Information is also included on the islands of Bornholm and Christiansø which are quite separate from the main Danish cruising areas but, because they are Danish, fall within the scope of this chapter.

The country

Of the total land area of 43,000km², 65% is devoted to farming with a further 12% used for forestry. Environmental considerations are given high priority. The countryside is generally flat, with the highest point only 173m above sea level. Motorways connect the main cities by means of high-level bridges or tunnels between the major islands. Bridges to the smaller islands are either of sufficient clearance, or open to allow the passage of yachts and other small boat traffic.

History

From the 11th to the 17th century the Danes were concerned to establish trading and territorial rights throughout the Baltic, a process in which contact often resulted in conflict. Denmark established trading posts in the east of the Baltic en route to Russia early (for instance, Tallinn in 1219) but she did not hold them for long. After a dispute, an act of union was signed at Kalmar in 1397, nominally uniting the three Scandinavian countries. However, the three tended to act as separate entities, and in due course the eastern part of Sweden established an independent existence.

When Denmark has not been involved with Norway and Sweden in their common objective of stemming German intrusion, her history has been largely that of her attempts to consolidate her own institutions and territories, and to ensure a revenue from the operations of her own traders and from her control of the Sound. This has at various times brought her into conflict, not only with Sweden and Germany, but also with the Dutch, who replaced the Hanseatic League as the carriers of the Baltic trade and were squeezed by dues at the Sound (see Copenhagen). Despite the difficulties which the Danes had with the Germans, by the end of the 17th century Denmark had a decidedly German stamp. German was the language of administration, of command in the army, and of the court. At the same time the navy and the academic world, including the church, were strongly nationalistic. A great interest in the country's own language, literature and history developed, as did interest in science and agriculture.

After a remarkable increase in Baltic trade in 1730, ship owners and merchants gained a new confidence. The combination of interest and confidence led to the establishment being questioned on such matters as its control of trade and its policy towards agriculture, which was badly in need of reform. At the end of the 18th century a series of reforms was started. Old monopolies were abolished, agriculture was further improved, the Danish peasant was released from his 'serfdom' and landowners were prevented from swallowing up small holdings – the effect of the last is noticeable in the landscape. Denmark insisted upon her right as a neutral to carry anyone's goods in her ships. This insistence was one factor which brought her into conflict with the British who, concerned with their fight with the French, claimed the right to search ships at sea. Although this was enforced after the Battle of Copenhagen in 1801, differences were not

The people, the church and the language

Some 90% of the population of over five million are estimated to belong to the Lutheran Church, which was established in 1536 and is the national church, under the direction of the state. Education has been compulsory since 1814, and there are three universities and two university centres, besides various other institutions of higher education. A comprehensive social security system covers health, pensions, industrial accidents, unemployment and certain other hazards.

Danish is one of the Scandinavian languages, and is most closely related to Norwegian and Swedish. The Danish alphabet is the same as the Norwegian, consisting of the twenty-six letters of the English alphabet plus æ, ø, and å at the end. English is widely spoken especially by the young and in the cities.

The Danes are friendly, tolerant and relaxed. They enjoy their pleasures and are happy for other people to enjoy theirs. Within sailing circles, however, they are under pressure from the recent great increase in visiting yachts.

settled and Nelson's bombardment of Copenhagen in 1807, together with the seizure of the Danish fleet, drove the Danish monarchy to side with the French, against the wish of the majority in both Denmark and Norway. The result was the ruin of trade, war with Russia and Sweden, the loss of Norway to Sweden and national bankruptcy.

It was difficult enough to recover economically, and internal reform was further slowed by the problem of Schleswig and Holstein, to which both Denmark and Germany had a claim through the two intermingled populations. Germany resorted to force, and in 1864 Denmark ceded both territories. Feeling that her aspirations were neglected by the rest of Europe, Denmark concentrated her efforts on internal matters, agriculture, economics and science. Politically there continued to be sharply different points of view, with the richer urban population sharing a position with the landowners and many of the civil and military leaders, and the producers, steadily coming up in the world, allied to liberal opinion in commerce and the professions. A constitution was not settled until 1915.

Denmark remained neutral in the First World War but sold her West Indian possessions to the USA in 1917, gave Iceland her independence under the crown in 1918 and, after a plebiscite, recovered northern Schleswig in 1920. Between the wars her agricultural and industrial efficiency was further improved despite a generally difficult trading situation. In the Second World War, Denmark

Formalities

Customs

Denmark is a member of the European Union and hence EU customs rules apply. See *Introduction*, page 8, for more information. In common with many other countries in the EU, customs offices are being closed and if one expects to need to report to customs it would be advisable to check availability before arrival. For enquiries telephone the head office in Copenhagen ② +45 7222 1818 or go to www.skat.dk
Be aware that customs allowances of tobacco and alcohol are small and large quantities are liable to be impounded and a receipt given so that collection can be arranged when leaving the country.

Immigration

Valid passports for all crew members are required. Visas are not required for citizens of EU countries, Scandinavian countries, the USA, Canada and many others. If in doubt check with any Danish Embassy. Visitors should report to the harbourmaster at the first port of call. Crew changes should be notified to the Harbourmaster where these take place.

The Royal Danish Embassy in London is located at 55 Sloane Street, London, SW1X 9SR ② 020 7333 0200 *Fax* 020 7333 0270 *Email* lonamb@um.dk www.denmark.org.uk.

The British Embassy in Copenhagen is at Kastelvej 36/38/40, DK-2100 Copenhagen ② +45 35 44 52 00 http://ukindenmark.fco.gov.uk/en

Practicalities

Time

Denmark uses UT+1 in winter and UT+2 in summer. The clocks change at the same time as UK, at the end of March and the end of October.

Money

The unit of currency is the Danish krone (Dkr) divided into 100 øre. In a referendum in 2002 the people of Denmark voted not to join the Euro.

Cash points (ATMs) are numerous and all major credit cards are accepted in shops and for fuel.

Shopping

Supermarkets in Denmark have a wide variety of foods. Prices fall between those in Norway and Sweden (where they are higher) and those in Germany. If approaching Denmark via the Kiel Canal it is worth stocking up with non-perishable stores in Holtenau. In particular it is worth stocking up on beer, wines and spirits as these are expensive in Denmark and even more so in Sweden.

Most shops, including hardware shops and some supermarkets, are closed on Saturday afternoon and all shops are closed on Sundays.

Public holidays

Official public holidays in Denmark include: 1 January, Maundy Thursday, Good Friday, Easter Sunday, Great Prayer Day (May), Ascension Day (May), Whit Sunday and Monday (May or June), 5 June (Constitution Day), 25–26 December.

Hotels and restaurants

There are many hotels and restaurants in the major cities, catering for all tastes and budgets.

Denmark is reputed to have a more relaxed attitude to alcohol, greater openness and more nightlife than the other Scandinavian countries.

Communications

All card and coin telephones can be used for international calls – dial 00 followed by the country code, area code (omitting any initial 0) and number. The country code for Denmark is 45. There is good coverage for mobile phones but this may not be the case if more than 1M offshore. For international directory enquiries dial 113.

Internet cafés are widely available and Wi-Fi is becoming much more common in marinas. Sometimes it is free.

Travel

Denmark can be reached very easily from most parts of western Europe by air, rail, road and sea. Until recently, air travel to Scandinavia was relatively expensive but low-cost airlines now offer connections to several cities including Esbjerg, Århus and Copenhagen (as well as Malmø, from which Copenhagen can be reached by train over the Øresund bridge). Train services are efficient and bicycles may be taken on board. Ferry services between Germany, Denmark and other Scandinavian countries can be very useful.

Holding tanks

In 2008 foreign visitors were not yet obliged to fit holding tanks but toilets must not be discharged within 2M of the shore and shore facilities used whenever possible. Danish registered vessels over 10·5m long or 2·8m beam and built after 1st January 2000 now have to be fitted with holding tanks with the means to be discharged through a deck fitting.

2. DENMARK

2a. Eastern Danish ports
2b. The Danish side of the Øresund
2c. Bornholm and Christiansø
2d. Approach to the Kattegat through the Limfjord
2e. Danish harbours & anchorages of the Kattegat
2f. Approach to The Baltic by the Lille Bælt
2g. Approach to The Baltic by the Store Bælt

Internet sites

www.amblondon.um.dk/en – Danish Embassy in London.

http://ukindenmark.fco.gov.uk/en/ – British Embassy in Copenhagen.

www.visitdenmark.com – Danish Tourist Board.

www.visitcopenhagen.dk/ – Copenhagen city website.

www.lolland-falster.dk – Tourist website for Lolland and Falster Islands.

www.visitvordingborg.dk – Tourist website for Møn Island.

www.visitfyn.com – Tourist website for Fyn Island.

www.bornholminfo.dk – Tourist website for Bornholm Island (includes harbour plans).

www.dmi.dk – Danmarks Meteorologiske Institut for weather forecasts.

www.kms.dk – Kort and Matrikelstyrelsen, national mapping and charting agency who do not sell direct to the public. Corrections to Danish charts are available on line.

www.skat.dk – Danish Customs. Not very user-friendly, but does give phone numbers for enquiries.

www.weilbach.dk – Chart and nautical book suppliers, *see under Copenhagen.*

submitted under protest to a German invasion in 1940, and the situation deteriorated into a state of war in 1943. Since then, and with some pain, Denmark has re-established her position as a leading agricultural producer, besides developing a significant manufacturing industry. The present constitution of Denmark is founded on the charter of 5 June 1953, which places the legislative power with the crown and a single chamber (the Folketing) and the executive power with the crown through its ministers. The judiciary is separate.

Denmark joined the European Community – now the EU – in 1973. However, the Danes have traditionally been suspicious of deeper political integration with the EU and negotiated several opt-outs from the Maastricht Treaty of 1992. Having rejected EMU membership in a referendum in September 2002, Denmark participates in the EU's revised exchange rate mechanism but has not embraced the Euro.

Cruising areas

This chapter aims to cover some of the harbours of Denmark in one of two ways. The majority of yachts visiting the Baltic Sea will approach it by the Kiel Canal and so the Danish harbours of the western Baltic are covered from west to east and then up the Sound (Øresund) from south to north to Copenhagen (København) and beyond. A minority will approach the Baltic through the Kattegat (including the Limfjord) and continue through the Little Belt (Lille Bælt) or the Great Belt (Store Bælt) so that these harbours are covered from north to south.

Additional reading

For more detail Brian Navin's *Cruising Guide to Denmark and Germany* is comprehensive, as is *Komma's Havnelods* harbour guide although it is in Danish but it has excellent harbour plans with

Charts and chart packs

Admiralty charts are excellent for the main channels around Denmark and for reaching all the passage harbours. In particular, details of the several shipping separation zones, firing practice ranges, windfarms, etc are given both on the charts and in notes. Large-scale charts will be needed for exploration of the fjords and the Limfjord and for the approaches to Copenhagen.

Danish charts give good large-scale coverage and these are enumerarated in the facts paragraph at the commencement of each harbour description.

There are two excellent series of German-published chart packs (size A2) which are readily available in Denmark. They are published annually and come with electronic versions on CD and complementary piot books.

NV Baltic Charts

Serie 1 Fünen – Kiel
Serie 2 Lübeck – Bornholm – Kopenhagen
Serie 3 Samsö – Sund – Kattegat
Serie 4 Rügen – Bodengewässer – Stettin
Serie 5 Schwedische Westküste
Serie 6 Poland – Litauen – Lettland
NOK Nord-Ostsee Kanal. A chart (A2) of the Kiel Canal.

Delius Klasing charts

Satz 1 Kieler Bucht und Rund Fünen (includes the Kiel Canal)
Satz 2 Mecklenburg - Vorpommern - Bornholm
Satz 3 Westküste-Schweden
Satz 4 Grosser Belt bis Bornholm
Satz 5 Kattegat
Satz 6 Limfjord, Sjkagerrak, Danische Nordseeküste
Satz 11 Ostküste Schweden 1
Satz 12 Ostküste Schweden 2

The advantages of the series type of chart are that one pack covers a large area and many harbour plans are included. However some people find the combination of large-scale and small size somewhat inconvenient and prefer to use normal charts.

Pilots and cruising guides

Cruising Guide to Germany and Denmark, Brian Navin, Imray Laurie Norie & Wilson Ltd.

Imray/Cruising Association *Cruising Almanac.* Imray Laurie Norie & Wilson Ltd.

Komma's Havnelods, Aschehoug Dansk Forlag. Comprehensive harbour information. In Danish. Two yearly*.

Dänemark I & 2, Jan Werner, DK Edition Maritim. In German.*

Hafenführer Dänemark, DK Edition Maritim. In German*.

Ankerplatz in Danemark, Gerti and Harm Claussen, DK Edition Maritim. In German*.

Der Grosse NV Hafen Lotse, Volumes 1, 2 and 3, Nautische Veröffentlichung (complements Serie 1, 2 and 3 of their charts). In German.

Hafenhandbuch Ostsee 1 covers all the harbours of Denmark apart from Jutland north of Grenå which are covered in the Nord See volume. Text in German and excellent harbour plans. Published by Delius, Klasing & Co. Complements their chart series.

Baltic Pilot Volume I (NP 18) covers the Danish islands in great detail but is not the most convenient publication for everyday pilotage.

See the *Appendix,* page 361, for sources.

2. DENMARK

symbols for the facilities available. Another useful publication are the *Sejlerens Marina Guides* Volumes 1, 2, 3 and 4 newly published at the beginning of each season and available free at marinas. They are in Danish and German but again have plans of marinas and easily understood symbols for the facilities available. Obtain a copy at the first Danish Marina you visit. Large scale charts are also essential.

Tidal streams and depths

There is little tide as such in Denmark and depths are generally quite shallow. But currents are unpredictable and are influenced by wind direction, but are usually modest other than in narrow channels such as at the north end of the Lille Bælt and in the Sound north of Copenhagen. Water levels can vary quite substantially – by up to 2m – due to atmospheric and wind conditions. Strong offshore winds in particular can reduce stated depths in harbours. Many of the harbours are quite shallow with depths of less than 2m, so it is necessary to check charts and plans carefully before entering a new harbour. Mean level is used for chart datum and the wind effect may result in charted depths differing by as much as 1m and very occasionally more.

Yacht services and chandlery

Chandlery and engine spares are widely available, although they sometimes have to be delivered from Copenhagen. Sailmakers are not generally found – most are centred around Copenhagen – but repairs may be arranged via yacht clubs (see below).

Re-filling non-Danish gas cylinders is likely to be difficult, especially blue (butane) *Calor Gas* bottles. It may be possible to re-fill propane bottles at service stations which supply gas powered cars. *Camping Gas* cylinders on the other hand are widely available.

Diesel is available in most harbours but petrol is not always available and may have to be carried from a filling station.

Costs for laying up in Denmark over the winter are very reasonable by UK standards and should be taken into consideration when planning a Baltic cruise lasting more than one season.

Berths

Danish harbours can be very crowded during the peak summer months of July and August, as German and Swedish yachts join the ever expanding fleet of Danish yachts and small motor boats. However in late May, June and late August they can be almost deserted.

Berthing is usually in box berths with bow to a quay or jetty and the stern moored to a post on each quarter. Sometimes these posts are positioned too close together for beamy boats and nice judgement is required when entering the box. Normal fenders are useless when entering a box but thickish ropes strung along the topsides from bow to stern can save a lot of anguish if short-handed. An unoccupied berth is signalled by a green plaque at its head sometimes with the date on which its owner plans to return. A red plaque on the other hand indicates that the berth is only temporarily unoccupied and its owner will be returning soon.

Berthing fees

Overnight berthing fees are likely to be in the range Dkr 100–130 for a 10m boat, Dkr 120–160 for a 12m boat and Dkr 140–180 for a 15m boat.

Yacht Clubs

Yacht clubs in Denmark are generally an association of local yachtsmen who are based on a particular yacht harbour. In many cases the club or association is responsible for the operation of the yacht harbour and for the provision of the facilities. Visitors are usually offered temporary use of any club facilities during their stay.

Radio communications and weather information

Denmark's VHF coast radio stations are well organised and convenient to use, and all parts of the coastline have excellent coverage, see Appendix on page 367. All VHF stations are remotely controlled from Lyngby Radio (near Copenhagen).

Although gale and storm warnings are broadcast in English, normal weather forecasts are not, but may be obtained on request.

Excellent weather forecasts and information on depths and currents can be obtained on the website of the Danish Maritime Safety Administration on www.ifm.frv.dk

Five-day forecasts in English are available on the Danish Meteorological Institute (DMI) website. www.dmi.dk

NAVTEX is perhaps the best and most reliable method of receiving weather information in English and covers the whole of the Baltic. Denmark is covered by the Skagerrak, Kattegat, The Belts and Western Baltic areas. Bornholm is in the southern Baltic area. Otherwise, weather information is obtainable from local yacht clubs and marinas.

In most harbours VHF is not used and communication with harbourmasters is normally by telephone as in Germany.

A votive ship as found in many churches *E. Redfern*

2a. Eastern Danish ports

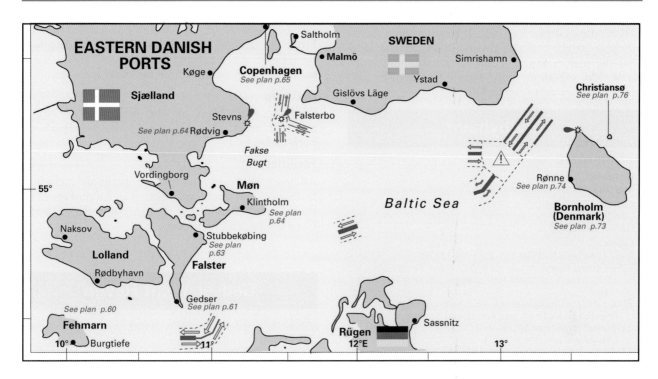

EASTERN DANISH PORTS

Sjælland

Køge

Copenhagen
See plan p.65

Saltholm

Malmö

SWEDEN

Simrishamn

Gislövs Läge

Ystad

Stevns

Rødvig *See plan p.64*

Falsterbo

Fakse Bugt

Vordingborg

Møn

Klintholm
See plan p.64

Baltic Sea

Christiansø
See plan p.76

55°

Rønne
See plan p.74

Bornholm
(Denmark)
See plan p.73

Naksov

Lolland

Rødbyhavn

Stubbekøbing
See plan p.63

Falster

Gedser
See plan p.61

See plan p.60

Fehmarn

10° Burgtiefe

11°

Rügen

12°E

Sassnitz

13°

2. DENMARK

These harbours are listed here as convenient harbours on the southern Danish Islands on the quickest route from the Kiel Canal to Copenhagen or southern Sweden. They are chosen as being at approximately day sailing intervals. The route is relatively exposed, may require overnight passages and will be close to main shipping routes. The information given is designed to be used with passage charts – large-scale charts should not be needed.

On leaving Kiel and heading towards Copenhagen or Sweden there are two main options – either to head east to Heiligenhafen (35M) and pass through Fehmarn Sund (see Germany, page 31) before crossing the shipping channels and heading for the

Free bicycle hire at Århus *J. Parkinson*

Evening view marina Stubbekøbing *C. Lassen*

Gedser peninsula, or to head northeastwards to Denmark, either to Rødbyhavn (45M) or Gedser (70M). In either case close attention to shipping lanes, practice firing ranges and crossing ferries will be needed.

Rounding Gedser Rev (shoal) requires due care to navigate safely between the shallows off the land and the major turning point in the shipping lanes some 9M offshore. Once round Gedser Rev the route north or east is straightforward.

Rødbyhavn

54°39'N 11°20'E

Distances
Kiel (Holtenau) 45M, Gedser 30M

Charts
UKHO 2113
Danish charts 196

Lights
Buoy **Landfall** 54°38'·3N 11°19'·4E RW LFl.10s
2216 **Central pierhead** Ldg Lts 045·2° Front 54°39'·2N
    11°21'E Iso.R.2s17m6M Red triangle on red framework
    tower
2216·1 Rear 300m from front, Iso.R.4s26m6M Red
    inverted triangle on grey framework tower
2218 **West molehead** 54°39'·1N 11°20'·8E F.R.8m5M Red
    framework tower 5m
2218·2 **East molehead** 54°39'N 11°20'·8E F.G.8m5M Green
    framework tower on hut 5m

Harbour communications
Rødbyhavn Harbourmaster ☎ +45 2025 0672
Port Control VHF Ch 74
Marina ☎ +45 5465 7180

General

Rødbyhavn, on the southwest coast of Lolland, is a busy port with a major ferry link to Germany. Access is straightforward with entry by day or night and, although not particularly yacht-friendly, it can be useful as a first stop in Denmark on passage from Kiel to Copenhagen or Sweden. Beware and keep clear of ferries on entry.

Approach

Approach waypoint 54°38'N 11°19'E

From the landfall buoy follow the (lit) leading line on 045·2°. After passing between the breakwaters turn due north and head for the inner harbour.

Berthing

Berth at a pontoon on the west side of North Harbour or on the west side of the west harbour both in 5m.

Facilities

All main harbour facilities are available including restaurant and diesel, with petrol at 500m. Ferries to Puttgarden (Fehmarn). Train connections with Copenhagen and Hamburg.

Gedser Yacht Haven

54°35'N 11°55'E

Distances
Kiel 70M, Rødbyhavn 30M, Stubbekøbing 30M, Klintholm 35M, Copenhagen 85M, Gislövs Läge (Sweden) 70M, Rønne (Bornholm) 100M

Charts
UKHO 2601, 2365
Danish 197

Lights
2186 **Gedser Odde** 54°33'·9N 11°57'·9E Fl(3)20s26m24M
    Racon (G) White hexagonal tower 20m
Buoy **West cardinal** 54°31'·7N 11°56'E Q(9)15s Yellow and
    black pillar buoy, W topmark
2188 **Gedser Odde S end** 54°31'·7N 11°56'·2E
    Fl(3)R.10s13m10M Red pillar and lantern 14m Floodlit
    Horn(3)30s
2196 Ldg Lts 350·5° Front 54°34'·3N 11°55'·7E
    Iso.2s17m9M 280·5°-vis-060·5° Red triangle on grey
    framework mast 15m
2196·1 Rear 376m from front Iso.2s26m9M 280·5°-vis-
    060·5° Grey framework tower 30m
    Note Buoyage in the entrance channel runs north to
    south (red buoys/lights to starboard on the approach
    from the South)
2205 **Yacht harbour N mole** 54°34'·9N 11°55'·2E F.R.4m2M
    Grey post 2m
2206 **Yacht harbour S mole** 54°34'·9N 11°55'·3E F.G.4m2M
    Grey post 2m

Harbour communications
Gedser Yacht Haven ☎ +45 5417 9245

General

The Gedser peninsula on the south end of the island of Falster is about half way between the Kiel Canal and Copenhagen or southern Sweden, with a major traffic separation zone some 9M offshore. It is a major ferry port and the yacht harbour is quite separate from the commercial harbour.

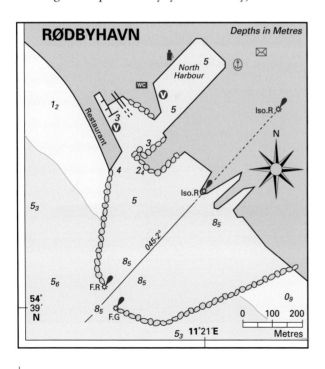

RØDBYHAVN — Depths in Metres

Approach

Approach waypoint 54°31'N 11°56'E

Approaching from the west, navigate to a position just east of the west cardinal buoy noted above, keeping clear of the offshore wind farm. Approaching from the east, keep clear of the shoals which run some distance south-southeast from the tip of the peninsula.

As Gedser has a major ferry terminal, there is a buoyed and lit channel and a lit leading line – red buoys to starboard. Follow the channel until just before the entrance to the ferry harbour, then turn to port and follow the next part of the marked channel for about 0·75M, when the yacht harbour will be seen to starboard.

Berthing

Berth in box berths. The southernmost berths carry a depth of 3m and the others 2·5m.

Facilities

All basic facilities are available including a restaurant and a diesel berth.

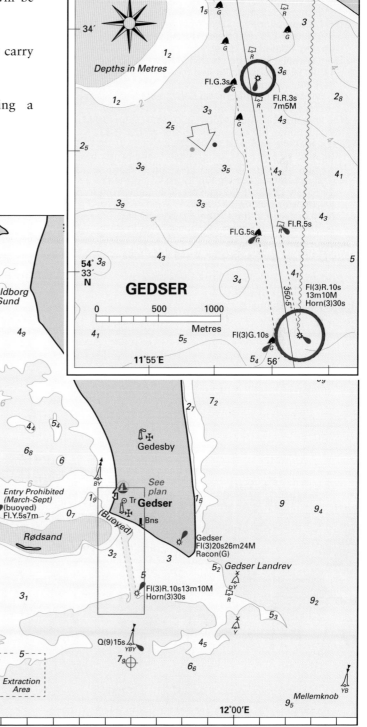

Stubbekøbing

54°54'N 12°03'E

Distances
Kiel 95M, Gedser 30M, Klintholm 20M,
Copenhagen 70M, Gislövs Läge 60M

Charts
UKHO 2115
Danish 198, 162

Lights
2152 **Hestehoved** 54°50'·1N 12°09'·9E
Oc(2)WRG.6s14m13–9M 216·5°-R-264°-G-290°-W-342°-R-007°-G-024° White house 4m
Red can buoy 54°49'·8N 12°11'·4E Fl(3)R.10s
2166 Ldg Lts 324° *Front* 54°53'N 12°07'·2E Iso.2s12m9M
319°-intens-329° Red triangle on white tower 13m
2166·1 **Skansepynt** *Rear* 520m from front, Iso.4s20m13M
319°-intens-329° Red inverted triangle, white bands,
on grey framework tower 19m
2154·9 **Hårbølle Pynt** Ldg Lts. 353·5° *Front* 54°53'N
12°08'·9E Iso.G.2s10m7M Red triangle, white bands on
grey framework tower
2155 *Rear* 480m from front. Iso.G.4s21m8M Red inverted
triangle, white bands, on grey framework tower
2178 **Borgsted** 54°54'·2N 12°06'·5E Oc.WRG.5s3m10–8M
White house, red band. 317°-G-320°-W-323°-R-332·5
2155·4 **Hårbolle** 54°53'·3N 12°08'·2E
Oc.WRG.10s6m12–9M Red triangle, white bands, on
framework tower. 064°-G-101·5-W-106·5°-R-117°
1857 **Stubbekøbing** Ldg Lts 176° *Front* W molehead
54°53'·5N 12°02'·7E F.G.3m Post. *Rear* 130m from front
F.G.7m Grey framework tower
Note Buoyage in the entrance channels runs
northwest to southeast (red buoys/lights to starboard)

Harbour communications
Stubbekøbing Harbourmaster ① +45 5444 1092

General

Stubbekøbing is a useful stop on the way from Kiel to Copenhagen or southern Sweden, although it is some 10M from the direct route. It is a pleasant small town and commercial port, with a friendly yacht club and comfortable yacht harbour immediately to the east of the commercial harbour.

Approach

Approach waypoints
Hestehoved Dyb Channel 54°49'N 12°12'E
Stubbekøbing Harbour 54°53'·8N 12°02'·7E

The dredged and well-buoyed approach channel – red buoys to starboard – with leading lights, starts to the east of Hestehoved light. The initial course is 324° from the waypoint near the red can buoy noted above, thereafter see plan. Leave the main buoyed channel opposite the harbour entrance and follow the buoyed channel southwards towards the commercial harbour and just before the entrance turn eastwards to follow the breakwater round to the yacht harbour entrance. Do not cut the corner.

Berthing

Berth in box berths (some of which are narrow) in outer part of yacht harbour which carries a depth of 2·3–2·7m. The inner basin has 1·5m or less.

Facilities

All main harbour facilities are available including diesel, with petrol at 500m. There is a kiosk selling a limited selection of groceries and drinks beside the commercial harbour, and a shopping centre in the town some 500m further away, where there are the usual banks, restaurants and hotels.

Stubbekøbing Marina *S. Carnegie*

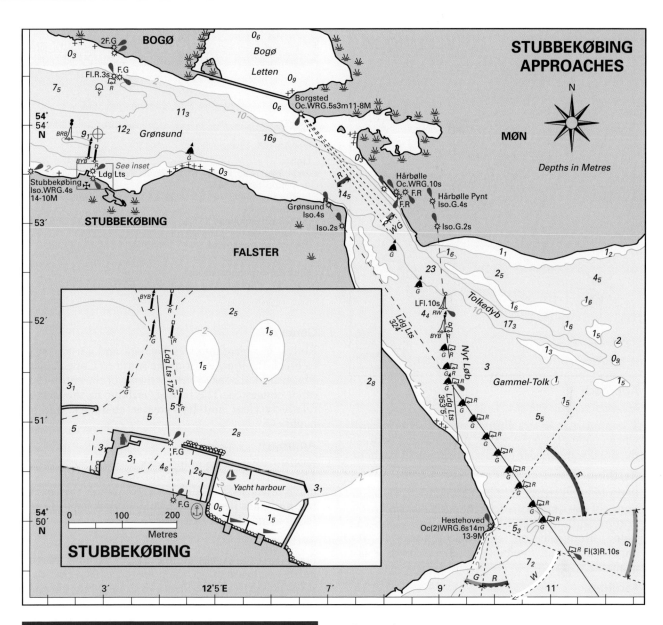

Klintholm

54°57'N 12°28'E

Distances
Gedser 35M, Stubbekøbing 20M, Rødvig 25M,
Copenhagen 55M, Gislövs Läge 40M

Charts
UKHO 2115, 2365
Danish 198

Lights
2142 **Møn SE Point** 54°56'·8N 12°32'·4E Fl(4)30s25m21M
214°-vis°071° Yellow square tower 13m
2146 **North molehead** 54°57'·2N 12°27'·9E Fl.R.3s4m4M
Post
2148 **South molehead** 54°57'·1N 12°27'·9E Fl.G.3s5m4M
White pedestal 3m

Harbour communications
Klintholm Harbourmaster ☎ +45 5581 9044

General
Klintholm provides a good passage harbour as it is
close to the direct route to Copenhagen and provides
a good starting point for the leg to southern Sweden.

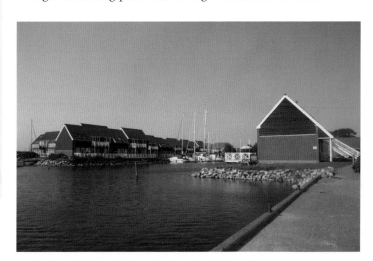

Sheltered berths in Klintholm
E. Redfern

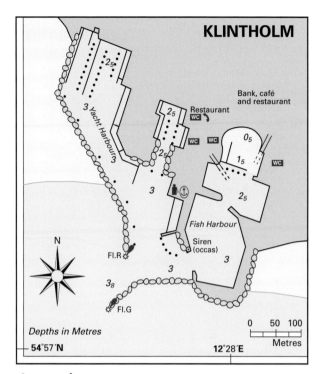

KLINTHOLM

Depths in Metres

Approach

Approach waypoint 54°56′N 12°28′E

The approach is straightforward with no hazards when coming from the south. After passing between the breakwaters, bear to port for the yacht harbour.

Berthing

Berth in box berths either in the smaller basin to the north of the entrance or in the larger basin to the northwest. Both carry 2·5m depth. Large yachts can moor alongside on the instructions of the harbourmaster if a suitably sized box berth is not available.

Facilities

All main harbour facilities are available including diesel, with petrol at 200m. A sailmaker works locally and there are banks and restaurants nearby.

Rødvig *P. Roach*

Rødvig

55°15′N 12°22′E

Distances
Gedser 55M, Klintholm 25M, Copenhagen 35M

Charts
UKHO 2115
Danish 198, 190

Lights
2094 **Stevns** 55°17′·5N 12°27′·2E LFl.25s64m26M White round tower 26m
buoy **Landfall** 55°14′·1N 12°23′·6E LFl.10s Red and white pillar buoy
2098 **East molehead** 55°15′·2N 12°22′·6E Fl.G.3s5m3M Red pedestal, white band
2099 **West molehead** 55°15′·2N 12°22′·5E Fl.R.3s5m3M Grey conical concrete hut 3m

Harbour communications
Rødvig Harbourmaster ☏ +45 56 50 60 07

General

Rødvig is a pleasant small harbour and a useful stop to break the journey from the south to Copenhagen. The yacht harbour to the northeast of the entrance is often congested. The fishing harbour to the west is relatively clear and has greater character, but no facilities.

Approach

Approach waypoint 55°14′N 12°23′E

The harbour entrance should be approached in a north-northeasterly direction to avoid the many fishing stakes just offshore, and entry at night is not recommended on a first visit.

Berthing

Berth in box berths in the yacht harbour to the north-northeast of the main entrance. The first two rows of berths carry a depth of 1·5m while the ones further in are deeper with 2·8m. If the yacht harbour is full there is alongside berthing for yachts in the fishing harbour to the northwest of the main entrance.

Facilities

All main harbour facilities are available including diesel and petrol in the main harbour. Wi-Fi.

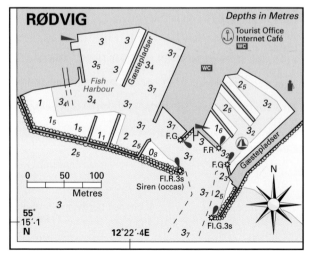

RØDVIG   Depths in Metres

2b. The Danish side of the Øresund (The Sound)

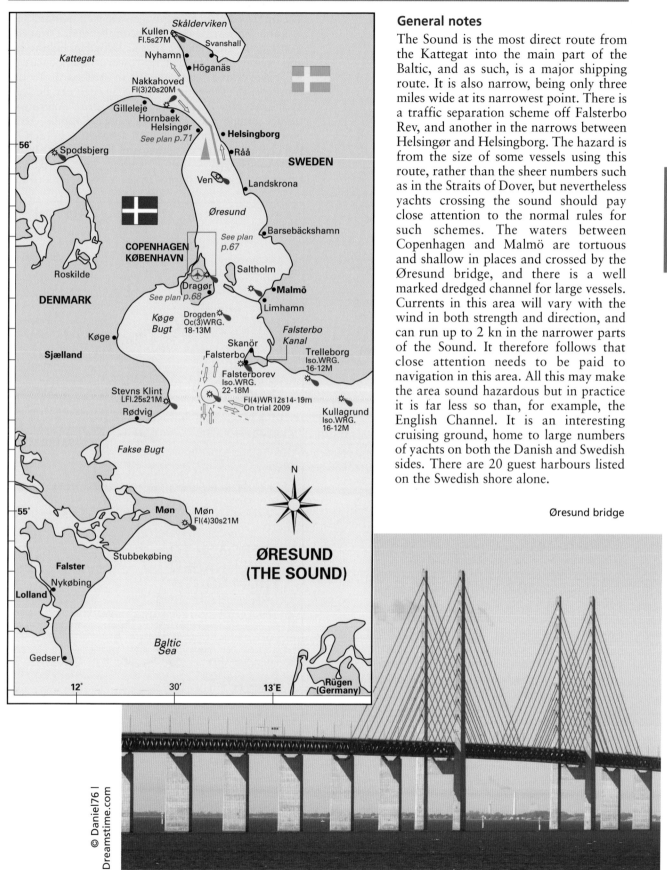

General notes

The Sound is the most direct route from the Kattegat into the main part of the Baltic, and as such, is a major shipping route. It is also narrow, being only three miles wide at its narrowest point. There is a traffic separation scheme off Falsterbo Rev, and another in the narrows between Helsingør and Helsingborg. The hazard is from the size of some vessels using this route, rather than the sheer numbers such as in the Straits of Dover, but nevertheless yachts crossing the sound should pay close attention to the normal rules for such schemes. The waters between Copenhagen and Malmö are tortuous and shallow in places and crossed by the Øresund bridge, and there is a well marked dredged channel for large vessels. Currents in this area will vary with the wind in both strength and direction, and can run up to 2 kn in the narrower parts of the Sound. It therefore follows that close attention needs to be paid to navigation in this area. All this may make the area sound hazardous but in practice it is far less so than, for example, the English Channel. It is an interesting cruising ground, home to large numbers of yachts on both the Danish and Swedish sides. There are 20 guest harbours listed on the Swedish shore alone.

Øresund bridge

2. DENMARK

© Daniel76 |
Dreamstime.com

Copenhagen

55°41'N 12°36'E

Distances
Helsingør 22M, Klintholm 55M, Gedser 85M,
Kiel 150M, Stralsund 85M, Falsterbo Kanal 21M, Gislövs
Läge (Sweden) 35M, Rønne 90M.

Charts
UKHO 902, 903, 2115, 2595
Danish 131, 132, 133, 134

Lights
964 **Middelgrunds Fort west** 55°43'·3N 12°39'·9E
Oc.WRG.5s11m12–10M 005°-R-069°-G-128°-R-173°-G-
184°-W-193°-R-225° Red block
1965 **Middelgrunds Fort east** 55°43'·2N 12°40'·1E
Oc(2)WRG.12s11m12–10M 204·5°-W-245°-R-290°-G-
346°-W-350°-R-056° Red block
1978 **Trekroner, east side** 55°42'·2N 12°37'E
Iso.WRG.2s20m17–13M 175°-R-195°-G-207°-W-210°-R-
214°-G-219·8°-W-222·9°-R-255°-G-316·5°-W-320°-R-
336° White round tower 12m
2024 **Prøvestenshavn oil jetty** 55°41'N 12°38'·3E
Oc(3)WRG.15s10m13–10M 160°-G-168°-W-171°-R-175°-
G-178·2°-W-180·4°-R-182·2°-G-203° White framework
tower, white hut, red band 8m
2042 **Nordre-Røse** 55°38'·2N 12°41'·3E
Oc(2)WRG.6s14m18–13M Racon (M) 140°-R-157·5°-G-
176·5°-W-181°-R-186°-G-030·5° Round granite tower
17m
2060 **Drogden** 55°32'·2N 12°42'·8E
Oc(3)WRG.15s18m18–13M 009°-R-021°-G-028·5°-W-
071°-R-256·5°-G-357·5°-W-009° Racon (X) White
square tower, red bands, grey base 20m Horn
Mo(U)30s (occas)

Harbour communications
Copenhagen Port Authority ✆ +45 3546 1111
VHF Ch 09, 10, 12, 13, 14, 16
Email cmport@cmport.com www.cmport.com
Copenhagen Harbourmaster ✆ +45 3546 1138
Langelinie Harbourmaster ✆ +45 3526 2338
Email havnefoged-llb@mail.dk
www.langeliniehavn.dk
Svanemølle Harbourmaster ✆ +45 3920 2221
(0900–1900 LT) *Email* info@smhavn.dk
www.smhavn.dk
Hellerup Harbourmaster ✆ +45 3962 0761
Email havn@gentofte.dk
Margaretheholms Havn (Lynette Sailing Club)
✆ +45 3257 5778 www.lynetten.dk

General

Copenhagen is a friendly city with a strong feeling of history. There is much for the tourist, better described in one of the numerous shore-based guide books than here. Sightseeing in the centre of the city can be done on foot.

After the treaty of Kalmar, Denmark controlled both sides of the Sound, and in 1429 King Erik, recognising its potential profitability, imposed a toll on all shipping passing through it. To administer and enforce this toll, he appropriated Copenhagen (then a Hanseatic town) to the crown and built a second fortification at Helsingør, opposite Helsingborg. The toll continued to be levied even after Denmark lost control of the Swedish shore and lasted until 1856, when, after increasing numbers of complaints from several countries, the United States simply refused to pay. The duties were abolished by treaty a year later.

Approach

Approach waypoints
From the north 55°45'N 12°39'·5E
From the south 55°34'N 12°42'E

The approaches to Copenhagen are well marked and lit but a large-scale chart is recommended. From the south gain the vicinity of the Drogden lighthouse and follow the channel northwards but beware – RED buoys and lights are left to **starboard**. To the northeast the Øresund Bridge to Sweden can be seen as it traverses Peberholm Island before entering a tunnel under the main shipping channel. After Nordre-Røse lighthouse is left to port, a branch of the channel to the city area (the Kongedybet) bears northwestwards – on a leading line of 317·8° towards Trekroner light – to leave the pylons of the

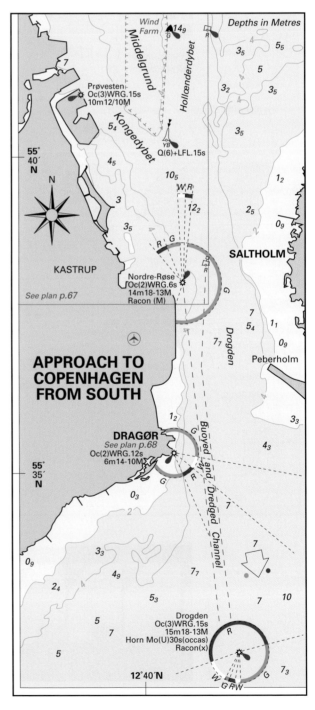

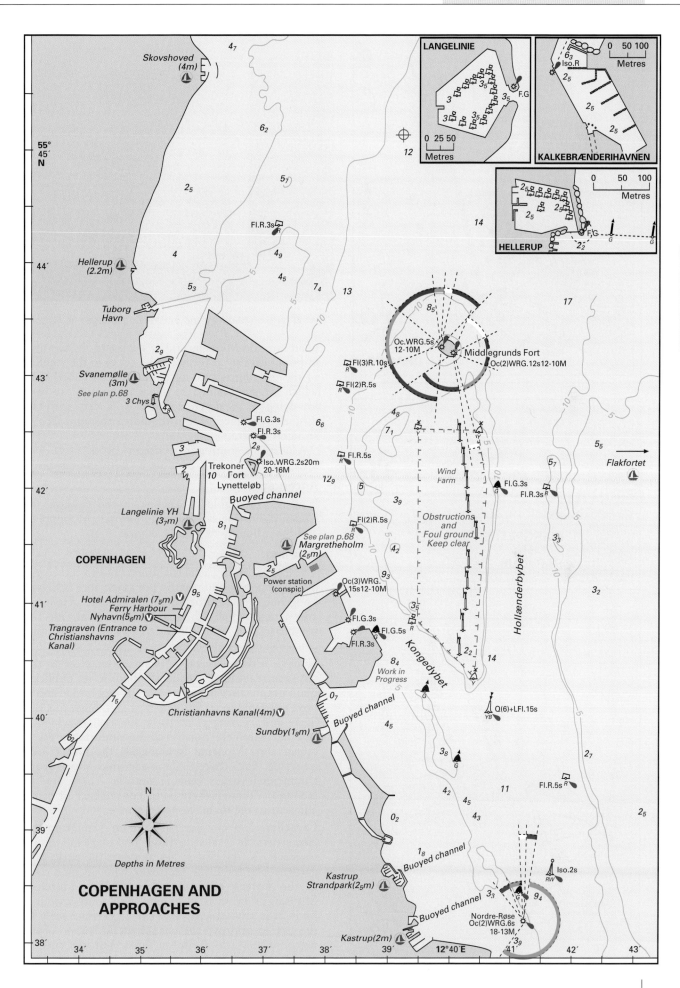

LANGELINIE

3
3₅
3₅
3
3₅
3₅
F.G
0 25 50
Metres

KALKEBRÆNDERIHAVNEN

6₃
Iso.R
2₅
2₅
2₅
2₅
0 50 100
Metres

HELLERUP

2₅
2₅
2₅
2₅
F.G
2₂
G
G
0   50 100
Metres

Skovshoved (4m)
4₇
6₂
5₇

55°
45′
N

2₅

Fl.R.3s
R

44′

Hellerup (2.2m)
4
4₉
4₅
7₄
13
5₃

Tuborg Havn

Svanemølle (3m)
See plan p.68
2₉
3 Chys

43′

Fl.G.3s
Fl.R.3s
2₈
Iso.WRG.2s20m 20-16M
Trekoner Fort
Lynetteløb
10
3
2

Langelinie YH (3₇m)

42′

8₁

COPENHAGEN

See plan p.68
Margretheholm (2₅m)
2₅
Power station (conspic)
Oc(3)WRG. 15s12-10M
Fl.G.3s
Fl.G.5s
G
Fl.R.3s
Work in Progress

Hotel Admiralen (7₅m)
Ferry Harbour
Nyhavn(5₆m)
Trangraven (Entrance to Christianshavns Kanal)
9₅

41′

Christianhavns Kanal(4m)
7₅
6₂
Sundby(1₈m)
Buoyed channel
0₇
Buoyed channel
4₅

40′

7
N
Depths in Metres

COPENHAGEN AND APPROACHES

39′

Kastrup Strandpark(2₅m)
0₂
1₈
Buoyed channel
4₂
4₅
4₃
11
Fl.R.5s
R

Kastrup(2m)
3₃
Buoyed channel
Nordre-Røse Oc(2)WRG.6s 18-13M
3₉
G
9₄

38′

Iso.2s
RW

12
6₆
6
12₉
5
Fl.R.5s
R
Fl(2)R.5s
R
4₈
7₁
3₉
4₂
9₃
3₅
2₂
8₄
5
Kongedybet
G
Q(6)+LFl.15s
YB
3₈
G

Middlegrunds Fort
8₅
Oc.WRG.5s 12-10M
Oc(2)WRG.12s12-10M
Fl(3)R.10s
R
Fl(2)R.5s
R
14
17

Wind Farm
Obstructions and Foul ground Keep clear

Hollænderbybet
Fl.G.3s
R
Fl.R.3s
R
5₅
5₇
3₃
3₂
2₇
2₅

Flakfortet

14

34′ 35′ 36′ 37′ 38′ 39′ **12°40′E** 41′ 42′ 43′

2. DENMARK

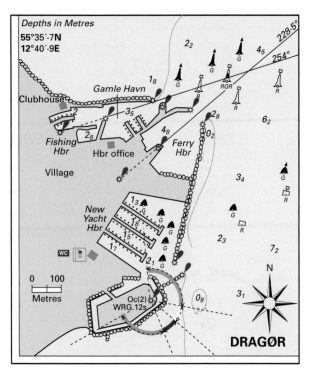

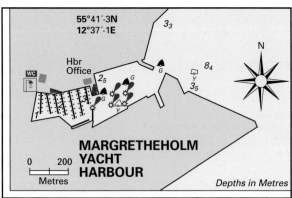

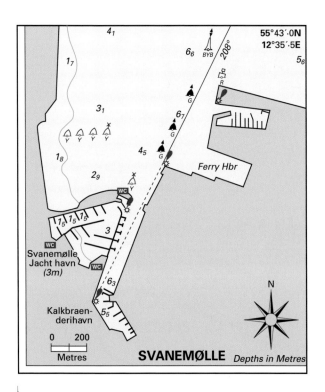

Wind farm on Middelgrund outside Copenhagen *R. Wilson*

wind farm on Middelgrund to starboard. By day and in poor visibility care should be taken in the vicinity of the offlying islands of Saltholm and Peberholm, which are surrounded by shoal water and are very low-lying – so much so that it is very easy to misjudge distances. From the north the approach is straightforward.

A north or south-going current can be up to 4–5 knots in the Sound depending on wind conditions.

Anchorage

It is not advisable to anchor in the environs of Copenhagen due to the large amount of shipping and the difficulty of getting ashore.

Berthing

There are several yacht harbours close to the centre of Copenhagen and details are given for: Nyhavn, Langelinie, Margretheholm, Svanemølle, Hellerup and Dragør. The Christianshavns Kanal, on the southeast side of the main harbour, is also very convenient for sightseeing.

Nyhavn is the picturesque old harbour, close to the city centre, which frequently figures in publicity photographs. Access is through a lifting bridge and is now restricted to traditional craft. Although this is a lively and exciting place to lie for a short while, it can be extremely noisy and uncomfortable for a longer stay. Mooring is alongside the rather high quayside and there is considerable wash from commercial vessels passing outside. There are no facilities, although there is the convenience of being adjacent to the main shopping centre.

Langelinie is a circular basin about 1km from the city centre. It is always busy, but is useful for its proximity to the city. It lies amongst the parks and gardens near the Little Mermaid, who sits on a rock at the water's edge near Langelinie promenade. Mooring is bows to the quay with stern line to a buoy. It is advisable to arrive at Langelinie early in the day to improve the chance of finding a vacant berth. There are basic facilities but no fuel is available. Berthing fees are high.

Nyhavn, Copenhagen *P. & G. Price*

Christianshavns Kanal, entered almost directly opposite Nyhavn, is a picturesque but crowded alongside mooring place with easy access to the city centre. This area, with its bridges and gabled houses, is reminiscent of Amsterdam's inner canals. Local people recommend it as *the* place to moor for sightseeing.

Margretheholm is run by Lynette Sailing Club who are very welcoming to visitors and have excellent facilities including a restaurant, a first rate chandlery and fuel. The approach is from the Kongedybet at 55°41'·6N 12°38'E.

Berthing is in box berths in 2·5–3·0m but these can vary up to 0·6m. The one disadvantage is that it is twenty minutes walk to the nearest bus stop.

Svanemølle is the largest of the Copenhagen yacht harbours and normally has space for visitors. It is approached in a southwesterly direction via a buoyed channel leading from the northern end of the dock complex. It is 4km from the main shopping centre, but the excellent public transport system makes travelling there easy, leaving one's boat in relative quiet and safety. Fuel is available.

Hellerup is a small yacht harbour 6km from the city centre and 500m north of the Tuborg harbour (which is out of bounds to yachts). It is administered by Hellerup Yacht Club and comprises a small square basin flanked by trees and overlooked by the yacht club. There is an obvious buoyed channel leading to the south-facing harbour entrance. Mooring is bows-to with stern lines to posts. Visitors are automatically made members of the yacht club for the duration of their stay.

Facilities include water and electricity on the quayside, toilets, showers and a sauna, and an excellent restaurant with umbrella-shaded tables on a balcony overlooking the sea. There is no fuelling berth. Berthing fees are mainly in the middle range, but in the upper range for large yachts.

Hellerup shopping centre is about 300m away, with a wide range of shops, banks, restaurants etc.

Langelinie *S. Carnegie*

2. DENMARK

Margretheholm with Langelinie in background   *P. Roach*

Dragør on the west shore of the southern end of the Drogden channel is a pretty mediaeval fishing village developed by the Dutch with easy access by public transport into the city (30 minutes) and very convenient for the airport (15 minutes). There is a new marina on the south side of the harbour complex but it is only suitable for smaller yachts, a ferry harbour in the middle which is forbidden to yachts and a *gamlehavn* on the north side where depths are 2·5–3·5m. The inner fishing harbour is

Where else but Copenhagen? The world-famous Little Mermaid *G. and M. Honey*

also forbidden to yachts. The gamlehavn has good facilities, is closer to the town and has an excellent supermarket. There is also a small boatyard.

Services for yachts

There are several chandlers in Copenhagen, and most repairs can be arranged. There are a number of sailmakers in and around the city.

Danish, Swedish, German and British charts and pilot books may be bought from:
Iver Weilbach & Co, Toldbodgade 35, DK 1253 København K
☎ +45 3334 3575 *Fax* +45 3334 3561
Email nautical@weilbach.dk www.weilbach.dk
Customs: Toldskat Kobenhavn, Tagensvej 135, 2200 Kobenhavn N. ☎ +45 7222 1818.

General facilities

The city provides many banks, restaurants and hotels. The main tourist information office, ☎ +45 7022 2442, is at 1 Bernstorffsgade, between the Central Station and Tivoli's main entrance. But only Dragør and possibly Hellerup are close to shops for provisioning.

Note The yacht harbours to the southwest of Copenhagen (such as Brøndby) also give easy access to the centre of Copenhagen by train, are near the airport and offer winter lay-up facilities which may be of interest.

Helsingør

56°02'N 12°37'E

Distances
Gilleleje 12M, Copenhagen 22M, Halmstad 43M.

Charts
UKHO 2108, 2115, 2594
Danish 102, 131

Lights
1908 **Kronborg** 56°02'·4N 12°37'·3E
  Oc(2)WRG.6s34m15–12M NE tower of castle. 129°-G-
  137°-W-145°-R-161°-G-214°-W-311°-R-349°-G-352°-W-
  356°-R-017°-G-027°
1913 Ldg Lts 257·8° *Front* 56°02'N 12°37'·1E FW.13m6M
  Grey mast. 337·8-vis-277·8. *Rear* 77m from front.
  FW.14m6M Square brick tower
1912 **S pierhead** 56°02'·1N 12°37'·2E FR.7m6M Red round
  metal tower
1914 **N molehead** 56°02'·1N 12°37'·2E FG.7m6M Green
  round tower

Communications
Harbourmaster ☏ +45 4928 1080
  www.nordhavn.helsingor.dk

General

Shakespeare's Elsinore Castle (or to give it its correct name Kronborg Slott) dominates Helsingør. Originally built in the 15th century to enforce the collection of tolls from all ships sailing up or down the Øresund, it played a major part in the creation of Denmark's wealth. Helsingør has two harbours with the large yacht harbour lying to the north of Kronborg Point and the commercial ferry port lying to the south of it. The latter is out of bounds to yachts. Beware of the many ferries running across to Helsingborg in Sweden.

Approach

Approach waypoint 56°02'·8N 12°37'·8E

The approach to the east-facing entrance to the marina should be from a northeasterly direction and is straightforward.

Kronborg Slott, otherwise known as Hamlet's Elsinore Castle
E. Redfern

Berthing

Berth in box berths at one of the many jetties. Depths are 2·5–3·0m.

Facilities

All facilities are available including Wi-Fi.

Helsingør from the northeast with Kronborg Slott on the left and the ferry port in the background *P. Roach*

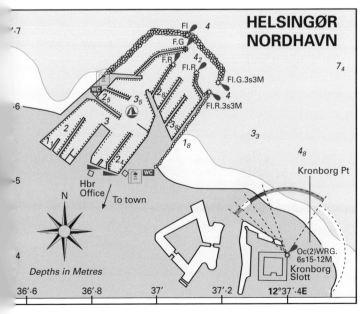

HELSINGØR NORDHAVN

Fl   4
F.G
F.R   4₂
Fl.R
  Fl.G.3s3M   4
  Fl.R.3s3M
7₄
3₃
1₈
4₈
Kronborg Pt
Oc(2)WRG. 6s15-12M
Kronborg Slott

Hbr Office → To town
N
Depths in Metres
36'·6   36'·8   37'   37'·2   **12°37'·4E**

2. DENMARK

Gilleleje

56°08'N 12°19'E

Distances
Grenå 50M, Anholt 50M, Lynaes 22M,
Falkenberg 48M, Lynaes 22M, Helsingør 12M,
Copenhagen 34M.

Charts
UKHO 2108, 2115, 2594
Danish 102, 129

Lights
1872 **Nakkehoved** 56°07'·2N 12°20'·6E Fl(3)W.20s54m20M
   White square tower
1866 **W Molehead** 56°07'·8N 12°18'·7E Fl.G.3s5m4M
   Green round tower
1867 **E Molehead** 56°07'·8N 12°18'·7E Fl.R.3s5m4M Red
   reflective post

Communications
Harbourmaster ☏ +45 4830 1663

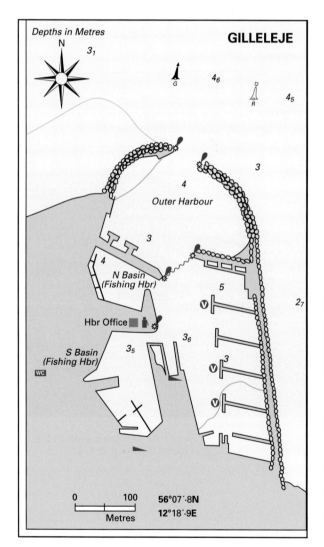

General

A busy fishing harbour which is gradually being taken over by yachts.

Approach

Approach waypoint 56°07'·9N 12°18'·7E

The approach is littered with shoals which can cause uncomfortable seas in onshore winds. From the west approach the waypoint on an easterly course leaving the South cardinal mark marking the southerly limit of the shoals to the north of the entrance to port. Then the two unlit port and starboard buoys marking the commencement of the short channel into the harbour will be seen. From the east approach the waypoint on a westerly course. This will clear the shoals to the north and south to reach the unlit entry channel buoys.

Berthing

Berth in box berths at jetties running out from the east breakwater or alongside in the south fishing basin.

Facilites

All facilities are available. Wi-Fi. All types of restaurant surround the harbour.

The quay alongside the old barracks at Christiansø (Bornholm), a lovely and fascinating stopover   *J. Parkinson*

2c. Bornholm and Christiansø

'When God had finished creating Scandinavia, he was left with a little of the best. He flung it into the Baltic, giving rise to Bornholm' – or so the legend has it.

Today Bornholm sets out to make visitors welcome. An excellent yacht harbour guide *Bornholm Yachting Guide,* available in Danish, German or English and written by the marina harbourmaster at Rønne can be obtained from the author or at tourist offices. Only a few of the available harbours can be mentioned here. The island claims the highest number of sunshine hours in the Baltic and has many excellent bathing beaches. There are good connections from Rønne to Sweden

by fast ferry to Ystad, with bus or rail connections to Copenhagen via the Øresund bridge.

Access to some of the harbours on the east coast of Bornholm and to Christiansø will be dependent on the weather, and significant currents can be generated round the island by strong winds.

All berthing fees on both Bornholm and Christiansø are in the middle range.

Firing practice areas

Firing practice takes place in Danish waters, notably from the southwest coast of Bornholm at Raghammer Odde and off the south coast of

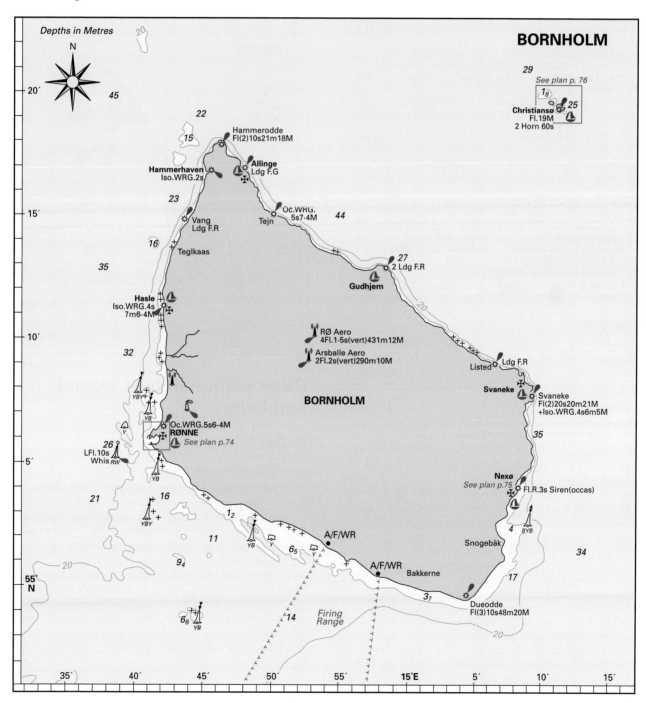

Sweden. When firing is taking place in daytime on Bornholm Q.Fl.W lights are shown at 55°00'·4N 14°57'·32E and 55°01'·4N 14°54'·5E. At night they show AlFl.WR. Guardboats will be present. No firing takes place in July. Contact with Danish Navy Control on Bornholm may be made on VHF Ch 16.

Rønne

55°06'N 14°41'E

Distances
Gedser 100M, Copenhagen 90M, Sassnitz (Germany) 50M, Gislövs Läge (Sweden) 55M, Simrishavn (Sweden) 30M, Karlskrona (Sweden) 75M

Charts
UKHO 2360, 958
Danish 189 (covers all Bornholm)

Lights
buoy **Fairway** 55°05'·1N 14°38'·6E LFl.10s Red and white pillar buoy Whistle
2483 **Ldg Lts 064·5°** *Front* 55°05'·9N 14°41'·8E Iso.2s16m9M 048°-vis-081° Framework tower 14m.
2483·1 *Rear* 229m from front Iso.4s24m9M 048°-vis-081° Red mast 12m
2484 **South shelter mole** 55°05'·6N 14°40'·9E Fl.G.3s11m8M Horn20s (on request) Green tower 5m Floodlit
2484·2 **East molehead** 55°05'·7N 14°40'·9E Fl.R.3s11m8M Red framework tower 5m Floodlit
2491 **Nørrekås** 55°06'·4N 14°42'E Oc.WRG.5s5m6–4M 045°-G-090°-W-105°-R-180° White hut, two red bands 3m

Harbour communications
Rønne Harbourmaster ☎ +45 56 95 06 78, *VHF* Ch 12, 13, 16 (0800–1600 LT) *Email* roennehavn@roennehavn.dk www.roennehavn.dk
Nørrekås Harbourmaster ☎ +45 56 92 23 20 (0900–1000 and 1600–1700 LT)
Email yachtroenne@mail.dk
www.bornholm.org/noerrekaas/default.htm

General

Yachts are expected to use the Nørrekås yacht harbour (to the north of the main harbour) and should only use the main harbour if the yacht harbour is full or weather conditions dictate.

Approach

Approach waypoint for Nørrekås 55°06'·5N 14°40'E
For Main Harbour 55°05'·5N 14°40'E

Nørrekås should be approached on a bearing of 100° approximately in the white sector of the Nørrekås light and leave the outer breakwater head with its green buoy to starboard. Beware the Hvidodde Reef 1M to the north marked by an East cardinal mark and a South cardinal mark. There is also an unmarked out-lyer on the south side of this reef with 3·7m over it, the Kasgaard Rev.

The approach to the main harbour is on 064·5° on the leading line.

Berthing

Berth in any vacant box berth not marked with a red plaque. Depths are 3m at the outer berths and 2m or less further in. The berths in the two small basins to the south of the main marina may be more comfortable in onshore winds and carry 2m depth

but the approach to them needs care and is close to the starboardhand quay.

If it is necessary to enter the main harbour there is possible alongside berthing for yachts on the southern quay of the northern basin or the western wall of the southern basin.

Facilities

All facilities are available at Nørrekås, including diesel and a sailmaker.

As the main town on Bornholm, Rønne has all amenities including a tourist office, supermarket, bicycle hire, bus tours etc. Wi-Fi. Ferries to Ystad, Køge and Świnoujście and an airport 5kms away. However unless these features are required it may be worth considering one of the other smaller yacht harbours around the island, some of which are listed below.

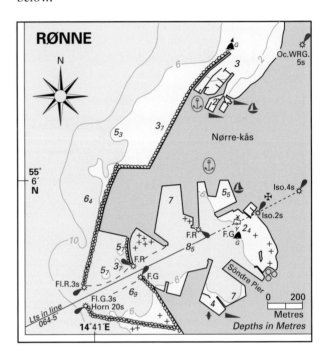

Other yacht harbours around Bornholm

Hasle

55°11'N 14°42'E
Approach waypoint 55°11'·5N 11°40'·8E

This fishing and yachting harbour is 5M north of Rønne and makes a good alternative to it. The yacht harbour is at the north end of the harbour complex and is very well sheltered. The outer and northernmost box berths carry a depth of 2·5m decreasing further in. Approach the harbour mouth on a bearing of 097° in the white sector of Hasle Lt. Beware of a shallow patch with 3·7m just north of the leading line close to the harbour entrance. Water and electricity on all quays, toilets, showers and laundry. Shopping facilities, restaurants in the town and buses to Rønne. Hasle harbourmaster ☎ +45 56 92 23 22.

Hammerhavn

55°17'N 14°46'E
Approach waypoint 55°16'·5N 14°44'·4E

This bay on the northwest tip of the island is protected by breakwaters and makes a change from built-up areas. It is well placed for a visit to the ruins of Hammershus Castle or for walking in the Hammerknuden nature reserve. Approach the harbour mouth on a bearing of 075° in the white sector of Hammerhavn Lt. Berth alongside the jetties of the inner harbour in 3m decreasing to 2m. The facilities are fairly basic but fuel is available. The nearest village with shops and restaurants is Sandvig 2km away. Hammerhavn harbourmaster ① +45 56 92 23 24.

Allinge

55°17'N 14°48'E
Approach waypoint 55°17'N 15°49'E

This picturesque ferry harbour on the northeast tip of the island provides sheltered alongside berthing in 3·9m in the inner harbour with most facilities, but the harbour may be closed by a shut gate between the outer and inner harbours in strong onshore winds. A black ball or three Vertical Red lights signal that the harbour is closed. Approach the harbour mouth on 208·9° on the leading line. Fuel is available. Easy passage to Christiansø (12M) and only 23M to Simrishamn in Sweden. Allinge harbourmaster ① +45 56 92 23 28.

Gudhjem South

55°13'N 14°58'E
Approach waypoint 55°13'·5N 14°58'·8E

Another pleasant harbour offering most facilities including diesel. However access to the inner harbour is closed by a gate in onshore winds of more than 10m/s (20 knots). This is signalled by a red ball hoisted on a flagpole or extinguished leading lights (F.R). Approach on 202°. Berth alongside or bow to quay with stern anchor in the inner harbour. Frequent ferries to Christiansø. Gudhjem South harbourmaster ① +45 56 92 23 36.

Svaneke

55°08'N 15°09'E
Approach waypoint 55°08'·5N 15°09'·5E

A charming and well preserved old market town with plenty going on and good bus connections to the rest of the island. Svaneke boasts Bornholm's largest fish smokery. The outer harbour gets rough in strong onshore winds and the inner harbour gate is closed in these conditions. Enter the bay on a course of 215° in the white sector of the sectored light at 55°08'·04N 15°08'·73E until the harbour mouth opens up and the leading line appears on 297°. Berth alongside or bow to quay with stern anchor in the inner harbour in 3·9m. All facilities available including diesel and a sailmaker. Svaneke harbourmaster ① +45 56 49 60 40.

The tight harbour at Gudhjem on the northeast coast of Bornholm *E. Redfern*

Nexø

55°04'N 15°08'E
Approach waypoint 55°04'·1N 15°09'E

Nexø is a fishing and commercial port and has a summer ferry connection to Poland. It is an all-weather port and is a useful landfall if coming from Poland. Approach on the leading line (F.G.) on 232°. Berth in 3m alongside or in box berths on the west quay of the old harbour (the second basin on the starboard side). All facilities including fuel, Wi-Fi and a sailmaker. Buses to other parts of the island. Nexø harbourmaster ① +45 56 49 22 50.

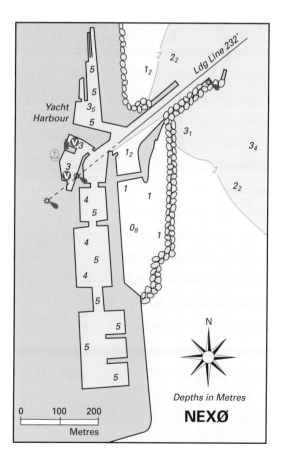

Depths in Metres
NEXØ

Nexø. Bornholm *J. Parkinson*

Christiansø

55°19'N 15°11'E

Approach waypoint 15°19'·3N 15°10'E

A gorgeous small island northeast (10M) from Bornholm. It has been a fortress and naval harbour since the 1600s. Enter from the south to moor alongside in the sound between Christiansø and Frederiksø. Approach the southern harbour from the west on the leading line on 103° leaving the red can buoy to port until the harbour opens up and enter in the white sector of the Light on Fredericksø. A black ball or three red lights signal that the harbour is closed either because of bad weather or because the harbour is full. Facilities are limited but diesel is available. Christiansø harbourmaster ☎ +45 40 45 20 14.

2d. Approach to the Kattegat through the Limfjord

The Limfjord provides a very pleasant shortcut for yachts sailing to the Baltic from Scotland or further north. It saves the long sail round the Skagen where the seas can be unpleasant and it provides sheltered sailing in beautiful surroundings in which to recover from the long passage across the North Sea. In fact one could spend a couple of weeks cruising in the area and still not have seen it all. Much of it is shallow but with a draught of less than 2m most of it is accessible. Minimum depth for the through route is 4m in the dredged channel west of Ålborg and maximum air draught 26m at the Sallingsund fixed bridge near Nykøbing.

Unfortunately the approach can be dangerous in onshore winds over Force 5 especially on the ebb when the current runs at up to two knots (but this can increase up to six knots in very strong winds) in which case diversion to Hanstholm, Hirtshals or round the Skagen may be necessary. But if intending to enter the Limfjord the two large scale Danish Charts *108* and *109* or their German equivalents are essential. Admiralty Charts do not cover the Limfjord further west than Løgstør. These Danish charts are difficult to obtain west of Ålborg and need to be purchased before arrival. An alternative would be the German Chart *Set 6* published by Delius Klasing which covers the whole of the Danish North Sea coast, the whole Limfjord and some of the western Kattegat as well.

Thybøron

56°42'N 08°13'E

Distances
Edinburgh 400M, Den Helder 250M, Helgoland 170M, Ålborg 80M, Esbjerg 90M, Christiansand 85M.

Charts
UKHO 426
Danish 93

Lights
Hanstholm 57°06'·7N 08°36'E Fl(3)20s65m26M
Lodbjerg 56°49'·4N 08°15'·8E Fl(2)20s48m23M
Ldg Lts 082° *Front* 56°43'N 06°14'·1E Iso.WRG.4s8m11M
   Rear 0·5M behind front Iso.4s17m11M
Landfall buoy 56°42'·53N 08°08'·65E LFl.10s Red and
   white buoy
Thybørøn 56°42'·5N 8°12'·9E Fl(3)10s16M
Bovbjerg 56°31'·7N 8°07'·1E Fl(2)10s62m16M

Tides
HW Esjberg +0120 – +0230 ML 0.0

Depths
Least depth in approach from seaward about 6m and inside the bar 5–8m.

Harbour communications
Harbourmaster ☎ +45 97 83 12 88
  www.thyboronport.dk/

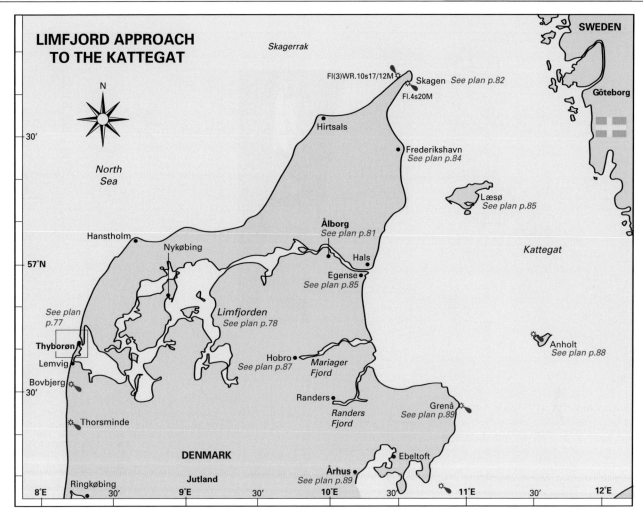

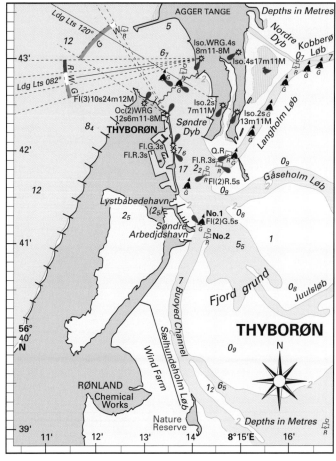

General

This small town has quite a large harbour which is mainly concerned with fishing and the ferry across the Limfjord. It is situated just inside the western entrance to the Limfjord. If arriving after a North Sea passage Lemvig would be more rewarding but it is 12M further on.

Approach

Approach waypoint from offshore 56°42'·75N 08°11'E

On arrival at the approach waypoint which is 1M from the entrance and 1·25M inside the landfall buoy make 082° on the leading line into the entrance and there pick up the starboardhand channel buoys and follow them round to the SSE and the harbour entrance. Once inside the breakwater turn northwards to the northernmost basin where there are berths for yachts in 3·5m.

The approach from the east involves picking up the narrow buoyed channel (some lit) which starts with a North cardinal mark and a South cardinal mark at 56°38'·1N 08°16'·7E and curves round northwards to join the main entrance channel past the harbour.

Facilities

All facilities are available including diesel which can be obtained from a barge in the main harbour.

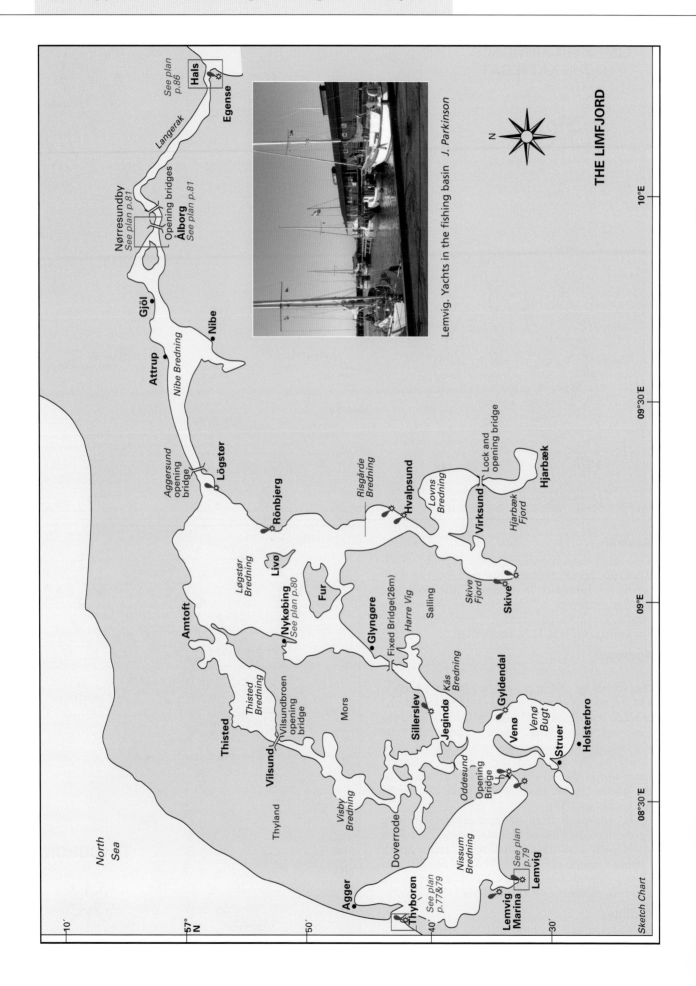

Lemvig. Yachts in the fishing basin J. Parkinson

THE LIMFJORD

Sketch Chart

Thyborøn and the west entrance to the Limfjord
P. Roach

Lemvig
56°33'N 08°18'E

This is a small and attractive town in the creek on the south side of the westernmost lake of the Limfjord, the Nissum Bredning.

It is approached through a long buoyed channel which is dredged to 4·4m

The dredged channel leaves a marina to starboard but it is a long way from the town and it is better to continue further and berth in the main harbour either alongside in the eastern Gammelhavn or bow to the quay and stern to a buoy in the western fishing harbour. The harbour has all facilities, the diesel pump being manned by the sea clothing/very limited chandlery shop in the restaurant/shower complex between the two basins.

Harbourmaster ☎ +45 9782 0106
www.visitlemvig.dk

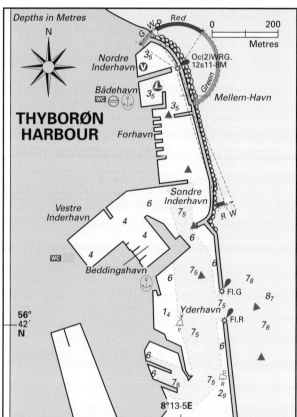

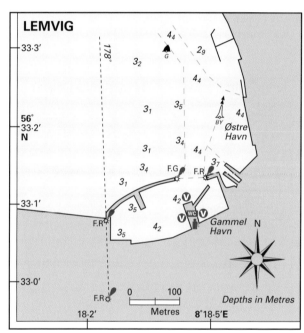

Oddesund Bridge
56°34'·5N 08°32'·5E

This combined rail and road bridge opens on demand (24 hours) but remains closed for 15 minutes before a train is due. Contact the bridgekeeper on ☎ +45 9787 5705, *VHF* Ch 12, 13 or hoist International Code Flag N in the rigging and wait.

Once through the bridge the more direct route to Ålborg and the Kattegat continues in a northeasterly direction but one can divert south into Venø Sund to visit Struer or take the northern route to Ålborg via a series of small lakes to Thisted Bredning and Thisted.

The Oddesund lifting road and rail bridge across the Limfjord will open for yachts even at rush hour *E. Redfern*

2. DENMARK

Nykøbing

56°48′N 08°52′E

Nykobing is a useful stop on the direct route to Ålborg as it is 30M from Thybøron and 35M from Ålborg.

2M southwest of the entrance channel is a fixed road bridge with a clearance of 26m.

Nykobing is an old fisheries town with many museums. It is entered by a a buoyed entrance channel dredged to 4·4m. It starts at the East cardinal mark just west of the point which forms the eastern side of the bay. Follow the buoyed channel on 345° with 2F.R Lts in line bearing round on to 323·6° (2F.G Lts in line) through the harbour entrance. Then berth either at pontoons in the marina in 3m on the porthand (but observe the porthand buoy when entering) or continue northwest up into the small Nordhaven in 3·5m.

All facilities are available but the fuel station is not always open when expected.

Harbourmaster ☎ +45 4076 7090.

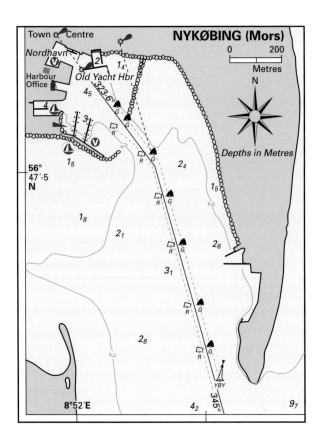

Ålborg

57°03′N 09°55′E

Ålborg is the capital of the region and the centre of communications as well as being a university town. It now has major industries but its original wealth came from the herring fisheries. The old part of the town, the Østerågade, is attractive and interesting.

Approach

The approach from the west by the Logstør Bredning starts at the red port-hand mark Fl(3)R10s at 56°58′·5N 09°09′·3E some 26M west of Ålborg. Leading Lights Iso.W.2s and 4s on 079·2° then lead up the channel to Løgstør where there is a marina with alongside berths in a canal which is entered just west of the main harbour.

The main channel to Ålborg then continues north-eastward to the Aggersund Lifting Bridge which opens on demand in theory but in practice seems to wait until there are a number of yachts waiting. At any bridge one can make one's wishes known by hoisting the N flag in the rigging and calling on VHF Ch 12 or 13.

The buoyed channel then continues for another 20 miles up to Ålborg. For the most part it is wide with depths over 4m but it is very narrow where it is dredged to 4m through the Drag Banke.

At Ålborg there is a big choice of marinas but the most convenient for the shops and for a bus or train to the centre is the Vester Bådehavn which is the last one on the south side before the railway bridge. It has restaurants and all facilities as well as an excellent chandlery but it is often crowded and a berth that is wide enough can sometimes be hard to find especially as the channels between the box berths are very narrow.

There are two lifting bridges in Ålborg. The western one is a railway bridge which seems to stay in the raised position until 15 minutes before a train is due. The eastern bridge is the Limfjord Road Bridge which opens at times displayed digitally on each side of the bridge. These times are sometimes two hours apart.

The route east from Ålborg to the sea at Hals and Egense is well buoyed and straight-forward. See page 85, Limfjord entrance.

Ålborg Bridge with rail bridge beyond
J. Parkinson

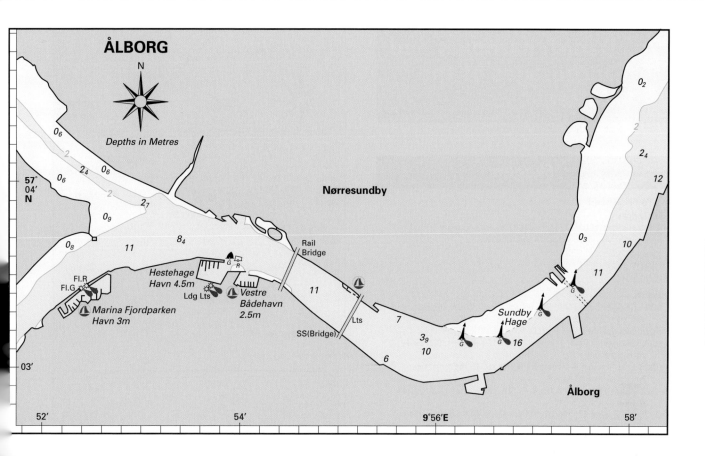

N

Depths in Metres

Nørresundby

57°
04'
N

Rail
Bridge

Hestehage
Havn 4.5m

Fl.R
Fl.G

Ldg Lts

Vestre
Bådehavn
2.5m

Marina Fjordparken
Havn 3m

SS(Bridge)

Lts

Sundby
Hage

03'

Ålborg

52'   54'   9°56'E   58'

Ålborg from the west with Hestehage Havn and Vestre Bådehavn on south shore *P. Roach*

2e. Danish harbours and anchorages of the Kattegat

Skagen

57°43'N 10°36'E

Distances
Kristiansand 100M, Göteborg 47M, Edinburgh 500M,
Fredrikshavn 20M, Copenhagen 145M.

Charts
UKHO 2107
Danish 101

Lights
0001 **Skagen** W 57°44'·9N 10°35'·7E Fl(3)WR.10s31m14M
White round tower 053°-W-248°-R-323°
Buoy **Skagen Shoal** 57°46'N 10°44'E NCM Q.Fl
0002 **Skagen** 57°44'·1N 10°37'·8E Fl.W.4s44m20M Grey
round tower
0005 Ldg Lts 334·5° *Front* 57°43'N 10°35'·4E
Iso.R.4s13m8M Mast
Rear 262m from front Iso.R.4s22m8M Metal framework
tower
0020 **Hirsholm** 57°29'·1N 10°37'·5E Fl(3)W.30s30m21M
Round granite tower

Communications
Port Authority ☎ +45 9844 1346 *VHF* Ch 12
Lystbådehavn (Marina) Harbourmaster ☎ +45 98 44 33 41
Mobile 23200941

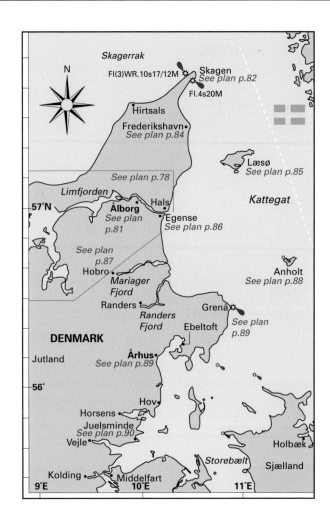

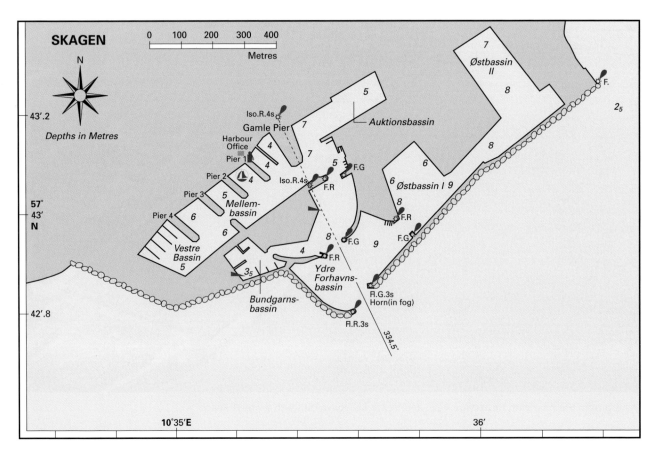

General

Skagen is a busy fishing harbour and a thriving holiday resort. The area is a favourite with Danish artists. The harbour provides good protection but it is not recommended in gales from the southeast when the approach can be dangerous.

Approach

Approach waypoints
From north and west 57°46′N 10°44′E
From south and east 57°42′N 10°36′·5E

The flat Skagen headland with its two lighthouses is extended for 2M in an east-northeast direction by a shallow reef marked by a North cardinal mark. In strong west and northwesterly winds the seas can be heavy and in addition there is usually much commercial traffic rounding the headland. Once rounded, course can be set for Skagen harbour entrance giving the shallows off the point a reasonably wide berth.

Berthing

Berth in the marina on pontoons between Piers 1 and 2 in 4m depths. Larger vessels berth alongside in the Bundgarnsbassin with depths of 3·5m but this is a long walk from town.

Facilities

All facilities are available including fuel.

Skagen from the northwest *P. Roach*

Frederikshavn

57°25′·6N 10°32′E

Distances
Skagen 20M, Laesø Vesterø Havn 15M, Limfjord entrance 30M.

Charts
UKHO 2107
Danish 101

Lights
0020 **Hirsholm** 57°29′·1N 10°37′·5E Fl(3)W.30s30m21M
  Round granite tower Also FRW.30m 007·6°-W-013·5°-R-016·4°
0028 **Commercial Port NE Breakwater Hd** 57°26′N
  10°33′·2E Iso.WG.8m13–9M Green Tower 302°-G-271°-W-278°
0029 **Commercial Port Approach Light** 57°26′·2N
  10°32′·5E Oc.WRG.10s14m9M 305·8°-G-308·3°-W-310·3°-R-312·8°
0033 **Marina E Mole Hd** 57°25′·6N 10°32′E Fl.R.3s4m3M
  Mast
0061 **Laesø Rende** 57°13′·1N 10°40′·3E
  LFl(2)WRG.20s25m17–13M White round concrete tower, black base 105·5°-G-179°-W-203°-R-252°-G-329·5°-W-337°-R-105·5°

Communications
Port Authority ☎ +45 9620 4700 *VHF* Ch 12, 13
Marina Harbourmaster ☎ +45 9843 2856
  www.Frederikshavnsejlklub.dk

General

Fredrikshavn Port is a very busy ferry and commercial harbour with ferries to Oslo, Larvik, Göteborg and Læsø. The *Søsporthavn* or marina is situated approximately 0·75M to the southwest of the entrance to the main port.

Approach

Approach waypoint 57°25′N 10°36′E

Approaching from the north the rocks and islands of Hirsholm guarded by the Hirsholm Lt must be left to starboard and the shallows to the east of Fredrikshavn which are marked by east and south cardinal marks and a green starboardhand buoy must be skirted in the same way. A westerly course from the South cardinal mark will then lead to the Søsporthavn entrance.

From the south the approach is straightforward although fish traps may be a hazard close to the shore.

2·5m in buoyed entrance channel but subject to silting.

Berthing

Moor in box berths with bow to staging.

Facilities

All facilities are available but the marina is some way from the city centre. Local food shops nearby.

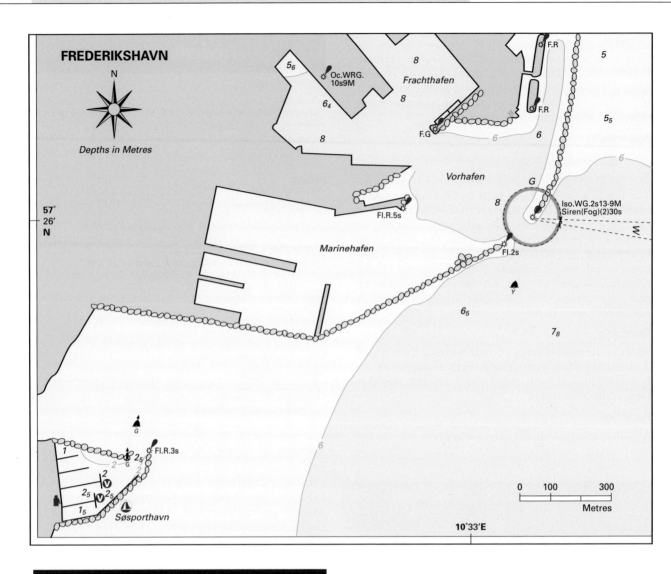

FREDERIKSHAVN

N

Depths in Metres

57°
26'
N

57° 18'N   10° 33'E

Frachthafen

Oc.WRG.
10s9M

Vorhafen

Marinehafen

Fl.R.5s

F.R

F.R

F.G

Iso.WG.2s13·9M
Siren(Fog)(2)30s

Fl.2s

Søsporthavn

Fl.R.3s

0   100   300

Metres

10°33'E

Vesterø

57°18'N 10°56'E

Distances
Frederikshavn 15M, Skagen 27M, Limfjord Entrance 30M, Göteborg 45M

Charts
UKHO 2107
Danish 123

Lights
0044 **Nordre Rønner** 57°21'·6N 10°55'·4E Fl.W.15s16m14M
 Round granite tower
0050 Ldg Lts 136·1° *Front* Outer E mole Head 57°17'·9N
 10°55'·4E Iso.R.2s7m3M Red triangle on red
 framework tower. *Rear* 364m from front.
 Iso.R.4s14m3M Red inverted triangle on framework
 tower
Buoy **Laesø** NW Rev 57°15'·7N 10°45'·4E Fl(2)R.5s Red can
 buoy
0061 **Laesø Rende** 57°13'·1N 10°40'·3E
 LFl(2)WRG.20s25m17M White round concrete tower,
 black base. 105·5°-G-179°-W-203°-R-252°-G-329·5°-W-
 337°-R-105·5°

Harbour communications
Harbourmaster ☎ +45 9849 9222
 www.laesohavn.dk

General

Laesø is a quiet and attractive island and Vesterø a fishing and ferry harbour. The coastline has extensive shallows so that an approach to gain shelter for anchoring would be quite difficult.

Approach

Approach waypoint 57°17'N 10°48'E

The leading line on 136·1° runs in from the northwest of the island with the Nordre Rønner reef with its light tower 2M to port and the northwest Laesø Reef (marked at its northwest corner by a red lightbuoy) 3·5M to starboard. The Nordre Ronner reef is extensively buoyed on the porthand but it is not until one is within 1M of the entrance that there are green starboardhand buoys. The entrance carries a depth of 3·4m.

Berthing

Berth in box berths bow to a jetty in the southwest basin.

Facilities

Facilities are good.

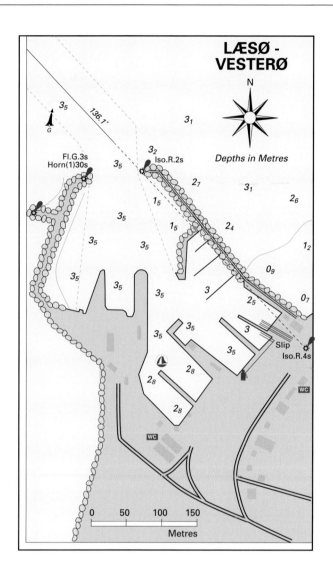

LÆSØ - VESTERØ

N

Depths in Metres

Fl.G.3s
Horn(1)30s

Iso.R.2s

Slip
Iso.R.4s

WC

WC

0   50   100   150
Metres

Vesterø Harbour, Læso *E. Redfern*

Limfjord entrance

General

The big ship channel for entry to the Limfjord begins 23M out in the Ålborg Bugt near the Svitringen South Light Tower but smaller craft can enter the channel much closer in, between the Hals Barre Light Tower and the twin Red and Green Light Towers marking the entrance.

Egense and Hals

56°59′N 10°18′E

Distances
Fredrikshavn 30M, Vesterø 30M, Ålborg 15M, Mariager Fjord 20M, Anholt 42M, Grenå 45M.

Charts
UKHO 2107, 894, 429
Danish 122, 107

Lights
0061 **Laesø Rende** 57°13′·1N 10°40′·3E
 LFl(2)WRG.20s25m13M White round concrete tower, black base. 105·5°-G-179°-W-203°-R-252°-G-329·5°-W-337°-R-105·5°
0066 **Hals Barre** 56°57′·3N 10°25′·5E Fl.W.10s18m18M Red tower, white bands
 Iso.WRG.2s15m10M 305°-G-313°-W-319°-R-323°
0066·8 **Svitringen Rende S** 56°51′N 10°36′·3E
 Fl.W.3s13m8M Red tower, white stripes marked SV S
0072 **Korsholm** Ldg Lts Egense N Front 294·3° 56°58′·4N 10°20′·1E Iso.G.2s5m9M Red 8-sided concrete tower
 Secondary Lt FlR3s5m3M Vis 139·5°-290·5° S *Front*
 IsoR2s5m9M Vis 290·3°-298·3° *Rear* 1·2M from front
 Iso.W.2s20m15M Red inverted triangle on red framework tower.
 All synchronised

Communications
Hals Harbourmaster ☎ +45 5152 6624
Egense Harbourmaster ☎ +45 9831 0057

Approach

Approach waypoint 56°57′·5N 10°24′E

The big ship channel is marked by a succession of red and green boys and light towers and can be entered anywhere along its length up to the twin light towers at 56°58′N 10°22′E. The channel continues with port and starboardhand buoys some lit and some unlit up to Ålborg. There is a succession of leading lights all the way up to Ålborg 15M inland.

Berthing

There are two harbours on opposite sides of the entrance; Hals on the north side, which is a fishing harbour, is lit and carries 3m depth but has only basic facilities and shops and Egense which is smaller, is unlit and carries 2·5m depth. It is a yacht marina with better facilities but no shops.

Alternatively there is a good anchorage with good protection from southwest through west to north and some protection from north through east to south in 2·3–3·1m in the area west of Korsholm. In the southernmost part of the anchorage is a narrow deeper part carrying 4m depth where a few yellow mooring buoys for visitors have been laid.

2. DENMARK

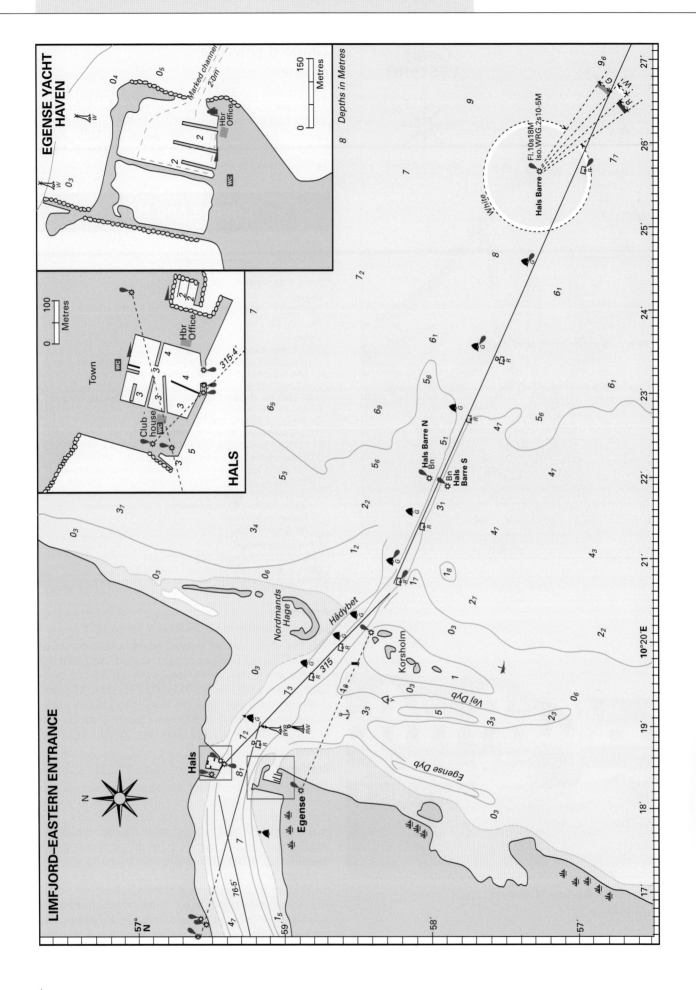

EGENSE YACHT HAVEN

Hbr Office

WC

Marked channel

2.0m

Metres

150

0

Depths in Metres

HALS

Town

Club house

Hbr Office

WC

WC

315.4°

Metres

100

0

LIMFJORD–EASTERN ENTRANCE

N

Hals

Egense

Nordmands Hage

Hådybet

Korsholm

Vel Dyb

Egense Dyb

315

76·5°

Hals Barre N
Bn

Bn
Hals
Barre S

White

Hals Barre
Fl.10s18M
Iso.WRG.2s10-5M

10°20E

57°
N

59'

58'

57'

27'

26'

25'

24'

23'

22'

21'

19'

18'

17'

Mariager Fjord

Distances
Limfjord Entrance 22M, Grenå 30M.

Charts
UKHO 894
Danish122, 110

Lights
Hals Barre 56°57'·3N 10°25'·5E Fl.W.10s18m18M Red tower, white bands

0066·8 **Svitringen Rende S** 56°51'N 10°36'·3E Fl.W.3s13m8M Red tower, white stripes marked SV S

0126 **Als Odde** Ldg Lts 261·9° *Front* 56°42'·7N 10°20'·8E Iso.W.2s7m9M Red triangle on grey framework tower. *Rear* 1511m from front Iso.W.4s24m10M Red inverted triangle on framework tower

0176 **Udbyhøj, Elkaer Bakke** 56°35'·4N 10°19'·2E Oc.WRG.5s33m15–12M White lighthouse, red band. 194°-G-228°-W-232°-R-254°-G-276°-W-279°-R-289°

Communications
Hadsund Lystbådehaven ☎ +45 98 57 24 39
Hadsund Bridge VHF Ch 12, 16
Hobro Havn Harbourmaster ☎ +45 96 57 65 00
Hobro Sailing Club Marina ☎ +45 98 52 38 75

General

Mariager Fjord is reputed to be one of the most beautiful fjords in Denmark with reed-lined vistas in its lower reaches and wooded hills further west. It is 20M long and is included here as it is a reasonable distance between the Limfjord and Grenå and offers good anchoring opportunities in attractive surroundings.

Approach

Approach waypoint 56°43'N 10°25'·5E

Pick up the buoyed entrance channel dredged to 5·7m and marked at its outer end by a green lightbuoy Fl(2)G.5s and make the approach on 262°. There can be a two knot current in the entrance when entry and departure in strong easterlies can be very rough. There is an opening bridge at Hadsund.

Berthing

Berth in Hadsund Harbour, Hobro Havn or at one of the smaller marinas, Mariager Marina or Hobro Sailing Club or anchor.

Mariager Fjord looking east from Hobro
P. Roach

2. DENMARK

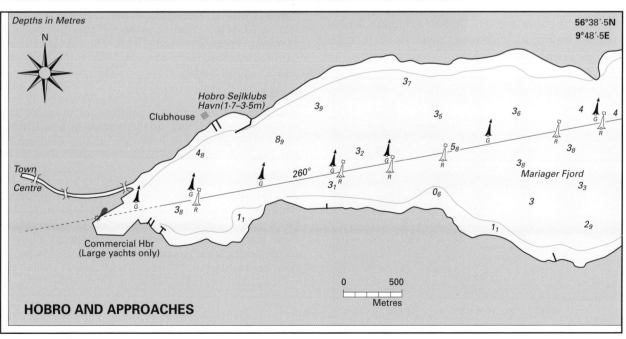

HOBRO AND APPROACHES

Anholt

56°43'N 11°30'E

Distances
Limfjord entrance 42M, Grenå 28M,
Falkenberg 35M, Helsingør 55M.

Charts
UKHO 2107, 2108
Danish 102, 124

Lights
Anholt Near E end 56°44'·2N 11°39'E Fl.W.15s40m14M
White round tower with upper part red
Anholt Harbour Outer N mole head 56°42'·9N 11°30'·5E
Iso.WRG.4s8m14–10M Red round metal tower 038°-G-
112°-W-130°-R-135°-G-160°-W-164°-R-038°

Communications
Harbourmaster ☎ +45 86 31 92 44
Mobile +45 20 30 07 08

General

This is a lovely little island with good beaches. Good
for walking and bicycling.

Approach

Approach waypoint 56°43'N 11°22'E

Easy approach from the west but the water is
shallow for a long way out and is rough in onshore
winds over Force 5. Beware shallow patches
extending 3M northwest of the harbour and the 5M
long Osterev Spit marked by an East cardinal mark
extending from the eastern end of the island. The
harbour entrance carries a depth of 3·5m.

Berthing

Berth bow to pontoons with stern buoys. Notices
warn that berthing alongside will be charged
double. This is not surprising as the harbour is very
crowded in season. Anchoring is possible in the
outer harbour but make sure the channel is clear for
the ferry from Grenå.

Facilities

All basic facilities and fuel. Anholt is famous for its
nightlife and music-making so don't forget to take
your earplugs!

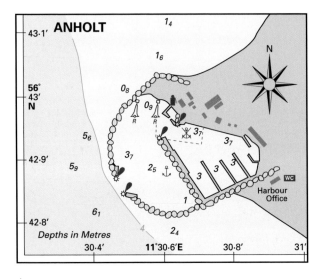

Grenå

56°24'·2N 10°55'·6E

Distances
Limfjord Entrance 42M, Mariager Fjord 30M, Anholt
28M, Ebeltoft 28M, Århus 38M

Charts
UKHO 2108
Danish 124

Lights
0204 **Fornaes** 56°26'·6N 10°57'·4E Fl.W.20s32m23M Round
stone tower
0208 **Grenå Harbour N approach** 56°24'·7N 10°55'·2E
Oc.WG.10s21m16–12M Grey framework tower 236°-G-
241°-W-246° synchronised with 0208·5
0208·5 **Grenå Harbour S approach** 56°24'·7N 10°55'·2E
Oc.WR.10s21m16–12M Grey framework tower 236°-
W-241°-R-246° synchronised with 0208
Lystbådehavn N Breakwater Hd 56°24'·2N 10°55'·5E
Fl.G.3s5m4M White pyramid green top. S Breakwater
Hd Fl.R.3s5m4M White pyramid, red top
0222 **Hesselø** 56°11'·8N 11°42'·6E Fl.W.15s40m14M White
round tower
0262 **Hjelm Summit** 56°08'N 10°48'·3E
Iso.WRG.8s61m14–11M White round tower 016·5°-G-
043°-W-051°-R-068°-G-088°-W-091°-R-110°-W-016·5°
1478 **Sjaellands Rev N** 56°06'N 11°12'·1E
Iso.WRG.2s25m16–13M White colomn, red band, black
pedestal. 025°-G-036°-W-039°-R062°-G-074°-W-077°-R-
105°-G118°-R-141°-G-205°-W212°-R-235°-G-256°-W-
283°-R-317°-G-350°-025°

Communications
Port Authority ☎ +45 8758 7600
Marina ☎ +45 86 32 72 55

General

The marina is 1M south of the entrance to the
commercial port from which ferries go to Varberg in
Sweden and Anholt.

Approach

Approach waypoint 56°24'·5N 10°58'E

If approaching from the north leave the Kalkgrund
North cardinal mark and South cardinal mark to
starboard before turning west towards the marina
entrance. From the south leave the Naveren East
cardinal mark to port. There is 3·5m in the entrance
and 2·5m just outside.

Berthing

Yachts over 13m berth alongside on the inside of the
east mole in 3·2m and smaller yachts in box berths
at the other jetties. The berths get smaller the further
one proceeds into the harbour.

Facilities

All facilities are available including restaurants,
Wi-Fi and fuel. The marina is some way from the
town centre but there are basic shops quite close.
Also close to the marina is the Kattegat Centre
Oceanarium which specialises in sharks. Grenå has a
ferry to Varberg.

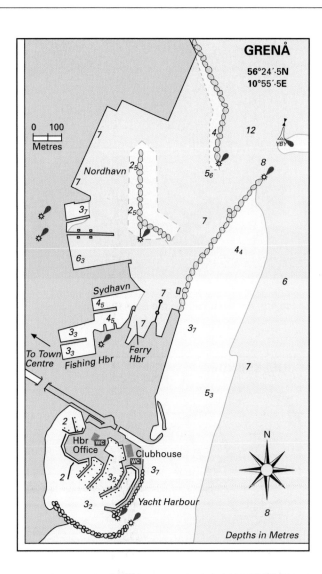

GRENÅ

56°24′·5N
10°55′·5E

Nordhavn

Metres
0   100

Sydhavn

To Town
Centre   Fishing Hbr   Ferry
Hbr

Hbr
Office   WC   Clubhouse
WC

Yacht Harbour

Depths in Metres

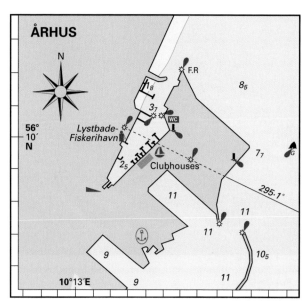

ÅRHUS

N

56°
10′
N

Lystbade-
Fiskerihavn

F.R

WC

Clubhouses

295·1°

10°13′E

Århus

56°10′N 10°13′E

Distances
Grenå 38M, Juelsminde 33M.

Charts
UKHO 2108
Danish 124

Lights
0786 **Helgenaes Sletterhage SW end** 56°05′·7N 10°30′·8E
  Oc.WRG.10s17m15–12M White round tower 250·9°-R-
  275°-G-297°-W-302·1°-R-320·5°-G-006·1°-R-060·2°-G-
  088·6°-W-117°-R-125·6°
0790 **Ldg Lts 295·1°** *Front* 56°09′·8N 10°13′·8E
  Iso.W.2s21m14M Grey framework tower *Rear* 421m
  from front Iso.W.2s42m14M Grey framework tower.
  Synchronised with front
0822 **Tunø** 55°57′N 10°26′·6E Oc.WRG.5s31m12–9M White
  church tower. 133°-G-157°-W-160°-R-175°-G-214°-W-
  220°-R-326°-G-345°-W-350°-R-045°

Communications
Commercial Port ☏ +45 9812 2777 *VHF* Chs 12, 13
Marina Harbourmaster ☏ +45 8619 1590
www.aarhuslystbaadehavn.dk

General
Århus is regarded as Denmark's cultural capital and
has plenty of sights to see and things to do. One of
its great joys from a yachtsman's point of view is the
excellent free bicycle service run by the council. One
can pick up a free bicycle (by inserting a 20DKr
deposit in the handlebars to release the chain) from
any of the rails round the city and leave it at a
different one where you chain it up again and get
your money back.

On the north side of Århus Bay is an area of
wooded bays and low hills with several small
harbours and attractive anchorages.

Approach
Approach waypoint 56°09′·3N 10°16′E

The entrance to the marina is open to the northeast
and lies immediately northwest of the entrance to the
commercial harbour. The entrance is straightforward
but, if following the leading line on 295° for the
commercial port in from the waypoint, the line must
eventually be left to the south to gain the entrance to
the marina.

Århus Marina J. Parkinson

2. DENMARK

Århus from northwest with commercial port in background
P. Roach

Juelsminde. Since the photo was taken a new marina,
Sandbjerg, has been built to the NW *P. Roach*

Berthing

Berth in box berths at marina on southeastern side of
harbour.

Facilities

All facilities available. Excellent Chandlery. Good
rail communications. Ferry to Kalundborg.
International airport.

Juelsminde

55°43'N 10°01'E

Distances
Århus 33M, Middelfart 20M, Bogense 10M, Horsens 16M,
Velje 21M

Charts
UKHO 2591
Danish 114

Lights
0884 **E mole Head** 55°42'·9N 10°01'·1E Fl.R.5s5m4M Red
    metal pillar
0893 **Aebelø NW Point** 55°38'·8N 10°09'·8E
    Fl.W.15s20m14M Round granite tower
0894 **Trelde Naes** 55°37'·5N 09°51'·5E
    Iso.WRG.2s26m8–6M Metal framework tower
    Shore-G-124°-W-128°-R-136·5°-W-232°-R-256°-G-276·5-W-
    010°

Communications
Juelsminde Port ☎ +45 75 69 35 81
Marina ☎ +45 20 28 82 48
    www.juelsmindehavn.dk

General

Juelsminde is a holiday town and its three marinas
are very crowded in season.

Approach

Approach waypoint 55°43'·2N 10°02'E

From the north the near approach is straightforward
but on passage from Århus Bay there are several
shoals to be negotiated including the Søgrund north
of Endelave. This carries a depth of only 3·5m and in
strong weather from the northeast or southwest it

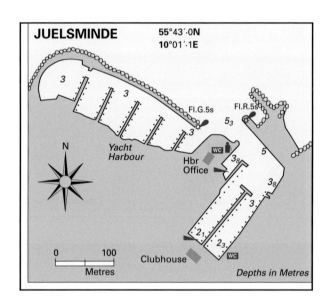

would be wise to take the long way round the west
coast of Samsø. From the southwest the Bjørnsknude
Rev SCM must be left to port.

Berthing

Berth in box berths either in the old harbour on the
porthand side after entering or in the new marina on
the starboardhand. Alternatively go past the harbour
entrance and enter the Sandbjerg marina which is
entered 100m to the northwest. If you still cannot
find a berth there is a good anchorage protected
from all directions except east in the bay off the
beach. In easterly weather there is an anchorage off
Hjarnø Sund leading into Horsens Fjord at
Borresknob on the east side of the Borre Peninsula.

Facilities

The marinas have all facilities but no craneage.

2f. Approach to The Baltic by the Lille Bælt

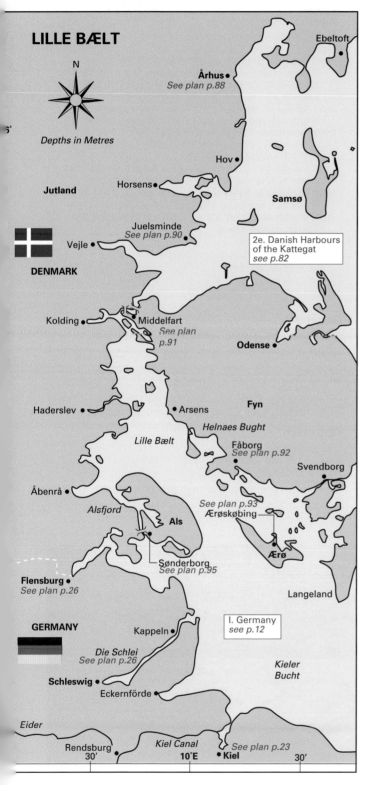

LILLE BÆLT

N

Depths in Metres

Ebeltoft

Århus •
See plan p.88

Hov •

Horsens •

Samsø

Jutland

Juelsminde •
See plan p.90

Vejle •

DENMARK

2e. Danish Harbours
of the Kattegat
see p.82

Kolding • • Middelfart
See plan p.91

Odense •

Haderslev • • Arsens

Fyn

Lille Bælt • Helnaes Bught

Fåborg
See plan p.92

Åbenrå • Svendborg

Alsfjord Als

See plan p.93
Ærøskøbing

Sønderborg
See plan p.95

Ærø

Flensburg •
See plan p.26

Langeland

GERMANY

Kappeln •

I. Germany
see p.12

Die Schlei
See plan p.26

Kieler Bucht

Schleswig •
Eckernförde •

Eider

Rendsburg •
30'

Kiel Canal
10°E

See plan p.23
• Kiel
30'

Middelfart

55°30'N 09°44'E

Distances
Juelsminde 22M, Assens 15M, Fåborg 38M, Svendborg 50M, Dyvig 35M, Sønderborg 40M

Charts
UKHO 2591, 2592
Danish 151, 158

Lights
894 **Trelde Naes** 55°37'·5N 09°51'·5E Iso.WRG.2s26m8–6M
   Metal framework tower Shore-G-124°-W-128°-R-136·5°-W-232°-R-256°-G-276·5°-W-010°
0922 **Strib** 55°32'·6 09°45'·4E Oc.WRG.5s21m13–10M
   White square tower 351°-G-007·5°-W-013·5°-R-135°-G-232°-W-238°-R-shore
0962 **Faeno** 55°28'·5N 09°42'·1E Fl.WRG.5s11m11–8M
   Gable of white house 338°-G-342°-W-346°-R-350°

Communications
Harbourmaster ☎ +45 8888 4910 for both harbours
www.middelfart.dk

General
Middelfart occupies a peninsula on the northwest tip of the island of Fyn. It has an old harbour, the Gammelhavn, on the north side of the peninsula and a large marina or lystbådehavn on the south side. The Gammelhavn is small and attractive and the marina is large and some way from the shops.

Approach
Approach waypoints From north 55°34'·5N 09°50'E
From south 55°25'N 09°44'E

Middelfart is at the narrowest part of the Lille Baelt and there is normally a two knot current flowing south with north flowing eddies in the bays. This current can increase to four knots in strong northerlies and with strong winds from the south the currents will be reversed. Enter the Gammelhavn from the north but make allowances for the current.

There are two fixed bridges and some electric cables across the sound with a minimum clearance of 33m.

The marina is entered from the Faeno Sund on a northeasterly course with the deeper water being nearer the east mole head.

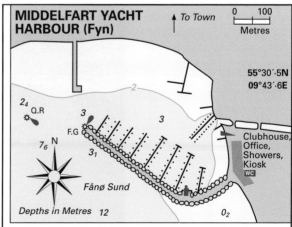

MIDDELFART YACHT HARBOUR (Fyn)

To Town

0   100
Metres

55°30'·5N
09°43'·6E

Q.R
F.G
N

Clubhouse, Office, Showers, Kiosk
WC

Fånø Sund

Depths in Metres

2. DENMARK

Middelfart Gammelhavn *E. Redfern*

Fåborg

55°06'N 10°15'E

Distances
Middelfart 38M, Assens 23M, Svendborg 15M, Marstal 28M, Sonderborg 27M.

Charts
Admiralty chart 2532
Danish charts 152

Lights
0988 **Helnaes**, Lindehoved 55°08'N 09°58'·7E
Fl.WRG.5s30m13–10M White square tower 302°-R-321°-G-330°-W-343°-R-030°-G-075°-W-125°-R-141°-G-179°
0991 **Bjornø** 55°03'·3N 10°15'·7E Iso.WRG.4s6m10–7M
White hut, red band. 040°-G-052°-W-060°-R-971°.
0992 **Sisserodde** 55°05'·7N 10°13'·7E
Dir.Iso.WRG.2s8m16–14M White hut, red band 350·7°-G-352·2°-W-354·2°-R-355·7°
1016 **Munke** 55°01'·4N 10°16'·3E Iso.WRG.4s10m14–10M
White hut, red band 259°-G-264°-W-268°-R-273°
1020 **Nakkeodde** 55°01'N 10°20'E Oc.WRG.5s9m11–8M
White hut, red band 115·2°-G-123°-W-130°-R-143°
1070 **Skjoldnaes** 54°58'·2N 10°12'·4E LFl.W.30s32m22M
Round granite tower

Communications
Harbourmaster ☎ +45 72 53 02 60
www.fåborghavn.dk

Berth

Berth either alongside and probably rafted out in the Gammelhavn or in box berths in the marina. The gammelhavn has 3–4m alongside and the marina 3m but less further in. There may be a few small commercial vessels in the Gammelhavn. It makes a useful stop for stores after a night at anchor.

There are nearby anchorages in Faenø Sund in the bay on the north side of Faenø and in Gamborg Fjord.

Facilities

Both harbours have basic facilities but the marina has a fuel station, laundry, restaurants and is better equipped.

General

Fåborg is a pretty little town with old houses and cobbled streets. Yachts berth in either the old harbour or the new marina 400m further north. There is a ferry to Gelting in Germany. The ferry berth is just south of the old harbour and classic Baltic Traders lie alongside the southern quays.

Approach

Approach waypoint
From north and south 55°02'·25N 10°13'E
From east 55°02'N 10°17'·5E

The approach into Fåborg Fjord is either by the buoyed main channel between the mainland of Fyn to the west and the island of Bjørnø to the east or

Fåborg from the west
P. Roach

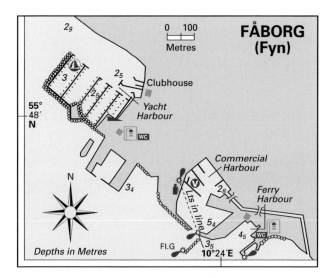

FÅBORG
(Fyn)

0   100
Metres

Depths in Metres

Fåborg (Fyn) *J. Parkinson*

through the narrow and buoyed Grydeløb channel to the east of Bjørnø which carries a least depth of 3·4m. The main channel is covered by a succession of leading lights and lightbuoys but the Grydeløb is unlit.

Once in the fjord by the main channel proceed on a course of 046° until the Højen porthand buoy is abeam when course can be altered to 336° for the harbour entrance.

Berthing

Berth in box berths either in the main harbour in 2·5–5m or in the marina which carries 2·5m in the approach and 3m inside. Vessels over 12m can berth alongside the south quay in the old harbour.

Facilities

Between them the two harbours provide all facilities including Wi-Fi. There is a good chandler close to the marina.

Ærøskøbing

54°54'N 10°25'E

Distances
Fåborg 15M, Svendborg 12M, Sønderborg 30M, Kiel 45M.

Charts
Admiralty chart 2532
Danish charts 152

Lights
1070 **Skjoldnaes** 54°58'·2N 10°12'·4E LFl.W.30s32m22M Round granite tower
1076 **Ærøskøbing Havn** Ldg Lts 196·3° W Mole Head *Front* 54°53'·5N 10°24'·8E F.G.11m5M also Fl.G.5s4m4M Red triangle on green metal mast, white top. *Rear* 145m from front F.G.15m5M Red inverted triangle on white metal mast

Communications
Harbourmaster ① +45 62 52 12 53

General

This is such a pretty place that, in spite of the difficulties of getting to it from the south, it should not be missed.

Approach

Approach waypoints
From north 54°54'·4N 10°25'·2E
From south 54°50'N 10°33'·8E

From the north the approach is straightforward and the leading line on 196° can be picked up just to the west of the landfall buoy. This takes one into the commercial harbour along a buoyed channel dredged to 3·8m. 0·3M from the commercial harbour entrance another buoyed channel dredged to 2·5m forks off to the marina entrance.

From the south there are extensive shallows to be negotiated by dredged and well buoyed channels

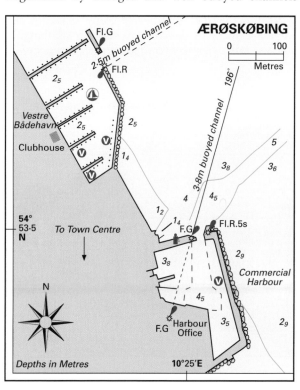

ÆRØSKØBING

0   100
Metres

2. DENMARK

Ærøskøbing from the south *P. Roach*

with a charted minimum depth of 2·3m. The channel takes one across the entrance to Marstal Harbour, then north for 0·7M before heading northeast to a RW safe water buoy from which one heads northwest to enter the Markedyb Channel at the Grensage South cardinal mark. The Markedyb continues north-westwards for 5M leaving the Bredholm and Birkholm islands close to starboard. At the next RW safe water buoy course can be set (leaving the Egholm Flak North cardinal mark to port) for the RW safe water buoy marking the commencement of the channel into Ærøskøbing. If courage fails when contemplating the complexity of this southern approach there is always the long way round up the west coast of Ærøskøbing or one can stop off at Marstal which is also a pretty place.

Berthing
Either in box berths in the marina or alongside and probably rafted up to the eastern breakwater in the old harbour. Large and classic vessels berth just inside the old harbour on the north pier.

But if the harbours are too crowded there is a good anchorage in any wind conditions except north and northwest in the bay just to the north and west of the town, the Revkrog, or in westerly conditions just to the east of the east breakwater of the commercial harbour.

Facilities
All facilities are available. Ferry to Svendborg.

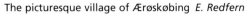

The picturesque village of Ærøskøbing *E. Redfern*

Ærøskøbing commercial harbour *S. Carnegie*

The Als Fjord and Sønderborg

54°54'N 09°47'E

Distances from northern entrance
Fåborg 25M, Middelfart 27M, Augustenborg 11M, Sønderborg 10M.

Charts
Admiralty chart 2532
Danish charts 155, 159

Lights
1030 **Nordborg** 55°04'·7N 09°42'·7E Oc.WRG.5s27m12–9M
  Yellow round tower. 065°-G-070°-W-073°-R-171°-G-
  184·5°-W-236°-R-254°
1066 **Ballebro** 54°59'·8N 09°40'·4E Iso.WRG.2s11m10–7M
  White round tower, red band. 128°-G-140°-W-152°-R-
  253°-G-262·5°-W-274-R-283°
1122 **Sottrupskov** 54°58'·3N 09°44'·6E Iso.WRG.4s9m6–4M
  White pedestal, red band. 151°-G-192·5°-W-201°-R-
  238°
1104 **Als. S Point. Kegnaes** 54°51'·2N 09°59'·3E
  Oc.WRG.5s32m12–9M Yellow round tower 217°-R-
  266·5°-G-273°-W-289·5°-R-337°-G-026°-W-044°-R-
  050·5°-G-075°-W-080°-R-102·5°
1113 **Kalkgrund** 54°49'·5N 09°53'·3E
  Iso.WRG.8s22m14–12M Red round tower, two white
  bands, three galleries. 012°-W-062°-R-084°-W-100°-R-
  120°-W-131·5-G-157°-W-164°-R-190°-W-252·6°-G-258°-
  W-265°-R-292°-W-308°-R-012°

Communications
Dyvig Kro Marina ☎ +45 74 45 14 90
Dyvig Yachthavn ☎ +45 74 45 02 00
Augustenborg Yachthavn ☎ +45 74 47 15 62
Yachtyard ☎ +45 74 47 10 86
Christian X Bridge ☎ +45 74 32 39 39 *VHF* Ch 12, 13
Sønderborg Harbourmaster ☎ +45 74 42 27 65
  Harbour office ☎ +45 74 42 93 92
  http://sonderborg.sonderborg.dk/marina/
Marina ☎ +45 74 42 93 92

General

This is an attractive and sheltered route through to Sønderborg and the Flensburg Fjord. At the northern end there is an almost totally enclosed anchorage at Dyvig and the Als Fjord leads eastward into the Augustenborg Fjord with Augustenborg at its eastern end. At the junction of the two fjords the Als Sund leads southwards to Sønderburg with its Christian X bridge where one usually has to wait for the next opening which is signalled on each side of the bridge by digital clock.

Approach

Approach waypoints
From north (Als Fjord) 55°03'·5N 09°37'E
From south (Als Sund) 54°53'N 09°47'E

From the north the approach is straightforward and from the south the ECM at the entrance to the sound must be left to starboard and the red porthand mark to port.

Dyvig Anchorage

The narrow entrance to the Dyvig anchorage is on the north side of Als Fjord. The buoyed entrance carries a least depth of 3·5m with 9·5m in the excellent anchorage in the middle. There are also two small marinas inside with the approach to Dyvig Kro marina on the north side having 5m depth and that of Dyvig Yachthafen on the south side 3m. There is a restaurant at Dyvig Kro and limited facilities at the Yachthafen. But no fuel at either.

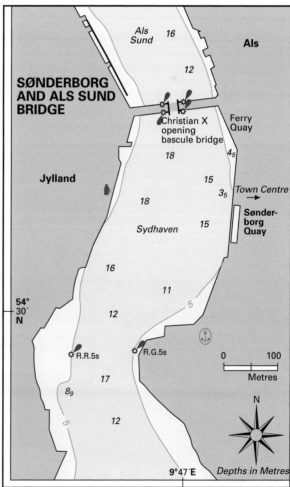

2. DENMARK

Christian X bridge at Sønderborg *J. Parkinson*

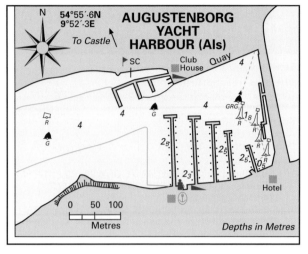

Augustenborg

Augustenborg is in the furthest southeast corner of Augustenborg fjord. It is reached by a buoyed channel dredged to 4m. On the south side of the fjord is an airfield and anchoring is forbidden within 600m of the south shore. Augustenborg has a large marina on the south side with a yachtyard, fuel station and restaurant whilst on the north side there is a very friendly sailing club which has basic facilities and welcomes visitors. The very neat village and the grandiose castle, now turned into a nursing home, are also on this side.

Sønderborg

Sønderborg is at the southern end of Als Sund and is dominated by the Christian X opening rail and road bridge whilst 1M further north is a fixed road bridge with a clearance of 33m. Opening times of the lifting bridge are supposed to be every hour but the trains seem to frequently interfere with this. Five horizontal F.R. lights signal no passage and five horizontal Fl.R. lights signal that the passage is open in both directions at which point vessels flood through the bridge in two columns in each direction. Keep to starboard!

There is a large marina on the east side of the southern entrance to Als Sund but the more interesting berths are alongside the staging on the east side just south of the rail bridge. But have a fender plank ready as there are awkward piles. Here there are basic facilities and it is close to the shops and supermarkets.

A 3km walk over the bridge takes one up to the Dybøl Mill and the Battlefield Centre which commemorate the battle of 1864 when the Danes lost most of Schleswig-Holstein to Germany.

Good anchorages outside the southern entrance to the Als Sund are Horup Hav 3M to the east and Vemmingbund 2M to the west.

Sønderborg from the northwest *P. Roach*

2g. Approach to The Baltic by the Store Bælt

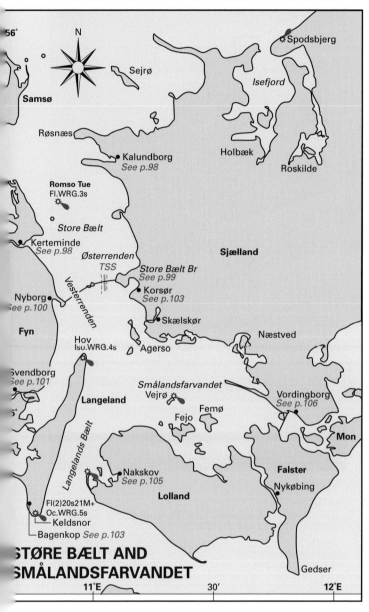

STØRE BÆLT AND SMÅLANDSFARVANDET

Porthand buoy
Danish-style
E. Redfern

Kalundborg

55°40'N 11°05'E

Distances
Århus 45M, Grenå 50M, Lynaes 60M, Nyborg 33M.

Charts
Admiralty chart 2596, 2108, 923
Danish charts 141, 145

Lights
1496 **Rosnaes** 55°44'·6N 10°52'·1E Fl.W.5s24m19M White square tower
1498 **Rosnaes Puller** 55°45'N 10°50'·6E Fl(2)W.5s9m8M Red mast on granite base
1500 **Asnaes**. NW point. 55°40'·3N 10°56'·1E Fl.W.3s12m4M White pedestal, red band
1507·3 **Anaesvaerket N** Dir Lt 116·52° 55°39'·90N 11°04'·73E Dir.Oc.WRG.10s13m12M Grey framework tower. 113·52°-G-115·52°-W-116·52°-R-118·52° Synchronised with 1507·4
1507·4 **Anaesvaerket S** 55°39'·89N 11°04'·72E Dir.Oc.WRG.10s13m12–8M Grey framework tower 114·52°-G-116·52°-W-117·52°-R-119·52° Synchronised with 1507·3

Communications
Harbourmaster ☎ +45 59 53 40 00
Port Control VHF Chs 12, 13

General

Kalundborg is a large town and ferry port with good shops and an interesting 12th-century church.

Approach

Approach waypoint 55°42'·5N 10°56'E

The buoyed entry channel on 116·5° commences at the green lightbuoy LFl.G.10s just east of the Approach waypoint. Follow the channel until just past a coal-fired powerstation on the southern side when course is altered on to 020° towards the ferry terminal between a red porthand buoy and a West cardinal mark. When the ferry terminal is abeam steer for a small red perch with a F.R light and solar panel which is difficult to see from a distance in daylight but it marks the eastern end of a breakwater some of which can be under water. The red perch must be left to port in order to enter the Westhavn.

Berthing

Berth in box berths along the south side the Westhavn in 2·8m with 1·7m further in. These berths can be made uncomfortable by the pilot boat going in and out so the small yacht harbour at Gisseløre is a good alternative. There is 2·5m in the dredged approach channel and between the two outside jetties. It is run by the sailing club.

Facilities

Showers/toilets on the ground floor of the harbour office. Water/electricity on the pier. Fuel station in the fishing harbour run by the Yacht Club which has to be phoned to arrange a time. The Yacht Harbour has good basic facilities but is a longer walk to town. Good rail connections with Copenhagen and ferry to Samsø.

2. DENMARK

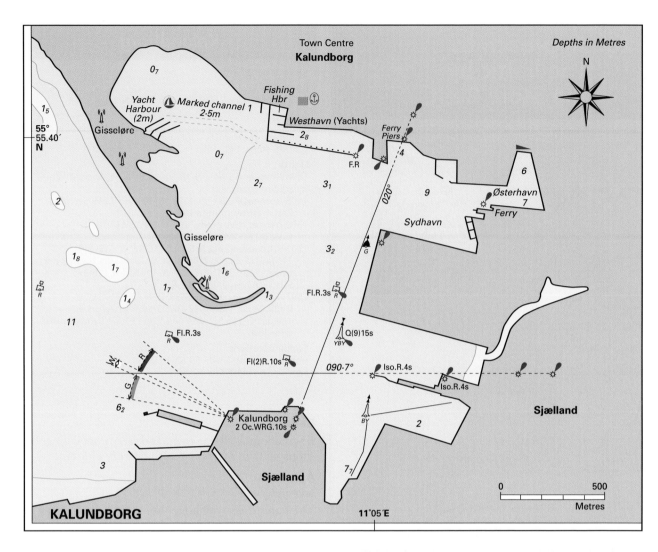

Kalundborg from the northwest *P. Roach*

Kerteminde

55°27'N 10°40'E

Distances
Juelsminde 30M, Kalundborg 25M, Nyborg 15M, Korsør 18M.

Charts
Admiralty chart 2596
Danish charts 141

Lights
1526 **Romsø Tue. No 24.** 55°33'·5N 10°49'·2E
Fl.WRG.3s10m11–7·5M Green tower 051°-G-132°-W-135°-R-150°-G-158°-W-169°-R-300°-G-325°-W-332°-R-051°
1531 Ldg Lts 253° *Front* 55°27'N 10°39'·7E Iso.R.2s6m5M
Yellow triangle on grey pillar. *Rear* 85m from front.
Iso.R.4s7m5M Yellow inverted triangle on grey pillar
1531 **Storebaelt Bridge, Westerrenden, E Passage.** W Dir
Lt 333·3° 55°18'·56N 10°53'·90E Iso.WR.8s26m10–8M
331·8°-R-334·8°-R-341·8°. E Dir Lt 336·3° 55°18'·57N
10°53'·93E Iso.WG.8s26m10–8M 327·8°-G-334·8-W-337·8°
Storbaelt Bridge, Westerrenden, W passage W Dir Lt
157·2° 55°18'·51N 10°53'·60E Iso.WG.8s26m10–8M
148·7°-G-155·7°-W-158·7°. E Dir Lt 154·2° 55°18'·51N
10°53'·63E Iso.WR.8s26m10–8M 152·7°-W-155·7°-R-162·7°

Communications
Marina Harbourmaster ☎ +45 65 32 37 33

Kerteminde looking west *P. Roach*

General

Kerteminde is a pretty holiday town which used to be the mediaeval port for Odense, Denmark's third city, and at one time harboured Fyn's largest fishing fleet. It has a large yacht harbour. The Danish version of the Nordic folk boat is built here.

Approach

Approach waypoint 55°27'.2N 10°40'.8E

Straight forward approach on 253° on the leading line which leads into the commercial harbour with a diversion northwards into the yacht harbour leaving the outer baffle breakwater to starboard.

Berthing

Berth in box berths with bow to jetties in 2–3m at outer ends and shallower further in. Larger vessels can berth on the north quay of the commercial harbour near the grain silo in 4·5m.

Facilities

The yacht harbour has all facilities including an excellent chandlery. Fuel in the commercial harbour next to the grain silo. Bus to Odense. Excavated Viking burial mound at Ladby 4km southwest.

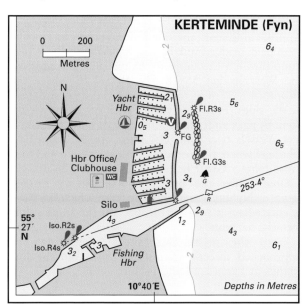

Store Bælt Bridge

55°27'N 10°40'E

Distances
Juelsminde 30M, Kalundborg 25M, Nyborg 15M, Korsør 18M

Charts
Admiralty chart 938
Danish charts 143

Lights
Westerenden buoy 55°19'·85N 10°52'·5E Iso.4s Red and white vertical stripes
1531·528 **Westerrenden, W passage** W Dir Lt 157·2° 55°18'·51N 10°53'·60E Iso.WG.8s26m10–8M 148·7°-G-155·7°-W-158·7°
1531·53 E Dir Lt 154·2° 55°18'·51N 10°53'·63E Iso.WR.8s26m10–8M 152·7°-W-155·7°-R-162·7°
1531·502 **Westerrenden, E Passage**. W Dir Lt 333·3° 55°18'·56N 10°53'·90E Iso.WR.8s26m10–8M 331·8°-W-334·8°-R-341·8°
1531·504 E Dir Lt 336·3° 55°18'·57N 10°53'·93E Iso.WG.8s26m10–8M 327·8°-G-334·8°-W-337·8°
Buoy 55°17'·25N 10°54'·1E Iso.4s Red and white vertical stripes
1532·2 **Sprogø** 55°19'·8N 10°58'·2E Fl.W.5s44m8M Red round masonary structure, yellow bands
Østerrenden buoy 55°22'·1N 11°02'·2E Iso.4s Red and white vertical stripes
1532·5 **Østerenden** N W26 Fl(3)G.10s10m8M Green lantern on green mast with platform
1532·606 **W Channel** Ldg Lts 180° N Side. *Front* 55°20'·49N 11°01'·82E Iso.W.4s74m10M 164·3-vis-194·3. S Side *Rear* 3FW(vert)95m6M
1532·608 **E Channel** Ldg Lts 000° S Side. *Front* 55°20'·54N 11°02'·46E Iso.W.4s74m10M N Side *Rear* 3FW(vert)95m6M
1534 **Østerrenden** S E28 55°19'·5N Fl(3)R.10s10m8M Red mast with platform
buoy 55°18'·88N 11°02'·2E Iso.4s Red and white vertical stripes

Communications
VTS Callsign Great Belt Traffic VHF Ch 10, 11, 16
All vessels over 20m LOA must use the Østerrenden TSS and report their intentions to GBT. Information is broadcast on *VHF* Ch 11 after prior announcement on *VHF* Ch 16

General

The bridge was opened in 1998 and is part of the motorway system which now connects Jutland with Sweden. The western end connects Fyn with the island of Sprogø and is a combined rail and road bridge with multiple spans and a clearance of 18m in the marked navigation channels while the eastern end is a motorway suspension bridge connecting Sprogø with Sjaelland. It has a clearance of 65m. The railway goes into a tunnel under the Østerrenden.

It is preferred that vessels under 20m LOA should use the Vesterrenden TSS or navigate outside the Østerrenden TSS (see plan on page 97) if possible but it is not compulsory to do so. If in any doubt discuss with Great Belt Traffic on VHF Ch 10, 11, 16.

The impressive Store Bælt Bridge *C. Lassen*

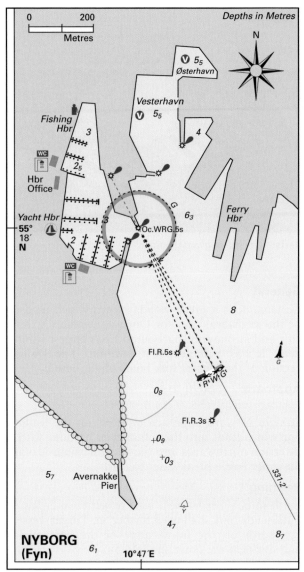

Nyborg

55°18'N 10°47'E

Distances
Kerteminde 17M, Kalundborg 35M, Korsør 14M,
Svendborg 24M, Bagenkop 42M, Naksov 36M

Charts
Admiralty chart 2596, 2597, 938
Danish charts 141, 142, 143

Lights
1532 **Sprogø** 55°19'·8N 10°58'·2E Fl.W.5s44m8M Red
round masonry structure, yellow bands
1556 **Knudshoved** 55°17'·4N 10°51'·1E
Oc.WRG.10s16m12–10M White square tower. 220°-G-
269°-W-276°-R-305·5°-G-359°-W-003·5°-R-095° (Partly
obscured 072°-080°)
1564 Ldg Lts 306° *Front* 55°18'N 10°46'·9E Iso.W.2s4m9M
White disc on beacon
Rear 55m from front Iso.W.2s13m9M White disc on
white beacon
1640 **Langelandsøre**, Omø 55°09'·6N 11°08'E
Oc(2)WRG.12s21m17–14M Yellow round tower 266°-
G-271°-W-283°-R-291°-G-296°-W-304·5°-R-006°-G-101°-
W-104°-R-118°-G-133°-W-138·5°-R-146°-G-162°-W-
164·5°R-183°-G220°
1656 **Frankeklint** 55°09'·6N 10°55'·9E Oc.RG.5s16m8M
Gable of white house 039°-G-047°-R-151°-G-178°-R-
219°
1668 **Hov** 55°08'·8N 10°57'·3E Iso.WRG.4s12m16–13M
White round tower, red band. 210°-R-226·5°-G-232·5°-
W-237°-R-308·5°-G-341°-W-346°-R-010°

Communications
Communications Port Authority ① +45 63 33 70 83
Marina ① +45 63 33 70 00, *Mobile* +45 20 46 05 66

General
Before the Store Bælt Bridge was built Nyborg was a
busy ferry port full of train ferries for the crossing to
Sjaelland but now they have gone it seems to have
slightly lost its way. However it is quite a pretty
town with a castle and some old buildings dating
from mediaeval times when it was the seat of the
Danish Parliament and used to collect dues from
ships sailing through the Store Bælt.

Approach
Approach waypoint 55°16'·3N 10°51'·1E (Landfall buoy)

Approaching from the north the western half of the
Storebælt Bridge must be negotiated and this is best
done through the buoyed channel in the middle of
the West Bridge 55°18'·5N 10°53'·7E where the
clearance is 18m in the centre of the span and 16m
at the sides. However yachts with local knowledge
seem to pass under it at other places but clearance is
less. Vessels over 20m OA must use the main East
Channel where the vertical clearance is 65m and they
must contact Great Belt Traffic on VHF Chs 10, 11.

Once under the bridge course can be altered
towards Nyborg Landfall buoy from which the fjord
is entered on a bearing of 306° on the leading line
into the harbour.

From the south the landfall buoy can be
approached directly taking care to avoid the low
islands at Langesand and its surrounding shoals.

Nyborg looking west *P. Roach*

Berthing

Berth in the marina in box berths in the southern part of the basin on the west side of the harbour with a maximum of 3m depth or larger vessels can berth alongside in the Vesterhavn in 7·5m or the Østerhavn in 5m.

Facilities

Nyborg has all facilities. Fuel is available in the fishing harbour in the northern part of the marina basin. Trains to Copenhagen, Odense and Hamburg.

Svendborg Nordre Havn looking southwest *P. Roach*

Svendborg

55°04'N 10°37'E

Distances
Nyborg 24M, Ærøskøbing 13M, Fåborg 15M, Bagenkop 15M, Kiel 45M, Sønderborg 35M

Charts
Admiralty chart 2532, 2597
Danish charts 152, 171

Lights
Buoy Thurø Reef SCM 55°01'·2N 10°44'E Q(6)+LFl.15s
1634 **Tåsinge**. Ldg Lts 283° *Front* 55°01'·7N 10°39'·4E
 Iso.R.2s11m11M Red triangle on red framework tower, white stripes. *Rear* 223m from front Iso.R.4s15m11M Red inverted triangle on red post with white stripes
1594 **Vindebyore** Ldg Lts 061° *Front* 55°03'·2N 10°37'·4E
 Iso.W.2s4m16M White post, red band. *Rear* 203m from front Iso.W.4s10m16M White post, red band.
1596 **Gaswaerk** 55°03'·3N 10°36'·8E Oc.WRG.5s8m6–4M
 White building 227°-G-232°-W-237°-R-252·5°-G-289°
1591 **St Jorgens** 55°02'·9N 10°35'·8E
 Oc(2)WRG.6s8m10–7M White hut, red band, on wooden piles. 053·5°-G-058·5°-W-060·5°-R-066°
1022 **Baekkehave** 55°01'N 10°32'·7E Oc.WRG.5s6m12–9M
 White hut, red band. 095°-G-100°-W-105°-R-107°

Communications
Harbourmaster ✆ +45 62 21 06 57

General

Svendborg is situated on a very beautiful sound and is attractive.

Approach

Approach waypoints
From east 55°01'N 10°44'·3E
From west 55°01'·3N 10°31'E

On approaching the eastern entrance to Svendborg Sound from the north the Thurø Reef South cardinal mark must be left to starboard before turning westward on to the leading line on 283°. (Be warned that many experienced sailors have inadvertently cut

2. DENMARK

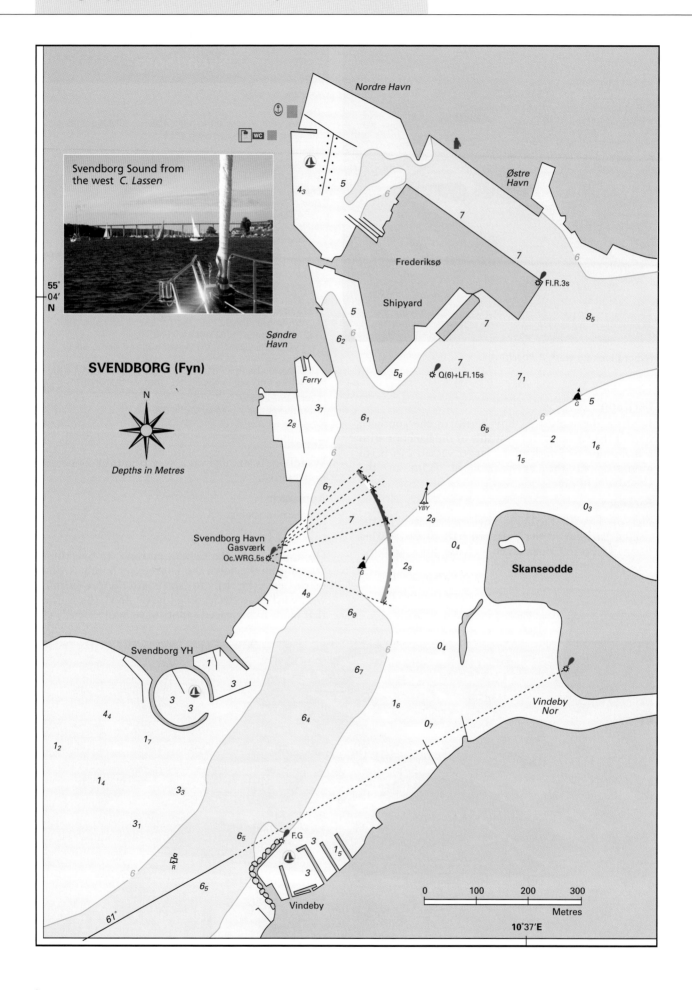

Svendborg Sound from the west *C. Lassen*

55°
04'
N

SVENDBORG (Fyn)

N

Depths in Metres

Nordre Havn

Østre Havn

Frederiksø

Shipyard

Søndre Havn

Ferry

Fl.R.3s

Q(6)+LFl.15s

Svendborg Havn
Gasværk
Oc.WRG.5s

YBY

Skanseodde

Svendborg YH

Vindeby
Nor

F.G

Vindeby

0   100   200   300

Metres

10°37'E

61°

the corner and hit rock). 283° leads into the sound which has a succession of leading lights and unlit buoys through the dog-leg which leads up into Svendborg.

The direction of buoyage changes at the most northerly point reached by the sound at 10°36′·8E and it is just west of this point that the Yacht Harbour in the northern basin of the commercial harbour can be entered.

The approach along Svendborgsund from the west is straightforward as long as one stays within the buoyed (unlit) channel. The fixed bridge just west of the town has a clearance of 33m. There is usually an east-going current of up to 2·5 knots in the sound.

Berthing

Berth in one of the several marinas on either side of the sound but the most convenient berth for the town is in the commercial harbour at 55°03′·5N 10°37′·1E. Yachts berth either in box berths or alongside in 4–5m but a strong current in the sound can sweep into the harbour and make it uncomfortable. (Most of the smaller marinas are served by a ferryboat into the town).

Facilities

A new shower and office block was opened in 2008 and most other facilities are available including a repair yard for traditional craft. There is a diesel berth on the north side of the basin.

Bagenkop

54°45′N 10°40′E

Distances
Svendborg 22M, Nyborg 43M, Kiel 30M, Vordingborg 55M.

Charts
Admiralty chart 2113, 2597
Danish charts 142, 195

Lights
1082 **Vejsnaes Nakke** 54°49′·1N 10°25′·5E
  Oc.WRG.5s24m7–4M White mast, red band. 007°-W-210°-G-252°-W-337°-R-352°-G-007°
1710 Ldg Lts 102·3° *Front* 54°45′·2N 10°40′·4E
  Iso.WRG.4s10m8–5M Red triangle on grey framework tower. 079°-G-099°-W-106-R-126° *Rear* Iso.W.4s13m6M red inverted triangle on grey framework tower. 077·3°-vis-127·3°
1705 **Kelsnor** 54°43′·9N 10°43′·3E Fl(2)W.20s39m21M White square tower 200°-vis-116° and in Marstal Bugt. Obscured 098°-135° when close to Langeland

Communications
Harbourmaster ① +45 62 56 18 61

General

Although situated on the west side of the southern tip of Langeland, Bagenkop is a useful stop if headed from the Store Bælt towards Kiel and vice versa or from Kiel to the Smålandsfarvandet. Bagenkop is a fishing village but at one time had a ferry to Kiel.

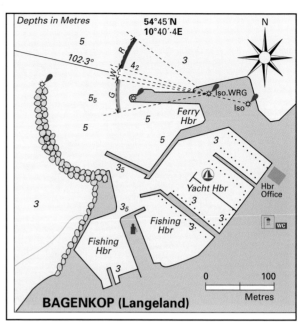

BAGENKOP (Langeland)

Approach

Approach waypoint 54°45′·4N 10°39′E

The approach is buoyed from the west on leading lights situated on the north pier on a bearing of 102°. Leave the western pierhead to starboard before heading southeast into the harbour.

Berthing

Berth in box berths in the northern basin.

Facilities

Most facilities are available together with small foodstores and restaurants. There is a diesel berth in the fishing harbour.

Korsør

55°20′N 11°08′E

Distances
Svendborg 22M, Nyborg 43M, Kiel 30M, Vordingborg 55M

Charts
Admiralty chart 2596, 938
Danish charts 141, 143

Lights
(For Store Bælt Bridge lights see page 99)
1532 Sprogø 55°19′·8N 10°58′·2E Fl.W.5s44m8M Red round masonary structure, yellow bands
1544 Commercial Harbour Ldg Lts 073·5° Front 55°20′·2N 11°08′·2E FR.8m11M Orange triangle on grey column. 068°-vis-080° Rear 164m from front FR.17m11M Inverted triangle on grey column
1552 Yacht Harbour N Mole. S Head 55°19′·7N 11°07′·7E Iso.WRG.4s5m6–4M Red Post 039°-G-049°-W-110°-R-039°
1553 Yacht Harbour S Mole. N Head 55°19′·7N 11°07′·8E Fl.G.3s4m2M Green mast
1534·6 Egholm Flak 55°15′·3N 11°05′·8E Fl.RG.3s10m8–7M Red metal mast with platform marked 30 158°-G-345°-R-158°

Communications
Port Authority ① +45 53 57 00 85
Marina ① +45 58 37 59 30
  www.korsoerlystbaadehavn.dk

2. DENMARK

Korsør looking north *P. Roach*

General

There is a large marina on the south side of a naval basin which is itself on the south side of the commercial harbour and ferry port. The town is old and has some interesting mediaeval buildings. Visitors may berth in the marina or alongside in the Gamle Havn.

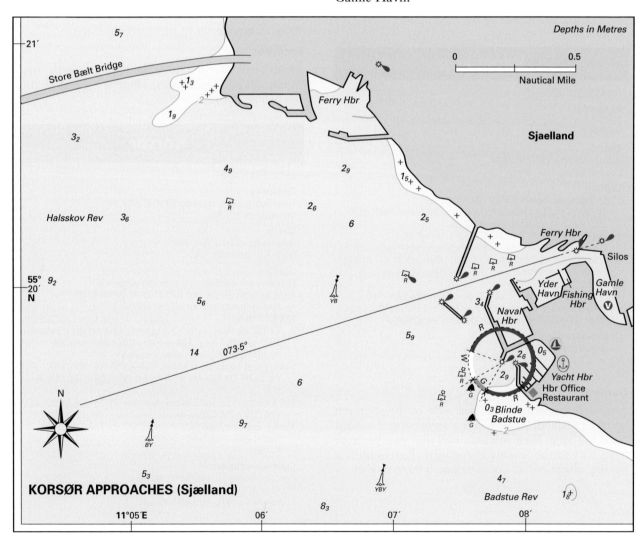

KORSØR APPROACHES (Sjælland)

Approach

Approach waypoints 55°19'·5N 11°04'·4E

The leading line for the commercial harbour leads north of the Nygrund North cardinal mark and north of the detached outer breakwater and into the old harbour. If heading for the marina head east after the Nygrund North cardinal mark to pick up the buoyed entrance channel. If approaching from the south or from the Agersøsund leave the Badstue Shoal West cardinal mark to starboard. The entrance to the marina carries a least depth of 2·9m.

Berthing

Berth in the marina in a box berth in 2·4 to 2·9m or alongside in the Gamle Havn.

Facilities

All the usual facilities are available in the marina including a restaurant and fuel berth. The town centre is a short walk away. Trains to Copenhagen, Fyn and Jutland.

Nakskov

54°50'N 11°08'E

Distances
Korsør 36M, Vordingborg 45M, Kiel 48M, Heiligenhafen 36M.

Charts
Admiralty chart 2597
Danish charts 142, 144

Lights
Buoy 54°51'·8N 10°56'·2E LFl.10s Red and white vertical stripes
1716·1 **Albuen** 54°50'·1N 10°57'·8E
 Iso.WRG.8s11m12–10M
1718 **Enehøje** Ldg Lts 120·1° Front 54°50'·3N 11°00'·9E
 Iso.W.2s16m8M Orange triangle on orange tripod.
 Rear 400m from front Iso.W.4s22m8M Orange inverted triangle on orange framework tower

Communications
Harbourmaster Nakskov Havn ☎ +45 54 67 73 32

General

Nakskov is some 8M east of the landfall buoy and is reached by a winding channel dredged to 6·3m. The town is old and has a long ship-building tradition although wind generators are now the main product. The entrance to the fjord provides several anchorages which could be useful in suitable conditions for those on passage between Kiel and Vordingborg for instance. However the depths are shallow so that a large scale chart and a draught of not more than about 1·5m are helpful.

Approach

Approach waypoint 54°51'·8N 10°56'·2E

The approach is made from the landfall buoy and then by the buoyed channel on a bearing of 120° on the Enehøje leading line. The buoyed channel twists and turns on a succession of lit leading lines eventually ending in the commercial harbour.

Berthing

Berth alongside on the north side of the harbour. There are two marinas to the north of the channel but for the visitor the commercial harbour is more convenient. Anchoring is possible for yachts of moderate draught just inside the bay formed by the Albuen peninsula or to the west or east of the southern end of Enehøje.

Facilities

Most facilities are available in the commercial harbour includig a diesel berth. Restaurants and shopping in the town. Train connections to Copenhagen.

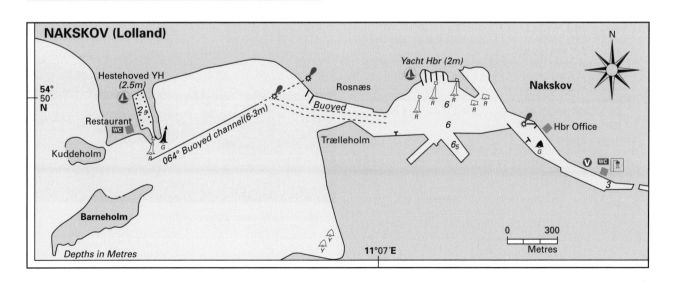

NAKSKOV (Lolland)

Smålandsfarvandet

This is a large area of water to the east of the Store Bælt and between the islands of Lolland and Falster in the south and Sjælland in the north. It provides a more interesting but slower route for those intent on reaching Sweden and Finland from Kiel but wanting a more intimate glimpse of Denmark on the way. There are several islands each with its own small harbour and three of them in particular, Vejrø, Femø and Fejø, are interesting to visit. They are all surrounded by shallow water making for intricate pilotage. In the right conditions anchoring in the lee of an island is possible provided the yacht's draught allows a close enough approach.

In the east the Baltic Sea can be rejoined via the Storstrøm with Vordingborg on its Sjælland shore and then through the Grønsund between Falster and Møn with Stubbkøbing on its southern side. The Storstrøm has a fixed bridge with 26m clearance on its east-going channel and 25m on its west-going side. However it can be by-passed by going through the Masnedsund with its opening bridge. The Grønsund also has a fixed bridge with a clearance of 26m. For those wishing to visit Copenhagen there is a northeast passage, the Bøgestrøm, from the Ulvesund which leads on from the Masnedsund providing a shortcut to join The Sound but there are two fixed bridges (clearances 20m and 25·6m). The well-marked but unlit Bøgestrøm channel is shallow and intricate and should be avoided in strong easterly conditions.

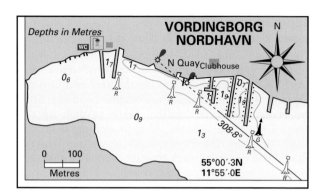

General

The Nordhavn is in an attractive and sheltered inlet off the Masnedsund. It is ten minutes walk from the town which is modern although it has an ancient history. But apart from the church the only remnant of that history are the remains of the 12th-century castle near the harbour.

Approach

From the west the approach can either be through the Masnedsund opening road and rail bridge and continuing as far as the Trellegrund East cardinal mark where the 2m buoyed channel into Vordingborg Nordhavn begins on 309°. Alternatively if having an air draught of less than 25m and a draught of less than 2·5m a yacht can pass beneath the fixed Storstrøm Bridge and then cross the shallow Middelgrund to pick up the Trellegrund East cardinal mark and buoyed channel into Vordingborg. This avoids having to wait for the Masnedsund bridge to open.

From the Grønsund in the south the fixed Farø-Falster Bridge (clearance 26m) will have been passed and again the shallow Middelgrund (2·5m) will need to be crossed to reach the Trellegrund East cardinal mark.

Vordingborg

55°00'N 11°55'E

Distances
Korsør 36M, Nakskov 45M, Klintholm 28M, Rødvig 28M, Copenhagen 60M

Charts
Admiralty chart 2115
Danish charts 162, 161

Lights
1798 **Ore** 55°00'·4N 11°52'·2E Iso.WRG.4s13m12–10M
   White square tower, red bands. 050°-G-091°-W-094°-R-108°
1797 **Masnedø**. W Dir Lt 119° 54°59'·8N 11°52'·9E
   Dir.Oc.WRG.5s11m10–8M Framework tower. 109°-G-118·5°-W-119·5°-R-124°
1814 **Vordingborg** Ldg Lts 309° *Front* 55°00'·2N 11°54'·9E
   FR.4m2M Mast on quay. *Rear* 103m from front.
   FR.8m2M Mast
1804 **Masnedø** E of railway bridge. Ldg Lts 294·6° *Front*
   54°59'·7N 11°53'·4E FG.8m4M Post. *Rear* 60m from front. FG.12m4M Post

Communications
Vordingborg Nordhavn ☎ +45 55 37 05 24
Masnedø Bridge ☎ +45 55 77 70 28
   VHF Ch 12, 13, 16

Vordingborg Marina *J. Parkinson*

View over Vordingborg *E. Redfern*

Berthing

Berth in box berths in the marina or, if the marina is full, alongside near the boatyard just west of the marina. Beware that some berths in the marina and the furthest alongside berths are shallower than 1·5m.

Facilities

Water and electricity on the jetties, showers and toilets onshore. Fish shop and marina kiosk. Yacht yard and restaurant. Fuel and chandlery are available at the Masnedø Marinecentre situated at the southern end of the Masnedsund opening bridge on its eastern side.

2. DENMARK

Vordingborg *P. Roach*

3. Sweden

The country

Physically and geologically Sweden comprises four distinct zones, three of which are founded on ancient rocks. The northern two thirds of the country has mountains to the west, along the Norwegian border, while to the east it is boulder-strewn bare rock, with peat bogs and spruce, pine and birch stretching northwards until they are beaten by the climate. South of this the land slopes down to the central lowlands, which are more hospitable, with prosperous agriculture and deciduous trees among the conifers. Stockholm and Göteborg are in this region. Southern Sweden has a central raised area with the same feel as the rocky north, bordered by coastal lowlands given over to agriculture and fishing. The fourth region, Skåne, in the extreme southwest, has the most recent rock, often covered with boulder clay, with beech and oak rather than conifers, and growing wheat rather than barley and rye. The mood of Skåne is much like that of Denmark.

The coast from north of Stockholm down to Kalmar is fringed by tens of thousands of islands – some inhabited, some not, some rocky and desolate and others green and fertile. It is a seductive area and immensely popular with both Swedish and foreign yachtsmen. The southern part of the Swedish coast, from Kalmar round to Malmö, is attractive, with an undulating coastline and a number of interesting harbours. In July and August, mosquitoes can be an irritation, especially in the remoter anchorages.

From early times, Sweden's economy has owed much to its geology and minerals. Iron and copper began to be of real significance in European markets at the end of the 16th century, and in world terms Sweden is still a leading exporter of iron ore. Building on these and other mineral resources, Sweden has developed an advanced engineering industry now capable of handling almost any category of work from heavy engineering to electronics, which produces more than half the value of all her manufactures. Another major resource is timber, which covers more than half of the country. A quarter of it is publicly owned, a quarter is owned by companies and the rest is in private hands – in all it produces some 20% of the total value of manufactures. Sweden's main lack is fuel – a little coal is mined in Skåne, but she depends on imports for oil and coal.

Fishing is significant to the economy, but is more important on the west coast than the east.

History

In common with most countries, Sweden's origins can be traced almost as far back as one wishes. However the country's name, Sverige, appears to be derived from the Svea people who inhabited the area around Lake Mälaren from the 7th century. A settled and prosperous way of life is thought to have led to an expanding population, and many Svea joined the Viking raids familiar to every British schoolchild. (It may surprise some 21st-century visitors to Scandinavia to encounter a breed of clinker-built smallcraft which are clearly direct descendants of the Viking longship).

Settlements in their homeland included the ancient city of Uppsala, site of a pagan temple where human sacrifice was practised before the country gradually converted to Christianity during the 11th century. This was also the period during which the various provinces gradually united under one ruler, though the struggle for power continued amongst the leading families. Throughout the 12th- and 13th-centuries power passed from king to minister and back to king again, until fratricidal fighting brought the already weakened ruling house down in 1317. Three year old Magnus Eriksson, already king of Norway, was offered the crown, eventually ruling an empire which extended from the North Sea to the Russian border. Further expansion appeared to be in prospect with the marriage of his son Håkon to Margarethe, daughter of the King of Denmark, and in time the crowns of Sweden, Norway and Denmark all went to her nephew Erik of Pomerania, who was crowned at Kalmar in 1397.

However the three countries were administered separately and the Swedes resented both the idea of the Union and the high taxes levied to fund wars against the powerful Hanseatic League. During the 15th century Swedish nationalism steadily developed and in 1435 a parliament was established – the second oldest in the world – which lasted unaltered for 500 years. The independence of Sweden was contested by the Danes, and there were many grim events until Gustav Vasa, helped by the Hanseatic town of Lübeck, established himself as king in 1523. His successors remained in place until the 19th century. There followed the Age of Greatness, when Sweden was involved in political and military alliances and adventures for reasons which had commercial, territorial and religious constituents involving all Europe. She established her presence, with varying success and for varying periods on all the shores of the Baltic, north, east and south, as well as in Norway and Denmark. She also developed her copper and iron mines, and expanded economically. Towards the end of the period, Sweden had established her present boundaries with Denmark and had withdrawn from overseas adventures, and during the 18th century architecture and other arts thrived.

However by the late 18th century the successors of Gustav Vasa were proving less able, and in 1810 one of Napoleon's marshals, Charles Bernadotte, a defector in modern terms, became by invitation Sweden's de facto leader. When the king, Karl XIII, died in 1818, Bernadotte took the throne as Karl XIV. Sweden remains a monarchy to this day, the present king Karl XVI Gustav having succeeded to the throne in 1973. Under the terms of the constitution, the monarch plays a mostly representative and ceremonial role. During the 19th century Swedish history became one of mainly social and economic development, with many Swedes moving from country to city and others emigrating, including about one million – a quarter of the population – leaving for the United States. Even so, industrial output increased steadily. Sweden remained neutral throughout both World Wars and offered sanctuary to many refugees in the 1940s. She joined the European Union in January 1995, after a close-fought referendum, but has remained outside the monetary union.

The people

Sweden has a population of around nine million, and a political system which includes a hereditary monarchy and a parliamentary democracy with a universal franchise, proportional representation and a single chamber of 349 members elected every three years. The established national church is Lutheran – non-Lutherans (including 130,000 Roman Catholics) make up less than 1·5% of the population.

Early on in the modern period, attention was paid to the welfare of all sections of the society, not just to the upper layers. Free education and poor relief started in 1807, old age pensions in 1890, employment injury insurance in 1901, and basic and disability pensions in 1914. Further benefits were added until, by the 1990s, an income tax rate of 45% was required to fund them and social expenditure, including health and social assistance, comprised about a third of the gross national product. Monetary problems during the early 1990s resulted in some services being cut back, allowing taxes to drop by about 25%. At the general election of 2006 the Social Democratic Party, which had governed Sweden for many years, was defeated by the Moderate Party in coalition with minor parties, thereby representing a swing to the right in politics. VAT is set at 25%, and Sweden remains a relatively expensive country for the visitor. The education system is excellent, one result being a well trained work force, another an appreciation of the arts, and a third, conveniently, widespread skill in the English language.

Friendly but sometimes formal, the Swedes have developed a regulated society which, from Gustav Vasa onwards, has looked after its environment and has avoided the worst squalors of industrialisation.

3. SWEDEN

Practicalities

Time

Sweden uses UT+1 in winter and UT+2 in summer. The clocks usually change on the last Sundays in March and September.

Money

The unit of currency is the Swedish *krona* (usually abbreviated to SEK, plural *kronor* and often spoken of as *crown*), divided into 100 *öre*. In early 2010 it stood at 10.7 SEK to £1 or 10.0 SEK to €1. Although within the European Union, it appears unlikely that Sweden will join EMU in the foreseeable future.

Major credit and debit cards are widely accepted, both in payment for goods and services and by banks, nearly all of which have ATMs.

Shopping

Both the standard and the cost of living are higher than in much of Europe, but there are few commodities which cannot be obtained. All daily needs can be met with ease other than in some parts of the Stockholm archipelago – the *skärgård* – where food stores may be few and far between. Throughout the country alcohol – other than beer at 2–3% – is expensive and available only from Systembolaget, the state-owned chain of liquor stores, www.systembolaget.se. There is much debate about the probable introduction of a 'Drink/Sail' law for vessels faster than 15kts or longer than 10m wef 01.07.10. The proposed limit of 0.02% is very low.

Public holidays

Official public holidays in Sweden include: 1 January, 6 January (Epiphany), Good Friday, Easter Sunday and Monday, 1 May (Labour Day), Ascension Day (May), Whit Sunday and Monday (May or June), Midsummer's Eve and Day (close to the summer solstice), All Saints Day (a Saturday in late October/early November), 24–26 December and 31 December.

Communications

The Swedish telephone system is of a high standard and mobile phones extremely popular. Direct dialling is available from all telephone kiosks, all of which are card-operated (and which generally display instructions in several languages, including English).

The international access code from Sweden is 00, followed by the country code, area code (omitting any initial 0) and number. Dialling within Sweden only the area code (including initial 0) and number are required, or number only for a local call. The country code for Sweden is 46, and if dialling from abroad the initial 0 of the area code is not required.

Fax machines are available at many marinas and larger hotels but not, generally, at post offices. Internet access is widespread, with free terminals in most public libraries (though often limited to 20 or 30 minute slots). Some tourist offices also have terminals, and a growing number of marina offices provide Wi-Fi sometimes with a charge. Letters normally take 2–3 days to or from the United Kingdom.

Travel

Sweden is well served by air, and some bus, rail and sea services from other parts of Europe. Internal bus, train and air services are exemplary. Various discounts are available to senior citizens on train services and some ferry routes.

Some useful internet sites

Sites directly connected with charts, pilot books and cruising guides are shown under that heading on page 113. Sites for harbours are shown under the harbour.

Many sites have English versions but often with only a summary of the content. Some browsers (e.g. Google) have automatic translators which, used with original language versions, can give more information despite occasional literal translations.

www.sweden.se – describes itself as the 'Official Gateway to Sweden', with many useful links

www.visit-sweden.com – the website of the Swedish Travel and Tourism Council

www.sverigeturism.se – the Swedish Tourism Trade Association, with links to tourist offices and on to marinas

www.tullverket.se – website of the Swedish Board of Customs. Includes regulations for 'Pleasure Boats' in English and links to other Swedish government sites

www.gotakanal.se – homepage of the Göta Canal Company's excellent and very informative website

www.stockholmtown.com – carries the excellent nine-language Stockholm Official Visitor's Guide

www.stockholm.se – the website of the City of Stockholm, designed primarily for local residents, slightly more formal than the above but with interesting parts – e.g. entertainment, theatres etc.

www.skargardsstiftelsen.se – the website of the Skärgårdsstiftelsen (the Archipelago Foundation)

www.ksss.se – the Kungl Svenska Segel Sällskapet, (the Royal Swedish Yacht Club), have marinas at Saltsjöbaden and Sandhamn

www.sxk.se – the Svenska Kryssarklubben (Swedish Cruising Club), currently in Swedish only

www.balticsunmarinas.net – the homepage of the Baltic Sun Marina group, which has guest harbours in a number of Baltic countries including Sweden. Each harbour rates a brief description and small plan

Cruising

The cruising areas

The varied nature of the cruising to be had around Sweden's coast is, to a large extent, a reflection of the country's geology. The southern part, from Malmö round to Kalmar, is very attractive, with an undulating coastline and a number of interesting (though sometimes shallow) harbours. In July and August mosquitoes can be an irritation, especially in the remoter anchorages but there is some evidence that the regular intake of vitamin B1 proves an effective deterrent.

The west coast varies from the busy and heavily populated Øresund, passing the fertile shores north of Kullen until the Göteborg Skärgård is reached. Then follows the wonderful cruising grounds of the Bohuslän before reaching the bare rocky foreshores backed by extensive forest towards the Norwegian border.

The coast from Kalmar to beyond Stockholm is largely a *skärgård* area. It demands careful navigation, but at the same time offers sheltered sailing in smooth waters dotted with hundreds of secluded anchorages and pretty visitors harbours (*gästhamns*). It is seldom crowded outside

Formalities

British passport holders do not require visas. Should one be required, contact the Swedish Embassy in your country of permanent residence or at 11 Montagu Place, London W1H 2AL ☏ 020 7917 6400
Fax 020 7274 4174
Email ambassaden.london-visum@foreign.ministry.se
www.swedenabroad.com. The British Embassy in Stockholm is located at Skarpögatan 6–8, Box 27819, 115 93 Stockholm, ☏ +46 8 671 3000, *Fax* +46 662 9989, Email info@britishembassy.se, http://ukinsweden.fco.gov.uk/en/. Passports may occasionally be requested when checking into marinas and guest harbours.

EU citizens coming direct from another EU country do not need to seek customs or immigration clearance on arrival unless carrying items which must be declared. In this context – and bearing in mind the very high cost of alcohol in Sweden – it is worth noting that the tax-free allowance if arriving from within the EU tax area is now:

No restriction on alcohol or tobacco, but must be for personal or family use. Age limits apply, 20 for alcohol and 18 for tobacco.

The tax-free allowance if arriving from outside the EU tax area – including from the Åland Islands – is:

1 litre of spirits or

2 litres of fortified wine

4 litres of table wine

16 litres of beer

200 cigarettes or equivalent.

People under 20 are not allowed to bring alcohol into Sweden.

Contact numbers for customs and immigration (which are normally handled by the same officials) are given in the text – of the harbours listed only Arkösund has neither, while Sandhamn has immigration but no customs. Further information can be obtained from the Swedish Board of Customs ☏ +46 771 520 520, Fax +46 820 8012 or email via form on website www.tullverket.se, or from any police station.

The yacht should carry the normal registration papers, including both ship's and operator's radio licences, but there is no requirement for the skipper to hold the International Certificate of Competence or any other formal qualification.

An EU-registered boat on which VAT has been paid can be kept in Sweden indefinitely. A non-EU registered boat can stay in the country for up to one year, but a bond may be payable whilst over-wintering and Customs should be notified before the yacht comes ashore.

The Swedish flag is blue with a yellow Scandinavian cross.

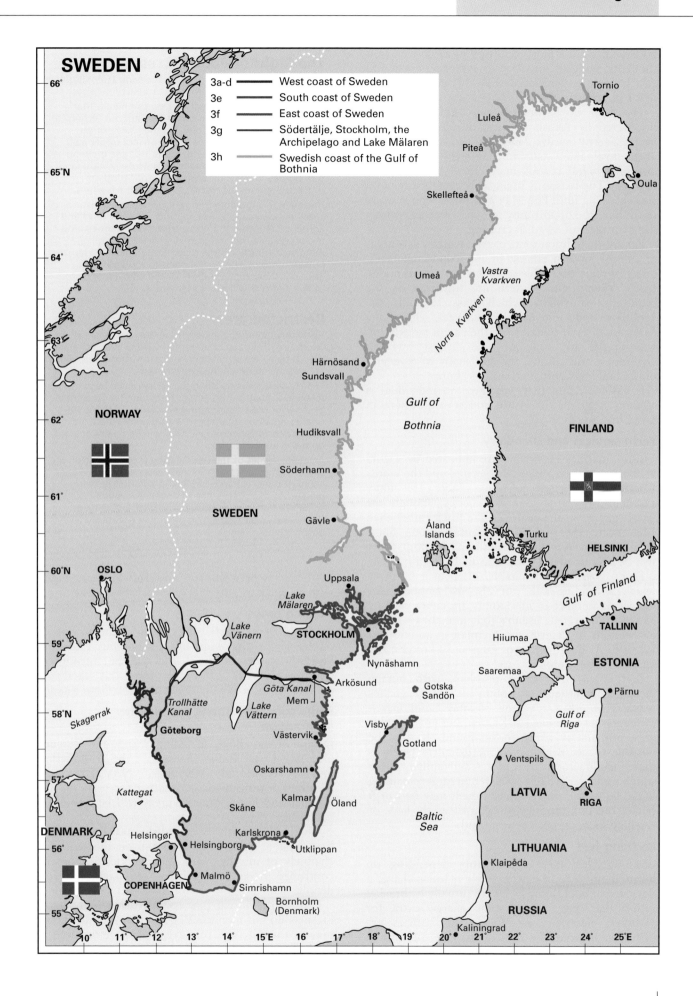

SWEDEN

3a-d	——	West coast of Sweden
3e	——	South coast of Sweden
3f	——	East coast of Sweden
3g	——	Södertälje, Stockholm, the Archipelago and Lake Mälaren
3h	——	Swedish coast of the Gulf of Bothnia

Tornio
Luleå
Piteå
Oula
Skellefteå

Umeå
Vastra Kvarkven
Norra Kvarkven

NORWAY

Härnösand
Sundsvall

Gulf of Bothnia

FINLAND

Hudiksvall

Söderhamn

SWEDEN

Gävle

Åland Islands

Turku

HELSINKI

Gulf of Finland

Uppsala

Lake Mälaren

Lake Vänern

STOCKHOLM

Hiiumaa

TALLINN

ESTONIA

OSLO

Nynäshamn

Saaremaa

Pärnu

Arkösund

Gotska Sandön

Trollhätte Kanal

Göta Kanal
Mem

Lake Vättern

Skagerrak

Göteborg

Västervik

Visby

Gulf of Riga

Gotland

Kattegat

Oskarshamn

Ventspils

Kalmar

LATVIA

Skåne

Öland

RIGA

DENMARK

Helsingør

Helsingborg

Karlskrona

Baltic Sea

LITHUANIA

Utklippan

Klaipėda

Malmö

COPENHAGEN

Simrishamn

Bornholm (Denmark)

RUSSIA

Kaliningrad

3. SWEDEN

midsummer but a fair proportion of those who visit the Baltic with the intention of exploring north and east become so entranced with this area that they never progress further.

The Gulf of Bothnia is only gradually being discovered by British cruisers, though it has long been sailed by Swedes, Finns and Germans. A glance at the invaluable *Gästhamns Guiden* (see *Pilots and cruising guides*) reveals many small harbours and marinas. The season is necessarily quite short, with ice remaining until late May and those who venture north have the opportunity to experience an entirely different facet of Swedish cruising.

Finally, in addition to its coastal waters, vast areas of central Sweden consist of interconnected lakes, many of them accessible to yachts with fixed masts. Lakes Vänern and Vättern are traversed by the hundreds of yachts which pass through the Trollhätte and Göta Kanals each year, while Lake Mälaren, directly inland from the city of Stockholm, was cradle to some of the earliest Swedish civilisation and culture and has many of Sweden's oldest buildings dotted around its shores.

It has been said that, whatever an individual is seeking, they are likely to find it somewhere in Swedish waters.

Yacht services and chandlery

Visitors marinas in Sweden are indicated by a gold anchor symbol on a blue background and the words *Gästhamn* or guest harbour. There are many excellent boatyards and chandleries, though the latter may be in the centre of the town rather than adjacent to the marina or yacht harbour. Some details are given in the text, but any harbour office will be able to advise what is available locally.

Diesel is readily obtainable, often at a berth at which a holding-tank can also be emptied. An increasing number of fuel points are either card or banknote operated, usually (but not always) with instructions in English and German in addition to Swedish. A small reserve of 20 and 50 krone notes may be found useful.

Bottled gas may be a problem, with butane increasingly difficult to obtain as one progresses north. *Camping Gaz* – and possibly *Calor Gas* – cylinders can be refilled at Kalmar, but north of this only propane is likely to be found. It may be possible to get British propane cylinders (such as those manufactured by *Calor Gas*) refilled, but a suitable adapter is likely to be required. If remaining in the Baltic for any length of time it may be worth buying one or more Swedish cylinders in the hope of reselling them on one's return south.

Berthing fees

Berthing fees vary considerably depending on location and time of season. Some marinas charge a flat rate per boat, some by length (usually by bracket rather than per metre); some charge extra for showers, electricity or Wi-Fi while others are inclusive. It would be difficult to give meaningful figures for the lifetime of this book but as a guide, in 2010 the majority would charge for a boat of

The Right of Public Access

Swedes are justly proud of their *Allemansrätten* (Right of Public Access) legislation.

From the yachtsman's point of view this means that a boat can be anchored anywhere (though not secured to a private jetty), and that one can then swim or go ashore, provided one respects the privacy of people's homes and does not enter gardens, trample growing crops, etc. Elsewhere one may walk across private land, pick berries, flowers or mushrooms (not those of protected species, of course), and even pitch a tent.

Naturally this freedom brings responsibilities. Disturbing wildlife – particularly nesting birds – leaving litter and lighting fires other than on purpose-built barbecues is not acceptable. Neither is driving or riding any motorised vehicle off the road, though pedal cycles (and horses) are fine. Fishing is limited to rod and line. Basically, show consideration for the enjoyment of others and one will not go far wrong.

Restricted areas

Notwithstanding the above, there are various areas which are off limits for all or parts of the year, normally due to being either Military or Conservation Areas. Both are clearly indicated on Swedish charts.

The regulations controlling the former have been relaxed, so that it is no longer forbidden for foreigners to enter or cross them during peacetime. If there are smaller areas or installations within them where entrance is forbidden to all, they will be clearly marked on the ground.

At certain times of the year landing is not permitted on wildlife sanctuaries, and in some cases approach within 100m of the shore is forbidden. In addition to being marked on the chart a line of linked buoys will sometimes be used to close off an inlet, but even in their absence all restrictions should be rigorously observed.

10–12m loa between 100 and 160 SEK per night with as much as 300 SEK in some city centres

Holding tanks

By 2012 it is likely that a law banning direct discharge or the emptying of holding tanks in Swedish waters of the Baltic will be introduced making the use of shore pump-out facilities mandatory as is already the case in the Göta Kanal.

Radio communications and weather information

Details of the above, including Search and Rescue, GMDSS, Coast Radio Stations, Weather Bulletins and Navigational Warnings, NAVTEX and Weatherfax transmissions, weather forecasts on the internet and Firing Practice areas will be found on pages 363–371.

Weather forecasts in Swedish and English are broadcast at 0800 and 2000 UT on the working channels of all the many VHF stations remotely controlled from Stockholm – see page 368 for details.

It is worth noting that an increasing number of marinas do not monitor VHF, so that mobile phone may be the only way to make contact before arrival (though few marinas seem perturbed at yachts arriving unannounced).

Charts and chart packs

Admiralty charts give good general coverage of the Swedish coast, quite sufficient for passage-making or cruise planning. However for cruising the intricate *Blå Kustens* (Blue Coast) either side of Västervik, or Stockholm's superb *skärgård*, the Swedish publications are essential. These, produced by *Sjöfartsverket*, (the Swedish Maritime Administration), are divided into small-scale 'Coastal charts', medium-scale 'Archipelago charts' and large-scale 'Special and harbour charts'. More details will be found on their website www.sjofartsverket.se.

Of particular appeal to the yachtsman are the excellent *Båtsportkort* series of chart-packs, effectively a combination of 'Archipelago' and 'Special' charts, mostly at scales of 1:50,000 or 1:25,000. These have recently been revised and now come as 15 Spiral bound A3 sized booklets. The series does not cover the entire Swedish coast, and neither does it run in sequence, but comprises:

Västkusten N (the west coast northern section, Svinesund – Måseskär)

Västkusten S (the west coast southern section, Måseskär – Varberg)

Dalslands Kanal

Vänern (Lake Vänern)

Göta Kanal (Mem - Sjötorp)

Hanöbukten (The southeast coast, Bergkvara – Simrishamn)

Kalmarsund (Västervik – Bergkvara)

Ostkusten (The east coast, Trosa – Västervik)

Stockholm S (Stockholm Skärgård, southern part, Dalarö – Trosa)

Stockholm M (Stockholm Skärgård, Central part, Möja – Dalarö)

Stockholm N (Stockholm Skärgård, northern part, Öregrund – Möja)

Mälaren (Lake Mälaren)

Bottenhavet S (Gulf of Bothnia, southern part, Sundsvall – Öregrund)

Bottenhavet N (Gulf of Bothnia, central part, Sikeå – Sundsvall)

Bottenviken (Northern part of Swedish Bothnia coast, Haparanda – Nygrån)

Each page in the booklet is clearly referenced to the next by a series of arrows, and an extract from the list of symbols is included.

There are also two useful series of German-published chart packs (size A2) which are readily available in Denmark. They are published annually and come with electronic versions on CD and complementary pilot books.

NV Baltic Charts

Serie 2 Lübeck – Bornholm - Kopenhagen. Includes the South Baltic coast of Sweden

Serie 3 Samsö – Sund - Kattegat. Includes Øresund to Göteborg

Serie 5 Schwedische Westküste

Delius Klasing charts

Satz 3 Westküste-Schweden

Satz 4 Grosser Belt bis Bornholm

Satz 11 Ostküste Schweden 1

Satz 12 Ostküste Schweden 2

Pilots and cruising guides

The Svenska Kusthandbok series which was produced by Sjöfartsverket (the Swedish Maritime Administration) aimed at the recreational market is no longer published, but copies are still available of two volumes only, Mälaren and Hjalmälaren and Vanern and Trollhätte Kanal. Further information can be found on the website www.sjofartsverket.se, but only on the Swedish version.

Gästhamns Guiden – (www.svenskagasthamnar.se) similar to the above and containing a little more information. Available in English at €17 (2010) or free on website.

Arholma to Landsort (Stockholm Archipelago) and *Landsort to Skanor.* Both pilots published in English by Norstedts Förlagsgrupp AB. Available from Imray.

Küstenhandbuch Schweden Volumes 2 and 3 DK Edition Maritim. In German. Based on the Swedish official pilots

Västkustens Naturhamnar (West Coast Natural harbours)

Naturhamnar på Ostkusten (Natural harbours of the East Coast)

Seglarhamnar på Ost Kusten (Sailing harbours of the East Coast)

Batleder på Ost Kusten (Small Boat Fairways of the East Coast)

Blå Kusten från Luften (The Blue Coast from the Air)

Skärgårdshamnar, Öskär–Landsort (Archipelago harbours, Öskär–Landsort)

Stockholms Skärgård från Luften (The Stockholm Archipelago from the Air)

Vol 1 Öregrund–Sandhamn

Vol 2 Sandhamn–Landsort

Kustguide Bottenhavskusten (Öregrund–Höga Kusten) (southern Gulf of Bothnia)

Bottenvikaren–Norrbottenskärgården (northern Gulf of Bothnia – produced annually by the local community)

Finally, three volumes of the *Baltic Pilot* are needed to cover the entire Swedish coast – *Vol I (NP 18)* for the west and south coasts; *Vol II (NP 19)* for the east coast from Ystad in the south to Norrtälje in the north; and *Vol III (NP 20)* for the Gulf of Bothnia. Although an important and definitive publication, it is often difficult to interpret and much of the practical information needed by yachtsmen is missing.

See the *Appendix*, page 361, for sources.

The coast near Varberg   *B. Weir*

West coast of Sweden

including the canals and lakes to the east coast of Sweden

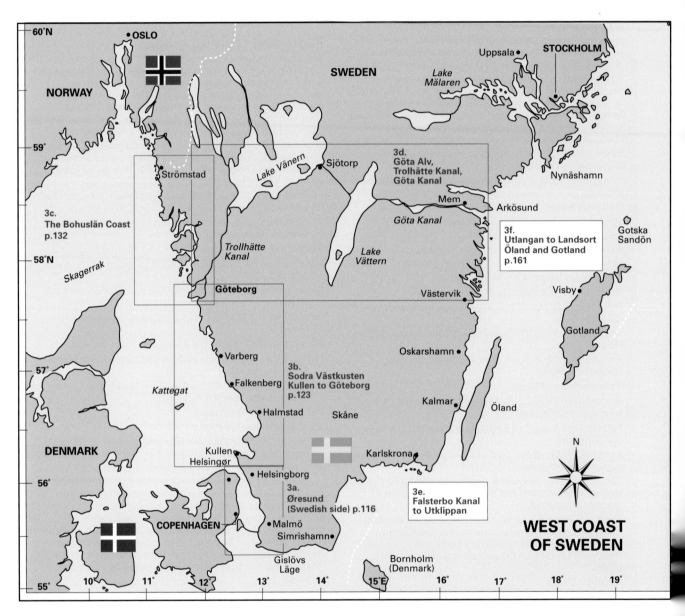

West coast of Sweden

3a. Swedish side of the Øresund, 116

3b. Södra Västkusten, 123

3c. The Bohuslän coast – Norra Västkusten, 132

3d. Göta Alv, Trollhätte Kanal and Göta Kanal, 142

Tylögrund lighthouse near Halmstad *B. Weir*

View from north Koster across Kostersundet towards south Koster *D. and P. Thorne*

Outer *skärgård* on a windy day *D. and P. Thorne*

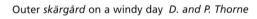

3. SWEDEN

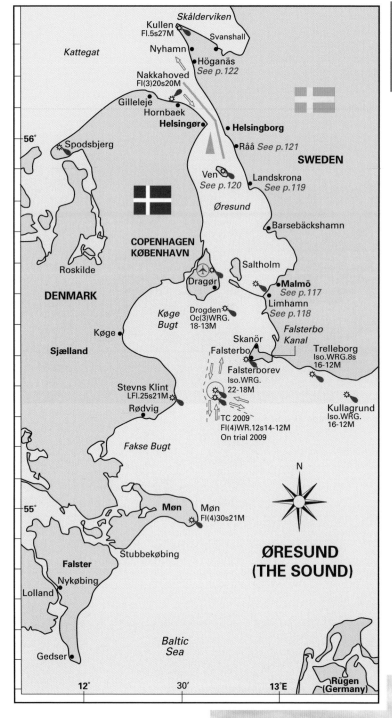

Kattegat

Skälderviken

Kullen
Fl.5s27M
Svanshall
Nyhamn
Höganäs
See p.122
Nakkahoved
Fl(3)20s20M
Gilleleje
Hornbaek
Helsingør
Helsingborg
Råå *See p.121*
SWEDEN
56°
Spodsbjerg
Ven
See p.120
Landskrona
See p.119
Øresund
Barsebäckshamn
**COPENHAGEN
KØBENHAVN**
Saltholm
Roskilde
Dragør
Malmö
See p.117
Limhamn
See p.118
DENMARK
Køge
Bugt
Drogden
Oc(3)WRG.
18-13M
*Falsterbo
Kanal*
Køge
Skanör
Falsterbo
Trelleborg
Iso.WRG.8s
16-12M
Sjælland
Falsterborev
Iso.WRG.
22-18M
Stevns Klint
LFl.25s21M
Kullagrund
Iso.WRG.
16-12M
Rødvig
TC 2009
Fl(4)WR.12s14-12M
On trial 2009
Fakse Bugt
N
Møn
Møn
Fl(4)30s21M
Stubbekøbing
**ØRESUND
(THE SOUND)**
Falster
Nykøbing
Lolland
*Baltic
Sea*
Gedser
12°
30'
13°E
Rügen
(Germany)

3a. The Swedish side of the Øresund

The Sound is the most direct route from the Baltic into the main part of the Kattegat, and as such, is a major shipping route. It is also narrow, being only three miles wide at its narrowest point. There is a traffic separation scheme off Falsterbo Rev, the southwest corner of Sweden, and another in the narrows between Helsingør and Helsingborg. The hazard is from the size of some vessels using this route, rather than the sheer numbers such as in the Straits of Dover, but nevertheless yachts crossing the sound should pay close attention to the normal rules for such schemes. The waters between Copenhagen and Malmö are tortuous and shallow in places and crossed by the Øresund bridge. But there is a well-marked dredged channel for large vessels. Currents in this area will vary with the wind in both strength and direction, and can run up to 2kns in the narrower parts of the Sound. It therefore follows that close attention needs to be paid to navigation in this area. All this may make the area sound hazardous but in practice it is far less so than, for example, the English Channel. It is an interesting cruising ground, home to large numbers of yachts on both the Swedish and Danish sides. There are 20 guest harbours listed on the Swedish shore alone.

Øresund Bridge
E. Redfern

Skanör

55°25′N 12°50′E

Distances
Stralsund 68M, Rostock 78M, Travemünde 110M, Kiel 125M

Charts
Swedish 921
UKHO 2595, 2115

Skanör is a popular holiday place on the southwest corner of Sweden. The harbour, which can be crowded at times, has pile moorings with some space alongside a quay, and makes a useful stopping place on a route between the north German coast at Rügen and Copenhagen.

Malmö

55°37′N 12° 59′E

Distances
Copenhagen 13M, Göteborg 136M, Falsterbo Kanal 13M, Stralsund 80M

Charts
Swedish 921, 8141, 9211
UKHO 903, 2115, 2595

Malmö is Sweden's third largest city, and as such has every facility which would be expected, including exciting architecture. It has excellent communications with the Øresund Bridge linking it to Denmark, as well as road, rail and air links to the rest of Scandinavia and beyond.

There are three main yacht harbours serving the city.

Malmö Dockan marina

55°37′N 12°59′E

☎ +46 703 40 19 18
Email marinan@dockan.se
www.dockan.se. Go to 'Guest'. Click tiny English flag.

Approach is deep water directly from harbour entrance. Moorings are pile or finger. Use a vacant mooring with green sign and pay at the machine. Services are limited to power and fresh water, it is small and expensive, but it is well placed close to the centre of the city.

A sunset view of Dockan Marina, Malmö

Malmö marinas *P. Roach*

3. SWEDEN

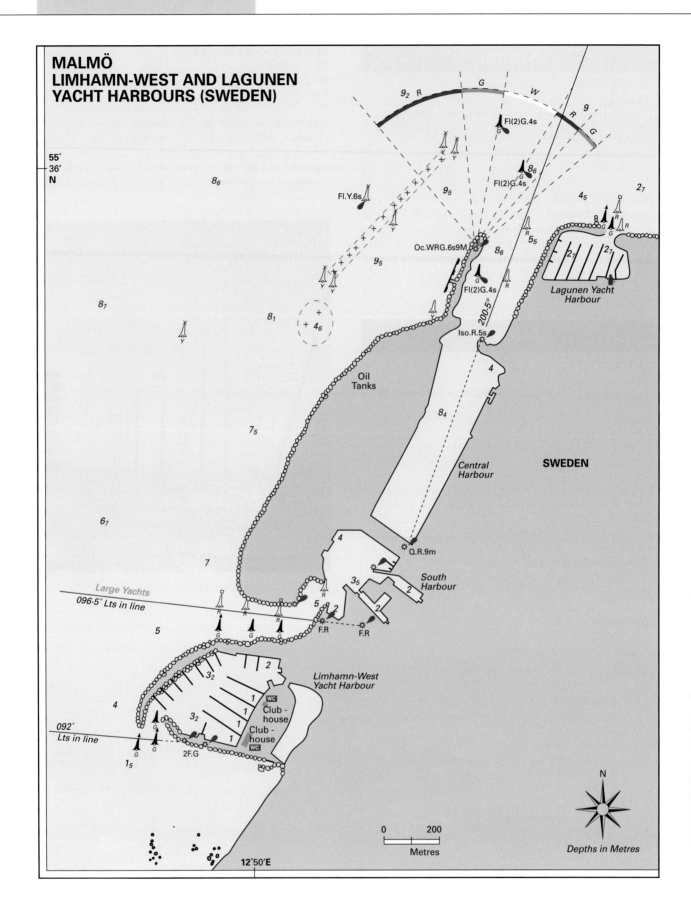

MALMÖ
LIMHAMN-WEST AND LAGUNEN
YACHT HARBOURS (SWEDEN)

55°
36'
N

9₂ R   G   W   R 9

8₆

Fl(2)G.4s

Fl(2)G.4s   8₆

4₅   2₇

Fl.Y.6s

9₅

8₆

Oc.WRG.6s9M

9₅

2₇   2₇

Lagunen Yacht
Harbour

8₇

8₁   4₆

Fl(2)G.4s

200·5°

Iso.R.5s

Oil
Tanks

4

7₅

8₄

Central
Harbour

SWEDEN

6₇

4

7

Q.R.9m

Large Yachts
096·5° Lts in line

5

5   2

3₅   South
Harbour
2

5

2

F.R   F.R

2

Limhamn-West
Yacht Harbour

2

3₂

4

1

WC

Club -
house
Club -
house

092°
Lts in line

3₂

1

1

1

WC

1₅

2F.G

0   200

Metres

N

Depths in Metres

12°50'E

Malmö Lagunen

55°36'N 12°56'E

☎ Harbourmaster + 46 40 16 04 30 Office + 46 40 16 04 18
Email kansli@lagunen.nu
www.lagunen.nu

This marina is home to many local boats, with all the usual facilities, and is particularly suitable for families, there being a nearby playground, beach and open surrounding fields. It is however nearly two miles from the city centre, but reportedly with a bus service. The approach is straight forward apart from a well marked reef charted at 3m depth about quarter of a mile offshore, except that the marina entrance is unlit. Depth in the marina is 2.7m. There are no dedicated berths for visitors, but they are welcome to use any vacant berth with a green sign. Payment is at the marina office.

Malmö Limhamn

55°35'N 12°55'E

☎ +46 40 15 20 24 Fax +46 40 15 18 95
Email info@smabatshamnen.nu
www.smabatshamnen.nu
Marina in Limhamn, Vågbrytarevägen 216 12 Limhamn

This is the best prepared marina for visitors, with all the usual facilities available, including Wi-Fi, but has the disadvantage of being some three miles from the city centre. Approach is straight forward, with depth up to 3m, but beware of the pontoons on the east side, which shallow to 1m at the shore end. Visitors berths are at pontoon F, or use any vacant berth with a green sign and pay at harbour office. If the harbour office is closed, ask for help at the Harbour Grill.

Landskrona

55°52'N 12°51'E

Distances
Copenhagen 13M, Helsingør 12M, Århus 93M, Kiel 140M

Charts
Swedish 922
UKHO 853, 869, 1402

Landskrona offers the choice of two different locations.

Landskrona Nyhamn This is in a yacht basin to port immediately inside the harbour entrance, which is the home of the Landskrona Yacht Club. Contact on mobile phone +46 70 669 41 87. Moorings are piles with bow to pontoon. Depth is 2.5m. There are some shore facilities, but the main advantage is that it is close to the magnificent citadel Castle, one of the best-preserved fortresses in the Nordic countries. It is also close to the town centre which has, as well as shopping, a number of impressive buildings.

Lundåkra yacht harbour This is a further 1.5M up the harbour, with a depth of 4–5m and possibly better facilities. It is however in an industrial area and is over a mile to shopping, or the castle. Contact is Lundåkra port association, ☎ +46 4 18 263 50, but could be a safe place to leave a yacht for a period.

Limhamn *P. Roach*

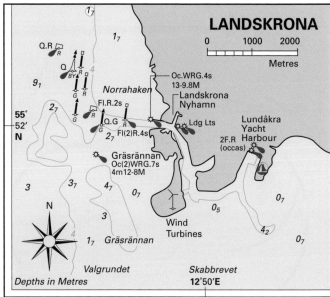

3. SWEDEN

Ven Island, Kyrkbacken Harbour   *P. Roach*

Ven Island

55°55'N 12°42'E
Charts Swedish 922, UKHO 877, 2115, 2594

Ven is a small Swedish island 3M from Landskrona and 4½M off the Danish coast. It is a pleasant holiday island with two small and one slightly larger harbour. Ven is 2·3M long and 1.3M across, the highest spot being a where Tycho Brahe built his castle, Uranienborg, 45m. above sea-level. The island slopes from south to north, the new Western

Lighthouse at the north western tip being 5m above the sea. Approach is simple from all directions, the only hazards being on the northwest corner of the island which are well-marked by cardinals.

Harbours are:

Kyrkbacken West coast. Depth is 2·7m, and there are is said to be 200 berths for visitors, both pile and alongside, with usual facilities, including fuel. Telephone contact for harbourmaster is +46 418 72 577, and harbour dues, must be paid at the office, under penalty of an extra payment if they have to come to find you! The harbour is popular with Danish boats.

Norreborg North coast. This is a small harbour, depth 2m, with minimal facilities and mooring head to quay, stern to a pile or anchor.

Bäckviken East coast. This is the main ferry harbour, which brings day visitors to the island from Landskrona. Depth is 1–2m and there are some pile moorings, or alongside but the ferry berth must be kept clear. Power is available, but not much else.
Anchorage is also possible almost anywhere round the shore, depending on wind conditions. It may however be necessary to make a precipitate departure in the event of a sudden increase or shift of wind.

Shore facilities include a convenience store and bicycle hire. The Tycho Brahe museum, which during 2007 was nominated for the 'European Museum of the Year Award', is a must. Here you can follow the famous scientist's life and how his research made Ven a scientific meeting place during the 16th century. There are several other interesting places to visit as well as a golf course and good beaches.

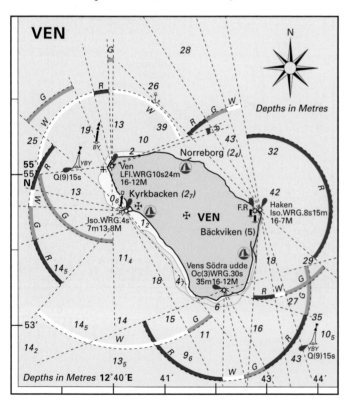

Råå

55°59'N 12°45'E

Distances
Copenhagen 22M, Malmö 29M, Falsterbo Kanal 40M, Stralsund 106M, Göteborg 103M

Charts
Swedish 922
UKHO 877, 2115, 2594

Communications
Råå Port Association ☎ +46 42 26 16 35 between 0900 and 1300
Email raa.hamnforening@telia.com

This is an alternative yacht harbour for Helsingborg, about 3.5 miles south of the main port. Entrance is most easily made at the northern end, which is the mouth of the river Råå. Beware of possible strong currents in the entrance where depth is 3·5–4·0m and in the harbour is 2·5m. Berths are all between

piles with bow to quay. Use vacant berth, preferably with green tag. Harbour office in fishing harbour is manned 0900–1300.

Ashore it is a pleasant, if unremarkable, small town with a shopping centre close to the yacht haven. Also nearby is the fishing harbour with a fishery and shipping museum.

Helsingborg (Norrahamnen)

56°03'N 12°41'E

Distances
Copenhagen 22M, Malmö 29M, Falsterbo Kanal 40M, Stralsund 106M, Göteborg 103M

Charts
Swedish 922, 9221
UKHO 877, 2115, 2594

Communications
Harbourmaster ☎/*Fax* +46 42 21 13 21
Mobile +46 708 18 48 93
Email norrahamnen@port.helsingborg.se
www.norrahamnen.helsingborg.se

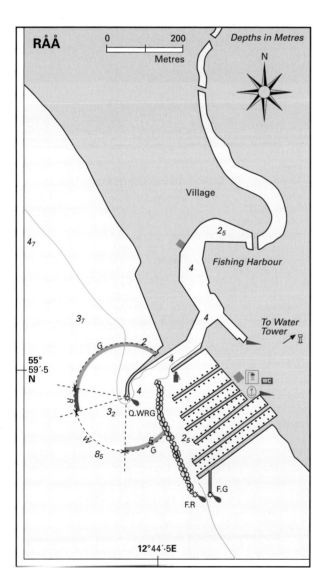

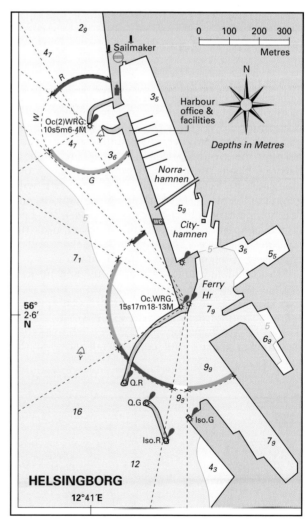

Helsingborg Marina   *P. Roach*

This recently constructed marina is half a mile north of the main ferry entrance to Helsingborg and a distance of 2·5M across the Sound from Helsingør, and thus offers an alternative, should that popular harbour be overcrowded. All other Helsingborg harbour basins are closed to private yachts. Moor alongside the East Quay, or use vacant berth with green tag. Depth is stated to be 4m throughout, and maximum beam in the finger moorings is 4·2m. Fuel is available from an automatic dispenser near the harbour entrance. There is a sailmaker and a chandlery at the north end of the harbour.

Ashore, the half mile walk up to the ancient part of the city and the Karnän tower gives a good view over the area from the top. The Fredriksdal open-air museum and gardens are said to be worth a visit. The usual attributes of a major city are available, including a theatre and concert hall close to the marina.

Höganäs

56°12′N 12°33′E

Distances
Helsingør 10M, Göteborg 96M, Copenhagen 30M

Charts
Swedish 922
UKHO 2594

Communications
Harbourmaster ✆/Fax +46 42 33 33 65
 Email hamnmastare@hbs.se
 www.hbs.se

Höganäs is seven miles south-southeast of Kullen Västra Point, the northern entrance to The Sound; a small town with the usual facilities and a marina with 2·5m draught and the usual facilities, including fuel and Wi-Fi, in pleasant surroundings. Berthing is stern to pile, and bow to quay. Use vacant berth with green tag. Öresundsmarin Boatyard with repair facilities is the main Beneteau importer for Sweden. Shore facilities include good bathing close to the harbour, bicycle hire, and local museum. Several flights daily from Heathrow via Stockholm to Ängelholm airport (13 miles).

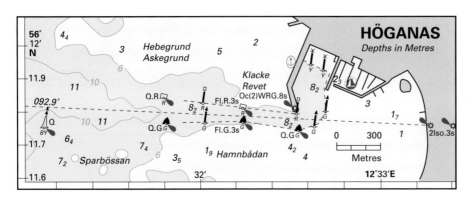

3b. Södra västkusten

From Kullen at the north end of the Sound to the frontier with Norway, the coast is of two distinct aspects. Starting from the south, the coast is low-lying and rather featureless. There is good agricultural land and there are beaches, golf courses and summer resorts. The principal towns are Halmstad, the provincial capital of Halland with a population of around 85,700; Falkenberg with a population of around 13,000; and Varberg with a population of about 19,000. All three places are commercial ports. About 25 miles south of Göteborg, the scenery begins to change from pastoral to rugged and the coast becomes broken and studded with the islands and rocks of the *skärgård*. The principal geological feature is that of gneiss intermingled with granite which forms extensive rock slabs.

Kullen to Göteborg

It is important to emphasise that the Kattegat is open water. The distance between the coast of Sweden and that of Jutland to the west varies from between 40 and 60 miles. A passage northwards is open to a very long fetch from the Skaggerak and likewise a southwards passage is subject to a long exposure to south or southwest winds. It follows that careful judgement must be made, particularly in unsettled conditions, as to when it is advisable to proceed. In favourable circumstances, a non-stop passage either way between Kullen and the sheltered waters of the skärgård south of Göteborg, a distance of some 80 miles, can be made with ease. But when strong winds prevail other than from an off-shore direction, it must not be forgotten that this open coast is liable to be a lee shore. There are a number of harbours which can provide good shelter but in certain cases entering may be hazardous in strong winds and heavy seas. Moreover, it cannot be assumed, particularly in the cruising season, that there will be a berth available, and contact should be made with the harbour or marina in question before deciding whether to attempt an entry.

Surface water travels from the Baltic Sea towards the North Sea but the rate is insignificant, being less than 1kn in the open sea. The tidal range is also of little account being not more than 0·3m (1ft) in the north Kattegat decreasing towards the south. However, strong winds either from an easterly or a westerly direction may cause the sea level along this coast to fall or rise respectively by as much as 0·9m (3ft). The climate in the Kattegat and in the Skagerrak is affected by weather conditions prevailing in the north Atlantic.

Despite the caution given, it would be unreasonable to disregard the coast south of the *skärgård*. There are pleasant harbours for those wishing to break the journey and a selection of these is given below, proceeding from south to north.

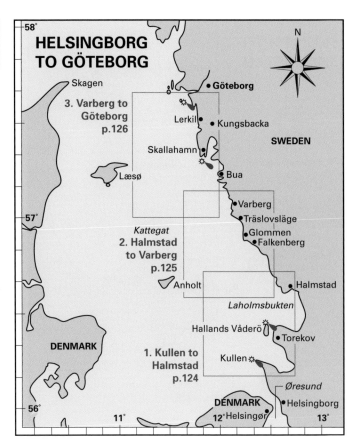

1. Kullen to Halmstad

Distance 25 miles

The promontory of Kullen is high and conspicuous. Approaching from the north it appears at first as an island until low-lying land to the east appears above the horizon. In 1941 the escape of the *Bismarck* from the Baltic was confirmed by the signalling station at Kullen

The coast trends to the north east and is indented by two large bays, Skälderviken and Laholms-bukten. For those wishing to make progress towards the north, it is more direct to proceed from Kullen towards Falkenberg or Varberg but this area is not without interest. (See plan on page 124).

Torekov

56°26'N 12°37'E
Charts Swedish 923 UKHO 875, 2108
☎ +46 431 364 207 *Mobile* +46 0705 924 423

Torekov lies between the two bays and is a convenient place at which to stop, if going south, before rounding Kullen. The north wall gives good shelter but the pontoon berths may be subject to swell in northerly or north westerly winds. It is a pretty place but apt to be overcrowded. Lying offshore is the only island in this part of the coast, Hallands Väderö, a nature reserve with shelter from westerly winds on its leeside.

3. SWEDEN

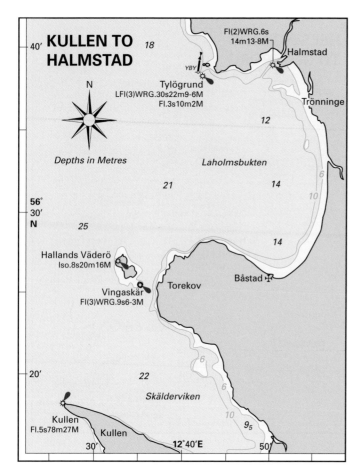

KULLEN TO HALMSTAD

40′
18
Fl(2)WRG.6s
14m13-8M
Halmstad
YBY
Tylögrund
LFl(3)WRG.30s22m9-6M
Fl.3s10m2M
Trönninge
N
12
Depths in Metres
Laholmsbukten
21
14
10
56°
30′
N
25
14
Hallands Väderö
Iso.8s20m16M
Vingaskär
Fl(3)WRG.9s6-3M
Torekov
Båstad
20′
22
Skälderviken
6
6
Kullen
Fl.5s78m27M
Kullen
10
9₅
30′
12°40′E
50

Typical view of the west coast of Sweden between Halmstad and Falkenberg   *B. Weir*

Torekov harbour looking north   *C. Lassen*

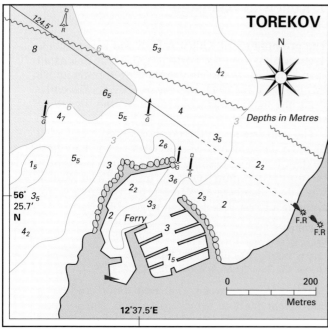

TOREKOV

124.5°
8
5₃
6
4₂
N
6₅
6
4
4₇
G
5₅
G
Depths in Metres
3
1₅
5₅
3₅
2₆
2₂
G
3₆
R
56°
25.7′
N
2₂
3₃
2₃
2
Ferry
3
4₂
1₅
F.R
F.R
0   200
Metres
12°37.5′E

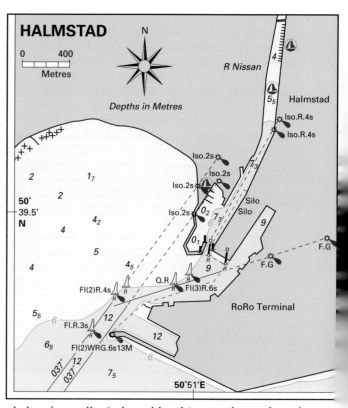

HALMSTAD

0   400
Metres
N
R Nissan
4
Depths in Metres
5₅
Halmstad
Iso.R.4s
Iso.R.4s
Iso.2s
Iso.2s
2
1₇
Iso.2s
Silo
50°
39.5′
N
Iso.2s
0₂
7₃
Silo
9
4
4₂
0₁
F.G
5
9
R
F.G
4
4₅
9
R
Q.R
Fl(2)R.4s
R
R
Fl(3)R.6s
RoRo Terminal
5₅
6
12
Fl.R.3s
R
12
6₅
R
037°
037°
12
Fl(2)WRG.6s13M
7₅
6
50°51′E

Halmstad

56°40′N 12°52′E

Charts Swedish 923, UKHO 875, 2108

Yacht club *Mobile* +46 702 05 71 27 *Fax* +46 35 18 47 75

Email info@bk-najaden.nu

www.bk-najaden.nu

This was a Danish town until the middle of the 17th century. It lies at the mouth of the river Nissan. A buoyed channel leads into the river where there is shelter from all winds and berthing on the starboard side in pleasant surroundings. Depth 3–7m. The town has all the facilities expected of a provincial capital.

2. Halmstad to Varberg

Distance 38 miles

Leaving Halmstad and after passing Tylögrund lighthouse and the very popular resort of Tylösand, the coast trends in a north westerly direction. With shallow water extending some distance off shore it is advisable to give this stretch of coast a good offing.

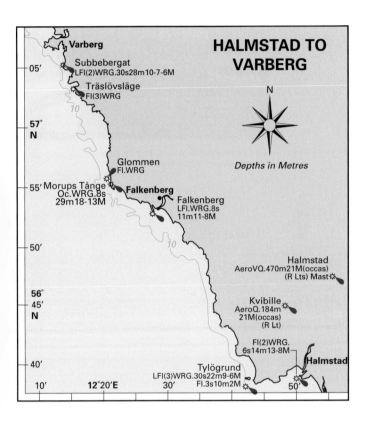

Falkenberg

56°54'N 12°30'E

Charts Swedish 924 UKHO 874, 2107

Sailing club ☎ +46 34 68 41 24 Evenings only

This is a useful stopping place at the mouth of the river Atran. Protected by two parallel moles and, at acute angles, long breakwaters there is good shelter and protection from any westerly swell caused by gales from the west or south west. Berthing is available at a small marina in the river on the southeastern side or possibly alongside the quay on the northwest side. There may be appreciable current from the river in certain conditions and there may be some risk in approaching or leaving the port in the event of strong wind outside.

Glommen

56°56'N 12°21'E

Charts 924 UKHO 874, 2107

Glommen is a picturesque harbour on the coastal plain open to the winds but safe enough inside either at the pontoon provided for yachts of moderate size, or alongside the quays. It is typical of other local harbours along this coast which are small but safe with tricky entrances.

Träslövsläge

57°03'N 12°16'E

Charts Swedish 924, UKHO 874, 2107

Sailing club ☎ +46 340 67 07 07 Fax +46 340 67 02 30
Email info@tbs-tbk.org

This harbour, 14M north of Falkenberg, is a large fishing port and provides good shelter, especially alongside in the fishing harbour provided a berth can be obtained. The yacht basin near the entrance may be subject to slight swell in strong westerlies. Depth is 2·4m and the moorings are pile with bow-to on fingers. Usual marina facilities and shops.

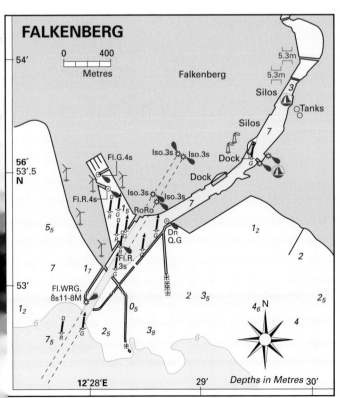

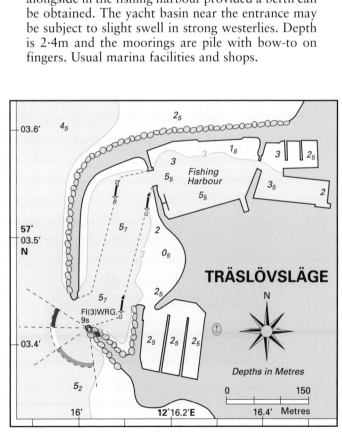

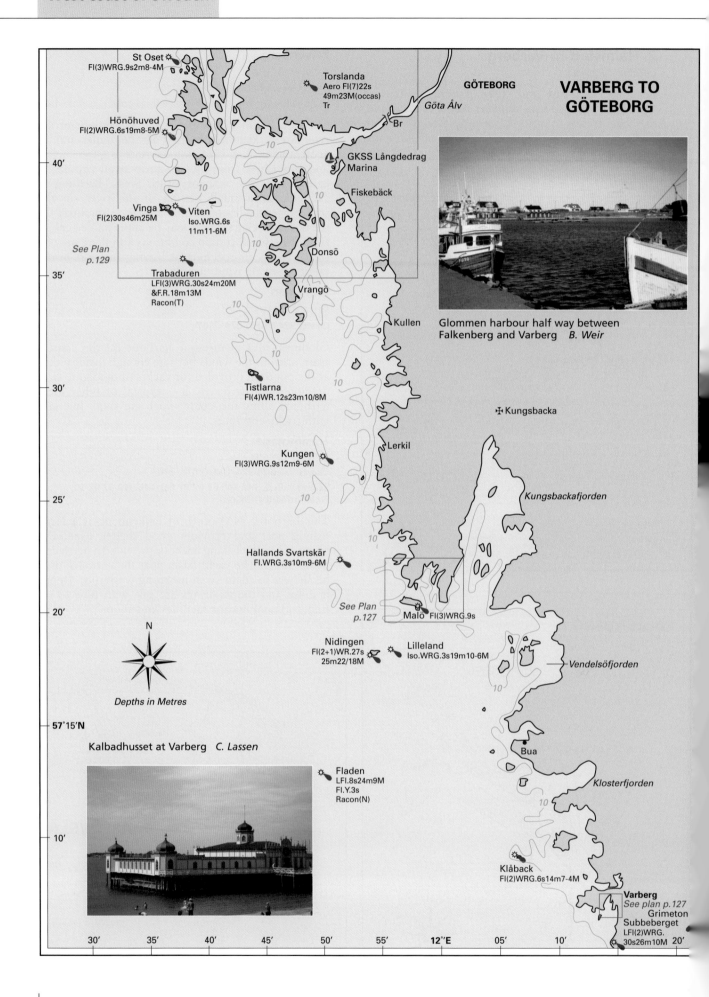

St Oset
Fl(3)WRG.9s2m8-4M

Torslanda
Aero Fl(7)22s
49m23M(occas)
Tr

GÖTEBORG

Göta Älv

Br

VARBERG TO GÖTEBORG

Hönöhuved
Fl(2)WRG.6s19m8-5M

GKSS Långdedrag Marina

Fiskebäck

Vinga
Fl(2)30s46m25M

Viten
Iso.WRG.6s
11m11-6M

Donsö

See Plan p.129

Trabaduren
LFl(3)WRG.30s24m20M
&F.R.18m13M
Racon(T)

Vrangö

Kullen

Glommen harbour half way between
Falkenberg and Varberg   *B. Weir*

Tistlarna
Fl(4)WR.12s23m10/8M

✠ Kungsbacka

Lerkil

Kungen
Fl(3)WRG.9s12m9-6M

Kungsbackafjorden

Hallands Svartskär
Fl.WRG.3s10m9-6M

See Plan p.127

Malö Fl(3)WRG.9s

N

Nidingen
Fl(2+1)WR.27s
25m22/18M

Lilleland
Iso.WRG.3s19m10-6M

Vendelsöfjorden

Depths in Metres

57°15'N

Bua

Kalbadhusset at Varberg   *C. Lassen*

Fladen
LFl.8s24m9M
Fl.Y.3s
Racon(N)

Klosterfjorden

Klåback
Fl(2)WRG.6s14m7-4M

Varberg
See plan p.127
Grimeton
Subbeberget
LFl(2)WRG.
30s26m10M

30'   35'   40'   45'   50'   55'   **12°E**   05'   10'   20'

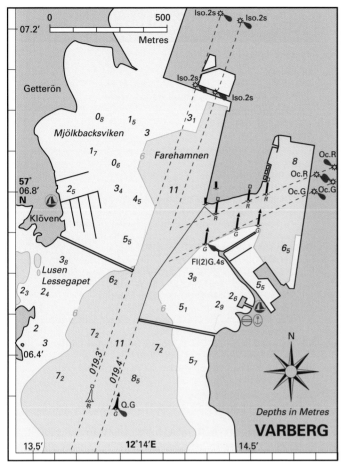

VARBERG

Depths in Metres

Varberg

57°06'N 12°14'E
Charts Swedish 924 UKHO 874, 2107
Yacht club ☎ +46 34 08 49 80
Email getteron@telia.com
www.gshvarberg.com

This historic town and spa built in the 17th century and dominated by a mediaeval fortress, is worth a visit. It is one of the most important harbours in Sweden for the export of timber. There is a ferry connection to Grenå in Denmark. On entering, a marina lies to port on Getterön and a second marina is to starboard. Both are sheltered and there are full facilities. The inner harbour is closer to the town but there is a regular ferry service there from Getterön. For the purpose of passage planning, Varberg is arguably the best half way house between the Sound and Göteborg. It is also a good landfall when crossing the Kattegat from the Limfjord (distance approximately 60 miles). In clear weather, the fortress is visible 15 miles from seaward and the Grimeton aero light tower can be seen from over 20 miles away.

3. Varberg to Göteborg (Langedråg)
Distance 40 miles

North of Varberg the character of the scenery begins to change and the first of many natural harbours is to be found. The channel proceeds northwards on a well-marked passage south of Malö and inside the lights at Lilleland (57°22'N 11°56'E), Hallands Svartskär (57°22'N 11°51'E) and Kungen (57°27'N 11°50'E). On reaching Tistlarna (57°30'N 11°44'E), the *skärgård* is entered with protection from the west and in another 12 miles the main channel into the port of Göteborg is reached.

Bua
57°14'N 12°07'E
Charts Swedish 925 UKHO 2107 only
☎ +46 340 66 20 20
Email info@batfjordenshamn.se
www.batfjordenshamn.se

Bua, 10 miles north of Varberg, is one of the largest fishing villages in this part of Sweden. There is an ample guest harbour although subject to some swell from strong onshore winds. Nearby are industrial buildings, notably the Ringhals nuclear power station.

Malö anchorages
56°21'N 12°58'E
Charts Swedish 925

For the north bound traveller, the bays just north of Malö will be the first experience of the scenery which will prevail in various forms thereafter. There are two possible anchorages. Skallahamn (57°21'N 11°59'E) gives shelter in moderate depths apart from the risk of swell in strong south westerly winds. To the west of Skallahamn snug anchorage is to be found between Hastholmen and Mönster (57°21'N 11°58'E). However, in these places, as generally on this coast, the quality of the holding ground cannot be relied upon.

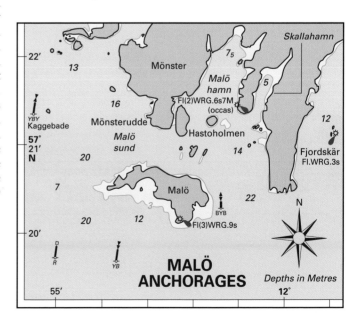

MALÖ ANCHORAGES

Depths in Metres

Lerkil

57°27′N 11°55′E

Charts Swedish 925 UKHO 2107 only

The last harbour before the shelter of the skargård, Lerkil is a sizeable yacht harbour which gives good shelter although the entrance may be difficult in strong north westerly winds. The harbour has recently been improved, and all the usual marina facilities are available.

Among the islands of the *skärgård* are many harbours, both natural and artificial, particularly in the vicinity of Vrangö, Donsö, Styrsö and Brannö. It was in the roadstead north of these islands that a Royal Navy fleet commanded by Admiral Sir James Saumarez in HMS *Victory* was stationed for several years after 1808 guarding the British Baltic convoy system. The enterprising yachtsman can spend a leisurely time exploring the various nooks and crannies of the archipelago but it is to be observed that owing to the vicinity of Göteborg the guest harbours are apt to be very busy. Apart from Vrangö, the islands mentioned above are within the commuter belt of Göteborg and frequent ferry traffic can create a disturbing wash.

Approach to Lilla Bommen *M. Lewin-Harris*

Göteborg (Gothenburg)

57°41′N 11°50′E

Distances
Arkosund 210M (390km) by inland waterway, Stockholm 350M (650km) by road, Copenhagen 130M

Charts and guides
UKHO 2107, 858, 857
Swedish 92, 93, 931, 9313, 9312
Båtsportkort series: Västkusten (S)

Lights
0569 **Trubaduren** 57°35′·7N 11°38′E
  LFI(3)WRG.30s24m20–17M
  005·5°-W-131·6°-R-163·5°-G-214·4°-W-237·2°-R-247·5°-G-005·5° Racon Helipad
  F.R.18m13M 064°-vis-131° Black tower, orange top, on grey base 25m
0570 **Buskärs Knotë** 57°38′·3N 11°41′·1E
  FI(3)WRG.9s12m7–4M
  012·6°-W-029·5°-R-088°-(partially obscd 065°-080°)-G-182°-W-190·5°-R-212°-G-234·4°-W-239·1°-R-270·5°-G-012·6° Racon Orange tower 12m Floodlit
0571·6 **Vasskärsgrund** 57°39′·2N 11°43′·4E
  IVQ.WR.8s11m13–10M Racon Red tower, white top, red roof on grey plinth 12m
0573 **Gäveskär** 57°39′·7N 11°46′·1E QR.10m4M White tower 10m Floodlit but obscured
0582·45 **No. 29 Channel Marker** 57°40′·7N 11°48′·9E
  FI(2)G.6s

Harbour communications
Göteborg Port Authority ☎ +46 31 731 2000, *VHF* Ch 16; 12, 13 (24 hours)
VTS Göteborg ☎ +46 31 125433, *VHF* Ch 16; 09, 13, 69 (24 hours)
Marieholmsbron and Götaälvbron bridges *VHF* Ch 09 (24 hours)
Lilla Bommen Marina ☎ +46 31 158082, *VHF* not monitored
GKSS Långedrag Marina ☎ +46 31 291145, *VHF* Ch 68

General

Göteborg is the second largest city in Sweden, and is a working port with a wide and busy river. The city is friendly and vibrant with much to offer both culturally and recreationally. Much of it is very attractive, with many fine buildings, canals and tree-lined avenues in the downtown area, good shops, and many excellent restaurants.

Overlooking the central (Lilla Bommen) marina is the impressive opera house and, a few hundred metres downriver, the aquarium and Göteborg Maritime Centre, whose moored museum ships are claimed to form the largest floating maritime museum in the world. The Natural History Museum is situated at Slottsskogen, and further out (about 25 minutes by tram from the city centre) are the Liseberg Amusement Park with its huge funfair and the nearby Universeum, an environmental museum.

Visitors generally use either the Lilla Bommen Hamnen, referred to above, or the Royal Göteborg Yacht Club (Göteborgs Kungliga Segel Sällskap or GKSS) Långedrag marina some 5M further downstream on the southern shore.

The Port of Göteborg maintains an interesting website at www.portgot.se.

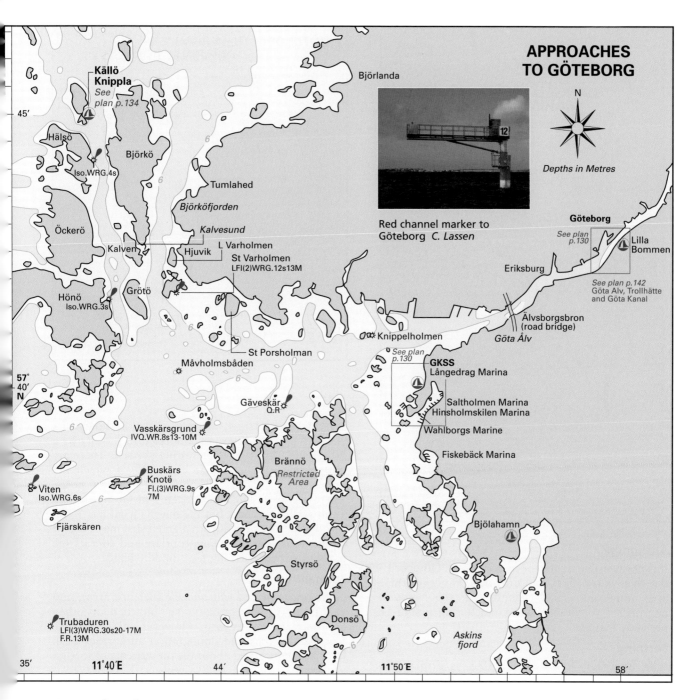

APPROACHES TO GÖTEBORG

Depths in Metres

Red channel marker to Göteborg *C. Lassen*

Björlanda

Källö Knippla
See plan p.134

Hälsö

Björkö
Iso.WRG.4s

Öckerö

Tumlahed

Björköfjorden

Kalvesund

Kalven

Hjuvik

L Varholmen

St Varholmen
LFl(2)WRG.12s13M

Grötö

Hönö
Iso.WRG.3s

St Porsholman

Knippelholmen

Göteborg

Lilla Bommen

Eriksburg

Älvsborgsbron (road bridge)

Göta Älv

See plan p.142 Göta Älv, Trollhätte and Göta Kanal

Måvholmsbåden

See plan p.130

GKSS
Långedrag Marina

Saltholmen Marina
Hinsholmskilen Marina

Wahlborgs Marine

Fiskebäck Marina

Gäveskär
Q.R

Vasskärsgrund
IVQ.WR.8s13-10M

Brännö
Restricted Area

Viten
Iso.WRG.6s

Buskärs Knotë
Fl.(3)WRG.9s 7M

Fjärskären

Bjölahamn

Styrsö

Trubaduren
LFl(3)WRG.30s20-17M
F.R.13M

Donsö

Askins fjord

45'

57° 40' N

35'   11°40'E   44'   11°50'E   58'

Approach and entrance

From the sea the main approach channel from the southwest, leaving the Trubaduren tower to port, is wide, well buoyed and, where necessary, dredged. The main hazard, so far as a yacht is concerned, is likely to be large commercial traffic. Other channels – all shown clearly on BA *858* – lead in from northwest, west and south. All these channels converge south of the prominent Knippelholmen tower to continue up the Älvsborgsfjorden into the city centre. The Älvsborgsbron road bridge (clearance 45m), which lies some 2·5M east of the towers, is conspicuous from well out to sea. Sailing is forbidden east of the bridge, though motor-sailing is permitted, and all moored ships must be given at least 25m clearance.

The Lilla Bommen marina lies on the starboard hand about 250m short of a tall (19·5m) bridge, the entrance conveniently marked by a most distinctive red and white building (*see photo*). The square-rigged sailing ship *Viking* lies close by. It is now an hotel and restaurant.

If arriving from the canal system inland via the Göta Älv, the conurbation starts several miles upstream. Notice of imminent arrival is heralded by a lifting rail bridge, the Marieholmsbron (clearance 5·9m). Opening times are displayed on a LED board. A bare 1·3M further downstream is the massive Götaälvbron (centre span 19·5m, side span 18·5m) which opens on request when called on VHF Ch 09, or may respond to a sound signal. The Lilla Bommen marina lies on the port hand some 250m beyond the Götaälvbron.

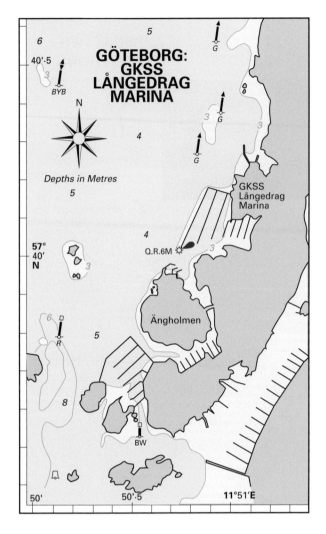

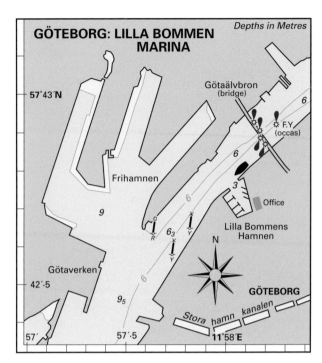

Anchorage

It is not possible to anchor in downtown Göteborg – the river is too busy and crowded. However there are numerous small islands in the western approaches to the city where anchoring would be perfectly feasible.

Berthing

Lilla Bommen ☎ +46 31 158082, is primarily a visitors marina with around 100 guest berths in depths of 2·5–3·5m, and is very popular due to its convenient location in the centre of the city. Enter with caution as passenger boats and small ferries berth on the east side of the basin and depart at speed. Movements are particularly intense in the morning between 0900 and 0930 and in the early evening. The marina basin should be exited slowly and carefully for the same reason. There are a few berths alongside but most are bows to pontoons with stern lines. It is also possible to moor alongside the quay just outside the marina, but there is constant wash from river traffic. Secure in any free berth on arrival and visit the marina office at the southeast corner, where the staff speak some English (open 0800–2200). Berthing fee – upper band.

GKSS Långedrag Marina ☎ +46 31 291145, www.gkss.se, is situated several miles southwest of the city, beside the GKSS clubhouse and close to

several other, larger, private yacht harbours. Its peaceful surroundings are connected to the city by a 40 minute tram ride – interesting in itself. There are 550 permanent berths, at least 100 of which are reserved for visitors. Berthing is between posts. There are areas in the approach with no more than 1·3m at chart datum, but the marina itself has 3–4m throughout. Any berth with a green sign may be used by a visitor – secure as appropriate and contact the harbour office. Berthing fee – middle band.

Formalities

Göteborg is in a *skyddsområde* (defence area), and yachts may occasionally be boarded as they approach from seaward. However on the whole Swedish customs and immigration authorities seem largely unconcerned about the movements of foreign yachts, particularly if EU registered. However if arriving from outside the country the formalities should certainly be observed – enquire at the marina offices for the relevant telephone numbers.

Services for yachts

The Lilla Bommen marina complex offers the usual showers, toilets and launderette, plus cafés, small shops and a chandlery in the office building. There is water and electricity to all berths. The GKSS Långedrag marina has water and electricity to all berths, with laundry facilities at the GKSS clubhouse and a small shop close by. A weather forecast is updated daily. The yacht club is friendly, with a pleasant clubhouse and several good restaurants nearby.

Diesel, petrol and bottled gas are available from a fuel barge (open 0800–2000 daily), moored on the north bank of the river between the Älvsborgsbron road bridge and the Eriksberg complex (marked by a

Göteborg. The view from the office tower beside Lilla Bommen, clockwise from *The Viking* are the ferry berths, the guest harbour with the Opera House behind   *E. Redfern*

massive overhead gantry), convenient for a yacht approaching or departing Lilla Bommen marina. The nearest diesel pump to the GKSS Långedrag marina is at Wahlborgs Marine (open 0900–1800 weekdays, 1000–1500 weekends), on the south side of Saltholmen island. Bottled gas is available at the GKSS Långedrag marina, and both have facilities for emptying holding tanks.

There is a boatyard with travel-lift and engineers at the GKSS Långedrag marina. For electronic or radio repairs at either marina ① +46 31 695100 or 909600, and for sail repairs ① +46 31 290021 or 291152. There is a small onsite chandlery at Lilla Bommen marina, also at Wahlborgs Marine and both the Hinsholmskilen and Fiskebäck marinas. Charts, sailing directions and books are available from Nautic AB, on the waterfront at Skeppsbron about 0·5M downstream from Lilla Bommen and from most bookshops in the city.

General facilities

From Lilla Bommen marina an elevated walkway leads to the Nordstan shopping mall with banks, supermarkets, delicatessen, bookshops, Systembolaget etc, with the city's train and bus terminals a short distance beyond. Cafés and restaurants abound, many with views out over the river. The Cityokutan hospital ① 031 101010, is about 1km distant.

If moored at the GKSS Långedrag marina and intent on major shopping, ride two stops on the No. 4 tram to the Konsum supermarket (open 0900–2200), with a bank with cash machine located about 400m beyond. Post Office. The nearest medical services are at the Sahlgrenska Hospital ① +46 31 342 1000.

Communications and travel

There are public telephones at both marinas and post offices in the city, though none very close to Lilla Bommen marina, and at least one internet access point in the city centre. The GKSS yacht club adjacent to the Långedrag marina will send and receive faxes, *Fax* +46 31 690048.

The proximity of Lilla Bommen marina to the city's bus and train stations makes it particularly convenient for crew arrival or departure. The Långedrag marina is served by the Nos. 4 and 9 trams, which run to the city centre (about 40 minutes). In addition, taxis or car hire are easily arranged. Göteborg's Landvetter Airport is some 25km east of the city, while the City Airport is about 20km to the north, both with good bus connections. Passenger ferries from Denmark and Germany visit the port regularly.

The Göta Kanal – Göta Alv, Trollhätte and Göta Kanals see page 142.

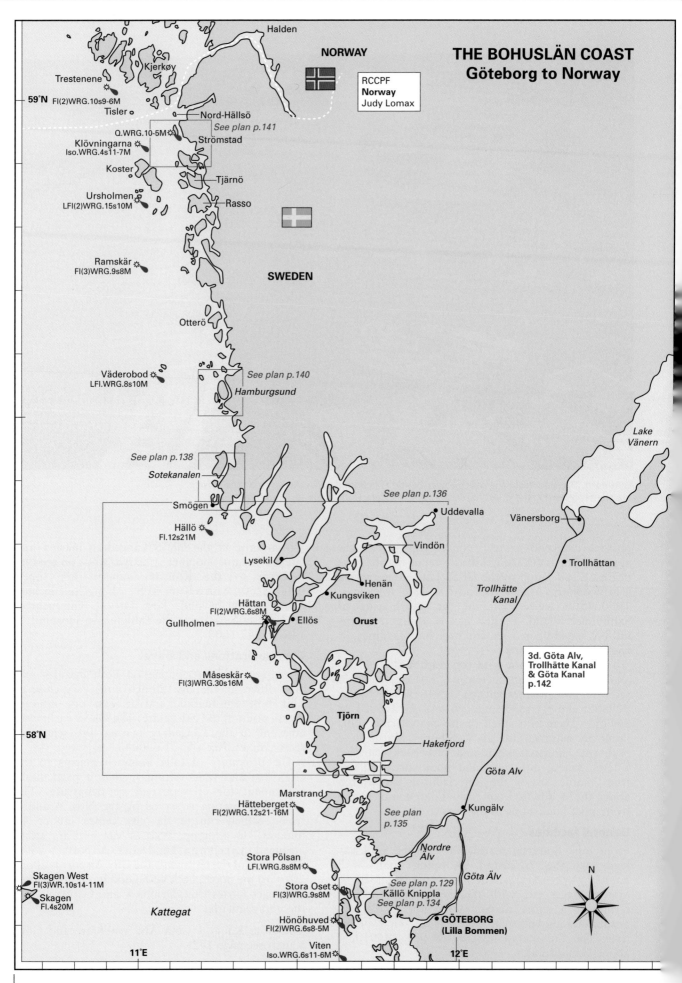

THE BOHUSLÄN COAST
Göteborg to Norway

RCCPF
Norway
Judy Lomax

Halden

NORWAY

Kjerkøy

Trestenene
59°N Fl(2)WRG.10s9-6M

Tisler

Nord-Hällsö
See plan p.141
Q.WRG.10-5M
Strömstad
Klövningarna
Iso.WRG.4s11-7M

Koster
Tjärnö

Ursholmen
LFl(2)WRG.15s10M
Rasso

SWEDEN

Ramskär
Fl(3)WRG.9s8M

Otterö

Väderobod
LFl.WRG.8s10M
See plan p.140
Hamburgsund

Lake
Vänern

See plan p.138
Sotekanalen

See plan p.136
Smögen
Uddevalla
Vänersborg

Hällö
Fl.12s21M
Vindön
Trollhättan

Lysekil
Trollhätte
Kanal

Henän
Kungsviken

Hättan
Fl(2)WRG.6s8M
Ellös
Orust

Gullholmen

3d. Göta Alv,
Trollhätte Kanal
& Göta Kanal
p.142

Måseskär
Fl(3)WRG.30s16M

Tjörn

58°N
Hakefjord

Göta Alv

Marstrand

Hätteberget
Fl(2)WRG.12s21-16M
See plan
p.135
Kungälv

Nordre
Älv

Stora Pölsan
LFl.WRG.8s8M
Göta Älv

Skagen West
Fl(3)WR.10s14-11M
Stora Oset
Fl(3)WRG.9s8M
See plan p.129
Källö Knippla
See plan p.134
Skagen
Fl.4s20M
GÖTEBORG
(Lilla Bommen)
Kattegat
Hönöhuved
Fl(2)WRG.6s8-5M

N

11°E
Viten
Iso.WRG.6s11-6M
12°E

3c. The Bohuslän coast – Norra västkusten

Göteborg to the Norwegian border

This 80 mile stretch of coast, known as the Bohuslän, is an attractive and interesting area on the route north from the Kattegat to south Norway, as well as being a popular cruising ground for Norwegians sailing south or east from their bases in Oslofjord or on the southeast coast. North of Göteborg, the coastline is largely devoid of trees and vegetation is sparse, although the inner channels feature some agricultural land and abundant pine and birch forests. It was originally settled by hunters and communication between settlements was by sea. Until the middle of the 17th century, it was part of Norway and this is reflected in place names and the local dialect. In time fishing became an important industry and fishing villages were settled up and down the coast. Fishing still has a significant role but many of the houses in picturesque places have become holiday homes. There are useful landfalls for those approaching from the North Sea across the Skagerrak. It is also a convenient shake down area for those collecting new boats from the prolific Swedish yards around Orust. The Skagerrak can be very rough in strong southwesterly weather, but virtually the whole distance can be sailed inside the relative shelter of the *skärgård*. In lighter weather winds can be fickle and a number of places are too narrow to sail.

The coastline of often pink Nordic granite is higher but reminiscent of the Åland Islands. A covering of houses in the south slowly gives way to trees approaching Norway.

Coast and harbours

The main towns, apart from Göteborg (population 460,000), are Uddevalla (population 49,000), Lysekil (population 14,800) and Stromstad (population 11,000). There are many sizeable villages or small towns of which the most notable is Marstrand, a well-known centre for sailing.

There are 65 *gästhamns* listed in the *Gästhamns Guiden* and innumerable anchorages in the many fjords and sunds. To do justice to these would require a book on its own, so this one is confined to a few suggested places to allow a leisurely transit of the coast. It must be emphasised that the use of the largest available scale of chart is advisable for anything other than a purely offshore passage. Minimal tidal differences make for easy bows-to mooring or anchoring.

In season supplies and services are plentiful but before June and after the middle of August a little more planning is required as many of the smaller harbours close their facilities, particularly restaurants and fuel points, around that time.

During the season, and particularly at weekends, the coast (including the islands) south of Smögen is likely to be very crowded. This is Göteborg's maritime playground with thousands of holiday or weekend cottages all of which seem to have their own mooring or ready access to small marinas.

To go north from Göteborg (see plan on page 129) there is a choice of routes, all clearly marked on both UKHO chart 858 and the *Båtsportkort B*, passing either side of the Måyholmsbåden light or the shortest passing immediately south of Stora Porsholmen and between Stora Varholmen and Lilla Varholmen. This brings one to the Öckerö archipelago, and, if taking the passage on between Kalven and Grötö, beware of unmarked outlying rocks, some awash, particularly on the south side. The Kalvesund channel leading north-northwest is narrow, but clearly marked. This group of 10 notable islands and numerous islets is less than half an hour by car from the centre of Göteborg and readily accessible by all kinds of boats and ferry, so it is not surprising that in places there is no space for any more houses or boats. There are ten *gästhamns* many of which will still give you a feel for this wild and magnificent Bohus countryside.

A typical bows-to *skärgård* mooring
J. Backus

Källö-Knippla

57°45'N 11°39'E

Charts Swedish 931 NW, UKHO 2107 only (scale 1:200,000)

Typical *gästhamn* in Ökeröarna.

Just 14M from the Lilla Bommen marina or 9M from the GKSS. Easily entered on a leading line from the south and just off the main route from Göteborg to Marstrand. Bows-to mooring from buoys and ample facilities for an overnight stop amid attractive, traditional Bohus houses. Fish available on the quay.

Marstrand

57°53'N 11°35'E

Charts Swedish 931 NW, UKHO 870, 873

Mecca of west coast Swedish yachting.

Only 12M further north from Källö-Knippla. The most attractive route is from the southeast through the narrow Albrektssunds kanal. Also there are well-buoyed entries from the open sea on the west and northwest. Mooring is bows-to with lazy lines. As most visitors will want to call here it is very crowded even during the week. Good services, restaurants and supplies with a small Watski chandlery and cash machine a short ferry ride away. The harbour is dominated by the conspicuous Carlstens Fästning fortress which is well worth a visit.

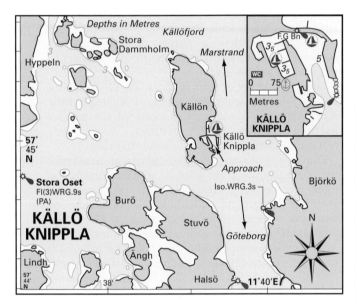

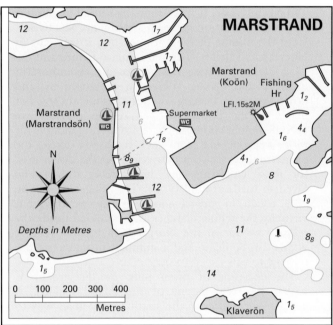

Left Källö Knippla berth
M. Lewin-Harris

Below Källö Knippla harbour looking south-southeast *M. Lewin-Harris*

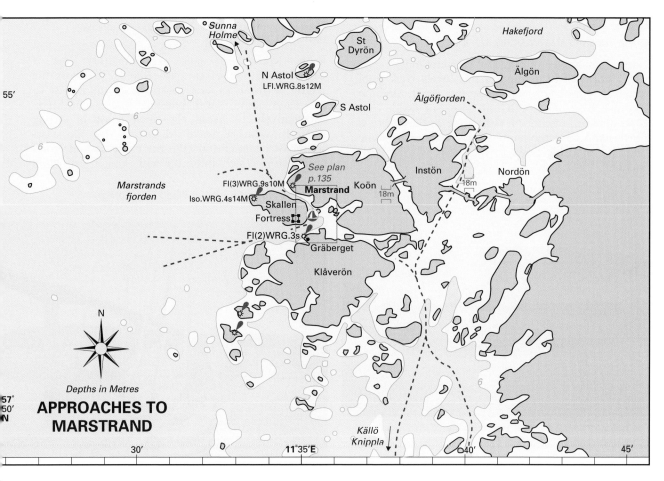

APPROACHES TO MARSTRAND

Depths in Metres

Sunna Holme

St Dyrön

Hakefjord

Älgön

N Astol
LFl.WRG.8s12M

S Astol

Älgöfjorden

Instön

Nordön

See plan p.135

Marstrand

Koön

18m

18m

Fl(3)WRG.9s10M

Iso.WRG.4s14M

Marstrands fjorden

Skallen Fortress

Fl(2)WRG.3s

Gräberget

Klåverön

Källö Knippla

55'

6

6

6

6

57° 50' N

30'

11°35'E

40'

45'

Left Marstrand Channel   *D. and P. Thorne*
Below Carlstens Fastning   *J. Backus*
Lower Marstrand. View looking east from fortress   *E. Redfern*

3. SWEDEN

Sunna Holme

58°00′N 11°31′E
Charts Swedish 9321 NW, UKHO 870, 873

Natural anchorage in beautiful surroundings.

9M north of Marstrand is this lovely rock pool which is typical of others along this coast. Shallow entrance from the south but with 6m inside and good holding. Anchor on either side as the centre is a little exposed to the south otherwise there are some rings for mooring bows to the rocks with a stern anchor.

Tjörn and Orust

Charts Swedish 932 SW, SE and NE, 933 SE and SW
UKHO 870, 873, 869, 853

From Marstrand make east-northeast for a circumnavigation of the two islands. Orust is the largest of Sweden's west coast islands and is base to at least four well-known yacht builders. Alternatively to avoid the open coast in strong westerly weather leave Marstrand by the east-southeast channel and take the route east of Koon and Inston which joins up with Hakefjord. Note

The boatyard and bridge at Vindo   *E. Redfern*

The quiet rock anchorage at Sunna Holme   *E. Redfern*

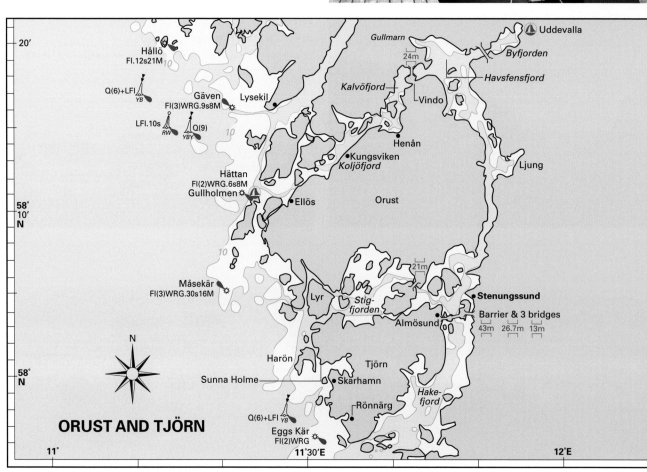

ORUST AND TJÖRN

Henan, home of Najad Yachts   *D. and P. Thorne*

Malo Strommar. The entrance to Malo yacht yard near Kunsviken   *D. and P. Thorne*

Gullholmen
58°11'N 11°24'E
Charts 932 NW, UKHO 853, 869, 870

Island *gästhamn* and holiday village.

On the north of Härmanö and 3M west of Ellös on Orust. Well buoyed approaches from both north and south. The harbour lies between two islands and is completely sheltered. Moor alongside or bows-to with lazy lines or stern anchor if crowded. Good facilities including an ICA mini-market. Bracing walks to the top are rewarded with spectacular views. The permanent population mushrooms from 140 to about 4,000 in season when the harbour is also extremely crowded.

Pretty holiday homes at Gullholmen   *J. Backus*

Entrance to Gullholmen harbour   *D. and P. Thorne*

there is a bridge with 18m clearance on this route. Head up Hakefjord under either bridge (min 26m) to Källön to the Askeröfjorden where the twisting route round the top of Tjörn joins. Then north through Halsefjorden and 11M of sunds to the top of Orust. Here in the Havstensfjord the important town of Uddevalla is found 4·5M to the northeast. If you turn to port just 3M to the west there are very capable yards at the Vindon bridge. There is excellent shopping at Henän only 5M further south. The route then heads southwest and through some narrow passages, passed Ellös to Gullholmen to the west or turn north 6M to the major tourist destination but useful town of Lysekil. Along this diversion of approximately 45M there are over 15 *gästhamns* and innumerable anchorages to explore for as long as time permits.

SWEDEN

Smögen

58°21'N 11°13'E

Charts Swedish 933 NW, UKHO 853, 869, 1402

Lively tourist town and fishing port.

Much prettier than Kungshamn half a mile to its east, Smögen lies some 15m northwest of Orust and close to the open sea but exposed only to the east. There is a very long wooden quay against which you moor or raft alongside. Less crowded is a new marina to port but it is a long walk round to the town. This is a picturesque and popular 'summer town' with many tourist shops in the wooden houses overlooking the quay. Good facilities but no fuel which is available at nearby Kungshamn. An important fishing harbour with fish market and large processing factories. Considerable modern development on its north side.

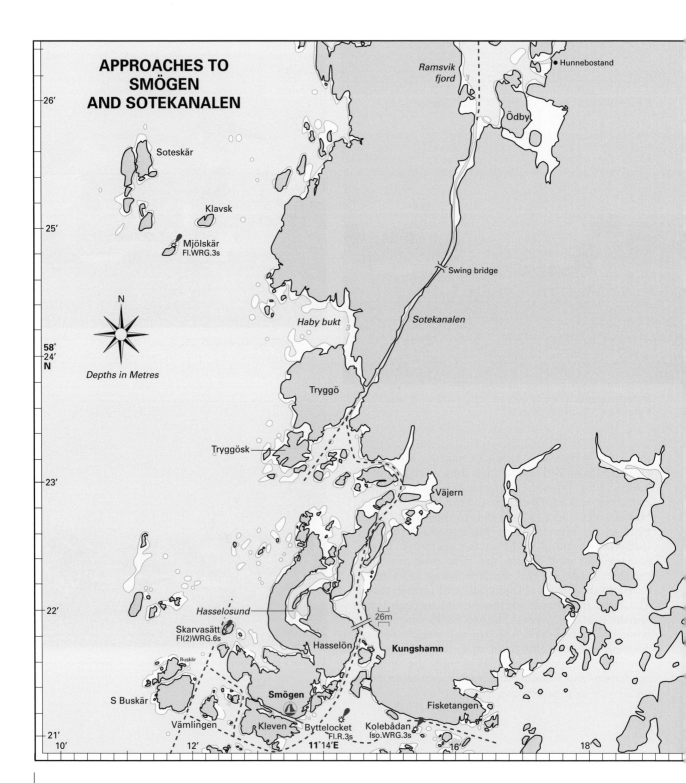

The summer town of Smögen   *E. Redfern*

Smögen quay   *D. and P. Thorne*

Smögen old boat harbour   *D. and P. Thorne*

If time is short, it is only a day's sail of about 40M outside all the off lying islands and skerries. There are 16 *gasthamns* and countless anchorages between Smögen and Strömstad, and many different routes which may be taken, depending on your vessel's draught and air draught (mast height) clearly marked on the *Båtsportkort*. However that would be to miss much of the variety of this coast.

Sotekanalen (southern entrance)

58°23'N 11°14'E (southern entrance)
Charts Swedish 933 NW, UKHO 869
http://kanaler.arnholm.nu/sotens.html

This partly artificial canal was opened in 1935 with the object of allowing local craft to avoid the exposed coast of the Sote peninsula which could be dangerous to small vessels in stormy southwest weather. Its length is just under three miles. Today it makes a convenient shortcut to the 200 berth *gasthamn* of Hunnebrostrand and is used by some 50,000 vessels of all sizes each year, the limitation being a beam of 15m and draught of 4·5m. It has one opening bridge and passes through typical more gentle Bohus countryside with a few houses and farms. There is no charge for transit, nor are there any suitable stopping places. Sailing is forbidden.

3. SWEDEN

Hamburgsund (Gästhamn)

58°33'N 11°16'E (Gästhamn)
Chart Swedish 934 SE. UKHO 1402

The sound is a natural waterway which, because of its totally sheltered position has been a centre of commerce and shipping for over 200 years. Sailing is forbidden and today its use is almost entirely leisure with some fishing activity which has attracted many holiday homes and boats. Despite this it is attractive, and there is much history to be found in the area by those so inclined. There is a well set up *gästhamn* in the centre which is popular in the season, and there is good basic shopping, including a supermarket.

There is a cable-operated vehicle ferry close to the marina which crosses at frequent intervals particularly at peak times and this needs care to pass safely. There are instructions on both approaches.

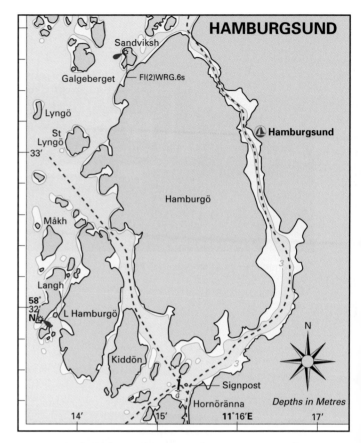

HAMBURGSUND

Sotekanalen bridge opening   *M. Lewin-Harris*

Hamburgsund marina   *M. Lewin-Harris*

Strömstad

58°56'N 11°10'E
Chart 935 E UKHO charts 879, 3160

Northernmost town on the Swedish west coast and yachting centre.

Barely 5M from the border with Norway and with very well-buoyed approaches from the north and west for the regular ferry to Larvik. There are also approaches from the south but these have restrictions on headroom and draught which are only clear on the detailed Swedish charts. The

Hamburgsund approach   *E. Redfern*

visitors' moorings are in the south harbour which is approached by leaving the islet of Skurve, which is now connected to the shore by marina berthing pontoons, to starboard. Berth on these or continue into the inner harbour which is more convenient to the shore facilities if space is available there. Otherwise use any vacant 'box' with a green label. The full facilities and services include an excellent Watski chandlery nearby. The community of 11,500 justify a first-class shopping centre which also serves the many visiting Norwegians, but it is not convenient to the marina and bicycles are an advantage as the town spreads northwards across the river. The 'Strömstad Marina' in the bay ½ mile to the north is normally full of local boats.

Left The busy harbour and shopping centre at Stromstad *D. and P. Thorne*

Above A signpost on the rocks. A missed sponsorship opportunity! *E. Redfern*

The route north to the Norwegian border is straightforward by way of the Långörännan channel giving access either up Oslo Fjord or towards Halden or Fredrikstad.

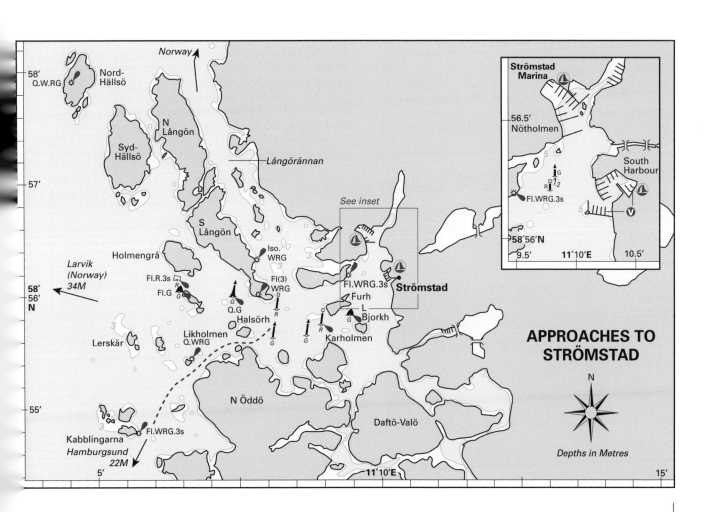

3. SWEDEN

3d. Göta Älv, Trollhätte Kanal and Göta Kanal

General

Though the name 'Göta Kanal' is often used to imply the entire 210M (390km) route between Göteborg on the west coast and Mem on the Baltic Sea, this is not technically correct. The westernmost stretch is actually a river, the Göta Älv, which is connected by the Trollhätte Kanal to Lake Vänern, by far the largest lake in Sweden and one of the largest in Europe. Between Lake Vänern and the smaller Lake Vättern runs the 35M (65km) western section of the Göta Kanal proper, which includes the canal's highest point at almost 92m (302ft) above sea level. The eastern section, between Lake Vättern and the Baltic Sea, is some 50M (93km) in length. Thus only about half the 'Göta Kanal' is actually canalised, and a good part of that is not the 'Göta' canal at all.

In spite of its numerous bridges, most yachts are able to pass through the entire system with masts in place, the minimum clearance being 22m at Norsholm on the eastern stretch. Maximum allowable length is 32m and the controlling width is 7·2m. Depths are nominally no less than 2·5m, though this does not always appear to be the case in practice. All except two of the 65 locks are hydraulically operated. It should be borne in mind that on occasions the locks can be extremely crowded and constant vigilance is required to avoid damage. In general it can be said that a minimum of three crew is desirable, one at the helm and the controls, and two to handle the lines and to fend off other craft. For a vessel of moderate size, a crew of

The Göta Kanal
'Sweden's Blue Ribbon'

Charts and guides
Swedish charts 13, 135, 134, 133, 132, 131, 1352, 1353, 121, 1331

Svensk Kusthandbok series: Vänern – Trollhätte Kanal
Båtsportkort series: Vänern (E)
Båtsportkort series: Göta kanal (Mem–Sjötorp)
The Göta Kanal, Mem–Sjötorp (in English), Sjöfartsverket 1993

two may suffice if strenuous work is not minded. In the Göta Kanal part it should be borne in mind that a crew member has to land at each lock to handle lines. Two lines of up to 10m in length are needed in the locks. Throughout its length the route is well provided with small harbours and marinas. Some of the older locks have rather uneven walls. Four large fenders each side might be considered a minimum, and some skippers favour carrying a plank (or two) to place outside them.

The western part of the system was the first to be canalised, the Trollhätte Kanal (bypassing the Trollhättan falls) opening in 1800 to allow access for shipping to Lake Vänern. Work on the Göta Kanal section began in 1809, under the direction of Baron von Platen and the civil engineer, Thomas Telford, architect of the Caledonian Canal; and took 23 years to complete, being officially opened in September 1832. Commercial traffic decreased markedly after the mainline railway link across Sweden was opened in 1862, but almost immediately the canal's potential for tourism was recognised, with several steamers plying its length. Now, as well as providing a second option for those wishing to reach or depart the Baltic Sea, the waterway is a popular holiday destination in its own right and home to the three historic vessels of the Göta Kanal Steamship Company in addition

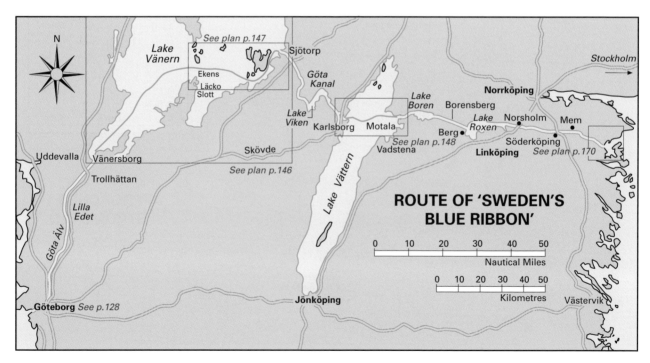

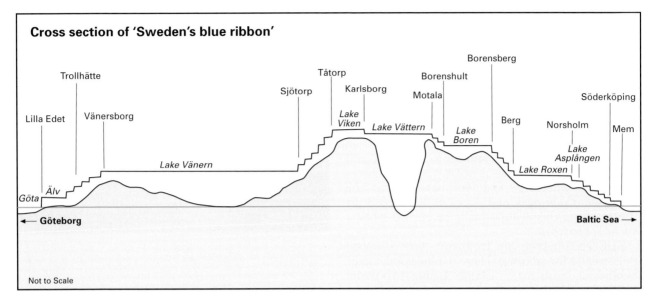

Cross section of 'Sweden's blue ribbon'

Trollhätte

Borensberg

Tåtorp

Borenshult

Sjötorp   Karlsborg   Motala

Vänersborg   Lake Viken   Lake Vättern   Lake Boren   Berg   Norsholm   Söderköping

Lilla Edet   Mem

Lake Asplången

Lake Vänern   Lake Roxen

Göta   Älv

← Göteborg   Baltic Sea →

Not to Scale

to many fleets of hire cruisers. Though originally in private hands the entire complex now belongs to the Swedish government.

The Trollhätte Kanal is regularly used by seagoing commercial ships of up to 4,000 tons and is open all the year round except at times in winter when lock maintenance is being carried out or the flow of water is affected by ice.

No firm prediction can be given as to how much time should be allowed for the passage from one coast to the other. There is a five knot speed limit on both the canals. With light traffic and an active crew it may be possible to make the journey in five to seven days if in a hurry.

The canal is open generally from May to September with small variations in dates from year to year. For instance, in 2010, it is open from 3rd May to 26th September. Before 6th June and after 20th August, advanced booking with three days notice is required but in the intervening high season, the canal operates between 0900 and 1800 daily.

Delays are liable to occur at both locks and bridges – the lifting road bridges at Töreboda, Karlsborg and Söderköping have fixed opening times, as do the railway bridges at Lyrestad, Töreboda, Motala and Norsholm, all listed in the information packs available on entering the system. Other bridges on the Göta Kanal are remotely controlled and will normally open within ten minutes of a yacht appearing. Rail traffic is invariably given priority. If taken slowly the passage offers plenty of variety – peace and quiet, but also plenty of interesting little towns and historical buildings to visit, not to mention several museums dealing with the canal's own history. Children almost invariably enjoy the passage, and many of the canal's small guest harbours are surrounded by fields and open countryside. The lock-keepers and bridge masters cannot be contacted by normal VHF marine radio.

The canals can become extremely crowded during the Swedish holiday season which straddles the month of July and there is much to be said for making the passage before or after that period. It is

a matter of opinion whether it should be tackled from east to west or the converse. Anyone planning a circuit of the Baltic and seeking to take advantage of prevailing south westerly winds will find it beneficial to return via the canal in a westerly direction. There will be the additional advantage of having a favourable current when the Göta river is reached. On the other hand it is to be observed that the current in this river is not likely to be significant to a craft of even moderate power unless an increase is caused by heavy rainfall or, early in the year, melting snow or ice. Moreover, a westerly wind will favour yachts making the direct passage of Lake Vänern and Lake Vättern whereas if the wind from that direction is fresh it may act as a delay to west bound yachts. In short no definite recommendation can be made about the preferred direction of the passage.

Dues of SEK 825 (about £80) are payable in the upper lock of the Trollhätte Kanal. For the Göta Kanal they are paid at Sjötorp (if eastbound) or Mem (if westbound). Though dues are relatively high – in 2010, a single passage along the Göta Kanal for a yacht of between 9 and 12m costs SEK 5600 (about £500) – but this includes up to five nights and services in each of the Company's 20 guest harbours. Dues for yachts of between 12 and 15m are SEK 7100 (about £635). Copies of the regulations for both canals are available when paying the dues.

The heads may not be used at any time in the canal system unless a holding tank is installed (there are now eight pump-out stations on the Göta Kanal alone). The safety regulations should also be given due attention, and a note made of the sound signals – a horn will be needed to give signals when approaching locks and bridges and at entrances to narrow sections. Even those already familiar with locks will find the written instructions on the subject, issued with the tickets at the first lock encountered, extremely useful.

The Company can be contacted by ☎ +46 141 20 20 57/ 58/ 59 or *Email* info@gotakanal.se.

3. SWEDEN

The Göta Älv and Trollhätte Kanal

A sketch plan of this stretch is available from the Lille Bommen office.

The approach from the west is via the port of Göteborg, the first lock being encountered at Lilla Edet, 26M (49km) upstream. Below the first lock the stream in the Göta Älv can be strong, running at up to three knots in the Göta gorge 2M below the lock. The average over the whole distance decreases from around two knots in early summer to 1·5 knots until autumn.

On the Göta Älv and Trollhätte Canal the approach to bridges and locks is monitored by cameras, and they will normally be opened when a yacht approaches.

Between Göteborg and Trollhätte, there is limited opportunity for mooring. There is a quiet anchorage behind a midstream island Ladugårdshlholm (58°1'·5N 12°8'·5E), 8M south of Lilla Edet for those who find the going tedious. There is a small harbour north of the lock at Lilla Edet but for scenic beauty and natural surroundings, it is better to proceed to the quays at Åkersvass below the original Trollhätten staircase.

This stretch of the system carries large (90m LOA) freighters, and movement by small craft after dark or in poor visibility is firmly discouraged. All six of its locks have a rise of between 6 to 8m, in contrast to the locks of the Göta Kanal the majority of which are 2·5m. In busy periods they may be filled by wall-to-wall yachts. Both sides of these large locks are fitted with small, recessed bollards some 3–4m apart vertically, so that those alongside can move lines up or down as the water level changes. Even easier is to secure to one of the ladders, generally against the south or southeast wall (the smoother of the two). Despite their impressive size, the locks are gentle in operation due to an unusual system of filling the chambers through gratings in their floors, which produces little turbulence.

It takes around 45 minutes to pass through the four giant locks bypassing the Trollhättan falls – or more accurately the three locks, holding basin, and single upper lock – and if time permits it is well

Moored at Åkersvass below the old Trollhättan locks   *B. Weir*

Top View from below Trollhättan Locks   *E. Redfern*

Above Trollhättan *gästhamn*   *E. Redfern*

worth pausing in the guest harbour beside the upper lock to visit the Trollhätte Canal Museum (open 1100–1900 daily) and explore the two flights of disused locks – the original 1800 flight, and larger replacements opened in 1844. Those currently in use date back to 1916. The final lock is at Brinkebergskulle, just short of Vänersborg where the canal merges with Lake Vänern, some 44M (82km) from the open sea.

There are five official guest harbours between Göteborg and Lake Vänern – Kungälv (about 10 miles upstream from the centre on Göteborg below the ramparts of the fortress of Bohus where there are a few berths approached by a narrow and tortuous channel); Lilla Edet; Åkerssjö (immediately above the Trollhättan locks, with 15 berths); Spikön (between Trollhättan's two bridges, the first lifting and the second a bascule, and close to the centre of the town: 25 berths with water and electricity, laundry facilities, showers and restaurant); and Vänersborg. Vänersborg is an unassuming but pleasant town with a wide range of shops in the pedestrian precinct. The marina is beside the railway station and 10 to 15 minutes from the shops and a large supermarket. It has most facilities including fuel, toilets, laundry and a good chandlery.

The lifting, railway bridge at Trollhättan *T. Aitken*

Lake Vänern

Vänersborg – Sjötorp

From Vänersborg to the start of the Göta Kanal proper at Sjötorp, the course is initially in a north easterly direction for just over 30 miles when the island of Kallandsö is reached. Passing through the Ekens *skärgård*, yachts proceed in an easterly direction for about 20 miles until Mariestad is abeam thereafter turning northwards under the bridge with clearance of 18m connecting the mainland with Torsö. The land is generally low-lying, the principal landmark seen for many miles around being a table mountain, Kinnekulle (305m) (58°36'N 13°25'E) on the southeast shore. The lack of elevation means that care must be taken to sight the channel buoys approaching Vanersborg, and with nothing more to the north east than an open horizon, the marks for the finger-like promontory of Hindens Rev and the marks at the approaches to the *skärgård*.

Between Vänersborg and Ekens *skärgård*, there are a number of inlets where shelter can be obtained. They include Sanneboviken (59°29'N 12°28'E), Dalbergsa (58°36'·4N 12°36'E), Jarlehusudden (58°37'N 13°1'E) and also in the bay to the east of Klitt island. Within the *skärgård* itself there is a free choice of a number of anchorages in calm and beautiful surroundings.

The channel going from west to east divides in the middle of the passage through the *skärgård*, one branch heading north towards open water and the other proceeding between two lines of concrete blocks (once used for pulling through sailing vessels) in a south easterly direction. Both channels are very well marked. The southeast channel leads past the small marina of Spiken (58°41'·5N 13°12'E) to the imposing mediaeval castle and grounds of Lackö which is open to the public. There is a marina to the northwest of the castle and it is feasible to anchor in the bay to the east.

The approach to Sjötorp passing Mariestad is by way of a winding buoyed channel which presents no difficulty provided a good look out is maintained. The fine city of Mariestad has an early 17th-century cathedral said to be a copy of Stockholm Cathedral. Guest berths are to be found at the southwest wall of the harbour. Full facilities are available and there is a main line railway connection.

At Sjötorp there is a marina in the outer harbour which is often crowded and is exposed to strong winds from the west and north. To avoid discomfort in strong westerly winds shelter may be obtained in the lee of the promontory to the west of the canal entrance.

Lake Vänern – General information

Although the majority of yachts in making their way across Sweden may be expected to take the direct route described above, Lake Vänern offers considerable scope for diversion. It is the largest expanse of fresh water in Sweden. The direction from southwest to northeast is about 80 miles and from northwest to southeast is about 40 miles. The depths shown on the charts are subject to variation of up to one metre depending on the amount of melted snow and rain or the lack of either. There are wide stretches of open water where conditions can become very uncomfortable in bad weather but the shoreline is much indented and provides many places of shelter.

The lake is conveniently divided by two promontories into sections, namely, Dalbosjön to the southwest and Värmlandssjön to the northeast. The channel between these peninsulas is restricted by the Lurö skärgård but the passage is well marked.

Two canals are found in the western region of Dalsland. The Dalslands Kanal starts at Köpmannebro (58°46'N 12°31'E) and ascends by way of 31 locks and a series of lakes almost to the Norwegian frontier. Passage is restricted to vessels drawing not more than 1.8 metres, not more than 22 metres in length, and a masthead height of not more than 12 metres. The other and longer canal, the

Above The rail and road bridges looking north from Vänersborg towards Lake Vänern *M. Lewin-Harris*

3. SWEDEN

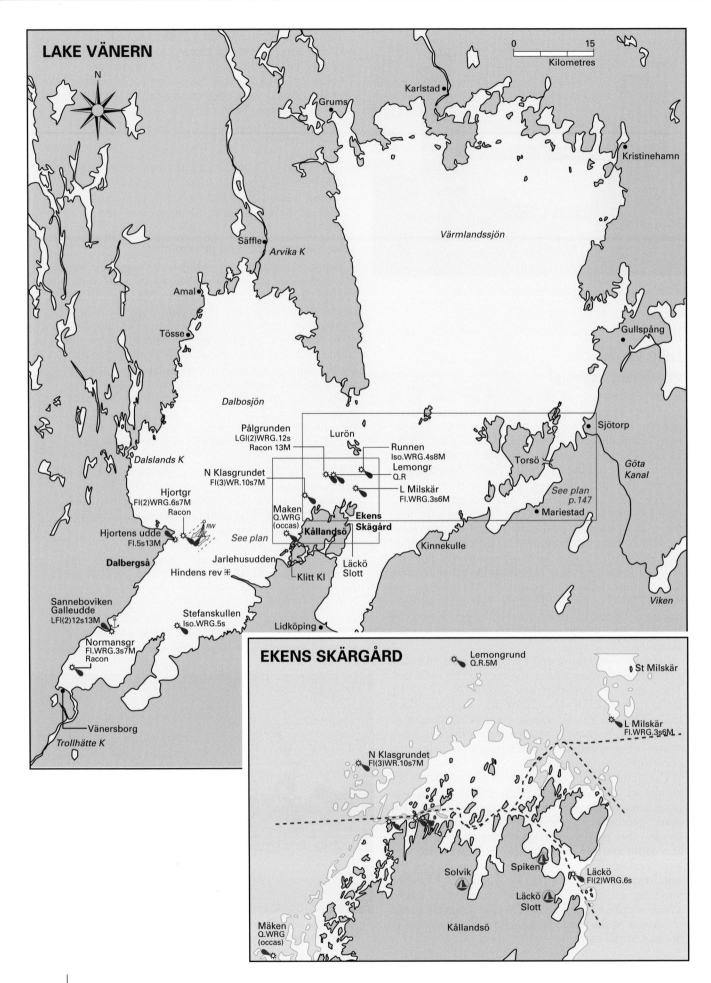

LAKE VÄNERN

N

0   15
Kilometres

Karlstad

Grums

Kristinehamn

Värmlandssjön

Säffle
Arvika K

Amal

Gullspång

Tösse

Dalbosjön

Pålgrunden
LGl(2)WRG.12s
Racon 13M

Lurön

Sjötorp

Runnen
Iso.WRG.4s8M

Torsö

Göta
Kanal

Dalslands K

N Klasgrundet
Fl(3)WR.10s7M

Lemongr
Q.R

Hjortgr
Fl(2)WRG.6s7M
Racon

L Milskär
Fl.WRG.3s6M

See plan
p.147

Maken
Q.WRG
(occas)

Ekens
Skägård

Mariestad

Hjortens udde
Fl.5s13M

Kållandsö

Dalbergså

See plan

Kinnekulle

Jarlehusudden

Klitt Kl

Läckö
Slott

Hindens rev

Viken

Sanneboviken
Galleudde
LFl(2)12s13M

Stefanskullen
Iso.WRG.5s

Lidköping

Normansgr
Fl.WRG.3s7M
Racon

EKENS SKÄRGÅRD

Lemongrund
Q.R.5M

St Milskär

L Milskär
Fl.WRG.3s6M

Vänersborg
Trollhätte K

N Klasgrundet
Fl(3)WR.10s7M

Solvik

Spiken

Läckö
Fl(2)WRG.6s

Läckö
Slott

Mäken
Q.WRG
(occas)

Kållandsö

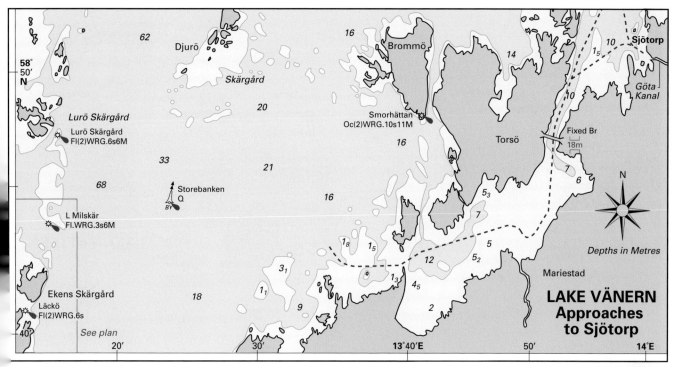

Arvika Kanal, leaves the lake just south of Säffle (59°08′N 12°55′E) and meanders north for about 40 miles through lakes and narrow channels. The maximum length, draught and masthead height are, respectively, 42 metres, 3m, and 16 metres. Maximum beam is 4·5m. Both canals were formerly used for the transport of timber and other cargoes but this traffic has now ceased. They are used, when open in the summer, by pleasure craft and are of great scenic beauty.

The principal town in Dalsland is Åmål (population 12,800). This well laid out town, with a fine 17th-century church overlooking it, has a sheltered marina. A few miles to the south lies the Tösse skärgård with scenery resembling the islands of the Stockholm archipelago. The *skärgårds* of Djurö, Ekens and Brommö lying not far north of the direct route between Vanersborg and Sjötorp are also popular with those seeking natural surroundings. But it has to be borne in mind that during summer weekends and the holiday month of July, there is liable to be activity, sometimes noisy, and wash from fast power boats and the like.

At the north end of Värmlandssjon are two sizeable towns. The larger of these, Karlstad (population 80,000) is a commercial port and capital of the province of Värmland. There are all the facilities of a large town as well as a substantial guest harbour. In the northeast corner of the lake lies Kristinehamn where there is a small marina. Between the two towns and indeed along the entire north shore of Värmlandssjon the coast is much broken up and there are numerous sheltered anchorages.

Yachts leaving the Göta Kanal's westernmost lock at Sjötorp, to enter Lake Vänern   *E. & M. Bonham Cozens*

Moored at the visitors' berths just west of the bridge at Karlsborg   *E. Redfern*

3. SWEDEN

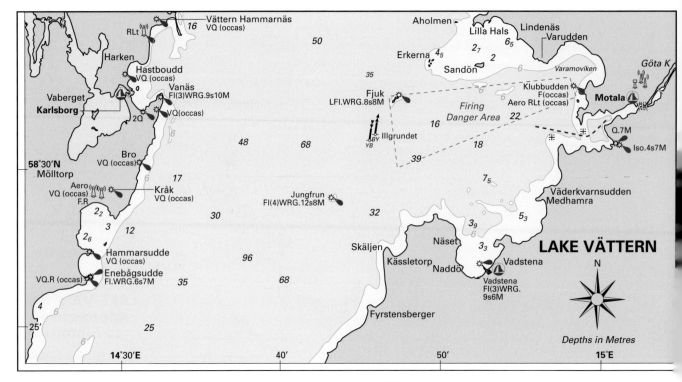

The Göta Kanal to Lake Vättern

This 35M section includes the route's highest point at Lake Viken, almost 92m (302ft) above sea level. Eastbound vessels climb 20 locks in 9M to reach the angular lake, which accounts for some 11M of the section, then pass through their first descending lock just beyond its eastern exit. A further 15M through attractive agricultural countryside without locks takes vessels through to Lake Vättern. There are eight guest harbours on the stretch between the two lakes – Sjötorp, Lyrestad, Hajstorp, Töreboda, Vassbacken, Tåtorp, Forsvik and Karlsborg – all with water, toilets and showers, but most without fuel pumps. Of the guest harbours mentioned above, Töreboda and Karlsborg are recommended for their facilities. Töreboda has supermarkets, a bank and is convenient for a crew change, being on the main line from Stockholm to Göteborg. Karlsborg has a fuel station and it also boasts an enormous citadel built in the early 19th century. There are guest harbours both in the canal and at Stenbryggen just below the fortress. A good museum is situated within the fortress.

The stretch between Lakes Vänern and Vättern is the wildest and most remote part of the canal – a landscape of lakes and fir trees, very different from further east where the waterway runs through lush pastures and carefully cultivated farmland. Lake Viken is particularly beautiful, with an abundance of possible anchorages in small bays and between islands. The lock at the west end of the lake is manually operated. At its eastern end is Forsvik Sluss (lock), which is both the highest and the oldest lock on the canal, and boasts the oldest iron bridge in Sweden. The walls of this lock are uneven and vessels should beware of unexpected protrusions.

Lake Vättern

This lake is about 60 miles in length running approximately north to south. Vessels making the transit of the canal will normally proceed directly between Karlsborg and Motala. The 17 mile passage is straightforward and the islet of Fjuk (58°30′N 14°46′·3E) provides a landmark two thirds of the way across the lake. A good lookout should be kept in approaching Motala from the west for the marks at Kävernöns Bk showing the entrance to the channel.

An alternative landfall is Vadstena, about eight miles southwest of Motala. The 16th-century castle provides a conspicuous landmark. The guest harbour is in the castle moat and is approached by a narrow canal. It has 15 berths in depths of 1·5 and 2·5m with a range of facilities. The castle is impressive as is the peaceful old town with its 13th-century convent and 15th-century abbey.

In comparison with Lake Vänern, Lake Vättern provides less incentive to divert those proceeding through Sweden by the canal. The lake is long, deep and unindented for the most part and is noted for its sudden squalls. However, a group of islands at Djäknesundet, 10 miles northeast of Karlsborg (58°37′·5N 14°34′E) provides a number of attractive and sheltered anchorages. The archipelago and the channels at the north end of the lake consists of over 200 islands and for those with the time to spare is well worth a visit.

There are firing ranges on the lake and for information about firing times, ☎ +46 505 40460 or call VHF Ch 14.

Lake Vättern to the Baltic Sea

On the 50M stretch between Motala on the eastern shores of Lake Vättern and Mem, where yachts lock out into the Slätbaken, an inlet of the Baltic Sea, there are 37 locks, all 'downhill' if eastbound. The distance is served by six guest harbours – at Motala, Borensberg where the lock is manually operated, Berg, Norsholm, Söderköping and Mem itself – where, again, up to five free nights may be spent. The guest harbour beside the canal entrance at Motala has 65 berths and all facilities, including fuel pumps and a holding tank emptying station. The nearby canal museum includes a working model of a lock – much enjoyed by children of all ages.

Less than three miles after leaving Motala, eastbound vessels reach a staircase of five locks at Borenshult. A wait of several hours may occur at this point. Lake Boren is six miles long and after Borensberg, a further 13 miles takes one through open agricultural country to Berg, where the canal descends four pairs of locks before reaching the small guest harbour, which has limited facilities but is handy for the small town's cafés and restaurants. Below the harbour basin is the spectacular Carl Johan flight – seven locks which lower the canal the 18·8m down to Lake Roxen. On summer days these locks are thronged with spectators who come to watch the yachts and river steamers pass up and down the flights. However waits can be long, and if one misses the 'traffic lights' it may be two hours or more before the direction of flow is reversed. Both Lake Boren and the 13·5M Lake Roxen are very pretty, and offer unhurried travellers the opportunity to anchor in unspoilt surroundings and off the beaten track.

Norsholm is at the east end of Lake Roxen. The busy main railway line from southern Sweden to Stockholm passes over the Canal at this point. At the lock beside the railway bridge, hanging warps are provided as the rise is only 0.9m. From Norsholm on

A yacht enters the first lock of the east-to-west transit, at Mem on the Slätbaken (an arm of the Baltic Sea) *A Hammick*

The reception quay at Mem on the Slätbaken, at the start of the east-to-west canal transit *E. Redfern*

a further 15M of canal (broken by the small and rocky Lake Asplången) and 15 locks connect to the Baltic Sea at Mem. East of Norsholm the canal is at its most rural, meandering along between cow pastures and past pretty cottages and gardens.

By Söderköping east-going yachts are almost at their journey's end, and many are tempted to stay for a day or two before heading out into the Baltic. The town is a favourite with the Swedes, and in July an almost Mediterranean atmosphere develops as people stroll in the sunshine. The canal is lined with tourist shops and restaurants, including a famous Ice Cream restaurant, many with live music, and some yachtsmen will find the 50 berth guest harbour, which lies along the canal just above the town's lock, both noisy and lacking in privacy. In compensation the town is most attractive with a fine 18th-century town hall and two mediaeval churches, both with beautiful interiors. Unlike Mem, (see page 171 and plan on page 170) Söderköping has many shops and is a good place for provisioning.

There are quays at Mem on both sides of the lock, with a 125m quay on the Slätbaken (Baltic) side where vessels entering the canal system wait to enter the lock and while dealing with paperwork. This berth can be uncomfortable in east or southeast winds. Inside the lock there is a second, longer quay with depths of 2·5–3m and space for about 20 visiting boats, with a further 10 bows-to berths on the (single) guest harbour pontoon. Showers and toilets, telephone, launderette, diesel pump, holding tank emptying station, café and a small general shop are all to hand, but there is no town nearby. The warehouse just above the lock was the venue for the canal's official opening ceremony, carried out by King Karl XIV Johan in 1832. Today it houses a shop, café and youth hostel.

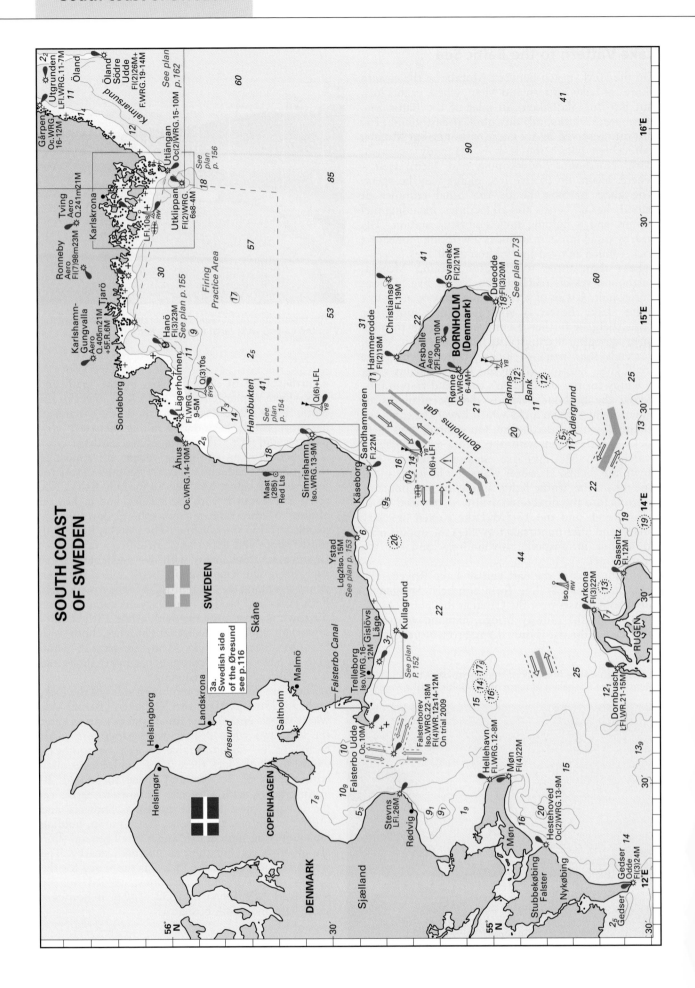

SOUTH COAST
OF SWEDEN

SWEDEN

Skåne

3a.
Swedish side
of the Øresund
see p.116

Landskrona

Helsingborg

Helsingør

COPENHAGEN

DENMARK

Sjælland

Saltholm

Malmö

Øresund

Falsterbo Canal

Falsterbo Udde
Oc.10M

Trelleborg
Iso.WRG.16
12M Gislövs
Läge

Gedser
Gedser Odde
Fl(3)24M

Stubbekøbing
Falster
Nykøbing

Hestehoved
Oc(2)WRG.13-9M

Møn
Fl(4)22M

Møn

Hellehavn
Fl.WRG.12-8M

Rødvig

Stevns
LFl.26M

Kullagrund

Falsterborev
Iso.WRG.22-18M
Fl(4)WR.12s14-12M
On trial 2009

See plan
P. 152

Ystad
Ldg2Iso.15M
See plan p.153

Sandhammaren
Fl.22M

Kåseborg

Simrishamn
Iso.WRG.13-9M

Mast
(285)
Red Lts

Åhus
Oc.WRG.14-10M

Lägerholmen
Fl.WRG.
9-5M

Hanö
Fl(3)23M
See plan p.155

Sondeborg

Karlshamn-
Gungvalla
Q.405m21M
+5F.R.6M

Ronneby
Aero
Fl(7)98m23M

Tving
Aero
Q.241m21M

Karlskrona

Utlängan
Oc(2)WRG.15-10M

Utklippan
Fl(2)WRG.
6s8-4M

See
plan
p.156

Gärpen
Oc.WRG.
16-12M

Utgrunden
LFl.WRG.11-7M

Öland

Öland
Södre
Udde
Fl(2)26M+
F.WRG.19-14M

See plan
p. 162

Firing
Practice Area

Hanöbukten

See
plan
p. 154

Christiansø
Fl.19M

Svaneke
Fl(2)21M

Dueodde
Fl(3)20M

See plan p.73

BORNHOLM
(Denmark)

Hammerodde
Fl(2)18M

Arsballe
Aero
2Fl.290m10M

Rønne
Oc.WRG.
6-4M

Rønne Bank

Adlergrund

Bornholms gat

Sassnitz
Fl.12M

Arkona
Fl(3)22M

Iso
RW

RUGEN

Dornbusch
LFl.WR.21-15M

THE BALTIC SEA

South coast of Sweden

3e. Falsterbo Kanal to Utklippan

The south coast of Sweden from Falsterbo as far as Simrishamn is largely low-lying, gentle, and with numerous sandy beaches. There are greater distances between significant harbours than on the rest of Sweden's coast line and the shore is open with few sheltered anchorages. Once past Simrishamn, the coastline starts to rise, and beyond Åhus it begins to assume the rocks and islands aspect, which is so typical of both the Kattegat and northeast coasts. There are firing ranges off this coast, see Appendix on page 363.

The Falsterbo Canal

55°25'N 12°50'E
Distances (north end) Copenhagen 21M, Gislövs Läge 11M
Charts Swedish 921, UKHO 2595, 2115, 2360, 2816
☎ +46 40 20 43 80 VHF Ch 73 (call *Falsterbo Canal*)

The mile-long Falsterbo Canal (pronounced *Fahlstehr-boo Kah-naal*) provides a convenient short cut from the Øresund to the Baltic, particularly useful to yachts coming from Copenhagen or beyond. Depth is 4.0 m. There are no locks, no dues and only one lifting bridge, which opens every hour on the hour from 0600 to 2200 except 0800 and 1700 Signal lights: fixed white or flashing red mean Stop, green means proceed. Both sailing and anchoring in the canal are forbidden.

The lifting bridge on the Falsterbo Canal *J. Mottram*

Höllviken

☎ +46 40 35 34 92

This is the small yacht harbour north of the bridge at the entrance to the canal. Pontoon moorings with piles or fingers have the usual basic facilities, and there are showers, a friendly club, free bicycle loan, and bus to Skanör peninsula. Café near bridge has waiting pontoon which can be used overnight. There is a grocery store and bakery about three blocks west on the main road.

Gislövs Läge

55°21'N 13°14'E
Distances
Ystad 21M, Simrishamn 50M, Copenhagen 33M (by Falsterbo Kanal), Gedser (Denmark) 70M, Kiel 135M, Rønne (Bornholm) 55M,
Charts and guides
Swedish 83, 839 UKHO 2115, 2360
Lights
2445 **Kullagrund** 55°17'·9N 13°19'·5E
   Iso.WRG.4s18m16–12M
   181°-R-244°-G-271°-W-105°-R-120°-G-181° Racon
   Red tower with black band, white lantern 20m
   Floodlit
2424 **Trelleborg** 55°21'·4N 13°09'·1E
   Iso.WRG.8s12m16–12M
   279°-G-311·5°-W-060°-R-082°-G-099°-G(unintens)-110°-W(unintens)-279° Racon Black tower with white band on grey conical base, white lantern 15m Floodlit
2436 **Gislövs Ldg Lts 022·5°** *Front* 55°21'·3N 13°13'·9E
   F.R.4m7M White ▲ with red border, on framework tower on inner east pierhead
2436·1 *Rear* 201m from front, F.R.11m7M White ▼ with red border, on framework tower. Inner pierheads Floodlit

Harbour communications
Harbourmaster ☎ +46 410 73 33 77
Marina office ☎ +46 704 807 692
VHF Ch 67 (Trelleborg commercial harbour)

General

Gislövs Läge (pronounced *Yeece-leuvs Lair-ge*) is a useful but somewhat featureless yacht harbour 3M east of the town of Trelleborg, itself a major ferry port and large commercial harbour but with no facilities for yachts. Several fishing boats are based at Gislövs Läge, but the harbour is mainly reserved for yachts and is administered as one of the civil amenities of Trelleborg.

In the wake of summer southerlies the entire south coast may be pervaded by a strong stench of rotting seaweed, so unpleasant that eventually a bulldozer is called in to clear it away.

Approach

On approach, the town of Trelleborg is very obvious from the sea, marked by the continual comings and goings of the ferries and other large vessels. Once within 3M of the coast, in normal visibility, the entrance to Gislovs Läge can be seen. Approach is on 022.5° with leading lights in line. Unlit channel markers indicate the last half mile of the approach. There is a small outer harbour with several small

3. SWEDEN

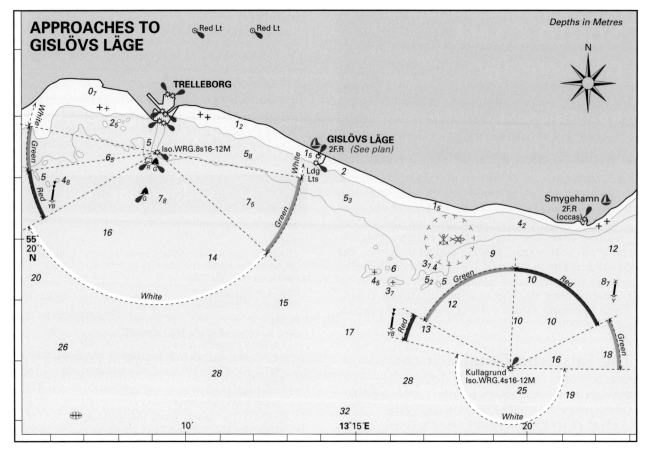

APPROACHES TO GISLÖVS LÄGE

Depths in Metres

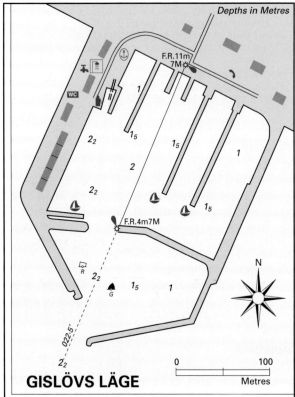

GISLÖVS LÄGE

The moorings at Gislövs Läge   *E. Redfern*

water have been known to be less than this. However the bottom is soft mud and it is usually possible to push through. Entrance should not be attempted in a strong southerly, when swell can penetrate the inner harbour.

Berthing

There are a total of some 30 guest berths – eight bows-on to a pontoon to port just inside the entrance with stern lines to posts, and a further 20 or so (rather narrow) slots at the outer ends of the two longer pontoons, again with stern lines to posts. Neither of the pontoons have hammerheads. Other available berths are marked by a green disc. It may also be possible to raft up alongside the western quay, provided yachts do not impede the working fishing boats.

green and red buoys just inside the entrance showing the way to the inner harbour. The southwestern part of the inner harbour has depths of 2m or more, shoaling to the north and east and at times of low

The harbour office is only open very limited hours but dues can be paid in cash into an honesty box.

Services

Water and electricity are on the pontoons. Toilets, showers and washing machines are in two small buildings between the clubhouse and a small café (tokens bought at the marina office required for washing machines can be a problem). Wi-Fi is free. Fuel is available from a self service credit card pump on the west quay (check depth).

General facilities

Ashore, there is a small village, partly serving as a residential area for Trelleborg and partly as a quiet location for holiday homes, though there is a restaurant and a small grocery store about 10 minutes walk up the road. Frequent buses go to Trelleborg which has all the attributes of a city

Ystad

55°25'N 13°49'E

Distances Gislövs Läge 21M, Simrishamn 28M, Copenhagen 58M,

Charts Swedish 839 *Båtsportkort:* Area not covered by the series, UKHO 958, 2360

Marina office ② +46 704 807 692

Email marinan@ystad.nu

www.ystadmarinan.com

This is a fishing harbour and busy ferry port to Bornholm and Germany, with a separate yacht

Ystad. Entrance to yacht harbour. Visitor moorings ahead on port side *S. Carnegie*

basin, depth 2·7m in entrance, to the west of the main harbour. These are protected from south to southeast by two outer breakwaters of rough boulders, but the yacht harbour entrance becomes difficult in strong southwest to west weather and should only be approached with extreme care in such conditions. It is also reported to be mildly affected by surge from incoming ferries. If a yacht will be left unattended for some time, Simrishamn is to be preferred, as it has a more sheltered marina and no large ferry traffic. In the approach the large green grain elevator on the west side of the main harbour stands out well from seaward. The outlying shallows are well buoyed and lit. Berthing (up to 30 berths for visiting yachts) in box moorings or alongside pontoons. The *gästhamn* can be very full in the season. Mooring fees include water, electricity, showers, Wi-Fi. Sauna and washing machine are available, as is a self service diesel pontoon. There is a shopping precinct including a small supermarket five minutes walk from the marina as well as a local museum and café/restaurant and 'Tacker o Tag', an excellent, old-fashioned chandlery with ancient and modern items including camping gaz exchange. Also there is a sailmaker in the town. Bike hire is available. Bus and train station is five minutes walk. The town with supermarkets, shopping, banks, plenty of pizzerias but not many good restaurants, is a 20 minute walk. It is a beautiful town with many interesting old buildings and in particular St Mary's Church should not be missed. Also Stenar standing stones dating from 600AD, thought to have been placed according to astronomical or astrological data, are worth a visit.

Ystad to Simrishamn or Bornholm

The passage from Ystad to either Bornholm or Simrishamn will pass through the Bornholmsgat. This is the main route for deep-water shipping entering the Baltic, and is controlled by a major Traffic Separation Scheme (TSS). All small craft must keep well clear of vessels using the TSS and if crossing to Bornholm, cross at right angles as required by international regulations. If making for Simrishamn, a yacht should keep in the inshore traffic zone on the Swedish side. Check firing times with marina office for range south and west of Sandhammaren light.

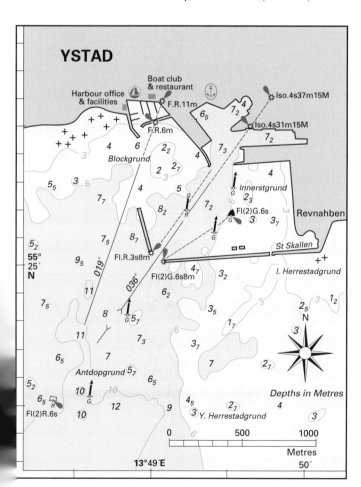

YSTAD

Boat club & restaurant

Harbour office & facilities

F.R.11m

Iso.4s37m15M

F.R.6m

Iso.4s31m15M

Blockgrund

Innerstrund

Revnahben

Fl(2)G.6s

St Skallen

Fl.R.3s8m

I. Herrestadgrund

Fl(2)G.6s8m

Antdopgrund

Y. Herrestadgrund

Depths in Metres

Fl(2)R.6s

0   500   1000

Metres

13°49'E   50'

Simrishamn

55°33'N 14°22'E

Distances
Gislövs Läge 50M, Rønne (Bornholm) 30M, Karlskrona 60M, Kalmar 100M

Charts and guides
Swedish 7, 74, 839 *Båtsportkort C: Hanöbukten*, UKHO 2360

Lights
2460 **Sandhammaren** 55°23'N 14°11'·8E Fl.5s31m22M Red metal tower, framework base 29m
7582 **Simrishamn** 55°33'·5N 14°22'E Iso.WRG.6s16m13-9M shore-G-160°-W-223°-G-238°-W-279°-R-285°-W-355°-R-shore White tower 15m
buoy **Långagrund** 55°32'·4N 14°30'·2E Q(6)+Fl.15s South cardinal pillar buoy, ⍌ topmark

Harbour communications
Commercial harbour ☎ +46 414 89 12 02
Marina office ☎ +46 708 16 58 81
Email Info@simrishamn-marina.se
www.simrishamn-marina.se
VHF Channel 11, 16

General

Simrishamn (pronounced *Sim-ris-hahmn*) is a pleasant town with a busy commercial and fishing harbour, leading to a well-equipped yacht harbour. It is a convenient stopping place on the way to or from the northern Baltic, though when the fishing fleet is active the harbour can be noisy and disturbed and particular care must be taken on entry and departure. The largely 19th-century town has pretty cobbled streets, painted houses and open market, and the 12th-century St Nicolai Kyrka (church) is particularly worth visiting. Small ferries run a regular service to Bornholm.

Approach

Both Simrishamn lighthouse and the gabled red-roofed church are good landmarks from offshore. When closer in, fluorescent orange leading marks will be seen on a bearing of 250°, keeping vessels well south of the 2·7m Nedjan shoal, itself marked by cardinal buoys. The harbour should only be approached with extreme caution in strong onshore winds, and unpredictable currents may be created

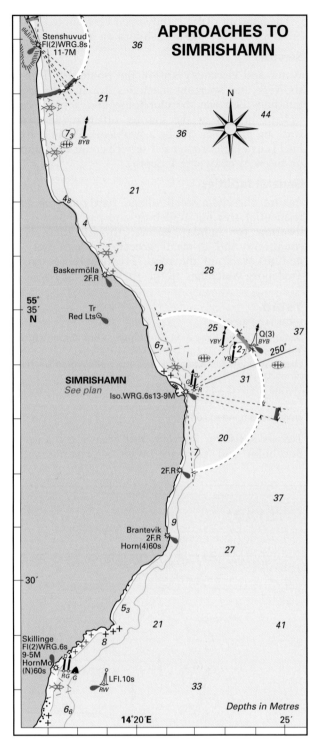

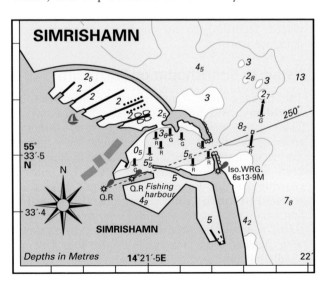

both inside and outside the entrance by prolonged easterlies. The yacht marina with all facilities is immediately to starboard after entering the main harbour. The entrance to the marina is marked by buoys. Do not stray outside the marked channel. Mooring is to pontoons with stern buoys or narrow fingers. The harbour is generally shallow, the first pontoon being the only one with depth significantly over 2m.

Simrishamn, once inside the outer breakwaters the *gästhamn* entrance is to starboard *J. Sadd*

Anchoring

The coast near Simrishamn is very exposed and steep-to, and anchoring outside recognised harbours is not recommended.

Berthing

The outer ends of the two southernmost pontoons are reserved for visiting yachts, berths on the nearer pontoon being alongside and reserved for those of more than 4m beam. The 26 visitors' berths on the second pontoon are bows-to between narrow metal fingers, both depth and width being indicated on posts on the pontoon itself. Yachts which are too large to use the marina may be able to berth in the fishing or commercial harbours – contact the harbour office before arrival.

Services and facilities

Normal facilities including washing machine near the marina office, fuel, propane and holding tank pump out are available. Engine and electronics repairs can be arranged – either the marina office or the sailing club may be able to assist. There is a large chandlery and sailmaker at Skillinge, 6M south of Simrishamn, Skeppshandel and Österlens Segelmakeri, ① +46 414 302 50 *Email* info@skepp.com, www.skepp.com. The Simrishamns Segelsällskap, ① +46 414 107 70, is an active sailing club with a pleasant clubhouse and a busy summer programme of racing and social events.

All normal facilities of a medium-sized town are available with the helpful tourist office close to the harbour. Bus and rail stations are within 0·5km of the marina, Timetables are available from the tourist office.

The coast from Hanö to Karlskrona and beyond

It is only eight miles north of Hanö that the east coast truly begins. This is an extraordinary coastline, consisting of thousands of islands with countless channels between them, many small harbours and myriad anchorages. Apart from Kalmarsund which runs inside the 70 mile long island of Öland, the *skärgård* runs to about 100M north of Stockholm. This provides a fascinating cruising ground which can take many years to explore to the full. A book such as this can only scratch the surface of what is available, and safe navigation demands the presence of the most detailed charts available.

Hanö

56°01′N 14°50′E

Distances Simrishamn 32M, Rønne (Bornholm) 55M, Karlskrona 28M, Utklippan29M

Charts Swedish 7, 74, 822 *Båtsportkort C: Hanöbukten* UKHO 2360, 2816, 2856

Marina office ① +46 456 53008, *Mobile* +46 768 993008 *Email* info@simrishamn-marina.se www.hano.nu

Hanö is a small artificial harbour on the west side of Hanö Island, and is a pleasant and convenient stopping place between Simrishamn and either Karlskrona or Utklippan. Approach is straightforward, but could be uncomfortable in north-west winds. Berthing alongside, or possibly rafting, particularly at weekends in the summer, where the harbourmaster will help. Depth is 2m anywhere, and 4m, alongside west or north piers.

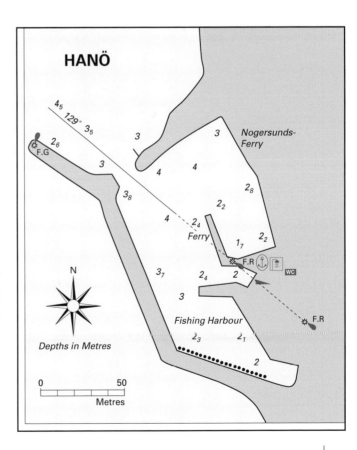

3. SWEDEN

Basic marina facilities are available, also shop, café (reported to produce a reasonable meal) and post.

There is an interesting walk up to the lighthouse and to the naval cemetery, where a cross was erected in 1973 in memory of the sailors of HMS *Victory*, who died there during the winter of 1810.

Karlskrona's Tallybryggan marina
J. Sadd

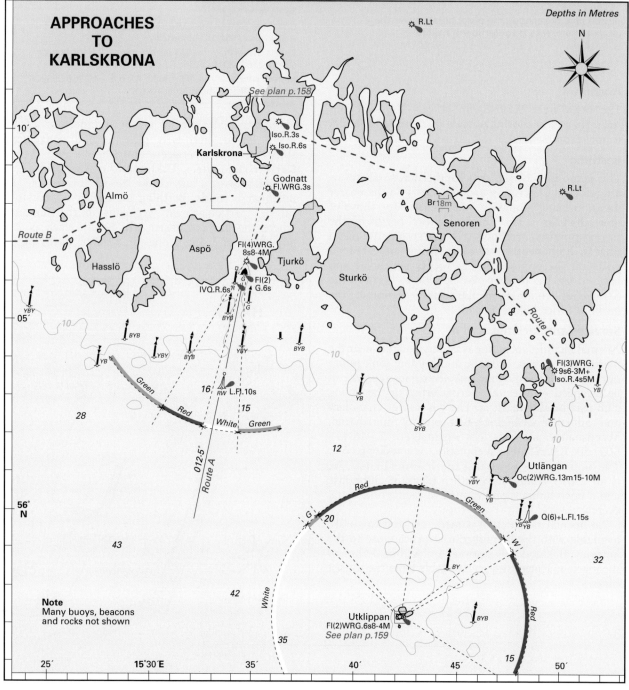

APPROACHES TO KARLSKRONA

Depths in Metres

R.Lt

See plan p.158

Iso.R.3s
Iso.R.6s

Karlskrona

Godnatt
Fl.WRG.3s

Almö

R.Lt

Br 18m

Senoren

Route B

Fl(4)WRG.
8s8-4M

Aspö

Tjurkö

Sturkö

Hasslö

Fl(2)
G.6s

IVQ.R.6s

Route C

YBY

BYB

BYB

BYB

BYB

YBY

BYB

Fl(3)WRG.
9s6-3M+
Iso.R.4s5M

YB

YB

G

16
RW L.Fl.10s

15

28

White   Green

Green

Red

BYB

12

Utlängan
Oc(2)WRG.13m15-10M

YBY

YB

56°
N

Red

Green

43

20

W

Q(6)+L.Fl.15s
YB YB

32

42

White

BY

BYB

Red

Note
Many buoys, beacons and rocks not shown

35

Utklippan
Fl(2)WRG.6s8-4M
See plan p.159

15

25'   15°30'E   35'   40'   45'   50'

Karlskrona

56°10′N 15°36′E

Distances
Hanö 28M, Simrishamn 60M, Rønne 75M, Kalmar 50M, Utklippan, 13M

Charts and guides
Swedish 7, 74, 821 *Båtsportkort C: Hanöbukten*
UKHO 2360, 2857, 2816

Lights
7442 **Utklippan south rock** 55°57′·2N 15°42′·2E Fl(2)WRG. 6s.30m W8/R5/G4M. Nov. to Mar. only.Red framework tower on old fort 30m
7460 **Karlskrona Ldg Lts 012·5°** *Front* Stumholmen, 56°09′·5N 15°36′E Iso.R.6s22m16M White round concrete tower 24m
7460·1 *Rear* 0·7M from front Iso.R.3s37m16M White round concrete tower 15m
7446 **Västra Försänkningen** 56°06′·5N 15°34′·5E Fl(4)WRG.8s6m8–4M
003°-W-115·5°-R-031°-G-204°-W-216·5°-R-350°-G-003°
Racon White and red dolphin Floodlit
7449 **Godnatt** 56°08′·5N 15°35′·8E
Fl.WRG.3s20m11–7M
003°-G-013·5°-W-017·5°-R-028·5°-G-056°-R-073·5°-G-079·5°-W-082·5°-R-125·5°-G-137°-W-139·5°-R-144°-G-189°-R-197°-G-234°-W-242°-R-302°-G-330°-R-003° Grey fort

Harbour communications
Karlskrona Port Authority ✆ +46 0455 303000,
VHF Ch 14, 16
Karlskrona Harbourmaster ✆ +46 455 21871,
Mobile +46 70 930 3151, *VHF* Ch 14, 16

General
The principal naval base of Sweden, Karlskrona occupies an easily-defended island site connected to the mainland by road and railway bridges, with an interesting 20M approach through the *skärgård*. The approach from the southeast is restricted by an 18 m bridge. In addition to an attractive, cobbled city centre, Karlskrona boasts a large maritime museum (www.marinmuseum.se) on Stumholmen island, where historic ships lie alongside the museum's own quay, the fortress of Kungsholmen and Drottningskär citadel on the island of Aspö. The naval port of Karlskrona is included in UNESCO's World Heritage list.

Approach and entrance
There are three principal channels, all of which require large-scale charts:

a. The main channel, which leads between the large islands of Aspö and Tjurkö on a bearing of 012·5° and is well buoyed and lit.

b. The southwest channel, which is entered at the Hyperionsgrund buoy (56°06′·7N 15°22′E) and is buoyed but not lit. There is a swing bridge between Almö and Hasslö Islands at 56°07′·N 15°27′·7E.

c. The southeast channel, which is entered east of Långören island at 56°03′·7N 15°50′E and is elaborately buoyed but not lit. It passes first through a wide shoal area studded with grass-

Hässlo swing bridge, west of Karlskrona
M. Lewin-Harris

covered islands (mostly designated nature reserves), then via a narrower, dog-legged channel and under a high level (18m) bridge north of the large island of Senoren (56°08′·2N 15°45′E), and thence to Karlskrona. If leaving the port to head eastwards, this route offers some interesting pilotage and saves many miles.

Even using the large-scale chart some of the buoyage is confusing, and calls for caution.

Berthing
Tallebryggan Marina (56°10′N 15°35′·3E)
Marina office ✆ +46 455 303150,
Fax +46 495 303151
Email info@batbolaget.se

This is the main yacht harbour for Karlskrona, and lies in a basin north of the city. It is very convenient for the city, but a motorway with its inevitable lights runs close along the side and the surroundings are not particularly attractive. In the final approach, the buoys marking the channel must be followed carefully. The visitors' berths are on the easternmost pontoon – some 60 or 70 places – mostly bows-to between fingers too narrow for walking though there are a few alongside berths near the pontoon's root

Karlskrona yacht harbour – large boats go alongside wall ahead, marina berths to starboard *S. Carnegie*

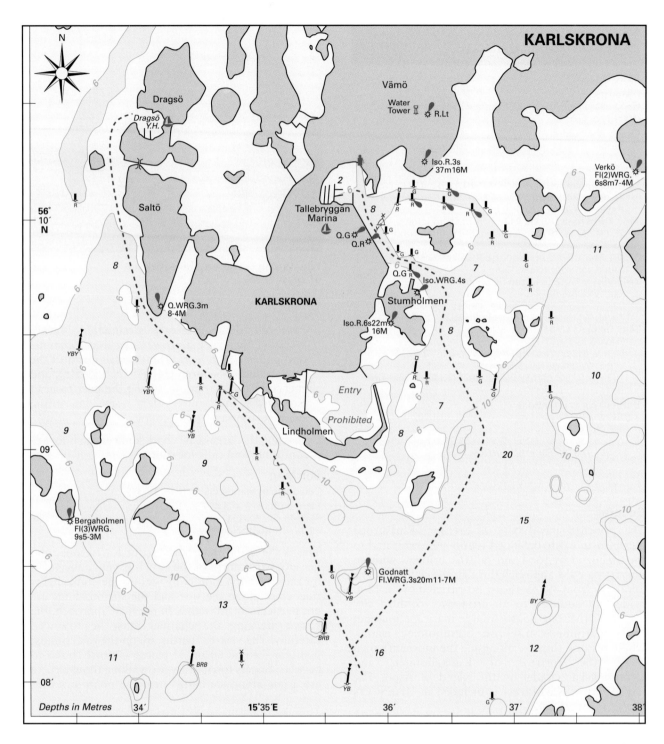

KARLSKRONA

and more against a floating pontoon on the south side of the basin east of the marina proper, particularly useful for larger yachts. Depths in the marina shoal from 4m in the south to 2m or less only a boats length off the ends of the pontoons.

The marina has all the usual facilities including fuel (diesel, self-service with card or 100 SEK notes) and Wi-Fi. Bottled gas is available at the filling station, and the office building nearby also houses a restaurant and the Tallebryggans Båtklubb, and is open 0700–2200 daily. A weather forecast is posted twice daily. Nearby chandlery – ask at office.

The town itself is pleasant, with good shops, a fish market; the outstanding maritime museum is a short walk away and by it the fascinating traditional wooden boat building school (Litorina Folkhögskola). The bus and railway station is 200m away. There are regular car ferries to Gdynia in Poland.

Dragsö Yacht Harbour

56°10'·4N 15°33'·9E

Marina office ☎ +46 455 10596, *Mobile* +46 709 283788
Email kss@knss.nu
www.knss.nu

Dragsö Yacht Harbour on Utkik island, administered by the Karlskrona Segelsällskap (sailing club), is quieter and much more scenic but is a long way from the city. Ten of its 130 berths are reserved for visitors. From any of the approach channels, pass north of the conspicuous Godnatt tower and follow the buoyed channel south of Lindholmen island, south of the Arsenal and west of Saltö island. The small islet northwest of Saltö must also be left to starboard. Once past this islet a buoyed channel opens to the east. Follow it, and the marina's two pontoons will soon come into view to starboard beyond the clubhouse. Berthing is bows on, stern to a buoy, in depths of 2–2·5m, with visitors placed at the ends of the two outer (westernmost) pontoons. A little swell may find its way in during strong north-westerly winds. The yacht harbour is in an almost enclosed lagoon surrounded by countryside, though some noise may penetrate from the nearby campsite. There is a children's play area and a barbecue area for the use of guests. There is water to all berths and electricity to most, with showers, sauna and laundry facilities ashore, a clubhouse with seasonal café, but no restaurant, shop or fuel. Slipway (with pressure hose and plenty of vacant cradles in summer) – enquire at the office. A diver is also available.

The Saltö Varv boatyard, ☎ +46 455 15511, where minor repairs might be undertaken, is about 300m to the south (though further by water). They will be able to help locate other tradesmen. The harbour is a on a bus route and bicycles can be hired from the nearby campsite.

Dragsö yacht harbour on wooded Utkik island, northwest of Karlskrona *A. Hammick*

Utklippan

55°57'N 15°42'E

Distances Karlskrona 13M, Bergkvara 29M, Kalmar 48M, Visby (Gotland) 135M, Christiansø 42M
Charts Swedish 7, 74, 81, 714, 821 *Båtsportkort C: Hanöbukten*, UKHO 2360, 2857
SXK 'harbourmaster' ☎ +46 702 18 71 27
Email info@sxk.se www.sxk.se

Utklippan consists of two small skerries situated 4·5M southwest of Utlängan, the nearest land. Four breakwaters nearly join the two skerries on their east and west sides, thus nearly enclosing the lagoon between them. In the north skerry a basin 90m x 40m was originally excavated for the use of the lighthouse tender, with two entrances, on the southeast and southwest sides. It is a delightful spot with perfect shelter and is capable – at a squeeze – of berthing up to 25 boats in 2·5–3m depths. There is a lighthouse 30m high on the south skerry (you will need a dinghy to reach this) and an automatic fog horn. Shoals extend both north and south of the islands, which should be approached with care and a large scale chart.

Final approach from either direction (favour the lee side) is via rock-fringed channels and thence between low moles, where strong currents can be encountered. At night, approach in the white sector of the Södraskär light from the northeast, or the

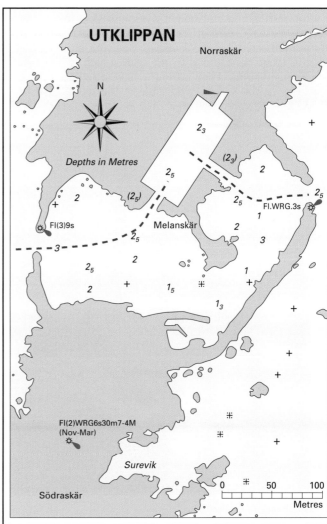

The rock harbour at Utklippan *J. Sadd*

green from the northwest. Utklippan provides an interesting and convenient overnight stop for yachts on passage along the Swedish coast and is administered by the Swedish Cruising club (SXK, not to be confused with the SKK which is Swedish Kennel Club!). They normally have a representative there in the season who collects the dues (cash in SEK – beware exchange rate in other currencies).

Facilities are limited to chemical toilets and refuse bins in season, reportedly with electricity to a few berths in the southeast corner and Wi-Fi, but the wild and attractive surroundings more than compensate. It is reported to be an outstanding spot for bird watching, though noisy in the nesting season when their young are vigorously defended.

Utklippan *E. Redfern*

East coast of Sweden

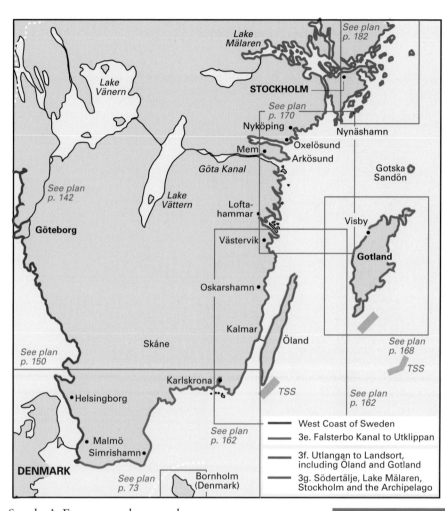

Sweden's East coast changes character as one moves north. For the first few miles it is open to the full width of the Baltic, and then comes under the influence of two major and one minor offshore islands. Oland, some 70 miles long is separated from the mainland by Kalmarsund, which is spanned by a bridge. Northeast of that lies Gotland, of similar length to Oland but wider, which is reputed to have some of the best summer weather in the Baltic. Visby is its only real harbour and is inclined to be busy during the peak month, but towards autumn the activity decreases and makes this an attractive time to visit. North of Gotland is the small island of Gotska Sandon which has no harbour, but is surrounded by superb sandy beaches off any of which one may anchor in suitable conditions.

North of Kalmarsund the skärgård begins with deep inlets and myriad offshore rocks and islands presenting a beautiful and interesting cruising area. The Göta Canal meets the Baltic at Mem, some 70 miles north of Kalmarsund, and the *skärgård* continues to Stockholm which is set between the lake and islands of Malaren to the west and the extensive Stockholm *skärgård* to the east and northeast.

There are firing practice areas on this coast – see Appendix page 363 for details.

3f. Utlangan to Landsort including Öland and Gotland

Kalmarsund

The Baltic coast of Sweden north of Utklippan offers superb cruising in relatively sheltered waters among islands. The first 20 miles or so is open until the entrance to Kalmarsund, the strait which runs for 70 miles inside the island of Öland. It narrows from about 10M wide at either end to 4M at its narrowest, and it can funnel the wind to provide some brisk sailing. The town of Kalmar is immediately south of its narrowest point, where it is crossed by a high level bridge with a clearance of 36m. The southern end of Gotland and Öland have a reputation for fog, but this tends to clear in summer as the sound is entered. There is a Traffic Separation Scheme off the southeast of Öland. A noticeable feature along parts of the low coasts of

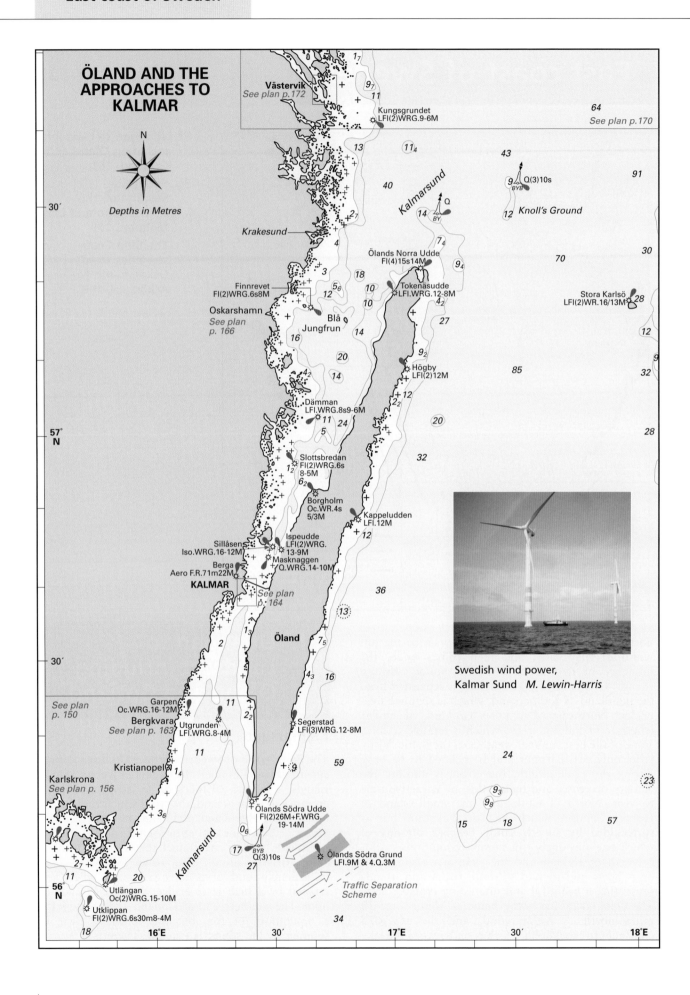

ÖLAND AND THE APPROACHES TO KALMAR

N

Depths in Metres

Västervik
See plan p.172

Kungsgrundet
☆ LFl(2)WRG.9-6M

64
See plan p.170

17

9₇
11

13

11₄

40

43

9₄ Q(3)10s
BYB

91

Kalmarsund

14
BY

Q
BY

12 Knoll's Ground

7₄

Krakesund

4

Ölands Norra Udde
Fl(4)15s14M

9₄

70

30

3

18

Tokenäsudde
☆ LFl.WRG.12-8M

4₂

27

Stora Karlsö
LFl(2)WR.16/13M ☆ 28

12

Finnrevet
Fl(2)WRG.6s8M

5₆

10

10

Oskarshamn
*See plan
p. 166*

12

10

Blå
Jungfrun

14

9₂

Högby
LFl(2)12M

85

32

16

20

14

4₂

+12
2₂

20

28

Dämman
LFl.WRG.8s9-6M

11
5

24

32

**57°
N**

Slottsbredan
Fl(2)WRG.6s
8-5M

1₂

6₂

Borgholm
Oc.WR.4s
5/3M

Kappeludden
LFl.12M

12

36

Sillåsen
Iso.WRG.16-12M

Ispeudde
LFl(2)WRG.
13-9M

Masknaggen
Q.WRG.14-10M

Berga
Aero F.R.71m22M

KALMAR
*See plan
p. 164*

13

Swedish wind power,
Kalmar Sund *M. Lewin-Harris*

2

1₃

Öland

7₅

30′

4₃

16

Garpen
Oc.WRG.16-12M

11

2₂

*See plan
p. 150*

Bergkvara
See plan p. 163

Utgrunden
LFl.WRG.8-4M

Segerstad
LFl(3)WRG.12-8M

24

Kristianopel

11

59

Karlskrona
See plan p. 156

1₄

9

23

3₆

9₃
9₈

Ölands Södra Udde
Fl(2)26M+F.WRG.
19-14M

15

18

57

0₆

17
BYB
Q(3)10s

27

Ölands Södra Grund
LFl.9M & 4.Q.3M

*Traffic Separation
Scheme*

11

20

Utlängan
Oc(2)WRG.15-10M

Utklippan
Fl(2)WRG.6s30m8-4M

**56°
N**

18

34

Kalmarsund

16°E

30′

17°E

30′

18°E

Sweden and Öland are the forests of wind turbines, only some of which are indicated on current charts. A wind farm in the middle of Kalmarsund has seven large windmills, while Öland is said to have around 400. Once north of Kalmar the *skärgård* begins to assert itself and the number of small harbours and anchorages increases far beyond the compass of this book. It is unwise to navigate anywhere on this coast without large scale (1:50,000 or greater) Swedish charts; from here northwards it becomes distinctly foolhardy. It is also wise to carry at least one of the local pilot books (see page 113) on board.

Bergkvara

56°23'·4N 16°26'·4E

Distances Utklippan 29M, Kalmar 19M

Charts
Swedish 7, 81, 713 *Båtsportkort F: Kalmarsund,* UKHO 2251, 2842

☎ +46 048 62 01 50 (Dalskärs Camping)

A pleasant and convenient stop between Utklippan or Karlskrona and Kalmar. There is a small marina in a natural basin, 300 metres north of the quay which has the usual basic services, including diesel fuel, restaurant and laundry. Mooring is bow to quay, stern to buoy. The approach is through a buoyed channel from a point 0.6M south-southwest of Garpen light, and there is a conspicuous grain elevator near to the quay which is in good condition and normally has space for a yacht not wishing to use the marina. Alternatively anchor off the quay. There is an another 3m depth channel marked with buoys from a point 1M north-northeast of Garpen light.

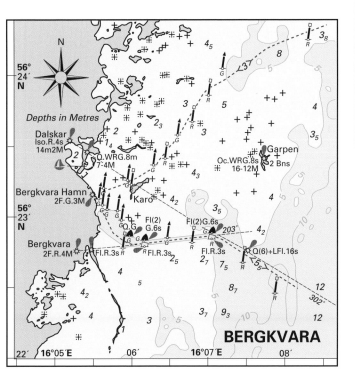

BERGKVARA

Kalmar

56°40'N 16°21'E

Distances
Simrishamn 100M, Karlskrona 50M, Visby 95M, Västervik 65M

Charts and guides
UKHO 2251, 3435
Swedish 81, 712
Båtsportkort F: Sydostkusten – Kalmarsund.

Lights

Southern approach
7280 **Ölands Södra Udde** 56°11'·8N 16°24'E
    Fl(2)30s41m26M+F.WRG.19m19–14M
    153·5°-G-159°-W-167·5°-R-to shore Round white stone
    tower, black band 42m Floodlit
7420 **Utgrunden (north end of shoal)** 56°22'·5N 16°15'·7E
    LFl.WRG.8s26m8–4M Racon
    019°-R-096°-G-153°-R-166°-G-185°-W-192°-R-265°-G-
    292°-R-316·5°-G-349°-W-019° Black tower, white band
    and lantern, grey conical base 28m
7390 **Skansgrundet** 56°39'·1N 16°22'·7E
    Oc(2)WRG.20s18m15–11M
    008°-G-019°-W-024·5°-R-032°-G-058°-R-150°-G-197°-W-
    202·5°-R-215°-G-217°-R-249°-G-256°-R-008° Black
    tower, green band, grey conical base, white lantern
    19m Floodlit
Northern approach
7324 **Dämman** 57°03'·4N 16°41'·7E
    LFl.WRG.8s9–6M
    010°-G-021°-W-024·5°-R-120°-G-169°-W-209°-R-010°
    Orange tower, black band, grey base 21m
7332 **Slottsbredan** 56°55'·7N 16°36'·3E
    Fl(2)WRG.6s20m9–6M
    018°-W-022°-R-048°-G-098°-R-184°-G-202°-W-208°-R-
    359°-G-018° Black tower, green band and lantern,
    grey conical base 21m
7352 **Krongrundet** 56°41'·4N 16°24'·5E
    Oc(2)WRG.8s10m15–10M
    023°-W-031°-R-058°-G-104°-W-184°-R-214°-G-222·5°-
    W-226·5°-R-284°-G-023° White tower, green and black
    stripe 11m

Communications

VTS Oxelösund ☎ +46 480 10719, *VHF* Ch 09.
Kalmar Commercial Harbour ☎ +46 480 451450
    VHF Ch 09, 12, 16
    Email kalmar.hamn@kommun.kalmar.se
Kalmar Guest Harbour ☎ +46 480 417700
    Email gasthamn@turistbyra.kalmar.se
    www.kalmar.se. Click on Tourism – Travel – Marinas.

General

Kalmar is one of Sweden's oldest towns, and the scene of the Union of Kalmar in 1397. It was originally a Viking stronghold, and became one of the major ports of the Hanseatic League. The present town, with a population of around 50,000, has many historic buildings dating back to the 17th century, a fine baroque cathedral and a picturesque and very interesting castle, which is a World Heritage Site, in a dominant position overlooking Kalmarsund. The castle museum has an outstanding exhibition of articles from the sunken 17th-century warship *Kronan*, while the maritime museum in the old quarter at the east end of the town is also worth visiting. A USSR submarine from the 1950s adds to the variety afloat. Kalmar has a very good shopping centre which, like all these attractions is within easy walking distance of the harbour.

3. SWEDEN

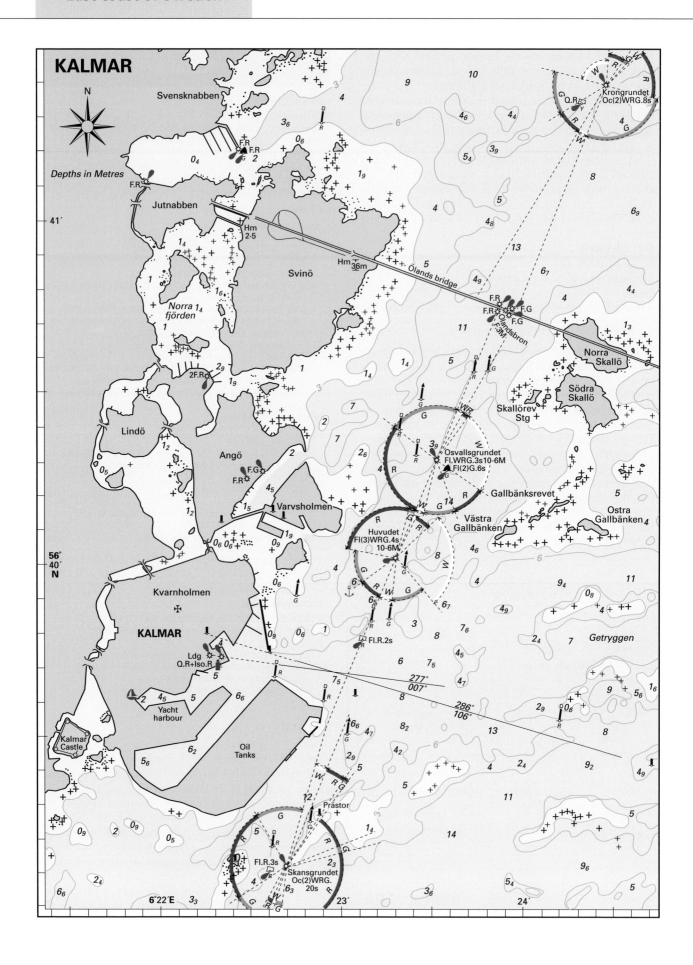

KALMAR

N

Svensknabben

Depths in Metres

F.R
F.R
G 2

F.R

Jutnabben

41´

Hm
2·5

Hm
36m

Öland bridge

Svinö

Norra
fjörden

2F.R

Lindö

Angö

F.G
F.R

Varvsholmen

56°
40´
N

Kvarnholmen

KALMAR

Ldg
Q.R+Iso.R

Yacht
harbour

Kalmar
Castle

Oil
Tanks

6°22´E

Krongrundet
Oc(2)WRG.8s

Q.R

Öland bridge

F.R
F.R
Ölandsbron
F.3M
F.G
F.G

Norra
Skallö

Södra
Skallö

Skallörev
Stg

Osvallsgrundet
Fl.WRG.3s10-6M
Fl(2)G.6s

Gallbänksrevet

Västra
Gallbänken

Ostra
Gallbänken

Huvudet
Fl(3)WRG.4s
10-6M

Getryggen

Fl.R.2s

277°
007°

286°
106°

Prästor

Skansgrundet
Oc(2)WRG.
20s

Fl.R.3s

23´

24´

Approach and entrance

From either direction, follow the main north - south shipping channel which passes close past the harbour. The entrance leads off it to the west at a point 1.2M south of the Öland bridge. Berthing is in the old northwest basin, the Ölandshamnen, which is approached through the Gamlahamnen, itself directly opposite the harbour entrance. Mooring is mainly with bows to the quay and stern to a buoy, though a few alongside berths may be found on the starboard hand near the entrance. Depths vary from 4·5m near the entrance to 2m at the head of the harbour. As the basin is entirely reserved for visitors, any free berth can be taken on arrival. There are some 120 berths; the office is in the tourist centre and the marina is fully operational May to October inclusive. Out of season arrangements can be made by telephone. Anchoring is not permitted in the vicinity of Kalmar harbour.

Services for yachts

All the usual services are available including Wi-Fi and sauna. Launderette time slot must be booked at the harbour office. Fuel (diesel and petrol) is on the north side of the marina entrance. There is a holding tank pump-out station. Kalmar is home to a particularly good chandlery, Baltic Skeppsfournering AB, ① +46 480 10600), across the road from the marina basin. Gas bottles, including *Camping Gaz* and possibly Calor Gas, plus German, Danish and Swedish makes can be refilled. Engine repairs can be accessed. A weather forecast, updated twice daily, is displayed in the marina office, but is only accessible during office hours.

General facilities

There is a very good shopping centre with excellent facilities, within easy walking distance of the harbour. There are other supermarkets in the town, some of which stay open late, together with many banks, restaurants and hotels. The railway and coach stations are opposite the marina, providing easy access to the rest of the country. Car hire can be arranged by the chandlery. Taxis are readily available. The airport a short distance inland has several daily flights to Stockholm and Malmö. Altogether it is a good place for crew changes.

Kalmar approach to yacht harbour   *S. Carnegie*

Ölands Bridge just north of Kalmar   *B. Sheffield*

3. SWEDEN

Blå Jungfrun (The Blue Maiden)
57°15′N 16°47′E

Blå Jungfrun (pronounced *Blawe Yung-fruuhn*) is a National Park island in the northern part of the Kalmarsund. There are daytime only anchorages at Sikhamn in the northwest and Lervik in the northeast, where summer students act as welcoming wardens. The island has dramatic granite slopes and varied flora (including 200 species of lichen!), with an ancient stone maze on the south coast.

Kalmar Castle is a World Heritage Site   *S. Carnegie*

Oskarshamn

57°16′N 16°28′E

Distances Kalmar 36M, Västervik 30M, Visby (Gotland) 63M

Charts Swedish 6, 81, 624, 711, 6241 *Båtsportkort: Kalmarsund*, UKHO 2844, 2846, 2251, 2816

www.oskarshamn.se Click on Tourists – Marinas.

This is a busy, shipbuilding port but nevertheless pleasant, clean and tidy. Approach may be made either north or south of Finnrevet lighthouse which is 5M east x north of the harbour and is well marked, presenting no difficulty, even at night. However beware of ferries in the narrow channels. There are several alternatives for berthing:

a. Brädholmen Marina (☏ +46 705 74 79 90) at the head of the harbour, either side of the bridge to the island, mostly 3m, bow to with stern anchor, or larger yachts can go alongside a very nice wood piled wall (historical local boats sometimes moored) where there is about 4.5m depth. This marina has all the usual services available. There are all the shops, post, banks of a fairly large town and a small Watski chandler 350m away. The boatyard to the south of the main harbour has been recommended by locals.

b. Secure to SXK buoy close east of Badholmen Island or anchor in 5m to the south of it. This berth is disturbed by wash in the day time.

c. There are various anchoring possibilities near Oskarshamn to the northwest of Tillingeo and the neighbouring islands but beware of the cables running out to Tillingeo lighthouse.

d. Ernemar Marina (☏ +46 49 11 74 00), at the east end of the harbour in position 57°15′·6N 16°29′·E. This is a quieter place with less urban surroundings, most services, but more than a mile to the town facilities. There are 10 guest buoys, otherwise use a green marked space.

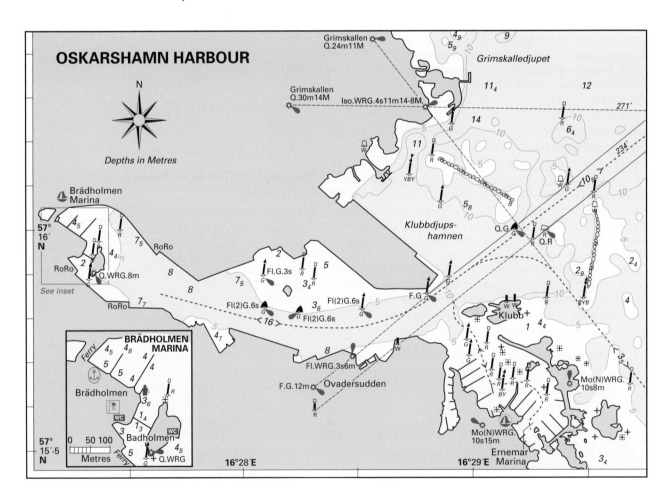

Visby (Gotland)

57°39'N 18°17'E

Distances
Kalmar 95M, Västervik 55M, Arkösund 65M

Charts and guides
UKHO 2251 (southwest Gotland), 2361
Swedish 72, 73, 731

Lights
7235 **Follingbo** 57°35'·6N 19°22'·6E Aero VQ.243m21M. Mast
Note This light is 4M inland with obstructions
7224 **Stora Karlsö, west side** 57°17'·5N 17°57'·8E
  LFl(2)WR.12s56m16–13M
  340°-W-193°-R-212°-W-233°-R-340° White tower on dwelling 18m
7236·5 **Visby, north breakwater** 57°38'·1N 18°16'·2E
  Q.R.9m9M White tower, green band, 6m Floodlit
7236 **Visby, south breakwater** 57°38'·1N 18°16'·4E
  Iso.WRG.4s11m12–8M 007°-R-044°-G-055°-W-087°-R-209°-G-239°-W-245°-R-296° White tower, red band 8m Floodlit

Harbour communications

VTS Oxelösund ☎ +46 855 42 45 50, VHF Ch 09
Visby pilots ☎ +46 498 21 01 38
Visby Guest Harbour ☎ +46 498 21 51 90
  Mobile +46 736 00 63 00
VTS & pilots VHF Ch 09 (0600–2200 LT)
Email info@visbygasthamn.se
www.visbygasthamn.se

General

Visby (pronounced *Vees-bu*) is the only town of any size on Gotland, and is a pleasant mixture of old and new. Its position led to it becoming one of the most important trading centres of Europe in the 10th and 11th centuries, and later a principal depot of the Hanseatic League. This strategic position and wealth

Visby's main marina, in the northeast of the harbour
F. and K. Williams

led to conflict, and the island of Gotland changed hands many times between the Swedes, the Danes and lastly the Russians, most recently in 1808. Visby's 13th-century towers and walls are a striking sight from the sea, and they and the ten early mediaeval churches stand witness to the city's former importance. A 'mediaeval week' is held in early August, particularly impressive on the Sundays at either end when many local people wear period costume. There is also an excellent museum. The island's website will be found at www.gotland.se.

Visby's harbour is deservedly popular with both yachtsmen and tourists. It can become very crowded and noisy on warm summer nights – particularly during the various festivals – with sidewalk cafés, a quayside amusement park and other yachts hosting cockpit parties late into the night. Gotland is claimed to have the best summer climate in Sweden, with only half the average rainfall of the mainland, but the south and west coasts may be subject to fog.

Approach and entrance

Both the water tower and the cathedral are conspicuous from offshore, as is the 343m Follingbo aero mast 4M southeast of the harbour. The entrance can be identified by the prominent oil tanks at its southern end, and often by the ferries berthed alongside. The outer harbour is large, with plenty of room to lower and stow sails once inside. After dark, approach using the sectored light on the end of the south breakwater, transferring to the two occulting red leading lights on 055° for final entry. The main north/south shipping lane runs some 4M offshore past Visby, carrying moderate to heavy traffic.

Berthing

Visiting yachts normally use the 200 berth marina in the extreme northeast of the harbour, where mooring is bows to a pontoon and stern to a buoy in depths of 3–6m, but it is crowded in the season. Local yachts have their own basin behind the ferry berth opposite the harbour mouth, but sometimes the harbourmaster will allow its use. When full, yachts have berthed against the northwest sea wall in the Imre Hamn but the walk to the harbourmaster's office and showers becomes a trek. In strong southwest-west winds the fishing harbour offers better shelter from the swell. All are administered from an office overlooking the northeast basin, open 0900–2100 in season. There are no suitable anchorages near Visby.

Formalities

There is a customs office near the harbour, if required. This should not be needed unless arriving directly from a non-Schengen country, such as Russia.

Services for yachts

The usual services and shops are available, including Wi-Fi. Toilets and showers, crowded at times, plus a launderette, are near the marina office. Fuel (diesel and petrol with cash or credit card) is beside the large slipway at the north end of the northwest

3. SWEDEN

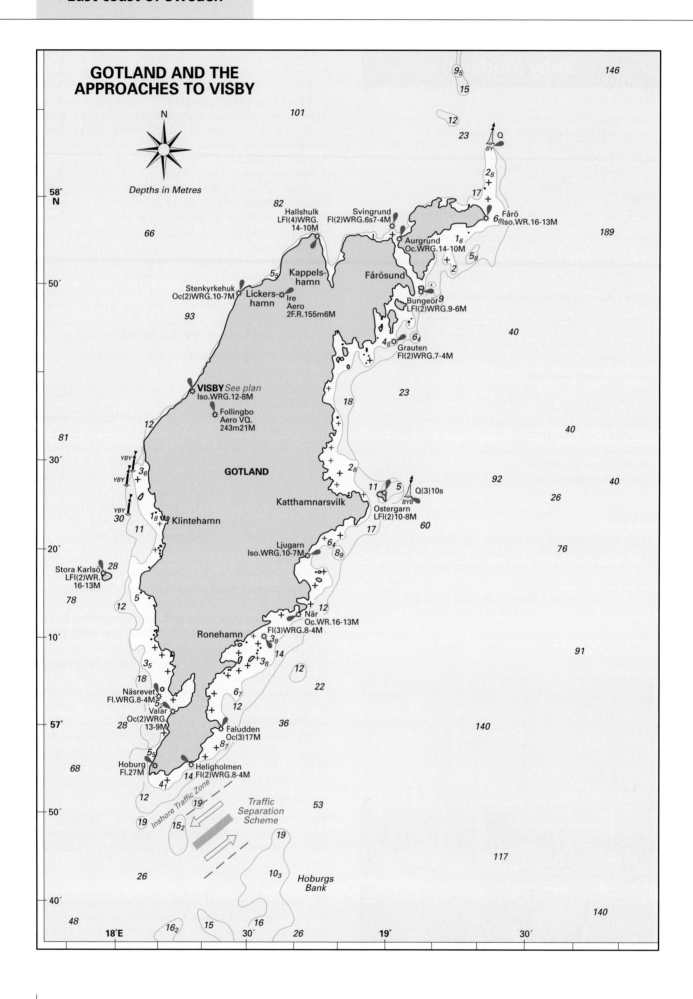

GOTLAND AND THE APPROACHES TO VISBY

N

Depths in Metres

58° N

50°

30°

20°

10°

57°

50°

40°

101

82

66

93

81

78

68

48

18°E

30°

19°

30°

146

9₅

15

12

23

146

189

Q
BY

2₈

17

Fårö
6₈Iso.WR.16-13M

Hallshuk
LFl(4)WRG.
14-10M

Svingrund
Fl(2)WRG.6s7-4M

Aurgrund
Oc.WRG.14-10M

1₆

5₈

2

40

Kappels-
hamn

Fårösund

5₅

Stenkyrkehuk
Oc(2)WRG.10-7M

Lickers-
hamn

Ire
Aero
2F.R.155m6M

Bungeör 9
LFl(2)WRG.9-6M

4₈

6₄

Grauten
Fl(2)WRG.7-4M

18

23

VISBY *See plan*
Iso.WRG.12-8M

Follingbo
Aero VQ.
243m21M

12

40

YBY

YBY

3₆

GOTLAND

2₈

11

5

Q(3)10s
BYB

Ostergarn
LFl(2)10-8M

92

26

40

YBY

30

1₈

Klintehamn

11

Katthamnarsvilk

17

60

Ljugarn
Iso.WRG.10-7M

6₄

8₉

76

Stora Karlsö
LFl(2)WR.
16-13M

28

5

12

Ronehamn

Når
Oc.WR.16-13M

12

3₈

14

3₈

12

91

18

3₅

6₇

12

22

Näsrevet
Fl.WRG.8-4M

5

Valar
Oc(2)WRG.
13-9M

28

Faludden
Oc(3)17M

8₇

36

140

Hoburg
Fl.27M

5₅

Heligholmen
14 Fl(2)WRG.8-4M

4₁

12

19

Inshore Traffic Zone

*Traffic
Separation
Scheme*

53

19

15₂

19

117

26

10₃

Hoburgs
Bank

16₂

15

16

26

140

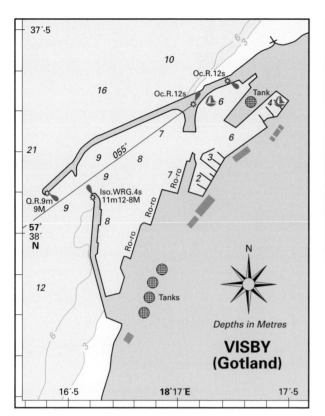

VISBY
(Gotland)

Depths in Metres

Visby is almost deserted by the end of August   *E. Redfern*

basin. The chandlery, Ljungs Skeppshandel, www.boatfittings.com, is conveniently near the harbour. Bottled gas and Swedish charts are available in addition to equipment. There are some excellent restaurants and a Systembolaget in town.

Communications and travel

There is internet access at the library. Cars and bicycles for hire. Frequent air and ferry connections with the mainland (the latter to/from Oskarshamn and Nynäshamn), and buses to all parts of Gotland.

Blå Kusten (The Blue Coast)

The Blue Coast is an extremely attractive area, characterised by thousands of small islands, many with interesting harbours or anchorages which stretches some 60M from Oskarshamn in the south to Arkösund in the north. Whilst providing the main coastal conduit from the southern Baltic to the northern cruising grounds, it also constitutes an attractive sailing area in its own right where one may linger in perfect shelter amongst the hundreds of wild islands, or venture up long leads to the several large and sophisticated towns.

Approaching the *skärgård* from the south through the wide and well marked Kalmarsund, considerable mental adjustment is required before one gains confidence when sailing fast in flat water only yards from rocks, winding down leads which appear to be dead ends, and keeping check of one's position where the marks are unnamed. But these are the joys and skills of *skärgård* sailing, which can be safe and relaxing provided one obeys the rules. These are few and simple but absolutely vital – to have a detailed chart, to stay in the marked channels, and ALWAYS

to know where you are. As so often, the key to safety and enjoyment lies in planning ahead. Decide where you are going and where you plan to stop. Do not rely on modern navigational aids, but do invest in some little red arrows to stick on the chart as you progress, so that if you are distracted you can find your place at a glance. To explore the many delightful anchorages a copy of the Swedish book *Naturhamnar på Ostkusten* is essential, and if tempted into an attractive area which does not feature in it be assured that there will be a good reason. It may have unmarked rocks, bad holding or some other drawback – if it was good it would be included in the handbook. *Naturhamnar på Ostkusten* is available from the Svenska Kryssarklubben (Swedish Cruising Club or SXK) – see page 110.

The Blue Coast is an important area for nesting birds, and many sites are out of bounds during the breeding season. These are marked both on the Swedish large-scale charts and on the water, where floating signs give the dates of prohibition. These vary between February to August, and must be respected. From the south one enters the *skärgård* at Krakelund (see plan on page 162) and is immediately confined to a testing fairway little over 200m wide. This winds north for about 4M, then widens into a thoroughfare where one can draw breath and take in the scenery. There are now 60M of leads ahead, which sometimes go deep into the islands and occasionally flirt with the open sea but which are almost always sheltered and provide flat water no matter where the wind. If you are already experienced in *skärgård* sailing, or are feeling particularly brave, you could stop for lunch at the delightfully tight anchorage at Strupo (57°31'·7N 16°44'·5E). The easy approach is from the south but don't miss the very narrow 2·3m western exit. Shops are scarce in the *skärgård*, so you might take the most attractive 5M fairway northwest to Blankaholm (57°35'·4N 16°31'·9E) where there is a modest marina and store. For more sophisticated

3. SWEDEN

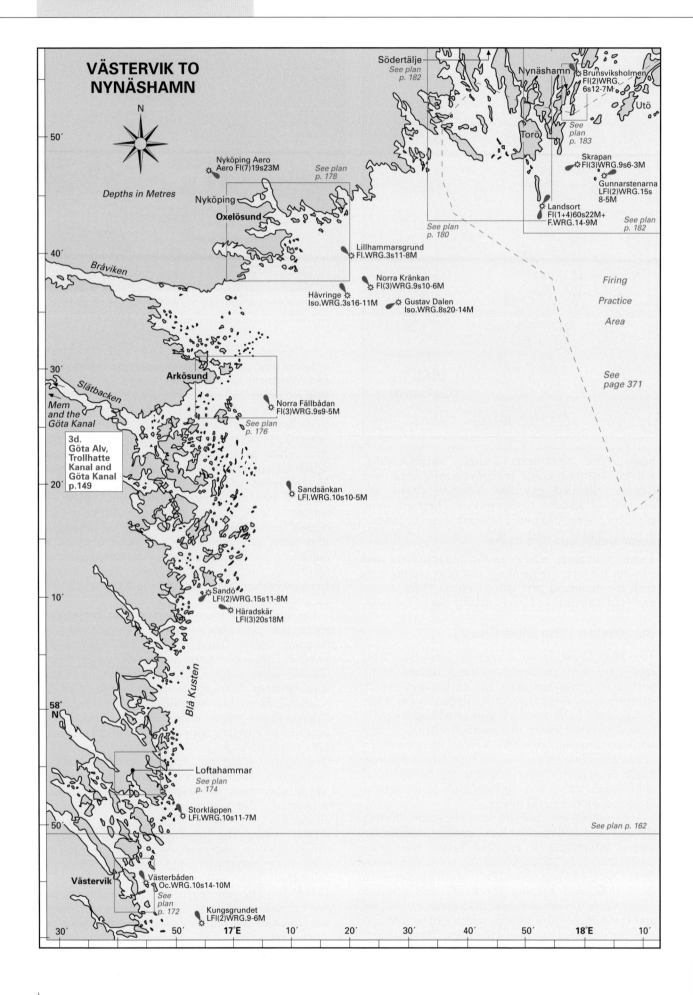

VÄSTERVIK TO NYNÄSHAMN

N

Depths in Metres

Nyköping Aero
Aero Fl(7)19s23M

Nyköping
Oxelösund

Södertälje
See plan p. 182

Nynäshamn

☼ Brunsviksholmen
Fl(2)WRG.
6s12-7M

Utö

Torö

See plan p. 183

Skrapan
☼ Fl(3)WRG.9s6-3M

Gunnarstenarna
LFl(2)WRG.15s
8-5M

☼ Landsort
Fl(1+4)60s22M+
F.WRG.14-9M

See plan p. 180

See plan p. 182

Bråviken

See plan p. 178

Lillhammarsgrund
☼ Fl.WRG.3s11-8M

Norra Kränkan
☼ Fl(3)WRG.9s10-6M

Hävringe ☼
Iso.WRG.3s16-11M

☼ Gustav Dalen
Iso.WRG.8s20-14M

Firing

Practice

Area

Arkösund

Norra Fällbådan
Fl(3)WRG.9s9-5M

See plan p. 176

See page 371

Slätbacken

Mem
and the
Göta Kanal

3d.
Göta Alv,
Trollhatte
Kanal and
Göta Kanal
p.149

Sandsänkan
LFl.WRG.10s10-5M

**58°
N**

Blå Kusten

☼Sandö
LFl(2)WRG.15s11-8M

☼ Häradskär
LFl(3)20s18M

Loftahammar
See plan p. 174

☼ Storkläppen
LFl.WRG.10s11-7M

See plan p. 162

Västervik

☼ Västerbåden
Oc.WRG.10s14-10M

See plan p. 172

Kungsgrundet
LFl(2)WRG.9-6M

30′   50′   **17°E**   10′   20′   30′   40′   50′   **18°E**   10′

needs Västervik provides all facilities and good communications. For those who find the close proximity of land oppressive the large, landlocked pool at Björkö (57°51'·7N 16°40'·2E) provides excellent security in beautiful surroundings. Continuing north, there is a small store and fish smokery at Stora Kallskär (58°03'·1N 16°49'·4E) where one can sometimes obtain fresh or smoked fish. One may secure to the small jetty beside the shop, or there is ample room to anchor just to the west. For total peace do not miss Harstena (58°15'·7N 17°01'·7E). One enters through a narrow channel between cliffs, emerging into a wide, enclosed bay to moor in typical Baltic style with bows to the rocks. Here is utter peace and security, with the added bonus that a short walk through the woods leads to a pretty fishing village where there is a modest store and a smokery. If there is a requirement for serious victuals and civilisation one could do no better than visit Arkösund (see page 175) where all requirements will be met in most pleasant surroundings. Finally, before leaving the Blue Coast to head north, consider making a last call at Lundarna (58°30'·3N 17°00'·5E), a delightful, tight little anchorage in a beautiful natural setting where one's new *skärgård* navigation skills will be well tested. Some of the main harbours which make convenient stops are listed below, but there are many others. Provided you have the Swedish charts and the Gästhamnsguiden, available free at any harbour, on board, you will be able to manage.

The Göta Kanal

The eastern entrance to the Göta Kanal is at Mem (see page 149) which is reached through the Slätbacken. Allow a mimimum of 4hrs for the attractive but tricky 21M from Arkösund to Mem if having to meet a particular lock opening time.

A *skärgård* mooring in the Blue Coast   *P. Bruce*

Västervik

57°45'N 16°39'E

Distances
Kalmar 65M, Visby 55M, Oskarsham 33M, Mem 50M, Arkösund 55M, Södertälje 95M, Nynäshamn 85M

Charts and guides
Swedish 6, 72, 623, 6231 *Båtsportkort C: Ostkusten–Kalmarsund*
UKHO 2816, 2361, 2848

Lights
buoy **Västerviks angöring** 57°44'·8N 16°55'·3E Q.Fl North cardinal pillar buoy, ↟ topmark
7078 **Kungsgrundet** 57°41'·1N 16°54'·2E
   LFl(2)WRG.27m9–6M
   005°-R-048°-G-088·5°-R-122°-G-193°-W-005° Racon Black tower, red band, white lantern. Helipad
7076 **Västerbåden** 57°44'·8N 16°44'·5E
   Oc.WRG.10s14m14–10M
   112°-G-133·5°-R-258·5°-G-268°-W-269·5°- R-309°-G-321°-R-011°-G-040° Racon Red tower, black base 15m Floodlit
7082 **Idö Stångskär** 57°40'·3N 16°47'·1E Q.WRG.13m8–5M
   145°-G-150°-W-152°-R-302°-G-321°-W-324°-R-338° White lantern, red base
7080 **Stickskär** Ldg Lts 236° 57°43'·3N 16°45'·3E
   Fl.WRG.1·5s10m7–3M White tower
7081 *Rear* Spårö 1M from front Iso.6s36m14M White tower 8m

Harbour communications
Västervik Commercial Harbour ✆ +46 490 16920/10690 VHF Ch 12, 16
Notholmen Yacht Harbour ✆ +46 490 12385 (0800–1200 and 1500–2000 LT)
Västerviks Gästhamn ✆ +46 490 36900, Mobile +46 70 459 3919 (0800–2000 LT)
Västerviks Marina ✆ +46 490 69800, Mobile +46 70 715 3200 (0800–1900 LT)

General

Västervik is a small industrial town with a modern harbour for small ships, many of them carrying timber. It is pleasant but unpretentious, with an attractive waterfront, some interesting old buildings and considerable charm. It has good shopping, including several large supermarkets and an open market, and a choice of three yacht harbours with several more in the approach. An outdoor song festival is held every July in the remains of Stegeholm Castle.

Västervik is an excellent base from which to explore the famous Blå Kustens archipelago to the south.

Approach and entrance

The approach to Västervik involves the negotiation of intricate, rock-fringed channels and a large-scale chart is essential. From seaward there are two main approaches, both well marked on the chart:

a. From the east, pass close to Västerviks angöring North cardinal buoy, which lies some 4M north of Kungsgrundet light, and head west towards Västerbåden light. Turn south-southwest and follow the buoyed and lit channel, turning west across Lusärnafjärden entrance.

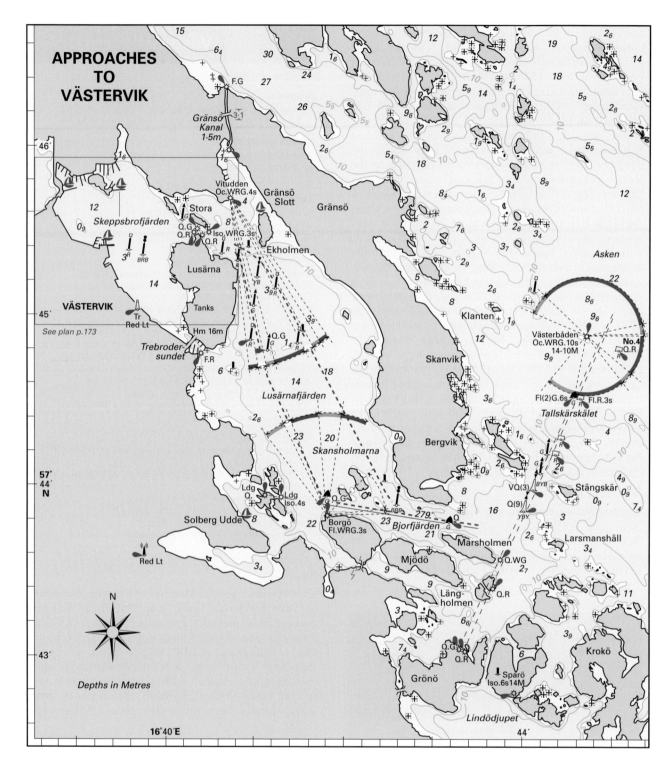

APPROACHES TO VÄSTERVIK

Depths in Metres

b. From the southeast head towards Ido Stängskär light on a bearing of 323° and pass close northeast of it. Head for the beacon on Spårö Island, and pass north through the Spårösund, to join the approach a. Turn west and cross the broad entry to Lusärnafjärden, to reach the port of Västervik.

There are no restrictions on anchoring in the area. It is also possible to continue through the lifting bridge to the Gamlebyviken.

Berthing

There are two yacht harbours on Lusärnafjärden both in quiet surroundings but at some distance from the town.

Solberg Udde

57°43′·7N 16°40′·7E
☎ +46 490 16291 *Mobile* +46 731 61 06 00

This is tucked behind a group of small islands on the south side close to the entrance. Around 20 of its berths are available for visitors, in depths of 2–5m, with a maximum beam of 3·5m and weight of 10

The narrow Sparösound, which separates the islands of Grönö and Sparö on the southern approach to Västervik
A. and A. Fleck

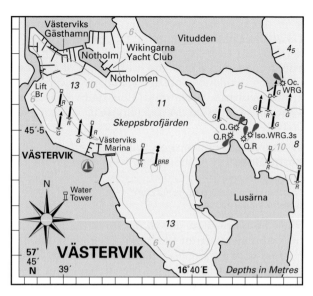

tonnes. The facilities are those of the nearby camping ground, restaurant and boatyard.

Gränsö Slott

57°45'·6N 16°40'·9E

☏+46 490 37080 *Mobile* ☏ +46 706 99 25 15

This is just north of Ekholmen Island, near the entrance to the Gränsö canal. It is run by the hotel and has 30 visitors berths in 1·5–2·3m, and has good basic services, plus use of the swimming pool and Wi-Fi. It is a pleasant stop

There are three yacht harbours near the town itself, which are reached by passing through the (very well marked) narrows close north of Lusärna island and across the Skeppsbrofjärden. Mooring in all three is bows-to, with stern to a buoy.

Västerviks Marina

This is on the south side of the harbour, has berthing for about 40 boats with the usual services and is more of a 'working' marina than those to the north, with a chandlery and boatyard ashore and a good

Right Looking southwest over Västerviks Gästhamn towards the city skyline   *A. Hammick*

Below The narrow but well-marked passage which connects the Lusärnafjärden and Skeppsbrofjärden on the final approach to Västervik, seen from the northwest
A. Hammick

electronics dealer nearby. The surroundings are industrial, and it is about 10 minutes walk from the town centre. It is possible to lie alongside (for free) whilst visiting the chandlery.

Västerviks Gästhamn

☏ +46 490 36900 *Mobile* ☏ +46 708 98 57 37
Email info@westervikwaterfront.se
www.westervikwaterfront.se

Sometimes known as the Blå Kustens marina, it is in the northwest corner of Skeppsbrofjärden and fills the space between the isthmus leading to the town and Notholmen peninsula. To add to the confusion,

it is the one listed as 'Västervik Marina' in the *Gästhamnsguiden* free national guide! There is berthing for over 300 yachts, good shelter from all but strong south winds and a full range of facilities including swimming pool and chandlery Reception is at the fuel berth, open 0800–1900 daily. Boats over 12m are requested to telephone in advance of arrival.

Westerviks Segelsällskap Wikingarna Yacht Club.

☏ +46 490 12385
Email sekreterare@wikingarna.com
www.wikingarna.com

They are on the east side of the tip of the peninsula of Notholmen, east of Västerviks Gästhamn. Do not confuse with a small boat marina to its north which does not take visitors. This friendly club has three pontoons, and keeps a few guest moorings on pontoons; much quieter than the town *gästhamn* and there is more chance of finding a berth. It is worth telephoning in advance of arrival to ensure a berth is available

General facilities

Västervik has all the facilities of a larger town, including good shopping, several large supermarkets, a wide variety of snack bars, restaurants and hotels, and an outdoor market in the square on Saturday mornings. For a short stay and quick shop, berth alongside the northwest end of the commercial quay in northwest corner of harbour. This is handy for the shops. The town centre is within walking distance of all three marinas, the path from the northern pair being across an attractive causeway complete with lifting bridge, next to which is the tourist office. Taxis are readily available if returning laden with shopping. Rail and coach services provide access to the rest of the country.

Loftahammar

57°54'·1N 16°41'·9E
Chart 623 NW & NE
Distances Västervik 16M, Arkösund 43M
Värd ☏ +46 493 613 15 or +46 70 530 8912

A large landlocked basin at the head of a long fjord; worth a visit being tranquil and picturesque.

There are narrow, twisting and shallow routes from the west and east in addition to the main approach from the southeast.

The basin is approached by a very narrow buoyed channel 3m deep. Several local yachts lie to buoys. Secure to a vacant mooring, anchor anywhere in the basin according to wind, or go alongside the small jetty northwest of the inner red prick in 2–3m. Good shelter and scenery. The locals are very helpful in the large village where there is an hotel, restaurant and some supplies. The marina has 50 guest berths with all facilities and although it is possible to lay up. Communications can be challenging.

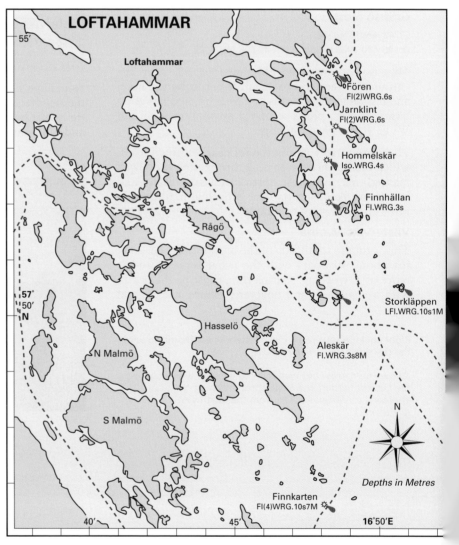

Arkösund

58°29'N 16°56'E

Distances
Visby 65M, Västervik 55M, Mem 20M,
Södertälje 60M, Nynäshamn 50M

Charts and guides
Swedish 72, 621 *Båtsportkort C: Ostkusten*
UKHO 2361, 2362, 3217

Lights
6866 **Norra Fällbåden** 58°26'·5N 17°06'·2E
FI(3)WRG.9s16m9–5M
108·5°-G-114·5°-W-116°-R-122°-G(unintens)-180°-
R(unintens)-240°-R-245°-G-253°-W-315°-R-333·5° Black
concrete tower, white top, yellow band, grey base
17m Wind generator
6868 **Arkö, Östra Kopparholm Ldg Lts** 292° *Front*
58°28'·4N 16°58'·4E Q.WRG.8m12–3M
119°-G-149°-W-156·5°-R-188°-R(unintens)228·5° White
intens on leading line. White lantern, red rectangle,
white stripe
6868·1 **Kälebo** *Rear* 0·9M from front Oc.6s27m16M
White lantern, red column, white stripe
6872·1 **Kuggviksskär** 58°28'·8N 16°58'·2E
FI(4)WRG.6s13m6–3M
307·5°-R-331°-G-009·5°-W-019°-R-051°-G-058·5°-R-090°-
G-129°-W-139°-R-253° White tower 12m

Harbour communications
Norrköpings Segelsällskap ① +46 125 20555
Arkösund Quay ① +46 125 20036
Badholmarna, Bäckmansviken and Nordanskog Yacht
Harbours ① +46 125 20684
Mobile ① +46 706 86 74 50

General

In addition to being a popular yachting centre in an attractive rural setting, Arkösund is less than 20M from Mem, the eastern gateway to the Göta Kanal. Although there are five possible places in which to berth, none are very large and the area remains relatively unspoilt, with only a few houses and hotels amongst the surrounding trees.

If heading up the long, narrow Slätbaken fjord which leads to Mem, allow time to combat the strong east-going currents which are sometimes encountered in the narrows at Ettersundet and Stegeborg.

Approach and entrance

From the open sea, pass close north of Norra Fällbåden lighthouse to enter the Arkö approach channel, marked at intervals with spar buoys on either side, on a course of 292°. The channel is also indicated by the Arkö leading marks, but these are not easily visible. However, the buoyage is clear in daylight, and once the Arkö light is reached the entrance becomes obvious.

Entry is not recommended by night or in poor visibility. It is also possible to approach from the north, via one of several buoyed channels, but this should not even be considered without a large-scale chart.

Berthing

Although in theory Arkösund boasts five guest harbours all within walking distance of one another, in practice a berth can be hard to find since all are relatively small with limited space for visitors. Berthing charges at all Arkösund's facilities are in the lower price band, (see page 112). The first berths to be seen on the approach from seaward lie below the handsome clubhouse of the Norrköpings Segelsällskap, and are helpfully labelled with a large GÄSTHAMN sign. Although only ten stern buoys are provided – lie bows to the staging which fringes the club's grounds – more yachts tend to be squeezed in between as beam allows. Depths range from 2·2m upwards. Facilities are limited to four electricity points (but no water) on the staging, with toilets and showers ashore. The area is occasionally closed to visitors when in use for club events. Many would consider this the most attractive of Arkösund's berthing possibilities. Next to be seen are the crowded berths on the old quay, or Kajen. Although around two dozen berths are claimed, many appear to be permanently occupied and depths in some parts are as little as 1·2m (a small red buoy marks an underwater rock between the inner berths and the Badholmarna pontoon). Only eight have access to electricity, though fresh water is readily available and there is a shower and laundry block nearby. Close beyond the old quay the first of the Badholmarna pontoons will be seen. This is the only one where visiting yachts may find a berth as the other pontoons, tucked between the low rocky islands, are in depths limited to small runabouts only. There is water on the pontoon, but no electricity. Shore facilities are shared with the Kajen berths.

Northwest of the three small, low islands lies Bäckmansviken guest harbour – effectively four pontoons set in a rough square, with a single narrow entrance and some 20 berths inside in depths of 1·5–3m. It is unsuitable for vessels of more than about 11m (unless exceptionally manoeuvrable), but larger yachts may find a bows-to berth on the

Hökö, north of Arkösund *P. and G. Price*

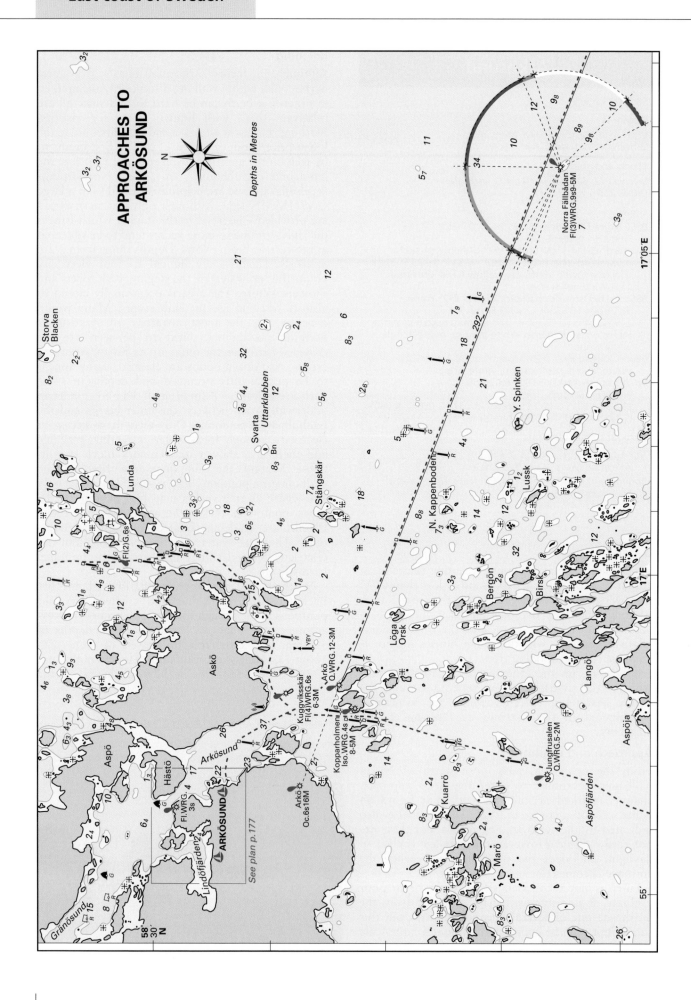

APPROACHES TO
ARKÖSUND

N

Depths in Metres

Norra Fällbådan
Fl(3)WRG.9s9-5M
7

Storva
Blacken

Lunda

Svarta
Uttarklabben

Stängskär

Askö

Kuggviksskär
Fl(4)WRG.6s
6-3M

Arkö
Q.WRG.12-3M

Kopparholmen
Iso.WRG.4s
8-5M

Jungfrusalen
Q.WRG.5-2M

N. Kappenboden

Y. Spinken

Lussk

Bergön

Birsk

Löga
Orsk

Langö

Aspöja

Aspö

Hästö

Arkösund

ARKÖSUND

Fl.WRG. 4
3s

Arkö
Oc.6s16M

See plan p.177

Lindöfjärden

Gränösund

Kuarrö

Marö

Aspöfjärden

58°
30′
N

17°05′E

17′E

55′

26′

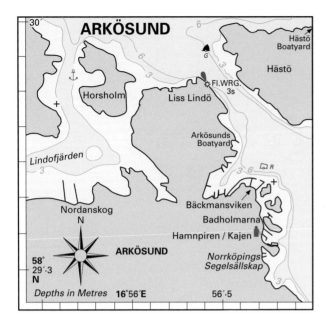

ARKÖSUND

pontoon just beyond. Shore facilities are shared with Kajen and Badholmarna. The red pillar buoy just off the guest harbour marks a rocky shoal and should be left to port on entry. Through the narrows between Liss Lindö and Hästö, and past the small island of Horshol, a channel to the southwest gives onto Lindöfjärden and the two long pontoons of Nordanskog yacht harbour. The 20 or so visitors' berths are at the outer ends of both pontoons in 2·5–3m, bows-to with the stern to a buoy. There is neither water nor electricity on the pontoons, though there are taps near their roots. Toilets and showers will be found at the nearby campsite Arkö Camp Strandgrillen where berthing fees are paid (open 0900–2100) and there is also a restaurant and small shop.

There are no restrictions on anchoring in this area. One recommended spot is west of Horsholm island.

Services for yachts

There is a fuel berth near the root of the old quay amongst the Hamnpiren/Kajen berths, the kiosk also contains a small shop. There are two boatyards in the area, the Arkösunds Båtvarv at Rökholmen on the Liss Lindö peninsula, and Hästö Båtvarv on the northern side of Hästö island. Arkösunds Båtvarv, ☎ +46 125 20053, open 0800–1630 weekdays only, can be reached on foot and has a 5·5 tonne crane and a small engineering workshop. Hästö Båtvarv, ☎ +46 125 20073, is larger if less accessible, though several buoys are available for visitors. It has an 8-tonne crane, open air and undercover storage, a diving service, large engineering workshop and GRP repair facilities.

General facilities

Arkösund is a very popular tourist spot, with several cafés and restaurants and at least one large hotel. The tourist office (open 1000–1200 and 1400–2000), at which berthing fees for both Badholmarna and Bäckmansviken guest harbours are payable, is within the hotel grounds. A

supermarket is situated near the root of the Bäckmansviken pontoon, but there is no bank or Post Office. There is a regular bus service to Norrköping, connecting with the railway system and convenient if changing crews.

Oxelösund

58°39'·3N 17°06'·1E
Chart Swedish 6211 SW
Distances Arkö Sund 14M, Nyköping 10M
Värd ☎ +46 70 213 40 66
Oxelösunds Båtvarv ☎ +46 155 308 27

General

A large town with a conspicuous ironworks on the east. Not the most attractive place but good for crew changes, stores and repairs.

Gamla Oxelösund is an island museum of restored buildings and there are well displayed remains of Cold War defences to the south of the entrance.

Approach and berthing

The prominent chimneys of the ironworks make a useful landmark, the entrance is very well buoyed and easy to follow to the two *gästhamns*.

First and to the south is the Fiskehamnen with 25 visitors' berths. Larger yachts will find greater depths of 2·5m to 4·5m here. Oxelösunds Båtvarv at the head of the Fiskehamnen offers all kinds of repair and has laying up facilities.

Half a mile to the north and closest to the town is the well laid out Badhusviken marina with 80 visitors' berths and fuel but with only 1·2–2·8m. There is a good chandlery at the offices and both *gästhamns* have a full range of services.

General facilities

Both marinas have their own restaurants and there is a tourist information office and excellent children's playground at Badhusviken. The shopping precinct has good shops, a very good supermarket and Systembolaget. A free 'Tuf-Tuf' train takes you the 1km up the hill to the town centre and back every half hour otherwise bicycles are an advantage. There is a very modern church on the hill in town.

Less than half an hour by taxi to the airport at Skavsta.

Nyköping

58°44'·6N 17°01'·3E
Chart 6211 NW
Distances Oxelösund 10M, Landsort 30M
Värd ☎ +46 155 21 72 30

General

An attractive small commercial and yachting harbour with the town marina on the west of the entrance and the large *gästhamn* and boat yard on the east.

The town itself is divided by a river and has a mediaeval castle.

3. SWEDEN

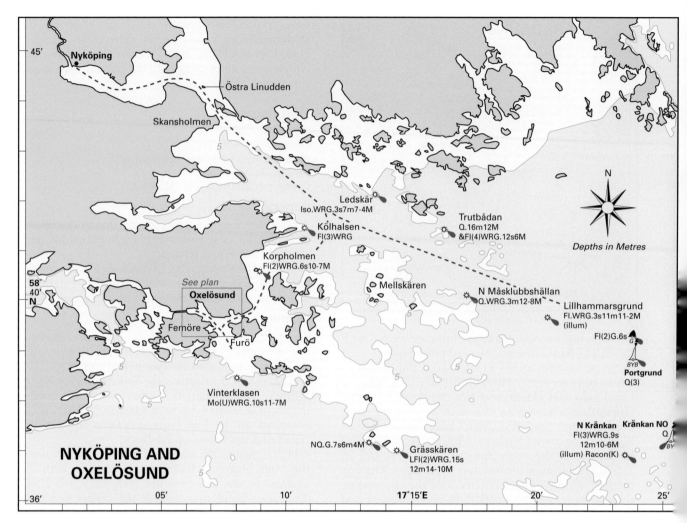

NYKÖPING AND OXELÖSUND

Ledskär
Iso.WRG.3s7m7-4M

Kölhalsen
Fl(3)WRG

Korpholmen
Fl(2)WRG.6s10-7M

See plan
Oxelösund

Femöre

Furö

Vinterklasen
Mo(U)WRG.10s11-7M

Trutbådan
Q.16m12M
&Fl(4)WRG.12s6M

Mellskären

N Måsklubbshällan
Q.WRG.3m12-8M

Lillhammarsgrund
Fl.WRG.3s11m11-2M
(illum)

Fl(2)G.6s

Portgrund
Q(3)

N Kränkan
Fl(3)WRG.9s
12m10-6M
(illum) Racon(K)

Kränkan NO

NQ.G.7s6m4M

Grässkären
LFl(2)WRG.15s
12m14-10M

Depths in Metres

Approach and berthing.

There is a well marked approach from the Lillhammarsgrund light (58°39′·7N 17°20′·3E) approx 4M off shore. This shoals to a 4m dredged channel at the Skansholmen Narrows, turns west at the Östra Linudden marker where it bears to port

again and is too restricted to sail unless you are lucky enough to have a favourable wind. The *gästhamn* provides 110 berths with the wider ones being first to starboard as you enter. The inside berths have a max width of 3·8m. Larger vessels can also tie up on the outside of the outside pontoons but passing high speed motor boats can create a tiresome wash. All the usual services are available and Wi-Fi at some berths. The very capable boat yard and a chandlery are a little further east

General

There is a substantial supermarket which will deliver to the boat, situated conveniently opposite the Systembolaget, and several good restaurants in the middle of the town. The *gästhamn* is only fifteen minutes by taxi from Skavsta airport which provides regular cheap flights to Stansted via Ryanair. Although a good place for crew changes or leaving one's boat it is further from the sea than Oxelösund.

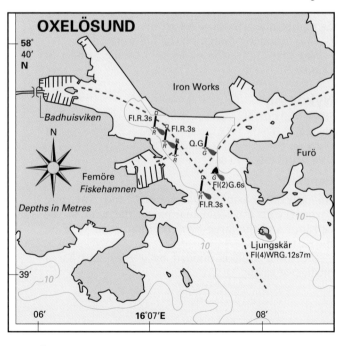

OXELÖSUND

Iron Works

Badhuisviken

Fl.R.3s

Fl.R.3s

Q.G.

Femöre
Fiskehamnen

Depths in Metres

Furö

Fl(2)G.6s

Fl.R.3s

Ljungskär
Fl(4)WRG.12s7m

3g. Södertälje, Stockholm, the Archipelago and Lake Mälaren

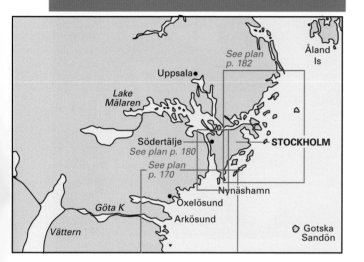

Södertälje and the Södertälje Kanal

59°12'N 17°38'E

Distances

Västervik 95M, Arkösund 60M, Nynäshamn 40M, Lake Mälaren (from Mälarbron bridge) 5M

Charts and guides

UKHO 2362, 3147, 3170, 3168
Swedish 11, 6172, 6181
Swedish *Båtsportkort*: Mälaren

Lights

6583·6 **Landsorts Bredgrund** 58°43'·9N 17°51'·9E
  Iso.WRG.4s18m16–12M
  001°-R-013°-G-047·5°-W-053°-R-086°-G-127°-R-159°-G-
  177°-R-210°-G-217°-W-219°-R-224°-G-234°-R-273°-G-
  321·5°-R-345°-G-356·5°-W-001° Racon. Orange tower.
  Floodlit
6584 **Landsort, south point** 58°44'·4N 17°52'·1E
  Fl(1+4)60s44m22M+F.WRG.27m14–9M
  323·5°-G-351°-W-358°-R-023° White tower, red top
  25m
6732 **Asenskallen** 58°47'N 17°42'·1E
  Fl.WRG.3s12m8–5M
  091°-G-106°-W-110°-R-238°-G-259°-W-267°-R-277°-G-
  294°-R-300° White tower, green band 9m
6675 **Granklubben** 58°47'·9N 17°44'·9E
  Iso.WRG.3s13m13–9M
  225°-G-298°-R-312·5°-G-317·5°-W-320°-R-329·5°-G-
  011°-W-054°-R-075° White lantern

Harbour communications

Södertälje Kanal ☎ +46 8 554 22720/22730/1/2
  Traffic Information Centre VHF Ch 68
  Smallcraft VHF Ch 14
Södertälje Commercial Harbour ☎ +46 8 550 23740/23750
  VHF Ch 11, 14, 16
Södertälje Guest Harbour ☎ +46 8 550 64712
  Mobile 070 310 6449
Järnvägs and Motorvägsbroarna bridges VHF Ch 16, 68
Slussbron lock and bridge VHF Ch 14, 16, 68
Mälarbron bridge VHF Ch 14, 16, 68

General

Södertälje (pronounced *Seu-dehr-tehl-je*) is a commercial port and town of about 25,000 inhabitants on the canal of the same name, the southern of Stockholm's two 'back entrances' (see page 184). First dug in 1819, and enlarged to take vessels of 7·5m draught in 1924, a surprising tonnage of commercial traffic still uses the Södertälje Kanal each year.

If heading northwards from the latitude of Nyköping, the *skärgård* is entered at the Landsort lights where a lumpy sea can build in northerly winds. In such conditions – and particularly if there are children or less enthusiastic sailors aboard – the well sheltered and interesting approach to Stockholm offered by the Södertälje Kanal may prove a real boon. This is the southern entrance to Lake Mälaren.

Approach and entrance

The long southern approach to the lock at Södertälje is intricate and poorly buoyed in places, making large scale charts a necessity. Rocks and shoals litter the area, though in good visibility the main channel – which is dredged to 9m – should not be difficult to follow. From a point west of the Landsort lights, the channel leads into the Himmerfjärden, a long and relatively straight fjord which trends northnorthwest for more than 30M before it reaches Lake Mälaren at Viksberg. Over its length the fjord changes its name several times before reaching Södertälje's two sections of canal, the Södra Kanalen and Norra Kanalen, separated by a single lock.

Approaching from the south, as the waterway narrows vessels pass under a railway bridge (40m clearance), before reaching the canal proper. Some 0·3M into the canal's narrow section lies a second railway bridge, with a motorway bridge just beyond (the Järnvägs and Motorvägsbroarna bridges, both clearance 25·9m), which open simultaneously. A request for opening, if required, should be made to Södertäjle VTS ☎ +46 8554 24500 or VHF Ch 68, who will advise times.

The guest harbour, lock and associated road bridge lie about 0·5M further on. The lock, which has a rise of less than 1m, accommodates vessels of up to 120m and 5·5m draught. It operates 0815–2115, opening southbound at 15 minutes past the hour and northbound immediately following the southbound lock, and is crossed by a low bridge which opens in conjunction with the lock gates. A third road bridge, the Mälarbron bridge, is encountered some 0·4M beyond the lock, close to the northern end of the canal. This bridge (clearance 13·8m) opens at approximately 2hr intervals 0900–2100 weekdays and hourly 0800–2100 weekends.

3. SWEDEN

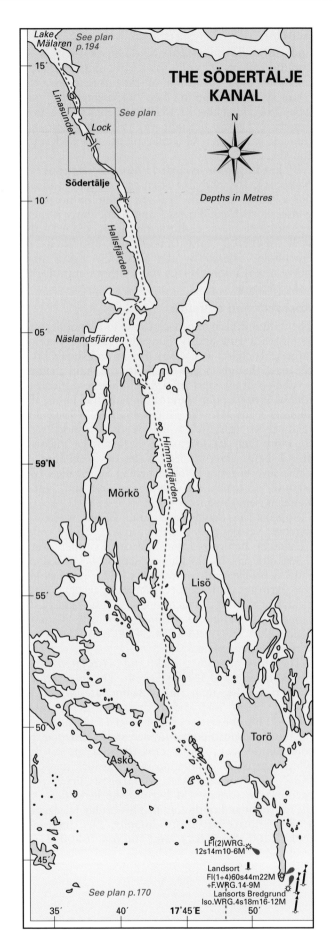

THE SÖDERTÄLJE
KANAL

N

Depths in Metres

Lake Mälaren
See plan p.194
15′
Linasundet
See plan
Lock
Södertälje
10′
Hallsfjärden
05′
Näslandsfjärden
59°N
Mörkö
Himmerfjärden
55′
Lisö
50′
Torö
Askö
45′
LFl(2)WRG.
12s14m10-6M
Landsort
Fl(1+4)60s44m22M
+F.WRG.14-9M
Lansorts Bredgrund
Iso.WRG.4s18m16-12M
See plan p.170
35′   40′   17°45′E   50′

Yachts heading south out of the single lock on the
Södertälje Kanal   *A. Hammick*

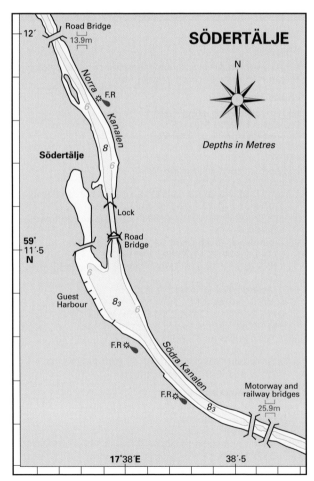

SÖDERTÄLJE

N

Depths in Metres

12′
Road Bridge
13.9m
Norra Kanalen
F.R
6
8
Södertälje
6
Lock
Road Bridge
59°
11′·5
N
6
Guest
Harbour
8₃
6
F.R
Södra Kanalen
F.R
Motorway and
railway bridges
25.9m
F.R
8₃
17°38′E   38′·5

Regulations

Sailing in the canal is forbidden between the south end of the Södra Kanalen and Linasundet to the north, and commercial shipping takes precedence over leisure craft at all times. It is recommended, but not mandatory, that smallcraft monitor VHF Ch 16 and 68 whilst in the canal section. There is no space for even a small yacht to pass a ship in the canal or lock, so all vessels must obey the light signals situated on the east bank at each end of the canal and at the lock – 2Iso.R.3s signifies STOP or DO NOT ENTER. Yachts may not pass through the lock at the same time as commercial vessels – permission to enter is given on VHF Ch 68 or by loudspeaker.

Berthing

There are waiting berths (to starboard on approaching) both below and above the lock, but for a longer stay use the guest harbour, ① +46 8 550 64712. *Email* info@sghc.net, www.sghc.net, on the west side of the channel just south of the lock. This has 90 visitors' berths in 2–8m depths, mostly bows-to between narrow, buoyed fingers. Enter any berth on arrival unless actually marked 'private' or 'reserved'. The harbour office, open 0730–2200 in summer, is situated in the café/shop about 50m south of the pontoons. Berthing fees are in the middle band (see page 112).

Services for yachts

Water and electricity are provided on the pontoons, with showers and launderette ashore. Fuelling berth (diesel and petrol) close south, near the café and shop. There is reported to be a good chandlery in the town.

General facilities

All the facilities of a good-sized town are within walking distance, with the bonus of an excellent swimming pool complex. The station, which has a frequent service to Stockholm, is only five minutes' walk from the harbour.

Nynäshamn

58°54′N 17°57′E

Distances

Västervik 85M, Arkösund 50M, Södertälje 40M, Saltsjöbaden 35M, Stockholm (via the Baggensstäket) 45M, Stockholm (via the *skärgård*) 70+M, Sandhamn 45M

Charts and guides

Swedish 11, 61, 72, 616, 6171
Båtsportkort A: *Stockholm Södra*
UKHO 2362, 3147, 3143, 3191

Lights

Southern approach

6583·6 **Landsorts Bredgrund** 58°43′·9N 17°52′·5E
Iso.WRG.4s19m16–12M
001°-R-113°-G-047·5°-W-053°-R-086°-G-127°-R-159°-G-177°-R-210°-G-217°-W-219°-R-224°-G-234°-R-273°-G-321·5°-R-345°-G-356·5°-W-001° Racon Orange tower Floodlit

6584 **Landsort, south point** 58°44′·4N 17°52′·1E
Fl(1+4)60s44m22M+F.WRG.27m14–9M
323·5°-G-351°-W-358°-R-023° White tower, red top 25m

6594 **Gunnarstenarna** 58°46′·5N 18°03′·3E
LFl(2)WRG.15s14m8–5M
000°-R-019°-G-038°-R-102°-G-142·5°-W-152·5°-R-180°-G-235°-W-000° White structure on red base

6596 **Måsknuv** 58°51′·4N 18°01′·1E
Mo(A)WRG.8s13m13–9M
008·5°-G-020°-W-024°-R-029°-W-156·5°-G-171°-W-182·5°-R-188°-G-195·5°-W-213°-R-217·5° White tower 10m

6602 **Trehörningen** 58°53′·5N 17°56′·8E
IVQ.WRG.6s8m10–6M
315°-G-358·5°-W-359·5°-R-025° White square metal framework tower

6606 **Bedarö** 58°53′·8N 17°56′·6E
Iso.WRG.4s2m7–5M 020·5°-G-033·5°-W-036°-R-043°-115°-G-163°-W-177°-R-195° White lantern

6610 **Strathmos Lts in Line** 315° *Front* 58°54′·8N 17°57′·7E
F.R.8m2M Red ▲ on pillar

6610·1 *Rear* 100m from front F.R.11m2M Red ▲ on pillar

Northern approach

6598 **Örngrund** 58°53′·8N 18°01′·5E
Q.WRG.10m10–6M
010°-W-020·5°-R-105°-G-131·5°-W-147°-R-195°-G-232·5°-W-246°-R-290°-G-340°-W-344·5°-R-358°-G-010° Black GRP tower, red band on concrete base

6614 **Brunsviksholmen** 58°55′·1N 17°58′·7E
Fl(2)WRG.6s8m12–7M
270°-R-279·5°-G-296·5°-W-306·5°-R-317°-G-323°-W-327°-R-000°-G-039°-W-043°-R-047·5° White tower 8m

Harbour communications

Nynäshamn Commercial Harbour ① +46 8520 10615, *VHF* Ch 11, 16

Nynäshamn Guest Harbour ① +46 8520 11635
Email info@nynashamn.se
www.nynashamn.se/gasthamn

General

If electing to take one of the outside routes north to Stockholm, leave Landsort to port and this is the first significant town to be encountered. A growing town with an attractive older centre near the large marina, the wide variety of shops and particularly good market make Nynäshamn (pronounced Nu-nairs-hahmn) a convenient place for storing up. Although large by Swedish standards, visitors

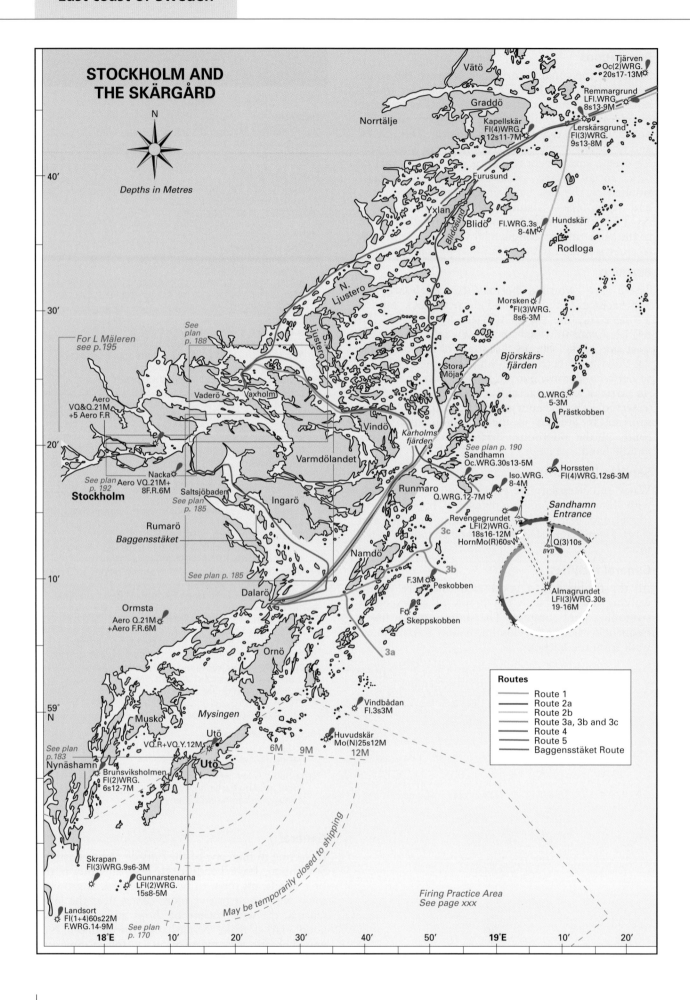

STOCKHOLM AND
THE SKÄRGÅRD

N

Depths in Metres

40'

Vätö

Graddö

Norrtälje

Tjärven
Oc(2)WRG.
20s17-13M

Remmargrund
LFl.WRG.
8s13-9M

Kapellskär
Fl(4)WRG.
12s11-7M

Lerskärsgrund
Fl(3)WRG.
9s13-8M

Furusund

Yxlan

Blidö

Fl.WRG.3s
8-4M

Hundskär

Rodloga

30'

N.
Ljustero

See plan p. 188

Morsken
Fl(3)WRG.
8s6-3M

*For L Mäleren
see p.195*

Ljustero

Stora
Möja

Björskärs-
fjärden

Aero
VQ&Q.21M
+5 Aero F.R

Vaderö

Vaxholm

Q.WRG.
5-3M

Prästkobben

Vindö

20'

Karholms
fjärden

See plan p. 190
Sandhamn
Oc.WRG.30s13-5M

Horssten
Fl(4)WRG.12s6-3M

Varmdölandet

Iso.WRG.
8-4M

*See plan
p. 192*
Stockholm

Nacka

Aero VQ.21M+
8F.R.6M

Runmaro

Q.WRG.12-7M

Sandhamn
Entrance

Saltsjöbaden

*See plan
p. 185*

Ingarö

Revengegrundet
LFl(2)WRG.
18s16-12M
HornMo(R)60s

Q(3)10s

BYB

Rumarö

Baggensstäket

3c

Namdö

3b

Almagrundet
LFl(3)WRG.30s
19-16M

See plan p. 185

Dalarö

F.3M

Peskobben

Ormsta

Aero Q.21M
+Aero F.R.6M

F.

Skeppskobben

Ornö

3a

Routes
— Route 1
— Route 2a
— Route 2b
— Route 3a, 3b and 3c
— Route 4
— Route 5
— Baggensstäket Route

Vindbådan
Fl.3s3M

59°
N

Musko

Mysingen

Utö

VQ.R+VQ.Y.12M

6M

9M

Huvudskär
Mo(N)25s12M

12M

*See plan
p.183*
Nynäshamn

Utö

Brunsviksholmen
Fl(2)WRG.
6s12-7M

May be temporarily closed to shipping

Skrapan
Fl(3)WRG.9s6-3M

Gunnarstenarna
LFl(2)WRG.
15s8-5M

*Firing Practice Area
See page xxx*

Landsort
Fl(1+4)60s22M
F.WRG.14-9M

*See plan
p. 170*

18°E 10' 20' 30' 40' 50' **19°E** 10' 20'

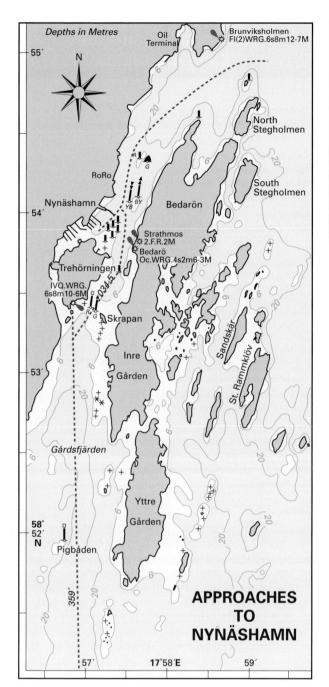

**APPROACHES
TO
NYNÄSHAMN**

The marina buildings at Nynäshamn, looking northwest
A. Hammick

sometimes report trouble in finding a berth in the marina, particularly if poor weather has driven yachts into the marina from the surrounding island anchorages.

Approach and entrance

The southern approach is straightforward, provided the red pillar buoy marking Pigbåden shoal is left well to port. The passage between Trehörningen and Skrapan islands, taken on 034·5°, is no more than 100m in width but is well buoyed and carries a minimum of 4m. The marina is approached around the north end of Trehörningen island, from which shoals extend nearly 400m to the northeast. No liberties should be taken with the buoyage.

From the north, approach can be made from the wide Mysingen passage which separates the island of Utö from mainland Sweden. There are two shoals to

be avoided once within a mile of the marina, but both are well buoyed. From the outer skärgård, and armed with the necessary large-scale Swedish charts, it is possible to sail through the gap between Utö and Ornö, either north or south of Långbäling and Marbäling. At one time closed to yachts entirely, some restrictions remain and anchoring, scuba diving and fishing are still forbidden in the area. There is a firing range to the southeast of Utö which extends up to 12M offshore and which may be temporarily closed to navigation – see page 363 for contact details.

Anchorage.

There is too much traffic to anchor off Nynäshamn itself, with commercial ships including cruise liners and ferries berthing north of the marina, but plenty of possibilities exist amongst the nearby islands.

Berthing

Nynäshamn marina, ☏ +46 8 520 11635, *Fax* +46 8 520 21306, office hours 0800–2200, is a large marina with some 200 visitors' berths in 4–10m depths. Most berths are provided with booms rather than stern buoys. Many of the berths are narrow by UK standards. All berths, other than those very close to the shore, are available to visitors. Berthing fees are in the middle band, but halve if the yacht is not occupied.

Services for yachts

Most, though not all, berths have access to water and electricity, with showers, a sauna and laundry facilities ashore. Fuel (diesel and petrol) from the Shell berth close north of the marina ☏ +46 8 520 11268, open 0900–2100 mid-season, otherwise 0900–1800) where bottled gas is also available. There are at least two boatyards near the marina, both with extensive chandleries. Charts are available from the chandleries as well as from the Bokia bookstore in town. Dyk and Marin, ☏ +46 8 520 13928, provide a dive service and will refill scuba tanks. A daily weather forecast is posted outside the marina office.

General facilities

All the usual facilities of a medium sized town, including good shopping, the aforementioned market and a Systembolaget liquor store. Many pavement cafés and restaurants near the waterfront, including two in the marina itself. There is an excellent smokery on the quay.

Communications and travel

The marina is immediately adjacent to the railway station with a direct line to Stockholm (about one hour), making it a convenient spot for crew changes or from which to explore the capital. Ferries run to Gotland, Poland and Russia from berths north of the marina. From beside the marina during the season but subject to the weather, there is a regular ferry to the Gotska Sandon National Park about 40M north of Gotland.

The marina office is happy to hold mail for visiting yachts (Nynäshamns Gästhamn, Fiskargränd 5, 14930 Nynäshamn, Sweden) and to send and receive faxes (*Fax* +46 8 520 21306). Internet access is available at the library and there is Wi-Fi at the marina.

Saltsjöbaden and the Baggensstäket

59°16'N 18°19'E

Distances
Nynäshamn 35M, Stockholm (via the Baggensstäket) 10M, Sandhamn 25M

Charts and guides
Swedish 11, 61, 6145, 6142
Båtsportkort A: Stockholms skärgård
UKHO 2362, 3143

Lights
6658 **Fjärdhällan** 59°09'·3N 18°33'·3E
    Fl.WRG.3s7m7–4M 006°-R-031°-G-063·5°-W-069°-R-109°-G-177°-R-199°-G-202°-W-205°-R-208°-G-255°-W-006° White round tower, black base 7m
6660 **Grönö** 59°12'·5N 18°34'E Iso.WRG.4s7m5–3M
    shore-G-246°-W-307·5°-R-331°-G-352°-W-358°-R-015°-G-053·5°-W-079°-R-092° Red tower, white top 8m
6654 **Boo** 59°18'·6N 18°17'·8E Fl(2)6s2m6M White hut, green band
6549 **Kingshamn** 59°20'·1N 18°12'·6E Fl.WRG.3s6m6-4-3M
    shore-G-058·5°-W-062°-R-076·5°-G-091°-W-098°-R-205°-G-219°-W-227·5°-R-shore White lantern

Harbour communications
KSSS Marina ☎ +46 871 70856
    Email ksss@ksss.se www.ksss.se
Pålnäsviken
Mobile ☎ +46 707 18 93 87
    Email kontakta@saltsjobadensbatklubb.se
    www.saltsjobadensbatklubb.se

The Baggensstäket, the southeastern passage into the centre of Stockholm *P. and G. Price*

General

Saltsjöbaden (pronounced *Sahlt-sheu-bahd-ehn*) has long been a popular spa and summer holiday resort, surrounded by attractive countryside and only half an hour by rail from Stockholm. It is the mainland headquarters of the Kungl Svenska Segel Sällskapet (Royal Swedish Yacht Club, better known as KSSS), whose extremely helpful staff also administer one of the two marinas. The narrow Baggensstäket (pronounced *Bahggehns- stairck-eht*) forms the southeastern – and smaller – of Stockholm's two 'back entrances'.

Approach and entrance

The approach up the wide Ingaröfjärden, giving onto the Ägnöfjärden and the Baggensfjärden, is largely unbuoyed, and if unfamiliar with the waters a large scale chart is essential. Saltsjöbaden lies at the south end of the Baggensfjärden and 2M short of the narrow entrance to the Baggensstäket and the Skurusundet – a long, winding but very attractive gorge which runs for 5M between high wooded banks to Kungshamn, less than 4M from the city centre. Depths in the Baggensstäket are least at its southeastern end, with under 3m in some sections. The channel has no locks and is crossed by a single bridge with 30m clearance. The narrowest sections are controlled by sound signals shown on boards.

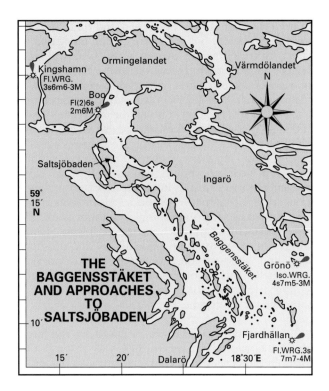

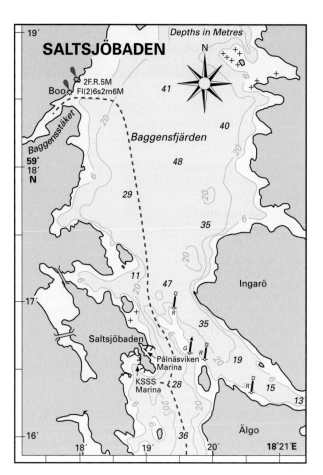

Anchorage

There are many possible anchorages in the Ingaröfjärden, Ägnöfjärden and Baggensfjärden, and possibly in the wider sections of the final stretch.

Berthing

Saltsjöbaden has two marinas – the Pålnäsviken (Saltsjöbadens båtklubb) and the larger KSSS marina to the west. The former is small with just five guest moorings but the KSSS marina reserves some three dozen berths for visitors (indicated by green buoys) in depths of 2·5–12m, though it has on occasion fitted in as many as 80 visitors. Although the marina has several different sections, visitors should pass south of the small central island when the pontoons will be seen to starboard. Mooring is, as usual, bows-to with a buoy astern.

Services for yachts

Water and electricity are provided on the KSSS pontoons, with a card phone, toilets, showers and launderette near the marina office. There is a small engineering workshop at their clubhouse, and the very helpful staff would doubtless assist in organising any other work which needed to be done. They will also advise regarding possible yards in which to lay up ashore. Fuel and bottled gas are available at the Pålnäsviken marina, east of the central island, and there are a number of boatyards in the area.

General facilities

A small kiosk near the station sells basic groceries, otherwise a 20 minute walk inland or three stops on the train (ask for directions at the marina office) takes one to the large shopping mall at Tippen, which also has Post Office, bank, Systembolaget and much more. The imposing Grand Hotel, with café

and restaurant (booking essential), overlooks the harbour. Fast trains run every 20 minutes to the centre of Stockholm – an attractive and interesting ride in itself which takes about half an hour. The station is only a few minutes' walk from the harbour.

The Kungl Svenska Segel Sällskapet (KSSS) marina at Saltsjöbaden, looking northwest towards the towering Grand Hotel   A. Hammick

3. SWEDEN

Stockholm and its archipelago – the *skärgård*

Charts and guides

Swedish 11, 61, 616, 615, 613, 612, 611, 719, 6161, 6145, 6144, 6143, 6142, 6141

Swedish *Båtsportkort: Stockholm S, M and N.*

UKHO 2362, 3143, 3144, 3127, 3163, 3157, 3156, 3155, 3114

Stockholms Skärgård från Luften (The Stockholm Archipelago from the Air) Vols 1 & 2

Principal lights

6584 **Landsort, south point** 58°44'·4N 17°52'·1E
Fl(1+4)60s44m22M+F.WRG.27m14–9M
323·5°-G-351°-W-358°-R-023° White tower, red top 25m

6576 **Huvudskär** 58°57'·8N 18°34'·1E Mo(N)25s26m12–5M
White tower, black band 15m

6465 **Almagrundet** 59°09'·3N 19°07'·5E Fl(4)WR.12s13m
045°-R-225°(180°)-W-045° Floodlit Helipad

6460 **Svenska Högarna** 59°26'·6N 19°30'·1E
LFl.15s31m15M Red metal tower 18m

6386 **Tjärven** 59°47'·5N 19°22'·2E
Fl(4)W.12s15M

General

Most yachtsmen working their way north along the east coast of Sweden will want to visit Stockholm, one of the most beautiful cities of northern Europe and offering a huge amount for all tastes. In particular, the incomparable Wasa museum must not be missed. Three entirely separate routes give access to the city, that through the offlying archipelago or skärgård being further subdivided into two major channels with potentially innumerable variations. The most southerly approach is the 'back entrance' via the Södertälje Kanal (see page 179), which leads from a point west of Landsort directly into Lake Mälaren west of the city. The southwesterly approach via the narrow Baggensstäket (see page 184) departs from the inner leads near Dalarö to emerge at Kungshamn less than 4M east of the city centre. The skärgård route from the western Baltic twists through a myriad of possible channels to pass close to Vaxholm and enter the city from the northeast.

The Skärgård (pronounced shair-gord)

The Stockholm Archipelago or skärgård is a vast area of islands stretching from Landsort in the southwest to Tjärven, on the edge of the Åland Sea, in the northeast. It is quite heavily populated, particularly during the summer, and is very popular with Swedish yachtsmen but, nevertheless, offers a most attractive cruising ground where one could wander for a month without ever repeating an anchorage or feeling crowded.

The inner skärgård is dotted with small guest harbours, though there are few marinas of any size other than those at Sandhamn – see page 190 – and Bullandö. The outer archipelago however, to the north and east of Sandhamn, presents a wild and challenging cruising ground. This area is well charted, though largely unbuoyed and quite heavily rock-encumbered, but with care can be navigated in safety to reach some of the most beautiful and remote anchorages in the whole of the Baltic. In the skärgård, as elsewhere on the Swedish coast, ensuring that one keeps a constant and accurate track of one's position among the numerous reefs and islands is vital, and all the advice given for the Blåkusten (Blue Coast) (see page 169) applies equally here. If following the well-charted routes you should have few problems but if you go 'off piste' take particular care. Cruising in the archipelago involves navigating within metres of rocks – electronics are of very limited use and 'eyeballing' is without doubt the only satisfactory approach to the problem. Strong winds can blow up quite suddenly, kicking up short seas, and although the numerous islands provide some shelter this is not a place where one can expect to find calm conditions inside them. The need for a complete set of current, large-scale Swedish charts is clear.

A further potential hazard is posed by the large modern ferries which weave their way through the tortuous passages which characterise much the inner approaches to Stockholm. At times a ferry's upperworks may be visible behind a nearby island, looking like a moving block of flats. It cannot be stressed too often that these ferries have absolute right of way AT ALL TIMES. Some of the 'pinch points' are so narrow that they do not allow room for a ferry to pass even a small yacht, and the vast difference in speeds should be taken into account whenever one of these gaps is approached – not forgetting to look astern as well as ahead, of course.

If intending the explore the skärgård in any detail, a copy of the two volume *Stockholms Skärgård från Luften* (The Stockholm Archipelago from the Air) published by the Svenska Kryssarklubben (Swedish Cruising Club) would be a very worthwhile investment. Ringbound and with text in Swedish, English and German, the two books – covering Öregrund to Sandhamn and Sandhamn to Landsort respectively – contain black and white aerial photographs of some seventy small harbours, islands and fairways with accompanying description. Two free publications produced by the Skärgårdsstiftelsen (Archipelago Foundation) are *Skärgårds Natur*, published annually in Swedish only but including some plans and colour photographs of use to all, and *The Archipelago Foundation*, an attractive little booklet printed in a number of languages including English. Although intended primarily for those visiting by ferry, it includes useful details of the facilities to be found on a number of the larger islands. Those with access to the internet should definitely explore the excellent, multi-language Skärgårdsstiftelsen website at www.skargardsstiftelsen.se

Top Stockholm's inner *skärgård* A. Hammick

Middle Rödlöga, in Stockholm's outer *skärgård*. The smooth rocks and red roofs are typical *E. and M. Bonham Cozens*

Above The well-protected anchorage at Ärholma in the northern *skärgård*. The island was off limits for some years but may now be visited *E. and M. Bonham Cozens*

Routes within the skärgård

Since the various routes through both inner and outer *skärgårds* are effectively limitless, the following brief descriptions barely scratch the surface of what is possible. (See plan on page 182).

Route 1 Dalarö to Vaxholm
Route 2 Dalarö to Söderarm
Route 3 Dalarö to Sandhamn and the
outer skärgård
Route 4 Sandhamn to Vaxholm
Route 5 Sandhamn to Söderarm
Route 6 Söderarm to Vaxholm

Route 1 – Dalarö to Vaxholm (the inner skärgård)

This route, the latter parts of which are much used by both international and inter-island ferries, leads northeastwards up the main channel inside the islands of Nämdö (59°12'N 18°42'E), and Runmarö (59°16'N 18°44'E) before swinging west along the north coast of Vindö (19°21'N 18°41'E). It branches to pass either north or south of Kavlön and Västerholmen – via the Grindafjärden to the north or the Sandöfjärden to the south – but the two rejoin at the narrows south of Vårholma (59°25'N 18°29'E). It then continues west-northwest via the Lindalssundet to the tiny island of Brödstycket (59°25'N 18°24'E), where larger vessels turn southwest to follow the main channel to Stockholm. Smaller craft – though including some sizeable inter-island ferries – continue west towards Hästholmen (59°25'N 18°21'·5E) to take the very narrow passage between Hästholmen, Resarö and the small islands which lie between, to approach Vaxholm from the north. The entire passage measures some 35M, and for much of its distance follows major shipping channels, well buoyed and lit. (For details of Vaxholm itself, see page 191.)

Route 2 – Dalarö to Söderarm

From Dalarö northeastwards through the Stockholm *skärgård* to Söderarm (59°45'·2N 19°24'·5E), where the Åland Sea begins, there is a choice of route. The early stages of both follow Route 1, diverging where that heads west around Vindö island. There is then a choice between inner and outer passages:

a. The inner route continues northeast across the Kanholmsfjärden to pass west of Södermöja (59°24'N 18°51'·5E) and Stora Möja (59°25'·5N 18°53'E), then north via an intricate but well-marked 8M passage between smaller islands to reach the south end of Blidösund (59°35'N 18°51'E), which separates Yxlan and Blidö islands. The north end of Blidösund gives onto the main Stockholm–Åland channel, known as the Söderarm. This route measures some 50M in total and includes some very attractive stretches, especially that between Stora Möja and Blidösund. It is well buoyed, but is not lit between Stora Möja and the northern end of Blidösund.

3. SWEDEN

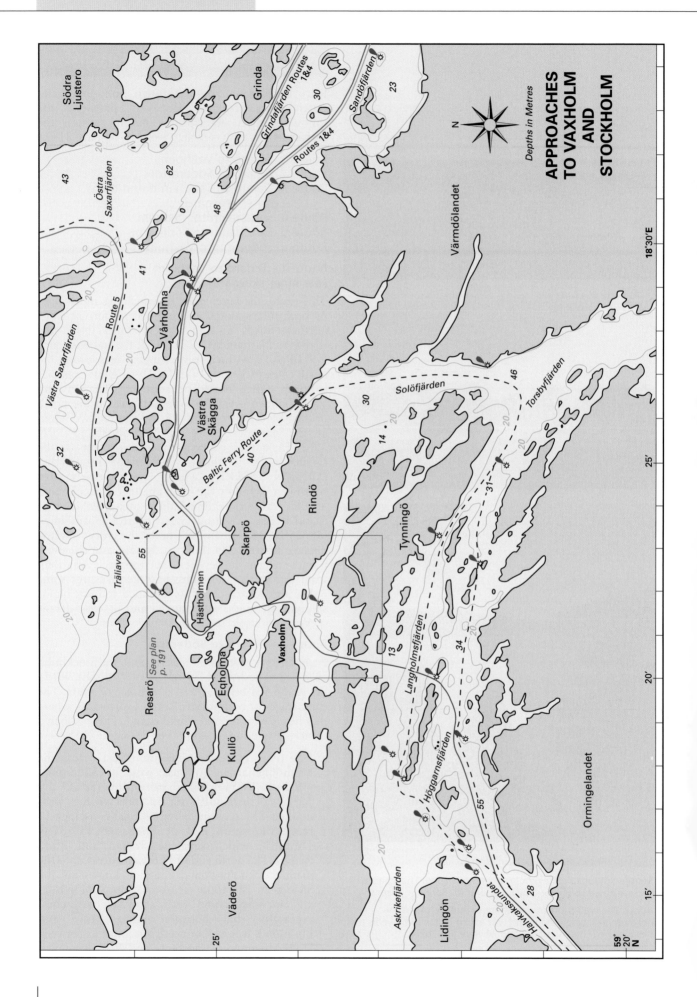

Södra
Ljustero

Grinda

Grindafjärden Routes
1&4

30

Routes 1&4

Sandöfjärden

23

Östra
Saxarfjärden

43

62

48

41

Värholma

Route 5

20

20

Västra Saxarfjärden

20

Västra
Skägga

32

Baltic Ferry Route

40

Skarpö

Rindö

Solöfjärden

30

14

20

46

Torsbyfjärden

20

20

31

Tynningö

Träliavet

55

Hästholmen

See plan
p. 191

20

20

13

34

Langholmsfjärden

55

Resarö

Eqholma

Vaxholm

Kullö

Höggarnsfjärden

Väderö

Askrikefjärden

20

Lidingön

Halvkakssundet

28

20

Ormingelandet

Värmdölandet

N

Depths in Metres

**APPROACHES
TO VAXHOLM
AND
STOCKHOLM**

18°30'E

25'

20'

15'

25'

59°
20'
N

b. The outer route follows that above as far as the south end of Södermöja, but passes east of both it and Stora Möja. It then continues northeastwards through a more open passage than that of 2a, past Morsken (59°30′·9N 19°05′·4E) and Hundskärsknuv (59°35′·9N 19°07′·5E) light structures, and rejoins the above in the vicinity of 59°43′·5N 19°10′·5E. The total distance is some 52M, and it is well buoyed and lit throughout.

Route 3 – Dalarö to Sandhamn and the outer skärgård

The outer *skärgård* is much more interesting than the inner part, with deciduous trees – birch and oak scrub – which makes a change from the monotonous fir of the inner areas. However the pilotage is considerably more difficult and demands great care. There are no floating marks – instead there are stone cairns, wooden triangles and marks painted on the rocks – but these are not shown on the charts and their significance is known only to the locals. The best routes eastward to the outer *skärgård* are as follows:

a. Via the sound south of Gillinge (59°06′·5N 18°39′E).

b. South of Mörtöklubb (59°09′N 18°37′E) a high, conspicuous islet south of the larger Mörtö, and then in a general east-northeast direction passing south of Orrön (59°10′·5N 18°42′E) and north of Måsskär (59°11′·7N 18°48′E), after which turn southeast and south.

c. To reach Sandhamn, follow the above route as far as Måsskär, continuing northeast to pass close east of Stora and Lilla Melskär (59°12′·5N 18°49′·5E). The route then leads northwest for a short distance, and then northeast again to pass west of the very conspicuous Algkobb (59°14′N 18°53′E). It then continues northeast up the Stora Skärgården between Hötterskär and Stora Hästskär, past Osterskär light (59°15′·5N 18°57′E), and finally approaches Sandhamn via the southeast entrance between Sandön and Korsö.

Route 4 – Sandhamn to Vaxholm

Leaving Sandhamn by its narrow northwest entrance, this relatively straightforward route heads northwest between Getholmen (59°15′N 18°52′·5E) and Smörasken (59°15′N 18°52′·2E) and south of Hasselkobben to emerge into the Kanholmsfjärden north of Runmarö, where it joins Route 1 towards Vaxholm. The total distance is approximately 22M.

Route 5 – Söderarm to Vaxholm

The main approach to Vaxholm from the northeast – the Söderarm – follows the main channel used by the Åland and Helsinki ferries, which are likely to pose a considerably greater threat to the average yacht than is the navigation. From the Tjärven light structure (59°47′·5N 19°22′·2E) the channels runs southwest and narrows to pass between Furusund and the north end of Yxlan island. It then splits either side of a group of small islands at 59°36′N 18°47′E, leaves the Södra Växlet shoal to the north, and continues southwest parallel to the mainland shore, north of the small islands of Långh (59°32′·2N 18°34′·4E), Huvön and beyond en route to the Trälhavet and Hästholmen (59°25′N 18°21′·5E) where it joins Route 1 for Vaxholm.

The scenery is less varied than that further south, consisting of long straight fjords fringed by long islands covered with monotonous fir trees, and there are fewer of the snug anchorages which are such a feature of the other routes. From Tjärven to Vaxholm is just over 40M.

Route 6 – Sandhamn to Söderarm

Not really a route at all …

The outer *skärgård* beyond Sandhamn is a fascinating and mysterious area. Within an area of 280M² there are some 13 individual groups of islets, each of which affords at least one beautiful, remote anchorage. As further south, the trees are mostly deciduous, and again there are no floating marks and the stone cairns, wooden triangles and painted marks are not shown on the charts. The soundings on the chart are much sparser than in the more frequented channels, but those shown can generally be relied upon. Dotted about between the main groups of islets are innumerable rocks just above or below water, so one has to pick one's way with caution. However given moderate weather and reasonable visibility the pilotage is not difficult – it simply requires great care. GPS is a very useful aid. The area may be entered either from Sandhamn, passing north of Högskär (59°17′·7N 19°01′·3E) and through the middle of the Björskärs *skärgård* (59°22′N 19°08′·2E), or from any convenient point on Route 2b northeast of Stora Möja.

Holiday cottages between Hästholmen and Skarpö just north of Vaxholm on Stockholm's outer *skärgård*   *E. Redfern*

Sandhamn

59°17'N 18°55'E

Distances
Nynäshamn 45M, Saltsjöbaden 25M, Vaxholm 20M, Stockholm 30M

Charts and guides
Swedish 61, 615, 6143, 6144
Båtsportkort: Stockholm M
UKHO 2362, 3144, 3157

Lights

Northwest approach
6495 **Yxhammarskobben** 59°18'·8N 18°48'·6E
  Fl(3)WRG.9s6–3M
  095°-W-166·5°-R-283°-G-292°-W-298°-R-022°
  Red housing on white base 7m. Floodlit
6481 **Smörasken** 59°18'N 18°52'·1E Q.6m6M Red
  structure Floodlit
6480 **Getholmen** 59°18'N 18°52'·5E Fl(2)WRG.6s11m5–3M
  shore-G-298°-W-307°-R-032°-G-102°-W-110°-R-shore
  White lantern, green band, on hut Floodlit
6478 **Farsfarsgrundet** 59°17'·7N 18°53'·3E
  Iso.WRG.5m6–3M 067°-G-122°-W-207°-R-336° Red
  structure
6472·1 **Sandhamn** 59°17'·4N 18°54'·9E
  Oc.WRG.30s10m13–5M
  294·5°-R-298·5°-G-304°-W-307°-R-314·5° & 108°-
  R(unintens)-119° Yellow tower on corner of pilot
  house 10m

Southeast approach
6470 **Revengegrundet** 59°15'·1N 19°00'·8E
  LFl(2)WRG.18s20m16–12M
  000°-W-005·5°-R-011°-G-110°-R-124°-G-137°-W-144°-R-
  160°-G-295°-W-307·5°-R-314°-G-000° Horn Mo(R)60s
  Racon Red tower, black base 21m. Floodlit
6471·6 **Svängen** 59°16'·2N 18°58'·5E
  Q.WRG.14m12–7M
  083°-G-117°-W-122°-R-186°-G-281°-R-083°
  Red tower, black bands 15m Floodlit
6472 **Prickgrundet** 59°17'·1N 18°55'·8E
  Fl(3)WRG.9s5m13–4M
  002·5°-W-084°-G-122°-R-246°-G-323°-R-002·5° White
  structure, yellow top

Harbour communications
KSSS marinas ☎ +46 857 15 32 85
  Mobile ☎ +46 702 13 20 68
  Email ksss@ksss.se
  www.ksss.se
KSSS Lökholmen ☎ +46 857 15 31 03
  Mobile ☎ +46 702 13 20 68

A seagull's eye view (courtesy of the Silja Line ferry) of Remmargrund light tower, one of the last major Swedish lights to be passed when heading for the Åland islands. Standing 20m high, it is floodlit after dark *A. Hammick*

General
Sometimes described as the 'Cowes of Sweden', Sandhamn has been the offshore home of the Royal Swedish Yacht Club, the Kungl Svenska Segel Sällskapet (KSSS) for more than a century. Additional berthing space on the adjacent island of Lökholmen was acquired in 1946. The whole area becomes very crowded in high summer, particularly in July at the time of the annual Round Gotland Race, which regularly attracts up to 500 yachts. It can, not surprisingly, be very noisy at night, particularly at weekends.

The island of Sandön is picturesque in the extreme, with clapboard houses, sanded roads and several good beaches. There is a permanent population of about 100 which increases vastly in summer, and a hotel/restaurant, the Sandhamns Värdshus, which is said to have been open throughout the year ever since 1672.

Approach and entrance
See *Routes 3 and 4* on page 189.

Berthing
Although in theory three separate marinas – the Västerhamn, the KSSS and the Österhamn – all are administered by the KSSS and share common shore facilities. Around 200 visitors berths are available on Sandhamn, in 2·5m or more, with a further 150 at Lökholmen, reached by water taxi. Berthing on one of the three marinas' six pontoons is mainly bows-to with a buoy astern, preferably as directed by one of the KSSS staff. Water and electricity is available at most berths, with showers etc ashore, and fuel from a jetty near the southeast end of the marina where holding tanks can also be emptied. Both mechanical and sail repairs can be carried out, but there would almost certainly be a considerable delay in the high season. There is a boatyard on the west side of Lökholmen but no chandlery on either island, the

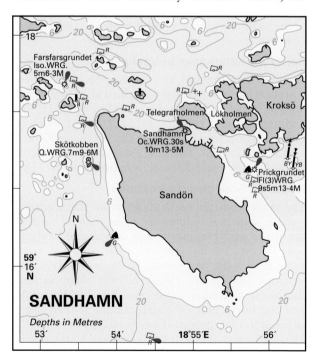

SANDHAMN
Depths in Metres

The western entrance to Sandhamn   *E. Redfern*

The Kungl Svenska Segel Sällskapet clubhouse at Sandhamn
F. and K. Williams

nearest (and that small) being close to the ferry berth at Stavsnäs.

General facilities

The island has adequate food shopping from two small supermarkets, a post office, numerous cafés, restaurants and boutiques – but no bank. There is an excellent, if expensive, bakery on the waterfront.

Vaxholm

59°24′N 18°21′E

Charts Swedish11, 61, 6142, UKHO 2362, 3155

The *skärgård* approach to Stockholm contains innumerable possible routes, but all come together northeast of Vaxholm. The main shipping channel passes east of Rindö, but most yachts will take the very narrow passage between Hästholmen, Resarö and the small islands which lie between. On approaching Vaxholm from the north, yachts are directed to pass east of the forbidding castle – which occupies an island in the centre of the channel – so leaving the western channel for the inter-island ferries.

There is a guest harbour, ☎ +46 8 541 33080, at the southeast corner of Vaxholm island which has some 100 visitors berths in depths ranging from 0·5–6m. The narrow entrance faces east and is well protected, but not surprisingly the harbour becomes very crowded and is very noisy in high summer, particularly at weekends. Berthing fees are in the middle band (see page 112). The marina has all the usual services, and there is a launderette nearby. Fuel is available at a jetty by the marina entrance or at a pontoon to the west of the castle which must be approached from the north (the last fuel before Stockholm, as neither of the city centre marinas have diesel pumps). There is good shopping close to the harbour, including one of the few Systembolagets in the *skärgård*, with more in the town proper. Frequent ferries run into central Stockholm or, for variety, take the bus over the bridges which link the island with mainland Sweden.

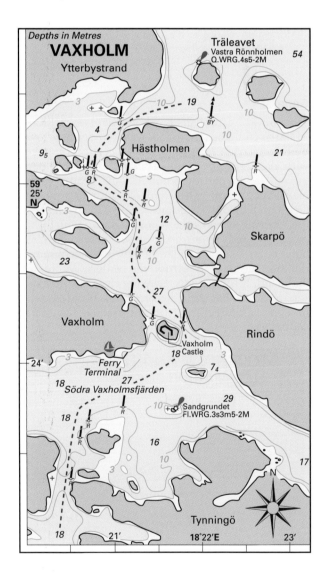

3. SWEDEN

Stockholm

59°20'N 18°04'E

Distances

Vaxholm 10M, Nynäshamn (via the Baggensstäket) 45M, Sandhamn 30M, Mariehamn 70M, Öregrund 85M

Charts and guides

Swedish 61, 11, 6142, 6141
Båtsportkort: Stockholm M
UKHO 2362, 3127, 3155, 3114

Harbour communications

Stockholm Port Authority ☎ +46 867 02600
  VHF Ch 09, 12, 16,
  Email info@stoports.com
  www.stoports.com
VTS Stockholm ☎ +46 855 42 45 00
  VHF Ch 16, 73 (yachts have no obligation to report but should maintain a listening watch on VHF Ch 73)
Wasahamnen Marina ☎ +46 866 19187
  Email info@wasahamnen.se
  www.wasahamnen.se
Navishamnen Marina ☎ +46 866 21127
(Information relating to the locks and bridges on the Hammarbyleden will be found on page 194)

General

Stockholm, established where access to Lake Mälaren could be controlled, was founded as a town by Birger Jarl in 1250, and was especially concerned with the metalwork industry which had developed inland. It was an important trading centre during Hanseatic times, when half its population was German. The old town and royal palace remain on the central island, the Gamla Stan, which has medieval and renaissance street plans. Modern Stockholm, with a population now approaching two million, has spread across the waterways to the mainland. It is a friendly, relaxing city with treelined squares and beautiful waterfronts blended with modern architecture, all intersected by busy waterways.

Stockholm has many places of cultural interest, including outstanding museums, palaces and churches. However for those of a nautical bent pride of place must go to the 17th-century man-of-war *Wasa*, raised in 1961 – seemingly almost undamaged – from the spot where she filled and sank within minutes of setting out on her maiden voyage more than 330 years earlier. The ship, together with the display of artefacts which surround her, are without equal anywhere in the world.

The website carrying the excellent nine-language *Stockholm Official Visitor's Guide*, with innumerable useful links, will be found at www.stockholmtown.com. The slightly more formal City of Stockholm website (also with English translation) is at www.stockholm.se.

Approaches

The three main approaches to Stockholm are detailed on pages 186–189.

Anchorage

Anchoring is not advisable in the main harbour area, though there are many possibilities in the approaches.

Berthing

There are several large yacht harbours in the Stockholm area, but only two which are both convenient for the city and accept visitors. There is also a public quay, normally used only by large yachts, with facilities geared to the requirements of sizeable vessels – contact the port authority before arrival. Visiting yachts of normal size have the choice of the Wasahamnen marina, sandwiched between the Vasa museum, the aquarium and the nearby Tivoli Gronalund, or the Navishamnen marina further east. Both are on the Djurgården, on the north side of the channel and well within walking distance of the city centre. As might be expected, they become very full during the holiday season and it is best to arrive early or telephone and reserve a berth in advance (preferably on an inner pontoon, as the outer berths

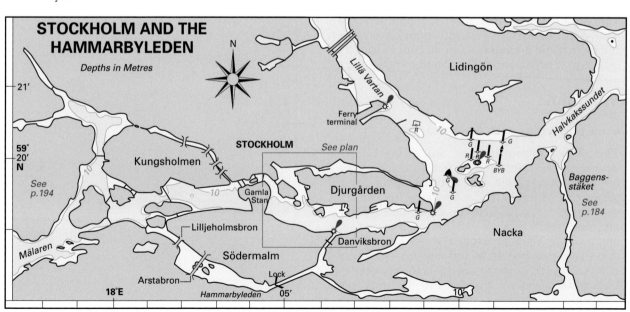

STOCKHOLM AND THE HAMMARBYLEDEN

Depths in Metres

N

Lidingön

Ferry terminal

STOCKHOLM

See plan

Kungsholmen

Djurgården

Baggens-stäket

See p.184

Gamla Stan

BYB

Lilljeholmsbron

Nacka

Mälaren

Södermalm

Danviksbron

Arstabron

Lock

Hammarbyleden

Halvkakssundet

Lillä Vartan

59° 20' N

21'

18°E   05'   10'

Might is definitely right during the final approach to Stockholm   *A. Hammick*

can be uncomfortable due to wash or strong winds). Berthing fees in both marinas are in the upper band (see page 112).

Wasahamnen Marina, ☎ +46 8 661 9187 (0800–1600), *Email* info@wasahamnen.se, www.wasahamnen.se, has around 150 visitors berths in 2–6m, arranged on two long pontoons lying parallel to the shore. Most berthing is bows-to with a stern buoy provided, though some (mostly narrow) berths have finger pontoons. On arrival, take any vacant space and report as soon as convenient to the harbour office on the inner pontoon.

Navishamnen Marina, ☎ +46 8 662 1127, about 900m southeast, has some 60 visitors berths in 2–7m depths, though more yachts may be squeezed in at times. Again, all berths are bows-to. Entry is from the east and the marina can be masked by the various houseboats and other large craft on the outer pontoon, though these do afford the inner berths some degree of protection.

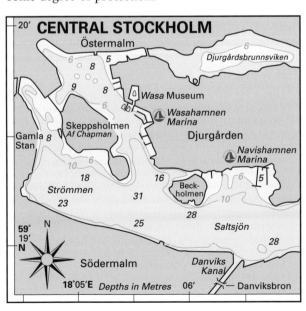

CENTRAL STOCKHOLM
20′
Östermalm
6
Djurgårdsbrunnsviken
6   8   5
9   8
Wasa Museum
6
Wasahamnen
Marina
Skeppsholmen
Af Chapman
Djurgården
Gamla 8
Stan
10 6
Navishamnen
Marina
18   16
Beck-
holmen
5
Strömmen
31
6
23
10
28
25
Saltsjön
59°
19′
N
28
N
Södermalm
Danviks
Kanal
18°05′E *Depths in Metres* 06′
Danviksbron

Formalities
Few yachts will require customs and immigration clearance on arrival at Stockholm unless non-EU registered or carrying large quantities of alcohol (perhaps following a visit to the Åland islands). If required, customs and immigration officials can be contacted on ☎ +46 771 520520.

Services for yachts
The Wasahamnen marina has electricity throughout plus a limited number of taps and hoses, with toilets, showers and laundry facilities ashore. Wi-Fi is available in most berths. There is a small foodstore in summer and many cafés and restaurants nearby. The Navishamnen marina has water and electricity on the pontoons, and toilets, showers and launderette ashore. There is a café and a small shop on site, and though there are no repair facilities as such the helpful manager will assist with organising such work as may be necessary. Neither marina sells fuel – the nearest yacht fuel is just south of Kungshamn at the north end of the Baggensskäket route – though both can arrange for propane (and possibly butane) cylinders to be refilled. Weather forecasts are displayed at both marina offices, and in addition a forecast is available, in English, on request from Stockholm Radio. Call on VHF Ch 16.

Royal Sails have a loft at Djurgården 46, directly behind the Wasahamnen marina, where all types of repair can be carried out ☎ +46 8 660 5505 *Fax* 08 662 8380, *Mobile* +46 70 589 5505, Email hans.segelmakaren@royalsails.se.   There are branches of the large Watski chandlery chain at Kommendörsgatan 26, ☎ +46 8 663 7777, (in the Östermalm area, north of Djurgården), and at Erstagaten 17 (in Södermalm on the south side of the harbour).

Swedish and foreign charts and other publications (including many books in English) are available from Nautiska Magasinet AB, at Slussplan 5 in the Gamla Stan (Box 15410, S-10465 Stockholm), ☎ +46 8 677 0000, *Fax* +46 8 677 0010, *Email* nautiska@nautiska.com, www.nautiska.com. More general maps are available from Kartcentrum Stockholm at Vasag 16 (opposite the Central Station).

Staff at the Svenska Kryssarklubben (Swedish Cruising Club) headquarters, at Augustendalsvägen 54, S–13127 Nacka Strand, ☎ +46 8 448 2880, *Fax* +46 8 448 2889, Email info@sxk.se, www.sxk.se, are very helpful and the club has a good range of yachting publications and charts on sale.

General facilities
Stockholm has all the shopping opportunities one might expect of a major European capital, including many familiar British names, and top quality goods of all types can be bought – at a price. There is a particularly helpful tourist office on the Hamngatan.

3. SWEDEN

Above right The rapids between Gamla Stan and Södermalm *E. Redfern*

Above The beautiful House of Nobility in central Stockholm with the distinctive steeple of the Riddarholmskyran (Royal burial church) on the right *E. Redfern*

Communications and travel

Telephone and fax facilities are widely available throughout the city, and there is a card-operated phone and Wi-Fi at the Wasahamnen marina. There are numerous cybercafés, and the internet can also be accessed free at the main library – the Stadsbiblioteket, Sveavägen 73 – from 1000 to 1700 Monday to Friday, though sessions are limited to 20 minutes. Travel within the city centre is made easy – even enjoyable – by the frequent buses and modern underground system (the same bus route serves both marinas, or one can get a waterbus across to the old town). Alternatively, as Stockholm is largely flat and appears to breed singularly considerate drivers, bicycles are a very practical way to get around. All three international airports can easily be reached by bus or train. Frequent rail, coach and ferry services run between Stockholm and other parts of Europe.

The incomparable *Wasa*, perhaps the greatest of Stockholm's many treasures *P. & G. Price*

Lake Mälaren

Charts and guides
Swedish 11, 111, 112, 113, 114, 1131
Båtsportkort D: Mälaren
UKHO 2362, 3142, 3141, 3145

General

Lake Mälaren, the third-largest lake in Sweden, stretches for some 70M to the west of Stockholm and provides a fine sailing ground in beautiful surroundings. Much of its charm lies in the fact that it is not one great sheet of water but is broken up by many large and small islands, forming a variety of channels through which to explore.

Water levels in Lake Mälaren are less than a metre above those in the Baltic, and it can be entered from the south via the Södertälje Kanal (see page 179) or from the east via the Hammarbyleden, just south of Stockholm. Prehistorically it was continuous with the sea. With the thawing of the ice sheet in the north of Scandinavia the whole country gradually rose, until the medieval settlements were cut off from the sea by the rapids which now separate Stockholm's Gamla Stan (old town) from the Södermalm.

Approach from Stockholm

To reach Lake Mälaren via the Hammarbyleden entails negotiating four bridges and a single lock which, taken from east to west, are:

Danviksbron (rail bridge, clearance 11.7m) ☎ 08 508 27911, VHF Ch 12, 16. Open 0000–0613, 0700–0718, 0903–1200, 1430–2400 LT weekdays, 24 hours weekends and holidays.

Skansbron (rail bridge, clearance 11.7m), ☎ 08 508 27912, Mobile 070 770 2812, VHF Ch 12. Open 0000–0630, 0700–0720, 0845–1630, 1800–2400 LT weekdays, 24 hours weekends and holidays, 0000–0630, 0700–0720, 0845–1200, 1430–2400 LT on days preceding holidays.

Hammarbyslussen (lock) ☎ +46 8 670 2815, VHF Ch 12, 16.

Årstabron north (rail bridge) now closed to marine traffic or Årstabron south (fixed rail bridge – clearance 26m).

Lilljeholmen (road bridge, clearance 13·7m; fixed span 15·5m), ☎ +46 8 508 27913, Mobile +46 70 770 2812, VHF Ch 12, 16, 68. Open 0000–0615, 0900–1600, 1830–2400 LT weekdays, 24 hours weekends and holidays, 0000–0615, 0900–1200, 1430–2400 LT on days preceding holidays.

Hammarbyleden entrance from Stockholm   *E. Redfern*

Local interest

The lake is home to or visited by large numbers of wildfowl and other birds. You would be unlucky not to see at least one Osprey or Sea Eagle most days. Though not as many sailing yachts are to be seen on Lake Mälaren as in Swedish coastal waters it is nevertheless a very popular cruising ground. There are nearly 30 yacht harbours on the lake itself and another dozen or so on its various extensions, as well as limitless possibilities for anchoring. However the surrounding land rises to more than 30m in places and is well wooded, sometimes making the wind flukey or non-existent.

There are many interesting and historic places on Lake Mälaren's shores, and a month or more could easily be spent visiting them all. A selection of the most well known follows

Bjorkö
59°20'N 17°32'·7E

Birka on this small island was the ancient Viking capital of Sweden and is now a World Heritage site. There are some supplies, an excellent museum, a good restaurant, lovely walks around the burial mounds and some reconstructed buildings. A fairly basic *gästhamn* with 40 visitors' berths can become very busy during the season.

The visitors' pontoon at Birka is almost deserted towards the end of August   *E. Redfern*

Drottningholm
59°19'·5N 17°53'·5E

Home of the Swedish royal family. The palace and gardens are well worth a visit as is the unique wooden 18th- century royal theatre. It is possible to moor bows-to or anchor nearby.

3. SWEDEN

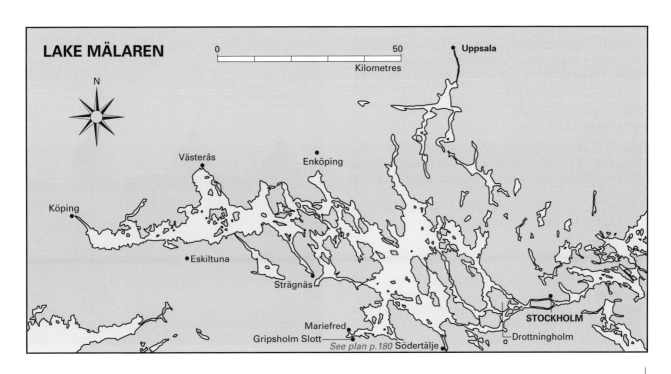

Mariefred on the Mälaren Lakes   *P. & G. Price*

Drottningholm Palace and gardens   *E. Redfern*

Gröneborg
59°32'7N 17°06'E

There is quiet anchorage in the bay on the west of this strategically placed island. Some stone remains of the 13th-century refuge citadel are still visible on the hill at the southern end.

Mariefred
59°15'·4N 17°13'·5E

The beautiful Gripsholm Slott, which houses the National Portrait Gallery, is within easy walking distance of the *gästhamn* and is certainly worth a visit. Limited depths but all facilities and 50 visitors' berths. A delightful little town which became established to service the royal castle.

Strägnäs
59°22'·7N 17°02'·5E

Although touristy this is a charming little Episcopal seat with a striking red brick cathedral. All the usual facilities are available at the 40 berth *gästhamn* just northwest of the Tosterbron swing bridge which opens on the hour for a maximum of 10 minutes.

Uppsala
59°51'·5N 17°55'E

There are 20 visitors' berths at the *gästhamn* but with restricted facilities although all services can be obtained nearby. This is Sweden's most famous university town and it also boasts the country's largest cathedral. See the Linnaeus Botanical Garden.

Västeräs
59°36'·2N 16°33'·5E

Said to be Sweden's largest freshwater port. With many miles of cycle paths it is ideal for a cycling break. 13th-century cathedral and close to the airport. 30 visitors' berths at the *gästhamn* which is about 800m from the shopping centre.

Many passenger boats ply the routes around the Lake, most notably the *Mariefred* which has been steaming between Stockholm and Mariefred continuously since 1903.

Gripsholm Castle at Mariefred on the Mälaren Lakes. The anchorage is near the castle, just off the attractive town
E. Redfern

The Gulf of Bothnia

Planning Charts
UKHO 2252
Swedish 5, 4
Finnish 5, 3
Larger-scale charts covering individual areas and harbours are listed in the text. *The Baltic Pilot Volume III (NP 20)* covers the whole of the Gulf of Bothnia.

Lights

Many lighthouses in the Gulf of Bothnia remain unlit between 20 May and 20 July – one month either side of midsummer – due to the almost continuous daylight.

Note that many more lights, buoys and beacons exist than are shown on the plans which accompany this section.

During the winter storms and ice can cause considerable damage to buoys which are sometimes not replaced in the early part of the season.

General

The Gulf of Bothnia is most often entered through the Södra Kvarken TSS between Sweden and the Åland islands, now that the Väddö Canal – which used to provide a convenient shortcut if coming from the Stockholm *skärgård* – has been blocked to many cruising yachts by the construction of a fixed bridge with 17m clearance at approximately 60°03′N.

The Gulf stretches northeast for some 350 miles with the Swedish/Finnish border neatly bisecting its closed end. Commercial shipping carries mainly paper, timber and iron ore with little evidence of commercial fishing activity. There is considerable local yachting all along the coast, particularly in the vicinity of the main towns of Hudiksvall, Sundsvall, Harnösand, Umeå, Skellefteå and Luleå, but though the area is popular with German and Finnish yachtsmen it has been less frequently visited by cruisers of other nationalities. However, for those who wish to get away from the beaten track, the Gulf of Bothnia provides excellent sailing often in *skärgårds*, and even in July when the southern cruising grounds are crowded one can still enjoy a solitary night at anchor in the most idyllic surroundings.

For many it is natural to want to reach the top of the gulf. However it is impossible for most cruising yachts to visit Haparanda on the Swedish side of the Tornio river because of the rock strewn approaches and fixed bridges but the sheltered harbour at Haparandahamn is

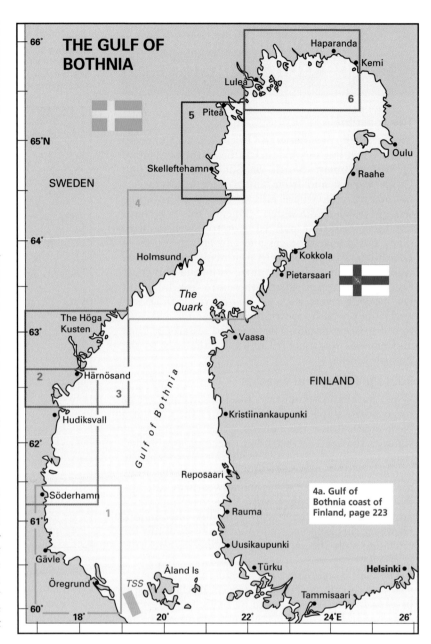

THE GULF OF BOTHNIA

4a. Gulf of Bothnia coast of Finland, page 223

18km southeast and is connected by bus. The northernmost point by water is at Töre, a little further west which can be reached with care and detailed charts. For the final part of the passage from Luleå to Haparandahamn, Swedish charts *411, 412, 413* and *414* are essential.

3. SWEDEN

3h. The Swedish coast of the Gulf of Bothnia

The coastline

The Swedish coast between Öregrund and Sundsvall is low lying, the only landmarks being the occasional factory chimney. North of Sundsvall the 'High Coast' begins, and from here to Örnsköldsvik is a fascinating area where hills of about 250m come straight down to the water. Scenically this is perhaps the most beautiful part of eastern Sweden, with many possible anchorages and *gästhamns*. North of Örnsköldsvik, The Quark is a difficult area of shoal waters requiring intricate navigation and the coast becomes flat again. Inland there are low hills and fast flowing rivers with various tourist attractions, and it may well be worth hiring a car for a day or two if weather-bound. The *skärgård* restarts at Piteå and extends for some 90 miles, all the way to the Finnish border.

Route planning and weather

When making a round trip, most yachtsmen prefer to go north along the Swedish side of the Gulf and back south down the Finnish, possibly because in summer the sea breeze tends to become established from the southeast on the west side and from the northwest on the east side. However northerly winds are also quite usual and the worst weather can come from that quarter, often with little warning. Gales are unusual in July, but fog is not uncommon. However this is considered to be the best month for cruising, with the weather improving as one sails north.

The Gulf is icebound for a considerable part of the year and though normally ice-free after May can still be very cold in June. It is fed by rivers from Sweden and Lapland, giving the Gulf as a whole very low salinity. There is no tide, but there are some local currents and water level is subject both to wind direction and to changes in atmospheric pressure. Most harbours are very shallow – and becoming more so due to continuing land rise since the last Ice Age.

1. Svartklubben to Söderhamn

Distance 90M
Båtsportkort H: Södra Bottenhavet
Skärgårdskort – 536, 535, 534, 5341, 533, 532
Specialkort – 5341, 5331

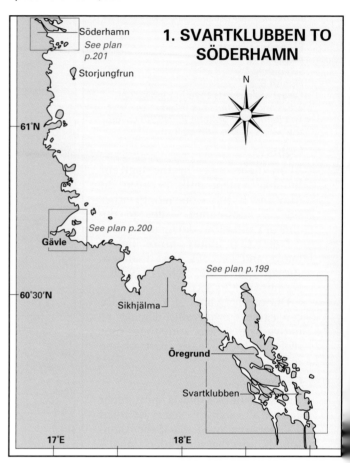

The southwest gateway to the gulf and Gävleborg coast.

If not in a rush take in the pretty *skärgård* from Svartklubben to Öregrund and some of the anchorages or 18 *gästhamns* up to Söderhamn. Uppland gives way to Gästrikland and Hälsingland to become Jungfrukusten – 'The Maiden Coast'. Apart from the infrequent mill chimney, landmarks are rare and you will come across progressively fewer yachts outside the main centres.

Svartklubben
60°10'·6N 18°48'·7E
Chart 536

Conspicuous light at entrance to Öregrund *skärgård* and small anchorage.

6.5M southeast of Understen and marking the southerly entrance to this attractive short cut inside Gräsö to Öregrund.

There is a pretty, settled weather anchorage nearby at 60°10'·5N 18°49'E. Anchor in good holding just east of the little used southern fairway. The northern fairway is used by a few pilot and fishing boats.

Öregrund
60°20'·5N 18°26'·8E
Charts 535 SW and 536 NW

Northern limit for many cruising yachts.

(Pronounced *Uhr-e-gruhnd*) The southeast approach is via the well buoyed, sheltered and sometimes tricky *skägård* route. From the northwest it is relatively easy through the Öregrunds Grepen. Both call for a large scale chart but are used by coastal shipping.

A busy harbour particularly in season with 80 guest berths ranging from 1–7m depth. The not unusual north winds can make the harbour uncomfortable when it is best to cross 1M to anchor, in clay, in the sheltered Kullbådaviken from where there is a nearby ferry back to town.

All the usual facilities are available from the *gästhamn* or quay with Öregrunds Båtvarv (☎ +46 173 30423) less than 1M to the south offering general boatyard engineering and lay up. Market on

The busy harbour at Öregrund   *E. Redfern*

the quay, good shopping which includes a Systembolaget and bookshop for Swedish charts. Wide selection of restaurants, interesting church and maritime museum.

Speedboat racing during the first week-end in June which is well supported but noisy.

Nearest station is Gimo some 30km distant but accessible by ferry and bus. The latter also run direct to Stockholm.

Sikhjälma
60°34'·5N 17°49'E
Chart 534 SE

Small holiday village.

30M from Öregrund towards Gävle is this collection of week-end or holiday homes. Very limited facilities and only four guest berths bows-to wooden staging from a stern anchor in 2·5m.

A delightful week-day or out of season spot which is reasonably sheltered.

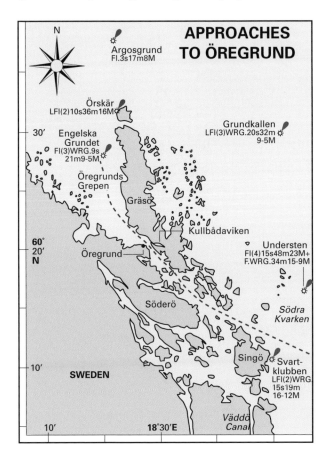

Alongside the tiny *gästhamn* at Sikjalma south east of Gävle *E. Redfern*

3. SWEDEN

Gävle

60°40'·4N 17°13'·1E
Charts 534 and 5341

Large regional, commercial and shopping centre with docks, industry and a university.

(Pronounced *Yairv-leh*). The main channel from the northeast is very well marked for shipping. There is an alternative route for leisure craft from the east between the islands of Limön and Orana.

Visiting yachts generally berth in the large, sheltered marina at Fliskar just beyond and opposite the docks. However there is little more than 2m and a limited number of guest spaces between metal booms. There is a 10 minute walk to the No. 12 bus which then takes half an hour to reach the centre of town. It may also be possible to berth further west at the sailing club to port just short of the canalized river entrance.

The Fliskar marina includes a yacht club, all the usual facilities and access to boatyard services.

Gävle centre has excellent shopping and all services of a town of nearly 70,000. The most attractive part is of older wooden houses, close to the River Gavleän.

Gävle, looking northeast (seawards) through the northeast entrance   *F. and G. Cattell*

Storjungfrun

61°10'·1N 17°20'·3E
Chart 533 NW

'Large Virgin Island'!

Take care to avoid the well marked Storgrundet shoal 2M to the east of the prominent black and white lighthouse just above the small *gästhamn*. Moor bows-to the wall from a stern anchor in 2·4m but crowded at week-ends and in season.

Here there are the first clear signs of rising land. The seaward side of the island is strewn with lichen covered, rounded rocks or large stones. Wood plank pathways have been laid to picturesque wooden houses and the delightful old chapel.

Probably a little exposed to the southeast but much more attractive than the mainland *gästhamns* at Vallvik or Ljusne. Excellent walks to the west side.

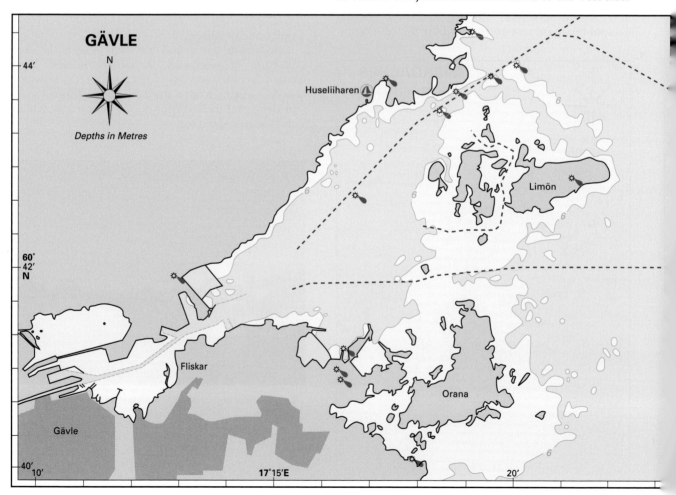

GÄVLE

N

Depths in Metres

Huseliiharen

Limön

Fliskar

Gävle

Orana

The attractive holiday island of Storjungfrun   *E. Redfern*

2. Hudiksvall to Härnösand

Distance 85M

Båtsportkort – Serie H Södra Bottenhavet
Skärgårdskort 532, 525, 524
Specialkort 5232

North from the Hornslandet peninsula to the start of 'The Höga Kusten'.

There are a series of small fishing villages along the north Hälsingland and Medelpad coasts. The wide Sundsvallbukten leads into Sweden's largest river delta. There are useful anchorages in addition to the 20 *gästhamns* covering this area, mainly around Hudiksvall and Sundsvall. As you sail north the land starts to rise where the High Coast begins between Sundsvall and Härnösand.

Söderhamn
61°17'·6N 17°04'·7E
Charts 532 SW and 5331 N

Gästhamn in the centre of town.

7M west of the Norrutharet light (61°15'·7N 17°18'E) with a large scale chart will take you passed the tiny harbour at Sandarne on your port hand to this not much larger *gästhamn* with eight bows-to berths from stern buoys in 2m.

Well serviced with all the facilities of a municipal centre nearby.

The main railway and E4 highway pass through town.

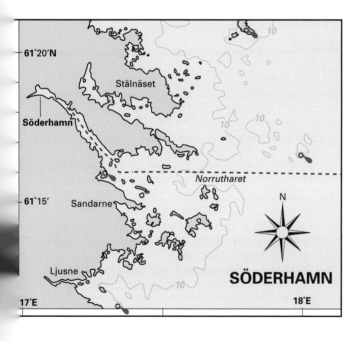

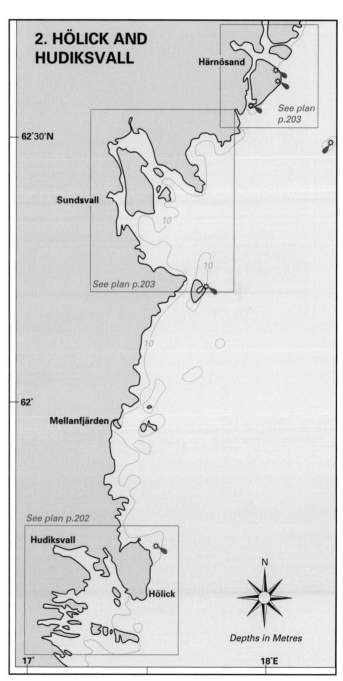

3. SWEDEN

Hölick

61°37'·5N 17°26'·1E
Chart 532 NE

Marina and holiday camp.

Having passed either side of the Olofsgrund shoal 1M north of Ago, Hölick is in an old fishing harbour on the southwest corner of Hornslandet 3M further north. Be sure to enter between the approach buoys outside the harbour breakwaters to the west of the lighthouse. Now equipped with 70 berths on finger pontoons in 2m but which suffer weed growth by late July.

Few services apart from a café/restaurant across the harbour as most facilities are 500m away at the camp site. Very attractive church high on the rocks above the village and excellent walks.

Road access only to Hudiksvall 14km away.

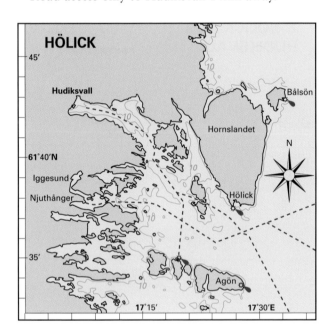

Holick's shallow *gästhamn*   *E. Redfern*

Hudiksvall

61°43'·5N 17°07'·1E
Charts 532 NW and NE

Large municipal centre with docks and deep-water berths.

15M along well marked channels from the open sea but with some shipping.

As you enter there is a large marina to starboard with 12 guest berths with booms or stern buoys in 3·5–7m.

The usual guest services are to hand and there is useful shopping in the town centre some 10 minutes walk away. A good place to hire a car to explore the Hälsingland coastline and hinterland. Interesting farm museum at Bjuraker of old wooden farm houses with painted rooms.

The E4 highway, mainline railway and airport all make this a good crew change harbour.

Mellanfjärden

61°57'·4N 17°20'·5E
Chart 525

Attractive old fishing village.

The easiest approach is from the south of Jättholmarna 5M to the east. The routes from the southeast and north require large scale Swedish charts. There is a lit leading line and then unlit buoys to the *gästhamn* just passed a local boat marina to port. Well sheltered with 20 berths, bows-to a wooden quay from stern buoys.

Village style facilities serve this attractive collection of red-painted wooden houses with an hotel on the quay.

Some 7km from the E4 highway but a convenient harbour on this stretch of coast.

Sundsvall

62°23'·6N 17°17'·8E
Chart 524

Rebuilt deep-water marina in neo-Renaissance town.

Avoiding the well charted shoals make for Draghällan light (62°20'4N 17°26'7E) and follow the deep-water channel into town. The Båt-och *gästhamn* is on the port hand and has 40 berths in 3–12m either to stern buoys or between booms but could be a little open to the east.

The usual visitors services are to hand and all the facilities expected of a town of nearly 50,000 are nearby including a chandler. Situated at the head of its own fjord the town has some richly ornamental buildings and nearby beaches.

Well served by the mainline rail network and E4 highway. It is closer to the local airport than Härnösand.

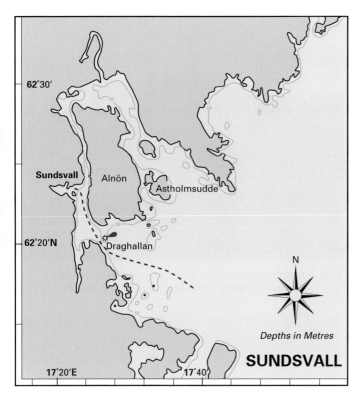

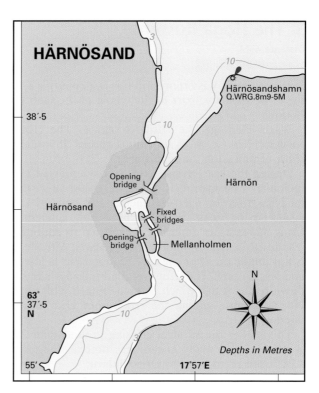

Härnösand

62°38'·1N 17°56'·2E
Chart 523

Regional and shopping centre with commercial port.
(Pronounced *Hair-neu-sahnd*). Deep water approaches from south, east and north all leading to the narrow fjord inside of Härnön island. Well placed lighthouses make this an easy landfall if sailing straight up from Öregrund or from the Åland Islands but note the 20m cable across the south entrance.

There are three *gästhamns* one of which will always be sheltered whatever the wind. Södra Sundet is below the lifting bridge, Norra Sundet is above the swing bridge and Nattviken between the two bridges. The north swing bridge is only 8m wide and is immediately north of a 90° turn to port. The bridges open at limited times by telephone request to ☎ +46 611 156817 pre 1600 and to ☎ +46 601 20184 post 1600.

Each of the *gästhamns* has the usual facilities although fuel is perhaps most easily obtained from the fuel station on the mainland north of Norra Sundet.

There is a large shopping centre spread across both banks of the fjord, a university and multi-faith cathedral.

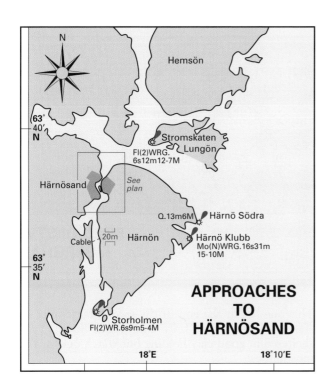

Härnösand, looking south-southeast towards the bridge from the western corner of the inner basin
F. and G. Cattell

3. The Höga Kusten

Distance 45M
Skärgårdskort 523, 522

In the centre of Västernorrland this is, in many ways, the most attractive part of the whole of the Gulf of Bothnia.

World Heritage Site status recognises The Höga Kusten (High Coast) as something special. If you are short of time, don't miss this area.

During the last ice age 3km of ice depressed the region by 800 metres. In the last 10,000 years the land has risen by over 400 metres and remains the fastest rising coast around the world. Currently rising at 9mm per annum it is expected to continue it's upward trend for another 5,000 years. Already it is not unlike the west coast of Scotland but is lower and less austere. The steep tree clad hillsides stretch down to the water which is often fringed with pink Nordic granite among the red houses with white windows.

This makes for an ideal cruising ground with 20 *gästhamns* and many anchorages dotted along the 45M from Härnösand to Örnsköldsvik.

Blue waters fringed with red Nordic granite and multitudes of green trees are typical in the Höga Kusten   *E. Redfern*

The Höga Kusten bridge was modelled on San Francisco's Golden Gate *E. Redfern*

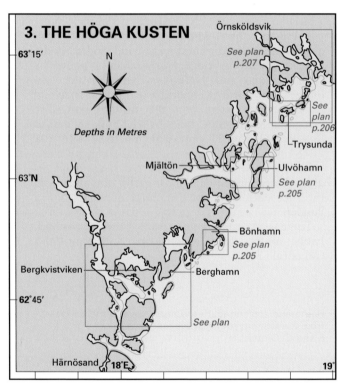

3. THE HÖGA KUSTEN

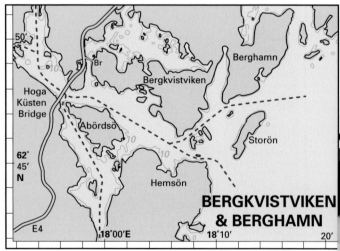

Bergkvistviken

62°48'·6N 18°04'·1E
Chart 523

Very quiet natural anchorage.

Just to the east of the impressive Höga Kusten bridge, 5M north of Härnösand is the entrance to Norafjärden. The ferry at Middags has been replaced with an 18m fixed bridge. There are buoys but a large scale chart is needed to find the way in.

Many south-facing houses have been constructed but it is still possible to find secluded anchorages.

This one lies at the end of the second large inlet to starboard in view of only one distant house. Very sheltered in good clay holding but watch out for the mosquitoes!

Berghamn
62°48'·4N 18°14'·1E
Chart 523

Tiny old fishing village.

Easy entrance from the open sea just below the 242m high Röåsen peak and providing good shelter from all but the east. An ideal lunch stop anchorage in 2–3m but less if mooring bows-to a small wooden jetty from a stern anchor. No visible facilities or services for the local houses in a rather agricultural setting but plentiful wildfowl and bird life.

Bönhamn
62°53'N 18°27'·2E
Chart 522 SW

A very pretty old fishing and holiday village, not to be missed.

1M inside the prominent Högbonden light (62°52'N 18°28'·8E) lies this most attractive harbour. The narrow southeast entrance is less easy than that from the north. It is difficult to argue with their claim to be the 'best kept *gästhamn* on this coast'. The berths off the new starboard breakwater are very shallow.

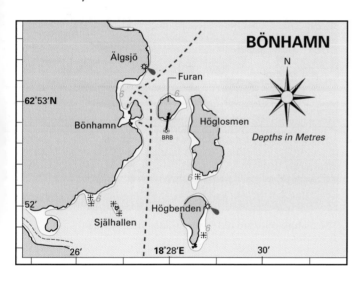

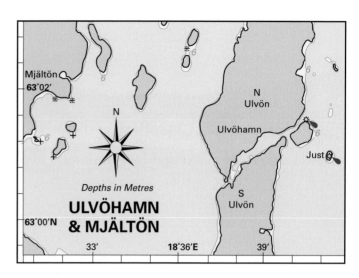

Picturesque Bönhamn *E. Redfern*

Nothing open out of season when it may be possible to moor alongside but usually crowded in season especially at weekends when bows-to from stern anchors can produce crossed lines.

Water, power, showers etc at the harbour. Post buses and the seamen's chapel are augmented in season by a café, kiosk, restaurant and art gallery. Good walks both north and south of the village giving wonderful views.

Ulvöhamn
63°01' 4N 18°39' 6E
Charts 522 SW and NW

A picture-perfect village with a splendid natural harbour.

Between the islands of north and south Ulvö lies the generally sheltered Ulvösund. Entry via the shallow and twisting southwest route is enlivened by the regular Ulvö ferry which has little respect for other vessels! The northeast and south entrances are more straight forward. Very deep water in the sound makes anchoring off difficult but there are three *gästhamns* with bows-to mooring from stern buoys or anchors and some rock moorings near the southwest entrance.

The large and attractive village has a permanent population, shop, pharmacy, hotel and restaurants. The usual facilities and fuel are available. Try to see the ancient wooden chapel with painted interior and taste the local fermented herring speciality of *Surströmming*. Very popular in season but well worth a visit.

Mjältön
62°02'·3N 18°32'·3E
Chart 522

A natural lagoon.

The narrow and shallow entrance reveals itself on the southeast side of the island. Totally protected and deep in the centre. Limited bows-to mooring to basic pontoons on the north side. If anchoring off, a trip line may be wise following extensive logging on the south side. Barbecue areas on the beach and latrine. Good walks into the nature reserve.

The very popular harbour at Ulvöhamn   *E. Redfern*

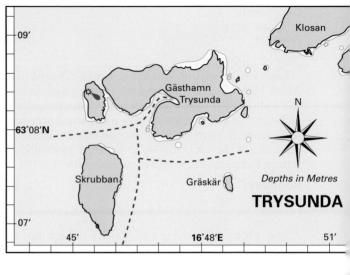

The natural lagoon at Mjältön   *E. Redfern*

The picture postcard old fishing village of Trysunda
E. Redfern

Set a new record by walking to the top of Sweden's highest island peak! Bastutoberger is about a 2km walk and reaches 236m above sea level but is rising at 9mm per annum.

Trysunda
63°08'·4N 18°47'·4E
Chart 522 NE

An enchanting holiday village in a nature reserve.

Easy entrance from the southwest to moor bows-to a substantial jetty from stern buoys in 3–7m. Exposed to the south when it may be possible to anchor on the north of the island. Power, water, washroom etc at the *gästhamn*.

This former fishing village is now almost entirely holiday homes with very few permanent residents. Beautifully maintained but nothing open before midsummer when a small shop and restaurants appear for the season. Interesting wooden seamen's chapel with painted interior. Excellent walks around the island.

Örnskoldsvik
63°17'·2N 18°42'·7E
Chart 522 NW

A regional centre and commercial port.

(Pronounced *Urn-sheulds-veek*). From the open sea the Skagsudde light (63°11'·3N 19°01'·4E) marks the start of a deep-water channel. After 4M this joins with the coastal route from the southwest from inside Trysunda. A sharp turn to port precedes 5M of well marked and lit channel right up to the extreme northwest corner of the harbour. The *gästhamn* of 35 berths in 3m offers boom or alongside moorings with all the usual services. There are many nearby anchorages from which to choose but all are well away from town.

This large and modern town centre which provides extensive shopping and services, is also Sweden's Ice Hockey centre. Well served by the E4 highway and buses but with no immediate rail link and there is an airport 20km away.

Örnsköldsvik, looking eastwards over the head of the harbour *F. and G. Cattell*

4. Husum to Bjuröklubb

Distance 110M

Charts *Båtsportkort K: Högbonden – Sikeå*
Skärgårdskort 514, 513, 512, 511, 422
Specialkort 5121

The Västerbotten coast and Norra Kvarken.

Well served by the E4 highway which links most of the dozen *gästhamns* but shallow midway and sometimes living up to its fearsome sounding name 'The Quark'. While signs of current or past industrial activities are spread along the coastline the island of Holmön just offshore claims to be Sweden's sunniest.

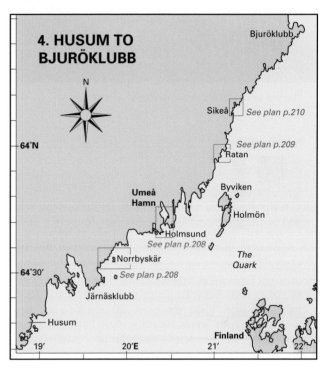

Husum

63°19'·8N 19°08'·5E
Charts 514 SW and NW

Safe harbour and commercial centre.

A well lit and buoyed entrance towards a dominating pulp mill.

This is a convenient first stop north of the Höga Kusten but the *gästhamn* is 3km away from the town. Six berths for alongside or bows-to from stern anchor moorings in 2–4m. Basic facilities as most services are in town.

E4 highway within 3km and airport 10km.

Järnäsklubb

63°26'·3N 19°40'·7E
Charts 513 SW and 514 NE

Sailing Club at old pilot station.

Situated 3M northeast of the Störbaden light (63°24'·5N 19°30'·36) which should be given a good offing. A large scale chart is essential to approach this tiny harbour. Alongside mooring for five rafted in 1–3m. To accommodate the claimed 10 boats all would have to be less than 7m LOA. Water and power only but very safe if there is space.

3. SWEDEN

The old pilot station at Järnäsklubb   *E. Redfern*

Norrbyskär

63°33'·8N 19°52'·5E
Chart 513 NW

Site of abandoned saw mill.

With the aid of a large scale chart make your way 8M west-northwest of the Bonden light (63°26'N 20°02'·5E) to this fascinating island. The small *gastbrygga* at Kalmarn on the northern end has space for no more than three alongside unless rafting. Take great care to avoid the sunken timbers at either end. Basic facilities and a 1km walk down to the village. Here there are 20 bows-to visitors' moorings from stern anchors with better facilities but close to the ferry quay from Norrbyn and exposed to the east.

In the 19th century this became the largest saw mill company in Europe and was set up as a model society. The management and workers' houses lining the street are now holiday homes. There are remains of its previous use all over the island and a miniature reproduction of the mill draws many day visitors from the mainland.

Holmsund, Umeå

63°49'N 20°16'E
Charts 512 NW and 5121 NW

Provincial capital, ferry port and yacht club marina.

The main entrance north-northeast from the Vaktaren light (63°36'·9N 20°25'·4E) is well buoyed and lit for the ferries to Finland. From the Lillbådan light (63°38'·9N 20°20'·8E) there is a straight forward deep water route to the north-northeast of

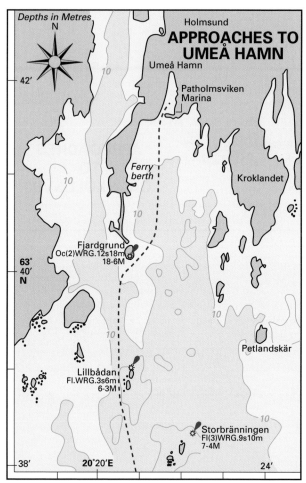

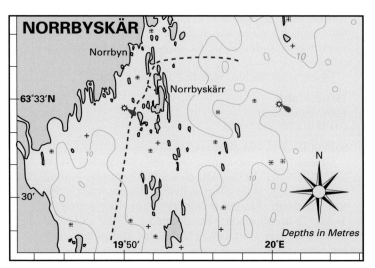

The Patholmsviken marina at Umeå Hamn, looking southwest   *F. and G. Cattell*

the long Fjardgrund peninsula. This leads passed the docks to starboard at Umeå Hamn but is then blocked by a 3·8m fixed bridge before going all the way 18km inland to Umeå.

Visiting yachts usually berth at the Holmsund, Patholmsviken Yacht Club and *gästhamn* to the east of Fjardgrund and north of the ferry terminal. However, north of the Lillbådan light can be very confusing with conflicting buoyage for different and cross channels. The large scale chart *5121* is essential.

There are 10 bows-to moorings from stern buoys in 1·5–6m. Water and limited power on the pontoon but there are excellent facilities and fuel at the Yacht Club boatyard, lift out and lay up services are available from the nearby yard.

There are adequate shopping and services at Holmsund 1km north and full services in a large shopping centre with a hospital and two universities 15km to the north by No. 124 bus at Umeå which is sometimes known as 'The City of Birches'.

The E4 highway, rail services and a busy local airport make this a good place to change crew.

Byviken

63°48'·4N 20°52'·5E
Charts 511 SW and 512 NE

Small guest and ferry harbour on the north of Holmön.

A straight forward entrance from the north to moor bows-to from stern buoys behind the east breakwater. There is 3m near the fairway but quickly shoaling towards the shore. Water and power on the quay with basic facilities nearby.

In season there are a café, kiosk, restaurant and the excellent boat museum between the ferry and prominent lighthouse on the west of the harbour. Small shop, chemist and Systembolaget 2km to the south.

Lying 6M off shore this is a popular weekend destination and good jumping off place for Finland just 45M to the east.

Ratan

63°59'·5N 20°53'·7E
Chart 511 NW

The best natural harbour on this coast.

Easy deep-water entrance from the southeast but more care is needed for the shallow north entrance. Mooring in 4·5m alongside or bows-to from stern anchors if crowded. Power, water and fuel on the quay with other facilities within 300m. Can be exposed to strong southeast winds when it is possible to anchor in the lee of Rataskar island further in.

Ratan was an important customs port and the site of a 'land uplift' experiment by Celsius and Linnaeus in the 19th century. The small building for their mareograph still stands. The excellent restaurant at Tullgårdens Gärtgifueri (closed Mondays) was previously a holiday home for worn-out housewives but was built for the Customs Chief Officer. Scene of a major battle with the Russians in 1809.

Go by dinghy for good walks on Rataskar.

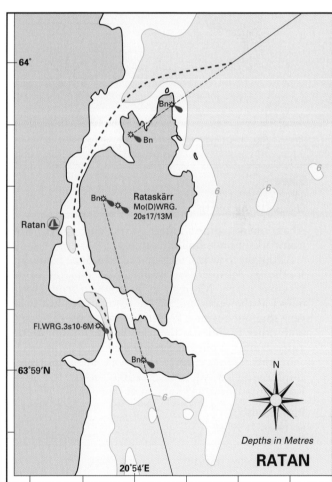

The very shallow harbour at Byviken on Holmön
E. Redfern

3. SWEDEN

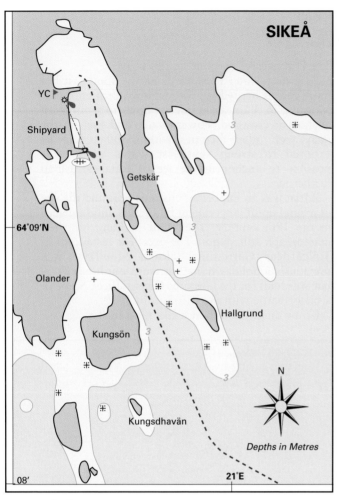

SIKEÅ

YC

Shipyard

Getskär

64°09'N

Olander

Kungsön

Hallgrund

Kungsdhavän

N

Depths in Metres

08'   21°E

Bjuröklubb lighthouse and Navtex station   *M. Bowyer*

Sikeå

64°09'·6N 20°58'·7E
Charts 511 NW and NE

Abandoned shipbuilding yard and port for ironworks, now a holiday camp.

A straight forward, well-marked entrance from the southeast. An operative leading light remains from previous usage. Moor in 2·5m bows-to from stern buoys at the outer end of the second jetty but it is very shallow beyond. Power and water on the quay with other facilities at the friendly yacht club 300m away. Some supplies at the campsite.

In the 18th century this was an important shipbuilding yard and trading port for the Robertfors Ironworks some miles inland.

Bjuröklubb

64°19'·8N 21°22'·5E
Chart 422

Tiny old pilot station.

Buoyed from the southeast and easy approach from the north to inside of Bjuron point. Unless there are small boats moored bows-to there is alongside berthing for four in 1–4m. In settled weather it is also possible to anchor off.

Basic facilities with a barbecue and free sauna but the invigorating walk up to the lighthouse is well worth the effort for spectacular views and the sunset.

In season there is a café near the lighthouse and fish for sale from a boat in the harbour.

Another old pilot station harbour at Bjuröklubb
E. Redfern

5. Skelleftehamn to Luleå

Distance 70M
Charts *Skärgårdskort* 421, 415, 414, 4101
Specialkort 4211, 4141, 4151, 4101

Norbotten and the north skärgård.

The waters are often shallower but the islands become more frequent throughout this area which becomes progressively more attractive. *Gästhamns* are less common and usually smaller but the opportunities to anchor increase.

Skelleftehamn, Kurjoviken

64°41'·2N 21°13'·7E
Charts 421 and 4211

Sailing Club marina and guest harbour.

Like Umeå, the town of Skellefteå is some 18km inland and cannot be approached by sailing yachts due to several low fixed bridges. Visiting yachts normally berth at the friendly Ursvikens Sailing Club at Kurjoviken.

From the south pass either side of Skötgrönnan beacon (64°35'·9N 21°30'E). From the north leave Gäsören light (64°39'·8N 21°19'·3E) to starboard. Then join the main buoyed channel just north of the Rakan light (64°38'·8N 21°18'E) and steer northwest to pass south and west of the prominent foundry on Rönnskär. Continue northwest approximately 2M through the buoys until the narrow entrance to Kurjoviken opens on the starboard beam. There is a leading line through this 2·7m channel to the marina which could be tricky in a strong on shore wind. A new *gästhamn* pontoon is immediately to port with bows-to mooring from stern buoys or anchors.

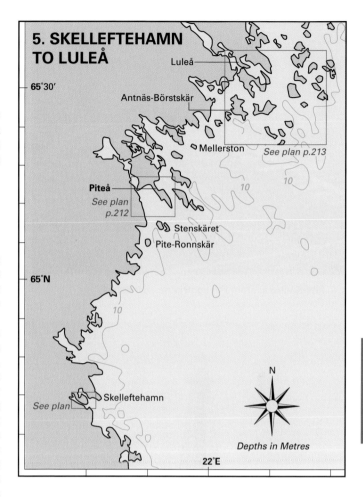

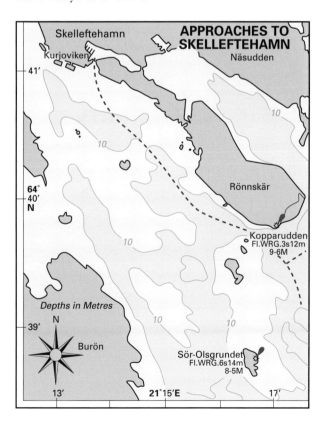

Water and power on this pontoon and all the usual facilities at the nearby clubhouse.

There is adequate shopping and some services within 2km and frequent buses to a large shopping centre in town. Boatyard, lift out services and lay up facilities at the marina. Pleasant walks around Kurjoviken.

Pite-Rönnskär

65°03'·2N 21°33'·4E
Chart 421

A prominent red lighthouse overlooks this old pilot station.

This little island lies 3·5M west of the Nygrån light (65°01'N 22°41'·5E). Even with a large scale chart the entrance looks unfriendly but round the buoy to it's north to pick up the leading line and creep into this spectacular spot. A small ferry from Piteå claims the immediate alongside berth leaving just enough space for six boats to moor bows-to from their own stern anchors in 2·5m. During the season and at weekends more than 10m LOA is likely to be too large. By July long weeds stream to the surface.

An ideal lunch stop with few facilities. Most of the wooden houses are now holiday homes handed down through the generations. Fishing nets used to be stored for the winter in the small wooden chapel. It is worth seeking out a guide to climb the unusual iron lighthouse for panoramic views.

Pite-Rönnskär from the lighthouse   *E. Redfern*

The iron lighthouse at Pite-Rönnskär   *E. Redfern*

Pite-Rönnskär
beacon
M. Bowyer

Stenskäret
65°07'N 21°43'E
Chart 415

Good anchorage and a small guest pontoon near an old fishing village.

Just 7M to the northwest of Pite-Rönnskär is this reverse L-shaped island. However approach from the north into a long gently shelving bay with the guest pontoon to port. You may moor bows-to from a stern anchor generally with many local boats but the rest of the bay is an easy anchorage open only to the northwest.

There are no facilities but extensive walks along sweeping sandy beaches backed by flowering sea peas, marram grass and wild flowers. Also large areas of multi-coloured stones cover the ground. On the seaward side these are coated with lichen. In the southwest corner behind the settlement are a number of fertility or good luck circles laid out by generations of fishermen.

Piteå, Haraholmen
65°14'·5N 21°37'·6E
Charts 415 SW and 4141S

Small marina beside commercial port.

Well buoyed and lit routes lead to the port and the small sailing club marina is just to the northwest. There are no facilities apart from water on hand but this could be a useful place from which to reach the large town of Piteå which is beyond a low fixed bridge. Nearby sandy beaches at Pitsundet seem to attract many Norwegians for their holidays. The *gästhamns* on the north side of this peninsula are only suitable for boats drawing less than 1·2m and 1·5m.

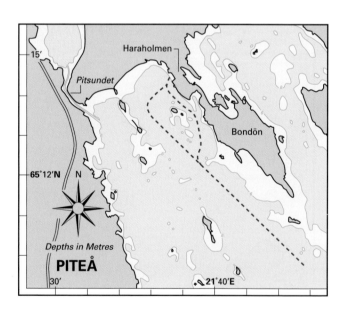

On the road from Luleå to Jokkmokk are the
Storforsen Falls   *E. Redfern*

The Icebreaker fleet laid up for the summer at Luleå
M. Bowyer

Mellerston
65°11′N 21°47′·4E
Chart 415

Lunch time anchorage.

Another 7M north and to the east of Bondön is the
large island of Mellerston. On its north shore are
several anchorages the west of which has a small and
shallow guest pontoon.

There are no facilities but this is a useful lunch
time anchorage in 1·5–2m open only to the
northwest.

Antnäs-Börskä
65°25′·7N 22°06′·5E
Chart 414

Small guest pontoon and anchorage by a friendly
village.

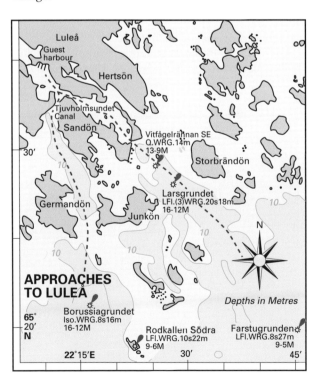

APPROACHES TO LULEÅ

There is an easy relatively deep-water entrance
from the northwest. The pontoon for 10 bows-to
berths has some stern buoys in 2·5m and is straight
ahead. Anchor in deeper water in the bay which is
exposed only to the northwest.

The few facilities include a free sauna provided by
the commune but please split replacement wood.

Luleå
65°34′·8N 22°09′·7E
Charts 414 NW and 4101 NW, NE

Regional capital, industrial, commercial, shopping
and yachting centre.

There are two main entrances to Luleå. Between
the airport and Sandön to the 1M long, dredged
Tjuvholmsundet canal is convenient for leisure boats
from the south. The very well-buoyed commercial
route from the open sea starts just north of the
Farstugr whistle buoy (65°19′·8N 22°45′E). After
16M to the northwest the narrows at Likskarët
(65°31′N 22°22′E) are reached. These two routes
meet just north of Sandön 5M later but still 2·5M
short of the marina. Pass the impressive icebreaker
fleet to starboard and head for the west end of the
marina for the Ettans Båthamn *gästhamn*. Berth
bows-to the jetty between booms in 3·5m. Larger
vessels can moor alongside further west on the town
quay.

The *gästhamn* is fully equipped with good facilities
and all the usual boatyard services. Dues are paid at
the comprehensive Granek chandlers behind and
there is a restaurant attached. The nearby major
shopping centre will meet all needs.

This town of nearly 75,000 is well served by road,
rail and air communications to make it a first class
crew change base.

The World Heritage site at Gammelstad Church
Village 10km to the northwest is well worth a visit
for its interesting history and good restaurants. Luleä
is also an excellent place from which to hire a car for
a short break to drive into the Arctic Circle, Lapland
and even Norway. Don't miss the spectacular
Storforsen falls en route.

3. SWEDEN

6. Luleå to Haparanda

Distance 65M
Charts *Skärgårdskort* 414, 412, 413, 411
Specialkort 4101

The top of the Gulf and border country.

The *skärgård* which started around Piteå continues all the way round to the Finnish border. In places it is shallow but there are enough *gästhamns*, anchorages and deep water to make this an attractive cruising area in its own right. Don't expect to find many visiting yachts but this leaves space for abundant wildlife and waterfowl.

The restored fishing village of Junkon south east of Luleå
E. Redfern

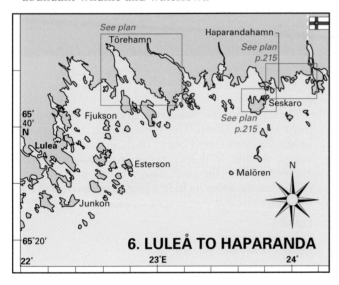

6. LULEÅ TO HAPARANDA

Junkon

65°27'·4N 22°24'·3E
Charts 414 NW and 4101 SE

Restored harbour with windmill and walks.

A straight forward approach from the north to the west bay on the top of the island. 10 berths for alongside, bows-to from stern anchors or between booms in 1·9–2·5m.

Since being declassified as a defence area the harbour and buildings have benefited from a make-over financed by the EU. There are a small café, museum, windmill and good walks on the island which is visited

by a day trip boat from Luleå. It is sometimes possible to buy fish from a local fisherman.

Esterson

65°32'·9N 22°47'·5E
Chart 414

Quiet natural anchorage.

Enter either end of the channel between the two islands. From the northwest there is a leading line. From the southeast stay south of the rocky shallows and mind the regular fishing nets. There is an overnight anchorage just west of the house in good holding or a lunch time stop on the east in more doubtful holding. Exposed to the northwest and east.

Fjukson

65°40'·9N 22°37'·3E
Chart 413

Well placed overnight anchorage.

Approach from the west and it is simple to anchor in 8m just west of the house on the north shore.

Windmill at Junkon   *E. Redfern*

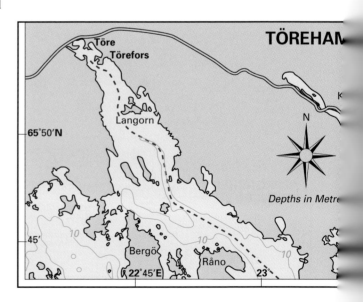

Good mud holding but exposed to the west. Well positioned if visiting Töre 15M further north.

Törehamn

65°54'·1N 22°39'E
Chart 413 N

Gästhamn at the top of the gulf.

Follow the transits and well-buoyed channel passed Törefors to the grain silos. There are six guest berths in 1·9m in the *gästhamn* or go alongside in deeper water outside. There are few facilities but a café serves the nearby camp site.

This is the most northerly point in the Baltic Sea so can be quite busy in season. Close by is a large yellow buoy with a letter box on its side. If you fill in the form provided you will receive a certificate recording that you have reached this landmark.

Malören

65°31'·6N 22°33'·5E
Charts 411 SW and 412 SE

Remote lighthouse island.

A bow shaped island with two lights and a Racon. Enter from the south and anchor off on the southwest of the pier but because of land uplift do not expect to find more than 1·5m. Exposed but safe in all winds except from the southwest. This is a convenient but shallow stop if crossing the top of the gulf. Popular at the weekends during the season.

Seskaro, Leppaniemi

65°44'N 23°44'·5F
Charts 411 NW and NE

Small guest harbour on attractive agricultural island.

Most yachts will have to approach from the northwest because of an 11·5m fixed bridge on the east side. There are several anchorages or harbours on the north side of this island. Leppaniemi is in the centre and easily entered with good buoyage and a leading line. Berth alongside or bows-to from a stern anchor at the jetty to starboard just north of the log pool or anchor off in 7m. Good holding and well sheltered except from the north when it would be quieter to tackle the tricky entrance to the east bay. Some facilities, campsite and limited provisions but daily buses to Haparanda.

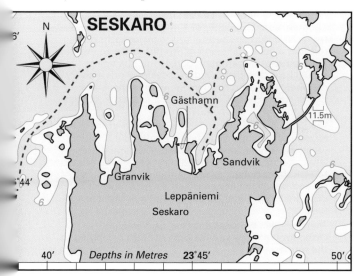

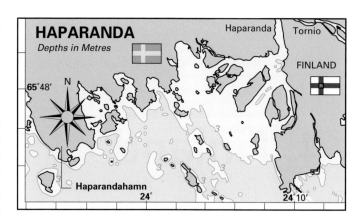

Looking north across Haparanda harbour
F. and G. Cattell

The buoy at Töre at the top of the Gulf of Bothnia
E. Redfern

Haparandahamn

65°46'·3N 23°54'·5E
Charts 411 NE and 4101 SE

Guest harbour for the northern border town.

A sheltered *gästhamn* with ten berths in 3m and the usual facilities run by a friendly Sailing Club. Not the most interesting spot but convenient if visiting Haparanda some 18km to the northeast, access to which is restricted by rocky shallows and fixed bridges. Haparanda lies on the Swedish side of the River Tornio and is best visited by bus.

3. SWEDEN

4. Finland

The country

The Finns call their country Suomi, which means the land of lakes and fens. A narrow coastal plain which supports limited farming is backed by a rocky, forested plateau some 100m above sea level where the wildlife is largely undisturbed. The plateau contains thousands of lakes, which drain westwards into the Gulf of Bothnia and south into the Gulf of Finland. The Lappi uplands of the far north comprise a third physical region. The continuous low temperature makes life there difficult to sustain, though reindeer farming and latterly tourism (hiking and skiing) support a limited population. The highly indented Baltic coastline is fringed with thousands of islands, including the remarkable Åland islands which stretch more than half way across the Gulf of Bothnia towards Sweden.

Finland's highly export-orientated market economy is based on private ownership. The chief natural resource is wood, and its derivatives – paper, paper board, wood pulp, veneers, plywood and timber – are important to the economy. Other natural resources include copper, iron and nickel, and there is also a smaller but significant agricultural industry. A quarter of the country's electricity is derived from water power.

There is much high-tech industry, producing electrical and electronic equipment (including Nokia mobile phones), machinery, and specialised shipbuilding such as ice-breakers. Finns have long had a standard of living matched by few other countries, but the economy is dependent upon world trade and has been particularly affected by developments in the former USSR, which used to take about 20% of her exports.

History

From 1154 until 1809 Finland was part of the kingdom of Sweden, after which it became a Russian possession. At first, when it was a grand duchy in the Russian empire, Finland was treated liberally, but late in the 19th century a Greater Russia chauvinistic movement resulted in the suppression of Finnish institutions. During the First World War the Finnish students surreptitiously turned to Germany for military training and formed a so-called Jääkäri battalion. At the time of the Russian revolution of 1917 all parties in Finland were agreed on their desire for independence, but after they had taken advantage of the new Soviet constitution to make it so by a unilateral declaration, the division between the socialists, who wanted close ties with the USSR, and the conservatives, who wanted complete independence, led to civil war. As elsewhere in the region, one side was supported by the USSR, the other by Germany. In the event, the conservatives won, due primarily to the superior leadership of Mannerheim and the support of the Jääkäri battalion.

In the interwar period great economic and social progress was achieved and a sound democratic system consolidated, but Finland was unable to allay

The language

Finland is home to several distinct ethnic groups and at least three major languages. Some 93% of Finns speak Finnish as their native tongue while between 6% and 7% are Swedish speaking, mostly in the coastal districts and around Åland. Fewer than 0·1% speak one of the Sami languages. In many places road signs, as well as names on street maps, will be in more than one language.

Finnish is an agglutinative language related to Hungarian and is very difficult. Lacking the common Latin or Teutonic origins of the majority of European languages it appears totally alien – almost no words can be guessed, even when seen written. Fortunately the excellent Finnish educational system means that almost everyone, from marina executives through to bus drivers, speaks passable and often fluent English (and often German and/or French as well).

Swedish is somewhat easier and again almost all Swedish-speaking Finns also speak excellent English. Although the national percentage is relatively small, a disproportionate number of Finnish yachtsmen come from this group and several of the major yacht clubs consider a good command of Swedish to be an essential requirement for membership. (Even so, the visitor should be aware that Swedish-speaking Finns are very definitely Finns and not Swedes, even in the Åland islands where Swedish is the official language, spoken by up to 90% of the population).

The Samis (Lapps) live in the northern half of the country so are unlikely to be encountered by cruising yachtsmen unless travelling inland. The Lappish language (which has several distinct variants) is related to Finnish, as is their culture. Although the Samis of Finland now number no more than 7,000, they maintain close links with those resident in Norway, Sweden and Russia.

There are two national churches, Lutheran and Orthodox, with the vast majority of Finns belonging to the former.

Practicalities

Time

Finland uses UT+2 in winter and UT+3 in summer.

Money

Finland has used the Euro since January 2002, replacing the Finnish mark (finmark or FIM). Major credit and debit cards are widely accepted, both in payment for goods and services and by banks, nearly all of which have ATMs.

Shopping

Food is plentiful, and there are many well-stocked supermarkets as well as small local shops throughout the archipelago. Prices are higher than in England, with fish – perhaps the most notable food speciality of Finland – somewhat cheaper.

Beer with an alcohol content of around 4·5% is available in supermarkets and other shops, but full-strength beer (5·2–8%), wines and spirits can only be purchased at branches of ALKO, the state alcohol company. In both cases prices are higher than in the UK.

Public holidays

Official public holidays in Finland include: 1 January, 6 January (Epiphany), Good Friday, Easter Sunday and Monday, 30 April (May Day Eve), 1 May (May Day), Ascension Day (May), Whitsunday (May or June), Midsummer's Eve and Day, (third weekend in June), 1 November (All Saints Day), 6 December (Independence Day), 24–26 December.

Local festivals and other events are held in many towns throughout the summer, listed in the Finland Festivals booklet and on the internet at www.festivals.fi.

Communications

The Finnish telephone system is excellent and mobile phones almost universal – as befits one of the world's leading manufacturers. Most telephone kiosks are card-operated (occasionally using more than one type of card). For international calls dial +, followed by the country code, area code (omitting any initial 0) and number. Dialling within Finland only the area code (including initial 0) and number are required, or number only for a local call. The country code for Finland is 358, and if dialling from abroad the initial 0 of the area code is not required.

There are fax facilities at commercial bureaux, most large post offices and many marina offices. Internet access is widespread, with free terminals in almost every public library. Other options are included in the text for each harbour. Letters normally take 2–3 days to or from the United Kingdom. It is essential to quote the correct postal index (post code) when addressing letters to Finland.

Travel

Helsinki has good communications by air with all parts of Europe, and Mariehamn and Turku can be reached from Stockholm. There are ferry services linking Helsinki with Turku, Mariehamn, Stockholm and many other destinations, including Tallinn in Estonia. The rail/ferry and coach/ferry services to western Europe are good, as is the rail service within Finland.

A mainline train service links Helsinki to St Petersburg, for which coaches also depart several times each day.

---

the USSR's fear for the security of her western flank – a fear not lessened by the long memory of the damage done to Russian interests by the British navy operating in Finland during the Crimean War. In 1939 the USSR followed up the demand for a frontier adjustment and a base in Finland by invasion, and forced a settlement in 1940. With the intervention of the Germans, hostilities soon restarted. The Finns, who again rallied under Mannerheim, recaptured their territory only to be thrown out once more when the tide turned against Germany. During this period a small British force was for a time sent to help the Finns.

An armistice in October 1944 settled the present Karelian (eastern) border west of its original line, transferring the Finnish city of Viipuri – now known as Vyborg – to Russia. Since then the Finns have maintained a fine balance between their democratic instincts and their powerful eastern neighbour, at the same time working actively to promote better relations between east and west.

With a stable population of just over five million, Finland is a parliamentary democracy, with a president elected for six years and a single-chamber 200-seat parliament, elected every four years by proportional representation. In 1906, Finland was the first European country to grant women the vote. It joined the EU in 1995 and was among those countries which embraced the common currency in January 2002.

Cruising

The cruising areas

Cruising in Finland means meandering amid tree-clad islands, with clear, tideless and sheltered waters, colourful villages, well run marinas, secluded anchorages, warm summer days, rich and fertile land and fragrant forests carpeted with pine needles. The people are extremely friendly and wildlife abounds – wild swans, eider, deer, sea trout, turbot and many other species. There is a special satisfaction in being able to navigate in complete confidence through the myriad channels between the islands, often only a matter of feet from the rocks, with the use of the Finnish charts. In complex areas where each island looks much like its neighbour, a small, removable adhesive marker will be found useful to keep track of one's position on the chart – see *Coastal Navigation*, page 9.

To the north the Gulf of Bothnia extends almost to the Arctic Circle. The further north one goes, the less it is populated and the fir trees predominate. Yachts going that way will have to be aware of this and carry adequate supplies on board. There are however good harbours from time to time, and scattered sheltered anchorages.

The Åland Islands, a favourite cruising ground for yachtsmen from Sweden and Finland – not to mention further afield – are of particular interest, not only because of their beauty, but also because of their connection with the sailing traders. The Åland Sea is only about 22M wide if measured between the

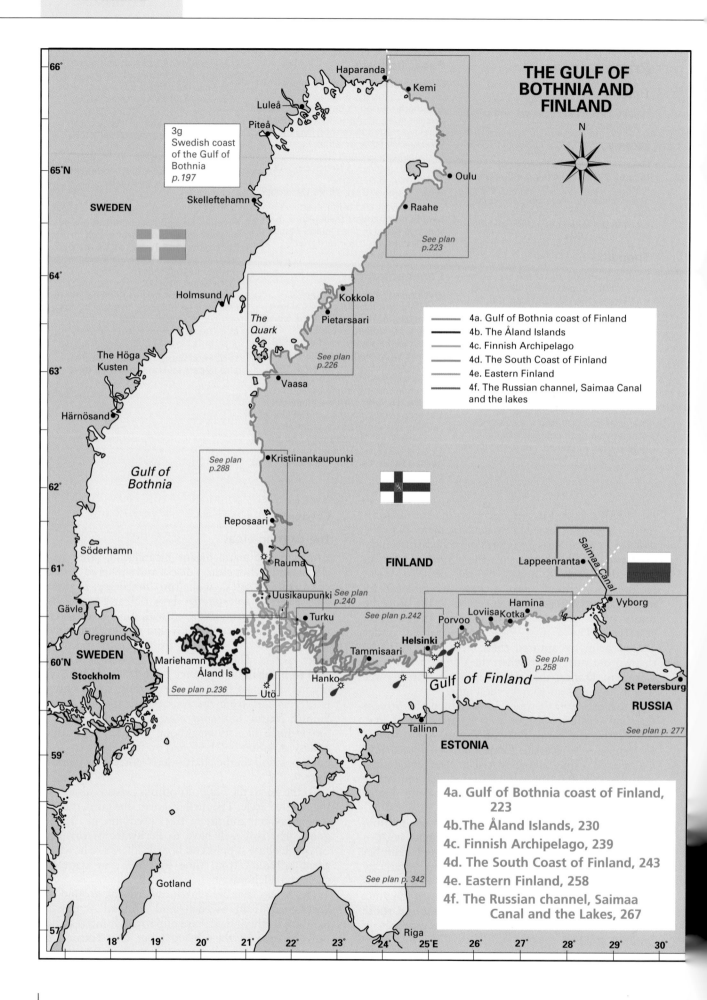

THE GULF OF BOTHNIA AND FINLAND

N

66°

Haparanda
Kemi

Luleå

Piteå

3g
Swedish coast
of the Gulf of
Bothnia
p.197

65°N

Oulu

SWEDEN

Skelleftehamn

Raahe

See plan
p.223

64°

Holmsund

Kokkola

The
Quark

Pietarsaari

63°

The Höga
Kusten

Vaasa

See plan
p.226

4a. Gulf of Bothnia coast of Finland
4b. The Åland Islands
4c. Finnish Archipelago
4d. The South Coast of Finland
4e. Eastern Finland
4f. The Russian channel, Saimaa Canal
and the lakes

Härnösand

See plan
p.288

Kristiinankaupunki

62°

Gulf of
Bothnia

FINLAND

Lappeenranta

Saimaa Canal

Söderhamn

Reposaari

Vyborg

61°

Rauma

Gävle

Uusikaupunki

See plan
p.240

See plan p.242

Hamina
Loviisa Kotka

Öregrund

Turku

Porvoo

See plan
p.258

St Petersburg

SWEDEN

Mariehamn

Helsinki

Stockholm

Åland Is

Tammisaari

Gulf of Finland

RUSSIA

60°N

See plan p.236

Utö

Hanko

See plan p. 277

59°

Tallinn

ESTONIA

4a. Gulf of Bothnia coast of Finland, 223
4b.The Åland Islands, 230
4c. Finnish Archipelago, 239
4d. The South Coast of Finland, 243
4e. Eastern Finland, 258
4f. The Russian channel, Saimaa Canal and the Lakes, 267

Gotland

See plan p. 342

57°

Riga

18°   19°   20°   21°   22°   23°   24°   25°E   26°   27°   28°   29°   30°

Formalities

British passport holders do not require visas. Should one be required contact the Finnish Embassy at 38 Chesham Place, London SW1X 8HW, ☎ 020 7838 6200, *Fax* 020 7235 3680 (*Fax* 020 7838 9703 for visa enquiries), *Email* sanomat.lon@formin.fi www.finemb.org.uk/en/.

The British Embassy in Helsinki is located at Itäinen Puistotie 17, 00140 Helsinki ☎ 09 2286 5100, *Fax* 09 2286 5264, http://ukinfinland.fco.gov.uk. In addition there are Honorary Consuls in a number of the larger towns and cities, including Mariehamn (now a Consulate General), Turku, Kotka and Vaasa.

The Frontier Guard is responsible for border crossing and passport control, and the current regulations on who must seek them out and where follows in the *Entry by Yacht* Section (see page 220). The yacht is expected to carry standard safety equipment, but as of 2010 there is no requirement for the skipper to hold the International Certificate of Competence or any other formal qualification.

If carrying large supplies of duty-free drinks, the Frontier Guard should be told. Excess liquor will be sealed in bond aboard for the duration of the stay in Finland. However, if staying in Finland for some time, they may be reluctant to allow more than one bottle per crew member and have been known to refuse to bond and to confiscate the excess. Sailing whilst under the influence of alcohol is an offence under Finnish law, and the authorities have the right to stop a vessel at sea to check the alcohol levels of both the skipper and whoever is at the helm.

An EU-registered boat on which VAT has been paid can be kept in Finland indefinitely. A non-EU registered boat can stay in the country for up to one year, but a bond may be payable whilst over-wintering and Customs should be notified before the yacht comes ashore.

The Finnish flag is white with a blue Scandinavian cross; the Åland flag blue with a red cross on a yellow cross. Even Finnish yachts wear this courtesy flag when west of the Kihti (Swedish: Skiftet), the sound dividing the Åland islands from the Turku archipelago.

easternmost Swedish *skärgård* and the westernmost Finnish ones, but it has a reputation for difficult weather. During the summer months there is likely to be a continuous procession of car ferries and yachts all the way across.

The boundary between Åland and the rest of Finland, or between the Åland *skärgård* and the Turku archipelago (Turunmaan saaristo), is marked by the Kihti (Skiftet), a long, narrow sound only a mile wide in its northern part which runs north/south in longitude 21°09′E. West of this boundary the language spoken is almost entirely Swedish. East of it Finnish speakers and place names gradually become more frequent. The waters between the western Åland islands and Hanko are said to be the densest archipelago in the world.

From the Åland Islands to Hamina, just short of the border with Russia, the coast is a saaristo or *skärgård* coast, that is to say there is a sheltered route in smooth water behind the fringe of islands. It is difficult to convey the fascination of this kind of sailing to those who have never experienced it. One sails for hundreds of miles in smooth water through a vast forest or rock garden, stopping almost at will. At first the pilotage may seem difficult, especially if it is blowing hard, but the waters are excellently marked by buoys, lighthouses, and stone cairns and (in Finland) by pairs of wooden transits on shore. These cairns, or kummel are the oldest marks in the islands, and very skilfully sited. They show the general direction of the route but not, of course, every isolated danger.

Yachtsmen from elsewhere in Europe who are new to these waters often expend a great deal of nervous energy looking for 'the next mark'. It should be borne in mind, however, that the fairways are not like the rivers which flow into the Channel or North Sea, shoaling gradually to each side. The bottom is very uneven – the marks show the rocks, which are as likely to be in the centre of the fairway as at the sides. If there are no rocks there will be no marks, sometimes for several miles. Therefore, as a general rule, one is better off if one cannot see a mark than if one can – provided one is in the fairway, which means on the correct side of the relevant island. There are exceptions, of course…

An entirely separate cruising ground is the Saimaa Lake area, an immense landlocked complex of lakes entered through the Saimaa Canal. The Canal starts near Vyborg (see page 279), and runs through territory secured by the Russians in 1944 and leased back to the Finns in 1963 in return for the latter undertaking the upkeep of the canal. The Saimaa lakes are a favourite cruising ground for local yachtsmen, especially at the time of the Savonlinna Opera Festival in July, but are little visited by foreign yachts. The Board of Management of the Saimaa Canal issues a well produced booklet of instructions for small-boat traffic in the Saimaa Canal.

There are many beautiful and interesting harbours in Finland and it is only possible in this guide to mention a small selection of them.

The cruising season

Finland has an even shorter cruising season than Sweden, and it should be noted that some services are only provided between mid-June and mid-August – if that. Numbers of Finnish cruising yachts are already falling off by the third week of July, and decreasing markedly by early August. By late August most local yachts are already laid up ashore.

Private islands

Most smaller Finnish islands are privately owned, many sporting a single house, and although anchoring off seems to cause no problems it is polite to do so out of sight of the house. The owners of islands guard their privacy jealously and landing is seldom allowed.

In one reported incident, a yacht anchored off an apparently uninhabited island a few miles east of Hanko and two members of the crew went ashore at about 2100 for a short walk along the shore. The owners saw them but chose not to make any contact, and instead summoned the police who arrived by launch at 0100 – from 60M away. The policemen asked to see the passports of those aboard and said

Restricted areas

There are 17 military Restricted Areas in Finnish waters, some of which contain smaller Military Areas and all of which are marked on current Finnish charts. They range in size from a single island to an area west of Helsinki measuring, at its extremes, some 18M by 19M. Although movement within Restricted Areas is no longer forbidden or even limited, certain activities are, in particular scuba diving and bottom fishing (though use of a rod or a towed line appears quite acceptable). Pleasure craft under 24m can anchor where they wish. No Military Area may be approached within 100m unless within a marked fairway. These regulations apply to all, regardless of nationality. Further details can be found on the Finnish Defence Forces website at www.mil.fi.

In addition to the military Restricted Areas, there are Conservation Areas – most often to ensure that breeding birds remain undisturbed – where limitations on movement and/or anchoring may be in force for part of the year. Like the military areas they are clearly marked on the Finnish charts and should be rigorously observed.

they were required to investigate all complaints of trespass. They eventually left, but the lesson is clear: going ashore on a private island can cause a disproportionate amount of trouble.

The position throughout the Åland archipelago appears to be somewhat different to that in the rest of Finland. Relatively few islands are privately owned, and even those few normally take the Swedish attitude – that the owners' privacy must be respected but that anchoring, and a stroll ashore, are perfectly acceptable provided no damage is done.

Entry by yacht

Until recently, all yachts arriving in Finland had to check in at a Frontier Guard station before proceeding to their chosen berth or anchorage. This requirement has now been relaxed in the case of pleasure craft arriving directly from any co-signatories of the Schengen Convention i.e. Denmark, Estonia, France, Germany, Latvia, Lithuania, Sweden, Poland.

If arriving from a country not party to the Schengen Convention – effectively, Russia or directly from the UK or Ireland – or if the yacht has goods to

declare, it is still necessary to approach via the prescribed fairway and then visit the Frontier Guard and Passport Control point. Until this has been done, no one should leave the boat and nothing may be unloaded. The same is true if departing for a non–Schengen Convention country when, having obtained outwards clearance, the yacht must leave by the most direct route along an official fairway without any detours. Both the 'official fairways' and the Frontier Guard stations themselves are labelled on Finnish charts.

In addition to the 'fairway' Frontier Guard stations listed below, Mariehamn has a station (clearly labelled PASSPORT CONTROL) close to the yacht marina in the west harbour.

Although Frontier Guard stations are open around the clock, yachts are recommended to visit between 0800 and 2000 having notified their approach at least one hour previously via telephone or VHF Ch 74. This is particularly important if approaching Haapasaari or Santio islands from the east – the vessel's approach will have been followed on radar, and officials at the border posts naturally prefer to know what they are looking at.

For further information about the customs clearance of pleasure craft, contact Customs ☎ +358 (0)20 690 600, *Fax* +358 (0)20 492 1812, *Email* via www.tulli.fi.

Yacht services and chandlery

Throughout Finland, visitors marinas are indicated by a white anchor on a blue background and the words '*Vierassatama*', '*Gästhamn*' or 'Guest Harbour' – or occasionally all three. There are numerous good boatyards and a chandlery at almost every harbour, though probably the largest and best-stocked are to be found at Mariehamn, Turku, Hanko and, of course, Helsinki.

Diesel is obtainable at nearly all marinas, often together with a station at which a holding-tank can be emptied. Bottled gas is more of a problem, with only Finnish and Swedish cylinders readily exchangeable.

Berthing fees

Most Finnish guest harbours charge a set fee per night irrespective of the size of the yacht. To give an indication of comparative costs in 2010 berthing fees have been bracketed as follows:
Lower: up to €15/night
Middle: up to €25/night
Upper: up to €35/night.

If electricity is required an additional set fee per night may be levied.

Yacht clubs

The principal club is the Nylandska Jaktklubben (NJK), which has extensive premises in Helsinki including a marina which welcomes visiting yachts. It also owns a number of islands and anchorages where its members carefully guard their privacy.

The Finnish Cruising Club (Merikarhut or Sea Bears) also owns islands and anchorages, and its rules forbid use by non-members.

Frontier Guard Stations for Pleasure Craft

Frontier station	Telephone	Fairway
Mariehamn 60°05′N 19°56′E	+358 2 0410 7230	Fairways past Körsö or Nyhamn
Hanko 59°48′·5N 22°55′E	+358 2 0410 6400	Fairways past Russarö or Morgonlandet
Suomenlinna 60°09′N 24°59′E	+358 2 0410 6900	Fairway from Helsinki lighthouse past Harmaja
Haapasaari 60°17′N 27°11′·5E	+358 2 0410 6050	Fairway past Haapasaari islands
Santio 60°27′·5N 27°43′·5E	+358 2 0410 2130	Coastal fairway past Santio island

Radio communications and weather information

Details of the above, including Search and Rescue, GMDSS, Coast Radio Stations, Weather Bulletins and Navigational Warnings, NAVTEX and Weatherfax transmissions, weather forecasts on the internet and Firing Practice areas can be found in the Appendix on pages 363–371.

Finland's VHF coast radio stations are extremely well organised and convenient to use, and all parts of the coastline have excellent coverage. All VHF stations are remotely controlled from Turku – see the Appendix page 369. Weather bulletins are broadcast in English at 0633 and 1833 UT, gale warnings on receipt and at 0233, 0633, 1033, 1433, 1833 and 2233 UT.

Maritime Search and Rescue

West Finland Coast Guard Distrcit is responsible for organizing and providing adequate maritime search and rescue (SAR) within its SAR area and for the required co-operation with other authorities. West Finland Coast Guard District is also responsible for keeping in touch with maritime SAR authorities in other countries

The Finnish Search and Rescue Region (SRR) Is shown on the map in blue. It is divided into to two sub-regions: West Finland (dark blue) and Gulf of Finland (light blue). The Finnish SRR is adjacent to the Swedish, Estonian and Russian SRRs.

Gulf of Finland Coast Guard District is responsible for the Gulf of Finland SAR sub-region.

Maritime Rescue Co-Ordination Centre

In West Finland Coast Guard District, SAR activity is led by two centres: Maritime Rescue Co-Ordination Centre in Turku (MRCC Turku) and Maritime Rescue Sub Centre in Vaasa (MRSC Vaasa). The centres are staffed 24/7, which ensures fast and efficient response to reports of distress. In the centres, the operations are lead by a Search and Rescue Mission Coordinator. (*See plan on right*).

MRCC Turku co-ordinates the tasking of national assets in rescue efforts when the need arises. It also co-ordinates the use of national and internationl assets when important SAR units are needed simultaniously in several incidents. (*See page 369*).

Coastguard stations

1. Santio
   Coastal fairway past Santio
   ☎ +358 (0) 71 872 6110 *Telefax* +358 (0) 71 872 6119
2. Haapasaari
   Fairway past Haapasaari
   ☎ +358 (0) 71 872 6130 *Telefax* +358 (0) 71 872 6139
3. Suomenlinna
   Fairway from Helsinki lighthouse past Harmaja
   ☎ +358 (0) 71 872 6310 *Telefax* +358 (0) 71 872 6319
4. Hanko
   Fairway past Russarö or fairway past Morgonlandet
   ☎ +358 (0) 71 872 6450 *Telefax* +358 (0) 71 872 6459
5. Maarianhamina
   Fairway past Korsö or Nyhamn
   ☎ +358 (0) 71 872 7230 *Telefax* +358 (0) 71 872 7239

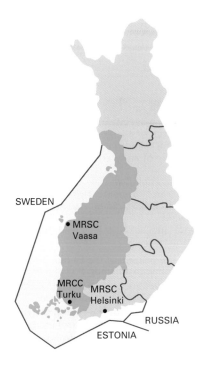

Charts and chart-books

Although Admiralty charts are very good for navigating at sea, it is essential to obtain the relevant large-scale Finnish publications to enjoy the delights of cruising inside the archipelago. Both conventional charts and chart-books are available, the latter – the *Merikarttasarja* series – providing a considerable amount of additional detail and useful information. Charts and maps are produced by the Finnish Maritime Administration, ① + 358 2 04481, *Fax* + 358 2 0448 4500, www.fma.fi. However to obtain the charts – and particularly the convenient chart-books – orders must be palced with John Nurminen Marine Oy who have an exclusive distribution agreement with the FMA. John Nurminen Marine Oy, Heikkiläntie 8, 00210 Helsinki ① +358 9 682 3180 *Fax* +358 9 6823 1811

For some reason the *Merikarttasarja* series does not run in sequence but instead comprises:

Vol A *Viipuri – Helsinki*
Vol B *Helsinki – Parainen*
Vol C *Ahvenanmaa*
Vol D *Turunmaan saaristo 2010*
Vol E *Selkämeri*
Vol F *Merenkurkku*
Vol G *Perämeri*
Vol J *Vesijärvi – Päijänne*
Vol K *Keitele ja Keiteleen kanava*
Vol L *Saimaan vesistö*

At first sight both charts and chart-books may look a little strange, employing colours and symbols different to those in the UK and Sweden – for example, a breaking rock is shown as a horizontal line with a stroke projecting upwards, a covered rock as a horizontal line with a stroke projecting downwards. However, once familiar, these charts make navigating the many narrow channels a straightforward if intricate affair. The channels have both obvious leading marks (typically red with a vertical yellow stripe) and black-and-white spar buoys with cardinal stripes but no topmarks.

Some of the many thousands of islands which fringe the routes described in this section have been renamed over the past few decades. Usage in this book follows that of current Finnish charts and *Merikarttasarja* chartbooks, but any attempt at correlation with older publications is likely to be met with failure or, at the very least, confusion.

Pilots and cruising guides

There is surprisingly little detailed information for yachtsmen published in English, though some of the following (and particularly the first) may be found useful:

The Sea of Archipelago and the Gulf of Finland, text in English, German and Russian. Not much detail in the text, but useful plans and stunning aerial photographs, 2002
The Suuri Satamkirja (Stora Hamnboken) series:
Vol 1 *Skärgård (Åbo skägård)*
Vol 2 *Ahvenanmaa (Åland skärgård)*
Vol 3 *Suomenlahti (Finska Viken)* (The Gulf of Finland) which between them cover some 350 harbours and anchorages in the Åland Islands and southwestern Finland. Although in Finnish and Swedish only, the text is short and subsidiary to the large-scale plans.
Käyntisatamat Besökshamnar, published annually in May, is a compilation of the harbour plan booklets enclosed with each of the *Merikarttasarja* chart-book series and could be very useful to supplement the latter, which are not updated annually. The text is in Finnish and Swedish, though the harbour information symbols are also explained in English. See the publisher's website at www.finnlake.com for further details.
Baltic Pilot Volume III (NP 20)
See the *Appendix*, page 361, for sources.

Internet sites

Seemingly everyone in Finland has their own website, and this is certainly true of nearly all companies and government organisations. The following are just the tip of the iceberg and even brief use of an internet search engine will uncover hundreds more.

Inclusion of an English version – along with Swedish, German and others – is apparently so standard on Finnish websites that this option can be assumed unless specifically stated otherwise.

Websites of individual towns and harbours are listed throughout the text.

www.fma.fi – the website of the Finnish Maritime Administration with all kinds of useful links

www.rvl.fi – the website of the Frontier Guard, responsible for border crossing and passport control

www.fmi.fi – the website of the Finnish Meteorological Institute, containing everything from today's weather forecast to long term climate statistics

www.mek.fi – the homepage of the Finnish Tourist Board.

www.finland-tourism.com – the Official Online Travel Guide to Finland, maintained by the Finnish Tourist Board and containing much of direct relevance to visitors, including travel information and many useful links

www.festivals.fi – the website of the Finland Festivals organisation, with details of thousands of local festivals and events, all with relevant e-mail and/or website addresses

www.visitaland.com – The official tourist gateway website

www.finlandarchipelago.org – the well-constructed website covering the Turku archipelago (the Turunmaan saaristo or Åbolands skärgård) – effectively those islands east of the Kihti (Skiftet)

www.lappeenranta.fi – the homepage of the City of Lappeenranta website, with an excellent section on 'Boaters' Lappeenranta' including the Saimaa Canal

www.marnet.fi – a useful site providing links to the homepages of most yacht clubs and marine-related business in Finland and beyond

www.balticsunmarinas.com – the homepage of the Baltic Sun Marina group, which has guest harbours in a number of Baltic countries including Finland. Each harbour rates a brief description and small plan

4a. Gulf of Bothnia coast of Finland

Heading south from Tornio on the Finnish coast of the Gulf of Bothnia there are many small anchorages or *gästhamns* and several important towns of sailing interest – Kemi and Oulu in the north; Pietarsaari (home of Nautor, the builders of Swan yachts) and Vaasa in The Quark; and Kristiinankaupunki, Pori (with its world famous jazz festival), Rauma and Uusikaupunki further south. The coastline is mostly flat and with shallow water, necessitating passage-making at a considerable distance from the coast. There is a small *skärgård* around the area of The Quark, but the *skärgård* proper does not start again until south of Rauma.

1. Tornio to Raahe

Distance 70M

Charts *Merikarttasarjat – G Perämeri, Ohtakari – Tornio Rannikkokartat 59, 55*

The northeast Finnish corner of the Gulf.

An inhospitable coast in bad weather where extensive shoals often call for long diversions, however there is more of interest here than ever expected.

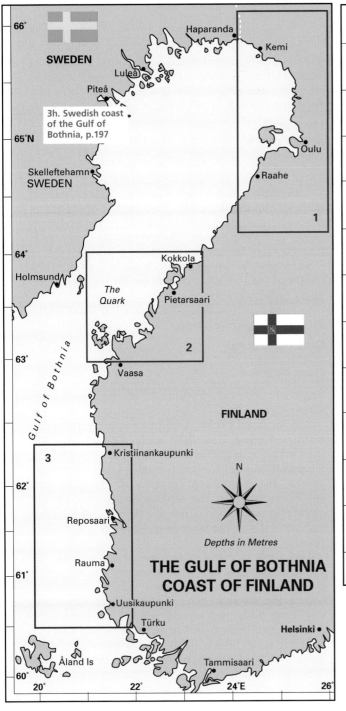

THE GULF OF BOTHNIA COAST OF FINLAND

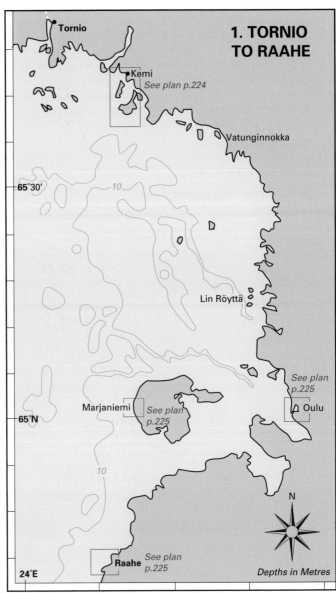

1. TORNIO TO RAAHE

4. FINLAND

Kemi

65°44'N 24°33'E
Charts 855 and 59

Lapland's deep-water port.

This port in the northeast corner of the Gulf is kept open throughout the winter by icebreakers to serve two pulp mills, the timber trade and a chromium mine. The commercial and ferry port is at Ajos 4M to the south.

Mind the fishing nets off the entrance, pass the docks at Ajos and the channel is deep for the first 1M beyond. Thereafter follow the narrower but still buoyed channel up to the town. The *gästhamn* provides well sheltered mooring with 25 bows-to berths from stern buoys in 2·4m. The two yacht clubs seem to take it in turns to collect fees. Between the two all the usual facilities are provided and all the services of a town of 35,000 are within 1km.

Kemi was very severely damaged during the Second World War but was rebuilt with rather little imagination during Russian occupation. The unremarkable church was restored in 2003. Excellent fish restaurant just along the quay if not eating at the friendly yacht clubs.

Vatunginnokka

65°33'N 25°07'E
Charts 851, 853 and 58

Safe harbour on exposed coast.

Easily identified by the surrounding wind turbines. Straightforward entrance with a lit leading line to 12 berths between booms or alongside in 2–4m

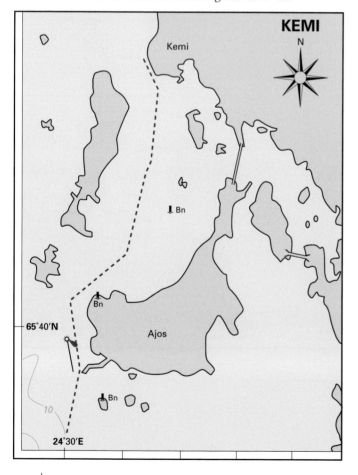

Wind turbines are not difficult to live with at Vatunginnokka harbour   *E. Redfern*

This small service harbour has better than expected facilities provided by the power company, Vapo and are shared with the underused caravan site. Café and good walks. It may be possible to buy fish from the fish farm on the south side.

Lin Röyttä

65°16'N 25°13'E
Charts 847, 850, 57 and 58.

Popular holiday island and nature reserve.

This excursion harbour was previously a loading port for the timber trade. The deepest approach is from the west and it now has 40 guest berths in 2–3m with stern buoys. The substantial stone walls give excellent shelter in all winds.

There is a narrow gauge track along the top of the southeast wall which is used to trolley luggage to the many holiday homes.

Limited facilities and no supplies but good walks on a very attractive island.

Oulu (Uleåborg)

65°01'N 25°27'E
Charts 846 and 57

Regional shopping and commercial centre with deep water port.

A 2·5m fixed bridge prohibits approach from the northwest but a 10M deep water channel from the west leads to the port which is easily identified by the large pulp mill. Beyond that is unlit but well buoyed passed the Hietasaari marina to port to the *gästhamn* close to the striking art centre by the market square. In 2007 the otherwise good facilities did not include the ablutions block in the market square.

This sixth largest city in Finland can provide all services, shopping and entertainment. The attractive wooden buildings on the south side of the market square are all that remain of the once important wood tar trade and salmon market but have been adapted into some excellent restaurants and cafés.

There is a Nokia factory, university and the workforce have embraced the high technology age. Well worth the long trip in from the open sea.

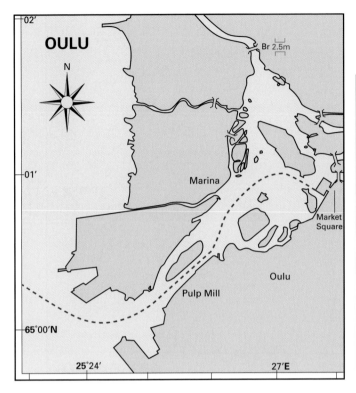

Good walks along the foreshore but mind the protesting turnstones if you stray a little inland. This is an excellent jumping off place for Sweden.

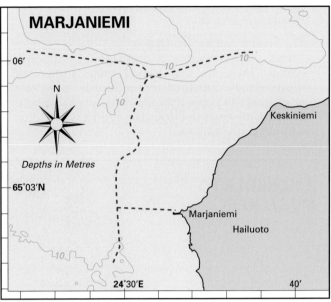

Raahe (Brahestad)
64°41'N 24°28'E
Charts 841, 842 and 55

Convenient service harbour.

South of Hailuoto there are other but shallower and smaller *gästhamns*. Raahe is a convenient overnight stop with nine guest berths from stern buoys or alongside in 2·4m. Facilities do not include power and shopping is limited.

Oulu from the *gästhamn* looking towards the Market Square   *E. Redfern*

Marjaniemi
65°02'N 24°32'E
Charts 844, 56 and 57

Safe harbour on the west of Hailuoto island.

Over 30M to the west of Oulu and requiring a careful approach from north or south is this well sheltered harbour. The three surrounding wind turbines can be seen from many miles off and channels are well buoyed to the leading line.

Now a small fishing harbour, active pilot station, campsite and *gästhamn* with up to 50 berths. Moor bows-to from stern buoys or alongside pontoons in 4·1m. Water and power available but at 100m, otherwise good facilities with an hotel and campsite kiosk. Sometimes possible to buy fish from the local fish processing shed.

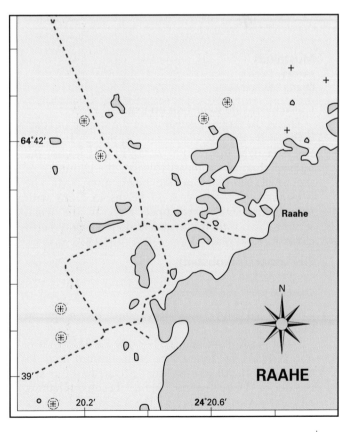

4. FINLAND

2. Kokkola to Vaasa

Distances
Raahe to Kokkola 75M, Kokkolato Vaasa 75M

Charts *Merikarttasarjat – F Merenkurkku, Siipyy – Himanka Rannikkokartat 54, 48*

The Finnish side of The Quark.

This covers another archipelago of attractive islands. There are well buoyed routes inshore of many islands. Excellent transit boards make this much easier to cover than the charts might suggest. The thriving cities of Pietarsaari and Vaasa contrast with natural anchorages.

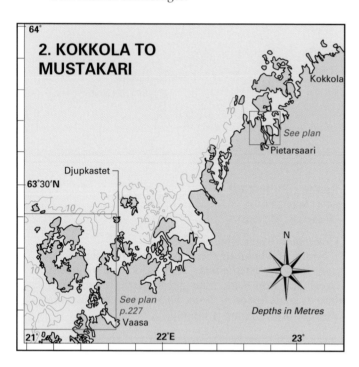

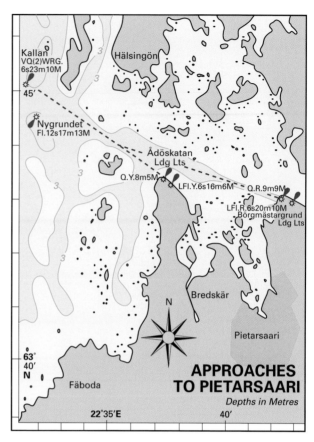

Mustakari
65°52'N 23°07'E
Charts 833 and 52

Convenient safe *gästhamn* on exposed coast.

This is the largest *gästhamn* on the stretch of coast between Raahe and Pietarsaari. Approach from the Kokkola light (63°59'·8N 22°52'E) and follow the buoyed channel southeast towards the chimneys of the town before branching north after 8M. The Mustakari *gästhamn* has 35 berths in 2·5m with stern buoys and is equipped with all the usual services. This is more convenient than trying to berth closer to Kokkola.

Pietarsaari (Jakobstad)
63°41'N 22°22'E
Charts 831, 832 and 51

Commercial port, busy town and the home of Nautor Swan.

From the Kallan light (63°45'·1N 22°31'·5E) it is not difficult to follow the well buoyed and lit channel southeast past Nautor's private harbour and the docks. Thereafter the channel becomes shallow and narrow all the way to the Yacht Club where

there are 30 bows-to moorings with stern buoys in 1·8–3m. All the usual services are on hand and the Yacht Club benefits from a good restaurant although still 1km north of the town.

There is an attractive old part of town with wooden houses but considerable late 20th-century development has transformed the shopping centre where every facility is available. Nautor would be more than capable of every kind of yacht repair and maintenance and are happy to show visitors round their impressive Boat Technology Centre. Baltic Yachts were due to move to here in late 2008.

The Yacht Club at Pietarsaari *M. Bowyer*

Djupkastet

63°18'N 21°37'E
Chart 49

Excellent safe anchorage.

The entrance is well marked with buoys and transits. Somewhere in this small natural harbour it would be possible to find good shelter to anchor in any wind.

There is also a small pontoon with stern buoys which can be used with prior agreement from the WSF in Vaasa.

Vaasa (Vasa)

63°06'N 21°35'E
Charts 819 and 48

Completely sheltered harbour in a modern industrial town.

There are various well charted and buoyed routes from the open sea to the Nagelprick light (63°06'·1N 20°25'·2E). Follow the main channel 3M southeast to the ferry terminal and then turn north into the smaller buoyed channel round Vaskiluoto island into the leisure harbour. It is possible to anchor off or berth alongside the town wharf which is convenient for shopping but short of facilities. Opposite there

Looking northwards from the WSF marina in Vaasa
E. Redfern

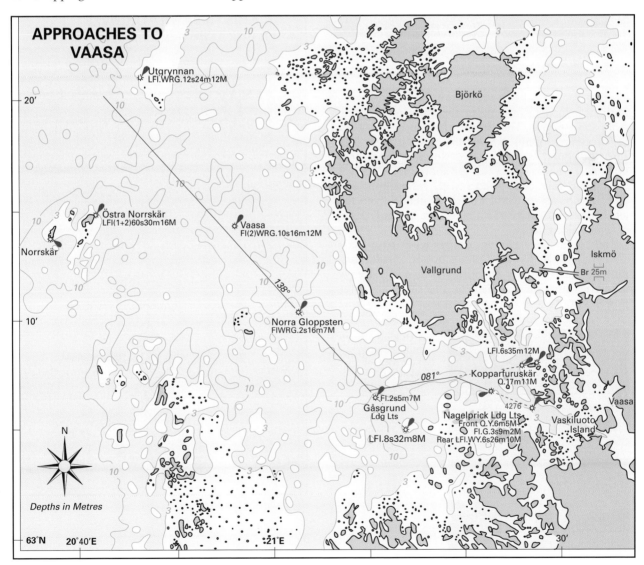

The Replot road bridge at Alskatintie is the longest in Finland   *M. Bowyer*

are two Yacht Clubs on the east of Vakiluoto island, both of which have 2·5–3m for bows-to mooring from stern buoys. The club to the south, the Wasa Segelförening (WSF) is Swedish speaking, very well run, with good facilities and is closer to town. It is possible to borrow bicycles for shopping. However both have fine club houses with restaurants and there are buses to town. Fuel is available from the jetty between the two yacht clubs but has only 1·5m of water alongside.

This is a busy sailing centre with first class shopping in the Remell Centre, hotels, restaurants, museums and Fantoy chandlers 1km away. Heavy industries provide employment and there are three power stations and three universities.

The striking lighthouse at Isokari west of Uusikaupunki *E. Redfern*

3. Kristiinankaupunki to Uusikaupunki

Distances

Vaasa to Kristiinankaupunki 65M
Kristiinanaupunki to Uusikaupunki 85M
Charts *Merikarttasajat – F Merenkurkku, Siipyy – Himanka E Selkämeri, Uusikaupunki – Kaskinen Rannikkokarten 47, 40*

The Finnish, southeast corner of the Gulf

More open and exposed in the north but once inside the islands south of Reposaari it is generally possible to find a protected route or sheltered anchorage. While less concentrated than the Turku archipelago this is nevertheless a challenging area for the navigator. First class buoyage and transits are a boon.

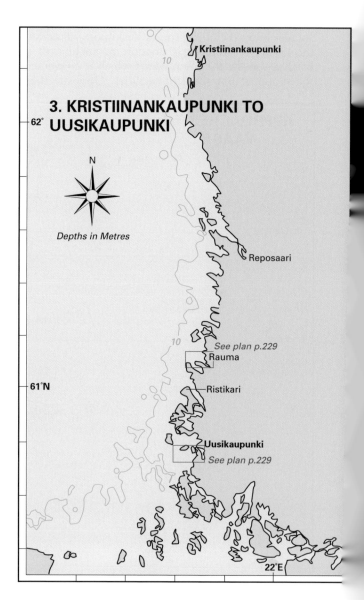

Kristiinankaupunki (Kristinestad)
62°16′N 21°22′E
Charts 812 and 44

Completely sheltered harbour by picturesque old wooden town.

There is a sizable oil terminal 2M to the west of the town with the appropriate well buoyed channels which should be avoided. From the south, west-northwest or west make for the Harkmeri light (62°11′·4N 21°20′E) and follow the 8M buoyed channel into the harbour. The main *gästhamn* is in the northeast corner by the bridge and has 30 berths from stern buoys in 2–3m and all the usual facilities except fuel.

Unlike most, the wooden town centre has escaped being burnt down and provides good services including a supermarket within two minutes' walk.

Reposaari (Räfsö)
61°37′N 21°26′E
Charts 807, 808, 809 and 42

Sheltered stopover west of Pori (Björneborg).

Surrounding fuel tanks will be seen long before reaching the Kaijakari light (61°36′·8N 21°22′·2E). Follow the transits and buoys to the 60 berth *gästhamn* to moor alongside or bows-to from stern buoys in 2–2·5m with good shelter. There are a wide range of facilities available on site. While the municipal centre of Pori, 22km away, can be reached by dredged channel it is probably best visited by bus or rail.

Rauma (Raumo)
60°08′N 21°28′E
Charts 804 and 41

A World Heritage Site and shipbuilding centre.

What a series of contrasts! The superbly marked deep-water approach then gives way to a confusion of buoys, leading lines and shallows to more than three *gästhamns*. Careful study of a large scale chart will show that the most accessible is at the east end of the harbour beyond the big ship berths. The moorings are alongside in 2–4m but the downside is the lack of facilities and the industrial surroundings.

There is at least one *gästhamn* with 10 berths in 2m with all facilities a little north at Petäjäs and another on the edge of the 400 boat Syväraumanlahti marina. The outside berths here are in 3·8m but you will be lucky to find much more than 2m in the twisting but well marked approach. Most facilities nearby but fuel and chandler at Petäjäs.

The very well preserved old wooden houses have been sensitively adapted for modern use and merit the World Heritage Site status which is bringing tourism and new prosperity to the town. Interesting church and good shopping but bicycles are an advantage.

Ristikari
61°00′N 21°17′E
Charts 803 and 41

Small natural harbour.

A short approach east, through buoys from the official north/south route leads to this safe harbour. Alongside pontoon moorings for 10 in 2·4–3·6m but with limited facilities.

Sometimes possible to buy fish from the single local boat on the quay. Good walks.

Uusikaupunki (Nystad)
60°47′N 21°24′E
Charts 735, 801, 802 and 40

Major yachting centre and attractive, large but industrialised town.

There are three main approach channels from north, west and south all of which are well marked and converge just northwest of Urpoinen island at 60°46′·8N 21°20′E. Then pass south of the power station and wind turbines to follow the buoys to the very narrow 2·5m deep channel which leads to the inner harbour. After a sharp turn to starboard the fully sheltered and award winning Pakkahuone *gästhamn* with up to 80 berths from stern buoys lies ahead to port. Up to 3m is claimed but this shoals to 1·5m beyond the café. Very good facilities on hand and within reach of two chandlers, boatyards, extensive shopping and services. Fuel available from a prominent jetty to port.

Bus and rail services are good to Turku (Åbo) about 40km to the southeast where the international airport makes either port useful crew changes.

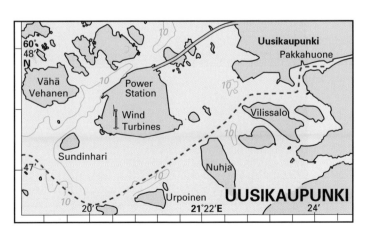

4b. The Åland Islands

Charts *Yleiskartat 953*
Merikarttasarjat – C Åland
The official tourist gateway website is
www.visitaland.com and that of the Turku
archipelago is at www.saaristo.org

See the Åland Islands and Saaristomeri plan on page 236.

Cruising the Åland and Turku archipelagos

Åland, an ancient realm of 6500 islands and skerries, is thought to be the oldest inhabited part of Finland. It is an autonomous province of Finland, within the EU but outside the EU tax area. It has its own parliament, police and flag (a red cross on a broader yellow cross on a blue background), prints its own stamps, registers its own ships, is a member of The Nordic Council and enjoys a large measure of autonomy. It is legally a neutral zone, and its citizens are therefore exempt from military service.

The culture and history of the Åland islands are closely bound up with the sea and shipping. In the 19th century Åland dominated the world grain-shipping trade, and its remaining sailing traders, owned by Gustaf Erikson, were still in commission in 1945.

Åland's east boundary is considered to be the Kihti (Skiftet), a long, narrow sound only a mile wide in its north part which runs north/south in longitude 21°09′E. To the east lies the Turku archipelago (the Turunmaan saaristo or Åbolands *skärgård*). In many ways this division is political rather than physical, and most visiting yachtsmen will have trouble telling them apart.

Navigation

The waters between Mariehamn and the Finnish mainland contain about 5,000 square miles of islands intersected by thousands of miles of navigable channels. It would require an entire summer to traverse the whole archipelago and a lifetime to sample all the secluded anchorages or 'nature harbours'.

For a detailed exploration it is necessary to carry Vols 1 and 2 of the Finnish *Suuri Satamkirja* (*Stora Hamnboken*), in addition to Vols C (*Åland/ Ahvenanmaa*) and D (*Turunmaan saaristo/ Åbolands skärgård*) of the *Merikarttasarjat chartbook* series and some or all of Finnish charts *903, 24–34* inclusive, *160* and *169*, but it is quite possible to sail through the area using only the latter. It is not mandatory for yachts and other small vessels to contact or monitor the Archipelago Vessel Traffic Service, ℡ +358 204 486 521, *VHF* Ch 71, but the information broadcast – which includes traffic movement reports, waterway and weather conditions and hazards – is of relevance to all.

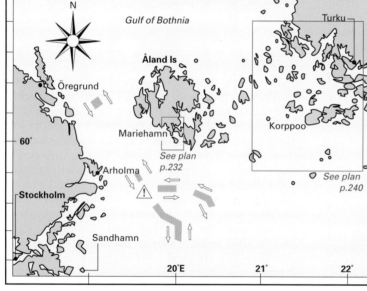

Sunset in an Åland anchorage *E. Redfern*

The spoken language varies between Swedish and Finnish. The majority of the near 28,000 population speak Swedish, the west being almost exclusively Swedish-speaking while more Finnish is encountered as one moves east. In many cases, place names are shown on the chart in both languages – usage here following that of the *Merikarttasarjat chartbook* series. There are a number of small private islands and, although these are not shown as such on the chart, the owners normally fly a national flag when at home. It is polite to recognise their privacy by not anchoring within sight of buildings or venturing ashore uninvited.

Åland is a paradise for sailing children. The innumerable islands are surrounded by waters which are tideless, sheltered and crystal clean. A short daysail will bring fresh adventures with each new anchorage – shoreline exploration followed by a barbecue, perhaps (but never on bare rocks). Man-made attractions are few, but much effort has been expended to make nearly every cultural site accessible to children.

Mariehamn (Maarianhamina)

60°06′N 19°56′E

Distances
Stockholm 70M, Hanko 105M, Turku 75M

Charts and guides
Merikarttasarjat – C Åland, Rannikkokarten 22–34

Lights
4490 **Marhällan** 60°01′·9N 19°52′·5E
Q(3)WRG.6s15mW9M 007°-W-120°-R-175°-G-219°-W-244°-R-333°-G-007° Round red tower, black bands. Floodlit
4494 **Tvibenan** 60°02′·4N 19°53′·3E Q.WRG.6m4M
184°-G-210°-W-212°-R-273·5°-G-330°-W-341·5°-R-070° White rectangle
4495·9 **Ldg Lts 052°** *Rear* 100m from front,
LFl.G.6s21m11M 046°-vis-058° Red rectangle, yellow stripe
4496 **Korsö** *Common front* 60°02′·4N 19°54′E
Iso.WRG.7m8M 318°-G-003°-W-009°-R-032·5°-G-062·5°-W-075°-R-179·5° Racon Red rectangle, yellow stripe
4496·1 **Ldg Lts 066°** *Rear* 180m from front,
LFl.6s17m15M 062°-vis-070° Red rectangle, yellow stripe
4510 **Granö** 60°03′·5N 19°55′·7E Q(2)WRG.5s6mW6M
146°-G-182°-W-185°-R-212°-G-332°-W-338°-R-006° Orange tower, white lantern
4500 **Lotsberget Ldg Lts 028°** *Front* 60°05′N 19°56′·2E
Iso.Y.2s31m10M 023°-vis-033°
Red rectangle, yellow stripe, on metal framework tower, white lantern
4500·1 *Rear* 457m from front Iso.Y.6s51m10M
023°-vis-033° Red rectangle, yellow stripe, on metal framework tower

Harbour communications
Mariehamn Port Authority ② +358 18 531 471
VHF Ch 12, 13, 16 (call *Mariehamn Port*)
Mariehamn website www.mariehamn.aland.fi

General

Mariehamn is by far the largest town in Åland with a year-round population of just under 11,000, though some 1·5 million tourists are estimated to pass through each year. It is the capital of the Department of Åland. Although the Åland Islands are within the EU they remain outside its tax area so Mariehamn provides a duty free shopping area easily accessible from both Sweden and the Finnish mainland.

Old wooden houses fringe wide tree-lined avenues, pedestrian areas full of small cafés, and a good shopping centre in this relaxed and spacious town. It stands on a tongue of land separating two arms of the sea and has two yacht harbours, West Harbour (Västerhamn) and East Harbour (Österhamn). Although less than a mile separates the two harbours by land, by sea it is some 15M so that when coming from the south the decision as to which to head for must be made before passing Nyhamn light, see plan on page 236. West Harbour is the deeper and more easily reached by visiting yachts unfamiliar with the area, but this advantage is balanced by East Harbour's proximity to the town centre.

Mariehamn is of particular interest to seafarers as the last home of square rig, having been the port of registry for Captain Gustaf Erikson's famous 'Flying P' line. The four-masted barque *Pommern*, which last sailed commercially in 1939, is now a museum ship in the West Harbour and is well worth a visit, as is the nearby Åland Maritime Museum (note the north Atlantic chart on display, published by James Imray & Son in 1864).

Near the East Harbour will be found the Maritime Quarter including museums, historic vessels and boatbuilding sheds. The 'Åland Sea Days', a five-day event held every July, is based in the Maritime Quarter and offers attractions for all ages including a busy programme for children.

Approach and entrance

The town is normally approached either from the southwest, most often from Sweden, or from the southeast, through the Åland Islands.

If coming from the southwest and making for the West Harbour the massive wind turbines at the Nyhamn light will be spotted a long way off and should be left well to starboard. Then approach the distinctive Marhällan light structure, turning onto a course of 028° to follow the main ferry channel into the south part of the harbour (aided after dark by the Lotsberget leading lights). The marina lies north of the ferry berths and the barque *Pommern*.

Large-scale charts are required for the southeast approach to West Harbour, though again the final approach follows the main shipping channel. From Stora Lökskär, some 2·5M northeast of Nyhamn light, pass between Järsö, Granö and Gåsö and the islets to their southwest, and thence continue on a course of 340° to converge with the southwest approach route.

There is also a buoyed (but unlit) approach channel from the west, which provides a convenient

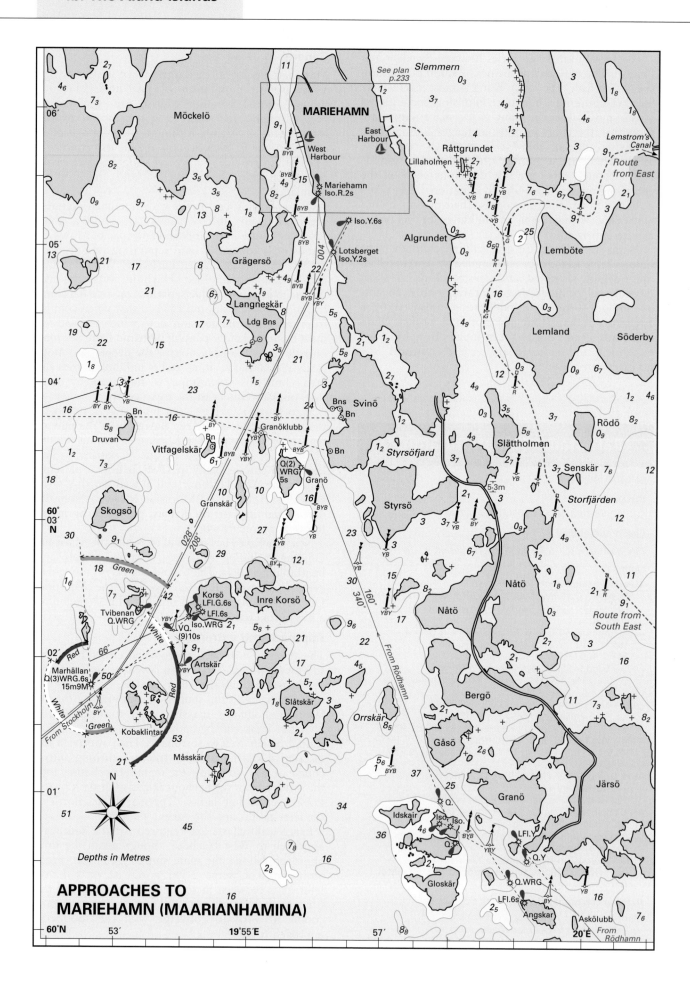

**APPROACHES TO
MARIEHAMN (MAARIANHAMINA)**

Depths in Metres

Marhällan lighthouse, which marks the southwestern approach to Mariehamn in the Åland islands *A. Hammick*

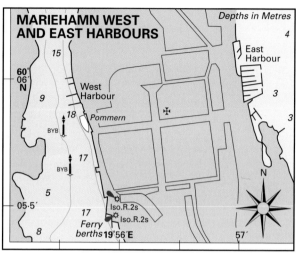

short cut for yachts coming from the west coast of the Åland Islands. It enters the archipelago in the vicinity of 60°04′N 19°47′E and joins the two main routes 4M to the east at 60°04′N 19°55′E.

The East Harbour is reached via a channel which is only partially buoyed and is, in places, shallow. Again, large-scale charts are a necessity. From a point midway between Stora Lökskär and Rödhamn lights the channel runs north to leave the island of Björkö to port, passes east of Gulskär, and thence northwest to leave Rönnakär to port. It then continues northwest between the northeast corner of Nåtö and the offlying islet of Senskär, leaves Slättholmen to port and the west extemity of Lemland to starboard, avoids the small Algrundet peninsula, and finally heads for East Harbour leaving the two small Råttgrundet islands to starboard – and all in 8M!

Alternatively if approaching from the east through Lumparn follow the buoys to the Lemstrom's Canal, through the swing bridge, round Lemböte and join the above route north of Lemland

Caution

It cannot be stressed too often that many of the channels used by the large ferries which ply from Stockholm to Turku via Mariehamn are narrow in the extreme, and that the ferries have priority AT ALL TIMES. If faced with the choice of running down a yacht or putting his ferry – complete with hundreds of passengers – aground on the rocks edging a narrow channel, there is little doubt which of the two evils most captains will choose.

Formalities

See Entry by yacht, page 220. If in doubt contact the Frontier Guard on *VHF* Ch 74 or ☎ +358 20 410 7230. There is a pontoon prominently marked PASSPORT CONTROL close south of the West Harbour marina where arriving yachts may be instructed to secure.

While it may be technically correct to fly both the Finnish and Åland courtesy flags the Åland Islanders appreciate not being reminded they are part of Finland.

Anchorage

There are no special restrictions on anchoring in the area of Mariehamn, but it will be difficult to find any suitable part of the shore which is not private property.

Berthing

The Västerhamn or West Harbour is run by the Åland Segel Sällskapet (ÅSS), ☎ +358 18 13610, *Fax* +358 18 19144, *Email* info@segel.ax www.segel.aland.fi. The ÅSS was founded in 1897 by the NJK (Nyländska Jaktklubben) of Helsinki and the KSSS (Kungliga Svenska Segelsällskapet) of Stockholm.

There are some 170 berths on four pontoons, where yachts lie bows-to from stern buoys in depths ranging from 2–18m. The outermost downstream berths are best suited to seriously large vessels, but the north pontoons provide better shelter for yachts of normal size. Take any vacant berth and call as soon as convenient to the harbour office (open 0800–2100 daily in season) directly below the ESSO Butik sign at the south end of the range of buildings. (Those to the north house club offices and an excellent restaurant). Berthing fees are in the middle band (see page 220).

Ferry rush hour, Mariehamn, from the Västerhamn pontoons *J.Sadd*

4. FINLAND

Mariehamn West Harbour, with the barque *Pommern* in the foreground *A. Hammick*

The Österhamn or East Harbour is run by the Mariehamns Seglarförening (MSF), Harbourmaster ☎ +358 40 8677 760, www.msf.aland.fi The harbour office is open 0800–1300 and 1500–2100 in June and August, 0700–2000 throughout July.

The visitors' berths are in and around the northern 'enclosure', that to the south being for local craft. The entrance is relatively narrow but it is reasonably spacious once inside. Moorings inside are between posts, those outside either bows-to from stern buoys or simply alongside, with space for 340 yachts in the marina plus a further 60 moorings. Depths shoal to 1·5m or less near the shore, though the outer berths have up to 3·5m. Shelter is good in strong southwest winds, which may cause problems for yachts in the West Harbour, but most would consider the surroundings less scenic. Berthing fees are in the middle band (see page 220).

Services for yachts

Both marinas provide water and electricity throughout, and showers, sauna, laundry and toilet facilities ashore. There are diesel pontoons (West Harbour: 0800–2200, East Harbour: 0900–2100) where holding tanks can be emptied. Finnish and Swedish propane bottles can be exchanged at both marinas. Weather forecasts are posted daily. There are small shops, cafés and restaurants near both marinas, plus a daily delivery of fresh bread every morning at around 0800.

The excellent Zetterströms Varv (boatyard), ☎ +358 18 22855, *Fax* +358 18 22856, about 0·75M upstream from the West Harbour, has long been a favourite spot for visiting yachts to have repairs carried out and to overwinter. There are two marine railways capable of handling vessels up to 16 tonnes, and repairs can be completed in GRP, steel and timber. There are marine engineers at the boatyard, and others may be recommended by the marina offices. Sail repairs can be arranged at the Västerhamn.

The Kalmers chandlery, is situated at Vikingagränd, about 3km north of Mariehamn ☎ +358 18 12012, *Email* info@kalmers.aland.fi (open 0800–1700 Monday–Saturday, 0800–1300 Sunday) A free minibus leaves the West Harbour at 1000 and 1200 calling at East Harbour 15 minutes later (or hire a bicycle – see below). The stock held is impressive, including general chandlery, rope, paint, electronics etc.

A few local charts are on sale at the West Harbour marina office, but for a full range of Swedish and Finnish charts and guides visit Lisco at 25 Skarpansvägen, ☎ +358 18 17177, *Email* bok@lisco.ax www.lisco.fi. More limited stocks are available from Mariehamns Bokhandel at 14 Torggatan, ☎ +358 18 19745, as well as the nearby Britas Bok & Papper (both in Mariehamn's pedestrian area).

General facilities

The main shopping centre lies on the east side of the peninsula, close to the Österhamn but about 1M from the Västerhamn. Small carts for carrying groceries can be borrowed from both places. All the facilities of a medium-sized town are available, including food stores, Alko, banks, restaurants and hotels, together with an excellent tourist information office and library. Parents with children aboard are recommended to visit the latter, which has an excellent children's area and play section with toys, books, CDs in English, storytelling and craft activities during July.

There are two excellent but expensive restaurants on the west side. One in the ÅSS clubhouse and the Restaurang Nautical above the Maritme Museum.

Communications and travel

Mail can be sent to both marinas – c/o ÅSS Marina, Strandpromenaden, Postbox 135, 22101 Mariehamn, Åland, Finland or c/o Mariehamns Seglarförening, Postbox 155, 22101 Mariehamn, Åland, Finland. There are several internet access points including Wi-Fi at the West Harbour, the tourist office (open 0900–1800 daily in summer) and the library.

There are regular flights and ferries from Mariehamn to Stockholm, Turku and Helsinki. An inter island ferry serves the archipelago, and all the islands can be reached from Mariehamn without difficulty.

Car hire is readily available, however Mariehamn might have been designed for the cyclist, having almost no hills and little traffic. Bicycles can be hired from both marinas, with a wider choice including tandems and children's bicycles available from a store opposite the ferry dock on the west.

Possible cruising routes

Cruising in Åland and beyond could follow any number of routes depending upon time constraints, final destination and personal interest, and those suggested below are just that – suggestions. Of course one can wander between them – indeed, it is possible to sail from Mariehamn direct to Hanko without stopping, but that would be to miss some of the best *skärgård* sailing in the entire Baltic.

Those routes which cover the area between the Ålands Sea in the west and the Kihti (Skiftet) in the east are taken first, followed by briefer notes on routes east towards the Finnish mainland. Refer to the plans on pages 236 and 240.

Route 1 Circumnavigation of the main island of Åland

Route 2 A southern route through the Åland Islands

Route 3 A northern route through the Åland Islands

Route 4 A figure of eight around the Åland Islands (the cultural route, but not shown on the plan on page 236)

Route 5 The Södö-Sälsö gap towards Hanko: a southern route

Route 6 The Södö-Sälsö gap towards Hanko: a central route

Route 7 The Södö-Sälsö gap towards Turku or Hanko: a northern route

Route 1 Circumnavigation of the main island of Åland (Ahvenanmaa)

A cruise round the main island of Åland is strongly recommended for anyone who does not have the time to venture further east. There are many beautiful, peaceful and remarkably unfrequented anchorages to be discovered, together with a cross-section of cultural and historical sights. A fair insight into Åland will be gained even with this limited visit. The route begins in Eckerö, heads southeast for Mariehamn (Maarianhamina), enters Lumparn through the Lemström's Canal, exits Lumparn via the Prästösundet, and finally skirts the northeast and

Karingsund Harbour map *J. Sadd*

northwest coasts of Åland before returning to Eckerö.

Käringsund (Käringsundet)
60°14′N 19°32′E

Charts

It is only 16M from Grisslehamn in Sweden to Signilskär off Eckerö, which makes the old fishing harbour of Käringsund a good starting point for a circumnavigation of Åland. This attractive little harbour behind the busy ferry terminal offers shelter from all directions, and contains a *gästhamn* with good facilities. The Mail Route Museum (see Route 4) and the Hunting and Fishing Museum are both in Eckerö which, doubtless due to its proximity to Sweden, receives the greatest number of tourists in the Åland Islands.

Lemström's Canal (Lemströmin Kanava)
60°06′N 20°01′E

Russian prisoners dug the 350m canal which is spanned by a swing bridge. Throughout June, July and August, this opens for 10 minutes on each hour between 0800 and 2200. It can be opened at other times, on payment of a fee, by contacting the operator on ☎ +358 18 33731. Strong currents may run through the canal in either direction.

Naset, a typical fishing village in the Åland Islands *E. Redfern*

Lemstron Canal swing bridge *J. Sadd*

4. FINLAND

THE ÅLAND ISLANDS
AND SAARISTOMERI

Continued on p.240

Depths in Metres

Sweden

Kastelholm
60°14'N 20°05'E

In the northwest corner of Lumparn is a wooded sound leading to Kastelholm Castle, the foundations of which were laid in the 13th century. From the end of the 1600s the castle was left to decay, leaving impressive ruins which have now been restored. Next door is the equally interesting Jan Karlsgården Open Air Museum, which has a collection of old Åland farm buildings and boathouses. There is a *gästhamn* with three pontoons and all the usual facilities close south of the castle.

Throughout July a ghost from the 16th century will lead children around Kastelholm Castle on a 'Ghostly Hour' journey with both sound and lighting effects (not suitable for children under six). All ages can play with old-fashioned toys in one of the old houses at the Open Air Museum.

Kastelholm Marina looking southwest   *J. Sadd*

Bomarsund
60°13'N 20°15'E

Bomarsund is spanned by a bridge with only 2·5m clearance and must therefore be entered from the north, after leaving Lumparn through Prästösundet. A fortress was built here by the Russians in the beginning of the 19th century, and was bombarded and captured by an Anglo-French fleet in 1854. The remains still stand. This delightful anchorage was a favourite of Tsar Alexander III and now has a *gästhamn* and a small holiday camp.

Nötviken
60°17'N 20°11'E

This long narrow fjord providing excellent anchorage at its head is now becoming more built up. A dinghy trip into the lagoon west of the anchorage is rewarding, but beware of boulders just below the surface in the narrows.

Hamnsundet
60°22'N 20°05'E

The north side of Åland is remote, so the fishing harbour of Hamnsundet is conveniently placed to offer protection in all winds. It has a small *gästhamn* with all the usual facilities, including fuel and kiosk with irregular hours.

Geta Djupviken
60°24'N 19°50'E

A long narrow inlet with an excellent anchorage carrying 7m at its head, well sheltered even from the north. From here it is possible to reach the wooden lookout tower on the summit of Getaberget, at 100m the highest hill in Åland.

Route 2
A southern route through the Åland Islands

Most of the vessels and ferry traffic between Mariehamn and Helsinki passes this way, even though parts of the route are open to south and southwest winds. However it does include Kökar, one of the most interesting of the Åland islands.

The route starts in Mariehamn, heads southeast into Rödhamnsfjärden and then north of Ledskär (59°58'N 20°10'E) to Degerby (60°02'N 20°23'E). Yachts drawing less than 1·8m may then take the most beautiful 10M Embarsund channel which leads east and south of Sandö (60°04'N 20°26'E), Nötö, Juddö-ö and Banö-ö, north of Berskär (60°04'N 20°40'E), between Ängo and Finö, and lastly between Södö and Sälsö (60°05'N 20°45'E). Yachts requiring over 1·8m should use the main channel via Enskär, some 3M further north. The route from Degerby to Kökar, which passes south of Degerö and north of Föglö, is barred to sailing yachts by a 5·3m bridge. The route then turns south, passes north of Kökar (59°58'N 20°55'E) and on across the Kihti (Skiftet).

Rödhamn
59°59'N 20°06'E

The beautiful old harbour of Rödhamn was an important anchorage for sailing ships en route from Sweden to Finland, as ships would sometimes lie for weeks waiting for favourable winds to carry them across the Åland Sea. A pilot station was built in 1818 and remained in use until the 1920s. In the late 1980s it was recreated using building plans from 1858. There is also a small museum depicting the history of the radio beacon, in use from 1937 until 1970.

In addition to the *gästhamn*, the Åland Yacht Club (ÅSS) has a marina and premises on the island – including a café offering fresh bread and freshly smoked fish, a sauna, and a boat-shed which doubles as an art gallery.

Degerby
60°02'N 20°23'E

Degerby, on the west coast of Degerö island, is considered to be the central point of the archipelago. There are two *gästhamns* with excellent facilities including shopping, restaurants and fuel, and everything is within walking distance. The keys to the community's modern indoor swimming pool

Brightly painted houses at Degerby *E. Redfern*

(unheated in the summer) are held at the restaurant overlooking the harbour. The north *gästhamn* although closer to the services is more disturbed by ferries.

Husö
60°04′N 20°48′E

Husö is in the municipality of Sottunga, the most sparsely inhabited community in Åland (though there are many holiday cottages). It is known for its rock formations and is well worth a visit. There is a small harbour where, as in most of the Åland harbours, fresh bread and cinnamon rolls are delivered every morning to your yacht.

Note There is an awkward transition between Charts 760 and 761 in Vol C of the *Merikarttasarja chartbook* series, which complicates pilotage north and south of Husö island. A larger scale and very useful Chart *758a* centred on Husö is bound a few pages earlier in the book, but it is not mentioned in the margins of Charts 760 and 761 so is easily overlooked.

Kökar
59°57′N 20°54′E

Kökar comprises Karlby, Finnö and Helsö islands, and is both Åland and Finland's most southern community. There are three *gästhamns* – Sandvik

The *gästhamn* at Sandvik, Kokar looking north *J. Sadd*

(59°56′N 20°53′E), Helsö (59°57′N 20°55′E) and Karlby (59°55′N 20°55′E). Sandvik and Helsö are both good natural harbours affording shelter from all winds, and have all the usual facilities ashore but mind the regular ferry. Karlby has a more difficult approach. Sandvik is convenient for exploration of the Franciscan Chapel on Hamnö and the Bronze Age settlement at Otterböte. The island of Källskär (59°53′N 20°54′E), in Kökar's south archipelago, boasts special rock formations known as Källskärskannan.

Route 3 A northern route through the Åland Islands

The waters of the northeastern archipelago are some of the most fascinating and least frequented in Åland, not least because they are off the beaten track from Mariehamn to Hanko or Helsinki. They can be approached from the southwest, from Vårdö after crossing Lumparn (Route 1) or from south, from Södö and Sälsö (Route 2). The route then wanders northeast through the communities of Kumlinge and Brändö which comprise many small islands and skerries.

Seglinge
60°13′N 20°43′E

The harbour at Seglinge, on the east side of the island, is very quiet and rural with mooring to wooden staging and stern buoys in about 2m. The walk up to the old windmill and the famous Stangnäs cauldrons – deep hollows in the rocks, where it is said that offerings were made for better fishing – offers excellent views of surrounding islands.

Remmarhamn, Kumlinge
60°15′N 20°44′E

There is a *gästhamn* at Remmarhamn in the bay south of Ljugarsholm and north of Snäckö, close to the village of Kumlinge but it is exposed to the south and there are strong currents from under the small road bridge. The unique St Anna's Church, which dates from the 15th century is less than 4km to the northeast. The walls have distinctive murals by an unknown artist of the period, a style not seen elsewhere. In strong southerlies it is better to use one of the *gästhamns* on the north of the island.

Lappo
60°19′N 21°00′E

This sheltered *gästhamn* formed by a wooden jetty, is surrounded by traditional boathouses and has good facilities nearby. A sandy beach and bird reserve lie west of the jetty. The Archipelago Museum contains fine examples of traditional boats and there is also a good restaurant.

Åva
60°27′·5N 21°04′E

Approached through Angskärsfjarden, Åva is a large, landlocked and somewhat bleak bay. Entry from the southeast is blocked by a 5·4m bridge.

Typical Finnish leading marks *P & G Price*

Jurmo
60°31'N 21°04'E

A most beautiful approach from the southeast suddenly reveals a large village with a fish quay. The *gästhamn*, which has all the usual facilities, is a short distance to the east.

Route 4
A figure of eight around the Åland Islands (the cultural route)

A yacht with plenty of time to soak up the culture and history of Åland could follow a figure of eight route around the islands. This would cover most of the historical sights and museums and travel along a section of the old post road, the great mail route between Sweden and Finland from 1638 until 1910.

If the old post road is of particular interest, a good starting point would be the Mail Route Museum in Eckerö. Then head south to Mariehamn with its plethora of cultural and maritime museums (see page 231). Join the old post road again at Kastelholm (Route 1) and follow it east, leaving Lumparn through Ängösund, across Delet to Kumlinge and Brändö, the northeast archipelago (Route 3). From here the mail route heads across Kihti (Skiftet) to the Åbo *skärgård* (see *The Mail Road Across Åland* by Jan Andersson).

The cultural route now heads south to Kökar, either by returning through the Kumlinge archipelago and joining Route 2 south of Sottunga, or by heading south through the Kihti (Skiftet), diverting southeast into the Åbo *skärgård* south of Fiskö (60°11'N 21°13'E) to avoid the restricted area east of Jungfruskär, and then finally turning southwest across Kihti (Skiftet) to Kökar.

From Kökar, Route 2 can be followed west to Degerby before heading northwest into Lumparn through Ängösund to Bomarsund (Route 1) and Värdö, crossing the old post road again. The southeast approach to the anchorage at Vargata on Värdö is spanned by Åland's longest bridge, of 7·5m. Route 1 now completes the passage back to Eckerö via the remote north coast of Åland.

4c. Finnish Archipelago

See plans on pages 236 and 240.

Route 5 The Södö-Sälsö gap towards Hanko: a southern route

After passing through the Södö-Sälsö gap, the southern route turns south to pass north of Kökar before heading southeast through the Kihti (Skiftet), the boundary between the Åland and Åbo skargards, towards Utö.

From Utö, Route 5 continues northeast to Jurmo and Borstö – possibly with a diversion north to investigate Björkö and Nötö – east past Yxskar (59°52'N 21°03'E) to Vänö, and finally north of Rosala (59°52'N 22°27'E) and Hiittinen (Hitis) (59°54'N 22°31'E) for the final leg southeast to Hanko.

The total distance from Mariehamn's West Harbour to Hanko's East Harbour by Routes 2 and 5 is approximately 122M.

Utö
59°47'N 21°22'E

Utö itself is isolated and rather barren, with a testing approach fairway off the main channel, but the *gästhamn* offers good shelter and has a single jetty with visitors' berths on the east side in 2–3m. There are basic facilities including two small shops, but fuel is not available. Utö boasts the oldest lighthouse in Finland, the original having been built in 1753.

Jurmo
59°49'N 21°35'E

Jurmo with a large *gästhamn* which is well buoyed, has up to 80 places in 1·8–3·8m on its northwest coast. Basic shopping facilities but no fuel. The island is known for its stone circles and mazes, some of which may date back to the bronze age. Their original purpose is unknown.

Borstö
59°52'N 21°58'E

The small and sheltered *gästhamn* lies in the gap between Borstö and Långskär, the islet to the south. The island is unspoilt and attractive, but has virtually no facilities other than a small museum which contains some interesting wreck artefacts. Doubtless the Borstö Gumma (Borstö Lady), an old ship's figurehead which resides on the top of the island's highest hill, has similar origins.

Björkö
59°54'N 21°41'E

The island has no harbour as such, but the long inlet which runs in from the southwest is one of the most popular natural anchorages in the archipelago. No facilities.

Nötö
59°57'N 21°44'E

Most of Nötö's quays are private, but visitors can anchor south of the ferry quay or use the few

4. FINLAND

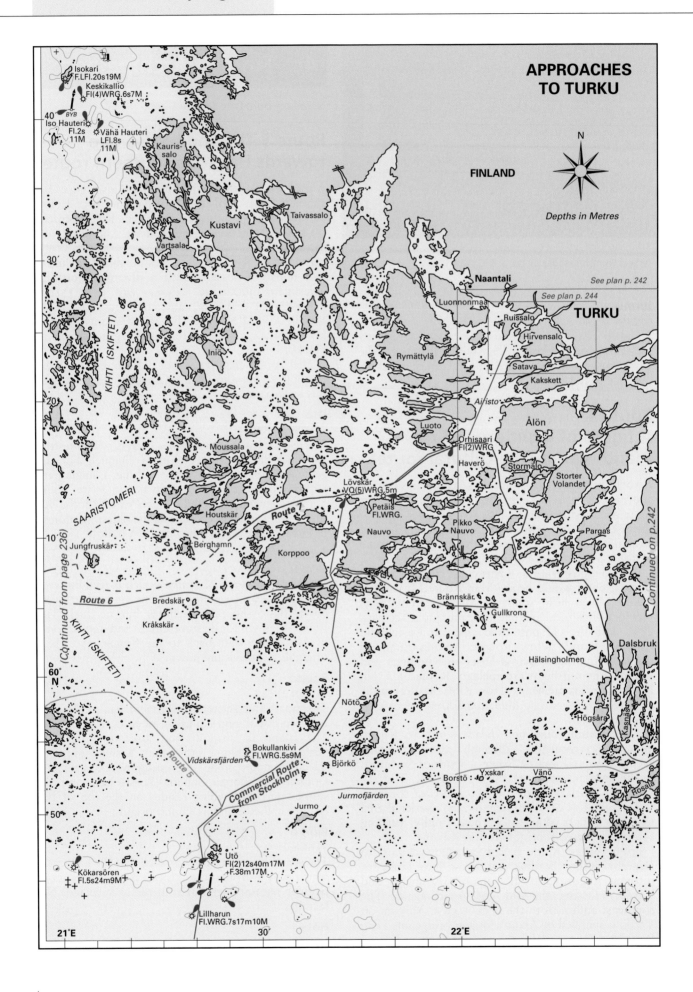

APPROACHES
TO TURKU

FINLAND

N

Depths in Metres

Isokari
F.LFl.20s19M
Keskikallio
Fl(4)WRG.6s7M
40′ BYB
Iso Hauteri
Fl.2s   Vähä Hauteri
11M   LFl.8s
        11M

Kauris-
salo

Taivassalo

Kustavi

Vartsala

30′

Naantali

Luonnonmaa

See plan p. 242

See plan p. 244

TURKU

Ruissalo

Hirvensalo

Rymättylä

Satava

Kakskett

20′

Airisto

Ålön

Iniö

KIHTI (SKIFTET)

Luoto

Orhisaari
Fl(2)WRG

Moussala

Haverö

Stormalo

Storter
Volandet

Lövskär
VQ(5)WRG.5m

Petäis
Fl.WRG.

Pikko
Nauvo

Pargas

SAARISTOMERI

Houtskär

Route 1

Nauvo

10′

Jungfruskär

Berghamn

Korppoo

(Continued from page 236)

Route 6

Bredskär

Brännskär

Gullkrona

Kråkskär

Dalsbruk

KIHTI (SKIFTET)

Hälsingholmen

60°
N

Nötö

Högsåra

Bokullankivi
Fl.WRG.5s9M

Vidskärsfjärden

Björkö

Route 5

Borstö Yxskar   Vänö

Commercial Route
from Stockholm

Jurmofjärden

Rosala

Jurmo

50′

Continued on p.242

Utö
Fl(2)12s40m17M
+F.38m17M

Kökarsören
Fl.5s24m9M

R

G

Lillharun
Fl.WRG.7s17m10M

21°E   30′   22°E

gästhamn berths. Another small *gästhamn* lies on the southwest coast of the island, sheltered by Koparholm islet, and facilities include shops and fuel.

Vänö
59°52′N 21°12′E

Vänö's old fishing harbour is on the island's south coast and consists of a single pontoon which has been converted into a small *gästhamn* whose facilities have been expanded .

Route 6 The Södö-Sälsö gap towards Hanko: a central route

After passing through the Södö-Sälsö gap (Route 2), the central route continues east past Kråkskär (60°04′N 21°15′E) and Bredskär (60°05′N 21°19′E), south of the large islands of Korppoo (Korpö) (60°08′N 21°36′E) and Nauvo (Nagu) (60°10′N 21°47′E), north of Ängsö (60°06′N 21°44′E) and Bergholm (60°07′N 21°46′E), and then east south-east to pass south of Brännskär (60°05′N 21°58′E) and close south of Gullkrona (60°05′N 22°05′E). The final leg is southeast via Hälsingholmen (Helsingholm) (60°02′N 22°17′E) and through the Jungfrusund (59°58′N 22°23′E), (the passage between Högsåra and Kasnäslandet) to join Route 5 north of Rosala.

Korpoström
60°06′N 21°36′E

Korpoström lies in the strait between Korppoo and Kaitholm. An old harbour, which once accommodated the entire Swedish navy fleet, it now contains a *gästhamn* showing 2·5–12m with good facilities including fuel.

Gullkrona
60°05′N 22°05′E

The sound north of Gullkrona is very beautiful. Approach either from east, leaving Gullkrona to port and two rocks above water to starboard or from south between Hamnskär and Gullkrona, leaving an islet to port and the wooded holm close northwest of Gullkrona to starboard. A heavy anchor will give good holding on weed in 2·5m in the bay immediately west of Furuskär. The guest pontoons were closed off in 2009 with little sign of life as the previous operators had moved away. Nevertheless a very peaceful anchorage and a good walk past the windmill to the lookout for splendid views. Small museum, nature trail and fish available at small shop.

Route 7 The Södö-Sälsö gap towards Turku or Hanko: a northern route

After passing through the Södö-Sälsö gap (Route 2), the north route continues east-northeast towards Jungfruskär (60°08′N 21°05′E) and Berghamn (60°09′N 21°19′E), passing either side of the two islands and the many islets between them. It then continues north of Korppoo (Korpö) (60°08′N 21°36′E) and Nauvo (Nagu) (60°10′N 21°47′E).

On leaving Nauvo astern the choice must be made as to whether to turn northeast for Turku, following the well-marked channel used by the Mariehamn–Turku ferries, or to make for Hanko. If the latter, head south through the gap between Haverö and Stormälö (60°15′N 22°06′E) to join Route 6 near Hälsingholmen and thence Route 5 to Hanko.

Caution

Parts of this route are used by the large ferries which ply from Mariehamn to Turku. Take particular care, not forgetting to check astern as well as ahead, as in places they have little room to manoeuvre and may be unable to alter course to avoid a yacht. Also if anchoring near the ferry routes it is best to find a spot sheltered from the frequent wash.

Verkan, Korppoo
60°10′N 21°33′E

In addition to Korpostrom (see Route 7), Korppoo has several harbours on its northwest coast. The large *gästhamn* at Verkan, which lies inside the small island of Sandholm, has good facilities including fuel, shopping and several restaurants. The very small *gästhamn* at Galtby (60°11′N 21°35′E) a little further east, is more exposed to the northwest and has few facilities.

Nauvo
60°11′N 21°55′E

The harbour of Nauvo is on the northeast coast of the island and is reached via a buoyed channel. There is a large *gästhamn* with 100 places on several pontoons and good facilities including shopping, restaurants and fuel. The island is popular as a holiday destination.

Pärnäinen, Nauvo
60°10′N 21°42′E

Pärnäinen lies in the passage between Nauvo and Korppoo. It is both a Passport Control station and a base for the commercial pilots who take ships through the intricate channels of the area. Facilities for yachts are limited.

4. FINLAND

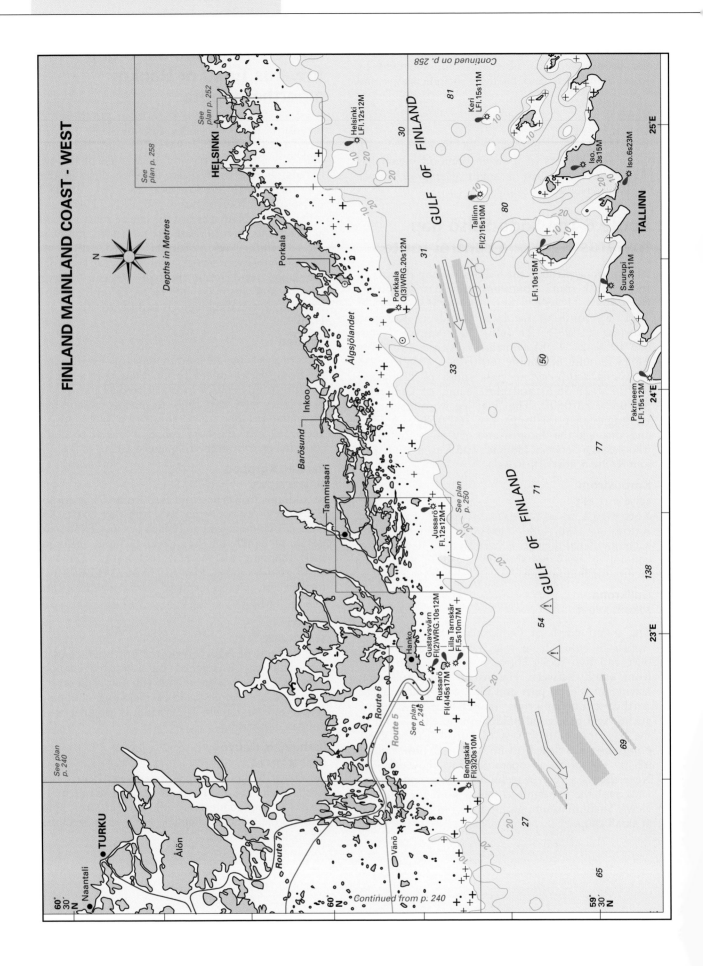

FINLAND MAINLAND COAST - WEST

N

Depths in Metres

TURKU

Naantali

Ålön

See plan p. 240

Tammisaari

Barösund   Inkoo

Porkala

HELSINKI

See plan p. 252

See plan p. 258

Helsinki
LFl.12s12M

Ålgsjölandet

Porkala
Ql(3)WRG.20s12M

GULF OF FINLAND

Keri
LFl.15s11M

Tallinn
Fl(2)15s10M

LFl.10s15M

Iso.
3s15M

Iso.6s23M

TALLINN

Suurupi
Iso.3s11M

Pakrineem
LFl.15s12M

See plan
p. 250

Jussarö
Fl.12s12M

Gustavsvärn
Fl(2)WRG.10s12M

Lilla Tarnskär
Fl.5s10m7M

Hanko

Russarö
Fl(4)45s17M

GULF OF FINLAND

See plan
p. 248

Route 5

Route 6

Bengtskär
Fl(3)20s10M

Route 70

Vänö

Continued from p. 240

Continued on p. 258

4d. South coast of Finland

Naantali (Nådendal)

60°28'N 22°01'E

Charts
UKHO 2297, 3439, 3436
Finnish 903, 912, 26

In a country where beautiful harbours abound, Naantali is nevertheless outstanding. The town, with its attractive old church, wooden houses and 19th century feel, is also highly popular with holidaymaking Finns. It has many good restaurants and hosts an internationally famous music festival every June. The town's website will be found at www.naantali.fi.

Sadly, access to Naantali is effectively denied to larger yachts – or at least those with taller masts. The convenient southeastern approach, between the mainland and the island of Luonnonmaa, is spanned by a bridge with a scant 12m clearance. The northwestern approach, which effectively circles Luonnonmaa, presents a 15·5m bridge between that island and Rymättylä. The western approach, which passes north of Rymättyla, is narrow, unmarked and shoals to 2·1m in places.

The guest harbour, ☎ +358 2 437 5512/02 435 0850, *Email* kari.rahja@naantali.fi, is operational from early June until the end of August only. Most visiting yachts berth on the long pontoon south of the small craft basin in 3–4m, where mooring is bows-to and water and electricity are available to most berths. There is also some space on the pontoon close north of the fuelling berth in 2m or less, and on the northernmost of the four pontoons north of the smallcraft area in 5m or more. Showers, saunas and laundry facilities are provided ashore. There is a fuel pontoon close south of the visitors pontoon where holding tanks can be pumped out and propane cylinders exchanged, though *Camping Gaz* is not available. The harbour office and tourist information centre share a small kiosk inland from the small craft basin. Berthing fees are in the middle band (see page 220).

The town offers reasonable shopping together with banks, Post Office etc, but Naantali is not the place to attempt to get serious work done. There is a card-operated telephone at the harbour office, plus others in the town. Internet access is available at the public library, on the second floor of the post office building. Regular buses run to Turku, where there is a mainline railway.

Turku (Åbo)

60°26'N 22°14'E

Distances
Mariehamn 75M, Naantali 20M, Hanko 65M

Charts and guides
UKHO 2297, 3439, 3436
Finnish 903, 912, 26, 190
Merikarttasarja D:
   Turunmnaan saaristo/Åbolands skärgård

Lights

4732 **Lillharun** 59°43'·6N 21°24'·2E Fl.WRG.7s17m10M 262°-G-340°-W-045°-R-101°-G-148°-W-156°-R-172° Racon Black concrete tower Wind generator

4736 **Utö** 59°46'·9N 21°22'·3E Fl(2)12s40m17M 235°-vis-100° Auxiliary F.38m17M 163°-vis-253° Square white granite tower, red stripes 24m. In centre of island

4743·2 **Bokullankivi** 59°50'·8N 21°25'·4E Fl.WRG.5s9m9M 009°-G-050°-W-054°-R-165°-G-232·5°-W-236·5°-R-009° Racon White tower, black band Wind generator

4779·4 **Lövskär** 60°13'·2N 21°43'·6E VQ(5)WRG.6s7m5M 197°-G-254°-W-258°-R-000°-W-197° Framework tower

4781·6 **Petäis** 60°14'·3N 21°48'·1E Fl.WRG.3s6m4M 030°-G-051°-W-055°-R-130°-G-209°-W-230°-R-240° Black concrete base, white lantern

4794 **Orhisaari** 60°16'·5N 22°00'E Fl.WRG.6s18m10M 019°-G-073°-W-158°-G-210°-W-217°-R-232°-G-246°-W-266°-R-284° White metal framework tower, concrete base

4798 **Rajakari** 60°22'·7N 22°06'E Fl.WRG.4s13m11M 166°-G-171°-W-173°-R-194°-G-203·5°-W-205°-R-257°-G-016°-W-024·5°-R-031° Red and white round concrete tower

Harbour communications
Turku Port Authority ☎ +358 2 267 4111
   VHF Ch 12,16, 71 (call *Turku Port Control*)
Turku Guest Harbour ☎ +358 2 267 4123
   Email turkuport@port.turku.fi

General

Turku, the capital of Finland until the early 19th century, is the country's third largest city, with a population of more than 160,000. It is also one of the most important ports in Finland, handling oil, containers and other freight, together with frequent ferry services to Stockholm. Its shipyards have constructed some of the world's largest cruise liners.

The modern city, built on a grid pattern, was rebuilt in 1827 after the old town was virtually wiped out by fire. The 13th-century cathedral, gutted by the fire, has been completely restored. Turku Castle, which stands near the mouth of the

Lovely Naantali *A. Hammick*

4. FINLAND

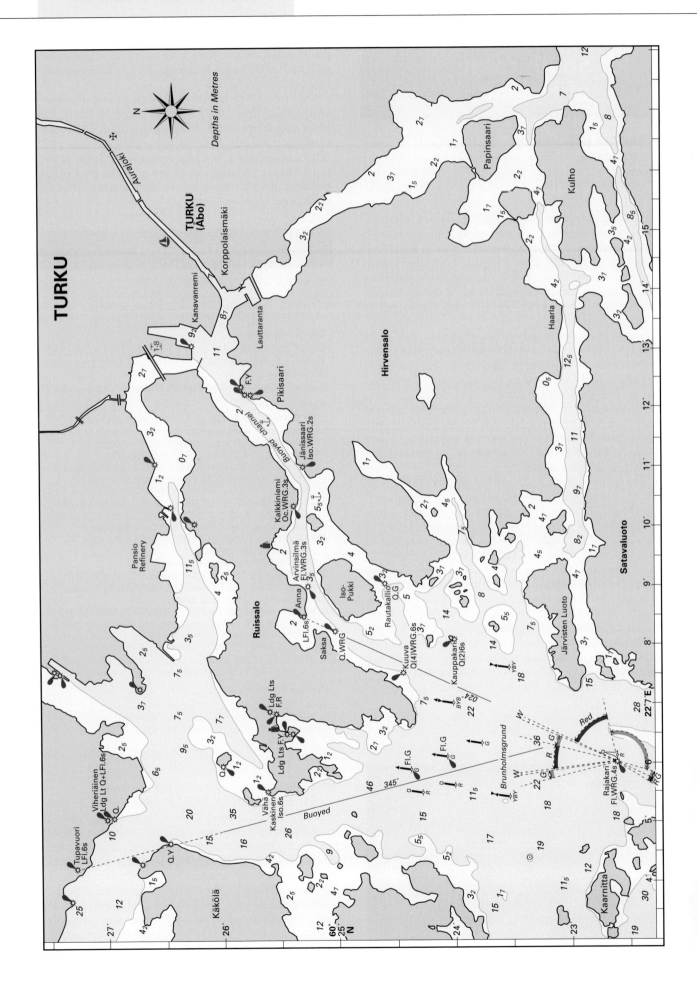

The well-buoyed final approach to Turku *A. Hammick*

Aura river, also dates back to the 13th century and now houses an interesting museum. There is also an excellent maritime museum, the Forum Marinum, www.forum-marinum.fi, with exhibits both ashore and afloat. All captions are in English as well as Finnish and Swedish, and an interesting river tour is included in the price.

The city's website is at www.port.turku.com.

Approach and entrance

The picturesque main approach channel to Turku is some 50M long, entering the archipelago at Utö (for routes see page 240) and leading through the islands in a generally northeasterly direction – though, as can be seen from the charts, there is a network of channels amongst the islands and a myriad of ways to approach Turku. On the chart, even the main channel's appearance may seem somewhat fearsome, but it is well marked, carries a minimum depth of 10m, and is regularly used by large ships. By day (and using the detailed Finnish charts which are essential) there is little difficulty, though navigation by night needs experience.

From Utö light the route heads north, then northeast past Bokullankivi light and again north to Lövskär, where it joins the 13m channel used by the ferries from Mariehamn by day and night. There are many places suitable for overnight anchorage in pleasant surroundings.

On nearing the city, proceed past Iso-Pukki and Hirvensalo to Turku docks, turn to starboard past the passenger and commercial wharves, and then to port up the river past the shipbuilding yards.

Formalities

See *Entry by yacht*, page 220.

Anchorages

Close to Turku itself most possible anchorages involve trespassing on private ground. However the more remote islands and channels offer many picturesque locations which can be used for overnight anchorage in good weather.

Berthing

There are several well-equipped marinas outside Turku, but visiting yachts will undoubtedly find it most convenient to moor at the small city-run guest harbour, ☎ +358 2 267 4111, *Email* turkuport@port.turku.fi, situated on the north bank of the Aura river, just downstream from the foot ferry and the three-masted *Suomen Jontsen* (Swan of Finland). The marina office (open 0800–2200 in season) doubles as a café, both occupying a small grey kiosk which also sells a few basic groceries. It has free internet access (for customers of the café/bar at least!)

Among the 60+ berths are several suitable for yachts of up to 3·5m beam and 2m draught, with larger yachts (up to 5m beam) berthing at the downstream end near an attractive sculptured fountain which resembles a giant goblet. Berthing is between posts, so there is no chance of squeezing a beamier yacht between two narrower neighbours. Although an occupied yacht is clearly quite safe, there is no security whatsoever and Turku might not be the ideal place to leave a yacht unattended for any length of time. Also, considerable disturbance is caused by wash from the many passing tourist boats. If there is no room on the northwest side, there are sometimes spaces alongside the quay on the southeast bank, below the foot ferry.

The guest harbour is often full to capacity from mid-June until mid-July, but it may be possible to lie alongside one of the charter vessels moored along the quayside.

Masted yachts are prevented from continuing up the river by a fixed bridge, but there are several public quays and landing places further up the river where a dinghy might be secured for short periods. Berthing fees are in the middle band (see page 220).

Services for yachts

The guest harbour has water and electricity on the pontoons (though washing boats down with fresh water is forbidden), with toilets, showers, sauna and laundry facilities in a block just across the road. Fresh rolls can be ordered at the marina office for morning collection.

Fuel is available from both Esso and Shell jetties on the north bank of the river in the dock area. Alternatively it may be found more convenient to call at one of the marinas in the approach – possibly Ruissalo's Santalanlahti (60°25'·5N 22°06'·6E) or Härkölänlahti (60°25'·6N 22°09'·6E) marinas.

For chandlery of all kinds visit Meredin-Ulkoiluaitta Oy at Puolalankatu 6, ☎ +358 2 275 275, *Fax* +358 2 275 2760, *Email* Meredin@meredin.fi, claimed to be one of the best chandleries in Finland. Amongst the items on offer are Finnish, Swedish and Estonian charts, electronics, clothing and shoes, and many leading international brands of hardware.

There are no boatyards – as against shipyards – in the immediate vicinity of Turku, but if repairs are essential enquiries could be made at the marina office or possibly the Forum Marinum.

4. FINLAND

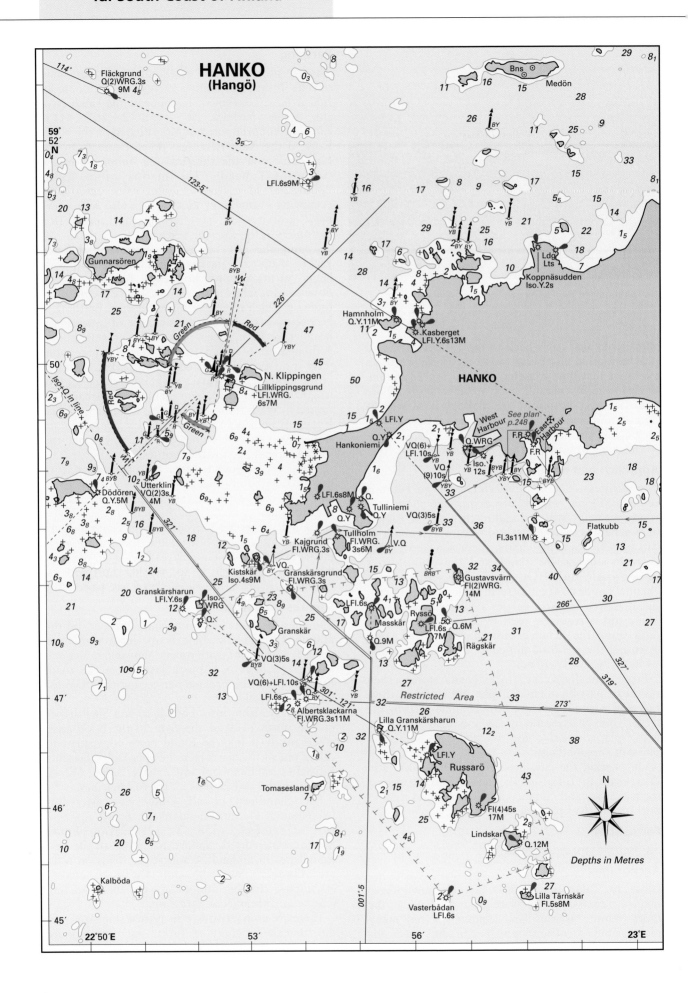

HANKO
(Hangö)

Fläckgrund
Q(2)WRG.3s
9M 4₅

Medön
Bns

LFl.6s9M

Hamnholm
Q.Y.11M

Kasberget
LFl.Y.6s13M

Koppnäsudden
Iso.Y.2s

Ldg
Lts

Gunnarsören

N. Klippingen
Lillklippingsgrund
LFl.WRG.
6s7M

HANKO

LFl.Y

Hankoniemi

Q.Y

West
Harbour

See plan
p.248

East
Harbour

F.R

F.R

VQ(6)+
LFl.10s

Q.WRG

Iso.
12s

Utterklin
VQ(2)3s
4M

Döderön
Q.Y.5M

VQ
(9)10s

LFl.6s8M

Q.

Tulliniemi
Q.Y

VQ(3)5s

Fl.3s11M

Flatkubb

Kajgrund
Fl.WRG.3s

Tullholm
Fl.WRG.
3s6M

V.Q

Kistskär
Iso.4s9M

Granskärsgrund
Fl.WRG.3s

Gustavsvärn
Fl(2)WRG.
14M

Granskärsharun
LFl.Y.6s

Iso.
WRG

Q.

Granskär

Masskär
Q.9M

Ryssö
LFl.6s
7M

Q.6M

Rägskär

VQ(3)5s

VQ(6)+LFl.10s

LFl.6s
Q.Y

Albertsklackarna
Fl.WRG.3s11M

Restricted   Area

Lilla Granskärsharun
Q.Y.11M

LFl.Y

Russarö

Tomasesland

Fl(4)45s
17M

Lindskar
Q.12M

Depths in Metres

Kalböda

Lilla Tärnskär
Fl.5s8M

Vasterbådan
LFl.6s

22°50′E   53′   56′   23°E

Turku marina, looking southwest (downriver) from the foot ferry *A. Hammick*

General facilities

The yacht harbour is about 20 minutes' walk along the riverside to the town centre, where all normal shopping needs can be met. There are excellent outdoor and covered markets and various supermarkets, including one in the basement of a shopping mall. The usual range of cafés, restaurants and hotels are to be found, many overlooking the water and several on historic vessels moored on the river itself.

Several enormous out-of-town shopping centres lie to the north of the town on the bus route to Naantali.

Communications and travel

There are good postal, telephone and fax services, though it should be noted that two different phone cards are in circulation – the national one and a 'Turku only' one – and of course each kiosk demands the correct card. Both are readily available throughout the city. There is a card-operated telephone just behind the guest harbour kiosk (which sells the required card). Internet access is available at the public library at 2 Linnankatu (open 1000–2000 Monday–Friday, 1000–1500 Saturday).

There is a bus stop in the road behind the marina, one way leading to the maritime museum, castle and docks, the other to the city centre and the airport. There is also a mainline station on the northern side of the city. Ferries leave the docks daily for the Åland Islands and Stockholm.

Direct charter flights operate from Turku to the UK, otherwise Helsinki airport is easily reached by train, bus or plane.

Dalsbruk

60°01'·2N 22°30'·6E

General

Dalsbruk is located in the east part of the Turku Archipelago, see plan on page 240. It is a small town with a large yacht repair and winter storage yard. It is the base for the 'Midnight Sun' Yacht charter Co. D-Marin Oy, which has 100 moorings for visitors.

There is fuel and septic tank pump out next to the marina. The harbour is in the centre of Dalsbruk and within walking distance of shops, the market and a pharmacy. There are two supermarkets, an Alko and a good chandlery. The berths are mostly stern to a buoy, bows to the quay. There is room to anchor off if no room to moor to the quay, but this would be exposed to southeast winds. The marina has two saunas, showers and washing machines. The harbour fees are in the middle bracket (see page 220) which includes water and electricity.

Harbour Office ① +358 2466 1125 has tourist information, free use of the internet, sailing clothes, charts.

Hanko (Hangö)

59°49'N 22°58'E

Distances
Turku 65M, Mariehamn 105M, Lehtma 50M, Haapsalu 55M, Tallinn 60M, Helsinki 70M

Charts and guides
UKHO 2241, 3443, 3437
Finnish 903, 912, 22, 21, 136
Merikarttasarja B: Jussarö – Parainen/Pargas

Lights
4872 **Fläckgrund** 59°52'·4N 22°50'·4E Q(2)WRG.3s6m9M 112°-W-115°-R-119°-G-170°-R-270°-G-307°-W-314°-R-020°-G-112° Red rectangle, yellow stripe
4906 **Bengtskär** 59°43'·4N 22°30'·1E Fl(3)20s51m10M Round granite tower and building 46m Wind generator
4919·4 **Hanko No.1** 59°44'·1N 23°02'·6E VQ(3)5s12m6M ♦ on black beacon, yellow band
4912 **Russarö** 59°46'N 22°57'·1E Fl(4)45s34m17M 174°-vis-115° Red octagonal tower 21m
4920·2 **Djubkobben Ldg Lts 327°** *Front* 59°48'·4N 22°58'·2E Fl.3s8m11M 324·5°-vis-329·5° *By day* 8M 321·5°-vis- 332·5° Red rectangle, yellow stripe, on framework tower
4920·21 *Rear* 59°49'·1N 22°57'·2E Iso.12s22m14M 324·5°-vis-329·5° *By day* 9M 321·5°-vis-332·5° Red rectangle, yellow stripe, on framework tower
4920·4 **Hankoniemi Pohjoinen Ldg Lts 319°** *Front* 59°49'·3N 22°55'·6E Q.Y.17m6M 315°-vis-323° Red rectangle, yellow stripe, on framework tower
4920·41 *Rear* 59°49'·4N 22°55'·4E LFl.Y.6s26m9M 315°-vis-323° Red rectangle, yellow stripe, on framework tower

Harbour communications
Hanko Port Authority ① +358 19 2203 801 *VHF* Ch 12, 13, 14, 16 *Email* port@hanko.fi
Hanko Guest Harbour ① +358 19 248 5617 *Email* itasatama@surfnet.fi/itasatama@hotmail.com
Marina Itameren Portti ① +358 19 2486 480

General

The pleasant town of Hanko, population 12,000, was founded in 1874 and quickly developed as a spa town popular with the dominant Russian ruling classes. A number of majestic 19th-century Finnish/Russian-style wooden villas are located to the northeast of the harbour amidst parks and tennis courts. However it had always been a useful

4. FINLAND

Looking southwest over Hanko East Harbour *E. Redfern*

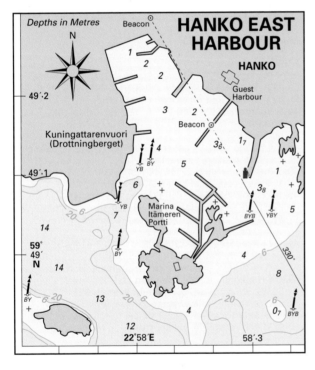

yachts. From the cruiser's point of view Hanko is a convenient port of call, since it involves practically no detour from the main coastal fairway. Facilities for children are particularly good, with playgrounds, beaches and plenty of open areas of rocks and short springy grass. Some visitors have likened the smooth, pinkish rocks to parts of North Brittany.

Both Finnish and Swedish are spoken on a ratio of around 53% to 46% (the odd 1% presumably speaking both with equal fluency). The town's interesting website will be found at www.hanko.fi.

Approach and entrance

The waters immediately around Hanko contain many hazards. However, the area is well supplied with leading marks, buoys and beacons and, using a large-scale chart, navigation in daylight is a great deal easier than appears at first sight. Entry by night should not be attempted unless familiar with the waters.

From northwest If coming from the Åland islands, Turku or elsewhere in the archipelago – see *Routes 5, 6 and 7*, pages 239 to 241 – the latter stages of the route pass close south of Fläckgrund lighthouse and then follow a somewhat circuitous path through a number of well marked channels around the western end of the Hanko peninsula. A choice of channels then link up with the southeastern route not far from the harbour entrance.

From southeast From Hanko No. 1 beacon follow first the Djubkobben leading lights on 327°, turning onto the Hankoneimi Pohjoinen leading lights on 319° in the vicinity of 59°46′N. Both sets of lights are marked by pairs of red rectangles with vertical yellow stripes. The channel is wide and all hazards are well marked.

anchorage, and its continued prosperity has been mainly due to the fact that its commercial port – the West Harbour – is closed by ice for shorter periods than most other Finnish ports. For some fifty years around the beginning of the 20th century Hanko was a major point of embarkation for Finns leaving their native country for new lives in the USA and Canada – up to 500,000 by some estimates. Hanko was leased to the Soviet Union in 1940 as a military base. This role was replaced by Porkkala in the armistice between Finland and Soviet Union in 1944 and returned back to Finland in 1956.

A century later Hanko remains popular as a holiday resort and tourist centre, with two marinas in its East Harbour, both of which accept visiting

In the vicinity of 59°48'·7N three cardinal beacons (east, west and north) will come roughly in line about 0·5M off to starboard on a heading of approximately 065°. Head towards them, leaving the east cardinal to port and the west and north cardinals to starboard, and pass between two further pairs of north and south cardinals to enter the harbour from the southwest, immediately south of the Kuningattarenvuori (Drottningberget) peninsula. Although very narrow, the entrance is well marked by further cardinals. Incoming vessels may be met by a reception boat.

From east The beautiful inshore passage from Helsinki to Hanko (see page 250) passes close north of the islands of Mulan and Andalskär, and leads directly to the well-marked southeast entrance on a course of 330°. The route is clearly shown on the large-scale Admiralty and Finnish charts. Again, incoming vessels may be met by a reception boat.

Formalities

See *Entry by yacht*, page 220. If clearance is required there is a Frontier Guard station at Tulliniemi (59°48'·5N 22°55'E) at the extreme southwest of the peninsula, about 1·5M west of the East Harbour.

Anchorage

Although there are few restrictions on anchoring, the depth of the water and the nature of the bottom make it impractical to anchor off in the vicinity of the town.

Berthing

Although there are other possibilities around the Hanko pensinsula, visiting yachts without local knowledge are recommended to use the East Harbour where there are two good-sized marinas, both of which have good facilities and excellent shelter. Hanko would be a very suitable place to leave a yacht whilst returning home, exploring inland, etc.

Hanko Guest Harbour, ☎ +358 19 248 5617, is located on the east side of the harbour and has some 180 visitors berths in depths of up to 3m. Mooring is bows-to with stern to pickup buoy, but the inshore berths are shallow (1·5m or less). If not met by a reception boat on arrival, take any suitable vacant berth and visit the marina office (open 0800–2400 in high season) as soon as convenient. Berthing fees are in the middle band (see page 220).

Marina Itameren Portti (Gateway to the Baltic), *Mobile* +358 400 544 164, www.itamerenportti.fi, is one of the Baltic Sun chain of marinas and welcomes visiting yachts. It is built astride several small islands in the southwestern part of the harbour and has a further 150 berths, most equipped with solid, UK-style finger pontoons. Depths range from 2m to 3·5m or more. Berthing fees are in the upper band (see page 220).

A regular ferry (free to berth-holders) runs between the marina and the shore.

Services for yachts

Both marinas have water and electricity on the pontoons, with toilets, showers, saunas, laundry facilities and restaurants ashore. There is a fuelling point at the end of the mole which forms the starboard side of the southeast entrance (it may be worth refuelling on arrival if there is no queue, as there can be a long wait on summer mornings) where holding tanks can be emptied and bottled gas (Finnish and Swedish cylinders only) and a few charts are available.

There is no boatyard at the East Harbour itself, but several in the wider Hanko area including Granströms Båtvarv, ☎ +358 19 248 6391, at Söderströmin on the west coast of the peninsula. There is a Volvo Penta service centre and a limited range of chandlery is available from one of the small huts near the root of the southeast mole.

Sail repairs can be carried out by Stig Sandberg, ☎ +358 19 248 6292, on Kapteeninkatu, about 2km northeast of the harbour, while Finnish charts are stocked by Tia's Bok at 15–17 Ratakatu (Bangatan), some 600m north of the harbour, together with some English paperbacks.

A daily weather forecast in Finnish and Swedish is posted outside the Guest Harbour office.

General facilities

General provisions may be bought from a small mobile shop at the harbour (open 0800–2100 weekdays, 0900–1900 weekends) or from the wide variety of shops and supermarkets in the town centre, approximately 1km away, where there is also an outdoor market. In addition the town centre has the usual banks, Post Office, tourist office, hotels and restaurants. Shopping trolleys can be borrowed from the guest harbour office against a deposit, and bicycles hired.

Communications and travel

There is a card-operated telephone near the Guest Harbour office, where a fax service and internet access are also available. Yachtsmen are welcome to use their own laptops, though a suitable phone plug adaptor may be required. The internet can also be accessed at the public library at 3–5 Vuorikatu about 500m north of the harbour (☎ +358 19 220 3380 to book a time slot), and several of the larger hotels. Letters for yachts visiting the Guest Harbour can be sent c/o Itäsatama/Satamatoimisto, 10900 Hanko, Finland.

Hanko is served by the Finnish railway system, and international air travel is possible via Helsinki or Turku. Car ferries run to Rostock in Germany. For more local exploration, bicycles and mopeds can be hired from several venues around the harbour, including the fuel berth.

4. FINLAND

Routes between Hanko and Helsinki

There are effectively two main routes, but as these come together in several places it is possible to 'mix and match' along the way. It should not need stating that current, large-scale, Finnish charts are a necessity when cruising this area. Parts of it pass through a national park which is home to elk, white-tailed deer and many bird species.

Between 23°20′E and 23°45′E the northern route passes north of Skärlandet, Torsö and Växär. It is a pretty, peaceful, easily-followed channel with some summer houses and many places to anchor, and fuel is available at several points. In unpleasant weather it provides a welcome alternative to the more interesting southern route. This passes south of Älgö and north of Busö, has some beautiful anchorages and is certainly the more popular of the two. The two routes converge at 59°55′N 23°45′·5E.

Between 23°45′E and 24°24′E the northern route through Barösund is relatively straight, well buoyed and lit. The Finns are justly proud of Barösund, which is narrow and has high rocky sides. It boasts a small shop, one of the few between Hanko and Helsinki not to involve a considerable detour, together with many summer homes and hence much small motorboat traffic. The southern route winds and twists between a number of small islands, sometimes open to the Gulf of Finland to the south. Although narrow in other places it is excellently marked by a profusion of buoys and white boards, but is not lit. It is quite possible to beat through in a yacht of 12m, though some of the tacks have to be very short. The southern route is very enjoyable from both the pilotage and scenic points of view. Both channels emerge to cross the Porkkalanselkä (Porkalafjärden).

Between 24°28′E and 24°45′E the inshore route, close off Porkkala, carries little more than 1·2m (4ft) for much of its length and is both intricate and narrow in places. However it is well marked and very beautiful. The outer route, which is the one usually followed, presents no difficulty and can be taken by yachts of any draught, but in places is exposed to south and southeasterly swell.

Tammisaari (Ekenäs)

59°58′·5N 23°26′E

Charts UKHO 2241
Finnish 903, 912, 21

Tammisaari, population 15,000, is a delightful, leafy town with many traditional wooden houses and a small guest harbour able to take around 120 yachts. Helsinki is some 100km by train, and if time is pressing it would be a good place to leave a boat while visiting the capital. There is a particularly appealing beach just south of the marina, backed by a children's playground, making Tammisaari an excellent port of call for those with young aboard. The town's website is listed under its Swedish name at www.ekenas.fi.

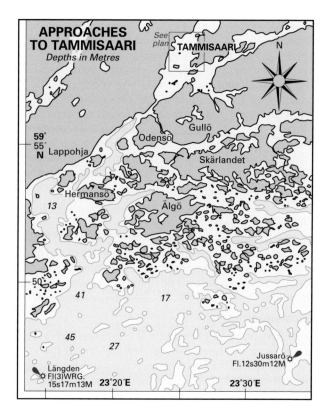

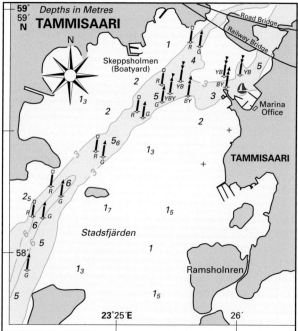

Although some 12M from the Gulf of Finland, the approach channels are well marked and present no difficulty. On reaching the guest harbour, ① +358 19 241 1790, just short of the Turku/Hanko road bridge, it is impossible to miss the amazingly ornate building which houses the Knipan restaurant – built on stilts in the harbour at a time when only one licensed premises was permitted 'on the soil of the town'.

Visitors berth on the east side of the main jetty (to which the restaurant is attached) and on the west and north sides of the shorter spur adjoining it. The pontoons either side of the fuel berth are private,

Looking southwest towards Tammisaari yacht pontoons, with the highly ornate restaurant building behind *A. Hammick*

though if the owner is away a green sign may be left at the berth to show it is free. Depths are said to be 3–4m off the end of the main quay though shoaling to 1·5m further in. There is some further space on the south side of a single pontoon north of the main harbour in 2–3m. There is now a new additional visitors pontoon which runs roughly north from near the white shed. Berthing is mainly bows-to with stern buoys, though it may be possible to lie alongside the northern pontoon if space permits. The marina office occupies a small building near the fuel berth which doubles as a café. Berthing fees are in the lower band (see page 220).

Berths on the main quay have access to water and electricity (though some berths would require long hoses and leads), and there are toilets, showers, sauna and laundry facilities ashore. The fuel pontoon, where holding tanks can be pumped out, has 2m+ depths. A weather forecast (in Finnish and Swedish) is posted at the marina office and is updated daily. There is a small chandlery, Marinboden, on Kustaa Vaasan katu (Gustav Wasas gata) just up the hill from the guest harbour. Kungsbokhandel, on Länggatan, stocks Finnish charts and chart-books.

Directly across the river, and clearly visible from the marina, is a large boatyard, Oy Eke Marin AB, ☎ +358 19 241 2670, *Email* telakka@eke-marin.fi, (open 0900–1700 weekdays, closed weekends), which also stocks a wide range of chandlery. The yard can handle yachts of up to 20 tonnes and 13·5m LOA and undertake repairs in all materials. There are engineers and electricians on site. There is extensive undercover storage and would be a definite possibility for over-wintering if booked well in advance.

There is good shopping of all kinds in Tammisaari, with a market on Wednesday and Saturday mornings. Internet access is available at the public library as well as several other places in the town. Bicycles can be hired from the marina office, and the town is linked to Helsinki and elsewhere by rail.

Barösund

59°59′N 23°53′E

There is a strong jetty to tie up to and a small supermarket on the south side of the bay This is one of the very few shops between Hangö and Helsinki. Fuel docks on both sides of the channel near ferry. Alternately, anchor north or northwest of Sparvholm at the northeast end of Barösund.

Älgsjölandet

59°58′N 23° 55′E

An outstanding City of Helsinki Island Park/Marina 40km west of the city. The entrance is ¾M southeast of the main channel which runs northeast–southwest between Barölandet and Orslandet. Shape a southeasterly course for the northeast corner of Morholmen until a 20′ wide channel (depth 2·2m) running south between Morholmen and Brataholmen opens up.

Moor to solid wooden staging, bows to with some stern buoys. There is a beautiful nature trail, campground, small kiosk and two classic wood-fired saunas.

Porkkala

59°58′N 24° 24′E

This is a useful place to leave for Tallinn, being the shortest distance at 34M. From the south enter through buoyed channel passing west and north of Högholmen or close east of this island. Berth alongside the Customs jetty to the north of the harbour to clear. Pick up a vacant buoy if staying. Shop at village quay. In strong easterlies there is a good anchorage 300m to the east by Kyrkogardson, shallow but sheltered and with sound holding.

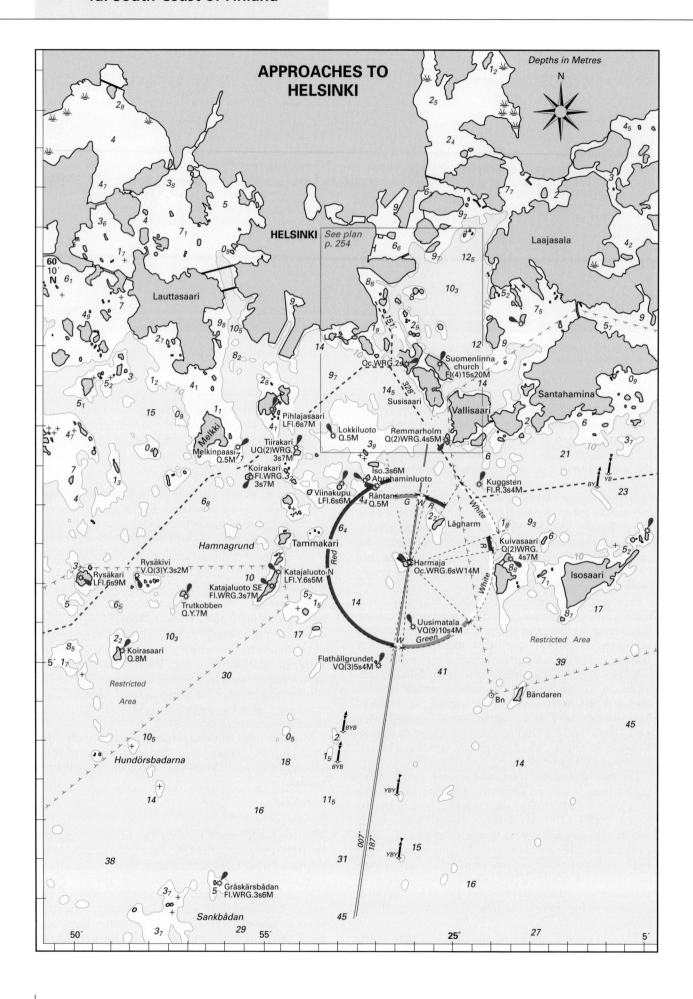

APPROACHES TO HELSINKI

Depths in Metres

N

HELSINKI

See plan p. 254

Laajasala

Lauttasaari

Suomenlinna church Fl(4)15s20M

Santahamina

Susisaari

Vallisaari

Pihlajasaari LFl.6s7M

Lokkiluoto Q.5M

Remmarholm Q(2)WRG.4s5M

Oc.WRG.2s

Kuggsten Fl.R.3s4M

Iso.3s6M Abrahaminluoto

Melkki

Melkinpaasi Q.5M

Tiirakari UQ(2)WRG.3s7M

Koirakari Fl.WRG.3s7M

Viinakupu LFl.6s6M

Räntan Q.5M

Lågharm

Kuivasaari Q(2)WRG.4s7M

Isosaari

Hamnagrund

Tammakari

Harmaja Oc.WRG.6sW14M

Rysäkivi V.Q(3)Y.3s2M

Rysäkari LFl.6s9M

Katajaluoto LFl.Y.6s5M

Katajaluoto SE Fl.WRG.3s7M

Trutkobben Q.Y.7M

Uusimatala VQ(9)10s4M Green

Restricted Area

Koirasaari Q.8M

Flathällgrundet VQ(3)5s4M

Bn Bändaren

Restricted Area

BYB

BYB

Hundörsbadarna

YBY

YBY

007° 187°

Gråskärsbådan Fl.WRG.3s6M

Sankbådan

Helsinki (Helsingfors)

60°10′N 24°58′E

Distances

Hanko 70M, Tallinn 45M, Porvoo 35M, Loviisa 60M, Kotka 75M, Haapasaari Island 80M, Vyborg 130M, St Petersburg 175M

Charts and guides

UKHO 2248, 1080, 2224
Finnish 902, 912, 18, 191
Merikarttasarja Z: Pellinki – Inkoo/Pellinge – Ingå

Lights

5184 **Helsinki** 59°56′·9N 24°55′·7E LFl.12s25m12M Racon
White round tower, upper part red, three galleries, aluminium lantern 25m. Helipad

5186 **Gråskärsbådan** 60°02′·2N 24°53′·6E
Fl.WRG.3s12m6M 153°-G-175°-W-180°-R-153° Red concrete column

5190·4 **Flathällgrundet** 60°05′N 24°58′·1E VQ(3)5s12m4M
Black diamond on black metal structure, yellow band, on piles (East cardinal)

5190 **Harmaja Ldg Lts 007°** *Front* 60°06′·3N 24°58′·7E
Oc.WRG.6s24m14M 004·5°-W-010·5°-R-168°-G-187°-W-193°-R-212°-W-250°-R-260°-W-312°-G-004·5° Racon
Red round tower, white band, square base

5190·1 **Suomenlinna Church** *Rear*, 60°08′·9N 24°59′·4E
(2·6M from front) Fl(4)15s54m21M Racon Cupola on church tower

5168 **Särkkä** 60°09′·1N 24°58′·2E Fl.WRG.2s2m6M 175°-G-186°-W-191°-R-280° White lantern, red band

5170 **Valkosaari (Luoto) Ldg Lts 356·5°** *Front* 60°09′·6N 24°58′·2E Q.R.2m6M 286°-vis-018°
White lantern, red band

5170·1 **Valkosaari** *Rear* 240m from front,
Iso.WRG.4s7m7M 135°-W-213°-G-137°-W-260°-R-271°-G-283°-W-293°-R-006° White lantern, red band

Harbour communications

Helsinki Port Authority ☎ + 358 9 310 1621
(Harbourmaster ☎ + 358 9 310 33676) *VHF Ch 12, 16 Email* port.helsinki@hel.fi

Helsinki Vessel Traffic Service ☎ + 358 9 310 33655, VHF channel according to sector (all vessels more than 12m in length must maintain a listening watch on the relevant VTS channel)

VTS Sector 1 (Western border: a line drawn from Helsinki lighthouse to Kytö and due north from there; Eastern border: a line drawn from Helsinki lighthouse to Kuiva Hevonen and due north from there), *VHF Ch 71, 11*

VTS Sector 2 (Western border: a line drawn from Inkoo 2 to Merholm light in Barösund and due north from there; Southern border: a line drawn from Inkoo 2 through Porkkala Kalbådan and Helsinki lighthouse to Kalbådagrund; Eastern border: a line drawn from Kalbådagrund to 60°05′N 25°40′W and due north from there, excluding the area of Sector 1), *VHF Ch 09, 11*

VTS Sector 3 (Western border: the line of longitude passing through Fläckgrund (22°50′·4E) south to 59°39′N, east to Hanko and east-northeast to Inkoo 2), *VHF Ch 67, 11*

Nylandska Jaktklubben (NJK) Marina ☎ + 358 9 636 047 *Fax* + 358 9 692 3194

Helsingfors Segelsällskap (HSS) Marina ☎ + 358 9 633 637, *Email* hss@hss-segel.fi

Katajanokka Visitors Marina ☎ + 358 9 4110 4000 *Fax* + 358 9 278 2571

Helsingin Moottorivenekerho (HMVK) Marina
☎ + 358 9 135 5313 *Fax* + 358 9 135 5130

Suomenlinna Marina ☎ + 358 96 926 45

General

Helsinki, the capital of Finland, has a population of over 500,000. It was founded in 1550 by the Swedish king, Gustav Vasa, and became the capital in 1812 at a time of Russian domination. It is a prosperous, well planned and pleasant city with the relaxed and friendly atmosphere typical of most major Scandinavian capitals. Nearly everyone speaks fluent English and the standard of living is as high as that anywhere in the world. The shopping centre is comprehensive with stores of every description. There are excellent outdoor and indoor markets close to the harbour.

The historic buildings, in particular both Lutheran and Orthodox cathedrals and the university in the old part of the city, are aesthetically and historically pleasing – but perhaps it is the wide-ranging examples of modern architecture in the centre which contribute most to the atmosphere of life and excitement which the city exudes. One of the many city guide books will add greatly to the enjoyment of a visit.

South Harbour (Eteläsatama), the main harbour for passenger ships and yachts, is conveniently close to the city centre and is always full of interest and activity.

The offshore fortress of Suomenlinna (Sveaborg), a World Heritage Site on five connected islands outside the harbour, is well worth a visit for its museum, galleries, heavy stone walls and beautiful buildings. It has a small guest harbour and is the site of the Helsinki Frontier Guard station (see below). Alternatively it can be reached by ferry from Helsinki's South Harbour.

A more distant objective, which can also be visited by passenger ship as well as train, is St Petersburg. (If by the former no visa is required). One tour operator is Kristina Cruises, www.kristinacruises.com, which also runs opera cruises to Savonlinna.

The Helsinki Port Authority maintains a website at www.portofhelsinki.fi which, though intended for commercial shipping, is of interest to all who visit the harbour. The outstanding City of Helsinki website is at www.helsinki.fi.

Approach and entrance

Helsinki is surrounded by water on three sides, and there are many possible approaches through the hundreds of nearby islands. However, although local yachtsmen appear to sail where they wish, the visitor is advised to use only the main routes indicated, at least until familiar with local hazards. Whichever approach is used, it is essential to be equipped with Admiralty chart 2224, Finnish chart 18 or 191, or Volume Z of the *Finnish Merikarttasarja* chart-book series.

From south This is the main approach from the open sea and is heavily used by shipping, including cruise liners and fast ferries. A good watch must therefore be kept at all times. From Helsinki light, the channel runs slightly east of north with Harmaja light house in line with Suomenlinna Church. It then passes close east of Harmaja light, but yachts should leave

4. FINLAND

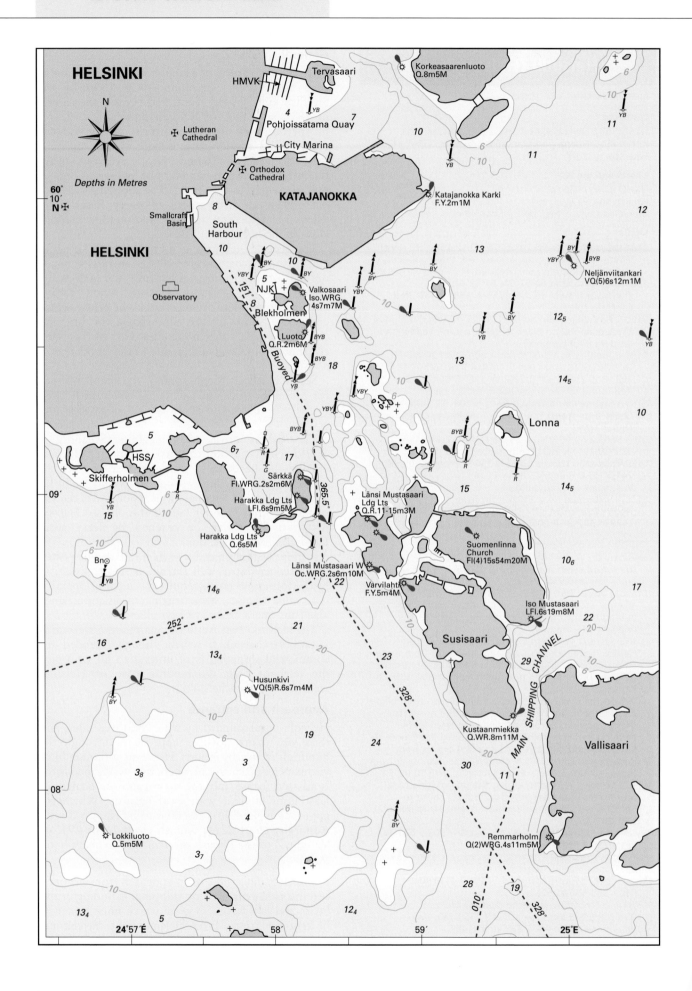

HELSINKI

N

Depths in Metres

60°
10′
N

HELSINKI

⌖ Lutheran
Cathedral

Observatory

Tervasaari

HMVK

Pohjoissatama Quay

City Marina

⌖ Orthodox
Cathedral

4

7

Korkeasaarenluoto
Q.8m5M

10

6

10

11

11

YB

YB

YB

KATAJANOKKA

Katajanokka Karki
F.Y.2m1M

12

Smallcraft
Basin

South
Harbour

8

10

10

13

12

BY

YBY

BY

BY

YBY

BYB

Neljänviitankari
VQ(5)6s12m1M

5
NJK

8

Valkosaari
Iso.WRG.
4s7m7M

Blekholmen

Luoto
Q.R.2m6M

BYB

BYB

18

Buoyed

YB

13

12.5

14.5

10

YB

YBY

BY

YB

6

13

Lonna

5

HSS

Skifferholmen

15

6₇

17

R

G

BYB

BY

R

R

R

BYB

14.5

Särkkä
Fl.WRG.2s2m6M

Länsi Mustasaari
Ldg Lts
Q.R.11-15m3M

15

YB

6

R

10

365.5°

Harakka Ldg Lts
LFl.6s9m5M

Harakka Ldg Lts
Q.6s5M

Suomenlinna
Church
Fl(4)15s54m20M

10.6

Bn ⊙

YB

Länsi Mustasaari W
Oc.WRG.2s6m10M

22

Varvilahti
F.Y.5m4M

Susisaari

17

14.6

252°

16

13.4

21

20

23

328°

Iso Mustasaari
LFl.6s19m8M

22

20

29

10

6

Vallisaari

Husunkivi
VQ(5)R.6s7m4M

19

24

Kustaanmiekka
Q.WR.8m11M

30

20

11

010°

MAIN SHIPPING CHANNEL

09′

08′

3₈

3

4

BY

Lokkiluoto
Q.5m5M

3₇

Remmarholm
Q(2)WRG.4s11m5M

28

19

328°

10

13.4

5

12.4

59′

25°E

24°57′E

58′

Passing Harmaja island on the southern approach to Helsinki *A. Hammick*

the main shipping channel before it continues northeast between the islands of Susisaari and Vallisaari.

Yachts are better advised to keep west of Susisaari island and enter South Harbour by the southern entrance, between the islands of Sarkkä and Länsi Mustasaari. If heading for the Helsingfors Segelsällskap (HSS) marina this will be followed by a sharp turn to port; if continuing to the Nylandska Jaktklubben (NJK) pontoons on Blekholmen island follow the buoyed channel west of Luoto island. For any of the marinas north of the Katajanokka peninsula, pass east of Luoto and Valkosaari (Blekholmen) islands before skirting Katajanokka, observing the buoyage throughout.

From west The inshore passage through the islands from the west passes either side of Rysäkari before heading northeast between the islands of Melkki and Pihlajasaari to the north and Koirakari and Tiirakari to the south. It then continues in a northeasterly direction to converge with the southern approach west of Länsi Mustasaari. It is very clearly marked, but it is easy to be confused by the plethora of beacons, lights and leading marks. The tower of Suomenlinna Church is a useful landmark throughout.

From east The deep-water channel for vessels using the inshore route from the east passes south of the islands of Santahamina and Vallisaari, joining the main channel from the south approximately one mile north of the Harmaja light. However, a slightly shorter but more interesting route, that carries 2·4m, passes north of Santahamina through the opening bridge, operating at HR+15 and HR-15.

Below The northeast view over the NJK, Helsinki *E. Redfern*

Formalities

See *Entry by yacht*, page 220. If clearance is required there is a Frontier Guard station at the western end of the narrow channel between Suomenlinna (Sveaborg) and Susisaari islands at 60°08'·8N 24°59'·1E, with a small guest harbour directly opposite.

Anchorage

Although there are few official restrictions on anchoring in the Helsinki area, in practice it is almost impossible to find a spot which does not involve landing on private property.

Berthing

There are at least fifteen yacht harbours and clubs in the immediate vicinity of Helsinki, but the visitor will normally find it most convenient to berth at the attractive Nylandska Jaktklubben (NJK) club pontoons on the tiny island of Blekholmen (Valkosaari) in South Harbour; at the Helsingfors Segelsällskap (HSS) distributed over Skifferholmen (Liuskasaari) and other small interconnected islands to the southwest; at the new, city-run Katajanokka Visitors Marina on the north side of the Katajanokka peninsula (the site of the magnificent Orthodox Cathedral); or at the Helsingin Moottorivenekerho (HMVK) on the south side of the causeway to Tervasaari island, itself north of Katajanokka.

Larger, traditional yachts may find a welcome alongside the Pohjoissatama quay between the Katajanokka and HMVK marinas, but should contact the Port Authority, ☎ +358 93 101 621, before arrival. The marina on the north side of the Tervasaari causeway does not accept visitors. There is a diminutive smallcraft basin close to the covered market in the northwest corner of South Harbour where a dinghy might be left during a shopping trip (subject to the two hour time limit).

The NJK, ☎ 09 6869 860, *Fax* 09 692 3194, *Email* kansliet@njk.fi, www.njk.fi/ (partially in English), is the oldest yacht club in Finland and has a most interesting Victorian clubhouse on Blekholmen island, though the sailing activities of the club is now situated some distance from the city on the island of Bjorkholmen (60°09'·7N 24°51'E). At Blekholmen there are some 125 berths, including a 25-berth visitors' pontoon in 3m depth. All mooring is bows-to with a stern buoy, berths marked 'P' being available for visitors. Berthing fees are in the upper band (see page 220).

The surroundings are very scenic and visitors are made most welcome, but it is not particularly peaceful since large ferries pass very close by, apparently still travelling at some speed. A two-minute ferry journey (every 20 minutes from 0800 until late in the evening) connects Blekholmen with the shore, from where it is a short walk into the city centre – or wait for a tram. Twice daily the ferry runs to the harbourside market.

The HSS, ☎ +358 9 633 637, *Fax* +358 9 633 603, *Email* hss@dlc.fi, www.dlc.fi/~hss, has berths for nearly 200 yachts in 5m depths. It is a little further from the city centre – though again near a tram route – but its berths are undoubtedly quieter than those at the NJK. A ferry runs every 30 minutes between the islands and the shore. Its protected waters, grassy islands and small beach make it particularly appealing for yachts with young children aboard. Berthing is, as usual, bows-to with a stern buoy. Berthing fees are in the middle band (see page 220).

The new, city-run Katajanokka Visitors Marina, ☎ +358 9 4110 4000 is closest to the city of all Helsinki's marinas. It occupies the westernmost pontoon on the north side of the Katajanokka peninsula – the two to the east are private – and offers berthing for 120 yachts in depths of 4m or more, some alongside finger pontoons and some with stern buoys. There is little wash to contend with, and security is good in the more expensive parts of the marina, but there is continuous noise from the nearby road. Berthing fees are in either the middle or upper bands depending on the berth (see page 220).

An information sheet in three languages can be downloaded in Adobe format by accessing the city website at www.hel.fi, entering Katajanokka Marina in the Search option, and choosing the first of the many possibilities listed.

The HMVK, ☎ +358 9 135 5313, *Email* hmvk@hmvk.fi, www.hmvk.fi/ (in Finnish only), has around 400 berths, all of them between piles (some of which are rather narrow) in 2–4·5m. The visitors' pontoon is the one nearest to the shore, alongside mooring mostly for bigger boats. There are a few boxes 15m x 5m and more boxes 13m x 4m.

Berths are available in July and first half of August as berth holders are away from their berths. The marina is peaceful and secure, if rather less picturesque than the two island marinas, and convenient for the city. Berthing fees are in the lower band (see page 220).

Helsingfors Segelsällskap (HSS) marina, looking northwest towards the city. Ballooning is very popular in both Sweden and Finland   *A. Hammick*

Yachts in Helsinki's Katajanokka Visitors' Marina, with Pohjoissatama quay in the background   *A. Hammick*

Services for yachts

All four marinas have water and electricity at their berths, with toilets and showers ashore and a station at which holding tanks can be pumped out. The NJK, HSS and HMVK marinas provide laundry facilities, while the NJK and HSS also have saunas on their islands, as well as first-class restaurants. Fuel is available at the HSS and HMVK, but not at the Katajanokka or NJK marinas. Instead of visiting the more distant chandleries it should be possible to exchange propane gas cylinders at these clubs.

Helsinki and its environs encompass many boatyards able to carry out work of almost any description, in addition to winter lay-up. The advice of a club secretary or marina manager should be sought as to which to approach first.

For a very wide range of chandlery it is worth taking the bus to Lauttasaari island to the west of the city, where three good-sized chandleries stand close together on Veneentekijäntie, the road paralleling the eastern shore. The largest of these is Oy Maritim, ☎ +358 9 681 631, *Fax* +358 9 692 7917, *Email* maritim@maritim.fi, www.maritim.fi (mainly in Finnish), which stocks an enormous range of paint, hardware, electronics, pilot books and charts. Nearby are the somewhat smaller ProSailor, ☎ +358 9 682 3900, *Fax* +358 9 682 3950, and the Captain's Shop, ☎/*Fax* +358 9 682 2512.

For worldwide charts visit John Nurminen Marine Ltd, Heikkiläntie 8, FI-00210 Helsinki, Finland ☎ +358 9 682 3180, *Fax* +358 9 6823 1811, *Email* marine@johnnurminen.com, www.johnnurminenmarine.com a few blocks west of the chandleries on Lauttasaari island. All the Baltic countries are fully covered, including Russia, together with a wide selection of pilot books for Baltic waters, some of them in English. The staff are particularly helpful.

Elvström Sails have premises near the HSS at 8B Laivanvarvstajankatu, ☎ +358 9 666 438, *Fax* +358 9 666 580, *Email* masa@elvstromsails.fi, where new sails can be ordered or repairs of all types carried out. Sailtex, ☎ +358 9 682 2283, *Fax* +358 9 682 2288, on Veneentekijäntie, mainly handle yacht upholstery work but will also undertake sail repairs.

General facilities

Helsinki has excellent shops of all kinds, as might be expected of a capital city.

The open-air and covered markets overlooking South Harbour can satisfy most needs, although it is perhaps for their wide variety of fish, fresh vegetables and fruit that they are most famous. The small delicatessens in the covered market – the 'Vanha Kauppahalli' or 'Gamla Saluhallen' – to the west are particularly tempting, but far from cheap.

There are many excellent supermarkets in the main shopping centre, a few minutes' walk from the harbour, and others beneath the main railway station. The large Akateeminin Kirjakauppa bookshop on Pohjois Esplanadi stocks books, magazines and newspapers in many languages including English.

There is a tourist information office near the harbour, and many excellent (but expensive) restaurants in addition to those at the Nylandska Jaktklubben and the Helsingfors Segelsällskap.

Communications and travel

There are card-operated telephones convenient to all four marinas. Fax services are available at the main post office near the main railway station and at all the marina offices by arrangement. Mail for visiting yachts can be sent c/o the Nylandska Jaktklubben, Blekholmen, 00140 Helsingfors, Finland; or the Helsingfors Segelsällskap, Skifferholmen, 00130 Helsingfors, Finland. Internet access is available at a number of places in the city including all public libraries – enquire at the marina office for the nearest.

There are good rail, air and coach services between Helsinki and all major European cities, plus regular ferries to Tallinn and Stockholm, the latter via Mariehamn.

4e. Eastern Finland

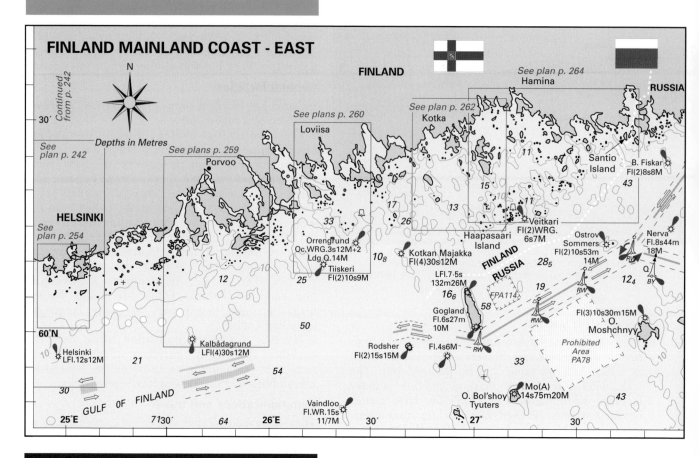

FINLAND MAINLAND COAST - EAST

Porvoo (Borgå)

60°23'N 25°40'E

Distances

Helsinki 35M, Tallinn 65M, Loviisa 40M, Haapasaari Island 65M

Charts and guides

UKHO 2248, 1083
Finnish 902, 17
Merikarttasarja Z: Pellinki – Inkoo/Pellinge – Ingå

Lights

5239 **Kalbådgrund** 59°59'·1N 25°36'·1E LFl(4)30s27m12M
    195°-vis-180° Racon Red concrete tower, white stripe
    25m Helipad
5239·4 **Porvoon Majakka Ldg Lts 016°** *Front* 60°05'·6N
    25°36'E Fl.WRG.2s10m6M
    004°-W-027°-R-105°-G-229°-W-237°-R-285°-G-004°
    Racon Red tower, black band 10m
5239·41 *Rear Larsskär* 60°08'·7N 25°37'·8E LFl.8s36m9M
    014°-vis-018° Red rectangle, yellow stripe
5242·9 **Havsudden Ldg Lts 012°** *Front* 310m from rear,
    Q.R.14m10M 007·5°-vis-015·5° Red rectangle, yellow
    stripe
5243·1 **Varlaxudden Ldg Lts 340·5°** *Front* 1570m from
    rear, Q.Y.19m12M 331°-vis-351°
    Red rectangle, yellow stripe
5243 *Common rear* 60°12'·9N 25°37'·1E Q.R.28m12M
    001·5°-vis-021·5°+LFl.Y.6s32m12M 331°-vis-351° Red
    rectangle, yellow stripe

Harbour communications

Porvoo Guest Harbour ☎ +358 19 584 727

General

Porvoo is the second oldest town in Finland and was established in 1346. Its early 15th-century cathedral overlooks the town, and there are numerous museums and art galleries. It is worth rowing up river beyond the bridge to admire a most attractive row of fishermens' houses. If it is not possible to visit by yacht – and the harbour is shallow – it would make an interesting day out from Helsinki by either ferry or coach. There is no rail connection except for an occasional tourist steam train.

The imaginative Porvoo website is at www.porvoo.fi.

Approach and entrance

The harbour is approached from either south-southwest or south-southeast, leaving the large island of Emäsalo to starboard or port respectively. Larger yachts are restricted to the latter approach, however, as a bridge south of Tolkkinen on the south-southwest approach has a clearance of only 18m. Although well-marked, both channels shoal to less than 3m in places, and to a scant 1·9m after combining some 4M south of the town. The final stages are also very narrow – more reminiscent of a canal than of a river. The harbour is completely sheltered, and has no traffic other than yachts and the occasional tourist boat.

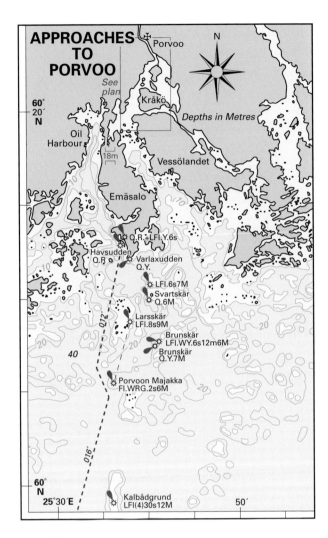

as well as a variety of marine engineers and other services – the marina office produces a useful booklet detailing local services, but sadly printed in Finnish and Swedish only. Familiar brands of clothing and chandlery are available from Meripuoti-Havsboden at Rihkamaatu 4, ☎ +358 19 585 808.

General facilities

Porvoo has good shopping, including a small outdoor market, within a short walk of the guest harbour. When tired of exploring the town, take the footbridge across the river to a pleasant, leafy park.

Communications and travel

There are many card-operated telephones throughout the town, with internet access available at the library. Porvoo is linked to Helsinki by bus and the occasional steam tourist train.

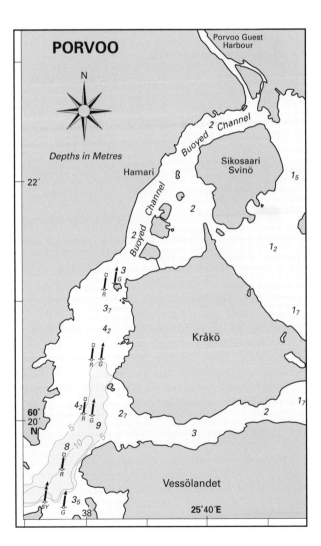

Berthing

Porvoo Guest Harbour, ☎ +358 19 584 727, occupies a single pontoon on the east bank of the river and is clearly marked with the usual white-on-blue anchor symbol. There are new visitors pontoons, some boxes and some alongside berths. Water and electricity are supplied to the pontoons. The marina office (open 1100–1700 daily) will be found in the small blue cafe slightly upstream. The services – which include laundry facilities and even a small kitchen in addition to the usual showers and toilets – are at the rear of the pink building directly opposite the pontoon walkway, the front of which is occupied by the customs office. A daily weather forecast is displayed at the marina office, but in Finnish and Swedish only. Berthing fees are in the upper band.

Formalities

See *Entry by yacht*, page 220.

Services for yachts

Fuel is available at Hamari, on the west bank about 2M downstream from Porvoo, and holding tanks can be pumped out at a facility about 0·5M downstream on the east side. There are several boatyards in the vicinity where repairs could be carried out and where it might be possible to lay-up,

4. FINLAND

Loviisa

60°27'N 26°14'E

Distances

Helsinki 55M, Porvoo 40M, Kotka 35M, Haapasaari Island 40M

Charts and guides

UKHO 2248, 1088
Finnish 902, 15
Merikarttasarja A: Viipuri – Pernaja/Viborg – Pernå

Lights

5318 **Tiiskeri** 60°09'·7N 26°15'·8E Fl(2)10s16m9M Racon
Black concrete tower and lantern

5321 **Tainio** 60°012'·7N 26°24'·7E VQ(5)6s17m6M Racon
White round concrete tower, black top, red lantern
17m

5322 **Orrengrund, W end** 60°16'·4N 26°26'·3E
Oc.WRG.3s12m12M 019°-R-082°-G-128°-W-138°-R-
151°-obsd-184°-G-197°-W-203°-R-212°-obsd- 288°-G-
355°-W-019° White concrete tower, black lantern.
Floodlit

5324 **Orrengrund Ldg Lts 022·5°** *Front* 60°16'·4N
26°27'·1E Q.16m14M 013°-vis-033° Racon Red
rectangle, yellow stripe

5324·1 *Rear* 520m from front Q.25m14M
013°-vis-033° (synchronised with front)
Red rectangle, yellow stripe

5328 **Skarven** 60°17'·8N 26°20'·91E Fl.WRG.3s7m4M 051°-
G-064°-W-068·5°-R-159°-G-241°-W-267°-R-310° Racon
Black concrete tower

Harbour communications

Loviisa Harbourmaster ① +358 19 555 730
   VHF Ch 12, 13, 14, 16
Loviisa Guest Harbour ① +358 19 555 445

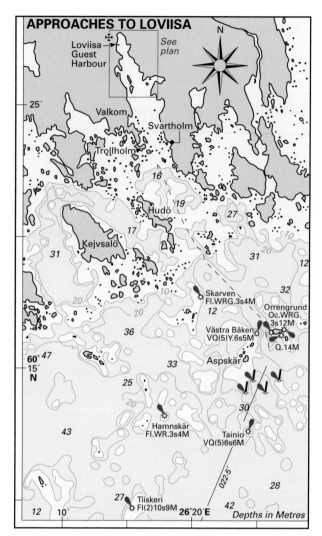

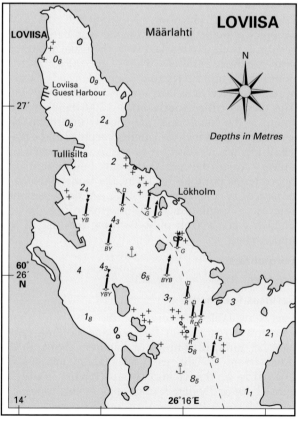

General

Loviisa is a small (population around 8,000) but interesting town at the head of a long, peaceful inlet. A thriving port during the 19th century and a resort town for the Russian nobility prior to 1914, it still contains much of interest including a fortress and picturesque wooden houses. Yachtsmen (and their children) will particularly enjoy the Museum of Seafaring, which overlooks the guest harbour and has a fine collection of models and old photographs. Also in the town is the house where Finland's greatest composer, Jean Sibelius, spent his childhood summers. Just beyond the church, on the junction of Sibeliuksenkatu and Mannerheiminkatu, it is open 1100–1600 Tuesday–Sunday from mid-June until mid-August. A Sibelius Festival is held in the town each summer.

The atomic power station on Hästholmen (60°22'N 26°21'E) is very conspicuous from the sea. About 1·5M northwest, on the starboard side of the main channel, lies the fortified island of Svartholma. The island is well worth visiting. Guided tours are available on both islands.

Loviisa's well-constructed website is at www.loviisa.fi.

Local dayboats berthed at Loviisa, with the single pontoon of the Loviisa/Laivasilta Guest Harbour beyond *A. Hammick*

Approach and entrance

The approach from the southeast is straightforward, leaving Lilla Hudö and Hudö to port and Yttre Täktarn to starboard. Though narrow where it passes between Hudö and some offlying islets, the channel is well marked with beacons and buoys. Further narrows are encountered between Trollholm and the mainland shore to starboard, before the reach opens out into a broad lake with depths of up to 12m where good anchorage is available. The final stretch is again well marked with lateral beacons, though shoaling to a bare 2m in some places as one approaches the marina.

At the entrance to the Loviisa inlet, to the right of the main channel, lies the interesting fortified island of Svartholm. There is a 40-berth marina on the east side of the island with plenty of depth in the outer berths. Free basic facilities and floods of tourists during the day. Café/restaurant on shore in season. Svartholm was bombarded by the British fleet during the Crimean War.

Formalities

See *Entry by yacht*, page 220.

Berthing

Loviisa Guest Harbour, ① +358 19 555 445, *Mobile* +358 40 740 7308 – sometimes referred to as Laivasilta or Skeppsbron marina – lies southeast of the town centre amid pleasant, park-like surroundings. There is a new visitors pontoon, mooring stern to buoys, bows to jetty. Berths in a claimed 2–2·5m, those reserved for visitors being on either side of a long pontoon aligned in an east/west direction. All are bow-to with a stern buoy provided. Deeper yachts can lie to a jetty at Tullisilta, about 0·5M further south, where there is a single pontoon offering 15 berths in up to 4m (though the inner ones are considerably shallower), but it is much less convenient for the town.

The harbour office at Laivasilta (open 0900–2100 daily) occupies a small kiosk near the fuel berth. Those berthed at Tullisilta should visit the Tourist Information office on the access road. Berthing fee – lower band at both facilities (see page 220).

Services for yachts

The guest harbour has all the usual facilities including showers, toilets, sauna and launderette, with cafés and restaurants nearby. Fuel is available at the service dock close south of the long visitor's pontoon, where holding tanks can also be pumped out. The jetty at Tullisilta has toilets, showers and a small shop.

There are several boatyards in the area, and mechanical and other work can be carried out by a variety of local companies – seek advice at the marina office. Limited chandlery is available at the Varvet Marina Shop, ① +358 19 535 149, near the town centre. Doyle Sails Finland, ① +358 91 533 167, *Email* info@doylesails.fi, handle sailmaking and repairs of all kinds.

General facilities

All normal shopping needs can be met in Loviisa town centre, a pleasant 750m walk from the guest harbour, where there are also the usual banks, cafés, restaurants etc.

Communications and travel

There are card-operated telephones at both the guest harbour office and at Tullisilta, and internet access at the public library at 24 Kuningattarenkatu.

Loviisa is on the railway network, though travelling to Helsinki would necessitate several changes. Buses run to Helsinki and Vantaa airport. Bicycles can be hired for forays into the hinterland.

4. FINLAND

Kotka

60°27'N 26°57'E

Distances

Helsinki 75M, Loviisa 35M, Haapasaari Island 15M, Hamina 20M, Santio Island 30M, Vyborg 65M, St Petersburg 110M

Charts and guides

UKHO 2248, 2264, 1089
Finnish 901, 902, 14, 138
Merikarttasarja A: Viipuri – Pernaja/Viborg – Pernå

Lights

5380 **Kotkan Majakka** 60°10'·3N 26°39'·2E
Fl(4)30s23m12M Racon Yellow metal column, blue band Helipad

5413 **Luppi** 60°14'·3N 27°01'·8E Fl.WRG.3s8m6M 247°-G-274°-W-048·5°-R-074°

5385 **Rankin Kivikari (Patricia)** 60°21'·2N 26°57'·4E
UQ(5)6s10m3M Racon White metal post, red band

5386 **Rankki** 60°21'·9N 26°58'·3E Fl(3)WRG.10s11m6M 225·5°-G-288°-W-295°-R-048°-G-096°-W-101°-R-127° Black round concrete tower on reef

5388 **Lelleri** 60°24'N 26°58'·5E Fl(2)WRG.5s5m7M 144°-G-167°-W-174°-R-244°-G-330·5°-W-336°-R-354° Yellow round tower, black top

5394 **Pirköyri** 60°27'·5N 26°58'·6E Fl.WRG.3s6m5M 000°-G-163°-W-166°-R-178° Red lantern on white concrete base

Harbour communications

Kotka Port Authority ① +358 20 790 8800
VHF Ch 16, 11, 13, 14
Kotka Harbourmaster ① +358 5 274 286
VHF Ch 16, 11, 13, 14
Kotka Vessel Traffic Service ① +358 204 485 604
VHF Ch 67 (all vessels more than 12m in length must maintain a listening watch while in the fairways of the Kotka pilotage area)
Kotka Guest Harbour ① +358 5 218 1417
(Kotka Yacht Club ① +358 5 213 349)

General

With a population of more than 55,000, Kotka is the largest city between Helsinki and the Russian border, and is an important port handling mostly timber. Originally it occupied only the island of Kotkansaari, but over the years has spread inland and to the adjacent islands. It is a useful point of departure from Finland to Vyborg or St Petersburg. Another reason for coming to Kotka is to visit the fishing lodge built in 1889 for Tsar Alexander III (open 1000–1900 daily in summer). It lies by the rapids at Langinkoski about 5km northwest of the town and is easily reached by bus. It is intriguing and well worth visiting.

The Kotka Maritime Festival is held annually in early August – details on the Kotka city website at www.kotka.fi. The commerical port's website is at www.portofkotka.fi.

Approach and entrance

The inshore approach from Helsinki passes north of the island of Kaunissaari, follows leading marks northeast between Mussalo and Viikarinsaari and thence north-northeast between Varissaari and

Kuutsalo, before turning northwest for the harbour entrance.

From the southeast the approach runs north of Haapasaari island, between the much smaller Vahakari and Merikari islands, turns northwest to leave Kirkonmaa to starboard, Rankki and then Lelleri to port and finally Kuutsalo to starboard, and so joins the route above in its final stages.

Formalities

See *Entry by yacht*, page 220. The Frontier Guard posts at Haapasaari and Santio islands are about 13M and 30M away respectively.

Berthing

Kotka's 50 berth visitors marina is situated on the southwest shore of the Sapokanlahti harbour and is administered by the city's yacht club – the Kotkan Pursiseura, ① +358 5 213 349 – with the harbour office (open 0900–2200 daily) sharing a small building with the nearby Café Segeli, ①/*Fax* +358 5 218 1417.

Visitors are normally berthed on the second pontoon on the left after entering the harbour (clearly identified with the usual white-on-blue anchor), which can take around 50 yachts. There is up to 5m at its outer end shoaling to 1·5m near the root, and mooring is the usual bow-to with a buoy provided astern. Yachts of up to 14m can be accommodated, and berthing fees are in the lower band (see page 220).

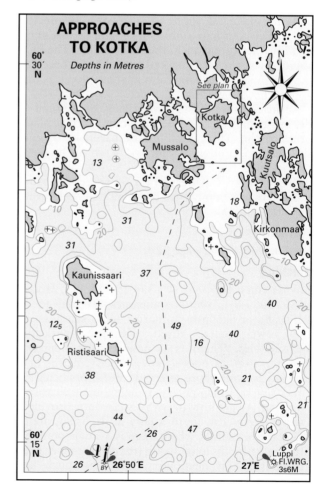

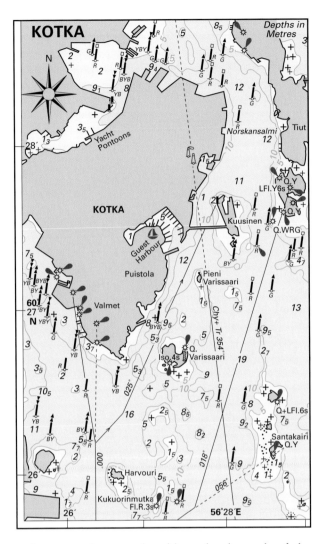

Larger yachts may be able to berth north of the city in the Vanhasatama area, beyond the old icebreaker *Tarmo* (built in Newcastle in 1907 and now a museum ship). The two pontoons can take up to 26 yachts, a few alongside but the majority bows-to. The area is a former passenger wharf and the water is deep. Like the visitors marina the pontoons are administered by the Kotkan Pursiseura, but there

is no office on site and it would be wise to check, ☎ +358 5 218 1417, in advance of arrival.

Services for yachts.

Water and electricity on both pontoons, with toilets and showers ashore. Laundry facilities at the yacht club marina, which has a fuelling berth (where holding tanks can also be emptied) at the end of the long, tree-shaded central mole (open 1000–1900 weekdays, 1000–1500 weekends). Finnish propane gas cylinders can be exchanged, but no others.

There are numerous boatyards and engineering workshops in the area – enquire at the marina office. Local charts and a small amount of limited chandlery are sold at the fuel berth, otherwise visit Veleiro Oy, just off the island to the north in the Puolanlaituri district, ☎ +358 5 210 9555. For sail repairs it is necessary to contact Doyle Sails in Loviisa.

General facilities

The shopping centre, where most food requirements can be met, is about 15 minutes' walk from the yacht harbour. There is also an outdoor market, as well as banks, restaurants and hotels in the town.

The Maritime Museum of Finland at the Maritime Centre Vellama, Kotka opened in 2008.

On the northwest side of Kotkansaari island, above the yacht pontoons, is a well-maintained and impressive water garden with pleasant walks.

Communications and travel

Card-operated telephone at the Café Segeli, near the root of the visitor's pontoon, plus many elsewhere. Postal services in the town and internet access at the public library on Kirkkokatu.

Good rail and express coach connections to Helsinki and elsewhere – or bicycles can be hired at the marina office.

Kotka, showing the visitors' pontoons on the southwest side of the harbour *A. Hammick*

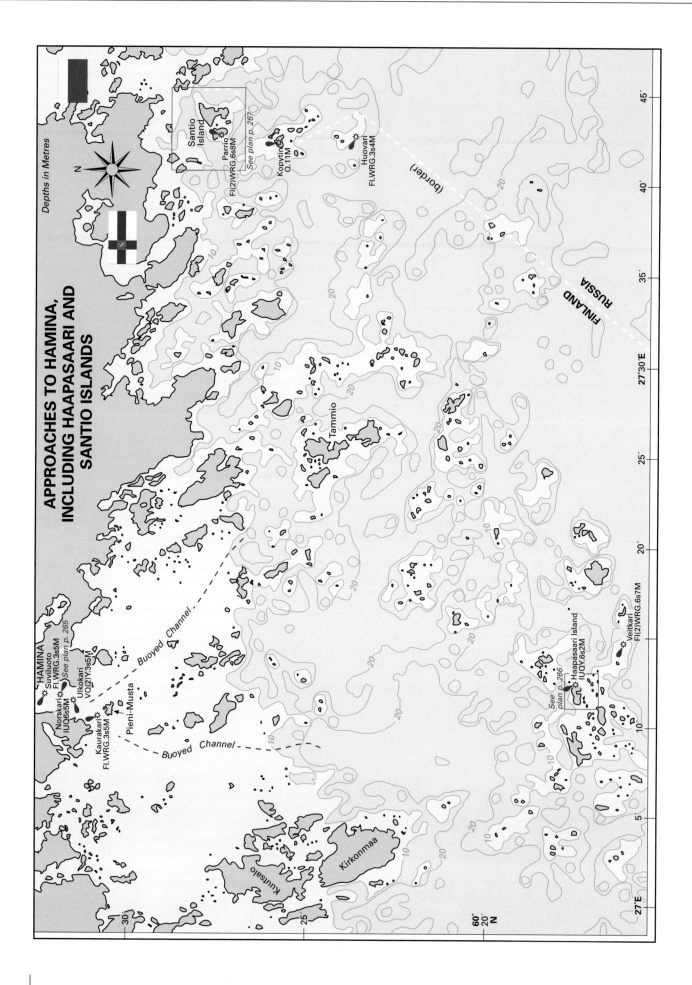

APPROACHES TO HAMINA, INCLUDING HAAPASAARI AND SANTIO ISLANDS

Depths in Metres

N

Santio Island

Parrio
Fl(2)WRG.6s8M

See plan p. 267

Kopytin
Q.11M

Huovari
Fl.WRG.3s4M

(border)

FINLAND
RUSSIA

27°30'E

Tammio

HAMINA
Suviluoto
Fl.WRG.3s5M
See plan p. 265

Norskari
IUQ6s5M

Ulkokari
VQ(2)Y.3s5M

Kaurakari
Fl.WRG.3s5M

Pieni-Musta

Buoyed Channel

Buoyed Channel

Haapasaari Island
IUQY.6s2M

See plan p. 266

Veitkari
Fl(2)WRG.6s7M

Kuutsalo

Kirkonmaa

27°E

60°
20'
N

Hamina (Fredrikshamn)

60°34'N 27°11'E

Distances

Kotka 20M, Haapasaari Island 15M, Santio Island 20M

Charts and guides

UKHO 2264, 1089
Finnish 901, 14, 134
Merikarttasarja A: Viipuri – Pernaja/Viborg – Pernå

Lights

5411 **Haapasaari** 60°17'·4N 27°12'·3E IUQ.Y.6s4m2M 133°-vis-310° Column

5412 **Kivikari** 60°17'·5N 27°12'·5E Q.WRG.8m7M 054°-G-154°-W-188°-R-205°-G-213°-W-217°-R-301° White lantern, white base

5420·4 **Kaurakari** 60°30'·8N 27°10'·5E Fl.WRG.1s4m4M 301°-G-320·5°-R-008°-G-135°-W-142·5°-R-162° Yellow rectangle, red border

5420·6 **Ulkokari** 60°31'·5N 27°11'·3E VQ(2)Y.3s4m2M Column

5422 **Norskari** 60°31'·8N 27°11'·5E IUQ.6s5m5M White post, red band

5428 **Suviluoto** 60°32'·3N 27°11'·8E Fl.WRG.3s3m5M 324°-G-005·5°-W-009·5°-R-027°-G-049·5°-W-056°-R-065°-G-078°-W-084°-R-105° Yellow rectangle, red stripe, on post

Harbour communications

Hamina Port Authority ① +358 5 225 5400
    VHF Ch 12, 13, 16
    Email office@portofhamina.fi
Tervasaari Visitors' Harbour ① +358 5 344 4828
Haminan Pursiseura Harbourmaster ① +358 5 572 1142
    Email uutela.jarmo@hotmail.com

General

Hamina is a pretty, spacious town with an unusual ground plan – eight roads radiate from the old town centre, with others forming concentric circles around them so that from the air it resembles a giant spider's web. Designed to fit inside a vast perimeter wall, Hamina has been a garrison town for most of its 350 year existence, and now lies only 40km from the Russian border. Its commercial port, which is some distance downstream, handles mainly container traffic and timber.

Both the town's website at www.hamina.fi and that of the port authority at www.portofhamina.fi have English versions.

Approach and entrance

The main approach is from the southeast, passing north of Tammio Island and thence northwest along a well-marked channel before turning north shortly after passing Pieni-Musta island to port. The final 2·5M are again clearly marked, with depths of 6m to within 1M of the town and 3m in its latter stages.

Formalities

See *Entry by yacht*, page 220.

Berthing

Yachts berth just short of two road bridges with 9·2m and 7·2m clearance respectively. There are two possibilities, the berthing fees at both of which are in the lower band (see page 220).

Tervasaari Visitors' Harbour, ① +358 5 344 4828, on the east bank has space for 25 yachts in 4m depths, with another 15 berths in 1·5m or less. Unusually, all the deeper berths are alongside. The office is at the southern end of the quay (in the bar), near the fuel berth.

Haminan Pursiseura (Hamina Yacht Club), ① +358 50 5721142, occupies the small island of Pieni Vuohisaari directly opposite the visitors harbour, and accepts visiting yachts on the southern of its two pontoons if space is available. Depths are shallower, at around 2m. A small ferry runs between the yacht club and the town.

Services for yachts

Diesel and water are available at the visitors harbour fuel berth (depth 2·5m), and both sites offer showers, but otherwise facilities are limited. Most of the guest harbour berths have access to electricity, and holding tanks can be pumped out at the south end of visitors quay (rather than at the fuel berth). There are several boatyards and other marine businesses in the locality, but Hamina is not a place to have major work carried out.

General facilities

Several cafés and restaurants overlook the harbour, and there is a good supermarket nearby. The town centre, which is about 15 minutes' walk from the visitors harbour, is well provided with shops and banks, and there is a large outdoor market.

Communications and travel

Card-operated phone at the visitors harbour and in town, where there is a Post Office. The internet terminal at the public library is well used and it may be necessary to book a slot well in advance.

The railway runs down the west bank of the estuary, some distance from the town, but the bus

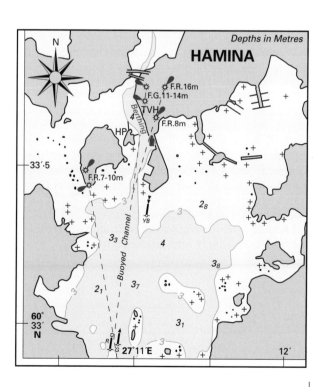

Approaching the visitors' quay at Hamina opposite the distinctive turreted clubhouse of the Haminan Pursiseura (HPS)   *A. Hammick*

station is much closer. Bicycles can be hired at the visitors' harbour office to cover the 1·5km into town.

Haapasaari Island

60°17'N 27°12'E

Charts
UKHO 2264, 1089
Finnish 901, 14

The most obvious reason to visit Haapasaari is to get Frontier Guard clearance to or from St Petersburg some 95M distant. However, it is an attractive, unspoilt island with well-kept wooden houses and cobbled streets, and well worth visiting in its own right.

The Frontier Guard occupy the smaller inlet near the western end of the island, where yachts can berth while clearance is being arranged, either alongside the outer quay in 4·5m on inside the bay in 2·5m as directed. See page 220 for details of Frontier Guard requirements.

The small guest harbour, ☎ +358 5 260 0227, is located in the larger inlet which almost bisects the island from south to north. Approach can be made via well-marked channels from either west or east, the entrance into the lagoon being no more than 12m wide and 3·5m deep. Berthing is bow-to on two pontoons, one each side of the lagoon near its head, which are also used by the island ferries. Water taps and toilets are available, but little else.

There is a fuel berth on the west side of harbour, near the surprisingly well-stocked shop.

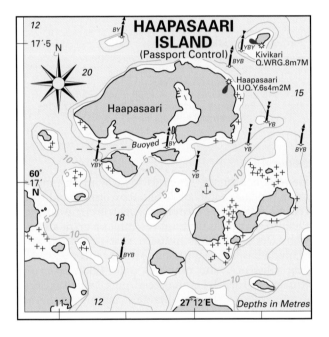

Approaching the inlet on Haapasaari island   *P. and G. Price*

4f. The Russian channel, Saimaa Canal and the Lakes

Santio Island

60°27'N 27°43'E
Charts
UKHO 2264
Finnish 901, 12, 13

Santio is a convenient island Frontier Guard station (see page 220) if heading to or from Vyborg, about 40M away. There is 2–4m at their solid pontoon (the inner side is well sheltered in strong winds) and yachts may be allowed to lie alongside overnight before a dawn departure. There is no fuel available and few facilities other than rubbish bins, toilets and a barbecue, and though the island appears attractive visitors are not permitted to leave the harbour area.

The Saimaa Canal and Lakes

Charts and guides
Finnish chart 921
Merikarttasarja L: Lappeenranta/Savonlinna

Instructions for Small-Boat Traffic in the Saimaa Canal (published annually, in English, by the Board of Management of the Saimaa Canal – Saimaan käyntisatamat), in similar format to the *Käyntisatamat Besökshamnar* (see page 222), gives details of nearly all Saimaa Lake harbours, plus information on transiting the Saimaa Canal in four languages including English. See the publisher's website at www.finnlake.com for further details.

Canal communications
Saimaa Canal Operations Centre, ☎ +358 5 458 5170, *Fax* +358 5 204 483110, *VHF* Ch 11, *Email* saimaankanavan.hoitokunta@fma.fi www.fma.fi/saimaacanal

General
The beautiful Saimaa Lake area is reached via the 23M (43km) Saimaa Canal, which is operated by the Finns under an agreement with Russia. Both lakes and canal are the highway for a great timber trade – log rafts, made up from felled timber piled on the ice during the winter and cleared from the south as the ice melts, are frequently encountered as they are moved under tow at an unstoppable 1–2 knots.

The lakes are navigable for deep-draught yachts with fixed masts for some 200M, as far as Joensuu (62°35'N 29°45'E) and Kuopio (62°50'N 27°40'E). There is good sailing on the larger bodies of water, but there are many sheltered and often tortuous channels. Those described locally as 'deep' – some 815km of them – carry 4·2m, the 1560km of 'main' channels at least 2·4m. The area is very well marked and even the smallest channels have transits.

Approach
See Vyborg (page 279) for the approach to the canal. A Russian visa is not necessary unless Vyborg is to be visited.

4. FINLAND

The Santio customs post with an interesting Finnish vessel in the foreground *P. and G. Price*

Approaching a lock on the Saimaa Canal
P. and G. Price

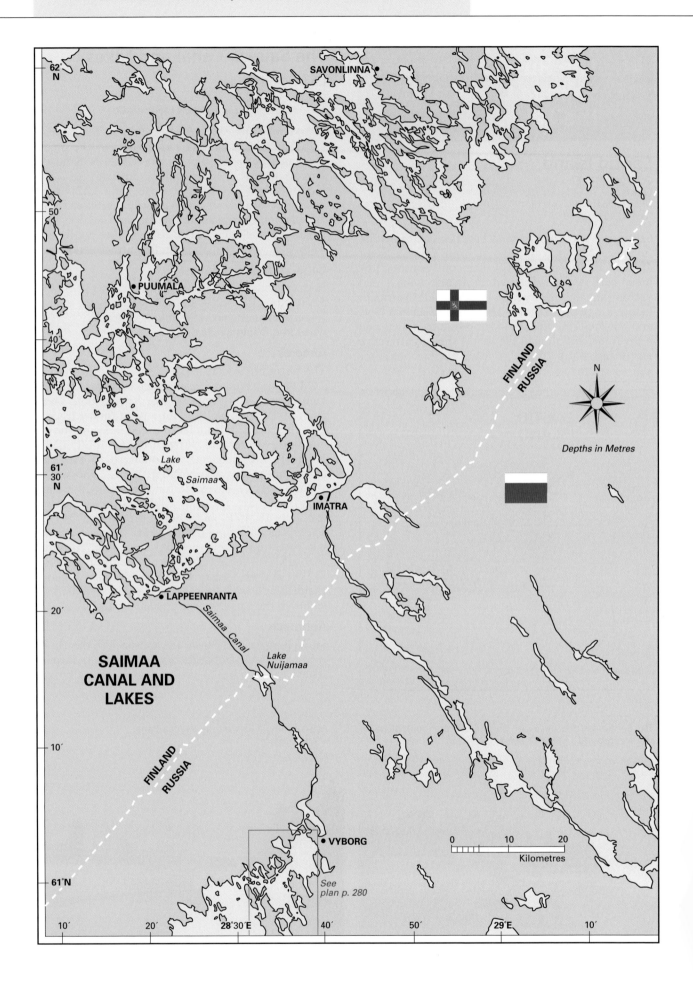

SAVONLINNA •

• PUUMALA

Lake

Saimaa

61°
30'
N

• IMATRA

FINLAND
RUSSIA

Depths in Metres

N

• LAPPEENRANTA

Saimaa Canal

Lake
Nuijamaa

**SAIMAA
CANAL AND
LAKES**

FINLAND
RUSSIA

10'

0   10   20
Kilometres

• VYBORG

See
plan p. 280

61° N

62°
N

50'

61°
30'
N

20'

10'

61° N

10'   20'   28°30'E   40'   50'   29°E   10'

The Saimaa Canal

It is absolutely essential to contact the Board of Management of the Saimaa Canal (as above or at Itäinen kanavatie 2, FIN – 53420 Lappeenranta, Finland) well before any intended visit, requesting a copy of their *Instructions for Small-Boat Traffic* in the Saimaa Canal which gives detailed instructions for passage of the Canal. This, together with copies of the necessary forms to be completed, will be sent immediately, without charge, to anywhere in the world. The completed forms must be received back by the Board of Management at least a week before the yacht arrives. There are strict regulations about safety equipment to be carried, all detailed in the *Instructions for Small-Boat Traffic*, though at present British yachtsmen do not need any formal qualification to transit the canal.

Outward clearance from Finland, most probably obtained at the Frontier Guard stations at either Haapasaari or Santio islands is necessary. Russian Customs control is at the first lock at Brusnitchnoe and passport control at Pälli. No entry visa is required if not calling at Vyborg but if you have a visa for a later visit to St Petersburg or Kaliningrad ensure that it is not stamped in the Canal. Finnish re-entry formalities take place at the Frontier Guard station at Nuijamaa, ① +358 2 0410 2370, about halfway along the canal where it crosses the frontier.

Yachts under 24m do not need a pilot provided that they have an English or Russian speaking person on board who can communicate on VHF Channel 11 with the Russian authorities. The VHF has to be switched on continuously.

Six copies of crew lists with passport information of each person, the name of the vessel and route from where to where should be prepared in advance. The skipper must carry a certificate stating his ownership of the yacht or authority of its use, and a copy of the yacht's certificate. Canal fees should be prepaid to Merenkulkulaitos, bank: Nordea 166030-107626, message: + name of vessel, paid by: the skipper (same person who has signed the paper announcing the intention of transit). If a Russian pilot is engaged he will remain on board until Brusnitchnoe, and his services will of course be charged for. Vessels under 25m are not required to carry a pilot in the Finnish-controlled section.

Engineless yachts may not use the canal, which varies in width from 34m up to 55m and carries 5·2m throughout. Eight locks – at Brusnitchnoe, Iskrovka, Cvetotchnoe, Ilistoe, Pälli, Soskua, Mustola and Mälkiä – handle the 76m difference in water level between the Baltic and the Saimaa Lakes, each lock 85m long and 13·2m wide. There are also seven opening bridges and six fixed ones (least clearance 24·5m), and transit normally takes between six and eight hours. No fuel is available on the canal – i.e. until reaching Lappeenranta – and skippers should ensure that they have plenty for the transit.

Lappeenranta

61°04′N 28°11′E

Harbour communications

Lappeenranta Port Authority ① +358 5 616 6070
   Email satamalaitos@lappeenranta.fi
Lappeenranta Harbourmasters
   Mobile +358 400 558 517 and +358 400 952 971
Linnoitusniemi (Rapasaari) ① +358 5 453 1482 (0800–2000)
Kasinonranta ① +358 5 616 7201

General

Following completion of the Saimaa Canal in 1856, Lappeenranta became the largest inland port in Finland. It remains a centre for the timber processing industry and is a thriving city with some 60,000 inhabitants. It is a friendly town, popular with both Finnish and Russian tourists and with several well-sheltered harbours which welcome foreign yachts. The paper mill is interesting, and the old military area of Linnoitus on a hill overlooking the harbour has a good museum.

The City of Lappeenranta website at www.lappeenranta.fi includes a well-presented section entitled 'Boaters' Lappeenranta', including brief details of the city's visitors' harbours and information about the Saimaa Canal.

Approach and entrance

All berthing for visiting yachts is in a large inlet west of the canal entrance, approach being made through the commercial port which can be quite complicated. There are overhead cables which are marked as having 18m clearance, but shown on some charts as having as little at 12m. Those with taller masts can make a detour.

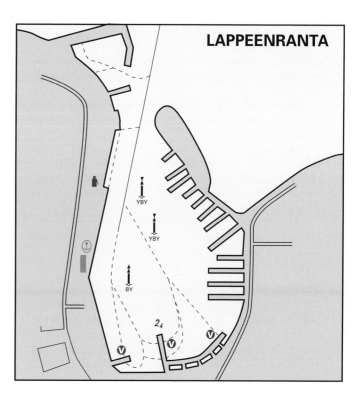

LAPPEENRANTA

4. FINLAND

Yachts berthed at Lappeenranta on the Saimaa Lakes
P. and G. Price

Timber barge on the way to the pulp mills at Lappeenranta
E. Redfern

Berthing

There are four guest harbours at Lappeenranta, all grouped around the Kaupunginlahti inlet at the western end of the city.

Linnoitusniemi sometimes referred to as Rapasaari, offers 20 visitors' berths on the west side of the bay near the entrance, all bows-to with a stern buoy provided.

Linnoituksen laituri, a little further south is a new facility, a 220m long dock intended for boats of more than 15m.

Maalaistenlaituri, in the southwest corner of the bay, has 10 visitors' berths and some additional space for short (maximum four hour) visits, particularly convenient as it is the closest to the shopping centre.

Kasinonranta, in the southeast corner, is the largest facility with 50 visitors berths, some alongside and some bows-to with a stern buoy, in 2·5m.

Services for yachts

All four berthing areas have water and electricity, with toilets, showers and sauna ashore. Linnoituksen has a washing machine. Fuel is available at Linnoitusniemi, where holding tanks can be emptied and there is also a small chandlery and a grocery store.

General facilities

Good shopping and several lively markets. Café at Linnoitusniemi and the usual restaurants in the city, together with two 'boat restaurants' at Maalaistenlaituri.

Communications and travel

There are bookable internet terminals at the library on Valtakatu, which is open daily. The airport lies about 3km outside the city, while mainline trains and express coaches run to Helsinki and elsewhere.

Imatra
61°13'N 28°43'E

A small town some 34M (63km) northeast of Lappeenranta, at the entrance to the Vuoski, the only river which flows from the southern Saimaa Lakes into Lake Ladoga, over the border in Russia. There are spectacular rapids, and a hydroelectric station just south of the town helps control lake levels.

There is a well-protected visitors marina on east side of the bay between Lammassaari island and the city, owned by the nearby Imatra Spa Hotel. Mooring is bows-to with a stern line to a buoy in 2m or more. All berths have water and electricity, with toilets and showers in the hotel, where fees are also paid.

Basic food items are available at the hotel shop, otherwise the town can provide for most needs. Fuel is available at the marina at the south end of the bay. Imatra's website is to be found at www.imatra.fi.

Puumala
61°50'N 28°11'E

A most attractive small town on the northern bank of the narrows through which larger traffic must pass en route from the southern and northern sections of the lakes. A road bridge spans the channel, but having 28·5m clearance can safely be ignored by yachts.

There is a municipal quay, also used by cruise and tourist boats, plus a guest harbour with all usual facilities including fuel, both close to the bridge in 3m or more. A good supermarket will be found five minutes' walk up the hill, where there is also a bank and other small shops.

The town maintains a website at www.puumala.fi, but much of it is in Finnish only.

Savonlinna
61°52'N 28°54'E

General

Savonlinna is a good turning point for a short cruise in the lakes, and can be reached in two days from the canal if time is short. It is a charming small tourist town straddling several islands which form a bridge across the Saimaa lakes, and stages an internationally famous Opera Festival in Olavinlinna Castle each July.

Saavonlina – the view from the castle down towards the harbour *P. & G. Price*

Olavinlinna Castle from the visitors' pontoons at Koulukadun *E. Redfern*

Savonlinna is also the home of many of the old boats still in use, which, though now converted from steam to diesel, still lend their own grace to the scene. There is an interesting maritime museum.

The city's website will be found at www.savonlinna.fi.

Approach and entrance
Savonlinna lies on one of the lakes' deep (4·2m) channels and the southerly approach is straightforward.

Berthing
Harri Westburg, a single quay and pontoon in an inlet on the south coast of the largest of Savonlinna's islands, in a rather dull area but handy for shopping. Mooring is bows-to with stern buoys.

Koulukadun, several pontoons able to take yachts up to 18m in an attractive spot close west of the castle. The outer hammerhead is much used by tourist boats and ferries.

Casinon, north of the town and requiring a circuitous and inconvenient passage for sailboats through several opening bridges. Mooring is bows-to with stern buoys, but larger yachts will find it somewhat cramped.

Services for yachts
Harri Westburg Water, electricity, fuel and a small chandlery, with a café nearby.
Koulukadun Water and electricity on the docks, with toilet and showers in the hotel 100m away. Free cars may be available for shopping or taking crew to bus, train or airport.
Casinon All facilities in the nearby Casino hotel.

General facilities
Shopping to meet all reasonable needs, plus a good daily outdoor market on the quay.

Communications and travel
There is internet access at the public library on Tottinkatu. Also well served by air, train (less than five hours to Helsinki) and express coach, making Savonlinna by far the best city in the northern lake area for crew changes. There is also a regular ferry to Lappeenranta.

Joensuu
62°35′N 29°45′E

Joensuu stands on an island at the narrows which, due to a bridge with 12·5m clearance, marks the northeast limit of navigation for most cruising yachts. There is smallboat marina, which is understood to accept visiting yachts, on the southwest coast of the island. The town's website is at www.joensuu.fi.

Kuopio
62°50′N 27°40′E

A large modern town in a beautiful area, Kuopio marks the northwest limit of navigation for boats with fixed masts of less than 12·5m. There are four guest harbours convenient to the city centre, though all are relatively small.

Maljalahti and the nearby Kuopio passenger harbour share a well-protected basin on the southeast side of the city, convenient to the city centre. The former has 21 visitors' berths, with showers, fuel, café etc on site, while the latter is better suited to larger yachts. Nearby are the Scandic Hotel harbour (10 visitors' berths) and Kuopionlahti, which has a 40m of landing stage.

Useful maps and photographs will be found on the city's website at www.kuopio.fi.

5. Russia

The country

That part of Russia which borders the far east of the Baltic Sea is almost entirely low-lying and backed by extensive marshes and lakes. The delta of the River Neva was an uninhabited swamp until the founding of St Petersburg in the early 18th century, and little of the city stands more than 5m above sea level. The 200m contour lies several hundred kilometres inland.

The seas in the eastern part of the Gulf of Finland are as shallow as the land is low, with the 10m contour running well to the northwest of Kronshtadt and much of the Nevskaya Guba 5m or less, other than where dredged. This may partly explain Russia's desire to retain Vyborg, close to the Finnish border, the approaches to which carry considerably greater depths.

Despite this, St Petersburg is home to a wide range of major industries – steel works, shipbuilding, mechanical equipment and heavy electrical engineering – as well as lighter industry such as timber processing, textiles and electrical goods. With minor exceptions, its only local fuel is some oil shale and peat, and its only mineral bauxite. The surrounding land grows timber and flax and not much else – nearly all fuel, food and other raw materials have to be brought from outside.

History and the future

This is not the place for a history of the entire Russian nation – just a few words about this small part of it.

After returning to Russia from his study of industry in Western Europe, Tsar Peter the Great (1672–1725) sought to give Russia secure access to the West, which meant access to the Baltic. It was necessary for him to break the power of the Swedes, who then dominated the Baltic, and in 1700 he began the war which lasted until 1721. By 1702 he already felt sufficiently confident to start building his fortress city at the mouth of the River Neva, and his position was further consolidated in 1709, after the Battle of Poltava, when Sweden ceded Latvia, Estonia, Karelia and part of Finland to Russia.

The Tsar took a direct personal interest in the development of the city. It was founded on a swamp, isolated from sources of labour and building materials, and mortality among the pressed labour force was high. And not only were the lower classes forced to become involved – the nobility were obliged to establish houses in the new city which, in 1713, became the capital of Russia and remained so until 1918. (Those who wish to learn more about this era are recommended to read *Peter the Great* by Robert Massie, which won the Pulitzer Prize and is probably the best account of the Baltic, and particularly Russia and Poland, in the late 17th century).

At much the same time that St Petersburg was founded, Kronshtadt was heavily fortified as a naval base and construction of the Russian Baltic Fleet was begun. However trade was also encouraged, and St Petersburg soon overtook Novgorod as the country's trade centre. The growing Russian presence on the Baltic shifted the balance of power in northern Europe irrevocably, but nevertheless St Petersburg has always been vulnerable. The most serious attempt at its destruction was made in the Second World War, when it was besieged by the Germans, indirectly assisted by the Finns, but held out despite very considerable privation.

Many changes have taken place since the break up of the Soviet Union, not least the 1991 referendum in which the residents of Leningrad voted to rename their city St Petersburg. In particular, foreign visitors are more numerous and made far more welcome than in the past, even though the formalities are complex and facilities for yachts are still somewhat

The people, the church and the language

Little need be said except to point out that even within the borders of what is now Russia there are many groups with customs, habits and languages quite different from those of the northwestern Russian. The Russian Federation contains, for instance, sixteen autonomous republics, five autonomous regions and ten autonomous areas, all based on ethnic differences. St Petersburg in particular is a cosmopolitan city where members of these groups may be encountered at any time, together with nationals of republics lying outside the Russian Federation.

With the abolition of communism as the state orthodoxy, the Russian Orthodox Church has enjoyed a major revival and now has more than 17,000 priests and 450 monasteries throughout the country as a whole. Churches and cathedrals are amongst the finest buildings in all Russia's Baltic cities, though many suffered vandalism during the Soviet era.

limited by western standards. The general consensus amongst those who have visited Russia by yacht over the past few years appears to be overwhelmingly in favour, and there is little doubt that future developments will improve the situation further.

Security

This is often a primary concern for those considering a visit to Russia, whether by yacht or conventionally. However modern sources maintain that St Petersburg is no more dangerous than any other large city, even though petty theft such as pocket-picking is rife. All the usual precautions should of course be taken – avoid carrying large amounts of money, conceal cameras etc inside nondescript, closed bags, be politely wary of over-friendly strangers, etc – but this would be equally true of most of the world's major cities.

Tales of mafia and other business-related crimes are undoubtedly true, but violence is invariably confined to others of the same ilk. A foreign visitor would have to be incredibly unlucky – or unwise – to become caught in the crossfire.

The Central River Yacht Club (CRYC) in St Petersburg is some distance out of town and has good security. Though thefts from flats and cars are frequent, thefts from foreign yachts appear to be rare. At Vyborg the pontoons of the Vyborg Sea Club's Terveniemi guest harbour have 24 hour security and there have been no reports of visiting yachts being targeted.

Finally, a few guidelines aimed at avoiding complications or embarrassments:

- A lost Customs declaration is not replaceable – without it you are allowed to leave Russia with US $3,000, but everything else is subject to confiscation

- Do not take unmarked taxis unless you are with a Russian friend

- Avoid making acquaintances without a Russian friend as intermediary

- Do not visit strangers' homes.

Foreign representation

The Russian Consular Section in London is located at 5 Kensington Palace Gardens, London W8 4QX, ☎ 0203 051 1199, 0845 868 1199 (ext. 930), *Fax* 0207 229 3215, *Email* info@rusemblon.org. Visa applications for UK residents are now handled by M/S VF services (UK) Ltd, 15–27 Gee Street, London, EC1V 3RD and 16 Forth Street, Edinburgh, EH1 3LH. For enquiries and information *Email* info.ruuk@vfshelpline.com or visit the website http://ru.vfsglobal.co.uk where instructions on obtaining visas are fully displayed.

The Russian Embassy in Helsinki is located at Tehtaankatu 1b, 00140, Helsinki, Finland ☎ +358 966 1876, *Fax* +358 966 1006, *Email* rusembassy@co.inet.fi or for the Consular Department, ☎ +358 966 1449, *Fax* +358 9622

Formalities

A great many yachtsmen are deterred from visiting Russia by the bureaucracy, and sadly the formalities do not appear to have relaxed in line with the general 'opening up' of the country to outside influences. Not only do all those aboard need visas – made out for pre-determined dates – but to obtain these it is first necessary to receive a voucher and confirmation (see visa section). This is, of course, in addition to the usual passports, vessel registration certificate, VHF licence and operators' certificate, and International Certificate of Competence (see page 8).

Yachts are best advised to sail to Russia from Finland rather than Estonia. Although it should in theory be possible to enter Russia directly from the latter, a few years ago a German yachtsman was arrested and detained for doing just this. Those responsible claimed doubts as to whether he was carrying the necessary charts – he was – but with the Finnish Frontier Guard posts at Haapasaari and Santio islands conveniently near the Russian border it currently seems wise to visit Finnish territory for clearance, even if only in passing. Also, since Russian formalities and practices change frequently, this provides the opportunity to check on latest procedures with the Finnish Frontier Guard personnel.

Surveillance is maintained over both foreign and Russian yachts, and most yachts will from time to time be called up on VHF (most likely on Ch 10, 11 or 16) or visited by a patrol boat. Normally a patrol vessel will approach to within 50m or so and ask on VHF for the name and nationality of the yacht, the number of people on board and the last and next ports of call. The first time this happens can be frightening, especially if the patrol vessel approaches without lights on a dark night and, without warning, focuses a powerful searchlight on the yacht. However, given the language problems, patrol vessel captains are not usually aggressive unless they believe that the yacht is being unco-operative.

The customs and immigration procedures on arrival are normally straightforward, provided all paperwork is correct. Yachts are generally boarded by two or three officials and sometimes an agent (if any) who tend to be concerned more with the appropriate forms than with inspecting the boat. Their main concerns are drugs and weapons and illegal migrants.

There are no specific rules restricting the temporary importation of yachts for wintering or repairs but one would be expected to prove the need for repairs to extend the temporary importation period if neccessary.

The Russian flag is a horizontal tricolour, white over blue over red.

NOTE – At the time of going to press in early April 2010 it was known that entry procedures and requirements were under active revision but the details were unavailable. For later information please visit www.rccpf.org

1812. Details of other countries' representation are listed on www.russianembassy.net.

The British Consulate in St Petersburg is located at PL Proletarskoy Diktatury 5, Smolinskiy Raion, 191124, St Petersburg, ☎ +7 812 320 3200, *Fax* +7 812 320 3211 ('00' for international calls is not used in Russia) www.ukinrussia.fco.gov.uk. It is open during normal business hours only.

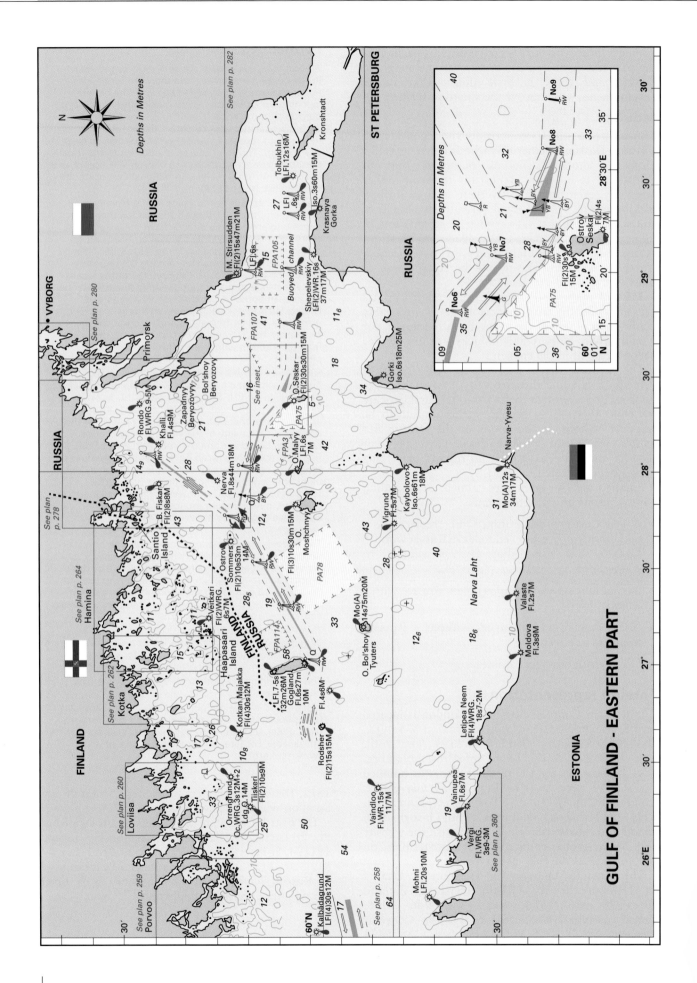

GULF OF FINLAND - EASTERN PART

Visas

Visas are granted by the Russian Consular Section (see page 273 for contact details), and come in various types. Most yachtsmen will travel on a tourist visa which is valid for a single entry of no more than one month – to visit both Kaliningrad and the St Petersburg area one would need a double entry visa. Application forms for UK citizens must be completed online at www.ru.vfsglobal.co.uk then downloaded and returned to one of the given addresses together with the following:

- One's passport which must be valid for at least six months after leaving Russia
- A passport photograph
- A postal order covering the fee, currently £50 plus service charge
- The voucher preferably as a fax print-out (although a signed and dated scanned email attachment is usually acceptable) plus confirmation of a berthing reservation at a nominated yacht harbour for the same period
- A self-addressed special delivery envelope for the return of your passport (one for each person).

Vouchers

The necessary voucher used to be issued by one of the St Petersburg yacht clubs, but changes in the regulations (mainly the requirement to register a Reference Number) have put this beyond the pockets of any of the yacht clubs. Instead yachtsmen are invited to contact Mr Vladimir Ivankiv, a Russian yachtsman who has for many years assisted visitors to Russia and who, for €30 per person (as of 2009) can make the following arrangements:

- the issue of a voucher and an accompanying confirmation document (limited to one month, as is the visa itself)
- a berthing reservation, also limited to one month (the equivalent of the hotel reservation required of conventional travellers)
- arrival and departure formalities
- any necessary support and assistance whilst in St Petersburg, including weather forecasts etc.

Russian regulations stipulate that an 'agent' must notify the Vyborg Pilot Station or, the Customs Control Post at St Petersburg, or the St Petersburg Coast Information Post at least 24 hours before the yacht's arrival, a task which Mr Ivankiv also undertakes. To do so he will require the following information:

About each person aboard:
- dates of the visit (can be extended to one month maximum)
- full name
- passport number
- date of birth
- nationality

About the yacht:
- full name
- sail number (if any)
- LOA, beam and draught

- registration number
- flag (ie country of registration)
- home port
- the number of people on board
- itinerary
- ETA
- hull colour
- call sign

Mr Ivankiv, who is based at the Central River Yacht Club (CRYC), can be contacted at Uchebnyj per 6-2-56, 194354 St Petersburg, Russia, ☎ +7 812 510 7602 (Initial zeros are used neither for international nor for local phone calls, *Mobile* +7 921 932 5831, *Email* vladimir@sailrussia.spb.ru or vladimirivankiv@yahoo.com (the latter is a reserve address which may not be checked regularly, but could nevertheless be useful if the primary one 'goes down' for any reason). Although arrangements can be made by email, a fax number will be necessary to which the final voucher can be sent. In theory the voucher can be arranged in a matter of days, but Mr Ivankiv suggests allowing at least a month for the paperwork to go through – in addition to the time taken by the Consulate's agent to process the visa itself.

A number of UK companies specialise in obtaining vouchers for tourists planning to visit Russia, amongst them CIBT (Thames Consular Services Ltd), PO Box 61745, London, SW1V 1UT ☎ 084 4736 0211 *Email* info@uk.cibt.com http://uk.cibt.com or Visa and Passport Services, 1 St Stephens Mews, London W2 5GQ ☎ 020 7229 4784 *Fax* 020 7229 7656 *Email* visa-passport@btclick.com

However, neither specialise in vouchers for yachtsmen, and it would clearly be wise to double check that whatever company is employed has experience of this aspect, and in particular of obtaining the necessary berthing reservation. It is not unknown for a western yachtsman to be turned back on arrival because his agent has omitted some essential aspect of the paperwork.

It is no longer possible to obtain a visa outside your country of permanent residence. The only exceptions being American citizens resident in the UK.

On arrival at the Customs Post one needs to have three copies of the crew list ready, passports with visas, proof of ownership of the boat, a copy of the skipper's passport (relevant page) and a copy of skipper's visa. A copy of the voucher may also be helpful.

If intending to stay in Russia for more than 72 hours plus a weekend, all visas must be registered at the Passport Office (OVIR), 1/3 Grota Steet, ☎ +7 230 8360, (for the Central River Yacht Club and the Petersburg Sea Yacht Club) or V.O. 19th Line, 12, ☎ +7 321 7534 (for the St Petersburg Navy Yacht Club), or via a tourist office (who normally charge around US $15/€30 per person). Again Mr Ivankiv has offered to assist if necessary.

Restricted Areas

Currently there are three Prohibited Areas (PA) which must not be entered at any time. These are Nos. 75 and 78 marked on the plan on page 274 and the area NE of the St Peterburgskiy buoy marked on the plan on page 282. All are outside official channels so should not prove a problem.

There are also four Firing Practice Areas (FPA) where firing times are announced on NAVTEX and VHF Ch 16. These are Nos. 3, 105, 107 and 114 each of which is marked on the plan on page 277.

All these Areas are shown on current charts and can be verified by Vladimir Ivankiv in advance or by VHF Ch 16 on entering Russian waters.

Firing range 107
Southeast of Bjorkesund Strait
60°10'.00N 28°45'.0E
60°07'.00N 28°34'.0E
60°04'.00N 28°34'.0E
60°04'.00N 28°55'.0E
60°10'.00N 28°55'.0E

Firing range 105
Southeast of Bjorkesund Strait
60°03'.5N 29°00'.00E
60°03'.5N 29°15'.00E
60°08'.0N 29°15'.00E
60°08'.0N 29°00'.00E

Firing range 114
East of Gogland Island
60°06'.3N 27°02'.5E
60°07'.5N 27° 07'.0E
60°03'.5N 27°11'.0E
60°02'.0N 27°06'.5E

Practicalities

Time

St Petersburg and its environs are on UT+3 in winter, with an additional hour of summer time between late March and late September.

Money

The Russian currency is the rouble (divided into 100 kopeks), the only legal tender even though Euro and US dollars are highly popular. In 2006 pounds sterling were not accepted even by banks.

It is now illegal to exchange western currencies on the street and there are no longer any private money changers.

Banks and other authorised exchange offices (in hotels, restaurants and some shops) are widespread, and cash advances can also be drawn on most major credit cards, though subject to the usual commission. Though a relatively recent innovation, ATMs dispensing roubles have become extremely popular and may be found in Post Offices, hotels and metro and other stations, as well as in banks. Most accept VISA, MasterCard and American Express as a minimum. ATMs dispensing dollars are much harder to find, though those of Alpha Bank are reported to do so.

Shopping

Though few people go to Russia specifically to shop, both basic commodities and more specialised items are now readily available at prices which seem exorbitant to a Russian wage earner but cheap to a Westerner. In particular, until the mid-1990s there were few DIY shops where one could buy tools, paint and other hardware items, but this has changed with the arrival of the IKEA, OBI, Maxidom and Iskrasoft chains, amongst others. Many shops now accept credit cards, though this should never be assumed. Shopping falls into several categories:

- Western shops, though only a few are actually run by Western

companies. Almost anything is available, though prices are expensive in line with Scandinavia as a whole. Credit cards are generally welcome.

- Local super (and hyper)markets which carry good quality food at reasonable prices, clothes shops and boutiques and European-type hardware stores sometimes with a chandlery section. Most still accept cash (roubles) only, though an increasing number accept credit cards.
- State shops, of which only a few are left. The range of goods is restricted, much queuing is necessary and prices are no longer kept artificially low. Not, on the whole, worth the effort.
- Kiosks by the thousand, with tempting prices but often poor quality (check for sell-by dates). Alcohol in particular should NEVER be bought at a kiosk. However if looking for a souvenir, the selection of nesting matryoshka dolls is immense and some bartering is generally acceptable.
- Markets sell meat, fruit, vegetables etc, usually of acceptable quality. Prices are often adjusted upwards when foreigners appear, so again it may be possible to bargain – always assuming that the language barrier can be overcome. Bags may not be provided.

Public holidays

Public holidays are flexible, but may occur on: 1 January, 7 January (Russian Orthodox Christmas), 23 February (Defenders of the Motherland, or Men's Day), 8 March (International Women's Day), Easter Sunday (note that Orthodox Easter may not be on the same date as Easter in the West), 1–2 May (International Labour Day), 9 May (Victory Day 1945), 27 May (City Day – St Petersburg only), 12 June (Russian Independence Day), the last 10 days of June (St Petersburg's White Nights – a festival rather than a public holiday), 7 November (Russian Unity Day), 12 December (Russian Constitution Day), 31 December.

Hotels and restaurants

St Petersburg has many hotels and restaurants at all levels, as befits a major city, some of the best ones being very expensive indeed. It is equally possible to get a good meal at a reasonable price, particularly if advised by a local.

The choice is much more limited in Vyborg although several adequate restaurants and hotels have been reported.

Communications

The Russian telephone system is generally good, and mobile phone coverage total in the St Petersburg area though charges are high. Internet access in the city is available at the Central Telephone Office, as well as at several hotels and cybercafés.

Card telephones with international dialling are now widely available in St Petersburg. All accept prepaid cards, which can be bought locally, and some also accept VISA or Mastercard.

International calls can usually be made during office hours from the two major yacht clubs, or from the tourist hotels though at much greater cost. To obtain an international line dial 8, wait for the second tone, then dial 10 followed by the country code, area code (omitting any initial 0) and number.

The country code for Russia is 7, the city code for St Petersburg and the surrounding area, including Vyborg, is 812 (if dialling from abroad the initial 0 should be omitted).

Travel

St Petersburg and its environs are well served by air, train, coach and ship – details will be found under the individual harbours.

Cruising

The attractions of a cruise to Baltic Russia are mainly concerned with St Petersburg, but there are several other possibilities.

Vyborg, about 85M northwest of St Petersburg, is an interesting old town with berthing for visiting yachts at the Vyborg Sea Club. It is close to the southern end of the Finnish-administered Saimaa Canal, which can only be approached through Russian territorial waters and which leads to a most attractive lake region in Finland.

Kronshtadt, which used to be the headquarters of the Russian Navy, is out of bounds to foreign yachts now that Customs and Immigration has moved close

to the Sea Passenger Terminal in St Petersburg. However with the completion of the barriers and bridges joining Kronshtadt to the northern and southern mainland shores the situation may change again and up-to-date information must be obtained.

The sea area between Kronshtadt and St Petersburg – the Nevskaya Guba – is a popular sailing area for Russian yachtsmen but recent changes in regulations have made any sort of local sailing practically impossible for foreign yachts and if one wants to view St Petersburg from the Neva at night it is best to take a river boat.

Finally, although the decision to open Gogland and the other nearby islands to foreign yachts

Internet sites

The internet is a rich source of information about Russia, and the following sites (in English unless otherwise stated) may well prove useful:

www.ellennet.com/english/ – then follow the Gulf of Finland link to access the Viborg, St Petersburg pages (note the spelling variants)

www.saint-petersburg.com

www.vyborg.ru – the very professional Vyborg city homepage

www.geocities.com/rusfortress/ – a commercial site offering tours of Kronstadt and its naval fortresses, but nevertheless interesting

www.port.spb.ru – the homepage of the St Petersburg Port Traffic Control Centre. The link to 'Why does St Petersburg need a new port?' is interesting

www.spb.ru/eng/ – the English version of St Petersburg's city homepage with links to everything from transport through festivals to restaurants (not all in English)

www.clubneva.ru – the website of the Central River Yacht Club

www.russia.net/country/stpetersburg – a potted history of St Petersburg, plus an interesting picture gallery

Charts, pilots and cruising guides

British Admiralty and Russian charts cover the area, the latter more detailed and in many cases to a larger scale. Russian charts are essential if planning to take any short cuts across the Nevskaya Guba between Kronstadt and St Petersburg. Those charts which are specific to an area or harbour are listed under individual harbour details. See *Appendix*, page 361, for sources.

There is little written information about the area in English, though the Finnish *The Sea of Archipelago and the Gulf of Finland* (with text in English, German and Russian) includes seven pages about Russia, most devoted to Vyborg. *The Baltic Pilot Volume II* (NP 19) is more suited to the needs of ships than of yachts.

continues to be deferred, unofficial sources report that yachts have used Suurkulan Lahti harbour on the island of Gogland, some 100M west of St Petersburg, as an overnight refuge on their way to and from St Petersburg. No landing is permitted, but there have been no reported problems with the border guards provided that all crew members have Russian visas. However this should definitely be regarded as a last resort, and Russian or Finnish advice sought if possible.

Caution

When sailing in the eastern Baltic, and particularly the shallow Nevskaya Guba, it is important to be aware that although the area has no daily tidal rise and fall, depths can vary considerably from those charted as a result of sustained strong winds from west or east. Changes of more than a metre in a few hours are not unusual. In addition to this, prolonged high pressure may result in a further decrease of up to 0·5m on charted depths.

Yacht services and chandlery

Services for yachts are limited in both St Petersburg and Vyborg, though improving in the former where there are now several chandleries, sail lofts and workshops where general repairs can be carried out. Diesel is available and there are several large DIY chains where tools and general hardware items can be purchased. But gas bottles are unobtainable at present and it is wise to assume that refilling is also not possible.

Yacht clubs

In Russia most clubs remain owned by organisations such as town councils, local business enterprises, trade unions or the military, though others are being privatised. They employ full-time staff for administrative and technical work, frequently have their own boatyard facilities including sailmaking, and often have round the clock security.

Radio communications and weather information

Navtex broadcast from Tallin and Helsinki is the most reliable means of getting weather information. Forecasts for the St Petersburg Harbour area can be obtained from the pilot station on VHF Chs 16, 09 20.

VHF radio is much used for marine communications, but no weather bulletins or navigational warnings are currently broadcast for the area.

Ostrov Sommers, near the 'roundabout' used to reach both Russian ports open to foreign yachts   *P. and G. Price*

5. RUSSIA

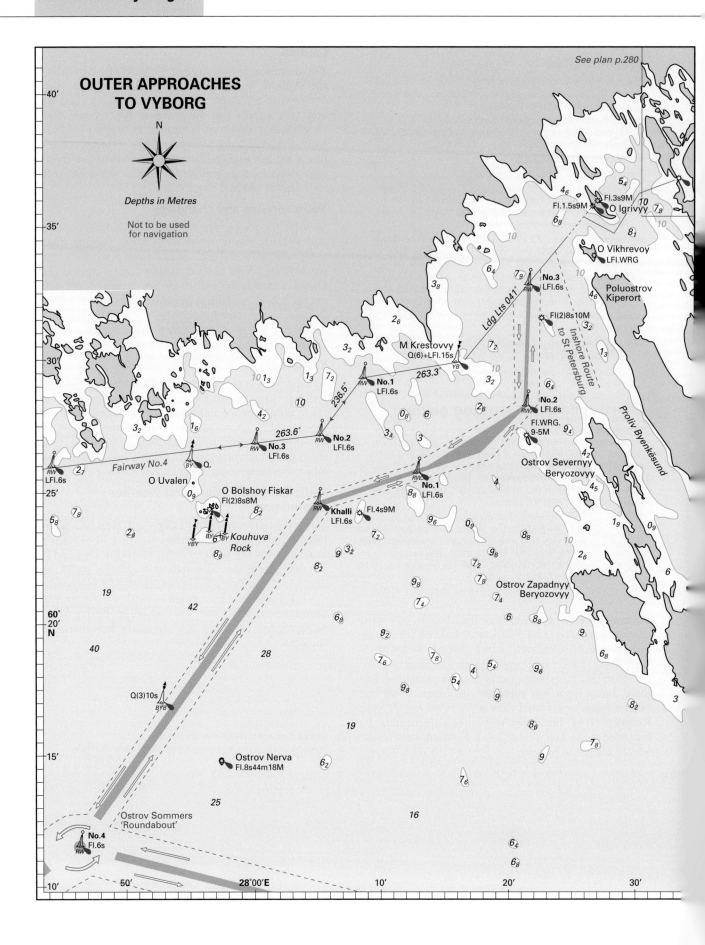

OUTER APPROACHES
TO VYBORG

N

Depths in Metres

Not to be used
for navigation

See plan p.280

Vyborg (Finnish: Viipuri)

60°42'·5N 28°44'E

Distances
Helsinki 130M, Kotka 65M, Haapasaari Island 60M,
Santio Island 40M,
Kronshtadt 95M, St Petersburg 110M

Charts and guides
UKHO 2264, 1090
Russian 28007, 28008, 28010, 28011Finnish 901, 11
Finnish *Merikarttasarjat* series:
  Viborg – Pernå/Viipuri – Pernaja (A)

Lights
5496 **Ostrov Khalli** 60°24'·2N 28°08'·3E Fl.4s16m9M Red
  metal framework tower, concrete base 12m
5500 **Ostrov Rondo** 60°27'·4N 28°21'·6E
  Fl.WRG.1·5s14m9–5M 063°-G-068°-W-077°-R-128°-G-
  162°-W-183°-R-201°-G-214°-W-234°-R-252°-W-063°
  White rectangle, black stripe, on red framework
  tower 10m
5505 **Vyborgskiy** 60°31'·6N 28°22'·7E Fl(2)8s14m10M
  Whis White octagonal tower, red bands 10m
buoy **Lotsmanskiy lightbuoy** 60°34'·5N 27°24'·5E LFl.6s
  Red and white pillar buoy, • topmark
5506 **Povorotnyy, N point** 60°34'·5N 28°25'·6E
  Fl.WRG.1·5s18m7–2M shore-G-359°-W-009°-R-020°-G-
  029°-W-231° 239°-G-249°-W-255°-R-270° White
  octagonal tower, red lantern 13m
buoy **Ostrov Igrivyy** 60°35'N 28°28'·75E Q(6)+LFl.15s
  South cardinal lightbuoy Yellow and black pillar
5518 **Vysotskiy-Yuzhnyy breakwater head** 60°36'·7N
  28°33'·2E Fl.WRG.1·5s8m5–3M 042°-G-063°8°-W-
  067·2°-R-087°-G-097°-W-111°-R-153°-G-201°-W-229°-
  R-266° White rectangle, red stripe, on mast 5m
Leading lights Five sets of leading lights plus many lit
  buoys guide a vessel through the Vysotsk narrows
  into the Vyborgskiy Morskoy Kanal, the buoyed
  channel leading to the junction of the Saimaa canal
  approach with the Vyborg final approach (see plan)
5539·4 **Dybovyy** 60°40'·2N 28°38'·9E
  Fl.G.2s6m2M Green column 3m
5544 **Saymenskiy** 60°41'·9N 28°42'·8E Iso.Y.2s8m3M
  White column, red stripe 4m
5544·1 **Vyborg Severnyy** 60°42'·6N 28°44'·1E
  Oc.R.3s23m4M White rectangle, red stripe, on white
  round concrete tower 9m
Many more lights and lit buoys exist in the approaches
and harbour area.

Harbour communications
Vyborg VTS Controller ☎ +7 812 789 3244
  VHF Ch 12 (call *Vyborg Radio 5*)
Vyborg Pilot Service ☎ +7 812 783 3449/93266
  VHF Ch 10, 74 (call *Vyborg Pilots*)
Vyborg Port Authority ☎ +7 812 782 0477
Vyborg Harbourmaster ☎ +7 812 782 0477/789 9650
  VHF Ch 12, 16
Vyborg Radio VHF Ch 02, 16, 24
Vyborg Sea Yacht Club Marina ☎/*Fax* +7 812 782 4536
  Email vyborg@baltic-region.net.ru

General

For centuries Vyborg was Finland's second most
important town and cultural centre. Already a
trading centre in the 12th century, it later became a
port of the Hanseatic League and was attacked by
Russia at least four times during the 14th and 15th
centuries. By the 18th century it was held by Peter
the Great as part of his programme to consolidate
his grip on St Petersburg. In 1812 it became part of
Finland, then under Russian control, and benefited
greatly from the opening of the Saimaa Canal in
1856. The port still handles timber, agricultural
products, minerals and ironware.

Vyborg reverted to Russia following fierce fighting
– and major damage – during the Second World War.
Almost all the Finnish population were evacuated
and the city resettled by Russians from elsewhere in
the country, with a current population of around
80,000. Both the castle and the large and attractive
Park Monrepo Reserve, beyond the bridge, are
worth exploring.

Approach

There are three routes to the Povorotnyy light tower:
- The inshore route along the Finnish coast from
  Kotka or Hamina, for which the Finnish charts are
  essential. Finnish emigration and customs
  procedures are carried out at the Frontier Guard
  station at Santio Island (60°27'N 27°43'E) – see
  page 267.
- The big-ship route south of Ostrov Gogland to the
  Ostrov Sommers 'roundabout' (60°11'·5N
  27°46'E), between Ostrov Bol'shoy Fiskar
  (60°24'·3N 27°56'·4E – Fl(2)8s22m8M) and
  Ostrov Khalli, past Ostrov Rondo and northwards
  to Povorotnyy. It is possible for a yacht to deviate
  from the main route but good charts are necessary.
  If leaving Finland, emigration and customs are at
  Haapasaari (60°17'N 27°12'E) – see page 266.
  After leaving Haapasaari yachts are expected to
  cross into Russian waters between buoys 15 and
  16.
- The inshore route from St Petersburg, the Proliv
  B'yerkësund (Koiviston Salmi in Finnish), which
  leads east of the three wooded islands of Ostrov
  Bol'shoy Beryozovyy, Ostrov Zapadnyy
  Beryozovyy and Ostrov Severnyy Beryozovyy. It
  would be wise to check with the Russian
  authorities before attempting this passage, as
  foreign yachts have sometimes been turned back.
  As of 2008 it was understood to be open, but
  yachts were not permitted to stop en route, either
  on the islands or at the city of Primorsk, as the
  entire area is military and is closed to foreigners.

The route then lies past the Ostrov Igrivyy lightbuoy
and through the narrows at Vysotsk, a sizeable
commercial town. It continues up an intermittently
buoyed channel to the Saymenskiy light tower, which
not only marks the junction with the Saimaa canal
but is also the front light for two sets of leading
lights (see plan on page 280). Once past Saymenskiy
a buoyed channel leads into Vyborg.

At least 24 hours' notice of arrival at the
Lotsmanskiy buoy (or six hours notice of departing
the harbour) is required.

All foreign vessels, including yachts, are required
to inform Vyborg at least two hours before entering
Russian waters. Details of the necessary telephone
numbers and/or VHF channels should be obtainable
from a number of sources including the Finnish
Frontier Guard, the Board of Management of the
Saimaa Canal (see page 269), or Mr Vladimir
Ivankiv (see *Vouchers*, page 274). Currently if a

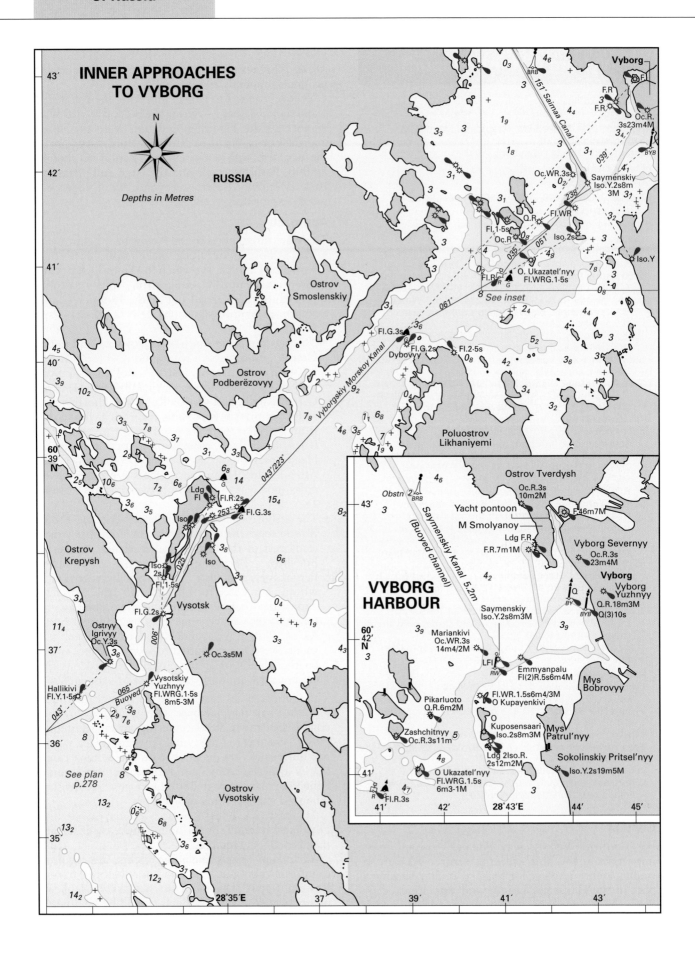

INNER APPROACHES TO VYBORG

N

RUSSIA

Depths in Metres

43′

42′

41′

40′

60°
39′
N

37′

36′

35′

Ostrov
Smoslenskiy

Ostrov
Podberëzovyy

Vyborgskiy Morskoy Kanal

Ostrov
Krepysh

Vysotsk

Ostryy
Igrivyy
Oc.Y.3s

Hallikivi
Fl.Y.1·5s

Vysotskiy
Yuzhnyy
Fl.WRG.1·5s
8m5-3M

See plan
p.278

Ostrov
Vysotskiy

151° Saimaa Canal

Vyborg
F.R
F.R
Oc.R.
3s23m4M
BYB

Oc.WR.3s
Saymenskiy
Iso.Y.2s8m
3M

Q.R
Fl.WR

Oc.R
Fl.1·5s

Iso.2s

Iso.Y

O. Ukazatel'nyy
Fl.WRG.1·5s

See inset

Fl.G.3s
Fl.G.2s
Dybovyy
Fl.2·5s

Poluostrov
Likhaniyemi

Ldg
Fl
Fl.R.2s
Fl.G.3s

Iso
Iso

Iso
2s
Fl.1·5s

Fl.G.2s

Oc.3s5M

VYBORG HARBOUR

60°
42′
N

60°
43′

Obstn
BRB

Saymenskiy Kanal 5.2m
(Buoyed channel)

Ostrov Tverdysh
Oc.R.3s
10m2M
F.46m7M

Yacht pontoon
M Smolyanoy
Ldg F.R
F.R.7m1M

Vyborg Severnyy
Oc.R.3s
23m4M

Vyborg
Vyborg
Yuzhnyy
Q.R.18m3M
Q(3)10s

Saymenskiy
Iso.Y.2s8m3M

Mariankivi
Oc.WR.3s
14m4/2M

LFI
RW

Emmyanpalu
Fl(2)R.5s6m4M

Mys
Bobrovyy

Pikarluoto
Q.R.6m2M

Fl.WR.1.5s6m4/3M
O Kupayenkivi

O
Kuposensaari
Iso.2s8m3M

Mys
Patrul'nyy

Zashchitnyy
Oc.R.3s11m

Ldg 2Iso.R.
2s12m2M

Sokolinskiy Pritsel'nyy
Iso.Y.2s19m5M

O Ukazatel'nyy
Fl.WRG.1.5s
6m3-1M

Fl.R.3s

28°43′E

yacht is passing straight through Vyborg en route for the Saimaa Canal a Russian visa is not required, but if a stay in Vyborg is contemplated a visa will be necessary. However, the regulations change frequently and advice should be sought three months in advance. It will, of course, still be necessary for all visiting yachts to call at the Customs and immigration quay at Vyborg (no need to stop at Vysotsk) for inward and outward clearance.

In 2010 it will be possible to clear Customs and Immigration here for both Vyborg and St Petersburg. Entry to St Petersburg may be made by the Sommers channel (see page 283) or via the Proliv B'yerkësund (see plan on page 278) where yachts may sail in sheltered waters for some of the way to St Petersburg. However VHF Ch 68 *Priorsk Traffic* must be monitored and advice given on entering and leaving the channel. Either way the authorities in Vyborg will advise their colleagues in Kronshtadt but to avoid being challenged there a call should be made when approaching Fort Konstantine on VHF Ch 6 *Granit* (pronounced *Graneeet*) to declare one's status.

Berthing

Visiting yachts normally berth at the Vyborg Sea Yacht Club – also called the Finnish Yachting Society of Vyborg
☎/Fax +7 812 782 4536,
Email vyborg@baltic-region.net.ru
www.baltic-region.net.ru.
Its Tervaniemi guest harbour, which has 80–100 berths on a long concrete pontoon, is situated on the port side of the entrance channel just short of the bridge, almost opposite the impressive island castle. The guest harbour has a café and kiosk near the landing stage, and there is 24 hour security. Berths on the starboard side of the entrance channel may appear less crowded and more convenient to the town but they have no security and few facilities.

General facilities

Vyborg is reported to have several restaurants where good meals can be had for very reasonable prices. Maps of the city and surrounding area are available from the bookstore at Pr Lenina 6.

Communications and travel

Vyborg is on the mainline railway between Helsinki and St Petersburg, and also on the principal coach and bus route. Trains to St Petersburg depart nearly every hour, taking about three hours for the journey.

Above Vyborg Sea Yacht Club from castle tower *E. Redfern*

Below Looking south over Vyborg harbour *E. Redfern*

5. RUSSIA

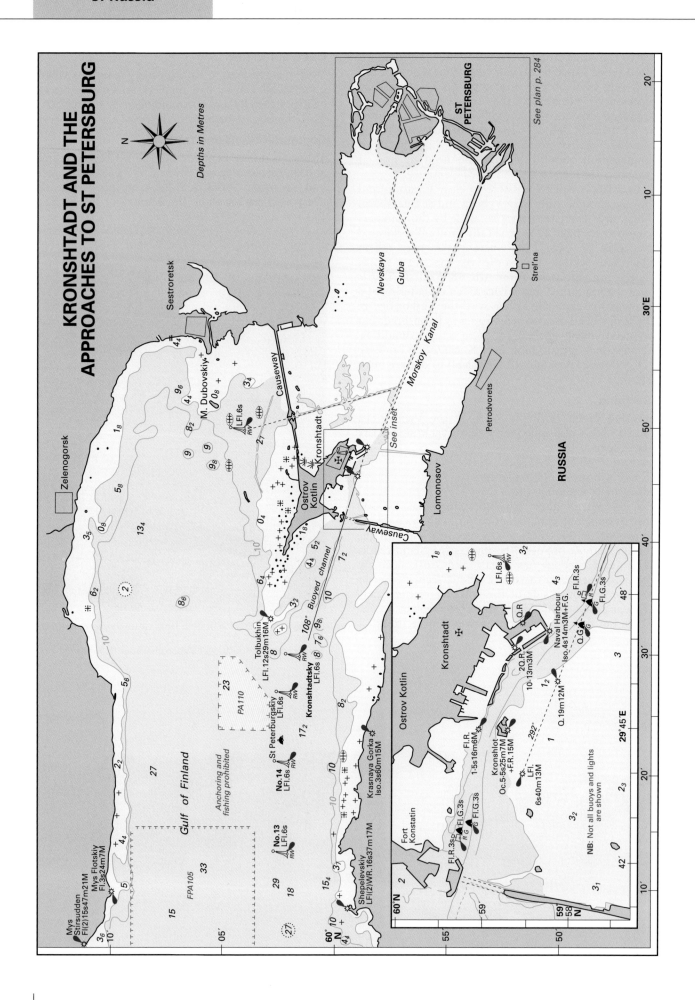

KRONSHTADT AND THE
APPROACHES TO ST PETERSBURG

N

Depths in Metres

See plan p. 284

ST
PETERSBURG

Nevskaya
Guba

Morskoy Kanal

Strel'na

Sestroretsk

RUSSIA

Petrodvorets

Lomonosov

Zelenogorsk

M. Dubovskiy

LFl.6s
RW

Causeway

Kronshtadt

Ostrov Kotlin

See inset

Causeway

Buoyed channel

Tolbukhin
LFl.12s29m16M

Kronshtadtsky
LFl.6s
RW

St Peterburgskiy
LFl.6s
RW

Anchoring and
fishing prohibited

PA110

No.14
LFl.6s
RW

Krasnaya Gorka
Iso.3s60m15M

No.13
LFl.6s
RW

Shepelevskiy
LFl(2)WR.16s37m17M

Mys
Stirsudden
Fl(2)15s47m21M

Mys Flotskiy
Fl.3s24m7M

Gulf of Finland

FPA105

Inset:

Kronshtadt

Ostrov Kotlin

LFl.6s
RW

Q.R

Naval Harbour
Iso.4s14m3M+F.G.

Fl.R.3s
R

Fl.G.3s
G

2Q.R.
10-13m3M

Q.G

Q.19m12M

Fl.R.
1·5s16m6M
+F.R.15M

Kronshlot
Oc.5·5s25m7M
+F.R.15M

LFl.
6s40m13M

Fort
Konstatin

Fl.R.3s
R

Fl.G.3s
G

NB: Not all buoys and lights
are shown

292°

29°45'E

60°N

St Petersburg

59°56′N 30°18′E

Distances
Helsinki 175M, Tallinn 185M, Haapasaari Island 95M,
Santio Island 85M, Vyborg 110M

Charts and guides
UKHO 2264, 2395
Russian 25002, 28030, 27047
Finnish 901

Lights
4004 **Shepelevskiy** 59°59′·5N 29°08′E
LFl(2)WR.16s37m17M Round white stone tower, red
bands. 053°-R-100°-W-265°-R-280°
4006 **Krasnaya Gorka** 59°58′·4N 29°23′·2E Iso.3s60m15M
Red rectangle, white stripe on red metal framework
tower 38m
Buoy Sankt Peterburgskiy 60°01′·5N 29°29′·8E LFl.6s Red
and white pillar buoy, B topmark
4010 **Tolbukhin** 60°02′·5N 29°32′·7E LFl.12s29m16M
Round white stone tower and building.
4042 **Kronshtadt Naval Harbour, south elbow** 59°58′·2N
29°47′·3E Iso.4s14m3M 218°-vis-150° Red framework
tower 12m
4060 **Severnaya Damba (north breakwater)** 59°54′·3N
30°05′·7E Fl.R.1·5s11m3M White column, red bands,
on base 9m
4061 **Yuzhnaya Damba (south breakwater)** 59°54′·1N
30°05′·9E Fl.G.1·5s11m3M White column, red bands,
on base 9m. There are Leading Lts on 108° through
the barrier at Kronstadt
Many more lights and lit buoys exist in the approaches
and harbour area

Harbour communications
St Petersburg Port Traffic Control Centre
☎ +7 812 251 0290 *VHF* Ch 09
St Petersburg Radar Guidance System (RASKAT)
VHF Ch 12
St Petersburg Vessel Movements Control System
VHF Ch 16, 78
St Petersburg Customs and Border Control
VHF Ch 06 (call *Graneet*). Call when in the vicinity of
the Sankt Peterburgskiy lightbuoy, giving ETA St
Petersburg
St Petersburg Port Authority ☎ +7 812 118 8951
VHF Ch 09, 16, 26
Central River Yacht Club Marina
☎ +7 812 235 6636
St Petersburg Sea Yacht Club Marina
☎ +7 812 322 6541
St Petersburg Navy Yacht Club Marina
☎ +7 812 351 1838

General

St Petersburg, with an estimated 4·2 million
inhabitants, is the second largest city in Russia. It is
built on a complex of waterways, and is a grand and
a spacious city. It is justifiably recognised as the
cultural capital of Russia – few cities in the world
have art galleries, concert halls, museums and
theatres which can compare with those of St
Petersburg.

No visitor should miss the Hermitage (the Winter
Palace), which undoubtedly contains one of the
world's greatest collections of art treasures, nor the
Russian Museum, actually an art gallery. The Peter
and Paul Fortress, the cruiser *Aurora*, St Isaac's
Cathedral, the Admiralty, Chesma Church, Kazanski
Cathedral, Smolny Cathedral, the St Petersburg
Philharmonia and the Kirov Theatre, to name a few,
all demand attention. A pocket guidebook such as St
Petersburg in the Lonely Planet series will prove
invaluable.

A few miles outside the city is the resplendent
Peterhof summer palace with its wonderful fountains
and gilded statuary, well worth a visit by hydrofoil
from behind the Hermitage.

Foreign yachtsmen, especially yachtsmen from
Western Europe, are still few and far between. In
consequence they receive a warm welcome, and the
facilities at the Central River Yacht Club are now
much improved.

Approach and entrance
Approach waypoint 60°01′·6N 29°29′E

From the Gulf of Finland, approach south of Ostrov
Gogland via the Sommers big ship channel
'roundabout' at 60°11′·5N 27°46′E and Ostrov
Seskar 60°04′N 28°20′E observing traffic separation
lanes throughout. A well-buoyed channel leads past
the Sankt Peterburgskiy Landfall buoy and thence
south of Ostrov Kotlin, at the eastern end of which
lies the city of Kronshtadt. The route is fringed by
various prohibited and restricted areas, and care
should be taken to remain within the buoyed
channel. At the time of writing entry is forbidden but
it is understood that the former Customs and
Immigration post at Kronshtadt is likely to be
reinstituted during 2010. For up to date information
please visit www.rccpf.org and consult Vladimir
Ivankiv.

Close south of Fort Konstatin 59°59′·7N
29°42′·3E, the former site of the Customs and
Immigration post for St Petersburg, the channel
passes through the southern flood defence barrier
which is not yet finished.

In the past foreign yachts have usually been
intercepted by a patrol vessel of some kind often
manned by crews who speak little English. Should
they wish to board, it would be best to heave-to and
put a boat over rather than risk them coming
alongside. As always a polite but firm approach pays
dividends.

When approaching Kronstadt yachts should
contact the local Coastguard Post on VHF Ch 6,
callsign *GRANIT* (pronounced *Graneeet*), to inform
them of the name of the boat and the destination, St
Petersburg, even though the boats agent will have
already informed the coastgard.

A pilot vessel, *St Petersburg*, is often stationed off
the Sankt Peterburgskiy lightbuoy but Port
Regulations do not require yachts to take a pilot at
any stage of the approach detailed here.

Once past Kronshtadt take the Deep Sea Channel
(Morskoy Kanal) to buoy 33 at 59°55′·17
30°00′·6E, then change course to 065° (two fixed
red Ldg Lts in line) to the GRG buoy at 59°56′·7N
30°06′·6E), from there take well-buoyed channel
dredged to 3·5m on 115° (F.WRG. Dir Lt) to the big
imposing building decorated with metal plates, with
a vessel sitting on the golden globe on top of the
spire. This is the passenger terminal where customs
and border control are situated. Berth alongside the

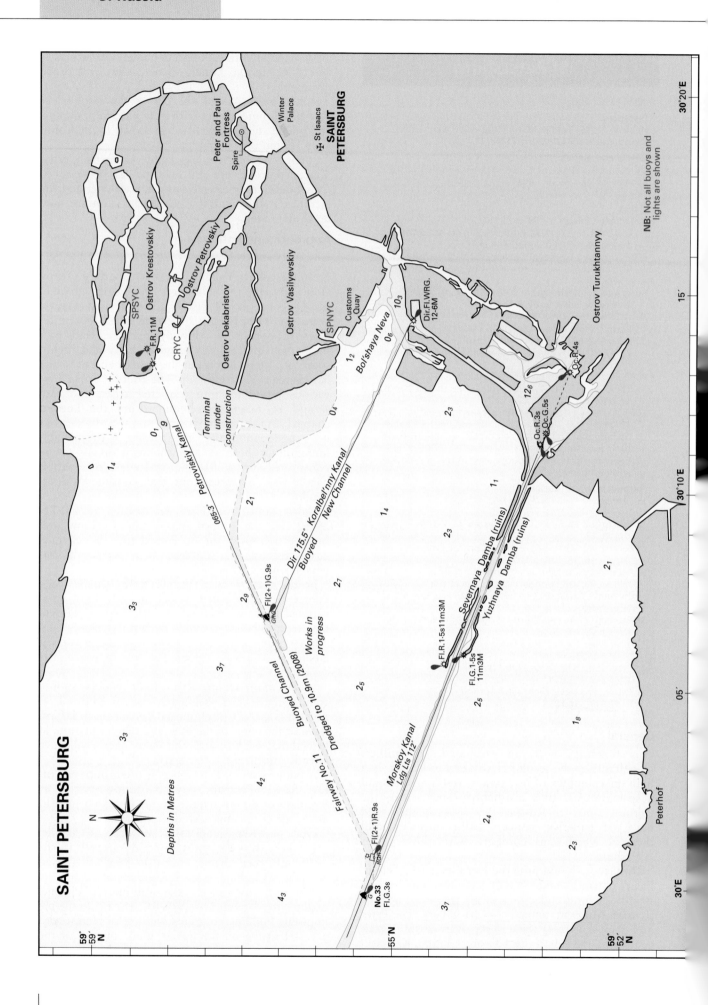

SAINT PETERSBURG

N

Depths in Metres

SAINT PETERSBURG

NB: Not all buoys and lights are shown

Peter and Paul Fortress
Spire

Winter Palace

✙ St Isaacs

SAINT PETERSBURG

SPSYC   Ostrov Krestovskiy

F.R.11M

CRYC   Ostrov Petrovskiy

Ostrov Dekabristov

Petrovskiy Kanal

Terminal under construction

Ostrov Vasilyevskiy

Customs Quay

SPNYC

Bol'shaya Neva

Dir.Fl.WRG. 12-6M

Ostrov Turukhtannyy

Oc.R.4s

Oc.R.3s
Oc.G.5s

065·3°

Dir 115·5° Koralbel'nny Kanal
New Channel
Buoyed

Works in progress

Fl(2+1)G.9s
GRG

Buoyed Channel
Dredged to 10·9m (2008)

Fairway No.11

Morskoy Kanal
Ldg Lts 112°

Fl.R.1·5s11m3M
Severnaya Damba (ruins)

Fl.G.1·5s
11m3M
Yuzhnaya Damba (ruins)

Fl(2+1)R.9s
RGR

No.33
Fl.G.3s

Peterhof

59° 59' N

55'N

59° 52' N

30°E   05'   30°10'E   15'   30°20'E

low quay, running northeast/southwest and about 50m long at 59°55'·43N 30°14'·3E. There is no legal alternative to the above given route to get to the Sea Terminal by sea. There are several buoyed channels much used by the hydrofoil ferries carrying visitors to the famous Tsars' Summer Palace at Peterhof but these fairways are not marked on British charts and should be ignored. Note the *Caution* on page 276. The relevant channels were slightly changed and the buoyage altered considerably in 2008 to accommodate vessels involved in new constructions so it is very important to have an up-to-date chart.

It is now possible to clear Customs and Immigration in St Petersburg for there and Vyborg. See but reverse the details given on p 281.

Formalities

As of April 2010 the berth used for clearance of yachts is a low concrete quay at right angles to the channel close east of the Sea Station, the main terminal for passenger ships. Clearance is usually relaxed and friendly, and generally one of the customs officers or border guards who will come on board will be able to speak a little English. In the daytime, at some point along the Morskoy Kanal yachts may be met by a port control launch and escorted to the passenger terminal. Be certain not to continue along the Morskoy Kanal after buoy 33. You will be fined for violation of the law as it is mandatory to have a pilot in the Morskoy Kanal further east than buoy 33.

Customs and Immigration Quay and Sea Passenger Terminal at St Petersburg   *T. Gunnersen*

Yachts are required to provide prior notice of arrival as detailed on page 274.

Anchorage

Anchoring is not prohibited outside the port area, the buoyed channels and the military areas around Kronshtadt, but there are no anchorages as such.

Berthing

After clearance, the customs officers will direct the yacht to whichever club she is booked into, and may telephone for a (free) pilot to guide her there. In 2008 foreign yachts were only allowed to berth at

Lenexpo Marina in the foreground is currently out of bounds but note route to the Customs Quay top right *Lenexpo Marina Company*

Customs Quay

the Central River Yacht Club (CRYC) but as this situation was under review in April 2010 details of the other marinas have been included. For up to date information please visit www.rccpf.org and consult Vladimir Ivankiv. To get to the CRYC from the Customs Pier sail back along the buoyed channel to the second GRG buoy at 59°56'·7N 30°06'·6E and then continue on 065° to the end of the fairway when a direct course can be set along the more northerly buoyed channel for the north-facing entrance of the CRYC avoiding the sandbanks created by the Neva River.

The CRYC, Petrovskaya Kosa 9, St Petersburg 197110, ℡ +7 812 235 6636, *Fax* +7 812 235 6636, *Email* info@yachtclub.spb.ru *VHF* Ch 16, www.yachtclub.spb.ru (with English translation), occupies the western part of Ostrov Petrovskiy (59°57'·9N 30°14'·4E).

The CRYC is largest yacht club in St Petersburg and one of the largest in Russia, with seven piers of up to 50m in length in its main harbour, a southern work harbour, and a separate guest harbour at the western tip of the island, next to which stands the easily identified clubhouse. The approach is straightforward. Depths are normally around 3m, and the guest harbour pontoons have water and electricity, with toilets and showers ashore, plus a kiosk and restaurant. There is good access to the city, including a nearby trolleybus which runs directly to the Nevskiy Prospekt and a metro station within about a 20 minute walk. In 2008 berthing fees were equivalent to €40 per boat for yachts of up to 20m doubling for larger vessels.

The following marinas are at present out-of-bounds to foreign vessels but are described here in case they are re-instated:

The St Petersburg Sea Yacht Club (SPSYC), (formerly The Baltic Shipping Company Yacht Club, and also referred to as the St Petersburg Marina), Nab Martinova 92, St Petersburg 197110, ℡ +7 812 3226540, *Fax* +7 812 331 7303, *Email* club@mycspb.ru, *VHF* Ch 09, 16, 26, is on Ostrov Krestovskiy, north of the CRYC (59°58'·6N 30°14'·9E).

Approaches to the SPSYC are difficult and poorly buoyed, and the club should not be approached without local guidance. Mooring is bows-to, on somewhat crowded pontoons with water and electricity available and the usual toilets and showers ashore. The club has its own bar/restaurant and chandlery, and security is reported to be good. More shopping is to be found about 1km away, but of the three clubs described this is the furthest from the city.

The St Petersburg Navy Yacht Club (SPNYC), Schkiperskiy Protok 12, St Petersburg 199106, ℡ +7 812 355 8301, *Fax* +7 812 355 8302 situated close north of the passenger terminal (59°56'N 30°14'·1E) on the west side of the same basin as the Lenexpo Marina. See photo on page 285.

A small club, particularly welcoming to ex-RN and other naval personnel, the SPNYC can take a maximum of 12 visiting yachts at the height of the season when some local boats are away. There are

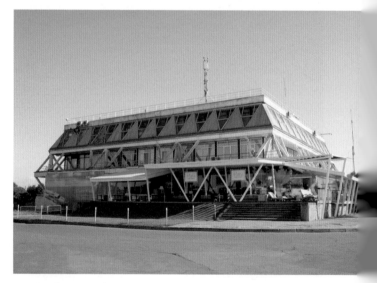

Top The Central River Yacht Club entrance *T. Gunnersen*

Middle Yachts on the pontoon of the Central River Yacht Club *V. Ivankiv*

Above The Central River Yacht Club at St Petersburg *T. Gunnersen*

four pontoons, all with 3–4m depths, water and electricity. Toilets are available ashore (but no showers) and there is reasonable shopping nearby. Diesel is usually available.

Services for yachts

Both the CRYC and the SPSYC have facilities for sailmaking and repairs, while the CRYC also had good general repair facilities (though electronic skills are limited). Both clubs also have chandleries, mostly selling imported equipment.

Diesel is available at the CRYC. Mr Ivankiv is very doubtful about the availability of gas and strongly advises that yachts arrive with full cylinders.

Visitors are recommended not to drink tap water without boiling it first – arrive with tanks full of Finnish or Estonian water, or buy bottled. This also applies to tooth brushing.

General facilities

St Petersburg offers cafés and restaurants at all levels, as well as street stalls selling blinis (pancakes) and all kinds of breads and pastries. See also *Shopping*, page 275.

City tours and guided visits to the many museums, art galleries and churches can usually be arranged for modest fees through the yacht clubs, or consult Mr Ivankiv. Tickets for the Kirov Theatre are extremely difficult to obtain through official channels, but are often obtainable outside the theatre immediately before the performance. Performances at the famous Philharmonia and other concert halls can usually be booked at the box office.

For medical care try the American Medical Centre ✆ (495) 933 7700, the American Cardiovascular Centre ✆ +7 812 558 8797; the Euromed Clinic ✆ +7 812 327 0301, the International Clinic ✆ +7 812 320 3870.

Communications and travel

All three yacht clubs have fax machines, as have the major hotels. The CRYC also has email facilities. Card phones with international dialling are now widely available in St Petersburg. All accept prepayment cards, which can be bought locally, and some also accept VISA or MasterCard.

St Peterburg's international airport is known as Pulkovo-2 (Pulkovo-1 handles domestic and some budget international flights, and lies some 17km south of the city). There are direct flights to/from many European cities, including London.

A mainline railway connects St Petersburg with Helsinki, for which coaches also depart several times each day. There is also a direct coach service to Tallinn, Estonia, with four or five departures daily.

Taxis are available everywhere, but taxi drivers are well attuned to the presence of foreign tourists and for major journeys it is as well to arrange a taxi through the yacht club to avoid being charged excessive prices.

Peterhof Palace fountains near St Petersburg *V. Ivankiv*

6. Poland

The country

The Polish coast extends some 250M from the quiet anchorages and small marinas of the Bay of Pomerania in the west to the Amber Coast and Bay of Gdansk in the east. The shoreline is mainly low-lying with few features, the result of the last glacial period when much clay, sand and other small debris was deposited, and is characterised by beaches, national parks and small protected harbours. The national parks have preserved large forested regions, though agricultural land begins not far inland, much of it growing cereals and still in the hands of small farmers.

There are extensive inland waterways and several navigable inland seas, including two major routes to Berlin, and boats drawing less than 1m can reach the Russian border at Kaliningrad, though as of 2008 this was still not open to privately-owned vessels. The eastern coastal area is known as the Amber Coast due to the large quantities of amber (petrified tree resin from some 40 million years ago) which are still washed onto the beaches following winter's northwesterly gales.

Poland's major industries include coal, copper and steel production, engineering, chemicals, shipbuilding, fishing and forestry. Almost all the previously state-owned industries have been privatised, and the most recent investments in Poland have centred on technology, automotive and industrial equipment, manufacturing, electronics, computers and banking. On the marine side, in addition to being a major builder and repairer of ships, Poland is now one of Europe's biggest moulders of GRP hulls for yachts.

History and the future

Poland is historically a land of transition between east and west, where different peoples and cultures have existed side by side. The Slavs, including the Polanians who gave the country their name, migrated north to the region which was then inhabited by the Balts and the Finns. These earliest cultures formed city-states with regional leaders, thus establishing from the 9th century onward the dynasties which were to rule Poland. From the 10th century the Catholic religion provided a further unifying force. In the 14th century the Piast dynasty united the Polish city-states, codified the common law, established the university in Kraków, built roads and fortified castles. The Golden Age continued following the Polish victory over the Teutonic Order in 1410.

During the Jagiellonian dynasty (1382–1572) the crowns of Poland and Lithuania were combined and the economy flourished, while intellectual and artistic growth were exemplified by the contributions to astronomy of Nicolaus Copernicus. At the end of the 18th century three successive partitions by Russia, Prussia, and Austria imposed outside rule on the country, but although foreign political rule dominated the geographical region, the Polish culture strengthened internally giving rise to figures such as the composer Frederic Chopin. As a legacy of her diverse history, the cruising yachtsman can detect Pomeranian influence in the western port of Szczecin, admire the medieval fortifications in Kołobrzeg, and see the Prussian influence most clearly within the restored old city of Gdańsk.

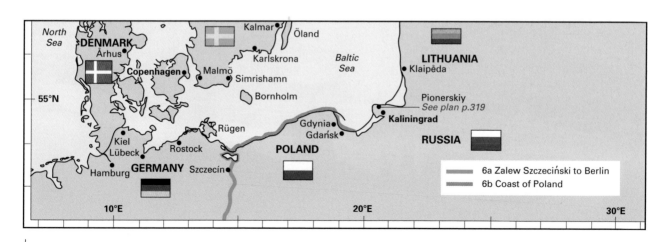

Formalities

All yachts are required to notify the customs and immigration authorities of their arrival in Poland only if coming from outside the EU or if there are people on board who hold non-EU passports and this can be done at any harbour that has a passport office. In practice this means only the larger ports which have ferry services from other Baltic countries. Visas are not required for any western European nationality, nor for citizens of the USA.

In addition to the normal registration papers, and ship's and operator's radio licences, the skipper should hold an International Certificate of Competence and the yacht's Certificate of Insurance should be available for inspection if required.

The Polish flag is equal parts of white over red.

Internet sites

Poland's presence on the web is growing steadily, and as of 2008 there is more information about marinas many of which have their own websites which are listed under the communications section of each harbour. Most sites are available in English translation unless stated otherwise.

www.poland.pl/ – the official Polish website, with some useful links

www.artmedialab.com/_portfolio/pnto/www/contact.html – the website of the Polish National Tourist Office in New York

www.cybersails.info.pl/ – homepage with links to many Polish suppliers and manufacturers of sailing-related equipment

www.hopn.mw.mil.pl – The official website of the Polish Hydrographic Office

http://www.port.szczecin.pl/eng/ – covers the port areas and operations of both Świnoujście and Szczecin. Interesting, but not particularly relevant to yachts

www.szczecin.pl – the Szczecin city website with some interesting history and photographs

www.szczecin.eu has some references to marinas but no detail

www.arkcharter.xt.pl – a commercial site advertising sailing and fishing charters out of Kolobrzeg in traditional sailing craft

www.leba.pl – the attractive Łeba town website, including a link to the harbour and marina, with some photographs but no plan

www.wladyslawowo.pl/index-en.html – the website of the Wladyslawowo region, which encompasses some eight towns and villages. Interesting, but very little about the harbour

www.gdynia.pl/eng/tourism/ – the Gydnia city website, including brief information about the yacht harbour in the tourism section

www.en.gdansk.gda.pl/ – the Gdansk city website, with English translation but no particular relevance to yachts and, surprisingly, no town plan

Following the end of the First World War in 1918 Poland regained her freedom, but in 1939 the invasion of the country by Germany, in co-operation with the USSR, signalled the beginning of the Second World War. With the defeat of Germany Poland came under the influence of the Soviet Union, and during the post-war period a communist regime was imposed. The Polish people were frustrated by the government, the economy deteriorated, and strikes became increasingly frequent. This led to the founding of the independent trade union Solidarity.

With Solidarity, hope for democratic reforms strengthened and eventually the Soviets were forced to negotiate. Another new factor for the regime was the increased influence of the Catholic Church headed by Polish Pope John Paul II. Unrest continued and the persistence of Polish citizens eventually forced the communists to talks in 1989. Following this meeting, democratic elections were held in Poland and Solidarity won 99% of the seats in the Senate. Changes following the election quickly re-established a free-market economy and social reform. This transition, although painful, has been fairly rapid, bringing change that has been welcomed by most Polish people. Now truly free from the influence of communist policies, Poland has experienced economic growth since 1989, sometimes in partnership with foreign investors, and is receptive to new ideas. Poland joined NATO in 1999 and became a member of the European Union in 2004.

Charts, pilots and cruising guides

British Admiralty and Polish charts cover the coast, though new editions of the former are apparently direct reproductions of the latter. However it may still be necessary to obtain Polish or German charts for detailed coverage of the smaller harbours. Those charts which are specific to an area or harbour are listed under individual harbour details. See the *Appendix*, page 362, for sources.

British Admiralty Charts may be obtained from Smart co Ltd, ① +48 58 661 1750, Gdynia & Szczecin offices. *Email* supply@smart.gda.pl, www.smart.gda.pl/shipchandler

Polish Charts and other nautical publications can be obtained from Biuro Hydrograficzne Marynarki wojennej in Gdynia. ① +48 58 626 6433 *Email* sprzedaz.wydawnictw@bhmw.mw.mil.pl http://hopn.mw.mil.pl/index.php?akcja=oferta

The German Hydrographic Office (BSH) *Small Craft Pack 3020* is very useful for navigation of the Zalew Szczeciński from Świnoujście to Dziwnów and up the Odra River to Szczecin and *Pack 3021* covers the rest of Poland from Swinoujscie to Gdańsk. *Pack 3007* covers the western German part Zalew Ozczeciński and the approach to it through the Peenestrom which are not covered by an Admiralty Chart. These can be obtained (with other nautical publications) from Sail-Ho who have a shop in Gdynia marina www.sklep.sail-ho.pl

Mapa Żeglarska (full name *Mapa veglarska Zalewu Szczecińskiego, Kamienskiego i J Dabie*) – a useful and detailed chart on a scale of 1: 85,000 which covers western Polish waters as far east as Dziwnów. Also contains information on customs and immigration, buoyage, VHF channels and telephone numbers, plus some photographs. In Polish, with English and German translations

Baltic Pilot Volume II (NP 19) – the British Admiralty pilot book for this area in English, but written with the big ship in mind, not a yacht with its comparatively shoal draught

Cruising in Poland by Gavin Goudie published by the Cruising Association.

Practicalities

Time

Poland uses UT+1 in winter and UT+2 in summer (from the last Sunday in March until the Saturday before the last Sunday in September).

Money

The Polish unit of currency is the złoty, divided into 100 groszy. Currency can be readily exchanged at most banks or at bureaux de change (kantor in Polish) within the major shopping areas, and ATMs (cash dispensers) are also widely available. Now that Poland has joined the EU there is talk of her joining the Euro but it has not happened yet (2010).

Shopping

Every town has its shopping area, usually in the centre where rows of shops offer a variety of goods. Big supermarkets such as Billa, Real, Minimal and Tesco are located at the edges of the towns and are similar to those in the UK. Most towns also have an open market where fresh food and other products are available at prices lower than those in the shops. Bakery goods can be bought at a *piekarnia*, sweet rolls and cakes from a *cukiernia* – try *sernik* (cheese cake).

Public holidays

Official public holidays in Poland include: 1 January, Easter Sunday and Monday, 1 May (Labour Day), 3 May (Constitution Day), Corpus Christi (occurs in May or June), 15 August (Assumption Day), 1 November (All Saints Day), 11 November (Rebirth of the Polish State), 25–26 December.

Hotels and restaurants

Most towns, especially seaside tourist resorts, have a range of hotels varying widely in quality and price.

Restaurants are similarly diverse, from high-priced speciality restaurants to pavement cafés and fast food outlets. If visiting one of those serving Polish food consider sampling *barszcz* (beetroot soup), *bigos* (a stew made with sauerkraut and a variety of meats, or *pierogi* (large dumplings usually stuffed with white cheese and potatoes, meat or fruit). In summer open air snack bars spring up selling grilled fish, sausage or other kinds of meat served with fresh bread and pickles – and of course there are the ubiquitous American burger and pizza chains.

Cafés (*kawiarnia*) serve rich desserts and a variety of drinks. Tea, Turkish, expresso and even iced coffee are popular, Polish beer is good (try Bosman, Żywiec or Warka) and imported wine plentiful. Vodka can be bought in a variety of forms and flavours including *wiśniówka* (sweet or dry cherry) and *Żubrówka* (flavoured with bison grass found only in one region of the country). Polish cognac is known as *winiak*. *Miód* (mead) is a delicious liqueur made from honey.

Communications

Great strides have been made during the past decade in modernising the telephone system. Mobile phone coverage is also good, and internet access available in the larger towns and cities.

National and international calls can be made from public call boxes, requiring cards available from shops or the post office (*poczta*). To obtain an international line, dial 00 followed by the country code, area code (omitting any initial 0) and number. Dialling within Poland all calls require the 2-digit area code.

The country code for Poland is 48, and if dialling from abroad the initial 0 of the area code must be omitted.

Travel

Major airports serve Warsaw, Gdansk and Kraków, with smaller airports near Poznan, Szczecin, Katowice and Wrocław. Crew changes may be most convenient in Gdansk or Gdynia as Poland's LOT Airlines has a direct service linking London Gatwick and Gdansk (dial 952 from anywhere in the country for toll-free airline information). The airport is 30 minutes by taxi from the marina in Gdansk city centre.

Railways connect most cities and towns – schedules are posted on large boards showing times, express services and track numbers.

Bus and tram travel requires one to obtain a ticket before embarking from a kiosk or stipulated newsagent and, once on the bus or tram, inserting the ticket into a machine to cancel it.

Foreign representation

The Polish Embassy, 47 Portland Place, London W1B 1JH ☎ 0870 7742700, *Fax* 0207 2913575, www.poland.embassyhomepage.com

The Polish Visa Section, 73 New Cavendish Street, London W1W 6LS, ☎ 020 7291 3900, *Fax* 020 7323 2320.

The British Embassy in Poland can be contacted on ☎ +48 22 311 0000, http://ukinpoland.fco.gov.uk/en/

The language

Polish words are often difficult to pronounce because of unfamiliar consonant groups. However, people in Poland are helpful and friendly to foreigners and language is seldom a problem. At most shops, hotels and customs offices and marinas some of the staff will be able to assist with at least basic English. English is now taught in schools instead of Russian so, for asking directions in the street for instance, a young person is likely to be more helpful than someone older. In the west, especially near Świnoujście or Szczecin, both German and English are likely to be understood since there are many visiting German yachts. As always, slow, careful pronunciation and basic vocabulary will aid communication.

Some useful phrases are: dzień dobry pronounced '*jin-dobry*' (good morning); dziękuję pronounced '*jin-ku-yea*' (thank you); proszę pronounced '*pro-sheh*' (please); przepraszam pronounced '*pseh-pra-sham*' (excuse me); tak (yes), nie (no), and toaleta (toilet). (One point regarding the latter is that the symbols WC and a circle indicate women, with a triangle for men. Showers use the international visual symbol or the words *natryski* or *prysznice*). At harbours, the word port is used, the harbourmaster is the *kapitan* working in the harbour office or *kapitanat*. The marina manager is the *bosman* (from the English bo's'un).

Cruising

The Polish coastline, which stretches for some 150 miles, is largely low lying with few features but there are harbours suitable for yachts every 30 to 50 miles and the unspoilt country is interesting. There are military ranges along the coast, as well as offshore exercise areas which are restricted when in use – dates and times are broadcast on VHF and are also available from the local harbour authorities.

There are two regions of particular interest to the cruising yachtsman – the inland 'Zalew Szczecinski' area between Świnoujście, Szczecin and Dziwnów, adjacent to the German border, and the Gdańsk/Gdynia area in the extreme east, just short of the border with Russian Kaliningrad.

The inland seas between and around Świnoujście and Szczecin provide interesting, sheltered-water sailing. The countryside is low-lying, and there are a number of unspoilt fishing harbours and several yacht harbours, though as a whole the area is still developing for yachts. It is possible to cross the border from (or into) Germany via the Peenestrom.

In contrast, Gdynia is a major city and container port and has a well-equipped yacht harbour with some of the best facilities – and certainly the best chandleries – in Poland. However since the mid 1990s when yachts were first able to berth in the centre of old Gdańsk, this has proved a greater magnet to visitors from all nations and, if cruising the southern Baltic, is undoubtedly somewhere which should not be missed.

Between these two areas lie some half dozen small harbours, several of which have either fully-fledged marinas or at least some provision for visiting yachts. On looking at charts of the north coast one sees quite large areas of inland water adjacent to the coast but all of them apart from the Zalew Szczecinski are too shallow for vessels drawing more than half a metre.

There seems little doubt that Poland, in parallel with its efforts to re-establish itself as a part of central rather than eastern Europe, can now lay claim to being a Baltic cruising ground in its own right rather than simply a curiosity which a few intrepid yachtsmen made the effort to visit on their way back west. In the last few years German and Scandinavian yachtsmen are cruising in Poland in increasing numbers. They like the improving facilities and modest prices.

Yacht services and chandlery

Drinking water is always readily available as are showers and toilets. But an electrical connection is sometimes some distance away and requires a long lead and not always with the 3-pin EU connector. A continental 2-pin adaptor can be useful. In 2008 Wi-Fi was still rare.

Fuelling berths are becoming more frequent but in an emergency a nearby filling station selling diesel can generally be found (a few 20 litre containers may prove useful). Fill up when you can! Local propane bottles can sometimes be exchanged or refilled at the larger filling stations such as Shell and BP, but *Calor Gas* is not available and *Camping Gaz* is rare. It is wise to make sure one is fully stocked up when entering the country.

The widest selection of chandlery is available in Gdynia – see page 310 – with more limited stocks at Świnoujście, Szczecin, Kołobrzeg, Władysławowo and Gdańsk. As of 2008 there was still no chandlery at Łeba. In the Szczecin area facilities for yachts are improving with marinas, boatyards, sailmakers and chandleries.

There are reasonable boatyards at Szczecin, Kołobrzeg, Łeba and Górki, and it is possible to lay up ashore in Gdynia, Górki, Łeba, Kołobrzeg and Szczecin though obtaining a cradle could be a problem. It is rare for a foreign yacht to lay up in Poland, so plenty of time should be allowed for scheduling and arrangements.

Weather information

Weather forecasts in Polish and English are broadcast by Witowo Radio on VHF Channels 24, 25 and 26 first announced on Ch 16 at 0133, 0533, 0933 1333, 1733 and 2133 UTC. Witovo Radio can be contacted on MMSI 002610210. In the of Gulf of Gdańsk weather bulletins and navigational warnings are broadcast by Zatoka Gdańska VTS in English on VHF Ch 71 at 0020, 0720, 1320 and 1920 LT.

Weather Bulletins for all sea ares in the Baltic are transmitted on NAVTEX twice daily. See Appendix page 369.

Meteorological information can also be obtained by telephoning offices at Gdynia ① +48 58 620 5493 (H24) or Szczecin ① +48 91 434 2012 (H24).

Firing Ranges

These is a particular problem between Darłowo and Ustka (Area 6) and less so off the Hel peninsula (Areas 10 and 11). There are also three small areas where navigation is forbidden at any time (Areas 3, and 15 north of Gdynia and Area 14 west of Hel). Firing times are broadcast on VHF Chs 24, 25, and 26 along with the weather forecast and other navigational warnings, after first being announced on VHF Ch 16. There are other less frequently used ranges as well and all must be allowed for. See diagrams of ranges on pages 292 and 308.

Up-to-date information can be obtained by phoning the Polish Navy 8th Coastal Defence Flotilla Operations Officer ① +48 91 324 2080. NAVTEX also carries information.

Firing times and other navigational warnings for the northwest coast are also broadcast by Radio Słupsk on VHF Ch 71 at 0715, 1245, and 1845 LT after first being announced on VHF Ch 16 or ① +48 59 814 4889 (H24).

See also the plan on page 315 and note on page 318 about Regulated Area 117.

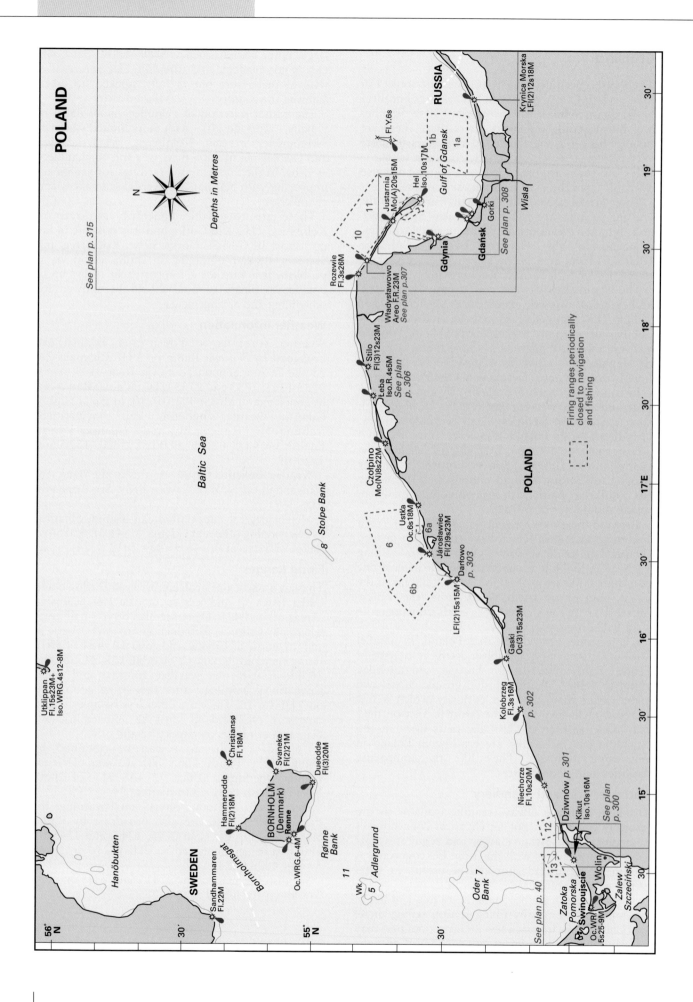

POLAND

See plan p. 315

N

Depths in Metres

Baltic Sea

SWEDEN

Hanöbukten

Sandhammaren
Fl.22M

56°
N

30'

55°
N

30'

Utklippan
Fl.15s23M+
Iso.WRG.4s12-8M

Hammerodde
Fl(2)18M

Christiansø
Fl.18M

Svaneke
Fl(2)21M

BORNHOLM
(Denmark)
Rønne

Dueodde
Fl(3)20M

Oc.WRG.6-4M

*Rønne
Bank*

Bornholmsgat

Adlergrund

Wk
5

11

Stolpe Bank

8

RUSSIA

Gulf of Gdansk

Wisla

Gdansk

Gdynia

Gorki

Krynica Morska
LFl(2)12s18M

30'

19°

Fl.Y.6s

Justarnia
Mo(A)20s15M

Hel
Iso.10s17M

1b

1a

11

10

Rozewie
Fl.3s26M

Wladyslawowo
Areo.F.R.23M
See plan p.307

Stilo
Fl(3)12s23M

Leba
Iso.R.4s5M
*See plan
p. 306*

Czolpino
Mo(N)8s22M

Ustka
Oc.6s18M

6a

6

6b

Jarostawiec
Fl(2)9s23M
*Dartowo
p. 303*

LFl(2)15s15M

Gaski
Oc(3)15s23M

Kolobrzeg
Fl.3s16M
p. 302

Niechorze
Fl.10s20M

Dziwnów p. 301

Kikut
Iso.10s16M

12

13

*See plan
p. 300*

Wolin

*Zatoka
Pomorska*

Swinoujscie
Oc.WR
.5s25-9M

*Zalew
Szczecinski*

See plan p. 40

POLAND

See plan p. 308

See plan p. 307

*Oder
Bank*

7

*Firing ranges periodically
closed to navigation
and fishing*

30'

15°

30'

16°

30'

17°E

30'

18°

30'

6a. Zalew Szczeciński to Berlin

Świnoujście

53°55'N 14°16'E

Distances
Stralsund 50M, Rønne 72M, Trzebież 15M, Szczecin 35M, Dziwnów 20M, Gdynia 190M

Charts and guides
UKHO 2150, 2679, 2677, 2676
Polish 252, 154, 75, 74, 36, 37, 15, 3020

Lights
2668 **Świnoujście** 53°55'N 14°17'·1E
   Oc.WR.5s68m25/9M 029°-R-057°-W-280° Yellow round tower on red building 65m
buoy **Landfall** 54°14'·7N 14°11'E Iso.10s Red and white pillar buoy
2892 **Kikut** 53°59'N 14°34'·9E Iso.10s91m16M 063°-vis-241° Grey round stone tower, white lantern 18m
2670 **Outer Ldg Lts 170·2°** *Front* Mlyny (west breakwater) 53°55'·6N 14°16'·6E Oc.10s11m17M White beacon resembling windmill 11m
2670·1 *Rear* **Galeriowa** 520m from front, Oc.10s23m17M White triangle on white round tower, three galleries 24m
2672 **East breakwater** 53°55'·9N 14°16'·8E Oc.R.4s13m10M Horn(3)60s Red tower with gallery 11m

Harbour communications
Świnoujście Harbourmaster ☏ +48 91 321 4394 (0730–1500 LT)
Świnoujście Port Control and VTS ☏ +48 91 321 6203 VHF Ch 12, 16, 70
Basen Stoczniowy (Basen Pólnocny) Marina ☏ +48 91 321 9177 VHF Ch 77 12 Mobile +48 502 443 954 www.osir.uznam.net.pl

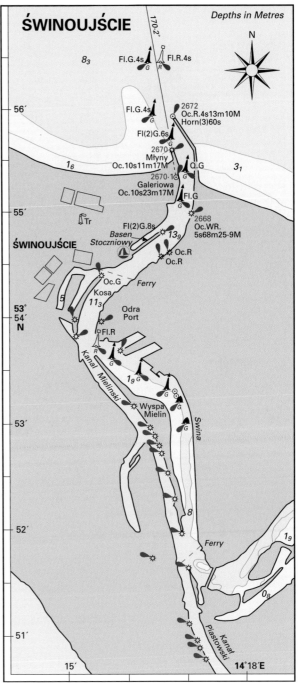

General

Świnoujście (pronounced *Sfeen-o-weesh-chey*) is the outer port of Szczecin. It lies at the mouth of the Odra River, which separates Uznam and Wolin islands, just east of the Polish/German border. It is a holiday resort with an esplanade and a blue flag beach as well as a commercial, fishing and naval harbour. A considerable amount of commercial traffic passes through the harbour en route to Szczecin, via the Odra River.

Approach and entrance
Approach waypoint 53°57'·0N 14°16'·2E

The main shipping channel is 14m deep and is well buoyed on a bearing of 170° from the landfall buoy (some 20M offshore) to the breakwaters. Yachts can safely take their own route but avoiding a shoal which extends 1M offshore close west of the entrance. Entrance is said to be safe in up to Force 9 onshore winds.

The eastern breakwater, the lighthouse and the harbour control tower are all conspicuous from well offshore. The entrance itself is obvious, well marked and free from obstructions. There can be currents across and into the entrance of up to two knots or an outflow current of up to four knots depending on the strength and direction of the wind.

Świnoujście can also be approached from the south via the Kanals Piastowski and Mieleński from the Zalew Szczeciński.

Anchorage

There is no anchorage within Świnoujście itself – continue some 10M southeast to the lake and island area of Zalew Szczeciński.

Berthing

Berth in the municipal marina at the southern end of Basen Pólnocny (Stoczniowy) on the west side of the harbour 1M south of the entrance. It has pontoon and alongside berthing in 4m depths. It is safe and comfortable and is about 1km from the town centre.

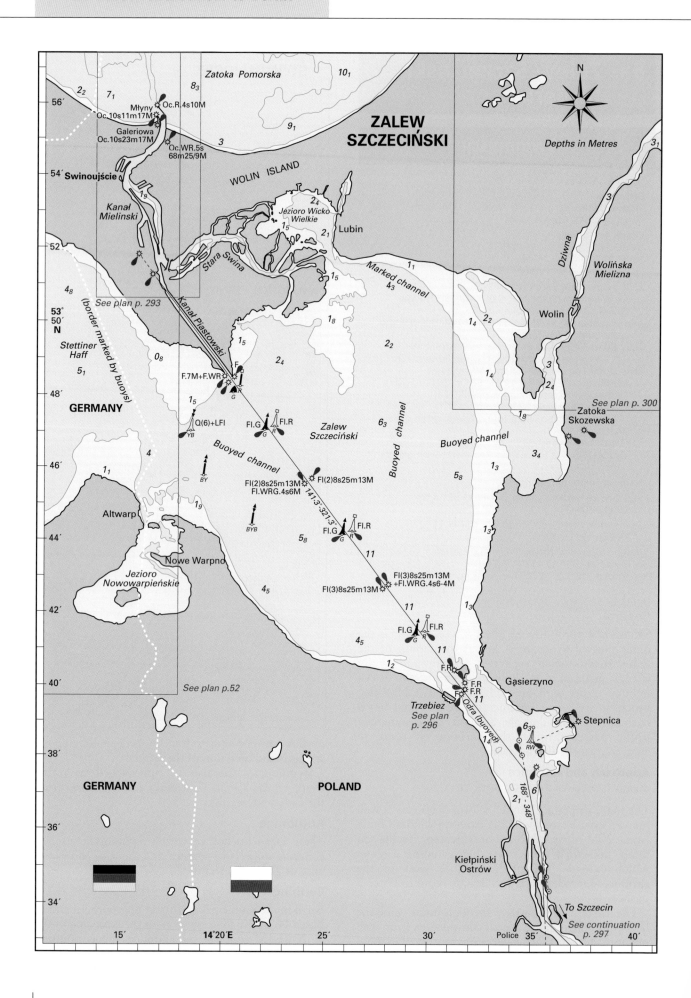

Zatoka Pomorska

10_1

8_3

2_2 7_1 Młyny ☼ Oc.R.4s10M
Oc.10s11m17M☼
Galeriowa
Oc.10s23m17M☼
☼ Oc.WR.5s
68m25/9M

9_1

3

**ZALEW
SZCZECIŃSKI**

N

Depths in Metres

3_1

56´

WOLIN ISLAND

54´ Swinoujście

Kanał
Mielinski

1_9

2_4

Jezioro Wicko
Wielkie

1_5

2_1 Lubin

Stara Swina

52´

1_1

Marked channel

4_3

Dziwna

Wolińska
Mielizna

See plan p. 293

1_5

1_8

Kanał Piastowski

Wolin

1_4 2_2

53°
50´
N

0_8

Stettiner
Haff

5_1

(border marked by buoys)

GERMANY

1_5

Q(6)+LFl
YB

F.7M+F.WR

F
☼
R
G

1_5

2_4

2_2

1_4

3

2_4

1_8

See plan p. 300

Zatoka
Skozewska

48´

Fl.G Fl.R
G R

Zalew
Szczeciński

6_3

Buoyed channel

Buoyed channel

3_4

46´

4

1_1

BY

Buoyed channel

1_9

Fl(2)8s25m13M
Fl.WRG.4s6M

Fl(2)8s25m13M
G R

5_8

1_3

5_8

4

Altwarp

BYB

5_8

Fl.G Fl.R
G R

11

1_3

44´

Nowe Warpno

Jezioro
Nowowarpieńskie

4_5

Fl(3)8s25m13M

Fl(3)8s25m13M
+Fl.WRG.4s6-4M

11

1_3

42´

4_5

11

Fl.G Fl.R
G R

11

1_2

F.R

Gąsierzyno

40´ See plan p.52

Trzebiez
See plan
p. 296

F.R
F.R
F
11

Odra (buoyed)

6_3
RW

☼ Stepnica

38´

GERMANY

POLAND

2_1 $168´ - 348´$

6

36´

Kiełpiński
Ostrów

To Szczecin

34´

See continuation
p. 297

15´   **14°20´E**   25´   30´   Police 35´   40´

Outer leading mark, Świnoujście *J. Mottram*

Both the canal and the buoyed channel across the Zalew Szczeciński are dredged to 10m, and there are 5m depths across most of the remainder of the area. The main channel is well buoyed and lit, with 25m towers at 2M intervals. The surrounding area is heavily forested and offers many quiet and scenic anchorages, though yachts venturing outside the fairway should keep a sharp watch for the many fishing nets, marked by stakes with red and white diamonds the red side indicating danger and the white pointing to safe passage.

The Zalew Szczeciński can also be accessed from both west and east – the former from Stralsund through the Greifswalder Bodden and the Peenestrom (see page 50), and the latter from the Baltic east of Świnoujście via Dziwnów, Kamien Pomorski and Wolin (see page 301).

Limited berthing may also be available alongside in the town centre by arrangement with the harbourmaster. But there are no facilities and there can be wash from passing traffic.

Facilities

Water and electricity are available at the Municipal Marina with toilets and showers in a new building. There is also a bar/café, fuel berth and sailmaker, but no laundry.

There is a small chandlery in the town centre which is about 1km from the marina along the harbourside. It stocks charts together with a reasonable selection of standard chandlery.

Bus, train and hydrofoil services to Szczecin where there are connections to Poznan and Berlin. There are also regular ferry services to Sweden via Rønne on Bornholm and to Copenhagen.

The Kanal Mieleński and Zalew Szczeciński

Leading southeast from Świnoujście is the Kanal Mielinski, which then becomes the Kanal Piastowski before opening into the wide Zalew Szczeciński.

Trzebież marina looking northwest, with the leading lights, the marina offices and the entrance to the yacht basin *J. Parkinson*

Trzebież

53°40'N 14°31'E
See plan on page 296

Distances
Świnoujście 17M, Szczecin 15M, Uckermünde 20M, Karnin (at S end of Peenestrom 26M

Charts and guides
UKHO 2678, 2677
Polish 75, 37, 38, 3020

Lights
From NW
Brama Tower No. 3 53°39'·92N 14°32'E Iso.2s25m7M Red tower with two galleries
Brama Tower No. 4 53°39'·83N 14°31'·83E Iso.2s25m7M Green tower with two galleries
N Landfall Buoy TN-A 53°40'·85N 14°29'·85E Fl.G.2s G buoy
Ldg Lights 150·2° *Front* 53°39'·6N 14°31'·1E Oc.4s11m 7M Red oblong shape on white framework tower *Rear* 433m from front Oc.4s21m 7M Red oblong shape on framework tower
From SE
Ldg Lts 301·2° *Front* 53°39'·8N 14°30'·9E Oc.Y.4s11m4M Orange square shape on white framework tower *Rear* 380m from front Oc.Y.4s18m4M Orange inverted triangle on white framework tower

Harbour communications
Harbourmaster ① +48 91 31 28 346
Marina Manager ① +48 91 31 28 294 *VHF* Ch 69
www.coz.com.pl

6. POLAND

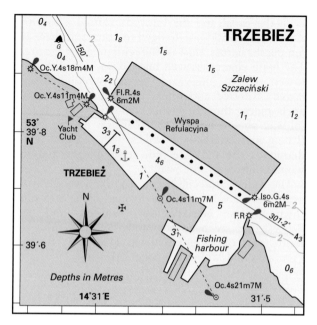

TRZEBIEŻ

53°25'N 14°33'E

Distances
Stralsund via the Peenestrom 85M, Świnoujście 35M, Trzebież 15M

Charts and guides
UKHO 2150, 2678, 2676
Polish 75, 38, 15, 3020

Lights
Night approach not recommended (the latter part is narrow and unlit)

Harbour communications
Szczecin Harbourmaster ☏ +48 91 433 6657/440 3596 (0830–1500 LT Monday–Friday)
Szczecin Port Control and VTS ☏ +48 91 433 0697/ 440 3510 *VHF* Ch 16, 69
Marina Gocław ☏ +48 91 423 0656
Pogon Marina (Zielona Marina)
☏ +48 91 461 4172
Marina Porta Hotele ☏ +48 91 461 2259
Yacht Club AZS Szczecin (Academic Yacht Club)
☏ +48 91 461 4739 www.azs.z.pl

General

At the southern neck of the Zalew Szczeciński, on the western shore, lies Trzebież (pronounced *Cheh-byeh*), an attractive small yacht and fishing harbour with berthing for approximately 60 yachts moored bows to the quay with stern buoys in two basins. The northern basin carries depths of 2·5–3m and the southern one, 1–1·5m. It can be approached either from the north or the south by buoyed channels off the main channel to Szczecin. Both channels have leading lights.

Facilities

Facilities include water, electricity, showers, toilets and a café/bar. The marina is the headquarters of the Polish Sailing Association and the café/bar serves as a club when the fleet is in. There is a fuel dock in the fishing and ferry basin 300m south of the yacht harbour, plus a 30 tonne hoist and some maintenance services. Yachts are also welcomed at alongside berths in the fishing harbour where there are facilities similar to the yacht harbour. Both harbours are subject to surge from onshore winds and passing ships.

General

Szczecin (pronounced *Sheh-chen-chin*) was a Slavic fishing and trading port from the 9th century, and today is the seventh largest city in Poland. In spite of its distance from the sea it remains one of Poland's major ports and is an important shipbuilding and ship repair centre. It has extensive waterways bordered by trees and fields and there are historic monuments dating from the 14th century, although the city was very severely damaged during the Second World War.

Approach

Approach waypoint 53°42'N 14°29'·1E

From the Zalew Szczeciński and Trzebież the ship channel follows the Odra River south to Szczecin. It is clearly marked and dredged to a minimum of 10m. Although some areas outside the fairway have adequate depths, shoal areas also exist just close to the main channel.

The Jezioro Dąbie, which has depths of 3–3·5m and where three of Szczecin's four marinas are located, can either be entered from the north at Mewia island or from the south via the Regalica Mienia. To reach the southern marinas, continue south along the River Odra past Marina Gocław (see below) and at Okrętowa island take the eastern channel, Przekop Mielenski. Large vessels signal their intentions at the junction with Kanaw Grabowski. Continue along Przekop Mielenski across its intersection with the Dunczyca and past Mielenski island until, some 0·8M further on, there is a four-way junction – the Parnica to the west, the Basen Górniczy (a deadend) ahead and the Regalica Mienia to the east. Northwards the Regalica Mienia leads directly into the Jezioro Dąbie, but by turning south at the first opportunity into the Regalica Odra yachts reach the Dąbska Struga, the canal serving Pogon Marina, Marina Porta Hotele and the AZS

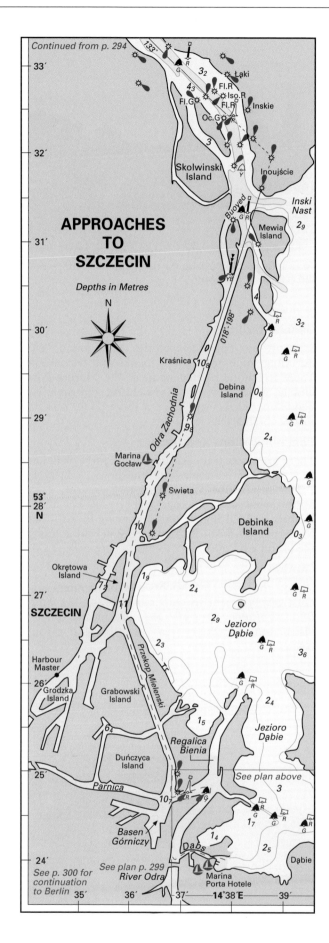

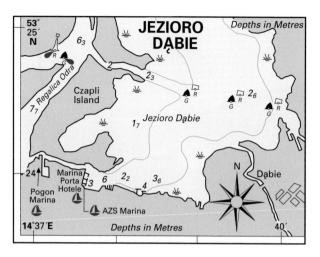

Yacht Club (see below). The entrance to the canal is distinctively marked on the starboard hand by the bridge superstructure of a large ship set on dry land, but beware the long spit which extends 20m into the river on the northern side of the entrance.

Anchorage

Anchoring is prohibited in the fairways, but the many creeks and harbours of the Jezioro Dąbie offer countless attractive anchorages.

Berthing

In 2008 yachts were permitted to moor for one or two nights only in Szczecin centre at the town quay opposite Grodzka Island amongst the trip boats and ferries if there was room but plans were being discussed for marina facilities to be set up alongside a quay further south with 3m depths just before the fixed bridge. There are already magnificent shower, toilet and laundry facilities which were put in place for the visit of the Tall Ships in 2007. They are situated under the south side of the steps leading to the Maritime Museum but across a very busy main road.

The city's four marinas are all located at some distance from the centre, Marina Gocław to the north and Pogon Marina, AZS Yacht Club and Marina Porta Hotele to the southeast, at the southern end of the Jezioro Dąbie. The latter can all be reached direct from the southern end of the Jezioro Dąbie but the approach is shallow and abounds with fishing stakes so it is wiser to use the canals.

Marina Gocław 53°28′·45N 14°36′E a pleasant yacht harbour situated at Gocław, on the west bank of the main channel about 2M north of the city centre and 20 minutes away by bus or tram (a frequent tram passes the marina gates). Mooring is bows to the quayside and stern to a buoy in about 4m. The marina is quiet and totally sheltered. Limited food is available in the hotel, part of the marina building.

Pogon Marina 53°24′N 14°37′·2E lies on the south side of the Dąbska Struga near its junction with the Regalica Odra and about 500m west of the Marina Porta Hotele. It is not as large as its neighbour, with

6. POLAND

Gocław Marina Szczecin   *J. Parkinson*

Szczecin city dock, showing the harbourmaster's office and the main pier   *R. Wilson*

fewer facilities but in equally pleasant surroundings, and is better suited to smaller yachts.

Marina Porta Hotele 54°24'N 14°37'·2E is situated in pleasant surroundings at the southern end of the Jezioro Dąbie. It is reached via the Dąbska Struga, passing the Pogon Marina en route. Moorings are the usual bow to quay, stern to a buoy, with about 4m of water outside the jetties and 2·5m inside. Transport to the city centre, about 4km by road, involves a change from bus to tram at Basen Górniczy where tickets for both the bus and the tram are sold.

YC AZS Marina is most welcoming and is in the two basins immediately south of Marina Porta Hotele. Depths are 2–2·5m in the northern basin and 1·5–2m in the southern one. Berths outside the basins carry depths of 3–5m.

Services for yachts

Marina Gocław has water and electricity on the quayside and showers ashore. It is possible to arrange for diesel to be delivered in containers. It has a crane for stepping and unstepping masts much used by German yachts exiting or entering the German canal system. There is a boatyard (with no marina facilities) a short distance to the south.

At Marina Porta Hotele there is water and electricity on the pontoons, a new shower block has been constructed, and there is a fuel berth. There is a crane suitable for stepping and unstepping masts.

Pogon Marina has the usual facilities as well as a fuel berth which sells *Camping Gaz*. It also has a marine electronics outlet.

AZS Marina has the usual facilities as well as a Taverna type bar/restaurant.

There is a sailmaker and a well-stocked chandlery in the boatyard close by. The same yard can store boats under cover in an enormous Dornier Flying Boat hanger dating from the nineteen twenties. For Admiralty charts there is a Smart chandlery in Szczecin.

General facilities

Szczecin has all the facilities of a major city, including some good shops, banks and restaurants. There is a hotel of that name at the Marina Porta Hotele, which also has a restaurant, and there is a good supermarket in Dąbie, a short (2km) bus ride east of the marina.

Communications and travel

There are good train services to all parts of Poland and, via Berlin, to the rest of Europe.

The airport for Szczecin is at Goleniow, 45km north. It has some international services but mainly handles internal flights, and if arriving by air it may be simpler to fly to Poznan or Berlin and complete the journey by train.

Caution

Within the port area, yachts and other small craft must always yield to ship movements. *The Baltic Pilot Volume II (NP 19)* includes extensive instructions for these areas and the ship turning basins.

Niederfinow ship lift*J. Sadd*

River and canal passage Szczecin to Berlin

NV Map/guides cover the passage. These are obtainable from Imray www.imray.com, www.hansenautic.de or www.sklep.sail-ho.pl at Gdynia

Many German yachts unstep their masts to make this trip twice a year, between their winter moorings near Berlin and their summer sailing ground of the Baltic. The usual route is by the West Oder and the Oder-Havel Kanal which then gives access to the German canal system.

Pilotage notes

Draught Passage may be made by either the West Oder (Odra) or the East Oder. The West Odra has much less current, and its recommended draught is officially 1·8 metres, though up to two metres is thought to be safe. There is a connection between the two rivers about 25 miles south of Sczecin which can provide a compromise, as the limiting section of the West Oder is the dredged section approaching the locks at Oder-Havel Kanal. There may be more depth in the East Oder, which is the main river, but as such is faster flowing and more subject to depth/current variations according to the weather further inland.

Advice should be sought before leaving Sczecin. There is lock access to the Kanal from either Oder.

Air draught The official recommendation is four metres, but a motor yacht with an air draught of 4·2m is known to have made safe passage in August 2008, reporting a minimum clearance of 30cm. This is despite markings of 3·45m and 3·75m on the first two bridges in central Sczecin, which is thought to refer to winter flood conditions. Any vessel contemplating passage should check the current conditions with the Sczecin harbourmaster before departure.

Distance and Time

106M (GPS distance) should take about four days cruising at 5½–6 knots.

Formalities

None, both countries being part of the Schengen area. 10M south of Szczecin is the now abandoned Polish/German border crossing where it is possible to stop overnight. There are no facilities.

Moorings and facilities

Hohensaaten Lock is 35M from Szczecin where you leave the West Oder River and join the Oder-Havel Kanal.

4M past the lock is Marina Oderberg www.marina-oderberg.de. Draught is restricted to 1·8m. Full facilities including a good restaurant. Overnight dues 20ZŁ. The town of Oderberg is 1½ miles further on, with basic shops and small supermarket.

6M beyond the marina is the ship lift at Niederfinow. This huge piece of canal engineering, built to replace a series of four conventional locks, is one of the biggest in Europe, lifting vessels something over 30 metres. Air draught is 4·4 metres with little prospect of ever increasing. Shortly after this there is a one-way section of canal which changes traffic direction at set times during the day. Leisure craft do not appear to be required to comply, the canal being wide enough to permit a yacht to pass an on-coming barge with care.

Near the town of Oranienburg there is an anchorage in the lake immediately south of the Schleuse Lehnitz lock in 3·5 metres. This is suitable for an overnight stop.

Leave the Oder-Havel canal after Henningsdorf and enter the lake area west of Berlin. One lock, then via a short canal to the River Spree. There is a wide choice of places to moor, some free, in and around Berlin. The central ones, though free and convenient, have no facilities and are subject to continual disturbance from passing river traffic. Generally more remote places are preferable, and most have readily available public transport to the city centre.

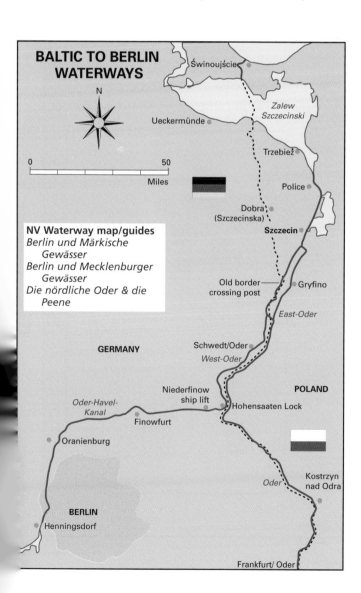

BALTIC TO BERLIN WATERWAYS

N

0   50 Miles

NV Waterway map/guides
Berlin und Märkische Gewässer
Berlin und Mecklenburger Gewässer
Die nördliche Oder & die Peene

Świnoujście
Zalew Szczecinski
Ueckermünde
Trzebież
Police
Dobra (Szczecinska)
Szczecin
Old border crossing post
Gryfino
East-Oder
GERMANY
Schwedt/Oder
West-Oder
Niederfinow ship lift
POLAND
Oder-Havel-Kanal
Finowfurt
Hohensaaten Lock
Oranienburg
Oder
Kostrzyn nad Odra
BERLIN
Henningsdorf
Frankfurt/ Oder

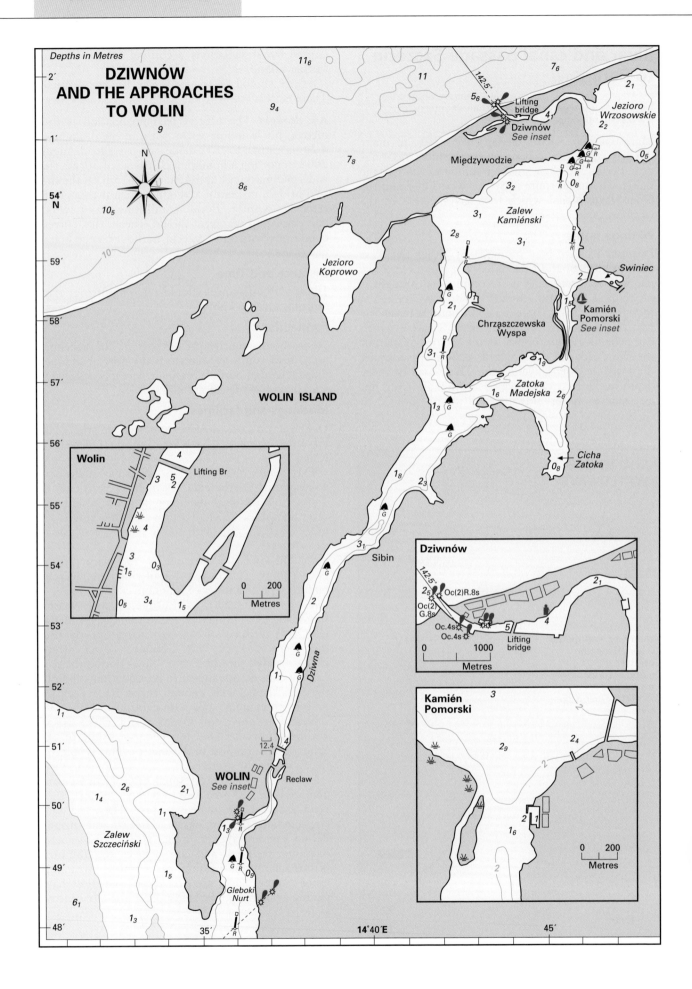

Depths in Metres

DZIWNÓW
AND THE APPROACHES
TO WOLIN

N

54°
N

11₆

11

9₄

9

7₆

7

5₆   Lifting
      bridge
      Dziwnów
      See inset

142.5°

2₁

Jezioro
Wrzosowskie

4₁

2₂

0₅

Międzywodzie

G R
G R
    R

Zalew
Kamiénski

3₂

3₁

2₈

3₁

2

Swiniec

Kamién
Pomorski
See inset

8₆

10₅

10

Jezioro
Koprowo

G
2₁

3₁
R

1₉

1₅

Chrząszczewska
Wyspa

Zatoka
Madejska

2₆

1₆

Cicha
Zatoka

0₈

WOLIN ISLAND

1₃
G

G

1₈

2₃

G

3₁

Sibin

Wolin

4

Lifting Br

3 5
   2

4

3

1₅ 0₃

0₅   3₄

1₅

0   200
Metres

Dziwnów

142.5°

2₅   Oc(2)R.8s

Oc(2)
G.8s

Oc.4s
Oc.4s

5

2₁

4

Lifting
bridge

0   1000
Metres

G
2

Dziwna

G

G
1₁

Kamién
Pomorski

3

2₉

2₄

2

1₁

2₆   2₁

1₄

1₁

WOLIN
See inset   Reclaw

12.4   4

2₁

2

2

2₉

2₄

Zalew
Szczeciński

1₅

1₃
G R

1₃
G R   0₉

2₁ 1

1₆

6₁

Gleboki
Nurt

0   200
Metres

1₃

35′   14°40′E   45′

6b. Coast of Poland

Dziwnów

54°01'N 14°44'E

Distances
Świnoujście 20M, Kołobrzeg 30M

Charts and guides
UKHO 2150
Polish 252, 154, 74, 75, 39, 3020

Lights
2668 **Świnoujście** 53°55'N 14°17'·1E
  Oc.WR.5s68m25/9M 029°-R-057°-W-280° Yellow
  round tower on red building 65m
2892 **Kikut** 53°59'N 14°34'·9E Iso.10s91m16M
  063°-vis-241° Grey round stone tower, white lantern
  18m
2904 **Niechorze** 54°05'·8N 15°03'·9E Fl.10s63m20M Grey
  octagonal tower and red building
2896 **Ldg Lts 142·5°** *Front* 54°01'·2N 14°43'·8E
  Oc.4s9m3M White diamond on white metal
  framework tower
2896·1 *Rear* 130m from front, Oc.4s13m3M
  White rectangle on red and white framework tower
2897 **West breakwater** 54°01'·4N 14°43'·5E
  Oc(2)G.8s11m7M Column
2898 **East breakwater** 54°01'·5N 14°43'·6E
  Oc(2)R.8s11m7M Column Horn Mo(A)60s

Harbour communications
Dziwnów Harbourmaster ✆ +48 91 3813 754 VHF Ch 10, 71
Dziwnów Port Control ✆ +48 91 381 3754/3642 VHF Ch 12, 16, 71
Opening bridge ✆ +48 91 381 3711 *VHF* Ch 10
Polmax marina ✆ +48 91 381 3634
  www.polmax.com.pl/tour/marina.htm

The fishing harbour at Dziwnów yacht basin where visiting yachts berth *S. Carnegie*

General

Dziwnów (pronounced *Jiv-noof*) set amongst trees, is an attractive small fishing and holiday resort at the mouth of the Dziwnów River, which links to the Jezioro Wrzosowskie and Zalew Kamienski lakes and thence to the Zalew Szczeciński. To the west lies Wolin island and to the east the Polish mainland.

Approach

Approach waypoint 54°02'N 14°42'·8E

The coastline on either side consists of low forested hills and sandy beaches, with no off-lying dangers. Entrance is straightforward using the 142·5° leading line although the leading marks can be difficult to see because of trees. Depths are 5m in the entrance and 4m inside.

Warning In winds over Force 5 from the west or northwest the entrance can be dangerous and should not be attempted. About 0·6M inside the entrance (beyond the yacht berths) lies a bridge which operates on request on every even numbered hour – call on VHF Ch 10 with anticipated time of arrival (24H).

Berthing

On the starboard hand close inside the entrance lies the small Polmax marina. It has a maximum depth of 2·5m. but it is some distance from the village. Most visiting yachts are directed to the fishing harbour on the porthand side 0.4M from the entrance. Preliminary contact may be made on VHF Ch 12. Here one lies alongside or rafted out between the fishng boats. Larger yachts can lie alongside on the north side of the river, beyond the bridge, east of the quay for excursion boats.

Facilities

All usual facilities are available in the Polmax Marina. In the fishing harbour access to a small shower block situated close to the former customs post is by key obtainable from the harbourmaster. Water and electricity on the quayside.

There is a fuel berth behind a fuel station to port beyond the bridge. General supplies, banks and small restaurants are available in the town.

The Zalew Szczeciński to Dziwnów

Yachts with limited water and air draughts can take the inland route from the Zalew Szczeciński to Dziwnów via Wolin and Kamien Pomorski. The marked channel carries a minimum depth of 1·7m, but two fixed bridges at Wolin limit height to 12·4m. The lower road bridge opens twice daily Monday to Friday 0900 and 1600 LT and once daily on Saturday (1000 LT), Sunday and Feast days (1300 LT).

Wolin 53°51'N 14°37'E is a small town and minor port with no specific facilities for yachts but there is a waiting quay on both sides of the bridge on the west side of the river.

Kamien Pomorski 53°58'N 14°45'E which is accessible from Dziwnów by yachts with a maximum draught of 2·1m is attractive and has a small marina and long quay backed by parkland overlooking a castle. General supplies are available.

6. POLAND

Kołobrzeg

54°11′N 15°33′E

Distances
Świnoujście 50M, Dziwnów 30M, Darłowo 30M

Charts and guides
UKHO 2150
Polish 252, 153

Lights
2904 **Niechorze** 54°05′·8N 15°03′·9E Fl.10s63m20M Grey
   octagonal tower and red building
2905·4 **Dźwirzyno** 54°09′·6N 15°23′·4E Oc.8s13m6M
   Concrete column
2906 **Kołobrzeg** 54°11′·3N 15°33′·4E Fl.3s33m16M Red
   round tower, black cupola
buoy **Koł lightbuoy** 54°13′·5N 15°30′·6E LFl.10s
   Red and white pillar buoy, • topmark
2910 **West breakwater** 54°11′·4N 15°33′·2E
   Oc.G.4s11m7M Green round column, two galleries
2908 **East breakwater** 54°11′·5N 15°33′·2E
   Oc.R.4s13m5M Red round column, two galleries Horn
   Mo(K)60s
2914 **Gaski** 54°14′·7N 15°52′·5E Oc(3)15s50m23M Red
   round tower, gallery and cupola

Harbour communications
Kołobrzeg Harbourmaster ☎ +48 94 352 2703
   (0730–1530 LT Monday–Friday)
Port Control ☎ +48 94 351 6765 *VHF* Ch 12
Kołobrzeg Marina ☎ +48 94 354 4301
   www.arkcharter.portkolobrzeg.pl

General

Kołobrzeg (pronounced *Co-wob-jeck*) is a tourist resort and commercial and fishing harbour, the largest on the long stretch between Świnoujście and Gdynia. The harbour entrance has a boardwalk, popular with tourists who gather to watch the maritime activities, and a long seafront promenade with shops and cafés. Near the marina stand parts of the walls of a fort built in 1774 and where there is a café and bar and music is played on summer evenings.

The entrance to Kołobrzeg. The Marriage to the Sea monument is to the left of the crane *J. Parkinson*

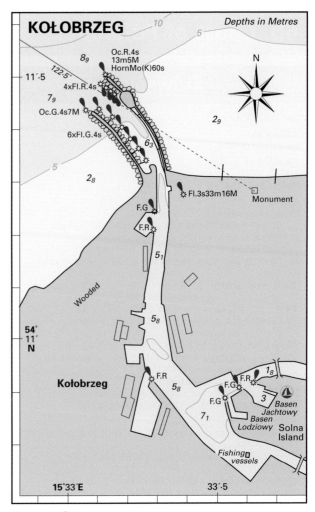

Approach

Approach waypoint 54°12′·7N 15°31′·4E

The approach channel lies on a bearing of 148° from the Koł landfall buoy, though the surrounding coast is clear of off-lying hazards. Two curved concrete moles extend from the entrance, the red structure on the port hand one being particularly prominent. When the eastern molehead is abeam to port turn on to 122·5° between the piers with the needle-like

monument 'Marriage to the Sea' directly on that bearing. The large brick lighthouse can also be seen from well offshore.

The entrance itself is narrow and is subject to swell from west through northwest. It can also be affected by strong cross-currents, depending on wind strength and direction. But there have been extensive alterations made to the pier ends recently with the aim of improving safety. Depths are 5–6m in the entrance and harbour, decreasing to 3m in the marina basin.

Do not confuse the illuminated pleasure pier 800m to the east with the entrance.

Request permission to enter or leave from Port Control on VHF Ch 12. If a vessel is leaving one is requested to wait because of the narrow entrance.

Warning In west or northwest winds over Force 5 the entrance is dangerous and should not be attempted. Also beware of fishing nets anywhere along the adjacent coast where there are small fishing villages. They can be found well out at sea.

Berthing

Kołobrzeg Marina lies 0·6M inside the entrance at the northwest end of Solna island. Most yachts berth in either the Basen Jachtowy or the smaller, adjacent Basen Lodziowy, with those requiring depths greater than 3m securing to the outside of the Basen Lodziowy quay. Mooring in both basins is bows to the quay and stern to a mooring buoy. The harbour office is clearly marked in English.

Facilities

Water, electricity and showers are available on the dockside. There is a fuel barge in the fishing harbour for fishing boats only but small quantities may be obtained in cans from a nearby garage.

There is a bar/restaurant at the marina and attractive open air cafés and good shops in the town, a short distance away. There is a sailmaker and a chandlery and yachts can be slipped and repairs carried out.

Darłowo

54°27'N 16°23'E

Distances
Kołobrzeg 32M, Ustka 22M

Charts and guides
UKHO 2150, 2369
Polish 252, 153

Lights
2914 **Gaski** 54°14'·7N 15°52'·5E Oc(3)15s50m23M red round tower with gallery and cupola
2918 **E. Mole near root** 54°26'·4N 16°22'·7E LFl(2)15s20m15M Red square tower with white gallery and dome
2926 **Jaroslawiec** 54°32'·3N 16°32'·6E Fl(2)9s50m23M Red round tower with white dome

Harbour communications
Harbourmaster ☎ +48 94 314 2683 *VHF* Ch 12
Marina Manager ☎ +48 94 314 5185
Opening Bridge ☎ +48 94 314 2976 *VHF* Ch 12
Radio Słupsk ☎ +48 59 814 4889

General

The port is a 10 minute ferry ride from the town which is up a canal and well worth a visit. The town is attractive with well-preserved historical sites. King Eric who was the last king of Scandinavia was married to a daughter of Henry V of England and made Darłowo his base for piratical raids on Scandinavia after he was banished from those countries.

Approach

Approach waypoint 54°27'·2N 16°21'E

In fair conditions the approach is straightforward, but the entrance itself is narrow and curved. Depths are around 4m, but an uncomfortable surge can enter in strong winds from between west and north. A bridge 0·5M inside the entrance opens every hour (24 hours) when craft are waiting.

Permission to enter or leave must be sought on VHF Ch 12.

Darłowo yacht berths *S. Carnegie*

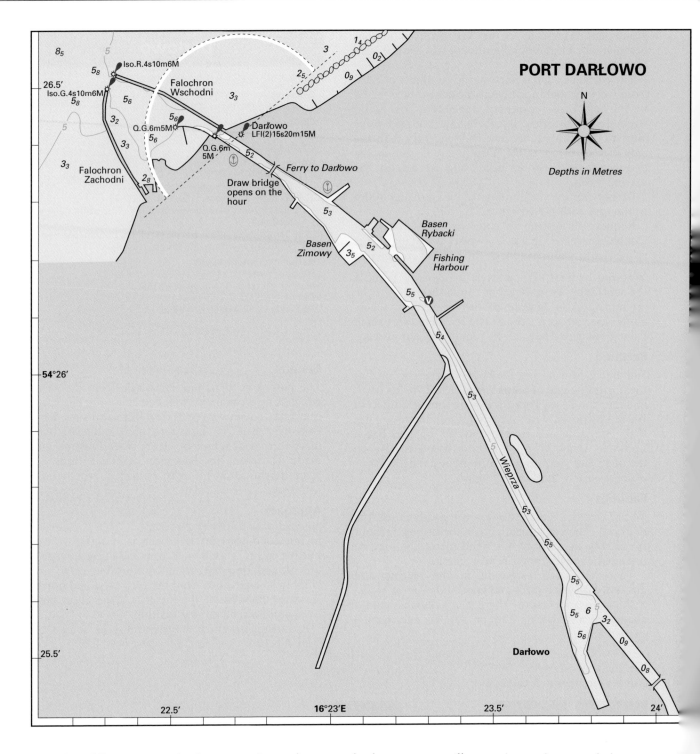

PORT DARŁOWO

Depths in Metres

Iso.R.4s10m6M

Falochron
Wschodni

Iso.G.4s10m6M

Darłowo
LFl(2)15s20m15M

Q.G.6m5M

Q.G.6m
5M

Falochron
Zachodni

Ferry to Darłowo

Draw bridge
opens on the
hour

Basen
Zimowy

Basen
Rybacki

Fishing
Harbour

Wieprza

Darłowo

Warnings The entrance is dangerous in onshore winds over Force 5 and beware of cross currents. Also beware the unlit isolated danger mark 6M southwest of the harbour at 54°22′·7N 16°12′·1E.

There are Firing Ranges, Areas 6, 6a and 6b between Darłowo and Ustka. See under Ustka for details.

Berth

Darłowo harbour caters mainly for commercial fishing, there is no marina as such; yachts lie against the north wall beyond the bridge and the ferry berth. The berths can be uncomfortable in onshore winds and a fender plank is useful. In severe conditions the harbourmaster will sometimes give permission to berth in the basin further east or up the River Wieprza which can be navigated up to 1·5M inland. Limited berthing may be available in the fishing harbour further in but in unattractive surroundings. Basic supplies can be obtained in the port area but the interesting town, which can be reached by the ferry, has plenty of shops.

Facilities

A small shower/toilet block has been built close to the yacht berths and the part-time marina manager has an office there and allows one to use his computer. No fuel berth.

Ustka

54°35'N 16°51'E

Distances
Darłowo 20M, Łeba 30M

Charts and guides
UKHO 2150, 2369,
Polish 252, 152, 153

Lights
2926 **Jaroslawiec** 54°32'·3N 16°32'·6E Fl(2)9s50m23M Red
round tower, white dome
2930 **Port Ustka** 54°35'·3N 16°51'·3E 22m8M Red
octagonal tower, white cupola.
2939 **Rowy** Ldg Lts 54°40'·1N 17°03'·1E Iso.Y.2s6m and 8m
2M
Czołpino 54°43'·1N 17°14'·5E Mo(N)8s75m22M Round
brick tower, black cupola

Harbour communications
Harbourmaster ✆ +48 598 144430
Port Control ✆ +48 59 814 4533 *VHF* Ch 12
Radio Słupsk ✆ +48 59 814 4889

Approach

Approach waypoint 54°36'·8N 16°49'·8E

The approach to Ustka is straightforward on a
bearing of 150° on the lighthouse or harbour
entrance. The entrance carries 5–6m, with 4–5m
inside the harbour. The harbourmaster's office,
clearly marked *Kapitanat Portu Ustka*, is situated on
the east pier – dues are paid at the office on the top
floor. Also on the first floor are the offices of Radio
Slupsk where the staff are helpful with enquiries
about the firing ranges.

Warnings Entry is dangerous in winds over Force 5
from southwest through north to east. And beware
of cross currents.

There are firing ranges (Areas 6, 6a and 6b)
between Ustka (pronounced *Oostka*) and Darłowo
where passage may be prohibited – dates and times
are broadcast on VHF accompanying the weather
forecasts and navigational warnings. See page 291
for details. In general firing takes place every day
between 0500 and 0200 the next day except on
Sundays, Mondays and public holidays. It may be
necessary to make a long diversion out to sea. Patrol
craft are in attendance.

The harbour office at Ustka *R. Wilson*

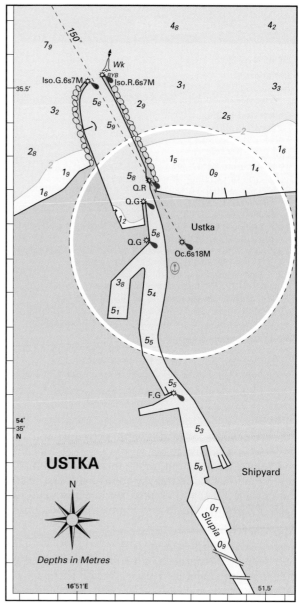

USTKA

N

Depths in Metres

16'51'E

Berth

The harbour is mainly devoted to fishing, with some
commercial traffic, and is also a popular holiday
resort. Although there is no marina, yachts can berth
alongside on the east side of the harbour clear of the
small crane used to launch an inflatable lifeboat.
Swell may enter the harbour in strong northerlies
and in these circumstances it may be better to berth
in the fishing basin on the west side of the harbour
where it is possible to raft up to the yachts of the
friendly Ustka Yacht Club, but it is a 2km walk into
town.

Facilities

There is a shower/toilet facility in one of the
buildings opposite the yacht berths. The key is
obtainable from the harbourmaster. Water on the
quay and electricity with a long lead. Fuel is
obtainable in the basin on the west side of the
harbour and there is a good selection of shops in
town.

6. POLAND

Łeba

54°46'N 17°33'E

Distances
Kołobrzeg 85M, Darłowo 55M, Ustka 30M,
   Władysławowo 30M, Gdynia 65M

Charts and guides
Admiralty 2369
Polish 251, 252, 152

Lights
2940 **Czołpino** 54°43'·3N 17°14'·6E Mo(N)8s75m22M
   Round brick tower, black cupola 25m
2944·5 **Dir Lt 203°** 54°46'·1N 17°33'N Dir.WRG.7m8–6M
   197°-Fl.G.3s-198°-F.G-201°-Al.WG-202°-F.W-204°-
   Al.WR-205°-F.R-208°-Fl.R.3s-209°
buoy **Łeba** 54°47'·2N 17°32'·5E LFl.10s Red and white
   pillar buoy, • topmark
2945 **West breakwater** 54°46'·2N 17°33'E Q(9)15s10m5M
   335°-vis-180°+Iso.G.4s10m5M 180°–vis-335°
2944 **East breakwater** 54°46'·2N 17°33'·1E
   Iso.R.4s10m5M Red column with gallery 7m
2948·2 **Marina breakwater** 54°45'·9N 17°33'E F.G.
2954 **Stilo** 54°47'·3N 17°44'·2E Fl(3)12s75m23M 050·5°-
   vis-290·5° Red, white and black banded tower 33m

Harbour communications
Łeba Harbourmaster ☎ +48 59 866 2973 (0730–1530 LT)
Łeba Port Control ☎ +48 59 866 1530 *VHF* Ch 12,
Łeba Marina ☎ +48 59 866 2873/1735 www.port.leba.pl

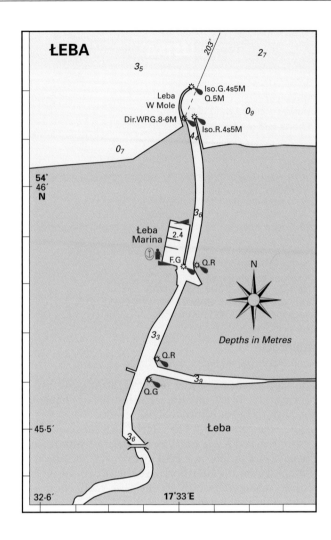

General

Like its neighbours to the west, Łeba (pronounced *Weh-ba*) is a tourist resort with a small commercial and fishing harbour, but unlike them has a relatively new yacht marina on the starboard hand just inside the entrance. Łeba is backed by a major national park of forest and lakes and impressive sand dunes.

Approach

Approach waypoint 54°47'N 17°33'·6E

The suggested approach is made on a bearing of 203° from the Łeba light buoy, though there are no offlying hazards and yachts can safely take their own line. Entry is made between two curved concrete breakwaters – the western one has recently been extended – in 2·5m depths, sometimes as little as 2m after storms. The Port Control Office with a signal mast is on the port hand close to the entrance, with the new marina just beyond it to starboard.

Request permission to enter or leave from Port Control on VHF Ch 12. Traffic Safety signals can also be shown on the signal mast on the east side.

Warning The entrance is dangerous in winds over Force 5 from west to northeast through north. Also beware of cross currents and there can be outflow of up to two knots from Lake Lebsko.

Łeba marina *S. Carnegie*

Berthing

Łeba Marina, website link from www.leba.pl, has 150 berths inside a long eastern wall which blocks any swell entering from the main harbour entrance. Mooring is alongside finger pontoons and yachts of up to 18m can be accommodated in depths of 2·5–3m. Berths towards the north side of the marina appear to be silting and are shallower. Larger yachts berth in the southwest corner. The marina office is clearly marked in English and staff will assist with mooring.

Facilities

Water and electricity on the marina pontoons, with showers, a sauna and laundry facilities. Fuel station in the marina. There is a boatyard nearby, and a winter storage facility is planned for the marina site, but as yet no chandlery. The marina and its facilities are notably well maintained and the staff, who speak English and German, will assist with information about the harbour and town.

There is a Post Office with telephones and a bar/restaurant in the marina complex, and some overnight accommodation on the upper floor. Shopping, banks etc are to be found in the town. Bicycles can be hired for exploration of the National Park.

Władysławowo

58°48′N 18°25′E

Distances
Kołobrzeg 115M, Ustka 60M, Łeba 30M, Hel 22M, Gdynia 30M, Gdańsk 32M

Charts and guides
UKHO 2369, 2288, 2688
Polish 251, 151, 152, 73, 35, 3022

Lights
2960 **Rozewie** 54°49′·8N 18°20′·2E Fl.3s83m26M Red round tower, red top, two galleries
Landfall buoy 54°47′·8N 18°26′·5E LFl.10sRW buoy
2961.4 **Ldg Lts 260°** *Front* E Breakwater 54°47′·7N 18°25′·2E Oc.R.6s14m2M Yellow framework tower
2961.41 *Rear* Ldg Lt 245m from front Oc.R.6s22m2M On roof of building
2965 **Jastarnia** 54°42′N 18°40′·9E Mo(A)20s22m15M White round tower, red bands, gallery

Harbour communications
Harbourmaster ① +48 58 674 0486
Port Control ① +48 58 674 0286 *VHF* Ch 10
www.szkuner.pl

General

Władysławowo (pronounced *Vwah-dih-swa-vo-vo*) is an artificial harbour near the root of the Mierzeja Helska (Hel peninsula) and some 4M southeast of Rozewie Point, a prominent headland which forms Poland's northernmost extremity. It is primarily a fishing port with some facilities for a small number of yachts but also a holiday resort.

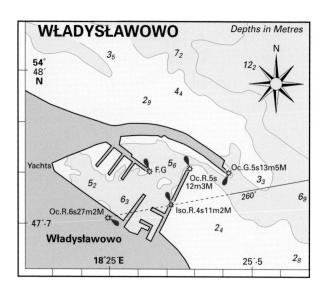

Approach

Approach waypoint 54°47′·8N 18°26′·4E

Straightforward approach and entrance on 260° from the landfall buoy (see plan) with the front leading mark, which is a column on the east breakwater 100m back from the east molehead, in line with the tower on the townhall though care must be taken not to stray north of the approach line on closing the north breakwater. Keep an eye on the depth sounder during the approach as the sandbanks sometimes change position. In 2008 there was a small green buoy and a red perch 300m east of the eastern end of the breakwater.

Warnings The approach is dangerous in winds over Force 5 from the north and east because of sand banks.

Between Władysławowo and the eastern end of the Hel peninsula are two Firing ranges (Areas 10 and 11) firing up to 10M out to sea. Firing times will need to be checked. See under firing ranges and navigational warnings on page 291.

Berth

Berth on the yacht pontoon with finger berths in the extreme west of the harbour clearly marked 'For Yachts Only'. Yachts can also lie alongside the breakwater in the outer basin although this berth is much less protected from swell and there are no facilities. The harbour carries a depth of 5m almost throughout.

Facilities

Water/electricity on the pontoons. Showers/toilets near shipyard/marina entrance opposite harbourmaster's office, with key from security guard on gate if office is closed. Diesel available.

Shops/restaurants in town 1km to northwest of shipyard gate. Shipyard with mechanical and electronic workshops. Trains to Hel, Gdynia and Gdańsk.

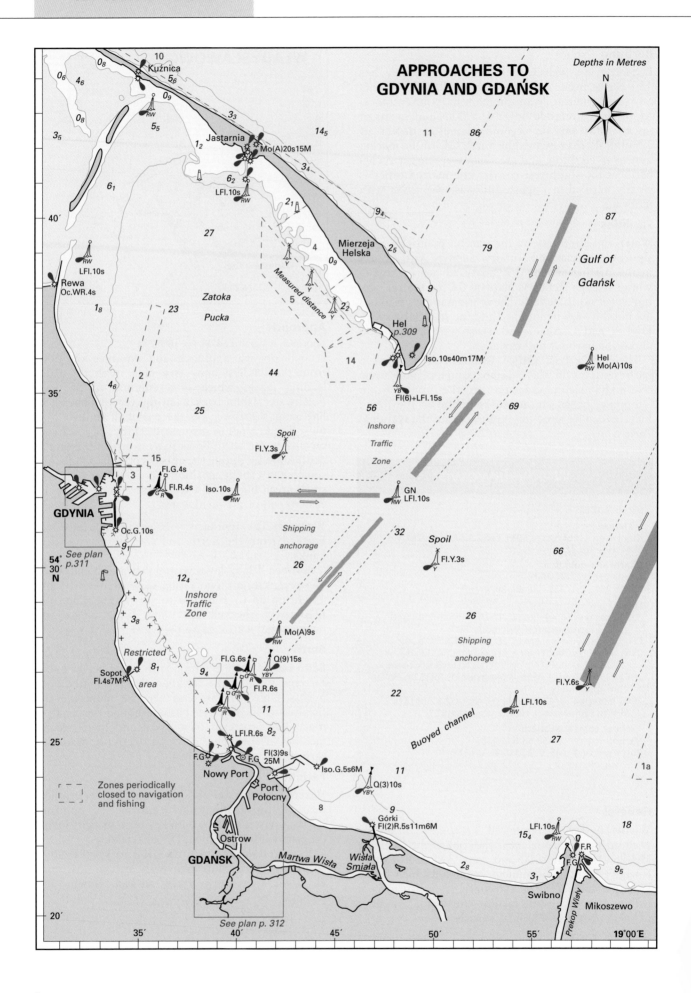

APPROACHES TO
GDYNIA AND GDAŃSK

Depths in Metres

N

0_8 10

0_6 4_6 Kuźnica 5_6

0_8 0_9

RW

3_5 5_5

3_3 14_5 11   86

1_2 Jastarnia 3_4

Mo(A)20s15M

6_1 6_2 2_1 9_4 87

LFl.10s 0_9 Mierzeja 2_5

RW   Helska   79   Gulf of

40'   27   4   9   Gdańsk

RW   Measured distance 2_2

LFl.10s   5

Rewa   Zatoka   Hel

Oc.WR.4s   Pucka   p.309

1_8 23   Iso.10s40m17M

RW

2   YB   Hel

35' 4_6 14   Fl(6)+LFl.15s   RW   Mo(A)10s

25   56   69

Spoil   Inshore

Fl.Y.3s   Traffic

15   Y   Zone

3   Fl.G.4s   GN

Fl.R.4s   LFl.10s

GDYNIA   G R   Iso.10s   RW

Oc.G.10s   RW

9_1 Shipping   32   Spoil

54°   See plan   anchorage   Fl.Y.3s   66

30'   p.311   26   Y

N

12_4 26

Inshore

Traffic

3_8 Zone   Mo(A)9s   Shipping

RW   anchorage

Restricted   Fl.G.6s   Q(9)15s

Sopot 8_1 G R   YBY   Fl.Y.6s

Fl.4s7M 9_4 Fl.R.6s   Y

area   G R   22   LFl.10s

11   RW

LFl.R.6s 8_2

25'   F.G   Fl(3)9s   Buoyed channel   27

F.G   25M   Iso.G.5s6M   11   1a

Nowy Port   Q(3)10s

Port   YBY

Połocny   8   9   Górki   LFl.10s   18

Fl(2)R.5s11m6M   RW   F.R

Ostrow 15_4 F.G 9_5

GDAŃSK   Martwa Wisła   Wisła 2_8

Śmiała 3_1

Swibno   Mikoszewo

20'

See plan p. 312   19°00'E

35'   40'   45'   50'   55'

Zones periodically
closed to navigation
and fishing

Hel

54°36′N 18°48′E

Distances
Łeba 52M, Władysławowo 22M, Gdynia 10M, Gdańsk 15M, Kaliningrad 30M, Klaipėda 105M

Charts and guides
UKHO 2369, 2688, 2688
Polish 251,151,73, 34, 12

Lights
2965 **Jastarnia** 54°42′N 18°40′·2E Mo(A)20s22m15M
    White round tower, red bands and gallery
HL-S SCM 54°35′·3N 18°48′E Q(6)+LFl.15s
2968 **Hel** 54°36′N 18°48′·75E Iso.10s41m17M Red
    octagonal masonry tower with gallery vis 151°-102°

Harbour communications
Harbourmaster ☎ +48 58 675 0618
Port Control ☎ +48 58 675 0624 VHF Ch 10
Marina Manager ☎ +48 58 675 0618

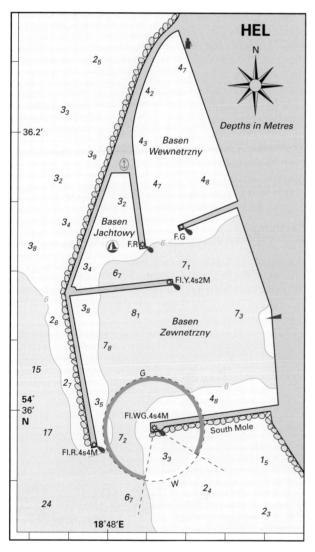

General

The small and pleasant fishing port of Hel is just inside the tip and on the southwest side of the Hel peninsula (Mierzeja Helska) which extends for 18M in a northwest/southeast direction, a line of wooded dunes no higher than 30m, and in places no more than 250m wide and quite steep-to. It carries road and rail links.

Warning Between the eastern end of the Hel Peninsula and Władysławowo are two Firing Ranges (Areas 10 and 11) firing up to 10M out to sea. Firing times will need to be checked. See page 291.

Approach

Approach waypoints
From north 54°40′N 18°52′E
From south 54°35′N 18°48′E

Approach from the south is straightforward but do not confuse the entrance with that of the naval harbour 1M to the northwest where entry is prohibited.

Approach from the north involves rounding the South cardinal mark at the end of a very shallow spit running out from the tip of the peninsula.

Commercial shipping in the area is moderately heavy, but yachts using the inshore traffic zone to Gdynia remain clear of the major separation scheme for the ports of Gdynia and Gdańsk. Yachts are required to monitor VHF Ch 12, but do not need to report their presence.

Berth

In the yacht basin on the west side of the harbour. Moor to pontoons or alongside in depths from 2·5–4·0m.

Facilities

Water on the quay and electricity on the pontoon. Showers/toilets in a new round building on the breakwater. Diesel in the fishing harbour. Workshops and mobile crane on harbourside. Shops and restaurants (including an Admiral Nelson and a Captain Morgan where there are menus in English) in the main street close to the harbour. Maritime Museum and a Baltic Seal aquarium. Trains to Gdynia and Gdańsk.

Yacht berths at Hel *S. Carnegie*

6. POLAND

Gdynia

54°32'N 18°33'E

Distances

Władysławowo 35M, Łeba 70M, Kołobrzeg 155M, Gdańsk 10M, Kaliningrad 45M, Klaipėda 115M

Charts and guides

UKHO 2369, 2288, 2688, 2680
Polish 251, 151, 73, 35, 12, 3022

Lights

2960 **Rozewie** 54°49'·9N 18°20'·3E Fl.3s83m26M
  Red round tower, red top, two galleries
2964·6 **Władysławowo** 57°47'·8N 18°24'·6E
  Aero F.R.78m23M Tower
2965 **Jastarnia** 54°42'N 18°40'·9E Mo(A)20s22m15M
  White round tower, red bands and gallery
2968 **Hel** 54°36'·1N 18°48'·9E Iso.10s40m17M
  130°-vis-080°+F.R Red octagonal tower with gallery
3018 **Ldg Lts 271·5°** *Front* 54°32'·2N 18°32'·9E
  Oc.Y.5s15m8M White metal framework tower 15m
3018·1 *Rear* 0·57M from front Oc.Y.5s27m8M
  White metal framework tower, black stripe 24m
3016 **South detached breakwater, north end**
  (main entrance) 54°32'·1N 18°34'·8E Iso.R.4s15m10M
  Round concrete tower with gallery and dome
3016·2 **South detached breakwater, south end** 54°31'N
  18°33'·7E Oc.G.10s12m9M Concrete tower with glass
  cupola
3037 **Basen żeglarski (yacht basin), east wall** 54°31'N
  18°33'·2E F.G.5m2M Green concrete column
3038 **Basen żeglarski (yacht basin), south wall** 54°31'N
  18°33'·2E F.R.5m2M Red concrete column on hut
3080·8 **Port Północny (Gdansk)** 54°24'N 18°41'·8E
  Fl(3)9s56m25M Blue square tower with white gallery
Note Lights for the central (main) and north entrances
  are not described

Harbour communications

Gdynia Harbourmaster ✆ +48 58 621 0705/7983
  VHF Ch 12
Gdynia Port Control ✆ +48 58 621 6636 *VHF* Ch 12, 16
  (Yachts are required to monitor *VHF* Ch 12, but need
  not report their presence)
Gdynia Yacht Club Marina ✆ +48 58 661 9366 *VHF* Ch 12
  www.marinagdynia.pl

General

Gdynia (pronounced *Guh-din-ya*) is a major commercial and shipbuilding port located in the Bay of Gdańsk. Most container traffic for Poland passes through Gdynia. It has a secure yacht harbour, with an approach south of that for the main harbour, together with several active sailing clubs which hold frequent regattas.

South of the city lies a popular beach area with pavement cafés, bars and local shops lining the seafront and main avenue. South again, by some 9km, is the city of Sopot where cultural events, concerts and seaside recreation are popular.

Approach and entrance

Approach waypoint 54°30'·8N 18°34'E

Gdynia is protected by north-south detached breakwaters more than 1·5M in length, pierced by three entrances. The leading lights direct shipping through the main (central) entrance and should be ignored by yachts.

Staying clear of the traffic separation scheme which begins 2M east of the Hel Peninsula, yachts should steer for the south end of the eastern detached breakwater. On rounding the breakwater the marina's east wall will be seen about 550m ahead, with a green column marking the entrance. It should be noted that a restricted area extends southwards from a point approximately 100m south of this. The entrance to the yacht basin (Basen Żeglarski) is narrow and the approach is marked by one starboardhand buoy and two porthand buoys quite close to the beach.

It is best to call the marina on VHF Ch 12 to notify arrival and request a berth.

Berthing

The marina master's office, ✆ +48 58 661 9366, is immediately inside the east wall and staff will direct an incoming yacht to a vacant berth. There are about 50 visitors' berths. Maximum length 20m and maximum draught 2·8m in the entrance. Berths

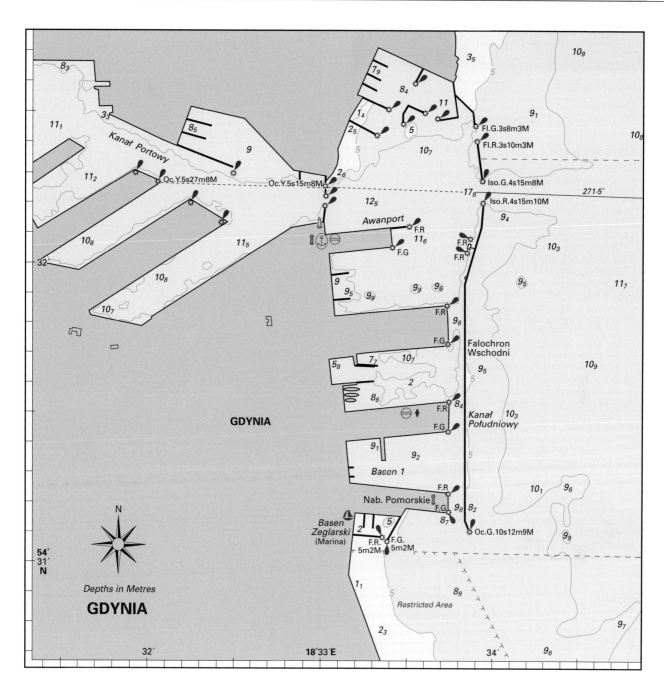

GDYNIA

Depths in Metres

GDYNIA

54°
31′
N

Kanał Portowy

Awanport

Falochron
Wschodni

Kanał
Południowy

Basen 1

Nab. Pomorskie

Basen
Zeglarski
(Marina)

Restricted Area

along the southern breakwater appear to be reserved for Polish Navy yachts. In season berths are often in short supply.

Facilities

Water and electricity on the pontoons. Toilets and showers at the marina office. Fuel is available in the eastern corner of the basin.

Gdynia undoubtedly has the best chandleries in Poland. They include SMART who are Admiralty chart agents and Sail-Ho who are agents for Imrays and NV-Verlag and Delius Klasing publications.

There is a three tonne crane for masts and small craft and a larger one can be arranged if required. Engineers, boatbuilders are also available. The nearest sailmaker is at Gdańsk. Winter storage

outside can be arranged although a cradle may be difficult to find.

Good shopping is available on the main avenue leading from the marina with further shops, including smaller speciality shops, along the main walkway. An open-air market is located adjacent to the multi-level Batory shopping centre about 10 minutes' walk up the avenue. For major provisioning it may be worth visiting the major Real superstore development approximately 20 minutes by taxi west of the city centre.

The railway station is about 15 minutes' walk from the marina. There is a frequent service to Gdańsk, 20km and about 25 minutes to the southeast, and good links with Szczecin and Berlin.

Gdańsk

54°21'N 18°39'E

Distances

Łeba 80M, Gdynia 10M, Kaliningrad 45M,
Klaipėda 110M

Charts and guides

UKHO 2369, 2288, 2688, 2680
Polish 251, 151, 73, 34, 12, 3022

Lights

2968 **Hel** 54°36'·1N 18°48'·9E Iso.10s40m17M
130°-vis-080° F.R Red octagonal tower with gallery

3080·8 **Port Północny** 54°24'N 18°41'·8E Fl(3)9s56m25M
Blue square tower with white gallery

3062 **Outer Ldg Lts196°** *Front* 54°24'·5N 18°38'·4E
Iso.Y.5s23m13M White triangle with red border, on
white metal framework tower 24m

3062·1 *Rear* 330m from front Iso.Y.5s31m13M Triangle
on black metal framework tower 36m

3064 **Inner Ldg Lts 147·7°** *Front* 54°24'·6N 18°39'·8E
Oc.G.5s23m8M Two white triangles with red borders,
on white beacon 20m

3064·1 *Rear* 370m from front, Oc.G.5s35m8M Black
triangle on dark grey beacon 32m

3068 **East breakwater** 54°25'N 18°39'·5E LFl.R.6s13m7M
Red tower 13m

3066 **West molehead** 54°24'·7N 18°39'·6E LFl.G.6s11m7M
Green framework tower

3082 **Górki** 54°22'·5N 18°46'·9N Fl(2)R.5s11m6M
Red round tower with gallery

3090 **Krynica Morska** 54°23'·1N 19°27'E
LFl(2)12s53m18M Red round tower, white lantern

Harbour communications

Gdańsk Harbourmaster ① +48 58 343 0610
VHF Ch 14
Gdańsk Port Control ① +48 58 343 0710
VHF Ch 14, 16
Gdańsk Marina ② +48 58 301 3378/302 6274
VHF Ch 17 www.marinagdansk.pl www.sailgdansk.pl

General

The historic city of Gdańsk (pronounced *Guh-dansk*), and the *Nowy* (pronounced *Novv-I*) Port is situated at the mouth of the Wisła River, the largest river in Poland, and at a strategic location on the old Amber Road, the city has long been a fortified trading settlement. It was a stronghold of the Teutonic Knights, and later a formidable member of the Hanseatic League. Prussian influence is strongly seen in the old waterfront buildings, especially the Crane Gate constructed in 1440, the largest goods lift of the 15th century. The Stare Miasto (old town) originally built with much Dutch influence has been carefully restored since the Second World War when 80% of the city was destroyed. It is now the site of cultural events and outdoor festivals during the summer, as well as numerous shops and cafés.

Amber is available from local artisans, and the National Museum houses an excellent collection of art, including a collection of Polish and Flemish paintings, relief panels and sculpture.

The local shipyards were the birthplace of Solidarity, the union movement which eventually led to the demise of Soviet control in Poland, and are

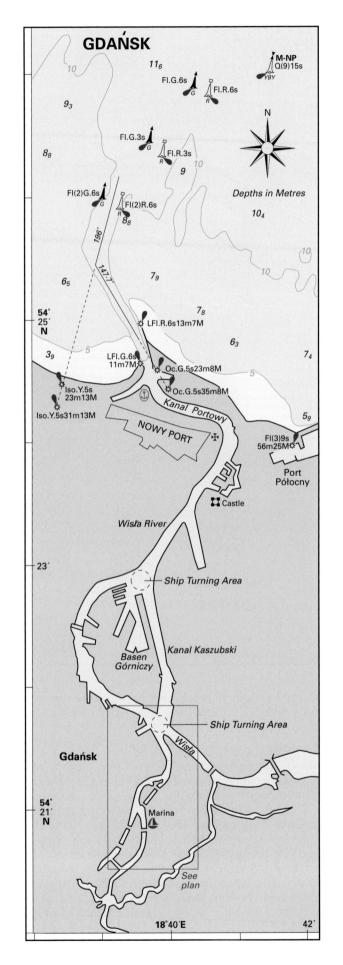

Gdańsk Marina from entrance *S. Carnegie*

now a World Heritage Site. The ship-building and bulk-shipping areas are to the north and east of the old town.

Approach and entrance

Approach waypoint 54°26'·3N 18°39'·4E

The approach from within the Gulf of Gdańsk is straightforward and can be taken in all but the severest of onshore weather conditions. Yachts should stay well clear of the TSS which begins 2M east of the tip of the Hel peninsula. The outer and inner leading lines can be followed although yachts can safely cut the corner and head directly for the eastern (outer) breakwater head.

Permission to enter (or leave) must be sought from Gdańsk Nowy Port Control on *VHF* Ch 14.

Just inside the entrance there is a large monument on the east side commemorating the men who died when the first shots of the Second World War were fired by a German battleship at the barracks on Westerplatte. It is customary to hold one's ensign at the dip when passing it.

The channel follows the Kanal Portowy and Wisła River for 3·7M through the commercial port and shipyards. At the ship turning area, north of Basen Gorniczy (54°23'N) follow the eastern channel, the Kanal Kaszubski. At the next ship turning area (54°21'·7N 18°40'E) follow the small channel directly ahead – the Motława River – which leads to the marina in the heart of the old city directly opposite the historic Crane Gate (54°21'N 18°39'E).

Berthing

Gdańsk marina has 70 berths. There are 2·8m depths in the main area but somewhat less near the

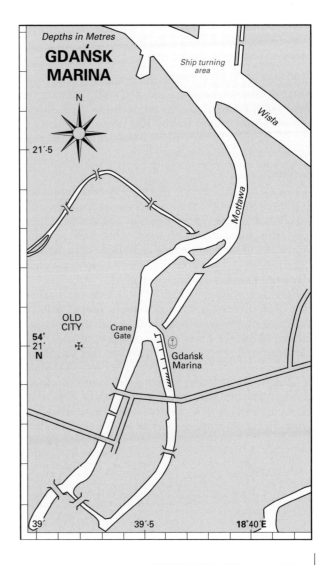

6. POLAND

Gdańsk Marina   *J. Parkinson*

bridge where smaller vessels are berthed. The marina office overlooks the pontoons, and staff (who are on duty around the clock during summer) will direct visitors to an empty berth. The office can also be contacted on VHF Ch 17. A yacht could safely be left here for several weeks.

Facilities

Water and electricity are provided on the pontoons and there are toilets and showers near the entrance. Diesel is available in the canal at Szczeciński Quay near the shipyards – marina staff will provide directions. There is a small chandlery with limited stock about 100m from the marina where Polish Hydrographic Charts are available.

Gdańsk has all the facilities of a long-established city. Restaurants, cafés and small shops will be found along the waterfront and in the Stare Miasto (old town) area. There is a small grocery near the marina, but it is necessary to travel further for major shopping.

Gdańsk Airport has international and national connections, and there are also good train services to Szczecin and Berlin. Marina staff can assist in arranging taxis to the airport or station if requested.

Yachts moored in the centre of old Gdańsk, with the Crane Gate in the background. The cream building on the right houses the city's maritime museum   *G. and M. Honey*

Górki

54°22'N 18°47'E

Charts
UKHO 2369, 2288, 2688, 2680
Polish 251, 151, 73, 34, 3022

The harbour of Górki (pronounced *Gor-key*) is located 5M to the east of the main entrance of Gdańsk, at the mouth of one of the channels which form the Wisła delta. See plan on page 308. The entrance is protected by breakwaters and is said to be dredged to 10m.

Warning Sand banks make the approach particularly dangerous in onshore winds.

Two small marinas lie to starboard just inside the entrance, with a boatyard 0·5M further on equipped with a 12-tonne crane where winter storage may be possible.

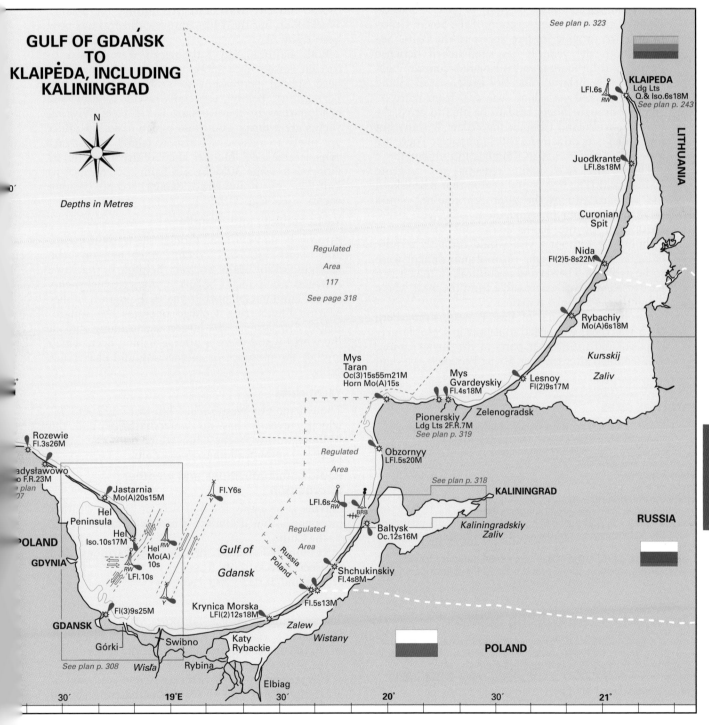

7. Kaliningrad

See location plan pages 298 and 322

The city and surrounding area

The Kaliningrad oblast (region) is part of Russia, retained after the disintegration of the Soviet Union in order to provide ice-free access to the Baltic Sea throughout the year. It lies sandwiched between Poland and Lithuania, and is isolated from the bulk of Russia by Belarus. The city itself is well inland and approached via a long sea canal from Baltiysk. Shallow-draught boats used to be able to cross the border into Poland through the Zalew Wislany but unmarked nets now make this impossible. There are also inland waterways to Klaipėda in Lithuania.

There are two main reasons for visiting Kaliningrad. The first is practical in that Baltiysk, at the seaward end of the approach channel, could serve as a harbour of refuge on an otherwise rather bleak part of the Baltic coast; but to arrive in Kaliningrad without a visa would certainly require being *in extremis* if some form of punishment were to be avoided. The second is cultural, in that it is a part of Russia easily accessible from the west where much that is Stalinist remains.

Formerly the capital of East Prussia, Königsberg (as it was then) was ceded to Russia in 1945, largely re-populated from other parts of the Soviet Union, and renamed after the then Soviet President, Mikhail Kalinin. However, it traces its roots back to the 13th century and during the middle ages was an important member of the Hanseatic League. Much of the old city was destroyed during the Second World War, but the 14th-century cathedral has now been restored.

Both Baltiysk and Kaliningrad were closed to foreign vessels until 1991, and foreign visitors still need special permission to visit the former (see *Formalities*, below) especially as it is now the headquarters of the Russian Baltic Fleet. Visiting yachts are a rarity, and those which make the effort are likely to receive a warm welcome and attract considerable local interest. There is also a harbour at Pionerskiy, some 30M by sea from the entrance to Baltiysk and Kaliningrad, which accepts visiting yachts – see page 319.

Internet sites

The internet is already a useful source of information about Kaliningrad, and is well worth searching for updated information. A good search engine may produce additional sites to those listed below:
www.kscport.ru
www.portinfo.htm
www.transmarine.ru/ – further information about the Port of Kaliningrad from the shipping agents TransMarine
www.ellennet.com/index.php?lang=english – a website maintained by the Swedish owners of the yacht Ellen, which covers many Baltic countries
http://www.klgd.ru/ – the official site of Kaliningrad City Hall
www.worldportsource.com General historical and port information

Charts, pilots and cruising guides

Admiralty charts *2288* and *2369* cover the approaches on scales of 1: 350,000 and 1:200,000 respectively. In addition the large scale Admiralty chart *2278* is essential if planning a visit.
Russian charts *25051, 27001, 27001, 27002, 27003, 27004, 27005,*
Baltic Pilot Volume II (NP 19)

Yacht services and chandlery

Effectively non-existent, though the harbourmaster and staff at the yacht harbour on the Kaliningradskiy Zaliv are very helpful. In a serious emergency help might be forthcoming from elements in the commercial port – the Kaliningrad Higher Marine Engineering College operates the square-rigged *Kruzenstern*, the largest sail training ship in the world – and there is a large fishing fleet, which implies the presence of engineering and electronics skills.

Yacht clubs

There is the Ost-West Yacht Club ① +7 112 443702 which currently has no waterside base and the Kaliningradskiy Yacht Club which runs the Yacht Harbour in the Kaliningradskiy Zaliv.

Radio communications and weather information

Navtex is probably the best way of getting weather information but doubtless it can be obtained at the Yacht Clubs.

Kaliningrad Radio broadcasts warnings and weather forecasts, in Russian, on VHF Ch 07 on receipt and at 0533 and 1333 UTC.

Caution

The situation in all Russian ports may change over the next few years, and every effort should be made to check current requirements while the cruise is still at the planning stage.

The security of both yacht and crew is plainly of great importance and all sensible precautions should be taken – see pages 273.

Practicalities

Time

The Kaliningrad *oblast* uses UT+2 throughout the year.

Money

As elsewhere in Russia, the rouble (divided into 100 kopecks), is the official currency and there are many exchange offices in the city, including one on the main street. (It is not worth exchanging currency prior to arrival as the exchange rate is likely to be much better on the spot.) Tips and other presents should always be made in roubles.

Shopping

Kaliningrad is not a place for major shopping, though there are an increasing number of supermarkets and all daily needs should be met without difficulty. Taxis are readily available for the 10km ride between the yacht harbour and the city centre.

Communications

Public call boxes, either coin or card operated, are widespread. Western mobile phones may function, but the charges will be high. To obtain an international line dial 8, wait for the dial tone, then 10 followed by the country code, area code (omitting any initial 0) and number. If dialling from abroad the country code for Russia is 7 and the area code for Baltiysk and Kaliningrad is 4012. VHF Ch 16 and/or 74 should be monitored on approach (see also *Harbour Communications*, opposite).

Travel

There are road and rail links to the surrounding countries, and a weekly ferry service to Sassnitz. Kaliningrad airport lies some 18km distant with regular flights to Moscow, Copenhagen and Hanover. However Kaliningrad remains an unlikely place to join or leave a yacht except in an emergency.

Formalities

Formalities are similar to those of the St Petersburg area – see pages 273–274 – and again Mr Vladimir Ivankiv, who speaks fluent English, has offered his assistance to those wishing to process the necessary papers. ☎ +7 812 510 7602 *Mobile* +7 921 932 5831 *Email* vladimir@sailrussia.spb.ru

Notice of arrival – including all the information in the list on page 274 – must be submitted to the Customs Post at Kaliningrad at least 72 hours prior to the yacht's arrival by the host yacht club or agent. Passport Control and Customs are located at the furthest northeastern corner of Basin No 3. Plenty of time should be allowed, as inward clearance procedures may take anything up to three hours. Outward clearance is of course mandatory, but is unlikely to take more than an hour.

As in St Petersburg persons staying in the country more than three days (or five if a weekend is included) must repeat their registration with the immigration department to avoid difficulties when leaving.

The Russian flag is a horizontal tricolour, white over blue over red.

See location plans on pages 288 and 322.

he entrance to Baltiysk   *K. Westersund*

Kaliningrad

Entrance 54°39′N 19°52′E
City 54°42′N 20°28′E

Distances
Gdynia 45M, Gdansk 45M, Klaipéda 80M

Lights
3096 **Shchukinskiy** 54°31′·6N 19°44′·5E Fl.4s50m8M Black and white metal framework tower 29m
3100·1 **Baltiysk Fairway** rear light, 54°38′·4N 19°53′·7E Oc.12s30m16M Round white tower, red top, two galleries 32m
3255 **Obzornyy** 54°49′·7N 19°57′·3E LFl.5s54m20M Triangle on orange round tower, white bands 22m
3256 **Mys Taran** 54°57′·6N 19°58′·9E Oc(3)15s55m21M Emergency light Iso.4s13M Red octagonal tower on building 30m Horn Mo(A)15s13m Red metal mast 4m120m NW of light
3100 **Baltiysk Fairway Ldg Lts 122·1°** *Front* 54°38′·6N 19°53′·1E Oc.12s12m12M 116°-vis-128° Two white rectangles with black stripes on red metal framework tower 21m
3100·1 *Rear* 770m from front, as above
buoy **Fairway No.1** 54°41′·3N 19°45′·1E LFl.6s Red and white pillar buoy
3100·11 **North mole** 54°39′N 19°52′·3E Fl.R.2·5s3M
3100·12 **South mole** 54°38′·8N 19°52′·1E Fl.G.4s1M
Many more lights and lit buoys mark the Kaliningradskiy Morskoy Kanal

Harbour communications
Baltiysk Traffic VHF Ch 16, 74. Call Sign Kaliningrad 47 or Voskod 16
Kaliningrad Port Authority ☎ +7 4012 44 43 06, Fax +7 4012 44 45 42 *VHF Ch 14*
Kaliningrad Radio VHF Ch 03, 07, 16
Kaliningrad Traffic (Call Kaliningrad Traffic or Kaliningrad 9) VHF Ch 67
Passport Control VHF Ch 74 Call Impools
Customs Control VHF Ch 74 Call Metch
Pilots VHF Ch 67 Call Kaliningrad 11

Approach and entrance

Approach waypoint 30°43′N 19°42′E

Beware of the Navy firing ranges to the north and northwest of the port of Baltiysk and the cape of Taran. It is recommended to stay away from the warships passing them by at a distance to avoid problems caused by possible missile launchings or artillery firings.

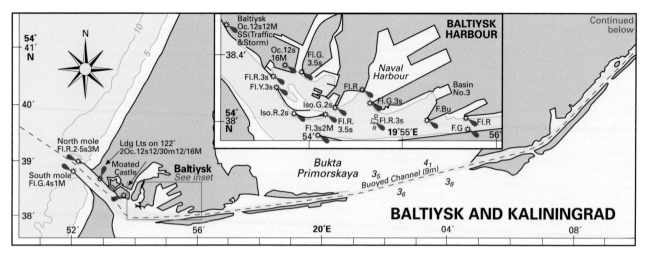

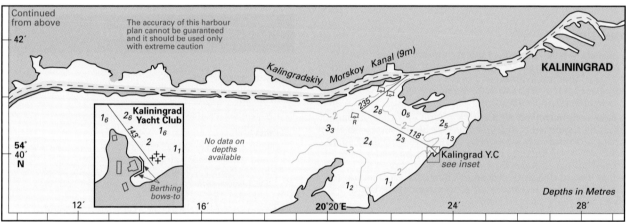

Particular attention should be paid to Regulated Area 117. See plan on page 315. In 2009 this area was intermittently closed and this affected several cruising yachts sailing between the Gulf of Gdańsk and Klaipėda. They had to round the northwest limit of the area at 55°54′N 19°03′E thus adding 45M to the straight-line route between Gdańsk and Klaipėda. Vessels approaching Kaliningrad from Klaipėda would also have to stay out of the area until given the all-clear. In this case clearing Customs at Pionerskiy could be an option but adequate notice of arrival would have to be given. (The northeast limit of Area 117 is 55°30′N 20°15′E and the southwest limit is 54°50′N 19°25′E and it extends on to the shore but all up-to-date charts show the limits). It is important to monitor VHF Ch 16 when sailing in or close to Russian waters so as to be able to respond to instructions as all vessels will be on their radar. Details of any closure of regulated areas are posted on Navtex with five days warning and can also be found on the website of the Swedish Maritime Administrative Co-ordinator Sub-area BALTICO at www.sjofartsverket.se

Approach is made from the Gulf of Gdańsk (see plan page 315). Though depths are generally good within 1M of the coast it would nevertheless be wise to keep well offshore until able to approach via the designated channel on 122°, passing Fairway Buoy No. 1 en route. Contact should be made with Baltiysk Traffic. For example: 'This is S/Y Name,

Flag, Final destination, Number of people on board going to Baltiysk for passport control, may I enter the port of Baltiysk?' Reporting is mandatory, and contact should be made when more than 7M (or one hour) from the entrance, and it is likely that an escort vessel will approach the yacht to check credentials and escort her in. Night approach could be hazardous due to a number of large, unlit ship mooring buoys within a few miles of the harbour mouth – and it might also cause needless difficulties with the authorities.

Final entry is straightforward, with the Passport Control and Customs berth on the north side of the channel 2M from the entrance in the northeast corner of Basin No. 3 (54°38′·25N 19°55′·45E). There is a duty-free shop within the secure area. From Baltiysk the well-buoyed Kaliningradskiy Morskoy Kanal runs some 22M (41km) between low-lying banks to the commercial port and city of Kaliningrad. Depths are dredged to a nominal 9m throughout its length, but shoal steeply on either side.

If heading for the yacht harbour in the southeastern corner of the Kaliningradskiy Zaliv (the large inland sea traversed by the Kaliningradskiy Morskoy Kanal) the main channel is followed as far as light beacon No. 30 (54°41′·4N 20°22′·4E). From there a course of 235° is followed for 1M, before swinging onto 118° towards the harbour and buildings of the Kaliningrad Yacht Club and 143°

for the final approach. Parts of the route are shallow – less than 2m – though the bottom is soft. Do not stray as there are unmarked fishing nets and wrecks in the Kaliningradskiy Zaliv.

At least four hours should be allowed between the Passport Control berth and the yacht harbour.

Berthing

Baltiysk There is a yacht harbour within the Naval Base area and it may be possible to obtain a permit to use it from the Kaliningrad or Baltijsk Sailing Federation but permission to use it was refused in 2007. Enquire at the Passport Control post, Kaliningrad. In the past yachts have berthed near the city centre, in the easternmost of the four basins. However the few foreign yachts which have visited Kaliningrad within the last few years have all used the yacht harbour, ✆ +7 4012 466 331, on the southeast coast of the Kaliningradskiy Zaliv with berthing for about 10 visiting yachts moored bows-to in 2·5m depths. This is the home of the Kaliningrad Yacht Club (54°40′N 20°23′·3E). Its members are most welcoming to visitors.

Yachts with a draught of over 2m may have to berth at Kaliningrad Sea Port, in the furthest basin on the south side (marked free harbour on Admiralty Chart 2278) at the Pier No. 3. Depth – 8m but large commercial vessels passing by often produce uncomfortable wash.

Toilet, shower, water. Public transport is nearby.

Services for yachts

Baltiysk Modest facilities, with water but no electricity. Berthing is free. There is a ferry across the entrance.

Kaliningrad Yacht Club Harbour The yacht club harbour has almost no services, though it is possible to get DC electricity aboard via a long lead from one of the sheds. There is water (but not for drinking unless previously boiled) but no showers, and toilet facilities are minimal – no more than a few holes in the ground in summer 2007. However, the harbourmaster and his staff are very helpful, and it may be possible to buy petrol or diesel in containers, get laundry done etc, with the assistance of local people.

Kaliningrad Yacht Club facilities are minimal *K. Westersund*

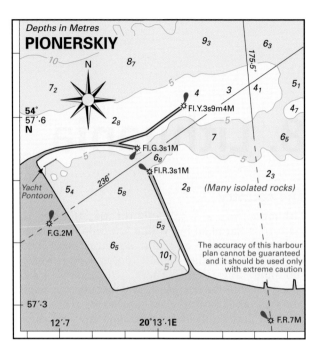

Pionerskiy

Approach

Approach waypoint 54°57′·7N 20°13′·5E

Little detail is available about the fishing harbour at Pionerskiy, which was opened to foreign vessels in 2000. It lies on the north coast of the wide peninsula which separates the Kaliningradskiy Zaliv from the Baltic Sea, about 30M by sea (41km as the crow flies) from the entrance to Baltiysk and Kaliningrad. In 2007 a party of seven yachts from Helsinki Sailing Club cleared Customs into Kaliningrad at Pionerskiy and this could be an option if Area 117 was closed. There is a nearby town of some size (Pionerskiy was long the home port of the Russian Baltic fishing fleet) and though it is likely that daily shopping needs can be met this should not be assumed.

Approach from offshore is made to the east of the harbour entrance, in theory turning onto a course of 236° to enter. However it is understood that shoaling has taken place off the end of the north breakwater, which is marked by a 5m red metal framework tower, and a careful watch must be kept on the echo-sounder. It is clearly not an entrance to be attempted in strong winds from between northwest through north to east, and certainly not in darkness or poor visibility.

It is reported that visiting yachts raft up to a quay in the harbour in 4m depths, where water and electricity are available. The Extel Yacht Club, ✆ +7 110 343 715, is understood to run the facility.

Customs and immigration officials will visit the yacht on arrival – indeed foreign yachts are so rare that they will probably be waiting before the crew have finished making fast. As elsewhere in Russia, the formalities are likely to be time-consuming, and will have to be repeated before departure.

8. Lithuania

The country

Lithuania has a total area of 65,300km², the majority a flat plain but with a few hills in the south and west. To the east and southeast the Baltic Highlands rise, the highest point being Mount Juoapine at 292m. There are many lakes, particularly in the northeast, and meandering rivers. Marshes and swamps are prevalent. The 99km coastline has sandy beaches backed by sand dunes and pine forest, while in the southwest the long Curonian sand spit almost encloses the Curonian Lagoon. South of Klaipėda lie the famous amber mines.

Lithuania has one of the fastest growing economies in Europe. Industry accounts for just over 25% of GDP, oil transit activity between Russia and Europe 12% and services 60%. Food processing, shipbuilding, electronics, machine tools and furniture are the main industries whilst IT is also developing. Main foreign trade is with the EU, mainly Latvia and Germany. About 50% of land is in agricultural use, agriculture employing some 20% of the workforce. Mineral oils and fuels, electric and electronic equipment, vehicles, machinery and transportation equipment form the major exports.

Formalities

EU passport holders do not require visas. The website of the Lithuanian Embassy (http://uk.mfa.lt) lists countries whose citizens do not need visas. If a visa is needed contact the Lithuanian Consulate at 84 Gloucester Place, London W1U 6AU. ✆ 0207 486 6401/2, Email amb.uk@urm.lt. The British Embassy in Vilnius can be contacted on ✆ 370 5 246 2900, Email be-vilnius@britain.lt, http://ukinlithuania.fco.gov.uk/en.

Formal reporting is no longer required for passages between Lithuania and another Schengen country. Vessels arriving from or departing to a non-Schengen country, such as Russia, must complete immigration procedures and should contact the authorities on arrival and departure.

Although nationals are required to have a 'boat driving licence', this does not apply to skippers of foreign flagged vessels. In practice, skippers and crew would be advised to carry any certificates of competence wherever they are sailing – see page 8.

The flag is a horizontal tricolour of – top to bottom – yellow, green and red.

The people, the church and the language

Of a total population of some 3·43 million, 83.5% are Lithuanians, 6.7% are Poles and 6.3% are Russians. The remaining 3.5% is made up of small numbers from Belarus, Ukraine, Germany and Latvia, as well as Jews and Tartars. 67% of the population is urban. The majority of believers (approximately 80%) follow the Catholic faith, but there are also large numbers of Russian Orthodox, Evangelical Lutherans and Baptists.

The national language is Lithuanian, in modern times similar only to Latvian but also said to bear a resemblance to ancient Sanskrit. There is still a strong Polish influence in much of the country – the capital, Vilnius, was a Polish city for many centuries – and the language is widely understood. Russian is also widely understood, but may not be welcome. German is a good alternative but the use of English is growing, particularly amongst younger people.

Visitors to Lithuania can be assured of a warm and friendly welcome.

Internet sites

The internet is a rich source of information about Lithuania, and the following sites (in English unless otherwise stated) may well provide links to others of interest:

www.travel.lt – compiled by the Lithuanian Tourist Board, with facts and figures on all aspects of tourism and travel

www.tourism.lt - the homepage of the Lithuanian State Department of Tourism with useful facts and figures about Lithuania

www.inyourpocket.com/lithuania/en/ – the homepage of the Lithuania in Your Pocket guide

www.online.lt – an index of various Lithuanian internet resources, most with English translations

http://ukinlithuania.fco.gov.uk/en – the British Embassy in Vilnius, Lithuania

www.nerija.lt/en – the homepage of the Kurši Nerija National Park, which includes much information on the Curonian Spit and the lagoon it shelters, including some of interest to sailors

History and the future

From the 14th to the 16th centuries Lithuania was a powerful independent state allied with Poland against the Teutonic Knights, the two countries becoming formally united in 1569, but by the 18th century this alliance had weakened and much of Lithuania was taken over by Russia. A brief spell of independence was enjoyed in the years between the two World Wars, but the Second World War brought first the Soviets and then the Germans, until in 1944 the Soviets took over once again and ruled until independence in 1991.

Since 1991 Lithuania has made enormous strides towards updating facilities and services. On the political front, Lithuania joined both the EU and NATO in 2004 and signed the Schengen agreement at the end of 2007.

Cruising

Lithuania has only the one Baltic Sea port of Klaipėda, although it is possible to explore the Curonian Lagoon as far as Nida, using well-marked channels. Small fishing harbours such as Mingė and Juodkrantė are being developed with facilities for yachts.

South of Lithuania lies the Russian enclave of Kaliningrad, for which visas are required.

Yacht services and chandlery

See under *Klaipėda*, page 323.

Yacht clubs

Sailing is popular both at Klaipėda and on the inland lakes. Although many yachts are privately owned, some still belong to yacht clubs. The Lithuanian Yachting Union is very active and organises training and regattas.

Radio communications and weather information

Details of the above, including Search and Rescue, GMDSS, Coast Radio Stations, Weather Bulletins, Navigational Warnings, NAVTEX, Weatherfax transmissions and weather forecasts on the internet can be found on page 370 in the Appendix.

Navigational and other information is broadcast on request by Klaipėda Traffic on VHF Ch 09.

VHF Ch 16 should be monitored while on passage as coastguard stations may call up passing craft including yachts.

Regulated Area 117

If sailing from Gdańsk to Klaipėda or vice versa the direct route is through this area. See plan on page 318 and details on page 315.

The Curonian Spit looking northeast over Nida   *E. Redfern*

8. LITHUANIA

Practicalities

Time

Lithuania is in the Eastern European time zone (UT+2 in winter/UT+3 in summer). Summer time starts and ends on the same dates as the rest of the EU.

Money

The Lithuanian currency is the litas (plural: lit), divided into 100 cent (singular: centas). All financial transactions are carried out in litas, but major currencies can readily be exchanged. Cash is easily obtained from banks or ATMs and credit cards are widely accepted although harbour fees have to be paid in cash.

Shopping

Food and other basic commodities are in plentiful supply in shops and markets.

Public holidays

Major public holidays occur on: 1 January, 16 February (Independence Day), 11 March (Restoration of Independence), Easter Sunday and Monday, the first Sunday in May (Mother's Day), 24 June (St John's Day), 6 July (Statehood Day), 15 August (Feast of the Assumption), 1 November and 25–26 December. There are also many 'commemorative days' on which most shops and offices remain open.

Hotels and restaurants

A variety of standards and prices are available. Bed and breakfast accommodation of good standard and at a reasonable price can usually be organised through the local tourist office.

Communications

There are efficient telephone and mail systems and full coverage of mobile phone networks. Internet access is widely available with many free Wi-Fi points.

National and international calls can be made from public call boxes, which require cards available from street kiosks or post offices. To obtain an international line dial 00, followed by the country code, area code (omitting any initial 0) and number. Lithuanian phone numbers now begin with a figure 8 but this is not always necessary. If difficulties are experienced the advice is to replace the 8 with the international code for Lithuania +370. Calling from one landline to another in Lithuania dial 8 + city code + the number. Calling from one Lithuanian mobile (i.e. if using a local simcard) to another dial +370 + the number (omitting the figure 8). Calling from a Lithuanian mobile to a Lithuanian landline dial +370 + city code + the number. Useful websites are www.vox.lt/en/domesticcodes and www.teo.lt

VHF Ch 16 should be monitored while on passage as coastguard stations may call up passing craft including yachts.

Travel

There are international airports at Vilnius, Kaunas and Palanga. Palanga is most suitably located for crew changes in Klaipėda and as at 2008 has connections to Oslo and Copenhagen. Comprehensive bus and rail network with trains running from Vilnius to Warsaw, Berlin, Budapest, Prague and Sofia. Ferries run from Klaipėda to Germany, Sweden and Denmark. www.lisco.lt and www.scandlines.lt

Charts, pilots and cruising guides

British Admiralty and Lithuanian Maritime Safety Administration charts cover the coast. Those charts which are specific to an area or harbour are listed under individual harbour details. See the *Appendix*, page 362 for sources.

Lithuanian Maritime Safety Administration. Six sheet charts covering the coast in the approaches to Klaipėda

Lithuanian Inland Waterways Authority. Curonian Lagoon and the Nemunas Delta

Baltic Pilot Volume II (NP 19)

Harbours of the Baltic States, F & G Cattell, available through the Cruising Association and major nautical suppliers in Scandinavia

Sailing Guide Kuršių marios Kaliningradskiy Zaliv 2007. Guide to harbours in the Curonian Lagoon as well as Kaliningrad, Baltiysk and the Kaliningradskiy Zaliv (lagoon south of Kaliningrad between Russia and Poland). In English.

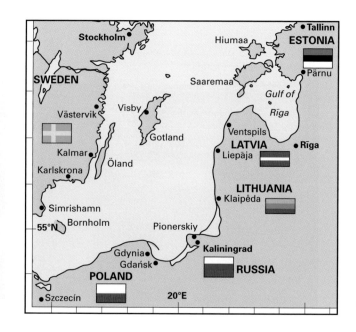

Klaipėda

55°42'N 21°07'E

Distances
Gdynia 115M, Gdansk 110M, Kaliningrad 80M, Liepāja 50M

Charts
UKHO 2288, 2276
Latvian 1253, 1024, 1023

Lights
C3334 **Juodkrantė** 55°33'·4N 21°07'·0E LFl.W.8s75m18M White square metal framework tower 20m

C3345·9 Ldg Lts 092.5° *Front* 55°43'·7N 21°05'·5E Q.W.31m16M White rectangle with black stripe and white diamond above on red metal framework tower 29m

C3346 *Rear* 285m from front Iso.W.6s44m18M 000° -vis-180° White round concrete tower, black bands and black stripe with balcony and lantern room 37m

C3382 **Šventoji** 56°01'·5N 21°04'·9E Fl(3)W.15s42m17M Red rectangle with white band on red square metal framework tower with balcony and lantern room 39m

C3348 **North breakwater** 55°43'·8N 21°04'·7E Fl.R.3s16m5M White square with red borders marked '2 B' on black metal cylindrical column with a viewing platform 12m

C3350 **South breakwater** 55°43'·6N 21°04'·6E Fl.G.3s15m5M White triangle with green borders marked '1 B' on black metal cylindrical column with viewing platform 12m

Harbour communications
Klaipėda Port Control ✆ +370 46 499799
Klaipėda Traffic VHF Ch 09, 16

General

Klaipėda is a pleasant, friendly town, not without charm. It was founded in 1252 and taken over by the Teutonic Knights who fortified it in 1404. Since then its ownership has been in constant dispute. Its industry was established by the Germans and it has a large port and shipbuilding complex. The waterway leads to the Curonian Lagoon, a large inland expanse of water separated from the sea by the narrow, sandy Curonian Spit.

There is an interesting maritime museum and an aquarium on the west bank of the river not far from the yacht club. On the east side an old three-master, now a restaurant, is moored near the centre of town. Amber is mined locally, and amber jewellery and ornaments are readily available. Small pieces can sometimes be found on the beach following onshore winds.

The town of Nida, some 48km from Klaipėda, is set among attractive surroundings on the sandspit which separates the Curonian Lagoon from the Baltic Sea. Nida is accessible by bus or taxi as well as water. It has a large harbour where yachts can berth and the World Heritage Centre makes an interesting visit.

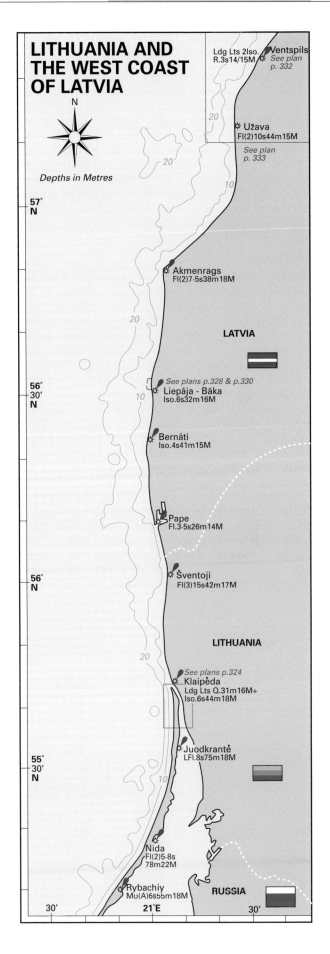

LITHUANIA AND THE WEST COAST OF LATVIA

N

Depths in Metres

Ldg Lts 2Iso.R.3s14/15M Ventspils *See plan p. 332*

Užava Fl(2)10s44m15M

See plan p. 333

Akmenrags Fl(2)7·5s38m18M

LATVIA

See plans p.328 & p.330
Liepāja - Bāka Iso.6s32m16M

Bernāti Iso.4s41m15M

Pape Fl.3·5s26m14M

Šventoji Fl(3)15s42m17M

LITHUANIA

See plans p.324
Klaipėda Ldg Lts Q.31m16M+ Iso.6s44m18M

Juodkrantė LFl.8s75m18M

Nida Fl(2)5·8s 78m22M

Rybachiy Mo(A)6s5m18M **RUSSIA**

Approach and entry

Approach waypoint 55°43'·78N 21°00'·00E

The town and the harbour entrance are clearly visible from seaward and the entrance, heavily used by commercial shipping, is well marked for entry at any time, though it would become hazardous for small craft in strong onshore (westerly) winds.

From the fairway buoy follow the leading line on 092·5°. It is important to keep to the centre of the channel at the entrance, as the remains of a wrecked ship lie to starboard and there is a danger of general industrial debris in the shallows on both sides. (By the time of publication of this book the well-marked wreck may have been removed).

Berthing

During 2008 the yacht harbours of Klaipėda underwent massive reconstruction and this is on-going in 2010. There will be two yacht harbours on the Klaipėda town side of the lagoon and another on the west bank. Visiting yachts should berth at the Cruise Terminal Marina which is clearly visible from the waterway and located just beyond the entrance to the River Dané. Smaller yachts may be directed to proceed into the River Dané (which is also used frequently by the ferry) and thence through the opening bridge into Old Castle Harbour. It is planned that there will be berths for visitors in both harbours. Berthing will either be alongside or to finger pontoons. Good shelter and all facilities are available in both harbours.

Alternatively yachts may berth at the Klaipėda Sailing Centre yacht harbour at Smiltyné, which is located in rural surroundings on the west bank about half a mile south of the ferry. There are two basins for yachts, the inner carrying up to 2m and the outer (upstream) basin slightly more. Mooring is bows-to with stern lines to posts. A yacht club member or official may indicate which berth to take and assist with mooring lines. The Harbour captain's office, located on the upper floor of the club building, is permanently staffed.

Whilst the Klaipėda Sailing Centre yacht harbour is thought to be safe in all weathers, strong onshore winds can send enough swell along the two miles of river to make the berths uncomfortable.

Klaipėda Harbour is a commercial waterway and anchoring is not permitted.

Services for yachts

Old Castle Harbour and Cruise Terminal Harbour

Water and electricity are available in both harbours with toilets and showers in facilities building which also houses the harbour office and a chandlery. Access with a keycard. Washing and drying machines also available. A fuel berth is planned – seek advice of harbourmaster. Otherwise fuel must be transported in cans from a local fuel station. Good repair and craning facilities.

Smiltyné Yacht Harbour

Water and electricity are available on the quay, with toilets and showers in the club building. Repairs and craning can be organised through the harbour captain, but the availability of parts and equipment is likely to be limited. Facilities and spares should be better at the Old Castle Harbour side.

General facilities

The town centre is very close to Old Castle and the Cruise Terminal harbours but on the opposite side of the river from Smiltyné (ferry a short walk from the club). Shops are well stocked and there is a good

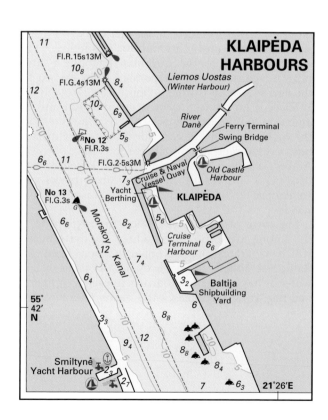

Smiltynė yacht harbour *F. and G. Cattell*

Modern architecture in Klaipėda *E. Redfern*

indoor/outdoor market. There are several restaurants in the town and a small café at the Smiltynė yacht club.

The capital, Vilnius lying over 300km to the SE, is accessible by bus but necessitates an overnight stay. It is a cosmopolitan city of over 550,000 inhabitants with many architectural traces of its changing history. In 2009 it was European Capital of Culture.

Communications and travel

For details of the phone system see *Communications*, page 322. Public Wi-Fi is available at the harbour charged by credit or debit card to obtain an enabling code. Internet access is available at both the public library and the telephone office.

Taxis and minibuses provide local transport, and Klaipėda is served by international bus and rail networks. The nearest major international airport is at Vilnius, with a smaller airport some 26km north near the coastal resort of Palanga.

Fisherman's markers on display at Nida *E. Redfern*

The grass mound, left, of the Old Castle beside the inner moorings at Klaipėda *F. and G. Cattell*

9. Latvia

The country

Latvia's total area of 64,589km² consists mostly of a low lying plain, though the east of the country becomes hilly. The land is crossed by a number of rivers, many of which drain into the Gulf of Rīga. The largest of these is the Daugava which rises in Russia. There are also numerous lakes, streams, marshes and bogs. Forest covers 43% of the country and peat bogs account for a further 10%. Nearly half the land is agricultural, small farms and fields often tucked away in forest clearings. The coastline extends some 500km along the Baltic Sea and the Gulf of Rīga, and is lined with sandy beaches, mostly backed by dunes and pine forest.

Latvia's harbours all lie in river mouths and in former times served fishing fleets and canning factories. With the demise of the Soviet Union the market for processed fish no longer exists and this, coupled with diminishing fish stocks, has left the fleets with little work. This has given some of the harbours opportunities to develop facilities for yachting. The major harbours Liepāja, Ventspils (which also has an oil terminal) and Rīga are ice-free ports and have commercial import/export work.

Services account for 71% of GDP and industry for about 25%. Major products are synthetic fibres, agricultural machinery, textiles, electronics, processed foods and timber. Agriculture is now of lesser importance but combined with forestry still provides about 15% of employment compared with 25% for industry and 60% for services. Forestry provides important exports such as paper and sawn timber, and both major and minor harbours export timber in all its forms. 78% of trade is with the EU and major exports comprise machinery, electrical equipment, wood, metal and mineral products.

History and the future

Present day Latvia devolves from the major tribes whose names live on in the regions – Kurzeme, Zemgale, Vidzeme and Latgale. By the 13th century the Teutonic Knights arrived, converting with the sword, followed by German merchants and traders. Rīga joined the Hanseatic League in 1282. Over the centuries the great powers of the region – Poland, Denmark, Sweden and Russia – fought wars over the area and each took parts of the country. During the 17th and early 18th centuries Latvia benefited from a period of beneficent rule under the Swedes, a time when universal education was introduced, but in the later 18th century Imperial Russia was in the ascendancy, Russian rule ending only with the 1917 revolution. A few years of independence came between the two World Wars, but with the outbreak of the Second World War Latvia came under first

The people, the church and the language

The total population of some 2·3 million is made up of 59% Latvians and 28% Russians, the remainder being Belorussians, Ukrainians, Poles and Lithuanians. Now 1.86 million (81% of the population) have the status of 'citizen', which is dependent upon both residency and proficiency in Latvian.

The majority of Christians are Lutherans, but many follow the Orthodox faith and in the east of the country there is a predominance of Catholics. The national language is Latvian although most speak Russian, many understand German, and English is becoming more widespread, particularly amongst the young.

English-speaking visitors to Latvia invariably receive a warm welcome.

Formalities

EU passport holders do not require a visa. The website of the Latvian Embassy (www.am.gov.lv/en/london) lists countries whose citizens do not need visas. If a visa is needed contact the Consular Office of the Latvian Embassy at 45 Nottingham Place, London W1M 3FE, ① 0207 312 0040, Email embassy.uk@mfa.gov.lv. The British Embassy in Rīga can be contacted on ① +371 6777 4700, Email british.embassy@apollo.lv, www.ukinlatvia.fco.gov.uk.

Formal reporting is no longer required for passages between Latvia and another Schengen country. Vessels arriving from or departing to a non-Schengen country, such as Russia, must complete immigration procedures and should contact the authorities on arrival or before departure.

Latvian Border guards are on duty in most harbours and now perform a role as coastguards. In some harbours (Pāvilosta and Liepāja) a yacht declaration form (essentially a crew list) has to be completed at the harbour office and this information is subsequently forwarded to the border guards.

Although nationals are required to have a 'boat driving licence', this does not apply to skippers of foreign flagged vessels. In practice, skippers and crew would be advised to carry any certificates of competence wherever they are sailing – see page 8.

The flag is a horizontal tricolour of maroon, white and maroon.

Practicalities

Time

Latvia is in the Eastern European time zone (UT+2 in winter/UT+3 in summer). 'Summer time' starts and ends on the same dates as the rest of the EU.

Money

The currency is the lats (plural: lati), divided into 100 santīmi (singular: santīms). All major currencies can be readily exchanged at banks or exchange booths, and cash is easily obtained from ATMs. Credit cards are widely used, but payment of harbour fees in most harbours must be made in cash.

Shopping

Food and other basic commodities are in plentiful supply in shops and markets. In smaller towns, supplies are available from small general stores where the choice is not as great as in the cities.

Public holidays

Public holidays occur on: 1 January, Good Friday, Easter Sunday and Monday, 1 May (Labour Day), 4 May (Declaration of Independence), the second Sunday in May (Mothers' Day), 23 June (Ligo, the midsummer festival), 24 June (St John's Day), 18 November (Independence or National Day), 25–26 December, 31 December.

There are, in addition, Remembrance Days on which some services may not be open.

Hotels and restaurants

Facilities of varying standards and prices are available, and many modern hotels have been built over the past few years. Restaurants of all types and price ranges can be found but in general the standard of cuisine is excellent and very well presented.

Communications

Public telephone, mobile phones and the mail system all function efficiently. Wi-Fi and internet access is available in Liepāja, Pāvilosta, Ventspils and Rīga. It is limited elsewhere on the coast, but available in major inland towns.

National and international calls may be made from public phone boxes which operate on cards (2 and 5 Lats) obtainable from shops or street kiosks. To ring abroad from Latvia dial 00 followed by the country code, area code (omitting any initial 0) and number.

The country code for Latvia is 371 followed by the 8 digits which comprise Latvian telephone numbers (this includes the area code).

Mobile numbers begin with a 2 and landlines with a 6.

VHF Ch 16 should be monitored while on passage as the coastguard at Pope and Kolka lights may call up passing craft including yachts.

Travel

Rīga has an international airport with direct flights to many European and Scandinavian cities, while the airport at Liepāja operates international flights to Denmark and Germany (AirBaltic) and domestic flights to Rīga. Rīga can be reached by bus and train from cities across Europe – it is possible to travel all the way to London by Eurolines – and there are bus connections to Berlin via Vilnius and Warsaw. There is also a good internal network for bus and train travel.

As of 2009 ferries sailed from Rīga to Lübeck (Germany) and Stockholm (Sweden), and from Ventspils to Rostock (Germany), and Nynashamn (Sweden). However routes and operating companies change frequently and the current situation should be checked before any plans are made. Useful website for ferry information www.ferrylines.com.

Soviet, then German and then Soviet rule again, the latter lasting until independence in 1991.

In the years since independence Latvia has made great strides towards improving facilities and services. In particular, yacht tourism is seen as a possible future use for its under-used harbours. Whilst some plans have not progressed, Pāvilosta and Liepāja, with financial help from the EU, have brought plans to fruition. There is some unemployment and problems with the economy, but while life can be difficult for the older generation living on small state pensions, the younger generation views the future with optimism. On the political front, Latvia joined both the EU and NATO in 2004 and signed the Schengen agreement at the end of 2007.

Internet sites

The Latvians were quick to establish their country's presence on the internet and the following sites (in English unless otherwise stated) only scratch the surface of what is available:

www.latviatravel.com – an impressive site compiled by Patricia Ltd, a Rīga-based tourism group, which contains much practical information for visitors plus other useful links

www.inyourpocket.com/latvia/en/ – the homepage of the Latvia in Your Pocket guide

www.latviatourism.lv – Latvian Tourist Department

www.rigathisweek.lv – the homepage of the Rīga *This Week* guide

www.jurasadministracija.lv – the Maritime Administration of Latvia, including the Latvian Hydrographic Service and current chart catalogue

www.am.gov.lv/en/london – the Latvian Embassy in London

www.ukinlatvia.fco.gov.uk/en – the British Embassy in Rīga, Latvia

Cruising

The Latvian coastline covers most of the Gulf of Rīga as well as part of the Baltic Sea. It is no longer possible for any other than shallow draught vessels to sail into the River Lielupe due to silting at the river mouth. Unmasted craft can enter the river via the Daugava and Bullupe rivers. Particular care should be taken when transiting the Irbensky Strait due to extensive shoals outside the buoyed channels.

There are few suitable places to anchor with the possible exception of the River Lielupe (but see comment about entry above).

Yacht services and chandlery

Fuel can generally be obtained either through special delivery organised by a yacht club or harbour captain, or by cans carried from the nearest filling station. There are fuelling berths in the River Daugava 5M north of Rīga and at Pāvilosta.

Charts, pilots and cruising guides

British Admiralty and Latvian Hydrographic Service
charts cover the coast. British Admiralty charts are
useful for passage planning but for detailed
navigation the Latvian charts should be used. Those
charts which are specific to an area or harbour are
listed under individual harbour details. See the
Appendix, page 362, for sources.

Set of Charts of Latvia for Yachts (16 charts covering the
coast from just south of Klaipėda (Lithuania) to the
southern end of Moon Sound including southern
coast of Saaremaa (Estonia). Also includes detailed
harbour charts for all Latvian ports)

Harbours of the Baltic States, F & G Cattell, available
through the Cruising Association and major nautical
suppliers in Scandinavia

Baltic Pilot Volume II (NP 19)

Pilot of Baltic Sea, Latvian Coast, Maritime
Administration of Latvia. 2002. Updated by *Notices
to Mariners* (www.lhd.lv/ATONLV/?gnotice=1).

Advice regarding craning and repair facilities
should also be sought from the yacht club or
harbour captain, but other than in Rīga the
availability of parts and equipment is likely to be
limited.

Local yachts are taken ashore during winter and a
few foreign yachts are beginning to overwinter.
Anyone planning to overwinter should check the
options early in the season and ensure that their
insurers are agreeable. At present the only problem is
the lack of suitable cradles although it is sometimes
possible to have a local cradle adapted. Twin keeled
craft can easily be accommodated.

Yacht Clubs

Yachts clubs are run as businesses and own a number
of yachts but private yacht ownership is also
increasing. The clubs at Rīga and on the River
Daugava are active and welcoming.

Radio communications and weather information

Details of the above, including Search and Rescue,
GMDSS, Coast Radio Stations, Weather Bulletins,
Navigational Warnings, NAVTEX, Weatherfax
transmissions and weather forecasts on the internet
can be found on page 370 in the Appendix.

Details of VHF channels and call signs will be
found under each harbour heading. In addition,
weather forecasts and navigational warnings are
broadcast in the Liepāja area on Ch 11 at 0805 and
2005 LT, by Rīga Port on VHF Ch 11 at 0805 and
2005 LT.

VHF Ch 16 should be monitored while on passage
as the coastguard at Pape and Kolka lights may call
up passing craft including yachts.

Regulated Area 117

If sailing from Gdańsk to southwest Latvia or vice
versa you may wish to pass through this area. See
plan on page 318 and details on page 315.

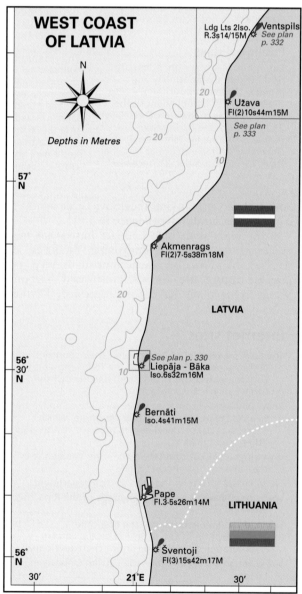

9a. Latvia
Baltic Sea coast

Liepāja

56°31'N 21°01'E

Distances
Klaipėda 50M, South Gotland 80M, Ventspils 55M

Charts
UKHO 2288, 2231, 2289
Latvian 1253, 1023, 1016, 2259, 3280, 3700 plus Set of
  Charts of Latvia for Yachts

Lights
C3390 **Bernāti** 56°22'·9N 20°58'·9E Iso.W.4s41m15M Red
  planking on metal framework tower 21m
C3396 **Liepāja-Bāka** 56°31'·0N 20°59'·5E Iso.W.6s32m16M
  000° -vis-180° Round tower, red and white bands
  30m
C3442 **Akmenrags** 56°49'·9N 21°03'·4E
  Fl(2)W.7·5s38m18M 000° -vis- 225° Red round stone
  tower 37m
C3396·2 **Central entrance, Ldg Lts 067·7°** *Front* 56°32'·7N
  20°59'·9E Iso.W.3s21m12M 064°-vis-072° White
  rectangle, black stripe on white framework tower
  20m
C3396·21 *Rear*, 984m from front, Iso.W.3s33m14M Red
  rectangle, white stripe on framework tower 30m
C3396·7 **Central entrance, north side** 56°32'·3N 20°57'·9E
  Iso.R.4s10m3M Red round column with platform 5m
C3396·6 **Central entrance, south side** 56°32'·2N
  20°57'·9E Iso.G.4s15m2M Green round column with
  platform 5m
C3397 **South entrance, Ldg Lts 112·4°** *Front* 56°31'·4N
  20°59'·7E Iso.G.2s33m9M White rectangle, black
  stripe on framework tower 30m
C3397·1 *Rear* 422m from front Iso.G.2s49m9M White
  rectangle, black stripe on framework tower 45m
  Both lights visible on leading line only
C3396·5 **South entrance, north side** 56°31'·8N 20°58'·1E
  Iso.R.2s9m3M Red round column with platform 5m
C3396·4 **South entrance, south side** 56°31'·7N 20°58'·1E
  Iso.G.2s11m2M Green round column with platform
  5m

Harbour communications
Liepāja 1 Harbour control VHF Ch 11, 16. (A reply is
  more likely on the former).
Harbour ① +371 634 88288
  Email yachting@promenadehotel.lv
  www.promenadehotel.lv

General

Liepāja (pronounced *Leea-pie-ya*) is Latvia's third major port, handling mainly grain and timber but also with a shipyard, naval base and fishing harbour. Under the Soviet system the city had many factories and was a centre for the manufacture of ladies' underwear, but most now lie idle and unemployment is high. The town centre, which has been refurbished, straddles the canal which connects Lake Liepāja to the Baltic Sea.

Approach and entry

Approach waypoint (fairway buoy) 56°30'N 20°49'E

The approaches to Liepāja harbour are shallow and should be regarded as unsafe in bad weather. Either the southern or the central entrances should be used, as the northern entrance is reported to be foul and unsafe. From the fairway, the leading line to the southern entrance is 112·4° and to the central entrance 067·7°.

The outer harbour, enclosed by the breakwaters, has numerous wrecks and is very shallow, particularly at the southern end. It is thus imperative to follow the buoyage and leading marks, and not to stray outside the marked channel.

For the yacht harbour, follow the Tirdzniecības Kanāls for about one and a half km towards the first bridge.

Anchoring is not permitted.

Permission is required to leave harbour in adverse weather conditions – Force 7 and above.

Berthing

The yacht harbour is located on the starboard side of the channel just below the first bridge, with berthing alongside wooden staging or a concrete quay. It may be necessary to raft up, depending on the space available although there are plans to lay out pontoons with finger berths.

Liepāja harbour visitors' pontoon *F. and G. Cattell*

9. LATVIA

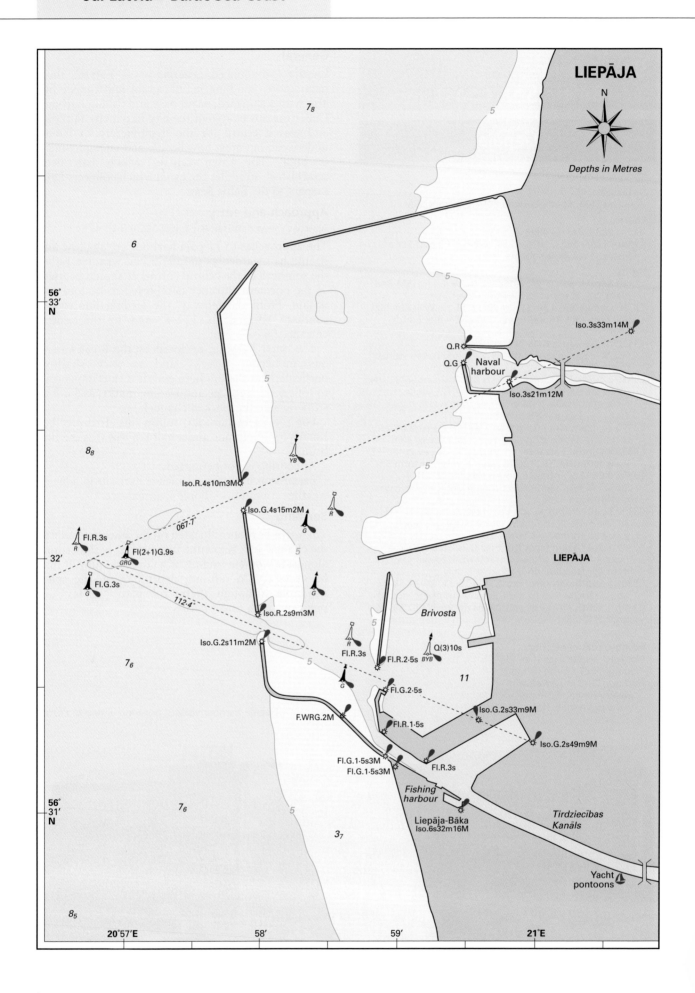

LIEPĀJA

N

Depths in Metres

7₈

5

6

56°
33′
N

Iso.3s33m14M

Q.R

Q.G · Naval
harbour

Iso.3s21m12M

8₈

YB

Iso.R.4s10m3M

5

Iso.G.4s15m2M

R

067·7

Fl.R.3s
R

Fl(2+1)G.9s
GRG

G

56°
32′

Fl.G.3s
G

LIEPĀJA

112·4

Iso.R.2s9m3M

G

5

Brivosta

Iso.G.2s11m2M

R

Q(3)10s
BYB

7₆

Fl.R.3s

Fl.R.2·5s

11

G

5

Fl.G.2·5s

F.WRG.2M

Iso.G.2s33m9M

Fl.R.1·5s

Iso.G.2s49m9M

Fl.G.1·5s3M
Fl.G.1·5s3M

Fl.R.3s

56°
31′
N

7₆

Fishing
harbour

Tirdziecības
Kanāls

3₇

Liepāja-Bāka
Iso.6s32m16M

Yacht
pontoons

8₅

20°57′E   58′   59′   21°E

Services for yachts

The yacht harbour now belongs to the Promenade Hotel situated facing the quay. Water and electricity are available on the quay, with toilets, showers, laundry facilities and sauna at the harbour office within the hotel complex. The harbourmaster advises that diesel from the fuel berth along the channel is not of suitable quality for yachts and it is preferable to obtain supplies in containers from a nearby filling station. For repair facilities consult the harbourmaster.

General facilities

Post Office, banks, restaurants and supermarket are all conveniently located in nearby streets. The shops are well stocked and the open air and indoor markets are full of excellent fresh produce.

Communications and travel

Card-operated telephones in the town, Wi-Fi in the hotel at the harbour and internet access at the public library.

Trains and buses run to Rīga and Ventspils but there are no longer any ferries. See *Travel*, page 327. The airport has international flights to Denmark and Germany and domestic flights to Rīga.

The Pape Light south of Liepāja *F. and G. Cattell*

Pāvilosta

56°53'N 21°11'E
UKHO chart 2288
Latvian chart 2101 plus *Set of Charts of Latvia for Yachts*.

A small port at the mouth of the River Saka on the Baltic Sea coast. Entry and exit considered dangerous in winds over Force 5 (20 knots). A new yacht harbour on the starboard side on entry opened in 2008. Alongside berthing. Toilets, showers, washing and drying machine available in harbour building. Wi-Fi at harbour. Fuel berth just upriver. www.pavilostamarina.lv.

Small shops and cafes in village on opposite side of river where there is also a small pontoon and shore facilities for visiting yachts.

Ventspils

57°24'N 21°32'E
See plan on page 332

Distances
Liepāja 55M, South Gotland 95M, Fårösund 85M, Roomassaare 65M, Roja 70M, Rīga 115M

Charts
UKHO 2223, 2226, 2277
Latvian 1252, 1022, 1023, 1014, 1015, 2257, 2100 plus Set of Charts of Latvia for Yachts

Lights
C3448 **Užava** 57°12'·6N 21°24'·9E Fl(2)W.10s44m15M 340° -vis-198° Racon White round stone tower with balcony 19m
C3450 Ldg Lts 143·7° *Front* 57°23'·7N 21°32'·5E Iso.R.3s28m14M 136° -vis-152° Red rectangle, white stripe, on framework tower 25m
C3450·1 *Rear* 0·5M from front, Iso.R.3s45m15M 128° -vis-160° Red rectangle, white stripe, on framework tower 35m
C3470 Oviši 57°34'·1N 21°43'·0E LFl.W.7.5s38m15M 010° -vis-223° Racon White round stone tower 37m
C3451 **North breakwater** 57°24'·5N 21°31'·6E Fl(2)R.3s14m4M White round concrete tower, red lantern 11m
C3452 **South breakwater** 57°24'·3N 21°31'·5E Fl(2)G.3s14m3M White round concrete tower, green lantern 11m

Harbour communications
Ventspils Vessel Traffic ☎ 371 6362 1040
    VHF Ch 09, 16
Ventspils Yacht Harbour ☎ +371 636 20151 and +371 294 21049

General

Founded in 1343 but with a castle dating from 1290, Ventspils is a substantial commercial port and oil terminal providing excellent shelter. It is the nearest Latvian port to Gotland, Sweden.

The town is attractive with wide, tree-lined streets and parks and has all the normal facilities. If time permits take a bus to the charming small town of Kuldiga, which has the widest waterfall in Europe.

Approach and entry

Approach waypoints
From north: fairway buoy 57°28'N 21°25'E
From south: fairway buoy 57°26'N 21°24'E

The approach is via a straight, buoyed channel to the harbour entrance. It would be unwise to stray from the channel due to a number of dangerous wrecks in the vicinity. Entry is straightforward by day or night, although a detailed chart is necessary for the latter.

Berthing

Yachts berth at the western end of the fish dock. Keep to the starboard side of the harbour, and head for a large grey/white building. Turn to starboard just before the building and moor at the head of the basin in front of the harbour office building, bows to staging and stern to a buoy. Anchoring is not permitted.

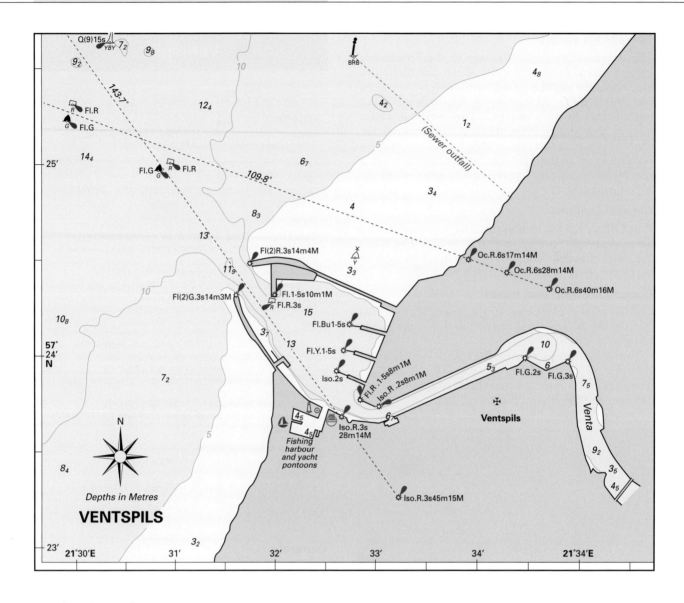

VENTSPILS

Depths in Metres

Services for yachts

Electricity is available on the quayside and water from the harbour building opposite the moorings (where there are also toilets, showers and laundry facilities). Fuel can be delivered in cans by arrangement with the harbour office. The harbour staff may also be able to assist with limited repair facilities.

General facilities

Bar in the harbour building, and small general store outside the dock gates. For shops, banks and restaurants, plus indoor and open air markets, it is necessary to go into the town some 2·5km away.

Communications/travel

Wi-Fi at the harbour. Card-operated telephones, and internet access at the public library and internet cafés. From Ventspils it is possible to travel by bus or train all over Latvia, or across Europe, via Rīga. Car hire can be arranged via the harbour office. Ferries to Nynashamn (Sweden), and Rostock (Germany).

The visitors' pontoon at Ventspils *S. Carnegie*

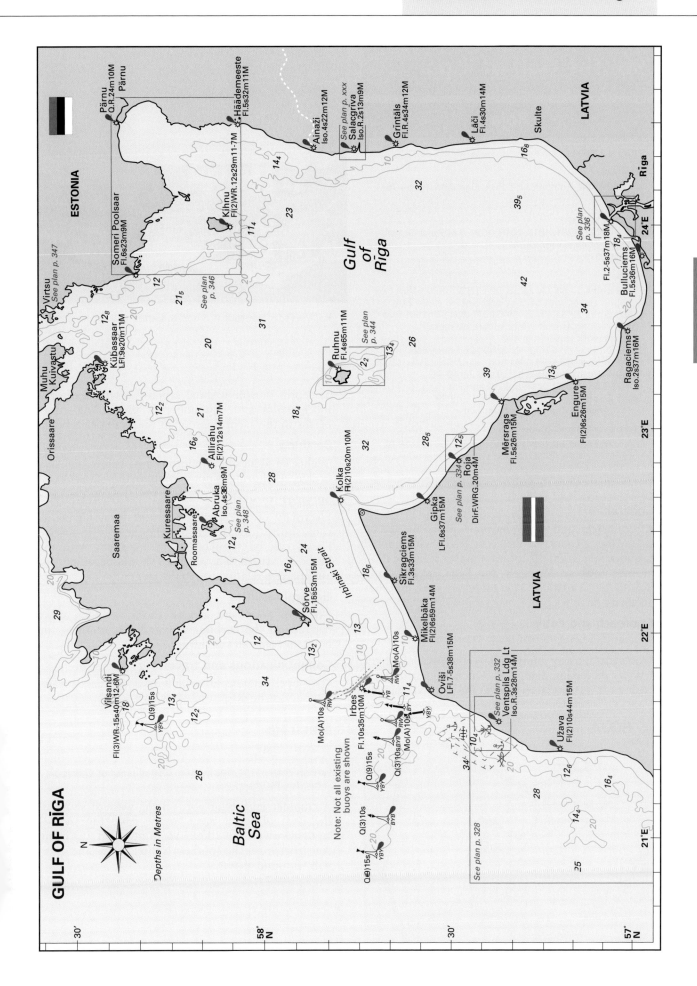

9. LATVIA

GULF OF RĪGA

Depths in Metres

N

Baltic Sea

Gulf of Rīga

ESTONIA

LATVIA

LATVIA

Rīga

Note: Not all existing buoys are shown

Pärnu
Q.R.24m10M
Pärnu

Häädemeeste
Fl.5s32m11M

Ainaži
Iso.4s22m12M

Salacgrīva
Iso.R.2s13m9M
See plan p. xxx

Grīntāls
Fl.R.4s34m12M

Lāči
Fl.4s30m14M

Skulte

Kihnu
Fl(2)WR.12s29m11-7M

Someri Poolsaar
Fl.6s23m9M

Virtsu
See plan p. 347

Muhu
Kuivastu

Orissaare

Saaremaa

Kübassaar
LFl.9s20m11M

Kuressaare
See plan p. 348

Roomassaare

Abruka
Iso.4s33m9M

Allirahu
Fl(2)12s14m7M

Sõrve
Fl.15s53m15M

Irbīnśki Strait

Ruhnu
Fl.4s65m11M
See plan p. 344

Fl.2.5s37m18M

Bulluciems
Fl.5s36m16M

Ragaciems
Iso.2s37m16M

See plan p. 336

Mērsrags
Fl.5s26m15M

Roja
DirF.WRG.20m4M
See plan p. 334

Engure
Fl(2)6s26m15M

Gipka
LFl.6s37m15M

Kolka
Fl(2)10s20m10M

Sīkragciems
Fl.3s33m15M

Mikelbāka
Fl(2)6s59m14M

Ovīši
LFl.7.5s38m15M

Ventspils Ldg Lt
Iso.R.3s28m14M
See plan p. 332

Užava
Fl(2)10s44m15M

See plan p. 328

Vilsandi
Fl(3)WR.15s40m12-6M

Q(9)15s
YBY

Irbes
Fl.10s35m10M

Mo(A)10s
RW

Mo(A)10s

Mo(A)10s
YB

Mo(A)10s
RW

Q(9)15s
YBY

Q(3)10s
BYB

Q(3)10s
YBY

Q(9)15s
YBY

Q(9)15s
YBY

9b. The Gulf of Rīga

Roja

57°30′N 22°48′E

Distances
Ventspils 70M, Roomassaare 45M, Rīga 50M, Pärnu 75M

Charts
UKHO 2215, 2226
Latvian 1022, 1251, 1012, 1013, 1021, 3215 plus *Set of Charts of Latvia for Yachts*
Estonian 519

Lights
C3478 **Kolka** 57°48′·0N 22°38′·0E Fl(2)W.10s20m10M Red round tower with balcony and lantern room 21m.
C3486 **Gipka** 57°34′·2N 22°39′·5E LFl.W.6s37m15M Two red rectangles over white square on metal framework tower 30m.
C3489 Dir Lt. 215° 57°30′·5N 22°48′·6E F Sectored WRG20mW7M R4M G4M Red triangular tower 18.5m.
C3489·3 **Northwest mole** 57°30′·7N 22°48′·7E Fl.G.3s6m2M White round column 3m
C3489·4 **Southeast mole** 57°30′·6N 22°48′·8E Fl.R.3s6m2M Red round column 3m

Harbour communications
Rojas Osta (Port Authority) ☏ +371 6 32 69315 *VHF* 10, 16

Roja, visitors' pontoons   *F. and G. Cattell*

General

A commercial and fishing harbour (pronounced *Roy ya*) in the entrance to the Roja River with limited facilities for yachts. Its location makes it useful if on passage between Ventspils and Rīga, or Rīga and Ruhnu or Saaremaa. The town is small but has adequate facilities.

Approach and entry

Approach waypoint (fairway buoy) 57°31′N 22°49′E

From the fairway buoy follow the sectored light F.WRG on leading line 215°. Once inside the outer harbour it is essential to keep to the marked channel, as depths outside it shoal rapidly. Pass between the inner moles and continue past the fishing vessel berths to the yacht pontoon at the head of harbour.

Berthing

Yachts lie alongside a pontoon just below the road bridge. Anchoring is not permitted.

Services for yachts

Electricity on the pontoon, water from tap at its root, showers and toilets in a mobile cubicle nearby. Diesel can be supplied by arrangement with the harbour captain, whose advice should be sought for any matters relating to repairs etc.

General facilities

Adequate food and general shops within a short distance of the harbour. Bar and restaurant at the hotel and a small café nearby.

Communications and travel

Card-operated telephones and internet access at café. Bus services to Rīga and elsewhere.

Mērsrags

57°20′N 23°08′E
UKHO chart 2215
Latvian charts 1251, 1021, 1273, 3250 plus *Set of Charts of Latvia for Yachts*

A commercial/fishing port on the western shore of the Gulf of Rīga, open to the east. Entrance is straightforward; in 2009 a yacht pontoon was being constructed on the southern shore. Shops and cafés will be found ashore.

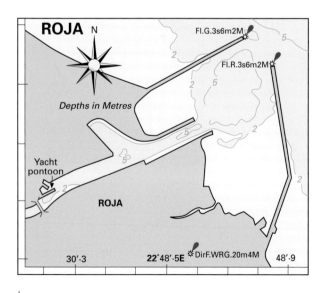

ROJA N
Fl.G.3s6m2M
Fl.R.3s6m2M
Depths in Metres
Yacht pontoon
ROJA
30′·3
22°48′·5E
DirF.WRG.20m4M
48′·9

The yacht moorings at Mērsrags on the Gulf of Rīga
F. and G. Cattell

Engure

57°10′N 23°14′E
UKHO chart 2215
Latvian charts 1021, 1273 plus *Set of Charts of Latvia for Yachts*

A small fishing harbour on the western shore of the Gulf of Rīga, open to the east. Due to silting in recent times the channel has shifted making the leading marks misleading. The buoyed channel must be followed but there are reports of yachts grounding in the approach. If attempted, entry should be in daylight and calm conditions only. Fishing nets may extend up to a mile eastwards on the north side of the entrance. Engure Yacht Club is a floating building. A few stern buoys are laid out for local craft and visitors should either lie alongside the yacht club or stern anchor. Shops and restaurants in village.

Engure yacht club and pontoon   *F. and K. Williams*

Jūrmala

56°59′N 23°53′E

This famous holiday resort/health spa is best visited by train from Rīga as the harbour entrance has silted and is dangerous to approach in anything but calm conditions. The last reported depth on the bar was 1m (2009) and still silting. For unmasted craft there is a possible entry via the River Bullupe from the River Daugava.

The shallow entrance to Jūrmala with the River Bullupe on the right   *F. and G. Cattell*

The rail bridge over the River Lielupe. In *Racundra's Third Cruise* Arthur Ransome describes having to wait for this to open on his way up to Jūmala   *F. and G. Cattell*

9. LATVIA

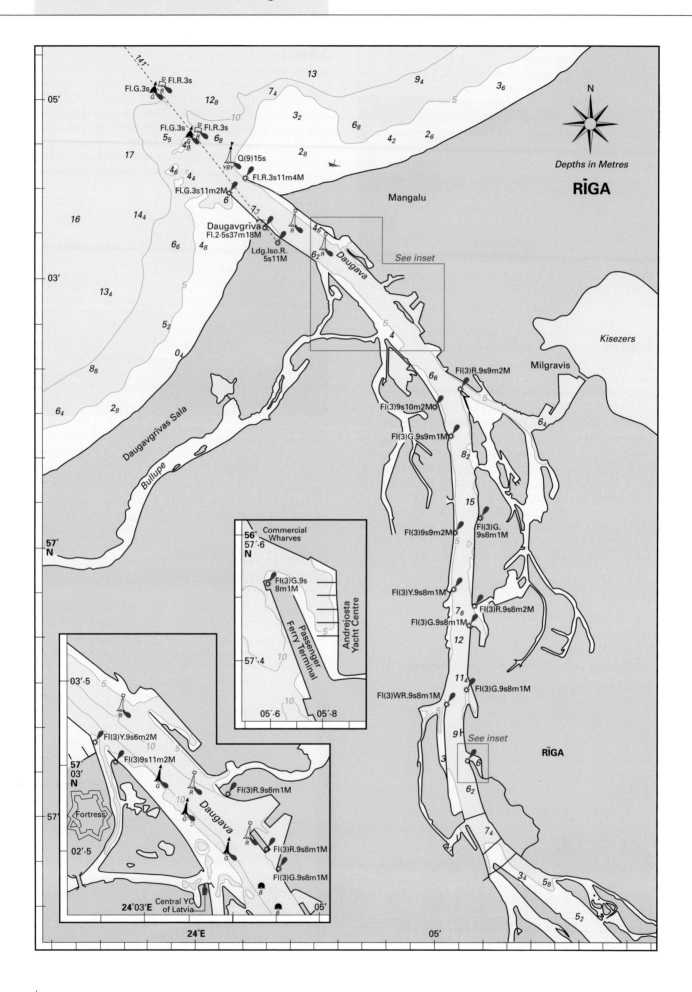

141°

Fl.R.3s
Fl.G.3s
G
R

13

9₄

3₆

12₈

7₄

3₂

10

6₈

5

Fl.G.3s Fl.R.3s
G R
5₅ 6₈
4₈

17

2₈

4₂

2₆

Q(9)15s
YBY

Fl.R.3s11m4M

4₆ 4₄

Fl.G.3s11m2M

6

16 14₄ 7₇

Daugavgriva
Fl.2·5s37m18M
Ldg.Iso.R.
5s11M

4₆ 4
R Daugava

6₂
R

Mangalu

N

Depths in Metres

RĪGA

See inset

6₆ 5

Kisezers

03'

13₄

5

4

Fl(3)R.9s9m2M
R

Milgravis

5₂

0₄

Fl(3)9s10m2M
R

6₄

8₈

2₈

Fl(3)G.9s9m1M

8₂

6₄ 2₈

Daugavgrivas Sala

Bullupe

15

56°
57'·6
N

Commercial
Wharves

Fl(3)9s9m2M

Fl(3)G.
9s8m1M

5

57°
N

Fl(3)G.9s
8m1M

5

Andrejosta
Yacht Centre

Fl(3)Y.9s8m1M

Fl(3)R.9s8m2M
R

7₆

Fl(3)G.9s8m1M

57'·4

Passenger
Ferry Terminal

10

12

57'

03'·5 5

11₄

Fl(3)WR.9s8m1M

Fl(3)G.9s8m1M

10

10

05'·6 05'·8

9

See inset

RĪGA

Fl(3)Y.9s6m2M

10 5

6

6₂

Fl(3)9s11m2M
G R

57°
03'
N

Fortress

Fl(3)R.9s6m1M
R

10
5

3

7₄

57'

Daugava

G
R

Fl(3)R.9s8m1M
R

4₄

3₄ 5₈

02'·5

G

Fl(3)G.9s8m1M
B

5₂

24°03'E Central YC
of Latvia 05'

B

24°E 05'

Riga

56°58'N 24°06'E

Distances
Roja 50M, Roomassaare 85M, Salacgriva 45M, Pärnu 80M

Charts
UKHO 2215, 2239
Latvian 1251, 1012,1021, 2253, 2102, 2103 plus *Set of Charts of Latvia for Yachts*

Lights
C3502 **Ragaciems** 57°02'·1N 23°29'·2E Iso.W.2s37m16M
    095°-vis-330° Red slatted daymark and skeletal mast
    on square framework tower 30m
C3503 **Bulluciems** 56°59'·6N 23°53'·2E Fl.W.5s36m16M
    Red and white planking on a framework tower 28m
C3526 **Daugavgriva** 57°03'·6N 24°01'·3E
    Fl.W.2.5s37m18M 035° -vis-245° Racon Round white
    concrete tower, black bands, balcony 35m
C3530 **Ldg Lts 141°** *Front* 57°03'·6N 24°01'·3E
    Iso.R.5s20m11M White daymark, red stripe, on red
    framework tower 15m
C3530·1 *Rear* 549m from front Iso.R.5s29m11M White
    rectangle, red stripe, on square red metal framework
    26m. Both lights visible on leading line only
C3528 **West breakwater** 57°03'·9N 24°00'·6E
    Fl.G.3s11m2M White concrete tower 7m
C3529 **East breakwater** 57°04'·1N 24°00'·9E
    Fl.R.3s11m4M Round red metal tower with
    balcony 7m

Harbour communications
Riga VTS VHF Ch 09, 14, 16 ☎ +371 6703 0861
Andrejosta Yacht Centre ☎ +371 6732 3221

General

Riga is the capital city of Latvia, with a population of about 800,000, and lies on the River Daugava about 8M from the sea. There is a busy port along the banks of the river between the city centre and the sea and a considerable amount of industry outside the central area. The old town remains extremely picturesque despite heavy bombing during the Second World War (a great deal of restoration is still taking place) while the newer city centre is spaciously laid out with tree-lined streets and parks.

The old town with its Hanseatic connections has many buildings of interest particularly the castle, Swedish Gate, the Powder Tower, the Dome Cathedral, St Peter's Church (take a lift to the top for a view over the entire city) and the restored House of the Blackheads. There are various museums including the Museum of the Occupation which is a chilling reminder of what this country has suffered in living memory. Riga has many fine examples of Art Nouveau.

Approach and entry
Approach waypoint (fairway buoy) 57°06'N 23°56'E

The wide river mouth with its powerful leading lights on 141° presents no problems at any time of the day or night. The river itself is wide and well marked, and normally has an outgoing current of around two knots.

Berthing

There are several yacht harbours along the river but foreign yachts normally stay at the Andrejosta Yacht Centre, which is located in a basin behind the passenger ferry terminal and just below the cable bridge. The harbour has long pontoons most with individual finger berths and one with stern buoys. It is sometimes possible for larger craft to lie alongside. Andrejosta Yacht Club owns the pontoons on the town side of the basin. There are other pontoons on the passenger terminal side but without adequate facilities and at higher cost.

The Andrejosta Yacht Harbour at Riga, looking northwest *F. and G. Cattell*

9. LATVIA

The House of the Blackheads   *F. and G. Cattell*

Below The Vansu Bridge   *E. Redfern*

Vansu Tilts and modern day Riga   *F. and G. Cattell*

Milda Freedom Monument
F. and G. Cattell

Other possibilities are the Marina Auda and Latvijas Jahta.

Anchoring is not permitted.

Services for yachts

Water and electricity are provided on the pontoons. Adequate toilet and shower facilities are available in cubicles. A washing machine in the clubhouse can be used by arrangement with the harbourmaster.

Fuel can be obtained from the fuel berth at Latvijas Jahta (Pildne) about five miles down river. The harbourmaster can arrange for repairs. *Camping gaz* bottles can be exchanged at Regate near the central market.

The Jana Seta Map Shop, 83/85 Elizabetes iela, Block 2, Rīga LV–1050, ℺ +371 6724 0894 *Fax* 6782 8039, *Email* veikals@kartes.lv, www.mapshop.lv is the largest chart supplier in the country and will despatch orders abroad. Most major credit cards are accepted.

General facilities

There is a bar in the clubhouse.

Rīga itself has all the facilities of a major city – many shops, a choice of restaurants, banks, Post Office etc. Currency exchange is readily available in hotels and kiosks and cash can be obtained from

ATMs. The market, which takes place in four ex-zeppelin hangars, is one of the largest in Europe and can provide almost anything edible.

Communications and travel

Card-operated telephones, Wi-Fi at the harbour and internet access at the public library and internet cafés.

International airport, railway and bus services within Latvia and to cities all over Europe, taxis and hire cars. Ferries to Stockholm (Sweden) and Lübeck (Germany) but routes are subject to constant change and availability should be checked in advance if necessary.

Skulte

57°19′N 24°25′E
UKHO chart 2215
Latvian charts 1012, 1021 plus *Set of Charts of Latvia for Yachts*

A small commercial harbour on the eastern shore of the Gulf of Rīga, open to the west. There is a small general store close by but little else. In 2009 the yacht pontoon had broken down and it was necessary to use the commercial quay at the head of the harbour.

Salacgrīva

57°45'N 24°21'E

Distances
Rīga 45M, Roomassaare 65M, Pärnu 40M

Charts
UKHO 2215
Latvian 1251, 1011, 1012, 1021, 3504 plus *Set of Charts of Latvia for Yachts*

Lights
C3587 **Ldg Lts 072·3°** *Front* 57°45'·4N 24°21'·2E
 Iso.R.2s13m9M White rectangle, black stripe, on
 framework tower. 10m Visible on leading line only
C3587·1 *Rear* 207m from front Iso.R.4s24m9M
 000° -vis-170° White rectangle, black stripe, on
 framework tower 18m

Harbour communications
Salacgrīva 52 (Port Authority) VHF Ch 12, 16

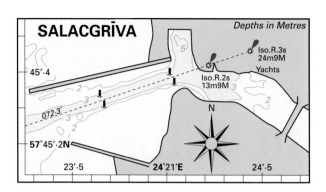

General

A small commercial port conveniently located midway between Rīga and Pärnu.

Approach and entry

Approach waypoint (fairway buoy) 57°44'N 24°17'E

The harbour entrance is well marked with buoys and leading marks on 072·3°, but becomes rough in onshore (westerly) winds. Entry/exit is restricted in winds over Force 7 (30 knots).

Berthing

There is a small pontoon for yachts with stern buoys. Anchoring is not permitted.

Services for yachts

Toilets in a portaloo are considered inadequate and it may be necessary to walk along the road to the bus station to use their facilities. Shops and restaurants in the village. Water and electricity on the pontoon.

General facilities

Bar and restaurant at the harbour, with shops and cafés in the nearby village. Internet access at the public library and Statoil fuel station.

Communications and travel

Buses to Rīga and elsewhere.

Salacgrīva *F. and G. Cattell*

Salacgrīva, looking west towards the entrance *F. and K. Williams*

10. Estonia

The country

Estonia consists for the most part of a low lying plain with higher ground towards the east. There are numerous streams and lakes including one of Europe's largest, Lake Peipsi, lying on the border with Russia. The coast is low lying and, particularly to the west, is fringed by islands which make up nearly 10% of Estonian land. The surrounding seas to the south and west are shallow.

Industry, mostly engineering and metalwork together with the mining of shale, accounts for 30% of GDP and 35% of total employment. Agriculture and forestry – about a quarter of Estonia is forested – account for 10% of GDP and 9% of total employment, forestry providing materials for the paper, timber and furniture industries.

The largest export (21% of total) is machinery and appliances, followed by mineral products (12%) and wood and articles made from wood (10%). The largest foreign investor is Sweden at almost 40% of total and Finland is the main trading partner at 25% of total.

Since independence Estonia has boosted its export trade within the European Union.

History and the future

Tacitus made mention of the Ests in the 1st century AD and their existence has been chronicled ever since. In the early 13th century the Danes invaded northern Estonia and founded Tallinn in 1219, but later sold their territories in the country to the Teutonic Knights. In their wake came merchants and traders from Germany, Tallinn becoming a member of the Hanseatic league in 1285.

In the mid 16th century the Swedes arrived, under whose rule Estonia enjoyed a period of social reform. However Sweden was defeated by Russia in the early 18th century and Estonia found itself under Imperial Russian rule. After the Russian revolution the country enjoyed a brief period of independence until the Second World War, when it shared the fate of the other Baltic States coming under Soviet, then German, and again Soviet rule, which lasted until the break up of the Soviet Union and independence in 1991.

In the years since independence the pace of change has been fast, progress rapid and Estonia has made great strides towards updating facilities and services.

Estonia orientates itself firmly towards the west and joined both the EU and NATO in 2004, signing the Schengen agreement in 2007.

Formalities

EU passport holders do not require visas. The website of the Foreign Ministry (www.vm.ee) lists countries whose citizens do not need visas. If a visa is needed contact the Estonian Consulate at 16 Hyde Park Gate, London SW7 5DG, ☎ 0207 589 3428, *Email* london@mfa.ee, www.estonia.gov.uk.

The British Embassy in Tallinn can be contacted on ☎ +372 667 4700, *Email* infotallinn@fco.gov.uk http://ukinestonia.fco.gov.uk.

Formal reporting is no longer required for passages between Estonia and another Schengen country and yachts may arrive or depart from any Estonian harbour. Vessels arriving from or departing to a non-Schengen country, such as Russia, should telephone the Border Guards on ☎ +372 619 1124 and +372 612 3411 for guidance on clearance.

According to the Estonian regulation 'Requirements for Operating Recreational Craft' skippers of recreational craft flying the Estonian flag (and skippers of foreign flagged craft whose flag state requires such) require a registration certificate and a certificate of a skipper of a recreational craft. For British-flagged craft there is no legal requirement to have such certificates when sailing in Estonian waters as there is no requirement for such under British law. In practice, skippers and crew would be advised to carry any certificates of competence wherever they are sailing – see page 8.

The Estonian flag is a horizontal tricolour of – top to bottom – blue, black and white

The people, the church and the language

Estonians are of the same race as the Finns and share a similar language. In the 20th century great numbers of the native population emigrated, and today Estonia has a total population of just under 1·4 million and an ethnic mix of which about 68% are Estonian and 26% Russian, the balance being made up of Ukrainians, Belorussians, Finns and Latvians. About 70% live in urban areas, nearly 30% in Tallinn alone. The official language is Estonian – a Finno-Ugric language – but most speak or understand Russian, though sometimes reluctantly. Finnish and German are commonly understood and many younger people are delighted to communicate in excellent English. Estonia suffered much from the Soviet policy of 'Russification', and since independence the government has introduced laws concerning not only citizenship requirements but also language ability for employment.

Estonians often describe themselves as pagan. Forcibly converted to Christianity by the Teutonic Knights, the majority of those still practising are split between the Lutheran and Orthodox churches with a smaller number adhering to the Catholic faith.

Visitors, whether they come by sea, air or land, can be assured of a warm welcome.

Practicalities

Time

Estonia is in the Eastern European time zone (UT+2 in winter/UT+3 in summer). 'Summer time' starts and ends on the same dates as the rest of the EU.

Money

The local currency is the kroon, often written as EEK, and divided into 100 sents. All major currencies can be readily exchanged at banks or exchange booths, and cash is easily obtained from ATMs. Credit cards are widely accepted but most harbours expect to be paid in cash.

Shopping

Food and other basic commodities are in plentiful supply in shops and markets. Supermarkets are popular and continue to increase in number. Tallinn is a centre for tourism, and also has a range of pricey international-style shops and boutiques.

Public holidays

Public holidays occur on: 1 January, 24 February (Independence Day), Good Friday, Easter Sunday, 1 May (May Day), Pentecost, 23 June (Victory Day), 24 June (St John's Day), 20 August (Restoration of Independence Day) and 24, 25, 26 December.

Hotels and restaurants

Facilities of varying standards and prices are available and modern hotels and restaurants continue to be built. It is still possible to obtain a decent meal for a reasonable price almost anywhere however prices throughout the country are increasing rapidly. Tallinn also has a range of high class high priced eating establishments.

Travel

Tallinn has an international airport only 3km from the city centre, with domestic airports at Pärnu and on the islands of Hiiumaa and Saaremaa (Roomassaare and Ruhnu). The country is served by a network of buses and trains, while Eurolines provides a link all the way from St Petersburg to cities in most European countries.

Tallinn has ferries and high speed jetfoil services to Helsinki and a ferry service to Stockholm. Other international ferries run from Paldiski to Kapellskär (Sweden). Internal ferries run between Rohuküla, Heltermaa (Hiiumaa) and Vormsi island; between Virtsu and Kuivastu (Muhu) and thence to Saaremaa; between Triigi (Saaremaa) and Sõru (Hiiumaa); and between Roomassaare (Saaremaa) and the small offlying island of Abruka.

Communications

There are efficient telephone and mail systems and full coverage of mobile phone networks. Internet access is widely available with many free Wi-Fi points.

National and international calls may be made from public phone boxes which operate on cards obtainable from shops or street kiosks. To obtain an international line, dial 00 followed by the country code, area code (omitting any initial 0) and number. Dialling within Estonia only the 7 digit number is required. There are no longer area codes nor an initial 0. All mobile numbers start with 5. The country code for Estonia is 372.

VHF Ch 16 should be monitored while on passage as the coastguard station at Paldiski may call up passing craft including yachts.

Charts, pilots and cruising guides

British Admiralty and Estonian charts cover the coast. British Admiralty charts are useful for passage planning but for detailed navigation the Estonian charts should be used. Those charts which are specific to an area or harbour are listed under individual harbour details. See the *Appendix*, page 362, for sources.

Charts of Estonia Vol. 1 Gulf of Finland from Narva to Paldiski. 2007

Charts of Estonia Vol. 2 Vainameri from Osmussaar to Saaremaa. 2009

Charts of Estonia Vol. 3 From Saaremaa to Ruhnu 2006

Recommended Recreational Craft Routes for Estonia

A series of small craft plans giving the recommended routes and contact information for Tallinn Bay, Haapsalu Bay, Pärnu Bay and Suur Katel Bay (Kuressaare area) have been produced and are downloadable from the Estonian Maritime Administration website www.vta.ee. Follow link to Recreational Craft

Harbours of the Baltic States, F & G Cattell, available through the Cruising Association and major nautical suppliers in Scandinavia

Baltic Pilot Volume II (NP 19)

Sailing Directions for Estonian Waters. Estonian Maritime Administration 2004. Updated by *Notices to Mariners*

Estonian Cruising Guide 2006.

Internet sites

A great deal of information about Estonia is available on the internet, much of it in English. However it should be remembered that not all sites are updated regularly.

www.tourism.ee – the well-presented website of the Estonian Tourist Board, with many useful links

www.inyourpocket.com/estonia/en/ – the homepage of the Estonia in Your Pocket guide

www.estonica.org/ – an interesting site containing well-written articles on Estonia's history, culture, natural history etc

www.ukinestonia.fco.gov.uk – the British Embassy in Tallinn, Estonia

www.estonia.gov.uk – the Estonian Embassy in London

www.marinas.nautilus.ee – website of the Estonian Cruising Guide

www.vta.ee – website of the Estonian Maritime Administration

Cruising

The most popular route for visiting yachts on passage between the Gulf of Rīga and the north coast of Estonia or Gulf of Finland is via Moon Sound, which runs between the mainland and the larger Estonian islands. Notwithstanding Arthur Ransome's well known 1923 voyage from Rīga to Helsinki described in his *Racundra's first cruise* passage through Moon Sound should not be attempted without large-scale local charts, as in places the navigable channels are narrow and the

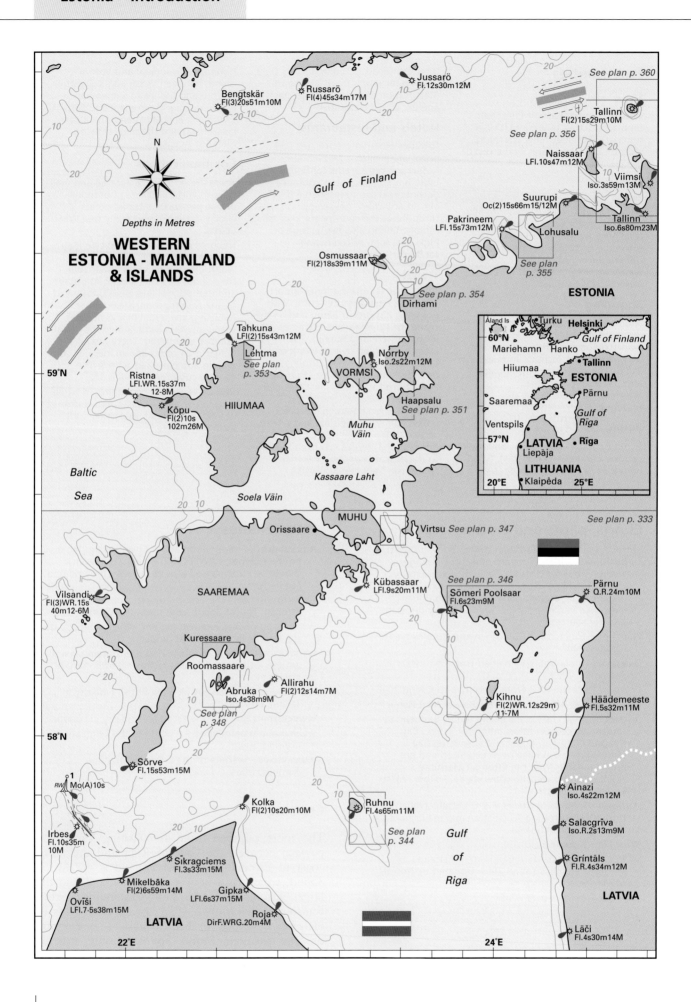

N

Depths in Metres

WESTERN
ESTONIA - MAINLAND
& ISLANDS

Gulf of Finland

Bengtskär
Fl(3)20s51m10M

Russarö
Fl(4)45s34m17M

Jussarö
Fl.12s30m12M

See plan p. 360

Tallinn
Fl(2)15s29m10M

See plan p. 356

Naissaar
LFl.10s47m12M

Viimsi
Iso.3s59m13M

Suurupi
Oc(2)15s66m15/12M

Pakrineem
LFl.15s73m12M

Tallinn
Iso.6s80m23M

Lohusalu

See plan
p. 355

ESTONIA

Osmussaar
Fl(2)18s39m11M

See plan p. 354

Dirhami

Tahkuna
LFl(2)15s43m12M

Lehtma

See plan
p. 353

Norrby
Iso.2s22m12M

VORMSI

Haapsalu
See plan p. 351

*Muhu
Väin*

Ristna
LFl.WR.15s37m
12-8M

Kõpu
Fl(2)10s
102m26M

HIIUMAA

Baltic

Sea

Kassaare Laht

Soela Väin

MUHU

Orissaare

Virtsu *See plan p. 347*

See plan p. 333

SAAREMAA

Kübassaar
LFl.9s20m11M

See plan p. 346

Sõmeri Poolsaar
Fl.6s23m9M

Pärnu
Q.R.24m10M

Vilsandi
Fl(3)WR.15s
40m12-6M

Kuressaare

Roomassaare

Abruka
Iso.4s38m9M

Allirahu
Fl(2)12s14m7M

See plan
p. 348

Kihnu
Fl(2)WR.12s29m
11-7M

Häädemeeste
Fl.5s32m11M

58°N

Sõrve
Fl.15s53m15M

1
RW Mo(A)10s

Kolka
Fl(2)10s20m10M

Ruhnu
Fl.4s65m11M

See plan
p. 344

Gulf

of

Riga

Ainazi
Iso.4s22m12M

Irbes
Fl.10s35m
10M

Sīkragciems
Fl.3s33m15M

Salacgrīva
Iso.R.2s13m9M

Mikelbāka
Fl(2)6s59m14M

Gipka
LFl.6s37m15M

Grīntāls
Fl.R.4s34m12M

Ovīši
LFl.7·5s38m15M

Roja
DirF.WRG.20m4M

LATVIA

LATVIA

Lāči
Fl.4s30m14M

22°E

24°E

Åland Is
Turku
Helsinki
60°N
Gulf of Finland
Mariehamn
Hanko
Hiiumaa
Tallinn
ESTONIA
Saaremaa
Pärnu
Gulf of
Riga
Ventspils
57°N
Rīga
LATVIA
Liepāja
LITHUANIA
20°E
Klaipêda
25°E

59°N

waters on either side are shallow and rock strewn. This applies particularly to the northern part of the passage between Vormsi and the mainland. The route is well marked with transit beacons and buoys where necessary, but it is dangerous to venture outside the channel. The complete coastline is covered by Estonian sheet charts but there are three small craft portfolios which cover the whole of Estonia and these are ideally suited for the cruising yachtsman.

Other than the major ports, caution should be exercised if approaching in darkness.

A rapid increase in privately owned yachts has lead to overcrowding, reduced spaces for visiting yachts and changed visitor locations in some harbours. This is particularly evident in Pirita (Tallinn).

Yacht services and chandlery

Fuelling berths have been established in more harbours – Pärnu, Roomassaare, Kuressaare, Haapsalu, Dirhami, Lohusalu, Tallinn (Pirita) and Vergi have facilities. Elsewhere fuel can be obtained by arrangement with the yacht club or harbourmaster.

Local gas refills are available in some harbours. Craning and repair facilities are available in the major harbours, otherwise seek advice from the harbourmaster. Chandlery and charts can be obtained at most major harbours, but it is wise to obtain charts before arrival as stocks may be limited.

Yacht Clubs

Yachting, both sail and motor, has become increasingly popular with Estonians. Many harbours have a yacht club but these are mostly owned by groups of businessmen and run as businesses, often with a hotel and restaurant open for tourists or conferences as part of the complex. The clubs may own a small fleet of racing yachts but many boats – including expensive motor yachts – are now privately owned.

Radio communications and weather information

Details of the above, including Search and Rescue, GMDSS, Coast Radio Stations, Weather Bulletins, Navigational Warnings, NAVTEX, Weatherfax transmissions and weather forecasts on the internet can be found in the Appendix on pages 370–371.

VHF radio is much used for marine communications – details of channels and callsigns will be found under each harbour heading. Weather bulletins and navigational warnings are broadcast at 0633 and 1533 LT on VHF Ch 69 by Tallinn Radio, in English and Estonian. See pages 370–371 for full details.

Formalities for those leaving or entering the Schengen area via an Estonian port

Border guard offices are now closed since Estonia signed the Schengen agreement. Skippers of yachts travelling between Estonia and Russia and thus needing clearance in or out, should telephone ☎ +372 619 1124 or +372 612 3411.

Ruhnu

57°47'N 23°16'E

Charts
Estonian charts 305, 516, 637
Charts of Estonia Vol. 3

Lights
C3482 **Ruhnu Lighthouse** 57°48'·08N 23°15'·6E
Fl.W.4s65m11M Dark brown metal tower with supporting pillars, balcony and lantern 40m

Approach waypoint on leading line 57°46'·50N 23°18'·20E
See plan on page 344.

A small island with Swedish cultural interest in Gulf of Rīga. The harbour has been redeveloped in recent years and now provides good shelter (in the inner portion) with individual finger berths. Additional alongside berthing inside the mole has less shelter from south and east. Outer part of harbour untenable in strong south easterly weather. The village is about 3km distant. Limited shopping, Post Office, bar, museum. No banks but most currencies accepted by harbour office. Leading line for approach 286·6°. Entry recommended in good visibility and moderate weather only. With the improvements Ruhnu has become a useful and convenient staging point on passages between Latvia and Estonia.

Ruhnu outer harbour mooring pontoon and, *below,* inner harbour moorings   *F. and G. Cattell*

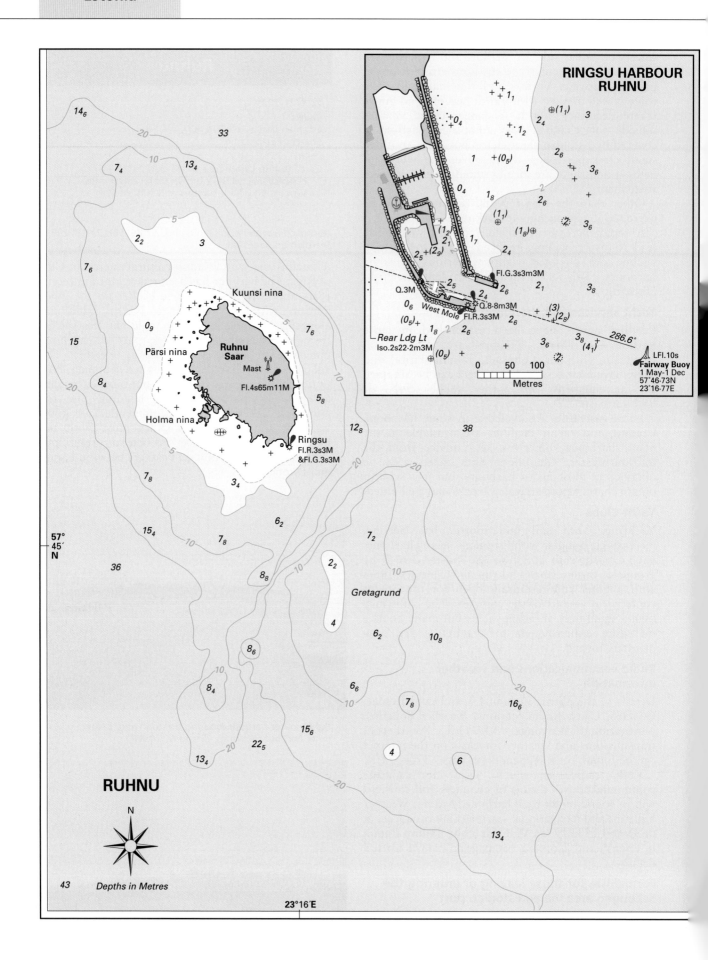

**RINGSU HARBOUR
RUHNU**

Fl.G.3s3m3M

Q.3M

West Mole
Q.8·8m3M
Fl.R.3s3M

Rear Ldg Lt
Iso.2s22·2m3M

286.6°

0   50   100
Metres

LFl.10s
Fairway Buoy
1 May-1 Dec
57°46·73N
23°16·77E

14₆

33

20

7₄   10   13₄

5

2₂   3

7₆

0₉

Kuunsi nina

15   Pärsi nina   **Ruhnu
Saar**

Mast
Fl.4s65m11M

7₆

8₄

5₈

Holma nina

Ringsu
Fl.R.3s3M
&Fl.G.3s3M

12₈   38

5   3₄

**57°
45′
N**

7₈   6₂   7₂

15₄   7₈   2₂   10

36   8₈   10   Gretagrund

4   6₂   10₈

8₆

8₄   10   6₆   7₈   16₆

15₆

13₄   22₅   4   6

20   13₄

RUHNU

N

43   Depths in Metres

23°16′E

Kihnu

58°08'N 24°01'E

UKHO chart 2215

Estonian charts 305, 516, 632, 781 *Charts of Estonia Vol. 3*

Approach waypoint on leading line 58°08'·45N 24°05'·20E

See plan on page 346.

A small island in the approaches to Pärnu surrounded by shoals up to 2M offshore. If approaching from the south keep at least 2M offshore leaving east cardinal mark to port and on reaching leading line sail in on 273°. (See *Estonian Small Craft Chart Vol. 3*, page 17). If approaching from north or east, well-buoyed channels lead in to join the leading line.

There is a fishing/ferry harbour with a pontoon and stern buoys for yachts. Facilities include bars and a few shops. The island has a very small permanent population. Ferries to Pärnu and Munalaid.

Pärnu

58°23'N 24°29'E

Distances
Rīga 80M, Salacgrīva 40M, Roomassaare 75M, Virtsu (inside Kihnu) 50M, Virtsu (outside Kihnu) 60M

Charts
UKHO 2215, 2816
Estonian charts 305, 516, 632, 780, *Charts of Estonia Vol. 3*
Latvian charts 1251, 1011

Lights
C3596 **Kihnu** 58°05'·8N 23°58'·3E Fl(2)W.R.12s28m11–7M 262° -W-225° -R- 262° Round white metal tower with balcony 32m
C3594·5 **Häädemeeste** 58°04'·4N 24°29'·2E Fl.W.5s32m11M White square metal framework tower 28m
C3602 **Sorgu Saar** 58°10'·7N 24°12'·00E Fl(2)WR.9s19m7M 101° -W-342° -R-101° Round red brick tower with balcony 16m
C3605 **Liu Light Beacon** 58°16'·6N 24°15'·9E Oc(2)5s30m7M White planking on metal framework tower 28m
C3606 **Pärnu Ldg Lts 023.9°** *Front* 58°22'·7N 24°27'·9E Q.R.24m10M White rectangle, black stripe, on red round metal tower 22m. Visible on leading line only
C3606·1 *Rear* 821m from front, Iso.R.6s37m11M White rectangle, black stripe, on metal framework tower 34m
C3611 **East breakwater** 58°22'N 24°28'E Fl.G.3s5m1M White metal column, green band, concrete base 3m
C3611·5 **West breakwater** 58°22'·1N 24°27'·7E Fl.R.3s4.5m1M White metal column, red band, on concrete base 3m

Harbour communications
Pärnu Jahtklubi Marina ☎ +372 44 71740
Pärnu Port VHF Ch 16 *Parnu Port*

General

Pärnu, an attractive small town and holiday resort in the extreme northeast corner of the Gulf of Rīga, is known as Estonia's Summer Capital. Timber is exported and there is a small amount of fishing. It is surrounded by beautiful sandy beaches – one of which is reserved for ladies only. The orthodox church is worth visiting.

Approach and entry

Approach waypoint 58°21'·50N 24°26'·90E

Straightforward approach on 023·9° – following the leading marks.

Berthing

Berth at the friendly Pärnu Yacht Club on the east bank of the river just round a bend. Mooring is bows-to pontoon and stern line to buoy or stern anchor in 2·5–3m depths and shelter is excellent. Visitors should use the first pontoon if possible, or otherwise tie up where space allows and seek advice at the yacht club.

Anchoring is not advised as the waterway is used by commercial shipping.

Services for yachts

Water and electricity on the pontoons, showers and toilets at the yacht club (which also has a bar and an excellent restaurant). There is a fuel berth beyond the yacht club pontoons and a chandlery.

General facilities

The small town is about a mile from the yacht club and has all facilities including shops, Post Office, banks and restaurants.

Communications and travel

Buses to Tallinn, Rīga and elsewhere. Airport for domestic flights. Ferry to Kihnu.

Wi-Fi at the sailing club and internet cafés in the town.

The yacht and small craft pontoons at Pärnu, looking west
F. and G. Cattell

10. ESTONIA

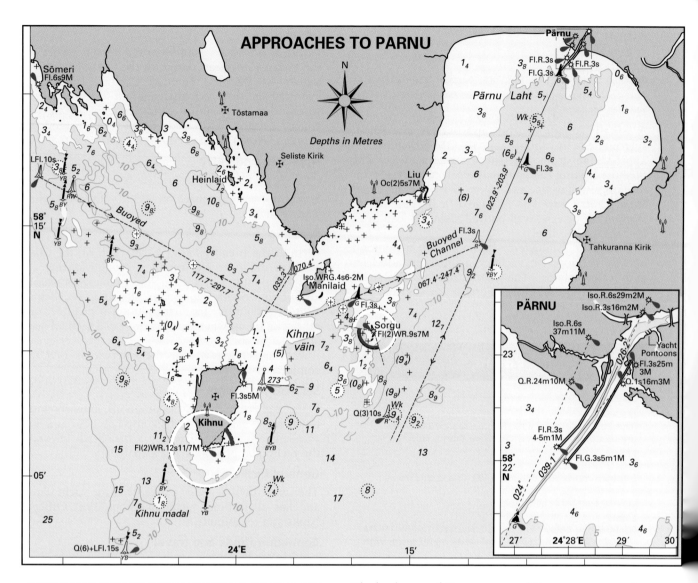

APPROACHES TO PARNU

Depths in Metres

Kuressaare (Saaremaa)

58°14'N 22°28'E

See plan on page 347

Distances
Ventspils 65M, Roja 45M, Rīga 85M, Virtsu 50M, Pärnu 75M

Charts
UKHO 2223, 2215
Estonian charts 305, 306, 513, 519, 628, *Charts of Estonia Vol. 3*
Latvian charts 1251, 1013

Lights
C3616·1 Abruka 58°08'·9N 22°31'·5E
 Iso.W.4s38m9M White round concrete tower, black bands 36m
C3626 Allirahu 58°09'·7N 22°47'·2E
 Fl(2)W.12s14m7M Metal framework tower with red planking on all sides 10m
Kuressaare Fairway buoy 58°12'·5N 22°28'·14E LFl.W.10s
C3612.3 Kuressaare Ldg Lts 1.3° Front
 58°14'·65N22°28'·23E Q.R.9m6M White rectangle with red stripe on red metal cylinder 7m
C3612.31 Rear 240m from front Oc.R.1·5s22m6M
 White rectangle with red strip on building – height above building 3m

The harbours of Kuressaare and Roomassaare on the southern shore of Saaremaa are located close together and are both based on the town of Kuressaare. Kuressaare harbour has the advantage of being within the town whereas Roomassaare, which has the advantage of a better location for onward passages, is some 4km to the east.

Kuressaare harbour F. and G. Cattell

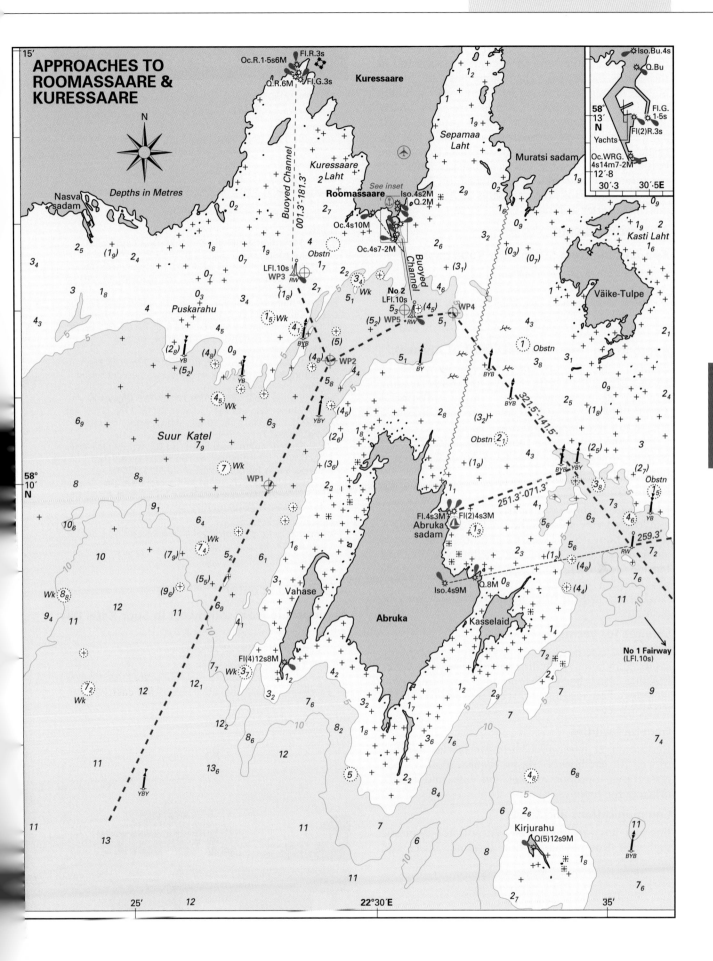

APPROACHES TO
ROOMASSAARE &
KURESSAARE

N

Depths in Metres

Kuressaare

Sepamaa Laht

Muratsi sadam

Kasti Laht

Väike-Tulpe

Nasva sadam

Kuressaare Laht

Roomassaare

Oc.R.1·5s6M   Fl.R.3s
Q.R.6M   Fl.G.3s

Iso.4s2M
Q.2M
Oc.4s10M
Oc.4s7-2M

Iso.Bu.4s
Q.Bu
Fl.G.1·5s
Fl(2)R.3s
Yachts
Oc.WRG.4s14m7-2M

58° 13′ N
30′·3   30′·5E   12′·8

See inset

Buoyed Channel 001.3°-181.3°

Buoyed Channel

Obstn

LFl.10s WP3   RW

No 2
LFl.10s

Wk

WP5   RW

WP4

WP2

BYB

BY

Puskarahu

YB

YB

Wk

Wk

Suur Katel

Wk

WP1

321.5°-141.5°

BYB   YBY

251.3°-071.3°

Obstn

Obstn

Obstn

YB

259.3°
RW

YBY

Wk

Vahase

Abruka sadam
Fl.4s3M   Fl(2)4s3M

Iso.4s9M   Q.8M

Abruka

Kasselaid

No 1 Fairway
(LFl.10s)

Fl(4)12s8M

Wk

Wk

Kirjurahu
Q(5)12s9M

BYB

25′   22°30′E   35′

10. ESTONIA

Kuressaare is the capital of Saaremaa the largest of the Estonian islands and the second largest island in the entire Baltic Sea. The island has one of the highest standards of living in Estonia and is highly popular with tourists. Kuressaare has many attractive buildings and a superb moated castle complete with large museum (it is claimed that the castle is the best-preserved medieval fortress in the Baltic) plus reasonable shops and many cafés and restaurants. Other places of interest on Saaremaa include Panga Pank, the windmills at Angla and the meteorite crater at Kaali.

Approach and entry

Approaching from SW in Suur Katel bay:

Waypoint 1 58°10'·00N 22°27'·00E
Waypoint 2 58°11'·60N 22°29'·20E
Waypoint 3 Kuressaare fairway buoy 58°12'·5N 22°28'·14E to join leading line of 01·3°
Waypoint 4 58°11'·9N 22°31'·7E

Approaching from southeast (east of Abruka):

Head for the Roomassaare fairway buoy No. 1 58°06'·77N 22°39'·44E. Follow the outer leading line for Roomassaare 321·5° until waypoint 4 58°11'·90N 22°31'·70E is reached then follow a course to waypoints 2 and 3 as above.

The approach is by a long, buoyed and dredged channel on a leading line of 01·3° from the fairway buoy. Channel dredged to 2·5m.

Berthing

Kuressaare harbour is a relatively new development and located very close to the small town. Berthing is to stern buoys and bows to pontoon with limited alongside berthing. There is no shelter to be obtained outside the harbour and the water is shallow outside the channel so anchoring off is not possible. Anchoring within the harbour would not be permitted.

Services for yachts

Water and electricity on pontoon, toilets, showers, sauna and laundry facilities in the harbour office building. Fuel berth and holding tank pump-out facilities. For repairs etc seek the advice of the harbourmaster.

General facilities

Restaurant at harbour. Charts for sale at harbour office. All facilities – shops, banks, Post Office, restaurants, outdoor market, car hire and tourist office in the town.

Communications and travel

Bus and ferry to Tallinn etc. Airport for domestic flights at Roomassaare (4km distant). Wi-Fi and internet access.

Roomassaare (Saaremaa)

58°13'N 22°30'E
See plan on page 347

Distances
Ventspils 65M, Roja 45M, Rīga 85M, Virtsu 50M, Pärnu 75M

Charts
UKHO 2223, 2215, 2816
Estonian charts 305, 306, 513, 519, 628, Charts of Estonia Vol. 3
Latvian charts 1251, 1013

Lights
C3616·1 **Abruka** 58°08'·9N 22°31'·5E Iso.W.4s38m9M White round concrete tower, black bands 36m
C3626 **Allirahu** 58°09'·7N 22°47'·2E Fl(2)W.12s14m7M Metal framework tower with red planking on all sides 10m
Fairway buoy No.1 58°06'·77N 22°39'·44E LFl.W.10s
C3622 **Outer Ldg Lts 321·5°** Front 58°12'·82N 22°30'·35E Oc.WRG.4s14m7–2M 276.5°-W-6.5° 15° -G-24° -W-30° -R-39° Black rectangle, white stripe, on red framework tower 12m
C3622·1 Rear 721m from front Oc.W.4s33m10M Black rectangle, white stripe, on metal framework tower 30m
Fairway buoy No.2 58°11'·97N 22°30'·78E LFl.W.10s
C3622·5 **Inner Ldg Lts 351·1°** Front 58°13'·17N 22°30'·43E Q.Bu.8m2M Black rectangle, white stripe, on red metal post 7m
C3622·51 Rear 107m from front, Iso.Bu.4s11.6m2M Black rectangle, white stripe, on red metal post 9·7m
C3622·55 **Yacht harbour West mole** 58°12'·97N 22°30'·42E Fl(2)R.3s4m1M Red metal post 2m
C3622·56 **Yacht harbour East mole** 58°12'·96N 22°30'·48E Fl.G.1·5s4m1M Green metal post 2m

Harbour communications
Roomassaare Port Control ☎ +372 455 5930
VHF Ch 14, 16

Approach and entry

Approaching from southwest in Suur Katel bay:

Waypoint 1 58°10'·00N 22°27'·00E
Waypoint 2 58°11'·60N 22°29'·20E
Waypoint 4 58°11'·9N 22°31'·7E
Waypoint 5 (Roomassaare Fairway buoy No. 2) 58°11'·97N 22°30'·78E to join leading line 351·4° to enter harbour

Roomassaare harbour   *F. and G. Cattell*

Roomassaare harbour looking northeast   *F. and G. Cattell*

Approaching from southeast (east of Abruka):

Head for the Roomassaare fairway buoy No. 1 58°06'·77N 22°39'·44E. Follow the outer leading line on a course of 321·5° until waypoint 4 58°11'·90N 22°31'·70E is reached then follow a course to waypoint 5 Fairway buoy No. 2 58°11'·97N 22°30'·78E is reached to join leading line 351·4° to enter harbour.

Berthing

Roomassaare has a small modern marina in the inner basin, beyond the commercial harbour. Berths are alongside individual finger pontoons in 2·5–3m. There is no shelter to be obtained outside the harbour, so anchoring off is not possible.

Services for yachts

Water and electricity on pontoon, toilets, showers and sauna in the harbour office building. Fuel berth which also has holding tank pump-out facilities. For repairs etc seek the advice of the harbourmaster. Arcona Yachts have a factory just north of the harbour.

General facilities

Bar, restaurant and small shop in the harbour area, with all facilities – shops, banks, Post Office, restaurants, outdoor market, car hire and tourist office – in Kuressaare.

Communications and travel

Bus to Kuressaare from outside the marina, and thence bus and ferry to Tallinn etc. The island also has an airport handling domestic flights.

Orissaare (Saaremaa)

58°34'N 23°06'E
UKHO chart 2215
Estonian charts 305, 621, 622 *Charts of Estonia Vol. 2*

A shallow harbour with stern buoys behind a concrete mole. Water and electricity available, nearby small town with shops and restaurants.

Virtsu

58°34'N 23°31'E

Distances
Roomassaare 50M, Pärnu (inside Kihnu) 50M, Pärnu (outside Kihnu) 60M, Haapsalu 30M

Charts
UKHO 2215
Estonian charts 305, 513, 621, 974 Charts of Estonia Vol. 3
Latvian chart 1251

Lights
C3630 **Kübassaare** 58°25'·70N 23°17'·99E
  LFl.W.9s20m11M 228° -vis-048° Round concrete tower, black upper white lower with balcony and lantern 18m
C3631 **Pöörilaid** 58°27'·68N 23°37'·77E
  Fl(4)WRG.18s14m6–2M 007° -W-141° -R-160° -W 340·5° -G-007° White round concrete tower with balcony and lantern 13m
C3636 **Viirelaid** 58°32'·68N 23°26'·58E Fl.WR.8s15m9–7M
  163° -W-349° -R-163° Red round concrete tower with balcony and lantern 11m
C3632 **Virtsu** 58°34'·03N 23°30'·09E Fl.W.5s19m11M Red upper and white lower – square concrete tower 18m
C3632·4 *Ldg Lts 087·7° Front* 58°34'·58N 23°31'·38E
  Iso.W.3s10m5M White rectangle, red stripe, on metal framework 8m
C3632·41 *Rear* 292m from front Iso.W.3s16m5M White rectangle, red stripe, on metal framework 13m. Both lights visible on leading line only
C3632·6 **Pierhead** 58°34'·57N 23°30'·49E
  Fl.WR.2s7m5–3M 072·5° -W-099° -R-072·5° Red metal column with balcony 5m

Harbour communications
Virtsu Port Control ✆ +372 477 5019 *VHF* Ch 14

General

Ferry harbour on the east side of the southern end of Moon Sound with limited facilities for yachts.

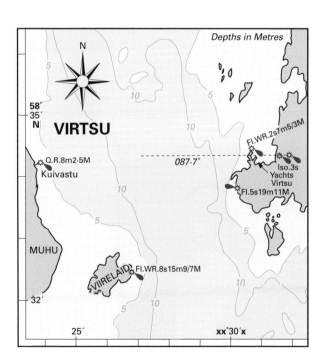

Virtsu, yacht moorings   *F. and G. Cattell*

Approach and entry

Approach waypoint 58°34'·50N 23°28'·65E on leading line.
Straightforward entry from Moon Sound with the leading marks in line on 087·7°.

Berthing

Yachts berth behind the inner mole, where a limited number of finger berths have been installed. It is possible to lie alongside the outer berths but these have no shelter and are exposed in north and northwest winds. The yacht berthing area has been dredged, but depths shoal rapidly outside the dredged area. Anchoring is not an option.

Services for yachts and general facilities

Water and electricity are available on the pontoon, though hoses are not provided.

Toilets in the ferry terminal building, where there is also a small café.

Boats drawing less than 1m can obtain diesel from the fishing jetty, otherwise it must be collected by can.

Communications and travel

Wi-Fi at harbour. Buses to Tallinn and other towns in Estonia. Ferry to Muhu island and thence to Saaremaa.

Virtsu lighthouse
F. and G. Cattell

Haapsalu

58°57'N 23°32'E

Distances

Virtsu 30M, Lehtma 30M, Hanko 55M, Lohusalu 45M, Tallinn 65M

Charts

UKHO 2241
Estonian charts 302, 513, 616, *Charts of Estonia Vol. 2*

Lights

C3651 **Paralepa Ldg Lts 152·7°** *Front* 58°56'·04N 23°28'·96E Q.W.15m9M White round concrete tower with balcony and lantern 16m

C3651·1 *Rear* 802m from front, Iso.W.4s38m9M Round white tower, black bands on upper part. Balcony, black lantern 34m

C3656 **Kajakarahu Ldg Lts 094·2°** *Front* 58°57'·18N 23°30'·82E Q.R.7m4M Red triangle, yellow stripe, on metal column 8m

C3656·1 *Rear* 595m from front Iso.R.3s12m4M Red triangle, yellow stripe, on metal framework yellow disk on top 13m

C3657 **Holmi Ldg Lts 073·2°** *Front* 58°57'·58N 23°30'·67E Q.G.8m2M White rectangle, black stripe on metal framework 7m

C3657·1 *Rear* 396m from front Iso.G.3s14m3M White rectangle, black stripe on metal framework 12m

C3658 **Tahu Lts in Line 049·8°** *Front* 58°58'·40N 23°32'·14E Q.W.4m4M White rectangle, black stripe on metal framework 6m

C3658·1 *Rear* 233m from front Iso.W.2s10m4M White rectangle, black stripe on concrete post 9m

Note All four pairs of lights visible on leading lines only

Harbour communications

VHF Ch 12 'Grand Holm'
Haapsalu Yacht Club ① +372 502 9540

General

Haapsalu lies on a small peninsula, on which also stand the ruins of an old castle with a high tower. It is a pleasant old town of about 15,000 inhabitants with medieval roots. At the end of the 19th century it was a popular resort for the wealthy of St Petersburg and their grand wooden villas dominate the scenery – it is still a health spa famous for mud baths. There are several museums, including the restored railway station which is now a museum and tourist office. Side by side are the Yacht Club, Grand Holm Marina and other private mooring facilities. Visitors may use both the Yacht Club and Grand Holm Marina facilities. Outside the channel the water is shallow but there are plans for some dredging.

Approach and entry

Approach waypoint in Haapsalu Laht (Bay) 58°57'·30N 23°27'·70E on leading line.

Whether coming from south or north it is essential to have detailed plans of the approach. Consult either *Charts of Estonia, Vol 2*; *Harbours of the Baltic States* or *Recommended Routes for Recreational Craft on Haapsalu Bay*, for the buoyage and leading lines. Provided the latter are followed closely a vessel

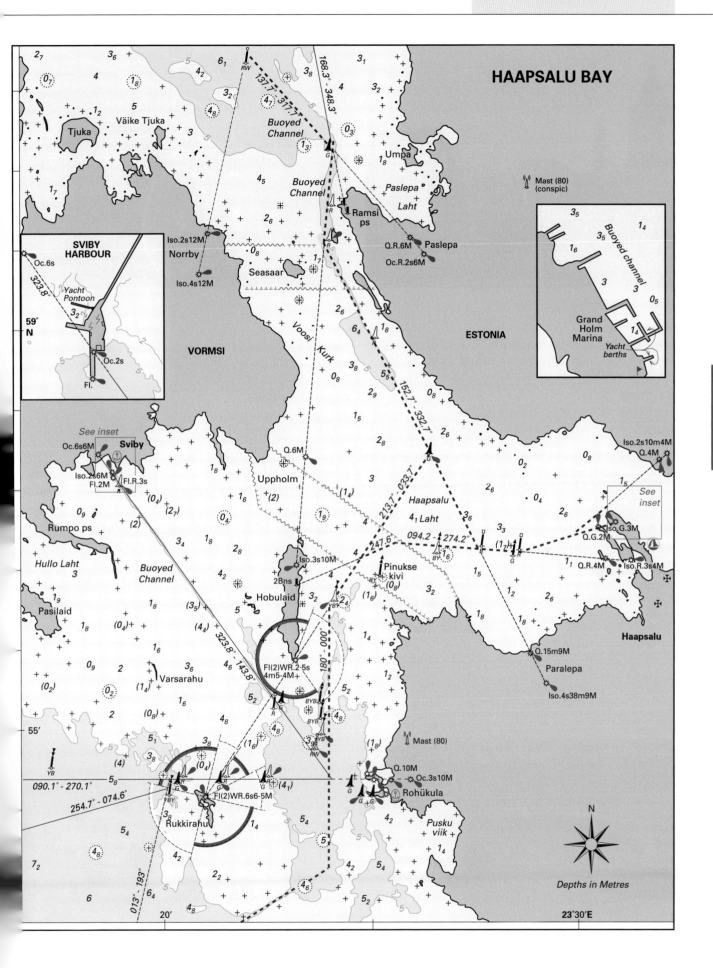

HAAPSALU BAY

HAAPSALU BAY

Haapsalu Castle   *F. and G. Cattell*

Locomotive Museum, Haapsalu   *F. and G. Cattell*

with 2m draught can approach Haapsalu without problem, the shallowest part being next to the harbour itself.

Berthing

At Grand Holm Marina mooring is to a concrete quay, bows to quay and stern to buoys and also to some newly installed pontoons. The harbour has no shelter from the east or northeast and in strong wind conditions can become very uncomfortable.

At the Yacht Club berthing is alongside a wooden pontoon.

Depths either side of the channel and in the harbour surroundings are extremely shallow and anchoring should not be attempted.

Services for yachts

Water and electricity available on quay or pontoon. Good showers, toilets and all facilities including restaurant at Grand Holm Marina. Restaurant at Yacht Club whose facilities are shared with the motel. Fuel berth in outer harbour.

Local gas cylinders are available in the town – enquire at the yacht club, which can also advise on repair facilities, sailmaker etc.

General facilities

The harbour is located about 2·5km from the town – take the bus from the end of the short lane leading from the yacht club gate. Haapsalu has all the usual facilities of a major town – banks, post office, shops, restaurants, etc.

Communications and travel

Wi-Fi at both Grand Holm Marina and Yacht Club.

Card-operated telephone kiosks in the town, and internet access at the public library (prior booking essential).

Regular bus service to Tallinn and other Estonian towns, but no rail connection. Hire cars can be arranged either through the yacht club or the tourist office.

Haapsalu Grand Holm left and sailing club right   *F. and G. Cattell*

Lehtma (Hiiumaa)

59°04'N 22°42'E

Distances

Mariehamn (Åland) 115M, Hanko 50M, Haapsalu 30M, Lohusalu 50M

Charts

UKHO *2241*
Estonian charts 302, 305, 511, 513, 618,
Charts of Estonia Vol. 2

Lights

C3746 **Kõpu** 58°54'·95N 22°11'·98E Fl(2)W.10s102m26M
White square stone tower with retaining walls, balcony and red lantern 36m

C3754 **Tahkuna** 59°05'·48N 22°35'·17E
LFl(2)W.15s43m12M 095° -vis-253·5° White conical tower with balcony 43m

C3755 **Ldg Lts 272·4°** *Front* 59°03'·92N 22°41'·31E
Iso.W.3s9m3M White rectangle, black stripe on metal framework 7m

C3755·1 *Rear* 81m from front Iso.W.3s13m3M White rectangle, black stripe on metal framework 11m. Visible on leading line only

C3755·3 **Breakwater** 59°03'·93N 22°42'·14E Q.G.10m2M
Red metal column with balcony 8m

Harbour communications

Lehtma Port Control & Harbour ① +372 462 2714
VHF Ch 10, 16

General

A small fishing and commercial harbour exposed to south and southeast winds, surrounded by excellent beaches. Kärdla, the island's capital and the nearest town, is 12km away. The island of Hiiumaa has a number of interesting places to visit, including the coastal boulder at Kärdla, the Hill of Crosses, Kõpu Lighthouse and the monument to the Estonia at Tahkuna.

Approach and entry

Approach waypoint 59°03'·90N 22°43'E

Approach on the 272·4° leading line, turning close around the end of the single long breakwater. Some protection from southerly swell is afforded by a submerged reef which curves into the harbour inside the breakwater. Anchoring is not feasible.

Berthing

Mostly bows to the quay and stern to a buoy, or possibly alongside.

Services for yachts

Water and electricity on quay. Toilets, showers and washing machine at harbour office. Fuel by arrangement with the harbour office.

General facilities and communications

There is a hotel nearby. Buses run along the coast to Kärdla.

LEHTMA

Depths in Metres

Lehtma, looking northwest *F. and G. Cattell*

10. ESTONIA

THE BALTIC SEA **353**

Sõru (Hiiumaa)

58°41'·50N 22°31'·50E

Estonian charts 305, 306, 513, 515, 622, 752, 856, Charts of Estonia Vol. 2

Approach waypoint 58°41'·30N 22°31'·30E in dredged channel

Note It is important to follow the channels marked on the chart as the area is very shallow.

Harbour used by ferries from Triigi (Saaremaa) with limited facilities and good shelter for yachts in inner harbour. Limited facilities ashore but useful as an arrival or departure point for Sweden.

Sviby (Vormsi)

58°58'·20N 23°18'·70E

UKHO chart 2241

Estonian charts 302, 305, 513, 616, 744, Charts of Estonia Vol. 2

Harbour for ferries from Rohuküla on the mainland. Two pontoons for yachts behind the jetty. Limited facilities. The island is interesting as there are many remains from the time when it was inhabited by Swedes. Useful now Heltermaa and Rohuküla are closed to yachts.

Dirhami

59°13'N 23°30'E

UKHO chart 2241

Estonian charts 302, 509, 614, Charts of Estonia Vols 1 and 2

A commercial/fishing harbour with limited berthing facilities for yachts. Entry/exit dangerous in strong northwesterly winds. Useful point of arrival/departure for Finland. Toilets and showers available. Fuel berth. Small shop nearby. Plans to expand the yacht facilities. Internet at harbour office.

Paldiski Nord (port of refuge)

59°21'N 24°03'E

UKHO chart chart 2241

Estonian charts 302, 305, 507, 612, 827, Charts of Estonia Vols 1 and 2.

A commercial harbour also available to yachts as port of refuge. Good shelter in all winds but it can be uncomfortable due to swell. All facilities in the town. Arthur Ransome's Baltic Port.

Note The commercial quays are high.

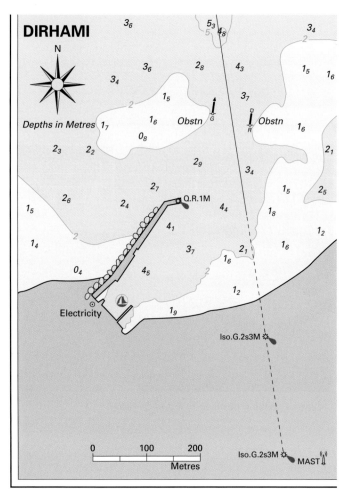

Dirhami. Since this photo was taken in 2006, the main harbour wall behind has been extensively rebuilt
E. Redfern

Lohusalu

59°24'N 24°12'E

Distances

Lehtma 50M, Haapsalu 45M, Hanko 45M, Tallinn 25M

Charts

UKHO 2241, 2248
Estonian charts 302, 507, 612, *Charts of Estonia Vol 1*

Lights

C3774 **Pakri Lighthouse** 59°23'·24N 24°02'·26E
   LFl.W.15s73m12M 011° -vis-243° Red round brick
   tower with balcony 52m
C3786·1 **Suurupi** 59°27'·81N 24°22'·82E
   Oc(2)W15s66m12–15M 056° – vis – 261·5° (vis 15M)
   245°–248° (vis 12M) White round stone tower with
   balcony and black lantern 22m
C3783 **Ldg Lts 233·3°** *Front* 59°24'·15N 24°12'·39E
   Iso.R.2s5m6M White rectangle, red stripe on metal
   post 3·5m
C3783·1 *Rear* 134m from front, Iso.R.4s6m6M White
   rectangle, red stripe on white metal post 5m

Harbour communications

Lohusalu Port Control ☎ +372 677 1640
VHF Ch 10, 16 'Lohusalu marina'

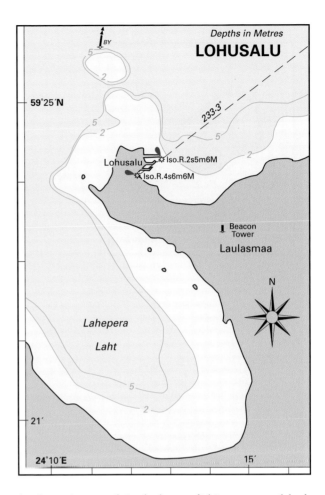

General

A small, modern yacht harbour with very few spaces for visitors, surrounded by forest and superb beaches.

Approach and entry

Approach waypoint 59°24'·95N 24°14'·40E on the leading line of 233·3°

The leading line on 233·3° is marked with two boards.

Berthing

Visitors may berth in the southern part of the harbour bows to the quay and stern to a buoy if space available. Alternatively there is a small number of stern buoys outside the end of the northern breakwater. Although there is a rocky outcrop, these moorings have very little protection if the wind is between north and south east. Anchoring outside the harbour is not advised, due to fishing nets and lack of shelter.

Services for yachts

Showers, toilets, laundry facilities. The fuel berth at the head of harbour has only 1·5m depth. For other services seek advice at the harbour office.

General facilities

Restaurant at the yacht club, plus a small rural café. Shops in the town of Laulasmaa, a short walk inland.

Communications and travel

Buses to Tallinn and elsewhere.

The small harbour at Lohusalu *F. and G. Cattell*

10. ESTONIA

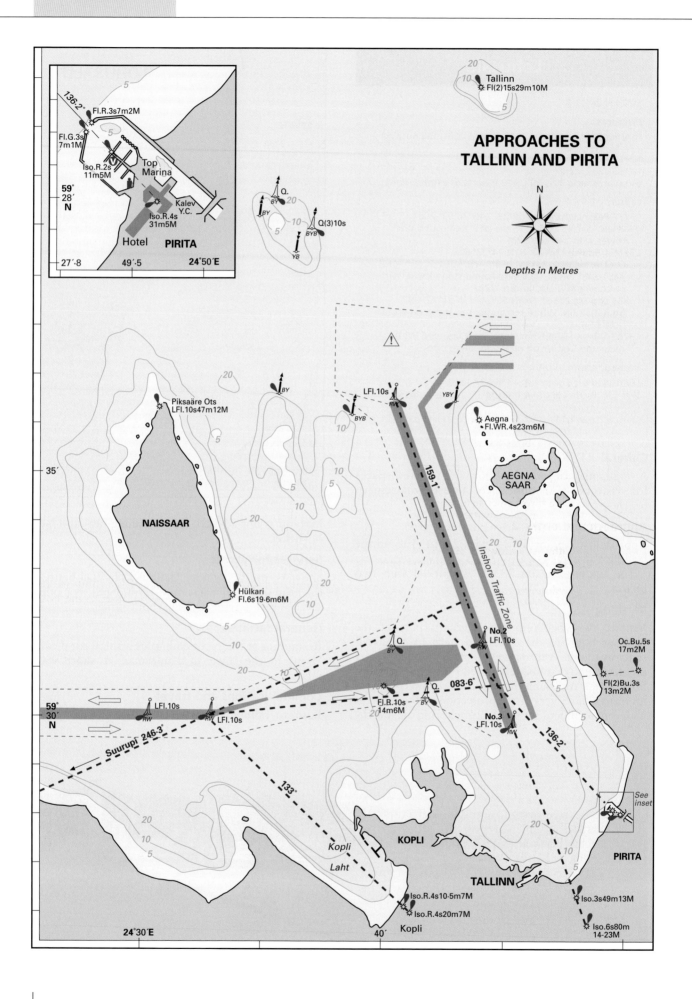

APPROACHES TO
TALLINN AND PIRITA

Depths in Metres

Inset (top left):

136·2°
Fl.R.3s7m2M
Fl.G.3s 7m1M
Iso.R.2s 11m5M
Top Marina
Kalev Y.C.
59° 28′ N
Iso.R.4s 31m5M
Hotel
PIRITA
27′·8
49′·5
24°50′E
5

Main chart:

Tallinn
Fl(2)15s29m10M

Q.
BY
BY
Q(3)10s
BYB
YB

Piksaäre Ots
LFl.10s47m12M

BY
BYB
LFl.10s
RW
YBY

Aegna
Fl.WR.4s23m6M

AEGNA SAAR

NAISSAAR

Inshore Traffic Zone
159·1°

Hülkari
Fl.6s19·6m6M

No.2
LFl.10s
RW

Oc.Bu.5s 17m2M

35′

Q.
BY
083·6°
Fl.R.10s 14m6M
Q.
BY
No.3
LFl.10s
RW

Fl(2)Bu.3s 13m2M

59° 30′ N
LFl.10s
RW
LFl.10s
RW
246·3°
Suurupi

133°
136·2°

See inset

Kopli
Laht

KOPLI

PIRITA

TALLINN

Iso.R.4s10·5m7M
Iso.R.4s20m7M
Kopli

Iso.3s49m13M

Iso.6s80m 14-23M

24°30′E
40′
24°50′E

Tallinn (Pirita)

59°28'·07N 24°49'·55E

Distances
Haapsalu 65M, Lohusalu 25M, Hanko 60M, Helsinki 45M, Vergi 55M

Charts
UKHO 2241, 2248, 2227
Estonian charts 302, 507, 610, 929,
Charts of Estonia Vol. 1

Lights
C3790 **Naissaar Lighthouse** 59°36'·22N 24°30'·63E
  LFl.W.10s47m12M 025° -vis-335° Octagonal white conical concrete tower, red top and balcony 45m
C3806 **Aegna** 59°36'·04N 24°43'·8E Fl.WR.4s23m6M
  053·5° -R-101° -W-053·5° Yellow latticed rectangle on grey metal post 21m
C3805 **Vahemadal** 59°30'·61N 24°39'·97E Fl.R.10s14m6M
  Red octagonal truncated pyramid with white band and two galleries 13m
C3842 **Tallinnamadal** 59°42'·72N 24°43'·89E
  Fl(2)W.15s29m10M Racon Red round metal tower, yellow top, black base, with three galleries 31m
C3810 **Outer Ldg Lts 159.1°** Front 59°26'·23N 24°47'·91E
  Iso.W.3s49m13M 154·5°–165° Conical red tower on building 18m
C3810·1 *Rear* 1,112m from front Iso.W.6s80m23M 157·1°
  -vis- 161·1° to 23M, 139° -vis-187·5° to 14M Round white stone tower, black top with balcony 40m
C3840·8 **Pirita Ldg Lts 136·2°** *Front* 59°28'·13N 24°49'·24E
  Iso.R.2s11m5M Red round concrete tower, three white balconies 9m
C3840·81 *Rear* 407m from front Iso.R.4s31m5M White square concrete tower on building 28m
C3841·2 **Pirita northeast breakwater** 59°28'·23N
  24°49'·01E Fl.R.3s7m2M Red metal column with balcony 5m
C3841 **Pirita southwest breakwater** 59°28'·20N
  24°49'·05E Fl.G.3s7m1M Green metal column with balcony 5m

Harbour communications
Pirita Port Control and Marina ☎ +372 639 8980
Email sadam@piritatop.ee No VHF
Kalev Jahtklubi Marina ☎ +372 623 9154
  www.kjk.ee

General

Tallinn, the capital of Estonia, has about 400,000 inhabitants and is a busy commercial harbour and industrial centre. It was part of the Hanseatic league from the 13th century and the town hall is the oldest surviving Gothic town hall in northern Europe. The city was fought over and badly damaged by both the Russians and the Germans but the old town in particular has been skilfully and tastefully restored. There are no facilities for yachts in the harbour at Tallinn itself, which is purely commercial, and instead yachts berth at Pirita, 6km east of the city. Pirita Marina (now known as TOP Marina) was built for the yachting Olympics in 1980 and has subsequently become the main yachting centre for Estonia.

There is a good beach beyond the river east of the harbour, with the impressive and well preserved ruins of St Birgitta's convent just inland.

Approach and entry

Approach waypoint 58°28'·35N 24°49'·00E

The approach is straightforward, with the television tower visible from many miles offshore and the gable end of the convent ruins coming into view on closer approach. The harbour entrance with its double breakwater is conspicuous and there are no offlying hazards.

Berthing

Yachts may berth at either TOP Marina or further in at the Kalev Yacht Club. For the TOP visitors' area, on entering harbour turn to starboard and berth in the area bounded by the first two quays. Berthing at Kalev Yacht Club is limited but if space is available, access is by turning to port on entering the harbour and proceeding towards the road bridge. Kalev Yacht Club is on the starboard side before the bridge. Pirita now has reduced space for visitors due to the demands for berths from local yacht owners.

Services for yachts

Water and electricity at all berths and plenty of rubbish skips, with toilets and showers at both TOP Marina and Kalev Yacht Club.

Fuel is available from the fuel berth at the head of the western basin, where local gas bottles can also be exchanged and the pump out station is situated.

There is a boatyard run by the marina and the Kalev Yacht Club has skilled shipwrights and well-equipped workshops where repairs can be carried out, as well as a small sail-loft. There are several chandleries within the complex.

Weather forecasts are displayed at the harbour office.

General facilities

Good restaurants both at the Club and in the Olympic Building, plus a snack bar next to the small

The ancient rooftops of Tallinn, seen from the old city on the hill *A. Hammick*

ESTONIA

10. ESTONIA

Above Pirita visitors' berths   *F. and G. Cattell*

Left The yacht harbour at Pirita – the leisure harbour for Tallinn – looking northwest towards the entrance showing residents' moorings   *A. Hammick*

Below Looking southeast over the Kalev Yacht Club marina at Pirita, with both the Birgitine convent ruins and television tower prominent in the background   *A. Hammick*

general shop. Other facilities, including an ATM and small post office, in the foyer of the Pirita TOP Spa Hotel.

The large Selver supermarket (on the opposite side of the main road a few hundred metres southwest), stocks most items, and there are other shops and kiosks in the vicinity. All facilities – banks, post office, restaurants, tourist office and souvenirs – are available in Tallinn itself.

Communications and travel

Several card-operated phones in the marina area, including one near the shop/café. Faxes can be sent from the central post office in the city or possibly from the Pirita TOP Spa Hotel (reception is on the ground floor). Wi-Fi is available in the area of the harbour but unlikely to work in the visitors' area. Internet access is available at the harbour office and in Tallinn at various internet cafés or at the public library (which is some distance out of town and often heavily booked).

There is an international airport, frequent ferries to Stockholm and Helsinki, and rail and bus links throughout Estonia and to many cities in Europe via Eurolines. Local buses run along the main road behind the harbour. It is necessary to purchase tickets in the local kiosk or TOP spa Hotel before boarding. Bicycles can be rented from a shop opposite the Olympic building.

Tallinn Harbour   *F. and G. Cattell*

Tallinn television tower seen from the horticultural gardens
E. Redfern

Vergi

59°35′N 26°06′E

Distances
Tallinn 55M, Helsinki 50M, Kotka 60M,
St Petersburg 145M

Charts
UKHO 2248
Estonian charts 302, 504, 606, *Charts of Estonia Vol. 1*

Lights
C3872 **Vergi light beacon** 59°36′·09N 26°06′·05E
Fl.WRG.3s11m7M 120°-G-167°-W-267°-R-356° White
round concrete tower with balcony 10m
Ldg Line 261·8° Daymarks only, lights missing

Harbour communications
Vergi Port Control VHF Ch 10, 16 *Vergi 32*
Mobile +372 55 567 349.

General

A small former fishing harbour. Due to the Russian requirement that yachts follow the shipping lane into St Petersburg, Vergi has effectively replaced Narva–Jõesuu as the port of departure and return for yachts travelling between Estonia and St Petersburg.

Approach and entry

Offshore waypoint 59°30′·5N 26°08′·00E
Approach from east-northeast on 261·8°, curving somewhat south before reaching the breakwater end to avoid a shoal patch. Do not attempt to close the harbour in darkness.

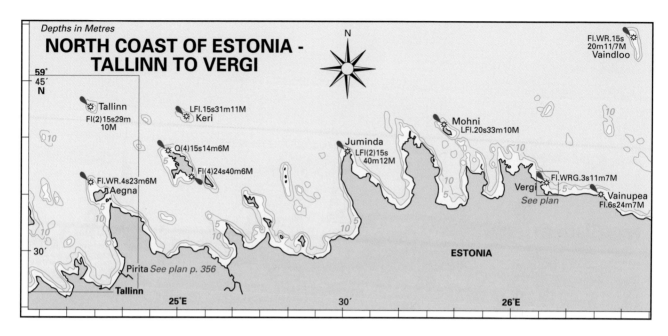

Depths in Metres

NORTH COAST OF ESTONIA - TALLINN TO VERGI

Fl.WR.15s 20m11/7M Vaindloo

Tallinn Fl(2)15s29m 10M

LFl.15s31m11M Keri

Q(4)15s14m6M

Fl(4)24s40m6M

Juminda LFl(2)15s 40m12M

Mohni LFl.20s33m10M

Vergi Fl.WRG.3s11m7M *See plan*

Vainupea Fl.6s24m7M

Fl.WR.4s23m6M Aegna

ESTONIA

Pirita *See plan p. 356*

Tallinn

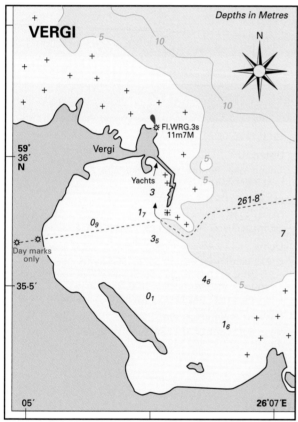

VERGI *Depths in Metres*

Fl.WRG.3s 11m7M

Vergi

Yachts

261·8°

Day marks only

Berthing

Yachts berth near the root of the breakwater, either bows to the pontoon and stern to a buoy, or occasionally alongside. Anchoring is not an option due to rocks and shallows.

Services for yachts and general facilities

Water and electricity on the pontoon, toilets and showers in the harbour building where there is also a small shop and restaurant. Fuel pump on the quay. Seek the advice of the harbourmaster if repair or other services are necessary.

Communications and travel

Buses to Tallinn and elsewhere in Estonia. Wi-Fi at harbour.

Narva-Jõesuu

59°28'N 28°03'E
Admiralty chart 2264
Estonian charts 300, 502, 601, *Charts of Estonia Vol. 1*
Approach waypoint 59°28'·68N 28°00'·96E (Fairway buoy).

A port on the Estonian border with Russia, formerly used as the port of entry/exit for St Petersburg. It has become less useful due to Russian regulations about the entry route and in any case has a dangerous approach due to shallows and silting. There is a small pontoon with stern buoys. No shore facilities. It is possible to proceed 18km upriver to the town of Narva where there are very basic facilities for berthing alongside. The centre of the fast-flowing river marks the Estonian/Russian border. Great care needs to be exercised not to accidentally cross the border and become involved with the Russian border guards who patrol the river. The town of Narva is of interest, particularly Narva Castle and the fortress of Ivangorod on the Russian shore.

Looking east over the single breakwater at Vergi
F. and G. Cattell

Appendix

I. Suppliers of charts and publications

British Admiralty charts are excellent for passage-making, but as a major part of the attraction of the Baltic is exploring the coastal islands and navigating through inshore channels, detailed local charts or chart packs/books are necessary, as listed in the text.

Many yachtsmen prefer to leave home already equipped with all the charts and other publications which they expect to need, either by ordering through one of the British suppliers listed below or arranging for charts to be shipped from a supplier in the country of origin. Others prefer to buy their charts on reaching the area, possibly from Nautischer Dienst (Kapitän Stegmann) in Kiel or Nautic Center in Göteburg.

Most of the charts and publications listed in the introductory section of each country are available through Imray (below) whose staff are able to advise on availability and and local agents.

UNITED KINGDOM

Imray Laurie Norie & Wilson Ltd
Wych House, St Ives, Huntingdon
Cambridgeshire PE27 5BT
℡ +44 (0)1480 62114
Fax +44 (0)1480 496109
www.imray.com

Kelvin Hughes Ltd
Kilgraston House
Southampton Street
Southampton SO15 2ED
℡ +44 (0)23 8063 4911
Fax +44 (0)23 8063 0014
www.bookharbour.com

United Kingdom Hydrographic Office

www.ukho.gov.uk – homepage of the United Kingdom Hydrographic Office, including free, downloadable weekly Notices to Mariners and the entire Admiralty Chart Catalogue. Orders for UKHO charts and publications must be placed with official agents.

GERMANY

Nautischer Dienst
Kapitän Stegmann, Makler Strasse 8
Postfach 80, D–24159 Kiel
℡ +49 (0)431 331772/332353
Fax +49 (0)431 331761
Email naudi@t-online.de

HanseNautic
Herrengraben 31, D 20459 Hamburg
℡ +49(0)40 374842-0
Fax +49(0)40 374842-42
www.hansenautic.de

www.bsh.de/ – homepage of the German Hydrographic Office, including a complete listing of German charts and official publications. English translation.

NV-Verlag
Lange Str. 95, 24399 Arnis
℡ +49 (0)4642/ 92 46 0
Fax +49 (0) 4642/ 92 46 92
www.nautische-veroeffentlichung.de

Delius Klasing
Siekerwall 21, D-33602 Bielefeld
℡ +49 (0)521 - 55 90
Fax +49 (0)521 - 55 98 81 14
www.delius-klasing.de

DENMARK

Iver Weilbach & Co A/S
Toldbodgade 35, PO Box 1560,
DK 1253 København K
℡ +45 331 35927
Fax +45 339 35927
Email nautical@weilbach.dk
www.weilbach.dk
www.kms.dk – homepage of Kort & Matrikelstyrelsen, the national mapping and charting agency. Includes pilotage, corrections to Danish charts and the entire map and chart catalogue

SWEDEN

www.sjofartsverket.se – homepage of the Swedish Maritime Administration, which is responsible for the country's hydrographic service

Nautiska Magasinet AB
Shop address: Slussplan 5, Gamla Stan,
Box 15410, 104 65 Stockholm
℡ +46 (0)8 677 0000
Fax +46 (0)8 677 0010
Email nautiska@nautiska.com
www.nautiska.com

Nautic Center
Klangfärgsgatan 16
SE-426 52 Västra Frölunda
℡ +46 (0)31 100885
Fax +46 (0)31 7115357
Email office@nautic-center.se
www.nautic-center.se

Svenska Kryssarklubben
Augustendalsvägen 54, S–13127 Nacka Strand,
Box 1189, Stockholm
℡ +46 (0)8 448 2880
Fax +46 (0)8 448 2889
Email info@sxk.se
www.sxk.se
(The Svenska Kryssarklubben (SKK) – Swedish Cruising Club – sells a wide range of Swedish charts, guides and other yachting publications)

FINLAND

www.fma.fi – homepage of the Finnish Maritime Administration.

Nautical charts are published by the Hydrography and Waterways Department of the Finnish Maritime Administration. John Nurminen Marine Oy are exclusive agents for the sale and nautical charts. Other publications can be purchased direct from the Hydrography.

Finnish Transport Agency
Hydrography, P.O. BOX 185
FIN-00101 Helsinki
☎ +358 (0)20 637 373
Email karttamyynti@liikennevirasto.fi

John Nurminen Marine Oy
Heikkiläntie 8, FI – 00210 Helsinki
Finland
☎ +358 9 682 3180
Fax +358 9 6823 1811
www.johnnurminenmarine.com
(Also stocks Russian, Latvian and Estonian charts, amongst others)

RUSSIA

Morintech Ltd
6 Prospekt Kima,
199155 Saint Petersburg
☎/*Fax* +7 812 3254048
☎ +7 812 3238528
Email support@morintech.ru
www.dkart.com/ & www.morintech.spb.su

POLAND

Polskie Biuro Hydrograficzne Marynarki Wojennej w Gdyni
ul. Jana z Kolna 4–6
81 – 912 Gdynia
☎ +48 (0)58 620 7472/626 6208
Fax +48 (0)58 626 6203/626 3487
(Polish charts can be ordered direct from the Polish Hydrographic Office, which currently has no website)

SMART Sp. z o.o.
Al Zjednoczenia 7, 81 – 345 GDYNIA
skr. poczt. 224
☎/*Fax* +48 (0)58 661 1751/661 1752/620 4567
Email digital@smart.gda.pl
www.smart.gda.pl

LITHUANIA
Lithuanian sheet charts can be obtained from the Lithuanian Maritime Safety Administration, J. Janonio St. 24, 92251 Klaipėda, Lithuania. www.msa.lt. Chart of Curonian Lagoon available from The Jana Seta Map Shop, 83/85 Elizabetes iela, Block 2. Rīga LV-1050, Latvia ☎ +371 6724 0894 *Fax* 6782 8039 *Email* veikals@kartes.lv www.mapshop.lv.

LATVIA
www.jurasadministracija.lv – homepage of the Maritime Administration of Latvia, responsible for hydrography, Featuring the current chart catalogue
The Jana Seta Map Shop, 83/85 Elizabetes iela, Block 2. Rīga LV-1050, Latvia ☎+371 6724 0894 *Fax* 6782 8039 *Email* veikals@kartes.lv www.mapshop.lv. is the largest chart supplier in the country and will despatch orders abroad. Most major credit cards are accepted.

ESTONIA
Gotta OU, Uus Sadama 25, 10120 Tallinn, Estonia
☎ +372 646 0650, *Fax* +372 646 0651
Email chart@gotta.ee
www.gotta.ee

II. Abbreviations used on Russian charts

IALA System A	МАМС
List of Lights	список маяков
Light	свет/огонь

Structures

Lighthouse	маяк (Мк)
Light vessel	пл. Мк
Radiobeacon (RC)	РМк
Beacon	зн
Column	колонна
Framework tower	ажурная установка ферма
House	дом
Building	здание, домик
Hut	будка
Mast	мачта
Post	столб
Tower	башня (бня)
Concrete	бетон(ный)
Iron	желез(ный)
Metal	металл(ический)
Stone	камен(ный)
Wooden	дерев(янный)
Band	горизонтальная полоса
Stripe	вертикальная полоса
Destroyed	разруш(енный)
Occasional	случ(айный)

Lights

Temporary	времен(ный)
Extinguished	погаш(енный)
F	П
Oc	Зтм
Iso	Изо
Fl	Пр
Q	Ч. Пр
IQ	прер. Ч. Пр
AI	пер
Oc(...)	Гр. Зтм
Fl(...)	Гр. Пр
F.Fl	П. Пр
FlFl(...)	П. Гр. Пр
LFl	Дл. Пр
Sec	С
Leading light	Ств.

Examples

Fl.7s8M	Пр 7С 8М
Iso.7M	Изо 7М
Fl(3)WR.15s12/10M	Пр(3)15С12/10М
Q.5M	Ч. Пр5М
Leading light, Q	Ств Ч. Пр
Leading light, Iso	Ств Изо

Supplementary information

Whistle	(Рев)
Horn	(Н)
Gong	(гонг)
Bell	(К)
Explosive	(В)
Cannon	(П)
Reed	(Г)
Siren	(С)

Colours

Black	чр.
Violet	фл.
Blue	сн.
Green	зл.
Orange	ор.
Red	кр.
White	бл.
Yellow	жл.
Brown	кч.
Grey	ср.
Pale blue	гл.

Or abbreviated as in:

Black/red/black	ч к ч
Black/yellow/black	ч ж ч
Yellow/black/yellow	ж ч ж
Red/white	к б

Bottom

Bottom	грунт
Broken, cracked	б
Pebbles, shingle	гк
Clay	гл
Gravel, sand with small stones	гр
Mud, silt, sludge	И
Clay, mud, silt	гл. И
Lime	Изв
Stone	К
Small stones	мК
Large stone, boulders	кК
Shallow	м
Soft	мг
Coarse	к
Hard, firm	т
Sand	П
Fine sand	мП
Coarse sand	кП
Plate, slab	Пл
Shells	Р
Cliff, rock face	С
Medium, average	с
Weed	вд
Firm, fine sand and mud	тмПИ
Magnetic variation	Магн. скл
(former) spoil dumping ground	(бывшая) свалка грунта

III. Firing practice areas

Military firing takes place in the waters adjoining Denmark, Sweden, Finland, Poland and Russia:

Denmark

Firing practice takes place around Bornholm and off the south coast of Sweden, as well as in other Danish waters not covered by this book. Information for the waters southwest of Bornholm is available from the Raghammer Safety Office, ☎ 56 978 106, *VHF* Ch 06, 08, 16, 77; information for the waters elsewhere around the island and off southern Sweden is available from Bornholms Marine District, ☎ 56 942 400 (no VHF contact).

Sweden

Firing practice takes place in seven areas around the Swedish coast, as well as on Lake Vättern. Information is available from:

Ringenäs (56°40'·8N 12°41'·1E) ☎ +46 (0) 3169 2600
Kabusa (55°25'N 14°00'E) ☎ +46 (0) 411 522 180/550 652, *VHF* Ch 16 (call *Kabusa skjufält*)
Ravlunda (55°46'N 14°20'E) ☎ +46 (0) 4147 4180, *VHF* Ch 16 (call *Ravlunda skjutfält*)
Landsort/Utlängan (58°45'N 19°10'E – 58°15'N 18°10'E, the area joining Landsort, Utö and Huvudskär), ☎ +46 (0) 850 261 823
Utlängan/Falsterborev ☎ +46 (0) 45 586 880
Utö southeastward (58°57'N 18°15'·8E), ☎ +46 (0) 850 157 045 (24 hour recorded information), *VHF* Ch 16 (call *Utö skjufält*)
Tåme (64°59'N 21°21'E) ☎ +46 (0) 912 43036; *VHF* Ch 16 (call *Tåme skjufält*)
Junkön (65°26'N 22°21'E), ☎ +46 (0) 920 258 013.

Finland

Finland has only one firing practice area, in the vicinity of 60°06'N 24°55'E. Information is available from the Katajaluoto Safety Office, ☎ +46 (0) 9 1814 5173, *Mobile* 040 503 5570 (no VHF contact).

Poland

There are six areas in regular use and a further eight used occasionally (see pages 291, 292 and 308).

Firing times are announced on NAVTEX and VHF Ch 16 followed by Chs 24, 25 or 26.

Phone the Polish Navy ☎ +48 91 324 2080 or for the northwest coast Radio Słupsk ☎ +48 59 814 4889 for full details.

Radio Słupsk also broadcasts details on VHF Ch 16 followed by Chs 71 at 0715, 1245 and 1845.

The Baltic States and Kaliningrad

While there are no firing practice areas along the coasts of the Baltic States Regulated Area 117 off Kaliningrad should be noted. See page 318 and the plan on page 315.

Russia

There are seven Prohibited Areas (PA) or Firing Practice Areas (FPA) in Russian waters approaching St Petersburg. Further details are given on page 275 and plans on pages 274 and 282 as well as current charts.

APPENDIX

IV. Search and rescue

Germany

National SAR Agency: German Sea Rescue Service
Communicate via MRCC Bremen, VHF DSC
MMSI 002111240
☎ +49 (0)421 53 6870 (124 124 for Mobiles
within German network coverage).

Denmark

National SAR Agency: Ministry of Defence
Communicate via the three centres controlled by
Århus,
☎ +45 (0)89 433203, or coast radio stations
controlled by Lyngby Radio, VHF DSC MMSI
002191000,
☎ +45 (0)45 6663 4800.

Sweden

National SAR Agency: Swedish Maritime
Administration
Communicate via MRCC Göteborg, VHF DSC
MMSI 002653000
☎ +46 (0)31 699080
(emergency) ☎ +46 (0)31 699050
(ship) *Email* mrccgbg@amrcc.sjofartsverket.se
Inmarsat–C (581) 426 590 010; or
Stockholm SJD, VHF DSC MMSI 002652000,
☎ +46 (0)8 601 7906
Email maritime@stockholmradio.se

Finland

National SAR Agency: Finnish Frontier Guard
Headquarters, SAR Branch. The National Alarm
number ☎ +358 (0) 204 1000 always connects to
the nearest MRCC or MRSC.
Communicate via MRSC Vaasa, VHF DSC MMSI
002303000,
☎ +358 (0)204 1003 (emergency)
☎ +358 (0)718 720300
Email mrsc.vaasa@raja.fi;
MRCC Turku, VHF DSC MMSI 002301000
☎ +358 (0)204 1000 (emergency)
☎ +358 (0)204 107070, *Email* mrcc@smmv.rvl.fi,
Inmarsat–C (581) 423 002 211; or
MRSC Helsinki (Gulf of Finland CG District),
VHF DSC MMSI 002302000
☎ +358 (0)204 1002 (emergency)
☎ +358 (0)718 720200
Email mrsc.helsinki@slmv.rvl.fi.

Russia (Gulf of Finland)

National SAR Agency: MRCC Moskva
Communicate via MRCC Saint Petersburg, VHF
DSC MMSI 002733700
☎ +7 (0)812 327 4146/718 8995
Fax +7 (812) 327 4146, *Telex* 121512RCC.RU
Email mrcc@mail.pasp.ru
Inmarsat–C (581) 492 509 012, Inmarsat Mini–M
761 319 893.

Poland

National SAR Agency: Polish Ship Salvage
Company
Communicate via MRCC Gdynia, VHF DSC
☎ +48 (0)58 6205 551/6216 811/6610 196;
Email polratok.1@sar.gov.pl
MRSC Świnoujście, ☎ +48 (0)91 3215 929/
☎ +48 (0)91 3214 917;
Email polratok.2@sar.gov.pl
Witowo (SPS), VHF DSC MMSI 002610210,
☎ +48 (0)59 8109 425
Email radio.witowo@emitel.pl

Russia (Kaliningrad)

National SAR Agency: MRCC Moscva
Communicate via MRCC Kaliningrad, DSC MMSI
002734417
☎ +7 (0)4012 538470
Email mrsc@mapkld.ru
Inmarsat Mini–M 762 830 387.

Lithuania

National SAR Agency: MRCC Klaipėda
Communicate via MRCC Klaipėda, DSC MMSI
002770330
☎ +370 46 491015/019 (maritime medical centre)
☎ +370 391257/258.

Latvia

National SAR Agency: Sea Search and Rescue
Service, Maritime Administration of Latvia
Communicate via MRCC Rīga VHF DSC MMSI
002750100
☎ +371 673 23103 (emergency)/
☎ +371 294 76101/+371 670 82070 (mobile)
Email sar@mrcc.lv,
Inmarsat–C 581–427518510.

Estonia

National SAR Agency: Estonian Border Guard and
Ministry of Transport and Communication
Communicate via JRCC Tallinn, VHF DSC MMSI
002761000
☎ +372 6 692222/6925000 (MRCC Tallinn)
Email ncc_estonia@pohja.pv.ee
Inmarsat–C (AOR-E) 492480040.

V. Radio communications and weather information

Radio communications are detailed under a number
of section headings. Should further detail be required
the reader is recommended to obtain the current
edition of NP 291, *Admiralty Maritime
Communications – United Kingdom and the Baltic.*
All times are given in UT unless stated.

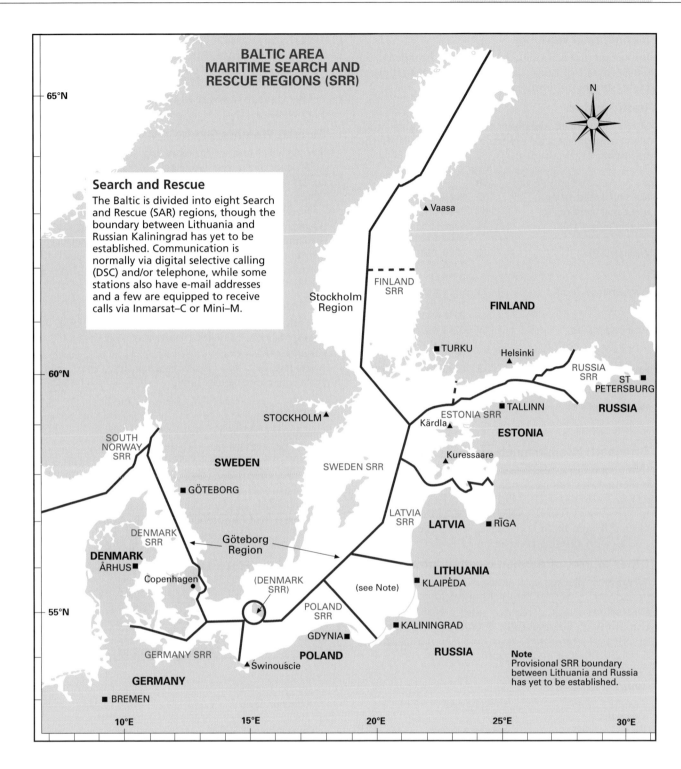

BALTIC AREA
MARITIME SEARCH AND
RESCUE REGIONS (SRR)

Search and Rescue
The Baltic is divided into eight Search and Rescue (SAR) regions, though the boundary between Lithuania and Russian Kaliningrad has yet to be established. Communication is normally via digital selective calling (DSC) and/or telephone, while some stations also have e-mail addresses and a few are equipped to receive calls via Inmarsat–C or Mini–M.

Note
Provisional SRR boundary between Lithuania and Russia has yet to be established.

GMDSS, Coast Radio Stations, weather bulletins and navigational warnings

Boundaries of forecast areas are shown on page 369. Details of port or harbour radio services on VHF will be found in the text relating to that harbour.

Note Some forecasts give wind speed in metres per second – multiply by two for the approximate equivalent in knots and divide by two for the approximate figure in Beaufort.

Germany

Bremen (MRCC) (53°05′N 8°48′E) (24 hours)
VHF DSC MMSI 002111240
VHF antennas and remotely controlled stations accepting VHF DSC are situated at:

		VHF Ch
Flensburg	54°44′N 09°30′E	16, 27
Kiel	54°25′N 10°11′E	16, 23
Lübeck	54°13′N 10°43′E	16, 24
Rostock	54°10′N 12°06′E	16, 60
Arkona	54°33′N 13°35′E	16, 66
Rügen	54°35′N 13°40′E	16

APPENDIX

Navigational warnings
Important navigational warnings are broadcast on Ch 16 by all stations, on receipt and repeated every H+00 and H+30 until cancelled.

Traffic centres
Storm warnings, weather bulletins, visibility and, when appropriate, ice reports are broadcast from the following Traffic Centres:

	VHF Ch	
Kiel Canal (east-going)	02	Every H+15 and H+45
Kiel Canal (west-going)	03	Every H+20 and H+50
Travemünde Traffic	13	Every 3 hours from 0600–2100 LT
Wismar Traffic	12	0230, 0630, 0930, 1230, 1530, 1830 and 2130 LT
Warnemünde Traffic	73	0115 then every odd H+15 from 0515–2115 LT
Stralsund Traffic	67	0235 then every even H+35 from 0635–2235 LT
Sassnitz Traffic	13	0230 then every even H+30 from 0630–2230 LT
Wolgast Traffic	09	0115 then every odd H+15 from 0515–2115 LT

Offenbach (Main)/Pinneberg
Offenbach/Pinneberg broadcasts detailed weather bulletins and navigational warnings in English on 4583, 7646 and 10100·8kHz. Full details are given in NP 291 *Admiralty Marititme Communications, United Kingdom and the Baltic*, which the owners of yachts with suitable receivers may wish to carry.

Other sources of German weather information
Weather bulletins and navigational warnings are broadcast by Deutschlandradio (Berlin), Deutschlandfunk (Köln), and Norddeutscher Rundfunk, in German only. Full details will be found in NP 291 *Admiralty Marititme Communications, United Kingdom and the Baltic*.

VHF transmission five times a day, provides a very comprehensive forecast in deliberately slow German. For times and frequencies see www.see-wetter.de/seefunk.

The website www.dwd.de is excellent for Baltic Sea areas

German Weather Service – Marine Weather
Strong wind and storm warnings (in excess of Force 6/22 knots) for the German North Sea and Baltic coasts are available on ☎ +49 (0) 40 6690 1209. When no warning is in operation a forecast is given.

Worldwide meteorological and routing advice via phone and/or modem is also available – for further information contact: German Weather Service – Shipping Department, PO Box 301190, 20304 Hamburg, Germany, ☎ +49 40 6690 1852, *Fax* +49 40 6690 1946.

Ice Reports
Ice information is available from the German Ice Report Service, ☎ +49 (0) 3814563787 *Email* ice@bsh.de, www.bsh.de or www.bsis-ice.de, from late November until early June.

Denmark
Lyngby (56°22′N 10°44′E) (24 hours)
VHF DSC MMSI 002191000
VHF Call Lyngby Radio. When traffic on hand, ship will be called by radio, DSC or satellite. Weather bulletins and navigational warnings as detailed below, both on working channels (bold type). Antennas and remotely controlled stations accepting VHF DSC are situated at:

		VHF Ch	
Karleby	54°52′N 11°12′E	16, 28, 61, 63	Areas 4, 5
Møn (Mern)	55°03′N 11°59′E	16, 02, 64	Areas 2, 3, 4
Åarsballe (Bornholm)	55°09′N 11°53′E	16, 04, 07	Areas 1, 2, 3
København	55°41′N 12°37′E	16, 03, 26,	Areas 3, 4, 5
Røsnæs	55°44′N 10°55′E	16, 04, 23	Areas 4, 5
Vejby	56°05′N 12°08′E	16, 83, 85	Areas 4, 5

WIND SCALES

Beaufort	Wind Description	Effect on Sea	Effect on Land	Wind speed (knots)	m/sec
0	Calm	Sea like a mirror	Smoke rises vertically	<1	–
1	Light air	Ripples like scales, no crests	Direction of wind shown by smoke	1–3	2
2	Light breeze	Small wavelets, crests do not break	Wind felt on face, leaves rustle	4–6	2–3
3	Gentle breeze	Large wavelets, some crests break	Wind extends light flags	7–10	3–5
4	Moderate breeze	Small waves, frequent white horses	Small branches move	11–16	5–8
5	Fresh breeze	Moderate waves, many white horses	Small trees sway	17–21	8–11
6	Strong breeze	Large waves form, white crests	Large branches move	22–27	11–14
7	Near gale	Sea heaps up, white foam from breaking waves	Whole trees in motion	28–33	14–17
8	Gale	Moderately high waves some spindrift. Foam blown with wind	Twigs break from trees, difficult to walk	34–40	17–20
9	Strong gale	High waves, dense foam, wave crests topple, spray may affect visibility	Slight structural damage	41–47	20–24
10	Storm	Very high waves, sea appears white, visibility affected	Trees uprooted, structural damage	48–55	24–27
11	Violent storm	Exceptionally high waves, long white patches of foam, crests blown into froth	Widespread damage	56–63	28–31
12	Hurricane	The air is filled with foam, visibility very seriously affected	Widespread structural damage	64+	32–

VHF RADIO STATIONS IN THE BALTIC

More detailed information is given in the text for individual countries

NORWAY

SWEDEN

FINLAND

Turku Radio
MMSI: 002300230

Stockholm Radio
MMSI: 002652000

St Petersburg Radio
MMSI: 002733700

Tallinn Radio
MMSI: 002761000

ESTONIA

(MRCC Göteborg)
MMSI: 002653000

LATVIA

Riga Radio
MMSI: 002750100

Lyngby Radio
MMSI: 002191000

DENMARK

Klaipeda Radio
MMSI: 002770330

Kaliningrad Radio
MMSI: 002734417

LITHUANIA

RUSSIA

RUSSIA

Witowo Radio
MMSI: 002610210

Gdynia Radio
MMSI: 002610310

Szczecin Radio
MMSI: 002610110

Bremen Radio
MMSI: 002111240

GERMANY

POLAND

Fornæs	56°27′N 10°57′E	16, 05	Areas 3, 4
Anholt	56°43′N 11°31′E	16, 07	Areas 4, 5
Læsø	57°17′N 11°03′E	16, 64	Area 5
Skagen	57°44′N 10°35′E	16, 04	Area 5

Weather bulletins

Gale and storm warnings are broadcast on the working channel on receipt, in Danish and English, for the area(s) indicated on page 369. Gale warnings are repeated, in English, on request.

Navigational warnings

Navigational and Mine warnings are broadcast at the end of the first silence period after receipt (0133, 0533, 0933, 1333, 1733 and 2133), in Danish and English. Ice reports are broadcast at 1305 and on request in English.

Other sources of Danish weather information

Weather bulletins and navigational warnings are also broadcast by Danmarks Radio, in Danish only.

APPENDIX

Sweden

Göteborg (57°28′N 11°56′E) (24 hours)
VHF DSC MMSI 002653000. For remotely controlled stations see under Stockholm.

Stockholm (59°17′N 18°43′E) (24 hours)
VHF DSC MMSI 002652000
VHF Calling vessels should give the name of the station and the channel number. An audible pulse is transmitted every 10 seconds to indicate that a working channel is occupied. Traffic lists are broadcast on working frequencies only at: 0200, 0600, 1000, 1400, 1800 and 2200.

Those stations which also accept remotely controlled VHF DSC traffic for Göteborg (see above) are indicated thus*. Antennas are situated at:

West coast (plus many others)		VHF Ch
Göteborg*	57°42′N 12°03′E	16, 24
Göta Canal and Lakes		
Trollhättan	58°17′N 12°17′E	16, 25
Kinnekulle*	58°36′N 13°25′E	16, 01
East coast		
Kivik*	55°40′N 14°10′E	16, 21
Karlshamn (Hörvik)	56°14′N 14°47′E	16, 25
Karlskrona*	56°10′N 15°36′E	16, 81
Ölands Södra Udde*	56°14′N 16°27′E	16, 27
Västervik*	57°43′N 16°26′E	16, 23
Hoburgen (Gotland)*	56°56′N 18°13′E	16, 24
Visby (Gotland)*	57°36′N 18°22′E	16, 25
Fårö (Gotland)*	57°52′N 19°02′E	16, 28
Gotska Sandön*	58°22′N 19°14′E	16, 65
Norrköping*	58°41′N 16°28′E	16, 64
Torö*	58°49′N 17°50′E	16, 24
Södertälje*	59°13′N 17°37′E	16, 66
Nacka (Stockholm)*	59°18′N 18°10′E	16, 03, 23, 26
Svenska Högarna*	59°27′N 19°30′E	16, 84
Väddö*	59°58′N 18°50′E	16, 78
Gävle*	60°38′N 17°08′E	16, 23
Hudiksvall*	61°42′N 16°51′E	16, 25
Sundsvall*	62°24′N 17°27′E	16, 24
Härnösand*	62°37′N 17°58′E	16, 23
Kramfors	62°57′N 17°57′E	16, 84
Mjällom*	62°59′N 18°24′E	16, 64
Örnsköldsvik	63°18′N 18°40′E	16, 28
Umeå*	63°50′N 19°49′E	16, 26
Skellefteå*	64°46′N 20°57′E	16, 23
Luleå*	65°36′N 21°56′E	16, 25
Mälaren		
Västerås*	59°39′N 16°24′E	16, 25
Hjälmaren	59°06′N 15°50′E	16, 81

Weather bulletins

24 hour forecast and synopsis for areas 1–15 are broadcast in Swedish and English on VHF working channels at 0600 and 1800 (see page 369).

Navigational warnings

Navigational warnings for all areas are broadcast in Swedish and English on VHF working channels at 0200, 0600, 1000, 1400, 1800 and 2200.

Ice reports

Reports for all areas are broadcast at 1400 and on request, in English.

Other sources of Swedish weather information

Swedish Meteorological and Hydrological Institute Weather bulletins and ice reports in Swedish and English are available on request (though at a charge) from the SMHI marine forecasting service at Norrköping, ℡ +46 11 495 8400/8532/8533/8535 *Fax* +46 11 495 8403.

Finland

Turku (60°10′N 21°43′E) (24 hours)
VHF DSC MMSI 002300230
All stations are remotely controlled from Turku. Weather bulletins and navigational warnings are broadcast on working channels by all stations

Those stations which accept remotely controlled VHF DSC traffic are indicated thus* and grouped according to Marine Rescue Co-ordination Centre – Vaasa, Turku and Helsinki. Antennas are situated at:

MRSC Vaasa (MMSI 002303000)		VHF Ch
Kemi*	65°47′N 24°33′E	26
Hailuoto*	65°02′N 24°35′E	27
Kalajoki*	64°18′N 24°11′E	84
Kokkola*	63°50′N 23°09′E	28
Raippaluoto*	63°18′N 21°10′E	25
MRCC Turku (MMSI 002301000)		
Kristiinankaupunki*	62°16′N 21°24′E	24
Pori*	61°37′N 21°27′E	26
Rauma*	61°07′N 21°31′E	28
Uusikaupunki*	60°49′N 21°26′E	01
Turku (MRCC)*	60°27′N 22°20′E	02, 26
Brändö*	60°25′N 21°03′E	86
Geta*	60°23′N 19°53′E	05
Korpoo*	60°10′N 21°33′E	23
Turku Radio	60°09′N 21°42′E	02, 26
Järsö*	60°01′N 20°00′E	25
MRSC Helsinki (MMSI 002302000)		
Utö*	59°47′N 21°22′E	24
Hanko*	59°50′N 22°56′E	03
Porkkala*	59°59′N 24°26′E	04
Helsinki*	60°09′N 25°02′E	05
Sondby (Porvoo)*	60°16′N 25°51′E	01
Kotka*	60°29′N 26°52′E	25
Virolahti*	60°36′N 27°50′E	24

Weather bulletins

Gale warnings are broadcast on receipt and at 0233, 0633, 1033, 1433, 1833 and 2223 in English, for Areas 1–5 and 7 (see page 369). Weather forecasts, including wave heights, are broadcast at 0633 and 1833, in English, for the same areas.

Navigational warnings

Local and coastal warnings in English for the Gulf of Finland are broadcast on receipt and at 0233, 0633, 1033, 1433, 1833 and 2233. Ice reports are broadcast, in English, at 1033 and 1833.

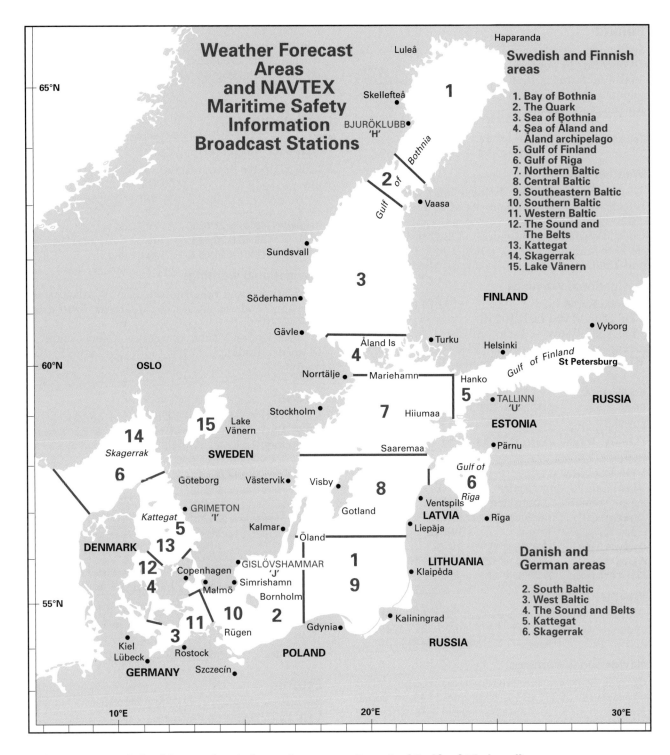

Weather Forecast Areas and NAVTEX Maritime Safety Information Broadcast Stations

Swedish and Finnish areas

1. Bay of Bothnia
2. The Quark
3. Sea of Bothnia
4. Sea of Åland and Åland archipelago
5. Gulf of Finland
6. Gulf of Riga
7. Northern Baltic
8. Central Baltic
9. Southeastern Baltic
10. Southern Baltic
11. Western Baltic
12. The Sound and The Belts
13. Kattegat
14. Skagerrak
15. Lake Vänern

Danish and German areas

2. South Baltic
3. West Baltic
4. The Sound and Belts
5. Kattegat
6. Skagerrak

Other sources of Finnish weather information

Weather bulletins and navigational warnings are also broadcast by Radio Vega and Radio Suomi, in Swedish and Finnish respectively.

Ice reports

Ice reports in Finnish, Swedish or English are available from the Finnish Institute of Marine Research (FIMR), ℡ +358 9 685 7659
Email ice_info@fimr.fi.
Services from www.iceservice.fi are charged for.

Russia (Gulf of Finland)

Vyborg (60°42′N 28°46′E) (24 hours)
VHF DSC MMSI 002734415 (60°42′N 28°43′E)
VHF Ch 02, 16
Saint Petersburg (MRCC) (59°33′N 30°13′E) (24 hours)
VHF DSC MMSI 002733700
VHF Ch 09, 16, 24, 27, 67, 71 (other channels may be used on request)
While some weather bulletins and navigational warnings are broadcast in Russian, the area is well covered by the English VHF broadcasts from Finland and Sweden.

Poland

Świnoujście (MRSC 53°55′N 14°17′E) (Ch 11, 16, 74 operates 24 hours)
VHF Call Szczecin Radio. Both stations also accept remotely controlled VHF DSC traffic for Szczecin. Antennas are situated at:

		VHF Ch
Zatoka Pomorska	53°57′N 14°16′E	16, 25, 26, 27
Szczecin	53°28′N 14°35′E	16, 24, 28

Weather bulletins

Weather bulletins in English and Polish are broadcast by Zatoka Pomorska at 0705, 1305 and 1905.
Coastal warnings are broadcast in English and Polish by both stations at 0200, 0600, 1000, 1400, 1800 and 2200. Ice reports are broadcast when relevant.

Navigational warnings

Witowo Radio (SPS) (54°33′N 16°32′E) (24 hours)
VHF DSC MMSI 002610210.
VHF Call Witowo Radio. All three stations also accept remotely controlled VHF DSC traffic for Witowo. Antennas are situated at:

		VHF Ch
Kolobrzeg	54°11′N 15°33′E	16, 24
Barzowice	54°28′N 16°30′E	16, 25
Rowokól	54°39′N 17°13′E	16, 26

Gdynia Radio (MRCC) (54°33′N 18°32′E) (24 hours)
VHF DSC MMSI 002610310
VHF Call Gydnia Radio. All three stations also accept remotely controlled VHF DSC traffic for Witowo (SPS). Antennas are situated at:

		VHF Ch
Rozewie	54°50′N 18°20′E	16, 24
Oksywie	54°33′N 18°32′E	16, 26, 27
Krynica Morska	54°23′N 19°27′E	16, 25

Weather bulletins

Weather bulletins are broadcast on VHF working channels at 0135, 0735, 1335 and 1935, in Polish and English, for Areas 7–11 (see page 369).

Navigational warnings

Coastal warnings are broadcast on receipt and at 0133, 0533, 0933, 1333, 1733 and 2133, in Polish and English. Ice reports, when relevant, are broadcast at 1035 and 1335 in Polish and English.

Other sources of Polish weather information

Weather bulletins and navigational warnings are broadcast by Polish (Polskie) Radio SA, in Polish only.

Marine Weather Telephone Service

Current condition reports and forecasts are available from Gdynia, ☎ 058 6203 422, and Szczecin, ☎ 091 4342 012.

Russia (Kaliningrad)

Kaliningrad (UIW) (54°42′N 20°30′E) (24 hours)
VHF DSC MMSI 002734417
VHF Ch 07, 16

Kaliningrad Radio-1 VHF Ch 07
While some weather bulletins and navigational warnings are broadcast in Russian, the area is well covered by the English VHF broadcasts from Finland and Sweden.

Lithuania

Klaipėda (MRCC) (55°43′N 21°06′E) (24 hours)
VHF DSC MMSI 002770330
Call Klaipėda Rescue Radio. Antennas are situated at:

		VHF Ch
Klaipėda	55°43′N 21°06′E	16
Nida	55°18′N 20°59′E	16
Šventoji	56°01′N 21°05′E	16

Navigational warnings

Navigational and other information is broadcast as necessary and on request by Klaipėda Traffic on VHF Ch 09.
JSC Navigation Center of Service Radio Centre of Klaipėda (Radio 5) (VTS) (55°43′N 21°06′E) (24 hours).

Latvia

Rīga (MRCC) (57°02′N 24°05′E) (24 hours)
VHF DSC MMSI 002750100. Call *Rīga Rescue Radio* (VHF Ch 71). Antennas are situated at:

Uzava	57°13′N 21°26′E
Jenupe	57°32′N 21°41′E
Kolka	57°45′N 22°35′E
Mersrags	57°22′N 23°07′E
Rīga	57°02′N 24°05′E
Vitrupe	57°36′N 24°23′E

Rīga (57°02′N 24°05′E) (24 hours)
VHF 70
Liepāja Radio (56°30′N 21°00′E) (24 hours).

Other sources of Latvian weather information

Gale warnings and local forecasts are broadcast by:

		VHF Ch
MRCC Rīga	0703, 1503 LT	71

Estonia

Kuressaare (MRSC) (58°15′N 22°29′E)
VHF DSC MMSI 002760120
Pärnu (ESP) (58°23′N 24°29′E) (24 hours)
VHF Ch 16, 10
Tallinn (MRCC) (59°24′N 24°40′E) and Tallinn (ESA) (59°28′N 24°21′E) (both 24 hours)
VHF DSC MMSI 002761000.
VHF All stations accept remotely controlled VHF DSC traffic on VHF Ch 70. Weather bulletins and navigational warnings are broadcast on VHF Ch 69 by all stations after prior announcement on VHF Ch 16.

		VHF Ch
Ruhnu	57°48′N 23°15′N	16, 03, 69
Tõstamaa	58°18′N 24°00′E	16, 01, 69
Torgu	57°59′N 22°05′E	16, 26, 69
Undva	58°31′N 21°56′E	16, 01, 69

Orissaare	58°34'N 23°04'E	16, 27, 69
Kõpu	58°55'N 22°12'E	16, 03, 69
Dirhami	59°12'N 23°31'E	16, 26, 69
Suurupi	59°28'N 24°23'E	16, 01, 69
Tallinn	59°24'N 24°40'E	16, 03, 27
Aabla	59°35'N 25°31'E	16, 27, 69
Eisma	59°34'N 26°17'E	16, 03, 69
Toila	59°25'N 27°32'E	16, 26, 69

Weather bulletins

Storm warnings for the Baltic Sea and Gulf of Finland are broadcast on receipt and at 0233, 0633, 1033, 1433, 1833 and 2233, in English and Estonian. Gale warnings, synopsis, and 24/48 hour weather and sea state forecasts are broadcast at 0433 and 1333 in English and Estonian.

Navigational warnings

Navigational warnings are broadcast on receipt and at 0233, 0633, 1033, 1433, 1833 and 2233 in English and Estonian.

Navtex

All broadcasts are in English. Boundaries of forecast areas are shown on page 369.

Sweden

Grimeton (57°06'N 12°23'E) Range 300M.
 Identification letter I
 Weather bulletins 0520, 1720.
 Navigational warnings 0120, 0520, 0920, 1320, 1720 and 2120
 Ice reports 1320

Gislövshammar (55°29'N 14°19'E) Range 300M.
 Identification letter J
 Weather bulletins 0520, 1730
 Navigational warnings 0130, 0530, 0930, 1330, 1730, 2130
 Ice reports 1330, 1730

Bjuröklubb (64°28'N 21°36'E) Range 300M.
 Identification letter H. (This station appears to broadcast only full gale warnings and ice reports).
 Weather bulletins 0510, 1710
 Navigational warnings 0110, 0510, 0910, 1310, 1710, 2110
 Ice reports 1310.

Estonia

Tallinn (59°30'N 24°30'E) Range 300M.
 Identification letter U.
 Weather bulletins 0720, 1920 for Areas 1–15
 Navigational and near gale warnings 0320, 0720, 1120, 1520, 1920, 2320 for Areas 4–8.
 Ice reports 1120, 1520 for Areas 1–15. (See page 369).

Weatherfax

A number of weatherfax transmissions cover the Baltic Sea, including those from Northwood (UK) and Offenbach (Main)/Pinneberg (DDH) (DDK) (Germany). Full details are given in NP 291, *Admiralty Maritime Communications – United Kingdom and the Baltic*, which the owners of all yachts equipped with weatherfax receivers are strongly advised to carry.

Northwood transmits on 2618·5, 4610, 8040, 11086·5kHz, with a schedule at 0236 and 1424, 24 hour forecasts at 0524, 0800, 1000, 1300, 1736, 2200, and gale warnings at 0348, 0600, 0700, 1148, 1548 and 1900. Coverage extends from the US East Coast across the North Atlantic as far as Russia.

Offenbach/Pinneberg transmits on 4583, 7646 and 10100·8kHz, Notices at 1110; outlook and 2-day forecast at 0905, 2105; outlook and 5-day forecast at 0330, 1505; marine weather reports at 0020, 0320, 0550, 0850, 1150, 1450, 1750 and 2050. Coverage varies from transmission to transmission.

Weather forecasts on the internet

An ever-increasing amount of weather-related information can be found on the internet. The following sites may be useful, though some information is duplicated at least once. Further investigation immediately before departure would be worthwhile, as new sites are coming online all the time.

www.cnn.com/WEATHER – worldwide weather coverage from CNN, with charts, satellite imagery and three day forecasts for principal cities. Cluttered with unrelated advertisements

www.ecmwf.int – the homepage of the European Centre for Medium-Range Weather Forecasts with links to almost every national met office in Europe. Fast and user-friendly

http://weather.mailasail.com/Franks-Weather/Home – a very interesting private site run by yachtsman and ex Met Office employee Frank Singleton. Particularly useful section (with links) devoted to Baltic Weather Forecasts

www.greatweather.co.uk – private site compiled by Ant Veal with hundreds of useful meteorological links for the UK and Europe, plus bookshop etc

www.metoffice.com – the homepage of the UK Met Office, with worldwide coverage in addition to the UK. Some services are subscription-based

www.sat.dundee.ac.uk – images from orbiting and geostationary satellites courtesy of Dundee University's satellite receiving station. Available free on completion of a registration form

www.foreca.se 5-day Swedish forecasts

http://weather.noaa.gov/ – site of the US National Weather Service, including highly detailed 24 hour weather reports (not forecasts) for many towns in Europe and beyond

http://weather.yahoo.com/ – Yahoo! Weather, an easy site to navigate (though with too many irritating advertisements) giving tourist-type weather information worldwide

www.wmo.ch – website of the World Meteorological Organization (a United Nations Specialized Agency) with information from many national met offices throughout the world. Text in English, French and Spanish

Index

Index